T0214195

Communications
in Computer and Information Science   1410

Editorial Board Members

More information about this series at http://www.springer.com/series/7899

Juan Antonio Lossio-Ventura ·
Jorge Carlos Valverde-Rebaza ·
Eduardo Díaz · Hugo Alatrista-Salas (Eds.)

Information Management and Big Data

7th Annual International Conference, SIMBig 2020
Lima, Peru, October 1–3, 2020
Proceedings

 Springer

Editors
Juan Antonio Lossio-Ventura (iD)
Stanford University
Stanford, CA, USA

Jorge Carlos Valverde-Rebaza (iD)
Visibilia
São Paulo, Brazil

Eduardo Díaz (iD)
University of Valencia
Valencia, Spain

Hugo Alatrista-Salas (iD)
Universidad del Pacífico
Lima, Peru

ISSN 1865-0929 ISSN 1865-0937 (electronic)
Communications in Computer and Information Science
ISBN 978-3-030-76227-8 ISBN 978-3-030-76228-5 (eBook)
https://doi.org/10.1007/978-3-030-76228-5

This Springer imprint is published by the registered company Springer Nature Switzerland AG
The registered company address is: Gewerbestrasse 11, 6330 Cham, Switzerland

Preface

SIMBig 2020, the 7th edition of the International Conference on Information Management and Big Data, aimed to present new methods fields related to Artificial Intelligence, Data Science, Machine Learning, Natural Language Processing, Semantic Web, and Health Informatics, among others, for analyzing and managing large volumes of data. The SIMBig conference series brings together national and international actors in the decision-making field to reveal new technologies dedicated to analyzing data.

Moreover, SIMBig 2020 encouraged all studies that proposed methods to extract meaningful insights from the COVID-19 crisis to influence policy and decision-making in the public and private sector (specially in South America). SIMBig is a convivial place where participants present their scientific contributions in the form of full and short papers. This book presents the entire proceedings of the 7th edition of SIMBig[1], which was fully virtual, held during October 1–3, 2020. In this edition, 32 full papers and 7 short papers were selected from 122 submitted.

Keynote Speakers' Resumes

Dr. Dina Demner-Fushman, from the National Library of Medicine, National Institutes of Health (NLM/NIH), USA, overviewed the efforts on retrieving information, answering questions, and detecting misinformation about COVID-19. One of the effects of the COVID-19 pandemic is a rapidly growing and changing stream of publications to inform clinicians, researchers, policy makers, and patients about the health, socio-economic, and cultural consequences of the pandemic. Leveraging this stream of information is essential for developing policies, guidelines and strategies during the pandemic, for recovery after the COVID-19 pandemic, and for designing measures to prevent recurrence of similar threats. Managing this information stream manually is not feasible. Automated approaches are needed to quickly bring the most salient and reliable points to the readers' attention. Leveraging the COVID-19 collection of scientific articles, data from government sites, and questions about SARS-CoV-2 asked by the researchers, clinicians and the public, in collaboration with the National Institute of Standards (NIST), Ai2, UTHealth, and OHSU researchers, Dina and her colleagues have developed datasets for retrieval of COVID-19 information and automatic question answering. These datasets allow researchers to (1) conduct a community-wide evaluation of the systems' ability to satisfy the needs for high-quality timely information about COVID-19; (2) develop deep-learning approaches to meeting information needs as they evolve during pandemics; and (3) develop approaches to detection of misinformation. Dina's talk presented the approaches to

---

[1] https://simbig.org/SIMBig2020/.

dataset development, their systems for question answering and misinformation detection, and some preliminary results.

Dr. Sophia Ananiadou, from the University of Manchester, UK, provided an overview of text mining methods for evidence-based medicine. Text mining methods have been used for the effective and timely identification of knowledge for evidence-based medicine. Evidence-based medicine seeks to answer well-posed questions using existing results by applying a systematic and transparent methodology. The evidence, e.g., results of clinical trials, should be collected and evaluated without bias, using consistent criteria for inclusion. Literature databases such as MEDLINE provide instant access to millions of research articles, obtained from an ever-expanding list of indexed journals. This progress comes at a cost. The majority of clinicians do not possess the expert literature search skills required to develop complex search strategies, and existing databases are manually updated. Sophia discussed methods for automating the process of systematic reviews, by automating the process of search, screening, and data extraction. These text mining methods have been integrated to the system RobotAnalyst currently used by NICE.

Dr. Maguelonne Teisseire, from the TETIS lab, France, presented her work focused on text mining activities in the context of the MOOD project. The MOOD project (https://mood-h2020.eu) aims at harnessing the data mining and analytical techniques to the big data originating from multiple sources to improve detection, monitoring, and assessment of emerging diseases in Europe. In her presentation, Maguelonne discussed some of the text mining activities conducted in the TETIS lab. In particular, Maguelonne explained how text analysis could help to detect weak signals for epidemic outbreak detection.

Dr. Ian Horrocks, from the University of Oxford, UK, presented the current methods of knowledge graph creation and curation. Knowledge graphs are increasingly important resources in science, medicine, and industry, and systems for storing and querying knowledge graphs are becoming increasingly capable. However, creating and curating high quality knowledge is still a hard problem, and this could impede their adoption. In his talk, Ian considered the nature of the problem and surveyed some recent (and not so recent) work that attempts to address it.

Dr. Andrew Tomkins, from Google, USA, talked about the incorporation of graph data into machine learning (ML). He said that at Google, they perform data mining tasks today over huge and growing datasets. To handle scale, we rely on a handful of highly optimized primitive operations. The current workhorse in training of ML models is stochastic gradient descent, which incorporates per-instance label data efficiently into a model's internal state. However, information is often available not just as labels but also through connections between data instances, often presented as graphs, sometimes in other forms. In his talk, Andrew Tomkins described a number of different approaches to incorporating such higher-order data into scalable training and inference, and suggested some open problems in this area.

Dr. Jiang Bian, from the University of Florida, USA, talked about the big shortcomings with AI in biomedical sciences and when actions do not follow predictions. Big data, high-performance computing, and (deep) machine learning are increasingly becoming key to precision medicine—from identifying disease risks and taking preventive measures, to making diagnoses and personalizing treatment for individuals.

Precision medicine, however, is not only about predicting risks and outcomes but also about weighing interventions. Interventional clinical predictive models require the correct specification of cause and effect, and the calculation of so-called counterfactuals, that is, alternative scenarios.

Dr. Francisco Rodrigues, from the University of São Paulo, Brazil, talked about predicting dynamical processes in complex networks through a machine learning approach. One of the most fundamental problems in network science is to understand how dynamical processes are influenced by the network organization. For instance, if we can understand how patterns of connections between coupled oscillators influence the evolution of the synchronous state, then we can change the network topology to control the level of synchronization of power grids and electronic circuits. In his talk, Francisco discussed how machine learning methods could be used to predict disease propagation in networks and the state of coupled oscillators. The current challenges in network science and some possible ideas for future research were also discussed.

April 2021

Juan Antonio Lossio-Ventura
Jorge Carlos Valverde-Rebaza
Eduardo Díaz
Hugo Alatrista-Salas

Organization

General Organizers

Juan Antonio Lossio-Ventura	Stanford University, USA
Hugo Alatrista-Salas	Universidad del Pacífico, Peru

SNMAM Track Organizers

Jorge Valverde-Rebaza	Visibilia, Brazil
Alan Valejo	University of São Paulo, Brazil

DISE Track Organizers

Eduardo Díaz	University of Valencia, Spain
Abraham Eliseo Dávila Ramón	Pontificia Universidad Católica del Perú, Peru

Local Organizers

Michelle Rodriguez Serra	Universidad del Pacífico, Peru
Cristhian Ganvini Valcarcel	Universidad Andina del Cusco, Peru

SIMBig Program Committee

Nathalie Abadie	COGIT IGN, France
Pedro Marco Achanccaray Diaz	Pontifical Catholic University of Rio de Janeiro, Brazil
César Antonio Aguilar	Pontifica Universidad Católica de Chile, Chile
Marco Alvarez	University of Rhode Island, USA
Alexandre Donizeti Alves	UFABC, Brazil
Erick Antezana	Norwegian University of Science and Technology, Norway
Smith Washington Arauco Canchumuni	Pontifical Catholic University of Rio de Janeiro, Brazil
Ghislain Auguste Atemezing	Mondeca, France
Victor Hugo Ayma	Universidad de Lima, Peru
Jérôme Azé	University of Montpellier, France
Riza Batista-Navarro	University of Manchester, UK
Patrice Bellot	Aix-Marseille Université, France
César Beltrán Castañón	Pontificia Universidad Católica del Perú, Peru

Thomas Guyet	AGROCAMPUS OUEST/IRISA, France
Patrick Happ	Pontifical Catholic University of Rio de Janeiro, Brazil
Zhe He	Florida State University, USA
José-Crispín Hernández	ITA, Mexico
Alexander Hilario-Tacuri	Universidad Nacional de San Agustín, Peru
Ian Horrocks	University of Oxford, UK
Marie Humbert-Droz	Stanford University, USA
Carlos Iniguez	EPN, Ecuador
Diana Inkpen	University of Ottawa, Canada
Clement Jonquet	University of Montpellier, France
Alípio Mário Guedes Jorge	University of Porto, Portugal
Frank Dennis Julca-Aguilar	University of São Paulo, Brazil/University of Nantes, France
Maulik R. Kamdar	Elsevier Inc., USA
Georgios Kontonatsios	Edge Hill University, UK
Yannis Korkontzelos	Edge Hill University, UK
Ravi Kumar	Google, USA
Nikolaos Lagos	NAVER LABS Europe, France
Juan Guillermo Lazo Lazo	Universidad del Pacífico, Peru
Yann Le Guen	Stanford University, USA
Huei Lee	Universidade Estadual do Oeste do Paraná, Brazil
Ulf Leser	Humboldt University of Berlin, Germany
Christian Libaque-Saenz	Universidad del Pacífico, Peru
Alncu Lopcs	University of São Paulo, Brazil
Cédric López	Emvista, France
Zhiyong Lu	NCBI, USA
Maysa Macedo	IBM Research, Brazil
Rocío Paola Maehara Aliaga de Benites	Universidad del Pacífico, Peru
Sabrine Mallek	ICN Business School, France
Ricardo Marcacini	University of São Paulo, Brazil
Marcos Martínez-Romero	Stanford University, USA
Florent Masseglia	Inria, France
Rosario A. Medina Rodríguez	Pontificia Universidad Católica del Perú, Peru
Héctor Andrés Melgar Sasieta	Pontificia Universidad Católica del Perú, Peru
André Miralles	Irstea, France
Pritam Mukherjee	Stanford University, USA
Denisse Muñante	Télécom SudParis, France
Nils Murrugarra-Llerena	University of Pittsburgh, USA
Nhung Nguyen	University of Manchester, UK
Jordi Nin	Universitat Ramon Llull, Spain
Miguel Nuñez-del-Prado-Cortéz	Universidad del Pacífico, Peru
José Eduardo Ochoa Luna	Universidad Católica San Pablo, Peru

Alvaro Talavera López	Universidad del Pacífico, Peru
Suzanne Tamang	Stanford University, USA
Silvia Lizeth Tapia Tarifa	University of Oslo, Norway
Maguelonne Teisseire	Irstea, France
Paul Thompson	University of Manchester, UK
Camilo Thorne	Elsevier, Germany
Andrew Tomkins	Google, USA
Juan-Manuel Torres-Moreno	University of Avignon, France
Turki Turki	King Abdulaziz University, Saudi Arabia
Willy Ugarte	Universidad Peruana de Ciencias Aplicadas, Peru
Alan Valejo	University of São Paulo, Brazil
Jorge Valverde-Rebaza	Visibilia, Brazil
Carlos Vázquez	École de technologie supérieure, Canada
Sebastian Walter	Semalytix GmbH, Germany
Chryssa Zerva	University of Manchester, UK
Hong Zheng	Stanford University, USA

SNMAM Program Committee

Alexandre Donizeti	Federal University of ABC, Brazil
Alonso Inostrosa-Psijas	Universidad Arturo Prat, Chile
Ankur Singh Bist	Signy Advanced Technology, India
Aurea Soriano Vargas	State University of Campinas, Brazil
Brett Drury	INESC TEC, Portugal
Carlos Andrés Ferrero	Instituto Federal de Santa Catarina, Brazil
Conceição Rocha	INESC TEC, Portugal
Daniela Godoy	UNICEN University, Argentina
Diego Furtado Silva	Universidade Federal de São Carlos, Brazil
Francisco Rodrigues	University of São Paulo, Brazil
Geraldo Pereira Rocha Filho	University of Brasilia, Brazil
Hugo D. Calderón Vilca	National University of San Marcos, Peru
Jorge Poco	FGV EMAp, Brazil
Josimar Chire	University of São Paulo, Brazil
Katarzyna Musial-Gabrys	University of Technology Sydney, Australia
Kiran Kumar Bandeli	Walmart Inc, USA
Leandro Anghinoni	University of São Paulo, Brazil
Luca Rossi	Queen Mary University of London, UK
Maria Lígia Chuerubim	Universidade Federal de Uberlândia, Brazil
Mathieu Roche	CIRAD/University of Montpellier, France
Muhammad Nihal Hussain	University of Arkansas at Little Rock, USA
Murilo Naldi	Universidade Federal de São Carlos, Brazil
Newton Spolaor	State University of Western Paraná, Brazil
Nils Murrugarra-Llerena	Snap Inc, USA
Paola LLerena Valdivia	Inria Saclay, France

Pascal Poncelet	University of Montpellier, France
Pedro Shiguihara Juárez	Pontifical Catholic University of Peru, Peru
Rafael Delalibera Rodrigues	University of São Paulo, Brazil
Rafael Giusti	Federal University of Amazonas, Brazil
Rafael Santos	National Institute for Space Research, Brazil
Renan de Padua	iFood, Brazil
Renato Fabbri	University of São Paulo, Brazil
Ricardo Campos	Polytechnic Institute of Tomar/INESC TEC, Portugal
Ronaldo Prati	Federal University of ABC, Brazil
Ryan Rossi	Adobe Research, USA
Sabrine Mallek	Université de Lorraine, France
Solange Rezende	University of São Paulo, Brazil
Sultan Orazbayev	Harvard University, USA
Thiago de Paulo Faleiros	University of Brasilia, Brazil
Tiago Colliri	University of São Paulo, Brazil
Victor Stroele	Federal University of Juiz de Fora, Brazil
Willy Ugarte	Universidad Peruana de Ciencias Aplicadas, Peru
Zhao Liang	University of São Paulo, Brazil

DISE Program Committee

Nelly Condori Fernández	Universidade da Coruna, Spain
Denisse Muñante Arzapalo	ESTIA, France
Carlos Gavidia Calderón	University College London, UK
José Ignacio Panach Navarrete	Universitat de València, Spain
Silvia Rueda Pascual	Universitat de València, Spain
José Fabián Reyes Román	Universitat Politècnica de València, Spain
Carlos Efraín Iñiguez Jarrín	Escuela Politécnica Nacional, Ecuador
Julio Sandobalin	Escuela Politécnica Nacional, Ecuador
Damiano Distante	University of Rome Unitelma Sapienza, Italy
Xavier Oriol	Universitat Politècnica de Catalunya, Spain
Silvia Lizeth Tapia Tarifa	University of Oslo, Norway
Otto Parra	Universidad de Cuenca, Ecuador
Jesús Edwin Bellido Angulo	Universidad de Ingeniería y Tecnología, Peru
Francisco Pino Correa	Universidad del Cauca, Colombia
César Pardo Calvache	Universidad del Cauca, Colombia
Mirna Muñoz Mata	Centro de Investigación en Matemáticas A.C, Mexico
Jezreel Mejía Miranda	Centro de Investigación en Matemáticas A.C, Mexico
Jose Antonio Pow-Sang	PUCP, Peru
Andrés Melgar Sasieta	PUCP, Peru
Edgar Sarmiento Calisaya	Universidad Nacional de San Agustín, Peru

Organizing Institutions

Universidad del Pacífico, Peru[1]
Stanford University, USA[2]

Collaborating Institutions

Universidad Andina del Cusco, Peru[3]
University of Florida, USA[4]
Universidad Nacional Mayor de San Marcos, Peru[5]
Universidade de São Paulo, Brazil[6]
Université de Montpellier, France[7]
Visibilia, Brazil[8]

Sponsoring Institutions

Google [9]
Consulado General del Perú en San Francisco [10]

---

[1] http://www.up.edu.pe/.
[2] https://www.stanford.edu/.
[3] http://www.uandina.edu.pe/.
[4] https://www.ufl.edu/.
[5] http://www.unmsm.edu.pe/.
[6] https://www.ffclrp.usp.br.
[7] https://www.umontpellier.fr/.
[8] http://visibilia.net.br.
[9] https://www.google.com.
[10] http://www.consulado.pe/es/SanFrancisco/Paginas/Inicio.aspx.

Contents

Social Networks

Data-Driven Software Engineering

Graph Mining

Semantic Web, Repositories, and Visualization

Natural Language Processing and Text Mining

Comparative Analysis of Question Answering Models for HRI Tasks with NAO in Spanish

Enrique Burga-Gutierrez[ID], Bryam Vasquez-Chauca[ID], and Willy Ugarte[✉][ID]

Universidad Peruana de Ciencias Aplicadas (UPC), Lima, Peru
{u201411972,u201413241}@upc.edu.pe, willy.ugarte@upc.pe

Abstract. Recent studies on Human Robot Interaction (HRI) have shown that different types of applications that combine metrics and techniques can help achieve a more efficient and organic interaction. This applications can be related to human care or go further and use a humanoid robot for nonverbal communication tasks. Similarly, for verbal communication, we found Question Answering, a Natural Language Processing task, that is in charge of capturing and interpret a question automatically and return a good representation of an answer. Also, recent work on creating Question Answering models, based on the Transformer architecture, have obtained state-of-the-art results. Our main goal in this project is to build a new Human Robot Interaction technique which uses a Question Answering system where we will test with college students. In the creation of the Question Answering model, we get results from state-of-the-art pre-trained models like BERT or XLNet, but also multilingual ones like m-BERT or XLM. We train them with a new Spanish dataset translated from the original SQuAD getting our best results with XLM-R, obtaining 68.1 F1 and 45.3 EM in the MLQA test dataset, and, 77.9 F1 and 58.3 EM for XQuAD test dataset. To validate the results obtained, we evaluated the project based on HRI metrics and a survey. The results demonstrate a high degree of acceptance in the students about the type of interaction that has been proposed.

Keywords: HRI · Question answering · NAO · SQuAD · NLP

1 Introduction

It is common for people to find information through some form of communication, such as verbal conversations. This is especially useful for work and daily life [32]. Thus, the creation of a conversational AI that simulates natural human communication, as well as, can answer questions on a variety of topics has become one of the most important goals in the field of natural language processing [11,25,31]. This is due to the great difficulty that machines have in reading and understanding texts [22]. A conversational AI can communicate with

© Springer Nature Switzerland AG 2021
J. A. Lossio-Ventura et al. (Eds.): SIMBig 2020, CCIS 1410, pp. 3–17, 2021.
https://doi.org/10.1007/978-3-030-76228-5_1

a user using the "System Ask, User Responds" paradigm to make the information transfer faster and more understandable [11]. It uses the data obtained from the user's request to return a possible valid answer, as many times as necessary, entering into a cycle of information collection and response [22].

Conversational AI has been widely used in the banking and insurance industries, including public transportation and retail [21], as well as biomedical text mining [14]. Likewise, the task of answering questions cannot be complete without the use of an user friendly interface. In [5], the authors describe the capabilities of the humanoid robot NAO in social scenarios and how can be improved by the combination between these class of AIs. Nowadays, robots are increasingly present in people's lives, either as support in manufacturing jobs or in scenarios where there is more personal interaction. The applications given to them aim to situations in which human-robot interaction is a very important point in development [1]. The fact that the robots have a complete and well-developed HRI, allow the user to be able to interact with it more easily, thus facilitating the use of these [2]. The applications in which humanoid robots stand out the most are assistance, so the main focus of the project is to develop a question and answer system that uses the NAO humanoid robot as an interface.

Our contributions are as follows:

- We trained and compared Question Answering pre-trained models using a Spanish datasets.
- We used the best model of the previous comparison with a NAO robot as interface and validate it with Human Robot Interaction metrics.

We have five main parts in this article, the background, the main contribution, related works, experiments and conclusion. In the background we describe all the main topics in this project. In the main contribution we describe what is our contribution with the project. In the related works part, we analyze the most important works of our state of the art. In experiments, we demonstrate how our project works and what are the results obtained. Finally, in the conclusion we analyze the results of the experimentation process.

2   Background

Question answering systems are a challenging activity for capturing a question and return a good representation of an answer based on a context [22]. However, large and high-quality datasets are lacking for languages other than English, hampering progress in multilingual quality control research [6].

2.1   Spanish Datasets

A new dataset translated into Spanish is proposed by [6]. Mainly, they developed a Translate-Align-Recover (TAR) method, based on MT and without alignment control algorithms to translate a Question Answering dataset from English to Spanish, automatically. They applied the TAR method to the famous SQuAD v1.1, the result was the first version of SQuAD v1.1 in Spanish. Then they prepared a Spanish quality control system adapting the multilingual BERT model [6]. Another dataset is Evaluating Cross-lingual Extractive Question Answering (MLQA) [15], made up of Wikipedia articles in 7 different languages, including Spanish. Finally, Cross-lingual Question Answering Dataset (XQuAD) dataset [4], which contains information from different languages that is useful for Question Answering tasks. This dataset is a subset of SQuAD v1.1, but translated into different languages (including Spanish) by professional human translators.

2.2   Model Architecture and Main Algorithms

Transformers. The first language model based completely designed with self-attention components to represent inputs and output without the use of a sequence structures just as the common recurrent neural networks or convolutional neural networks do [29]. The architecture has two principal structures, the encoder and the decoder. They are responsible for transporting and transforming the information from the input to the output. The Transformers' architecture established a new state of the art related to the use language modeling and machine translation [29].

BERT. An acronym for Bidirectional Encoder Representations from Transformers, this is because the BERT's architecture is based on the original implementation of the Multi-layer Bidirectional Transformer [10, 29]. And one of the most significant improvements of the model over others is how it works with its input and output representation, because it helps to differentiate from a single sentence and a pair of sentences using a token sequence technique, this especially useful in Question Answering approaches [10]. Here, a sequence means an input token that could be one or two sentences merged into one. The first token where each sequence begins is the Special Classification Token denoted as [CLS]. This token is widely used to connect sequence representations for classification tasks [10]. Also, another token used here to distinguish where a sequence is a combination of two sentences is the special token called [SEP], which is added between the two sentence sequences to create a new one. The use of a new input and output representation is very important in BERT, as mentioned, but also BERT has two main components in its representation. The first is called Pre-training, where it uses unlabeled data to feed the model in the beginning. And the second part is called Fine-tuning, where the model works by initializing the model with previously trained parameters, and all of them are fine-tuning using labeled data. BERT is a pre-trained model that was created using the English dataset BOOK-CORPUS [10]. But the same authors released a new version called Multilingual BERT (M-BERT) [10, 20], but this time using around 104 different languages using Wikipedia articles with similar contexts. The M-BERT pre-trained model has proven to stand out very well against Question Answering task with different languages, including Spanish [10, 20].

XLNet. A pre-training method based on autoregressive language modeling. First, instead of using a fixed forward or backward factorization order as in conventional AR models, XLNet maximizes the expected record probability of a sequence. Thanks to the permutation operation, the context for each position can consist of left and right tiles. In each position learns to use contextual information from all positions to capture the two-way context. Also, as a generalized AR language model, XLNet is not based on data corruption. So, XLNet does not suffer from the fine-tuning discrepancy to which BERT is subject. Meanwhile, the autoregressive objective also provides a natural way to use the product rule to factor the joint probability of the predicted tokens, eliminating the assumption of independence made in BERT [30].

SpanBERT. A pre-training method designed to better predict stretches of text. This method differs from BERT in both masking and training targets. Firstly, this method masks random contiguous stretches, rather than just random individual tokens. Second, a new Span Limit Objective (SBO) is introduced, with which the model learns to predict all masking, encompassing all tokens observed at its boundary. Stretch-based masking forces the model to predict integer stretches using only the context in which they appear. In addition, the SBO encourages storing information at the section level, giving accessibility at the adjustment stage [12].

ALBERT and RoBERTa. Acronym for A Lite BERT incorporates two parameters reduction techniques that lift the major obstacle in scaling pre-trained models. The first one is a factorized embedding parameterization. By decomposing the large vocabulary embedding matrix into two small matrices, we separate the size of the hidden layers from the size of vocabulary embedding. This separation makes it easier to grow the hidden size the architecture of ALBERT is similar to BERT because uses transformers encoder with GELU nonlinearities. There are three main contributions that ALBERT makes over the design choices of BERT. Factorized embedding parameterization. ALBERT uses a factorization of embedding parameters, decomposing them into smaller matrices. ALBERT proposes a cross-layer parameter sharing as another way to improve parameter efficiency. BERT uses additional loss called next-sentence prediction (NSP). NSP is a binary classification loss for prediction [13].

In the other hand, we have Robert for Robustly Optimized BERT Approach (RoBERTa), which is a new model based on BERT with improvements. RoBertA uses dynamic masking that generates a masking pattern every time we introduce a sequence in the model, which is very useful when we need to work with more steps in the model and larger data sets. RoBERTa uses larger batches in the training phase to improve the accuracy of the final task, which also helps facilitate the uses of parallel training. Finally, RoBERTa uses bytes instead of Unicode characters to store the information, with the use of bytes it is possible to work without the need for "unknown" tokens [17].

XLM and XLM-R. Cross-lingual language model (XLM) provides a general purpose for multilingual representations. Models are fine-tuned with multilingual classification datasets. Authors process all languages through Byte Pair Encoding (BPE). This encoding method improves the alignment of embedding spaces between languages. Also, one of the techniques used is to randomly sample 15% of the BPE tokens and replace them with the [MASK] token 80% of the time, by a random token 10% of the time [8]. Also, the creators of the model present a new Translation Language Modeling (TLM) objective to improve prior training in multiple languages, where parallel sentences are concatenated and randomly mask the input and output words [8].

In other hand, we have XLM-RoBERTa, this model works in multilingual classification, with better results than the m-BERT algorithm [7]. Especially in Question Answering tasks, getting good results using the MLQA dataset. And similar to m-BERT, XLM-R has been trained in 100 different languages. The authors apply subword tokenization directly to the plain text using the Sentence Piece with a one-word language model [7]. Use different factors that are important to pre-training large-scale multilingual models into downstreams tasks. The authors also mentioned that when the number of languages is increased in the dataset, the model can take advantage of the positive transfer that improves performance, especially in low resources languages. Finally, they argue that scaling the size of shared vocabulary can improve the performance of multilingual models in downstream tasks [7].

2.3   Human Robot Interaction (HRI)

Human robot interaction (HRI) is a field of research that focuses on the different ways in which humans work and interact with different types of robots. It aims to develop robots that aim to facilitate and improve IHR [2]. Interaction can be defined as the communication established between the robot and the human. Communication can take different forms. The application of this field within the project is essential [1].

Metrics. A variety of metrics have been proposed that allow us to quantify different groups of tasks performed by robots [2]. Among them we have:

- *the navigation metrics*, which allow us to measure how capable a robot is of avoiding obstacles, going from one path to another in a safe way.
- *the administration metric*, which allows verifying the ability of a robot to coordinate tasks between humans and robots;
- *the manipulation metric*, which measures the behavior of a robot in an environment.

For the aforementioned metrics, human-robot interaction is not fully linked. That is why a set of metrics that are completely related to human-robot interaction was proposed. Thus allowing to correctly quantify the results of events performed by robots. Among these we have [2]:

- *Task effectiveness*, this talks about how to measure the efficiency of a human-robot team to execute a task.
- *Interaction effort*, is more focused on human thinking, such as the time required and the cognitive potential it needs to interact with the robot.
- *Neglect tolerance* is directly related to measuring when a human completely changes their attention to a certain task and seeing how effective the robot is at following the task.
- *Robot attention demand*, this metric tells us about the level that a human needs to understand how a robot works.
- And finally, *the fan out* metric allows to measure the necessary number of robots that a human can manipulate in parallel.

Humanoid Robot. Humanoid robots are a type of robot that are aesthetically similar to human. Furthermore, they become able to fulfill tasks that are performed by humans, because they tend to have a motor similarity [18]. Most of the humanoid robots tend to be used in the cargo industry, but lately, They tend to be used to improve customer service, such as in hospitals and schools [18].

3   Main Contribution

Comparative Study of Question Answering Pre-trained Models over a Spanish Datasets

There are not many Question Answering oriented datasets in Spanish, so a new translated English dataset from SQuAD will be used. As mentioned in the background, the authors of [6] use the TAR algorithm to translate the English version of SQuAD1.1 into Spanish. One of the main proposals of this research project is to train a new model using a variety of pre-trained algorithms that work to answer questions, such as BERT, BERT-M, XLNet, ALBERT, etc., over the new dataset. And compare the results and verifying what works best based on the quality metrics that will be explained in detail in the Sect. 5.

User Experience (UX) in Human Robot Interaction (HRI)

The use of UX is increasingly important when creating or designing new technologies or solutions. These must completely ensure that the interaction that the user receives is not only safe or acceptable for him, but must ensure a positive experience [16]. This, in turn, applies in the context of social robots, whose main role is interaction with people. So, our proposal falls on the following categories of Human Robot Interaction (HRI): Human-centered HRI, which focuses on the person and the behavior design of the robot that must be oriented to the needs of the user; Robot-cognition HRI, focuses on equipping the robot with cognitive ability, as we can see in Fig. 1 [9].

As we have already mentioned, we are proposing an application, to be implemented on the NAO humanoid robot, whose main objective is to answer students' doubts. In the first category, our solution focuses on the needs of the student and tries, in turn, to adapt to them. The robot detects the user's question, and sends it to the service that we implement, which, based on the question or interaction, decides whether it will be answered by our Dialog Flow container or the machine learning model (see Fig. 2). Also, the fact of adding Dialog Flow as part of our solution allows us to provide a better interaction, covering the different flows that it can take, either at the beginning of this, in the case of the presentation of the robot and its functions; During the interaction, the question itself was not well understood; and at the end of the interaction.

The main objective we have with this project is to develop a complete and effective behavior that can be used as a university assistant. As explained previously, the robot must be able to interact with the student during verbal communication and must show the expected results to the student.

4   Related Work

Voice Controlled Humanoid Robot Based Movement Rehabilitation Framework

The use of non-automated methods in the rehabilitation and physical therapies of people, can lead to the loss of important data, which will influence the development of therapies. As well, the dependence of a person on a procedure that could be monitored by a robot generates an overload of work for therapists [24]. The main objective of this project is to create a rehabilitation application that is compatible with the Android-based voice-controlled humanoid robot can be an effective alternative in the rehabilitation of movement coordination and can be complementary to the existing therapeutic tools. They also present training software applied with the NAO humanoid robot that helps to rehabilitate disabled patients. The authors propose the development of an application for Android devices that serves as an interface to control the robot. The therapist programs

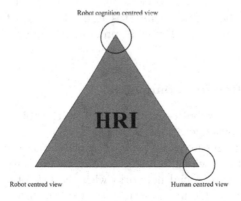

Fig. 1. The conceptual space of approaches for social interaction in HRI research (modified from Dautenhahn, 2007a, p. 685)

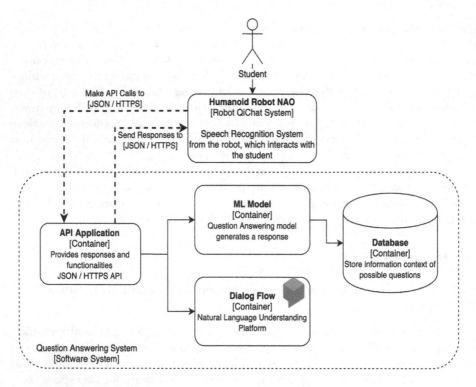

Fig. 2. Container diagram for our proposed solution.

a series of rehabilitation exercises that the patient will have to follow. The robot performs the movements so that the patient can imitate him. The robot is capable of detecting patient movements, allowing it to provide real-time feedback, in case the user is incorrectly performing the exercise. The mobile application gives the therapist the possibility of customizing routines and synchronizing them with the NAO, so that it can be controlled by voice. The solution is mainly based on the NAO robot, which generates an interaction between the robot and the patient verbally and visually, thus promoting the correct development of therapies [24].

Shopping with a Robotic Companion

The authors developed a robotic retail system with the ability to constantly learn and modify their knowledge about customers, thereby providing a noticeable improvement in shopping assistance [5]. The robot has the ability to connect to the store's database, which already contains a repository of users' digital data, or it can connect to social networks with the aim of consulting the user's profile, exposing their preferences, along with their cultural context. In this way, not only can the robot act as a purchasing assistant, it can also determine what the customer wants to buy, or will buy in the future. This form of robot interaction definitely changes the retail scene [5]. So, the main purpose of the authors in this project was to expose the capabilities present in humanoid robots, taking the NAO robot as an example. Considering all the capabilities of existing robots, they propose that these robotic solutions can carry out different types of activities, such as creating a shopping cart or determining if those products desired by customers are in the store. Through the document written by the authors, the aim is to test the functionalities of the NAO robot and document its response to a situation of real interaction with human beings.

Affective Touch in Human–Robot Interaction: Conveying Emotion to the Nao Robot

The authors present the first Human-Robot Interaction study that will allow measuring negative and positive emotions with respect to the NAO humanoid robot that will be based on the experimental selection of a human-human tactile communication study [3]. In this way, the authors develop a list of questions to verify if it is possible to determine what kind of emotions will be the result of the interaction with the humanoid robot NAO. The implementation method is based on three parts that allow closer interaction, generating the best results that will be received by users who interact with the robot. For this reason, the first part of the development method is responsible for determining what type of profile is necessary for the selection of questions and, in this way, understanding the appropriate behavior to be shown with respect to the results given with the humanoid robot. Finally, the authors create a plan for the implementation of the code, starting with the development on devices with touch screens where users interact with the robot. The results produced by the project are oriented to the user responses on the interface regarding interaction with humans. These results were analyzed on the criteria that evaluated the encoding of emotions in the HHI studies [3].

Automatic Spanish Translation of the SQuAD Dataset for Multilingual Question Answering

What the authors propose is to follow the dataset generation. Mainly, they developed the Translate-Align-Recover (TAR) method, based on MT and without alignment control algorithms to translate a QA dataset from English to Spanish, automatically. They applied the TAR method to the famous SQuAD v1.1, the result was the first version of SQuAD v1.1 in Spanish. Then they prepared a Spanish quality control system adapting the m-BERT model. In the end the results obtained were successful. Therefore, the SQuAD-es v1.1 dataset was used to train quality control systems, demonstrating the effectiveness of the TAR approach for the generation of synthetic Corpus. Therefore, the SQuAD-en v1.1 suite is now freely available to promote its use for multilingual quality control.

Context-Based Question-Answering System for the Ukrainian Language

The main objective of this project is to build Question Answering model for the Ukrainian language with an accuracy between 70% and 80%, trying to get a result very similar provided by Google Researches [25]. The first goal is to adapt a Question Answering dataset for the Ukrainian language based on the English dataset SQuAD 2.0. To make this possible, the authors use the API Translator from Google Cloud to transforms the dataset into an Ukrainian version. Although, they found errors in the translation in the content, because some translated phrases differs completely from the English context. To solve this error, the authors make a manual comparison of the answers in the English and Ukrainian version. In the second stage, a tokenization and lemmatization is applied to compare the results of the datasets. In the project, the authors use a pre-training model m-BERT and compare the results with some project working with slavic languages as Russian.

5   Experiments

In this section, we aim to demonstrate two purposes: i) *Train Question Answering pre-trained models using a Spanish datasets* and ii) *Human Robot Interaction.*

In one hand, there are a vast number of state-of-the-art Question Answering pre-trained models over the Spanish dataset created by [6] based on the original English dataset SQuAD 1.1 [22].

In the other hand, to demonstrate the efficiency of our proposal and, furthermore, that the Human-Robot Interaction hand in hand with UX is a key piece for a good adaptation of this new type of technology.

An apk file is available to enable further testing[1].

5.1   Train Question Answering Pre-trained Models Using a Spanish Datasets

Most of the pre-trained models were obtained from the HuggingFace's Transformers library[2], but a few of other models were obtained from the original repositories like XLNet[3] and SpanBERT[4]. Each model were trained using the default parameters found in the repositories and library.

Each training has two metrics in their evaluation [25]. The first of this metrics is the Exact Match (EM):

$$EM = \frac{\sum_{i=1}^{N} I(x_i)}{N} \tag{1}$$

---

[1] https://drive.google.com/file/d/1JgADUQ0F0x9-gePfiftf7AXtxVxFpOli/view.
[2] https://huggingface.co/.
[3] https://github.com/zihangdai/xlnet/.
[4] https://github.com/facebookresearch/SpanBERT/.

Table 1. Results of trained models using 50% Spanish SQuAD dataset

Models	Epochs	SQuAD-dev small		MLQA		XQuAD	
		F1	EM	F1	EM	F1	EM
BERT	2	60.1419	45.4352	49.0719	30.0971	59.7470	42.2689
m-BERT	2	73.8627	58.1954	**65.3695**	**43.5560**	**75.8487**	**57.1429**
XLNet	3	62.7840	46.9239	54.2081	32.9145	62.6688	42.6891
SpanBERT	4	66.7694	50.6000	56.0284	35.6749	67.0324	48.4874
ALBERT	2	64.8347	49.0202	54.4827	34.0187	64.5678	44.9579
RoBERTa	2	68.1290	51.9976	58.3300	37.4262	67.9618	48.5714
XLM	2	64.7773	50.0987	54.9992	35.5035	66.2386	48.4033
XLM-R	2	**74.3873**	**58.7726**	64.9041	43.0801	73.7640	55.0420

where N is the number of instances in the dataset and the input function $I(x_i)$ returns 1 when x_i is exactly equal to the original answer and 0 otherwise. Next, we have the metric F-score or F-measure (F1):

$$F1 = 2 \times \frac{precision \times recall}{precision + recall} \tag{2}$$

$$where \ precision = \frac{EM}{EM + false \ positive} \tag{3}$$

$$recall = \frac{EM}{EM + false \ negative} \tag{4}$$

We will train the model using the whole Spanish SQuAD and the 50% version Spanish, called SQuAD-small. Each result by model will be tested with the MLQA dataset and XQuAD dataset, but also with the test dataset by the half and whole SQuAD, this test dataset is called SQuAD-dev. First, we train the models with a small dataset with the results in Table 1, where we can notice that Multilingual BERT performs better than the others, only XLM-RoBERTa has a better performance but only in the SQuAD-dev dataset. Next, for the whole dataset, the results are shown in Table 2. Here, XLM-RoBERTa works better in all the Exact Match metrics, but Multilingual BERT has better results in the F-score metric for the SQuAD-dev and MLQA datasets.

5.2 Human Robot Interaction Experiments and Results

To carry out this experiment we asked 20 students from the University of Applied Sciences (UPC). Most of the participants were still undergraduate students with an age range of 20 to 26 years. None of these participants mentioned having had a previous experience with a NAO Humanoid Robot.

Participants were told what the purpose of the application was and asked to ask 5 questions at random or on the topics they wanted to know. Based on

Table 2. Results of trained models using the whole Spanish SQuAD dataset

Models	Epochs	SQuAD-dev		MLQA		XQuAD	
		F1	EM	F1	EM	F1	EM
BERT	2	64.8367	20.0668	54.0192	32.7241	63.9724	44.3697
m-BERT	2	76.7634	60.3027	67.6322	44.5269	78.2874	57.5630
XLNet	3	66.4660	48.9593	56.2023	34.4946	65.9436	44.7058
ALBERT	2	68.6729	51.9110	58.2788	36.6837	69.6446	48.4033
RoBERTa	2	72.0361	54.9479	61.6014	39.0633	73.2384	53.3613
XLM	2	65.7609	49.8108	56.0953	34.8372	66.7718	47.8151
XLM-R	2	**76.8075**	**60.5676**	**68.1052**	**45.2694**	**77.8576**	**58.3193**

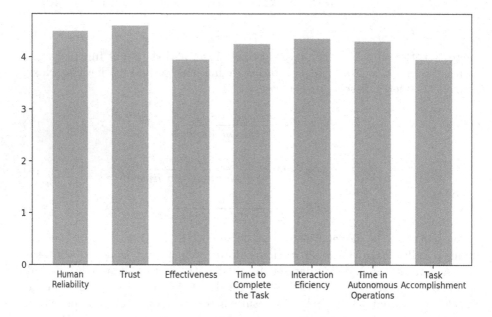

Fig. 3. Average results by HRI metrics

the previously conducted interaction, participants were asked to conduct a 12-question survey. These questions will help us validate our solution against the proposed metrics, which in turn are based on the metrics defined in [23] and [19]. These questions are divided into 3 sections, a section dedicated to the role played by the student; another dedicated to the role of the developed cognitive system; and the last one based on the robot and its development (see Fig. 3).

Part of the questions were simple yes or no questions, these questions were asked to measure certain features of the interaction developed. We asked the participants what they thought was the interaction regarding the difficulty in performing the tasks, did they find it difficult or not, and if the questions asked to the NAO were adequately resolved (see Fig. 4).

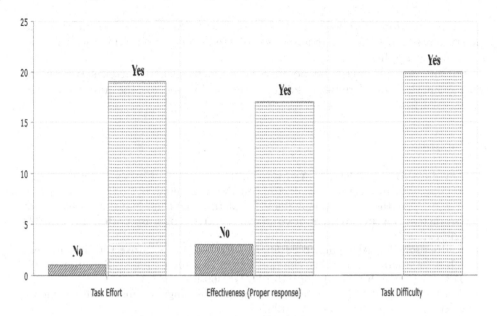

Fig. 4. System metrics results

6 Conclusions

In the Question Answering experiments, we observed the great potential of multilingual pre-trained models to obtain state-of-the-art metrics fine-tuning them with a new Spanish dataset [6]. The multilingual models are m-BERT, XLM-R and XLM, but only the first two had good performances, having as good results as the creator of the Spanish dataset. The authors fine-tuned the whole Spanish SQuAD 1.1 and obtained a result of 77, 6 for the F-score in the XQuAD test dataset. In our experiments, we passed this metric with the XLM-R, where we obtained a 77, 9 in the F-score. Although, we did not exceed all the metrics showed in [6], we have similar results to the authors for their fine-tuning with the m-BERT. For MLQA dataset they obtained a 68, 1 in F1 and 48, 3 in EM, and finally, for the XQuAD dataset, they got a 77, 6 in F1 and 61, 8 in EM. Our experiments took between 1 and 3 h to train the models in SQuAD-small, and between 3 and 7 h to train using the whole SQuAD.

In the HRI experiments part, we discussed the survey findings and the students' use of the application. As already mentioned, the questions asked were based on the metrics described in [23] and [19]. Our main discovery is that students received this solution in a positive way, finding it practical and easy to use and interact, as can be seen in Fig. 3. Also, according to Fig. 4, the interaction was adopted in a positive way by the participants, we identified two critical points during this, first of all, regarding what is the task effectiveness, all the questions were answered appropriately, and if a solution could not be found, the student was notified and regarding the interaction effort, due to being a simple interaction there were no major complications between the solution and the students, 100% of the participants indicated that they found it easy to interact with our application.

Furthermore, it might be possible to extract optimal patterns (i.e., itemsets) from the Squad dataset [28] or build a skycube for the aforementioned metrics [26,27].

References

1. Alenljung, B., Lindblom, J., Andreasson, R., Ziemke, T.: User experience in social human-robot interaction. Int. J. Ambient Comput. Intell. **8**(2), 12–31 (2017)
2. Aly, A., Griffiths, S.S., Stramandinoli, F.: Metrics and benchmarks in human-robot interaction: recent advances in cognitive robotics. Cogn. Syst. Res. **43**, 313–323 (2017)
3. Andreasson, R., Alenljung, B., Billing, E., Lowe, R.: Affective touch in human-robot interaction: conveying emotion to the nao robot. Int. J. Soc. Robot. **10**, 473–491 (2018). https://doi.org/10.1007/s12369-017-0446-3
4. Artetxe, M., Ruder, S., Yogatama, D.: On the cross-lingual transferability of monolingual representations. In: ACL (2020)
5. Bertacchini, F., Bilotta, E., Pantano, P.S.: Shopping with a robotic companion. Comput. Hum. Behav. **77**, 382–395 (2017)
6. Carrino, C.P., Costa-jussà, M.R., Fonollosa, J.A.R.: Automatic Spanish translation of the squad dataset for multilingual question answering. CoRR abs/1912.05200 (2019)
7. Conneau, A., et al.: Unsupervised cross-lingual representation learning at scale. In: ACL (2020)
8. Conneau, A., Lample, G.: Cross-lingual language model pretraining. In: NeurIPS (2019)
9. Dautenhahn, K.: Methodology and themes of human-robot interaction: a growing research field. Int. J. Adv. Robot. Syst. **4**, 103–108 (2007)
10. Devlin, J., Chang, M., Lee, K., Toutanova, K.: BERT: pre-training of deep bidirectional transformers for language understanding. In: NAACL-HLT (2019)
11. Gao, J., Galley, M., Li, L.: Neural approaches to conversational AI. Found. Trends Inf. Retr. **13**, 127–298 (2019)
12. Joshi, M., Chen, D., Liu, Y., Weld, D.S., Zettlemoyer, L., Levy, O.: SpanBERT: improving pre-training by representing and predicting spans. Trans. ACL **8**, 64–77 (2020)
13. Lan, Z., Chen, M., Goodman, S., Gimpel, K., Sharma, P., Soricut, R.: ALBERT: a lite BERT for self-supervised learning of language representations. In: ICLR (2020)
14. Lee, J., et al.: BioBERT: a pre-trained biomedical language representation model for biomedical text mining. Bioinformatics **36**(4), 1234–1240 (2020)
15. Lewis, P.S.H., Oguz, B., Rinott, R., Riedel, S., Schwenk, H.: MLQA: evaluating cross-lingual extractive question answering. In: ACL (2020)
16. Lindblom, J., Andreasson, R.: Current challenges for UX evaluation of human-robot interaction. In: Schlick, C., Trzcieliński, S. (eds.) Advances in Ergonomics of Manufacturing: Managing the Enterprise of the Future. AISC, vol. 490, pp. 267–277. Springer, Cham (2016). https://doi.org/10.1007/978-3-319-41697-7_24
17. Liu, Y., et al.: RoBERTa: a robustly optimized BERT pretraining approach. CoRR abs/1907.11692 (2019)

18. Mattioli, T., Vendittelli, M.: Interaction force reconstruction for humanoid robots. IEEE Robot. Autom. Lett. **2**(1), 282–289 (2017)
19. Murphy, R.R., Schreckenghost, D.: Survey of metrics for human-robot interaction. In: HRI. IEEE/ACM (2013)
20. Pires, T., Schlinger, E., Garrette, D.: How multilingual is multilingual BERT? In: ACL (2019)
21. Quarteroni, S.: Natural language processing for industry - ELCA's experience. Informatik Spektrum **41**, 105–112 (2018). https://doi.org/10.1007/s00287-018-1094-1
22. Rajpurkar, P., Zhang, J., Lopyrev, K., Liang, P.: SQuAD: 100,000+ questions for machine comprehension of text. In: EMNLP (2016)
23. Steinfeld, A., et al.: Common metrics for human-robot interaction. In: HRI (2006)
24. Szűcs, V., Karolyi, G., Tatar, A., Magyar, A.: Voice controlled humanoid robot based movement rehabilitation framework. In: CogInfoCom (2018)
25. Tiutiunnyk, S., Dyomkin, V.: Context-based question-answering system for the Ukrainian language. In: CEUR Workshop Proceedings (2020)
26. Ugarte, W., Boizumault, P., Loudni, S., Crémilleux, B.: Computing skypattern cubes. In: ECAI (2014)
27. Ugarte, W., Boizumault, P., Loudni, S., Crémilleux, B.: Computing skypattern cubes using relaxation. In: ICTAI. IEEE (2014)
28. Ugarte, W., Boizumault, P., Loudni, S., Crémilleux, B.: Modeling and mining optimal patterns using dynamic CSP. In: ICTAI. IEEE (2015)
29. Vaswani, A., et al.: Attention is all you need. In: NIPS (2017)
30. Yang, Z., Dai, Z., Yang, Y., Carbonell, J.G., Salakhutdinov, R., Le, Q.V.: XLNet: generalized autoregressive pretraining for language understanding. In: NeurIPS (2019)
31. Zaib, M., Sheng, Q.Z., Zhang, W.E.: A short survey of pre-trained language models for conversational AI-a new age in NLP. In: ACSW. ACM (2020)
32. Zhang, Y., Chen, X., Ai, Q., Yang, L., Croft, W.B.: Towards conversational search and recommendation: system ask, user respond. In: CIKM. ACM (2018)

Peruvian Citizens Reaction to Reactiva Perú Program: A Twitter Sentiment Analysis Approach

Rosmery Ramos-Sandoval(✉) ⓘ

Centre for Interdisciplinary Science and Society Studies – CIICS, Universidad de Ciencias y Humanidades, Lima, Peru
rramos@uch.edu.pe

Abstract. The internet is part of people's daily lives, and social networking sites (SNSs) may provide insights into how people perceive government actions. The present case study contributes to the debate concerning SNSs as an alternative communication tool between citizens and politicians in terms of information about the policies that rule citizens' lives. To reach this goal, we explored the role of Twitter sentiment analysis as a means of monitoring reactions to *Reactiva Perú*, a program implemented by the Peruvian Government in response to the COVID-19 economic crisis. The findings suggest that SNSs may become an alternative source of information for policymakers to capture citizens' reactions to implemented policies. Implications and possible strategies are discussed at an empirical level.

Keywords: Twitter sentiment analysis · Social networking sites · Natural language processing · Opinion mining

1 Introduction

Digital platforms and devices are part of daily life and are used for different purposes. According to recent reports, there are approximately 3.80 billion active social media users around the world, and the number of users is expected to reach 9.2% in annual average growth in the coming year [1]. Therefore, social networking sites are online environments where users can express their feelings and/or opinions about a particular topic, and users' shared content may contain extended reflections of what happens in society [2].

Currently, the COVID-19 crisis and lockdown measures have lead users to express their points of view and feelings. As a result of this, SNSs may capture politicians' and citizens' interactions as well as the acceptance of public policies related to the COVID-19 pandemic. For instance, previous research has found that SNSs could represent unprecedented real-time connectivity, monitoring almost every human activity [3]. Furthermore, in these particular times in which digital devices are part of peoples' lives, the massive use of SNSs (e.g., Facebook, Twitter, Instagram) may provide data about how governmental actions have been received by citizens during the pandemic.

© Springer Nature Switzerland AG 2021
J. A. Lossio-Ventura et al. (Eds.): SIMBig 2020, CCIS 1410, pp. 18–28, 2021.
https://doi.org/10.1007/978-3-030-76228-5_2

Due to social distance measures in the Peruvian context, people may be more likely to conduct internet-related activities. For example, according to the Digital 2020 report [1], there were 24 million internet users in Peru until January 2020, while the numbers of social media users from platforms like Facebook were around 22 million, or 1.24 million from Twitter. In this regard, SNSs may provide insights into how some government strategies are perceived by citizens.

Furthermore, recent evidence suggests that active Twitter users worldwide employ these platforms as alternative communication channels, showing Twitter's potential as a tool to follow meaningfully what is happening in real-time, becoming a place for debate surrounding news, politics, business, and entertainment [4–9]. Therefore, Twitter may represent an instrumental platform that captures the user's responses to public policies.

1.1 Sentiment Analysis with Twitter

SNSs such as Twitter hold increasing potential to enable the extraction of subjective information from the text in natural languages, such as opinions and sentiments, during specific periods of time. According to Fersini [10], the transition process from social networks to *online* social networks enables people to talk about their emotions, opinions, and thoughts. For this reason, the digital activity of individuals and companies is currently being studied by researchers and official institutions as a source of information to monitor and understand underlying socio-economic behaviors [11]. Furthermore, social media technologies such as Twitter, may "push" content to their users, becoming a complex and interactive systematization of different information flows [7]. Then, Twitter becomes an alternative tool for monitoring citizens' reactions, thoughts, and emotions, thus generating knowledge to support decision-makers in less time than it would traditionally take to evaluate the acceptance of public policies.

This is in line with Thelwall's [12, Ch. 7] point that the contributions of users to microblogging services like Twitter are particularly useful for monitoring public opinions because: (a) they can be analyzed from a temporal perspective; (b) they are easy to create, so in theory, anyone with access to the internet could create them; and (c) they are widely accessible to researchers. In addition, according to Gruzd et al. [13], Twitter connections tend to be less about friends or family and more about connecting with other people for information sharing purposes. Therefore, the sentiments expressed on Twitter may reflect the user's mood, public concerns, and spaces for discussion about the involved policies in a variety of contexts.

Identifying Twitter sentiments about any specific topic has been a growing area of research. In this respect, Twitter sentiments have been assessed through sentiment analysis (SA) classification techniques, which have the potential to create knowledge that could be employed by decision support systems or decision-makers [4, 9, 14]. Furthermore, the polarity classification in SA, which aims to quantify "what people think," detects positive, negative, or neutral text [10]. In line with this, Ceron et al. [9] state that the information that can be obtained from SA has benefits, such as low costs and the ability to obtain information about trends. Then, classifying opinions posted by people in SNSs may contribute to monitoring citizens' receptivity for public policy proposes, considering that positive or negative opinions of a given proposal could influence implementation success. In addition, these observations make Twitter SA an efficient, innovative tool to understand the underlying complexity of messages in SNSs and promote new approaches to using social networks as an information source in the Peruvian context.

1.2 Applicability of Sentiment Analysis in the Field of Public Policy

As mentioned before, the exponential diffusion of social media could facilitate the citizens' interactions with government representatives, becoming not only a channel of direct interaction but also a space where institutional barriers seem to disappear. According to Maireder and Ausserhofer [12, Ch. 23], political conversations on Twitter represent an opportunity for political actors to connect with other professionals as well as active political citizens. Likewise, Ceron and Negri [4], point to Twitter as a data source for "monitoring public opinion" toward proposed policies. The aforementioned positions highlight the opportunity that SNSs can provide, mainly for political actors, by having an immediate monitoring tool regarding the programs proposed as a response to societal problems.

Furthermore, policy processes are embedded in specific political actors. Previous studies have found that political opinion leaders can mobilize followers by re-tweets and amplify their opinions through SNSs [6]. In contrast, some scholars pointed on the risk about, how online communication ecosystems could open the door not only to polarizing messages but also to populist messages [15]. Thereby, it will become relevant monitoring the interaction between political opinion leaders and citizens, focusing on the effects of deliberative discourse through public discussion, and how these may drive citizens public acceptance or rejection to public policies.

This article aims to contribute to the debate on whether SNSs have the potential to discuss the formulation and implementation of public policies. For this purpose, a case study was designed to explore twitter user's opinions of current public policies proposed during the COVID-19 by the Peruvian Government, to reactivate the national economy. The paper is organized as follows. Section 2 describes the case study. Section 3 discusses the method for dataset collection and processing, also the sentiment analysis classification technique employed in the paper. While Sect. 4 presents the results on citizen's opinions about the public policy under review, and the contrast of the results with some results obtained through traditional surveys. Section 5 shows the conclusions of the case study.

2 "Reactiva Perú"

In March 2020, Peruvian President Martin Vizcarra declared a State of National Emergency as a result of the COVID-19 pandemic. Among the measures taken, the Government ordered the lockdown of the entire country, paralyzing all activities at a national level. In response to the economic impact of this measure, the Government proposed *Reactiva Perú* program [16]. The aim of *Reactiva Perú* was to give funds to companies facing payment delays to their workers and suppliers to ensure their continuity.

As a result of this, several opinions for and against the program have been spreading since its publication. According to The Central Reserve Bank of Peru, the first part of the program executed 30 billion *soles* (8.5 billion dollars approx.) in June. The program distributed funds among 51,440 micro and small businesses, representing 70% of the total beneficiaries. From this total, 4% of them were large and 26% medium-sized companies [17] respectively.

Because of this, an evaluation of users opinions and acceptance of this measure have been spread into SNSs such as Twitter. Consequently, this gives the baseline of the acceptance of *Reactiva Perú* proposed by the Peruvian Government.

3   Method

According to Boiy and Moens [18], Machine Learning techniques for sentiment classification gain interest in research because of their capability to characterize and model many features. The method proposed was based on the assumption that people's opinions posted on Twitter during the first phase of *Reactiva Perú* program, allow characterized polarity opinions about the government response to face the economic crisis.

This study used Machine Learning techniques to classify tweets according to their sentiment, which is one of the most prospecting methods in Natural Language Processing (NLP). It has been used a supervised sentiment classification technique, lean on machine learning whit Naive Bayes (NB), usually applied to reviews and Web discourses [19]. Whit this aim, the following steps were taken: (1) scraped #ReactivaPerú tweets posted on Twitter, (2) pre-processing datasets, and (3) classification process under a Naive Bayes approach.

3.1   Scraping Tweets #ReactivaPerú from Twitter

The first step is to get the dataset; tweets were downloaded with all the possible combinations of the hashtags: #ReactivaPerú, #ReactivaPeru, #Reactiva. From hereafter, *#ReactivaPerú* will be mentioned to refer to all hashtag options used in the study. The tweets were compiled by scrapping using the Python package named GetOldTweets[1]; this package allows us to retrieve tweets older than a week. The information extracted from each specific tweet was the date-time in UTC and text, mentions, and hashtags in str format.

The data gathering process proposed in this paper can be applied to specifying the query search from mentions and hashtags: "*#ReactivaPerú*", which were combined with the date-time specification, extracting tweets posted between April 6, 2020, and June 12, 2020. A total of 5,000 tweets related to "*#ReactivaPerú*" were extracted. Figure 1 shows #ReactivaPerú tweets frequency posted by day, exhibiting erratic patterns throughout the consultation period.

---

[1] https://github.com/Jefferson-Henrique/GetOldTweets-python

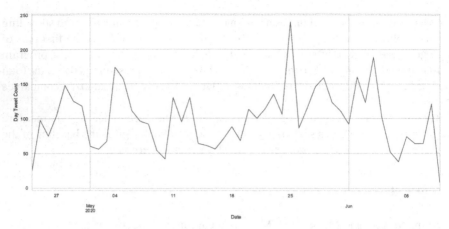

Fig. 1. #ReactivaPerú tweets frequency count by day, April 6 to June 12, 2020.

3.2 Pre-procesing

Pre-processing was to convert words to vectors. After the conversion, train text was imported from the Corpus TASS trained [20], and the texts from the #ReactivaPerú dataset. The Corpus TASS [20] contained over 70,000 tweets written in Spanish with topics of politics, economy, communication, mass media, and culture between November 2011 and March 2012. Tweets extracted were posted in Spanish as the pre-processing task is relevant when the dataset is classified as multilingual [21]. This step has the aim to reduce noise in the text and improve the performance and accuracy of the sentiment classification. With this in mind, NLP techniques as 1) tokenization, which are used to break the text down into words and symbols [22]; 2) stop words, to remove common words in the given language do not carry important meaning; and 3) stemming, which is a task used to transform words into their roots words [21], explores applying the Python's library, Natural Language Toolkit[2] (NLTK).

After classification processes, natural language analysis was used, such as tokenization and stemming. Tokenization process allows us to exclude the presence of special Twitter tokens like user names, hashtags, URLs, emoticons (e.g., @MEF_Peru; #Día40; https://; ☺), and punctuations (e.g., "¿"; "\"; "…"). Stemmers algorithms remove morphological affixes from words, leaving only the "stems" words. The stemming process applied to transform words in this study was supported by the Snowball stemmer algorithm, which is adequate for the Spanish language.

3.3 Polarity Classification

The study performs a subjectivity classification on individual sentences, obtained from people's opinions posted on Twitter, during the first phase of *Reactiva Perú* program. In this regard, it was proposed a machine learning method [23], which applies a binary classification task of labelling an opinionated text as expressing either an overall positive or an

---

[2] https://www.nltk.org/book/.

overall negative opinion, determining a polarity classification. The method employed to text polarity classification was the Naive Bayes technique, which is a supervised machine learning approach, that allows us to build classification models automatically. According to Dhande and Patnaik [24], Naive Bayes is simple and accurate on text classification. Although, Bird et al. [25], noticed that in Naive Bayes classifiers, every feature gets a say in determining which label should be assigned to a given input value. Whereas to Fersini [10], most of the work regarding polarity classification usually considers text as unique information to infer sentiments. Consequently, this technique provides an optimal and accuracy option in the process of polarity classification text under assessment.

Naive Bayes Classifiers. In Naive Bayes classifiers, every feature gets a say in determining which label should be assigned to a given input value [25]. Then, in text classification, Naive Bayes is a probabilistic classifier, where c is a specific class, and t is the text want to classify. The Bayes Theorem (1) predicted approach, were the baseline to the Naive Bayes classifier. In Bayes theorem $P(c)$ and $P(t)$ are the prior probabilities of this class and this text, respectably, while $P(t|c)$ is the posterior probability, the text t appears given this classification c. Therefore, based on Bayes theorem, it can find the probability of occurrence of c, since t has occurred.

$$P(c|t) = (P(t|c)P(c))/(P(t)) \tag{1}$$

Under independent assumptions of the Bayes Theorem, this case study it can be found the probability of the assignment of a sentiment class c, which might be positive or negative, given that tweet t occurrence, assuming that the predictors and features are independent, and the presence of one particular feature does not affect the other. Therefore, this study focus on the availability of the Corpus TASS [20] with polarity labels, to detect the polarity of the test text data, pointed on subjective parts of the text in which sentiment is explicitly expressed. Then, this learning method takes the training set m as input and returns the learned classification function γ (Fig. 2).

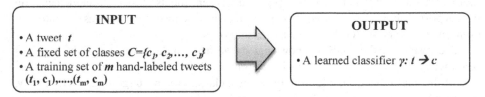

INPUT
- A tweet t
- A fixed set of classes $C=\{c_1, c_2,..., c_j\}$
- A training set of m hand-labeled tweets $(t_1, c_1),.....,(t_m, c_m)$

OUTPUT
- A learned classifier $\gamma: t \rightarrow c$

Fig. 2. The learning method modelled in the case study.

4 Results

The purpose of this Twitter SA study case was to determine the positive or negative user's response to the governmental program *#ReactivaPerú*. The author performed a classification technique over the opinions posted on twitter.

From the implementation of the first phase from *Reactiva Perú* program, this proposal, have been observed by citizens. In this regard, this study analyzed opinions posted on Twitter and distinguished polarity reactions concerning the program proposed by the Government as a response to the economic effects of the Covid-19 crisis.

As mentioned above, the frequency of #ReactivaPerú tweets exhibited erratic patterns throughout the consultation period. Then, from the pre-processing phase, Fig. 3, shows an idea of the frequency from the most common words mentioned on tweets posted by users about the #ReactivaPerú program.

Fig. 3. Frequently mentioned tweets from the #ReactivaPerú dataset.

4.1   What Do Citizens Think About #*ReactivaPerú*?

After training the model proposed, an accuracy rate of 80.47% was obtained, showing an optimal performance in terms of classification. Furthermore, Fig. 4 rating scores of 14.51% positive (P) and 85.49% negative (N) sentiments classification, detected on tweets posted about the *Reactiva Perú* program, quantifying the proportions on sentiment opinions predicted under the Naive Bayes approach.

The results of the analysis show that in the first phase of the program, Negative sentiment is prevailing over the positive opinions. Table 1 presents an overview of the lists of the randomized sample from tweets text classification, suggesting in a first view, the distribution of funding as the source of polarization.

The results of tweets classified as "Positive" or "Negative" summarized in Fig. 5, shows specific patterns in the first phase of the program. It is worth mentioning that it was only possible to identify patterns of positive positions until the first days of June, this period is adjusted with the beginning of the decrease in lockdown measures in Peru. In addition, the rebound of tweets activity is quite visible on May 24, 2020, which coincidently was the date of the last extension of the Peruvian lockdown announced by the Government. In conclusion, the publication of negative opinions was regular throughout the period under evaluation; nonetheless, since the reduction of the restrictions, it was possible to observe a continuous decrease in negative daily publications (Fig. 5).

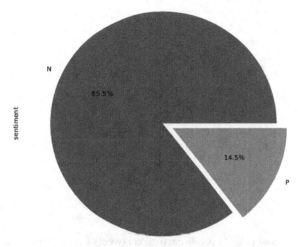

Fig. 4. Distribution of #ReactivaPerú Twitter Sentiment.

Table 1. Results from the Naive Bayes algorithm classification

Tweet text	Sentiment classification
('El programa Reactiva Perú es todo un éxito!!', nan)	P
('Reactiva Perú: Sunat facilita información a mipymes para acceder a créditos preferentes', nan)	P
('Reactiva Perú: BCRP completó la primera etapa de subastas del programa de garantías https://dlvr.it/RYSYhq #Economía', nan)	P
('Ayer recibí la noticia de que mi pequeña empresa, accedió al programa Reactiva Perú…pensé que no se daría. Gracias!!!', nan)	P
('El plan Reactiva Peru es una burla, los bancos le dan el dinero a sus clientes deudores para que no se hundan y sigan pagando su deuda con ellos… a los demás ni los miran.', nan)	N
('Y el reactiva Perú…. Cuantos millones los premiaron a estos sinvergüenzas desinformadores… Tienen miedo al socialismo que están implantando, por eso quieren fugar con sus millones.', nan)	N
('#ladrones políticos y mafias empresariales del Perú se reparten los fondos del estado con el cuento de reactiva Perú miles de millones de soles que a los.mas pobres…', nan)	N
('Los bancos y cajas están dando créditos sólo a "sus clientes" siendo que los fondos de #ReactivaPeru son fondos del Estado estos deben de abarcar a un abanico amplio de micro y pequeñas empresas sin discriminación con el cumplimiento de los requisitos de la norma legal', nan)	N

P = Positive; N = Negative.

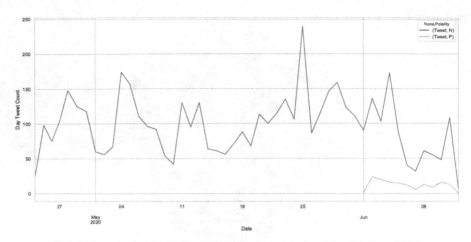

Fig. 5. Trends of polarity for #ReactivaPerú tweets from April to June 2020.

This finding has been in line compared with the output obtained by traditional surveys carried out by a survey company, reported in May [26] and June [27] 2020, the "National Urban Survey- *Encuesta Nacional Urbana*" (Ipsos Perú). Table 2 illustrates the comparison between the last surveys published and sentiment analysis reported.

Table 2. Comparison between traditional surveys and sentiment analysis of Twitter.

Item	Twitter SA	Survey[a] May-20	Survey[b] June-20
Date	6 Apr–12 Jun 2020	14–15 May 2020	11–12 Jun 2020
Rate of *Reactiva Perú* program opinions	- Positive: 14.51% - Negative: 85.49%	The Government main achievement: - 1%, having created the *Reactiva Perú* program as a support for companies	The Government performance in the field of economic reactivation: - 7%, are doing very well

[a] Ipsos Perú: Encuesta Nacional Urbana, May 2020.
[b] Ipsos Perú: Encuesta Nacional Urbana, June 2020.

From the comparison in Table 2, it has been identified low rates of positive response respect to the *Reactiva Perú* program and economic recovery policies overall, as patter commons. Therefore, it is possible to verify both traditional surveys, and information gathered from social networks, the citizen's low expectancies for the program in this first phase. The comparison between the results obtained and the traditional sources of information is used as a method of control [9], demonstrating whether the results obtained under the SA approach can be compared with widely accepted opinion polls.

5 Conclusions

The study gathered 5,000 tweets during 67 days, taking a quasi-real-time survey of the perception that citizens had of *"Reactiva Peru"* program. The study case has the expectancy to contribute with the professional debate concerning the potentiality of the SNSs platforms as an alternative communication model to empower the relationship that citizens could have with policy decisions.

The present study modelled an adaptation of Sentiment Analysis in the Peruvian context and obtained high rates of accuracy. The model monitored the first phase of the *Reactiva Perú* program and showed that negative opinions were prevailing through the consultation period, although, positive opinions were listed at the end. It is important to bear in mind the possible growth of negative responses among citizens because the Peruvian Government insisted on keeping the lockdown in the entire country.

These findings may help to understand that SNSs may become an alternative source of information for policymakers to capture citizen's reactions concerning the implementation of public policies. Although, further work is required to minimize biases inherent to social media data collection, considering that users' populations in social media may not be representative of the country's citizens, users of public policies in evaluation.

Limitations of the present study may concern the lower accessibility rates to SNSs from the target population in the study case. Moreover, since the study did not focus on the user's location, demographic information could be contrasted in future research.

References

1. We Are Social: Digital 2020: Global Digital Overview (2020)
2. Blazquez, D., Domenech, J.: Big data sources and methods for social and economic analyses. Technol. Forecast. Soc. Change **130**, 99–113 (2018)
3. Meshi, D., Tamir, D.I., Heekeren, H.R.: The emerging neuroscience of social media. Trends Cogn. Sci. **19**(12), 771–782 (2015)
4. Ceron, A., Negri, F.: The 'social side' of public policy: monitoring online public opinion and its mobilization during the policy cycle. Policy Internet **8**(2), 131–147 (2016)
5. Stier, S., Schünemann, W.J., Steiger, S.: Of activists and gatekeepers: temporal and structural properties of policy networks on Twitter. New Media Soc. **20**(5), 1910–1930 (2018)
6. Recuero, R., Zago, G., Soares, F.: Using social network analysis and social capital to identify user roles on polarized political conversations on twitter. Soc. Media Soc. **5**(2), 205630511984874 (2019)
7. Pond, P.: Twitter time: a temporal analysis of tweet streams during televised political debate. Telev. New Media **17**(2), 142–158 (2016)
8. Vergeer, M.: Adopting, networking, and communicating on twitter: a cross-national comparative analysis. Soc. Sci. Comput. Rev. **35**(6), 698–712 (2017)
9. Ceron, A., Curini, L., Iacus, S.M., Porro, G.: Every tweet counts? How sentiment analysis of social media can improve our knowledge of citizens' political preferences with an application to Italy and France. New Media Soc. **16**(2), 340–358 (2014)
10. Fersini, E.: Sentiment analysis in social networks: a machine learning perspective. In: Sentiment Analysis in Social Networks, pp. 20–25. Elsevier Inc. (2017)
11. Blazquez, D., Domenech, J., Garcia-Alvarez-Coque, J.-M.: Assessing technology platforms for sustainability with web data mining techniques. Sustainability **10**(12), 4497 (2018)

12. Weller, K., Bruns, A., Burgess, J., Merja, M., Cornelius, P.: Twitter and Society, vol. 52, no. 2. Peter Lang, Bern (2014)
13. Gruzd, A., Wellman, B., Takhteyev, Y.: Imagining Twitter as an imagined community. Am. Behav. Sci. **55**(10), 1294–1318 (2011)
14. Pozzi, F.A., Fersini, E., Messina, E., Liu, B.: Challenges of sentiment analysis in social networks: an overview. In: Sentiment Analysis in Social Networks, vol. 1, pp. 1–11. Elsevier Inc. (2017)
15. Gil de Zúñiga, H., Koc Michalska, K., Römmele, A.: Populism in the era of twitter: how social media contextualized new insights into an old phenomenon. New Media Soc. **22**(4), 585–594 (2020)
16. Diario Oficial El Peruano: *DECRETO LEGISLATIVO N⁰ 1455*. pp. 2–6, Lima (2020)
17. Banco Central de Reserva del Perú: Nota Informativa. Lima (2020)
18. Boiy, E., Moens, M.-F.: A Machine learning approach to sentiment analysis in multilingual web texts. Inf. Retr. **12**, 526–558 (2009)
19. Abbasi, A., Chen, H., Salem, A.: Sentiment analysis in multiple languages: feature selection for opinion classification in web forums. ACM Trans. Inf. Syst. **26**(3), 12 (2008)
20. Villena-román, J., Martínez-cámara, E., Lana-serrano, S., González-cristóbal, J.C.: TASS - workshop on sentiment analysis at SEPLN TASS - Taller de Análisis de Sentimientos en la SEPLN. Proces. del Leng. Nat. **50**, 37–44 (2013)
21. Dashtipour, K., Poria, S., Hussain, A., Cambria, E.: Multilingual sentiment analysis: state of the art and independent comparison of techniques. Cogn. Comput. **8**(4), 757–771 (2016)
22. Kouloumpis, E., Wilson, T., Moore, J.: Twitter sentiment analysis : the good the bad and the OMG!. In: Fifth International AAAI Conference on Weblogs and Social Media, pp. 538–541 (2011)
23. Pang, B., Lee, L.: Opinion mining and sentiment analysis. Found. Trends Inf. Retr. **2**(1–2), 1–135 (2008)
24. Dhande, L., Patnaik, G.: Review of sentiment analysis using Naive Bayes and neural network classifier. Int. J. Sci. Eng. Technol. Res. **03**(07), 1110–1113 (2014)
25. Bird, S., Klein, E., Loper, E.: Natural Language Processing With Python: Analyzing Text with the Natural Language Toolkit. O'reilly Media, Inc. (2009)
26. Ipsos Perú: Encuesta Nacional Urbana. Informe de Resultados Opinión Data – Mayo, Lima (2020)
27. Ipsos Perú: Encuesta Nacional Urbana. Informe de Resultados Opinión Data – Junio, Lima (2020)

Twitter Early Prediction of Preferences and Tendencies Based in Neighborhood Behavior

Emanuel Meriles[✉], Martín Ariel Domínguez[✉],
and Pablo Gabriel Celayes[✉]

FaMAF, Universidad Nacional de Cordoba, Córdoba, Argentina
{meriles,mdoming,celayes}@famaf.unc.edu.ar

Abstract. In recent years, social networks have become increasingly massive. Consequently, they are a fundamental source of information and a powerful tool to spread ideas and opinions. Based on Twitter, this paper studies the problem of predicting the retweet preference of a user for a given tweet, considering how the tweet has been shared by that user's environment. It also addresses the more global problem of predicting whether a tweet will be popular, based on the retweet behavior of central users. For both problems, we explore the evolution of prediction quality depending on the amount of information available over the time since a tweet is created, and derive insights about the trade-off between elapsed time and prediction performance.

For the user retweet preference problem, this social prediction model achieves, for example, around 63.76% on F_1 score by using the first 15 min information, 75.2% by 4 h, and 86.08% without considering any time window. In the case of popularity prediction, the model achieve scores of 65.67% with 60 min of information, 74.4% with 4 h, and 80.73% with no time window restriction, using the behaviour 15% of users considered as influencers. All these results are obtained without considering the content of the tweets. Next, we incorporate features based on FastText word embeddings to represent the content of tweets. While such models alone attain an F_1 of around barely 50% for preferences and popularity prediction, combined with social models, they improve the popularity prediction, generally, more than 4%. For preference prediction, the Fast-Text model is more useful in small time spans.

We conclude that it is possible to reasonably predict the preference of a user retweet or how massive a publication will be, using only the information available during the first 30–60 min.

Keywords: Retweet prediction · Social network analysis · Machine learning · FastText · Word embeddings

1 Introduction

In the last years, social media platforms such as Twitter, Facebook, and Instagram have gained massive adoption. They have become a central presence in

© Springer Nature Switzerland AG 2021
J. A. Lossio-Ventura et al. (Eds.): SIMBig 2020, CCIS 1410, pp. 29–44, 2021.
https://doi.org/10.1007/978-3-030-76228-5_3

everyday life and public discussions, with a strong impact in the way people express themselves, get informed, and influence each other. One of the most prominent of these social networks is Twitter, an online real-time microblogging platform that enables its users to post, read and share short messages of up to 280 characters, known as tweets. Every time a user publishes a tweet, Twitter attaches to it a unique identifier and a creation timestamp. A frequently used function on the bird net is the "retweet", which allows a user to republish a tweet from another user within her own message stream (the "timeline"). A feature distinguishing Twitter from other popular social networks is that most of the shared content is public by default. Therefore, structured data, both about the way users interact with each other and the content that they share, is easily accessible through the official API. This is perhaps one of the main reasons why most research work is done on Twitter.

The influence of social media can be studied both at an individual and at a collective level. In the first case, efforts are concentrated in understanding how the preferences and behavior of a given user are shaped by their previous social media activity. On the other hand, collective phenomena can also be studied and analyzed seeking to understand the mechanisms that cause publications to become popular among greater audiences. In our previous research efforts, we have worked on formulations of both of these targets as predictive modelling problems. In [2], we studied the problem of predicting the content preferences of a user based on the preferences of her neighborhood. Namely, given a tweet, how much we can predict whether or not a user will retweet it based on the retweets it gets among its nearby social connections. In [12], we took these ideas to the community level predicting popularity of tweets instead of individual preferences, and replacing the immediate set of neighbours of a user with a set of influencers. This can be regarded as a sort of common or global neighborhood in the sense that everyone is, to some extent, exposed to the activity of these very visible users. Regardless of whether the goal is predicting individual or global preferences, in both cases it is possible to base the predictions on social information (who shared which content, and how they are connected to other users) or on content information (what is the content about, which topics and concepts are discussed). Both our previous works started off focusing on what can be learned purely from social interaction information, to then extend the models with information about the content by means of diverse Natural Language Processing techniques.

Beyond social interactions and content characteristics, time is the natural next dimension to explore when trying to deepen our understanding of the formation of social preferences. *Who* shares a piece of information and *what* it is about are important, but the impact of these factors is strongly determined by *when* the activity happens. In the present paper, we tackle the problems of retweet and trend prediction using only information available within a limited time window since the creation of the analyzed tweet. For example: five minutes since a tweet was created, is it feasible to effectively predict if a user will retweet it? Or, 10 min later, can we give an accurate estimation of whether or not it will become popular? Temporal information can also be included among the features for prediction, considering not only whether or not users retweet a tweet, but also when they do so. Extending our research in this way not only gives us a more profound understanding of the dynamics of social influence, but also makes the results much more applicable in an online early prediction setting, by providing us with a quantification of the trade-off between elapsed time and predictability.

The rest of this paper is structured as follows: Sect. 2 gives an overview of related works. Section 3 describes how we build the datasets from Twitter for our experiments. Section 4 describes time constrained models for prediction of retweet preference for individual users, while Sect. 5 introduces time constrained model for the prediction of popularity of a tweet. Finally, in Sect. 6 we present our conclusions and possible lines of future research.

2 Related Work

Along with the increased popularity and impact of social media, the research interest has grown both on modeling the preferences of users and the distribution of popular content. Many initial works focused on analyzing characteristics of the content and how they can be used to predict popularity and outreach [5, 10, 14]. Among these, [8] is more closely related to our study. They develop purely content-based models for predicting the likelihood of a given tweet being retweeted by general users.

Another approach to study preferences and influence in social media is to focus on the interactions and connections between users. In [2] we studied the prediction of retweets for a given user, using the behavior of users in her second degree social neighborhood (followed, and followed by followed) to build a classifier that determines whether or not she will *retweet* a given post. These models, based purely on social information, achieved a high predictive performance, with an average F_1 score of 87.6%. In this work, we also explored extending the model with content features for the cases where the purely social models were not performing well. By using a topic modeling algorithm specifically adapted to tweets (TwitterLDA), an average performance improvement of 1.7% was obtained.

In [12], we extended the previous work to the problem of predicting popularity within a community of users, instead of just individual preferences. The target here was to build classifiers that could identify if a given tweet would become popular or not, based only on the activity a selected set of influencers (i.e.: highly central and active users) had on it. This work also explored improvements incorporating embeddings-based features to represent the content and different algorithms for selecting user influencers. Same as the previous work, we first studied the performance of a purely social prediction, obtaining an F_1 score of 79.2%, using only the retweeting behavior of the top 10% most central and active users as influencers. Considering the content of the tweet and adding features based on FastText embeddings, increased the performance up to 86.7%.

In the present work, we set off to refine the previous studies to take the time of retweeting activity in consideration. Similarly to the approach proposed in our paper, [15] develops models to predict the popularity of a given tweet based on temporal information about the first minutes of activity, using a Bayesian approach. These models only use observations on the retweet times and the structure of the graph of retweets between users. [13] also explores the problem of early prediction of social activity but with a different goal: distinguishing tweets that become popular in an organic fashion from those that are sustained artificially by advertising or coordinated efforts like groups of bots or trolls.

3   Dataset

In this section, we describe the dataset used in this work for all experiments. The base dataset from previous work [2] could not be reused as a whole, because no information about the precise moment of publication of tweets was persisted during its tweet collection phase. We explain the construction of our dataset in two steps: first, building the social graph of users and, then, getting content shared by them.

3.1   Social Graph

To perform the experiments in this paper, we collected our data following the same steps detailed in previous work [2]. Data consists of Twitter users and the who-follows-whom relation between them. Even though we could have reused the data from the who-follows-whom relation from our previous experiments, we decided to rebuild the network with more recent connections, since otherwise there would have been a considerable time gap (around 2 years) between newly collected tweets and older social interaction information.

Back in our previous work, the idea was to create a representative subgraph of Twitter where all users would have a similar amount of social information about their neighborhood of connected users. The decision was to build a homogeneous network where each user has the same number of followed users. To this end, a two-step process was performed. Initially, a large enough *universe graph* was built, which was subsectionquently filtered to obtain a smaller but more homogeneous subgraph.

The *universe graph* was built starting with a singleton graph containing just one Twitter user account $\mathcal{U}_0 = \{u_0\}$ and performing 3 iterations of the following procedure: (1) Fetch all users followed by users in $\mathcal{U}_i$; (2) from that group, filter only those having at least 40 followers and following at least 40 accounts; (3) add filtered users and their edges to get an extended $\mathcal{U}_{i+1}$ graph. This process generated a *universe graph* $\mathcal{U} := \mathcal{U}_3$ with $2,926,181$ vertices and $10,144,158$ edges.

For the second step, in order to get a homogeneous network, a subgraph was extracted following the procedure below. Note that many users added in the last step might have no outgoing edges.

- We started off with a small sample of seed users S, consisting of users in $\mathcal{U}$ having out-degree 50, this is, users following exactly 50 other users.

- For each of those, we added their 50 most socially affine followed users. The affinity between two users was measured as the ratio between the number of users followed by both and the number of users followed by at least one of them.
- We repeated the last step for each newly added user until there were no more new users to add.

This filtering produced the final graph $\mathcal{G}$ with $5,589$ vertices and $245,694$ edges, called the homogeneous K-degree closure ($K = 50$ in this case) of S in the universe graph $\mathcal{U}$.

3.2   Content

The content dataset is composed of $9,441,950$ tweets. These tweets result from extracting the content written in Spanish from user's timelines in $\mathcal{G}$ for dates between September and October 2018. Also, in the beginning of the tweet collection process, we fetched every tweet from the past that the Twitter API would give us, which at that moment were 200 tweets on their timeline per user.

Let's call $\mathbf{T}$ to our set of tweets. The main difference between this dataset and the ones used in our previous works is that we have a publication timestamp for tweets and retweets. Let's denote with $\mathbf{T}^\theta$ the set of content available at timestamp θ, this will be used in the next section for building the retweet-time-window.

3.3   Retweet-Time-Window

As mentioned before, the main goal in this work is to reproduce our previous works introducing the idea of time windows. To do so, for each "original" tweet (that is, a tweet that is not a retweet of any previous tweet) we take time windows of different widths, always with the publication timestamp of the considered tweet as a starting point. Let θ_0 represent the exact moment in which an original tweet t was published by its author user u, we call θ_0 the window start timestamp. So, for any time ω, we define the *retweet-time-window* $\mathbf{rtw}(t, \omega)$, for tweet t and width ω as the set of all the retweets of t made by any other user, that happen before $\theta_0 + \omega$. We also need to define $\mathbf{RTW}(\omega)$ which is the union of all retweet-time-windows of width ω. Formally, $\mathbf{rtw}(t, \omega) := \mathtt{retweets}(t) \cap \mathbf{T}^{\mathtt{timestamp}(t)+\omega}$ and $\mathbf{RTW}(\omega) := \bigcup_{t \in \mathbf{T}_o} \mathbf{rtw}(t, \omega)$, where $\mathtt{timestamp}(t)$ is the time when t was published, $\mathtt{retweets}(t)$ are all the retweets of t among the users in our graph $\mathcal{G}$ and $\mathbf{T}_o$ is the set of all original tweets in $\mathbf{T}$.

User Selection: Inactive users will be omitted in this experiment because they are unpredictable by nature. We consider that a user in our dataset is passive if she has less than ten retweets in her timeline. Filtering those out leaves us with a set of only $3,911$ active users in $\mathcal{G}$. We restrict the analysis to those users, also removing content shared only by inactive users from $\mathcal{T}$.

4 Early Prediction of Retweet Preferences

In this section we extend the experiments from the previous work, [2], for the different retweet-time-windows using the new dataset described in Sect. 3. We make a summary from the work mentioned about how to build the model for prediction. Later, we describe how to select the users for prediction and how to build all the necessary datasets. We finish the section with the results describing the variation of predictive performance depending on the size of the chosen time window.

4.1 Experimental Setup

We aim to predict, for a given user u and a given *tweet* t, whether or not u will share t based on information about which users in the environment of u have retweeted t *so far*. Since the process of feature extraction, modeling, and parameter tuning is computationally expensive, these experiments are performed on a selected subset of users. We begin by describing the criterion with which these users were chosen. We then describe how we generate, for each user u, a neighborhood of users E_u and a set T_u of potentially interesting *tweets*. Then, we describe the feature extraction process based on T_u and the partitioning into sets of *training, tuning* and *evaluation*. Finally, we explain the process of training classifiers and tuning their parameters.

Users for Prediction: Following the methods applied in [2], but with the new data obtained in Sect. 3, we take the top 1000 users with the highest Katz centrality coefficient [6] in the graph in $\mathcal{G}$ and, on the other hand, the top 1000 users with the highest retweeting activity. We restrict our analysis to users belonging to both sets, which leaves us with a set U of 211 users. For comparison, in the previous work this selection consisted of 194 users.

User's Environment: We consider as environment a second degree of users which are followed by u. This is, we take all users (other than u herself) to 1 or 2 steps forward from u in the directed graph G, formally:

$$E_u = \left(\bigcup_{x \in \{u\} \cup \texttt{followed}(u)} \texttt{followed}(x) \right) - \{u\}.$$

Visible Tweets: The Twitter API doesn't provide explicit information about whether or not a user viewed a given tweet, but we can at least take a universe of *potentially viewed* tweets. We simply define this to be the set of all the tweets written or shared by the users followed by u. We exclude from this set those tweets *written* by u herself, since our focus is in recognizing interesting external content, and not on studying the generation of content from a particular user. Formally this set is defined as:

$$T_u := \left(\bigcup_{x \in \{u\} \cup \texttt{followed}(u)} \texttt{timeline}(x) \right) - \{t \in T | \texttt{author}(t) = u\},$$

where $\texttt{timeline}(x)$ is the set of tweets in T that were written or shared by x.

In addition, we need to define the subsets of tweets that are visible at time ω since their creation. Formally:

$\mathbf{RTW}_u(\omega) := \{t \in T_u | t \in \texttt{timeline}(x, \texttt{timestamp}(t) + \omega)$ for some $x \in \{u\} \cup \texttt{followed}(u)\}$, where $\texttt{timeline}(x, \theta)$ is the set of all those tweets in $\texttt{timeline}(x)$ that were written or shared by x until time θ.

Features for Users' Environment. Now, we can build the set of features and target vectors needed for the predictive model centered in user u until the time ω. Given $E_u = \{u_1, u_2, \ldots, u_n\}$, we define for each tweet $t \in \mathbf{RTW}_u(\omega)$ the following vector of boolean features:

$$v_u^\omega(t) := [\texttt{tw\_tl}(t, u_i, \omega)]_{i=1,\ldots,n},$$

$$\text{where } \texttt{tw\_tl}(t, u, \omega) := \begin{cases} 1 & t \in \texttt{timeline}(u, \texttt{timestamp} + \omega(t)) \\ 0 & \text{otherwise} \end{cases}$$

Note that the content of tweet t is not considered, we only include the information about who retweeted t until time ω since its creation.

Finally, the target vector $y_u(t)$ is a boolean vector which indicates, for each tweet $t \in \mathbf{RTW}_u(\omega)$, whether the user u has retweeted t.

Building Training, Tuning, and Testing Sets: As usual for any machine learning problem, a training and test set should be available. We also build a tuning set, to validate the models using unseen data, but different from the test set. To do so, we decide to randomly split T_u in 3 datasets for every user u: training (T_u^{tr}), tuning (T_u^{tu}), and evaluation (T_u^{ev}). The resulting sets contain 70%, 10% and 20% respectively, against T_u dataset. Let y_u^{tr}, y_u^{tu} and y_u^{ev} be the corresponding target for each of these datasets. Now, let $T_u^{tr}(\omega)$, $T_u^{tu}(\omega)$, $T_u^{ev}(\omega)$ be the corresponding previously defined training, tuning, and testing set with the information of the retweet-time-window ω, as we defined in the previous Section. Next, we show the available retweet information in $T_u^{tr}(\omega)$ for different windows ω. In the following list, we show the percentages of retweets available against the total amount of retweets for the full T_u^{tr} set without windows. These percentages are averages of our test users which have a total retweet activity of $4,468.38$ in T_u^{tr}.

1 s	2 s	10 s	30 s	2 m	5 m	15 m	30 m	60 m	90 m	120 m	240 m	540 m
0%	0%	0.1%	2.18%	8.72%	15.93%	27%	35.47%	44.89%	51%	55.66%	66.72%	78.28%

Adding Content Features: To analyze the content of each tweet, we decided to use the FastText [4] implementation of *word embeddings*. One of its most interesting features for our work is the possibility of assigning vectors to words not seen in the vectorization model training, looking for matches at the n-gram level of characters to vectorize those words out of vocabulary. This makes our vectorization more robust for handling misspelled words that are common on social networks. We use a 300-dimension pre-trained model, included in the FastText[1] library. Even though FastText only provides vector representations of single words, a vector representation of a document (tweet) can be easily obtained by taking the average of the vectors of its component words. In our previous work for prediction of single user retweets [2], we did not use FastText, but in Sect. 4.2, we report those experiments.

4.2   Results

We will now analyze the results obtained from training and evaluating user-centered classifier models using the feature vectors described in the previous section. We start with the purely social models and we finish with models that also consider the content.

Social Prediction: For the social model centered in a user, we use SVC[2] included in the scikit-learn [9] Python package, with `GridSearchCV` for hyper-parameter optimization.

Then, for each user u in our set U of test users, we evaluate the classifier obtained on the evaluation set, obtaining the results that can be seen in Table 1. Then, we considered different widths for the retweet-time-window, ($\omega \in \{2, 5, 15, 30, 60, 120, 240, 540\}$ minutes). This analysis seeks to answer the question of how much time is needed to accurately predict the retweet behavior for user u. This set of experiments shows, on the one hand, that when no window is considered the F_1 score obtained is 86.08; this result is comparable to the results obtained in the previous work [2] of 87.68. On the other hand, analyzing the results obtained for the different values of ω, we see that with only 60 min of data, we start off with a high performance of 69.08. From these results we can say that 60 min are enough to ensure an acceptable prediction.

Adding Content-Based Features. As we see in the results shown in Table 1, adding content features barely increases the performance between 0.15 and 1.62% for bigger time windows. However, the content plays a more significant role in prediction performance for smaller windows. It's an interesting result, given that in presence of less social behaviour information, for example for 2 min of

---

[1] https://FastText.cc/docs/en/crawl-vectors.html.

[2] `Support Vector Classifier`, which is the name given in `scikit-learn` to `Support Vector Machines` (SVM).

Table 1. Performance of social models over the set U of selected users.

Social model				Social + FastText			
Time	Av. F_1	Av. Prec.	Av. Rec.	Time	Av. F_1	AV. Prec.	Av. Rec.
2 m	53.76	43.18	80.09	2 m	55.38	47.95	78.65
5 m	60.45	45.01	93.42	5 m	62.05	48.82	92.17
15 m	63.76	49.32	91.45	15 m	64.47	51.43	90.36
30 m	66.29	52.93	89.83	30 m	66.89	53.61	89.94
60 m	69.08	57.19	88.35	60 m	70.05	58.04	88.60
90 m	70.64	59.96	87.27	90 m	71.36	60.57	87.82
120 m	72.07	62.43	86.45	120 m	72.61	62.83	86.91
240 m	75.2	68.24	84.98	240 m	75.52	69.02	84.98
540 m	78.65	75.96	82.61	540 m	78.92	76.28	82.61
n. w.	86.08	94.56	80.17	n. w.	86.24	93.78	80.93

information, the content features improve the F_1 measure by 1.5. It is important to note that in the previous work [2] FastText had not been used.

We remark that in our current work when we combine the social model with FastText, it hardly obtains a 0.15% of improvement in the F_1 score, relative to the pure social model. In our previous work, the improvement achieved by the Twitter LDA model combined with the social one did not reach 0.3%.

5   Early Prediction of Tendencies

In this section, we explain how to extend the experiments from previous work in [12], for different retweet-time-windows using the new dataset described in Sect. 3.

5.1   Experimental Setup

This section describes how to build models capable of accurately predicting the acceptance that a tweet t could have over a general audience of users ($U_G \subset \mathcal{G}$), based only on the reaction of a set of influencers ($U_I \subset \mathcal{G}$) to the publication. Also, we show how to set up models for this purpose over a selection of users and tweets from the ($\mathcal{G}, \mathbf{T}$) dataset defined before. Similar to the previous section, we start with predictive models based only on social features and then we extend them to use word embeddings features.

Social Prediction. The focus of this work is to predict if a tweet t will have enough retweets from general users, to consider it as *trending*, based on information about which of the influencers from U_I has shared it until the time defined.

We begin this section with an explanation of our filtering processes to select relevant users and tweets. After that, we detail how we proceed to get the influencers U_I from $\mathcal{G}$ and which algorithms we use to that purpose. Finally, we explain the feature extraction and dataset splitting for training and testing the models without any data overlap between those tasks.

Trending Tweets. We call a tweet *trending* if we consider it popular enough to possibly become a trending topic. This term is related to the number of retweets it earns over the general public U_G. To get the *golden value* of retweets considered enough to take a given tweet as popular, we built and analyzed a histogram of how many retweets each tweet in **T** receives.

Initially, we wanted to use the value in the 90th percentile as our golden value, but given the fact that most tweets are shared only by their author, this value turned out to equal 1. So we decided to discard all the tweets with less than 3 retweets, which caused this percentile to increase to 14, allowing us to implement more accurate models. Therefore, we consider a tweet *trending* if it was retweeted at least 14 times[3].

On the other hand, it is important to remark that the experiments carried out make sense only within the context of U_G users, keeping in mind that the goal of this work is to analyze the influence of the U_I group over general users. That is why we are interested only in those tweets from **T** that showed up on the *timeline* of at least one user in U_G, defining $T' := \left(\bigcup_{x \in U_G} timeline(x) \right)$.

Influencers Detection: As in the previous work, we decided to use the ideas included in [1], which proposes a combination of three types of features: network centrality, activity level, and profile features. Since we didn't have any extended profile information in our dataset, we focused on centrality and activity. This has the advantage of making the results more generalizable to other social networks without depending on specific information that might be available only in Twitter, and for certain users.

To measure the *centrality* of a user, we apply an average of metrics computed by the following algorithms: PageRank, Betweenness, Closeness, Eigenvector centrality, and Eccentricity included in `igraph` Python package [3]. The *activity* level of a user is computed simply as the average of the number of tweets and the number of retweets posted by users.

In the same line as in [12], to decide the best option to rank users as influencers, we compared different weighted combinations of centrality and activity measures, $\alpha * Centrality + (1 - \alpha) * Activity$, where α controls the importance given to *centrality*. We found that $\alpha = 0.5$, is the best choice.[4]

---

[3] In the previous dataset used in the experiments in [12] this number was 13.

[4] To compare the performance of these options a subset of 500 random tweets from **T** was set aside, as a tuning set. This sample called T_{SI} is removed from **T** to avoid considering them as part of the test set, where trending prediction models will be evaluated later.

This analysis reveals that a very central user would be useless for this study if she has a low level of activity and, similarly, a very active user has no value as an influencer if she is not sufficiently well connected. The comparison of these results indicates that the best choice for measuring the influence level of users is the average of centrality and activity.

Now that we have selected our metric, we apply it to $\mathcal{G}$ without these 500 tweets from T_{SI}, to get a ranking of all users by level of influence. We take the top 25% as our set of *influencers* and call it U_I, the rest of the users are considered the general audience and called U_G. The goal of the social models described later is to predict the level of acceptance of tweets among the general audience U_G, based on knowledge about the activity of the influencers U_I on them. The idea for the experiments described in the following sections, is to vary the number of influencers taken from U_I to predict the popularity of tweets.

Social Features. As mentioned earlier, we need to train a classifier model to make predictions. To that purpose, it is necessary to define the feature vector and the target vector. For the feature vector, in the social based model, we only consider the retweeting behaviour the selected influencers have over tweets from the training set. For each tweet t, we can define a binary vector $V_t^\omega := \begin{bmatrix} i_{t1} & i_{t2} & \dots & i_{tn} \end{bmatrix}$, where n is the number of influencers, and each i_{tj} is 1 if the tweet t was retweeted by the influencer j before $\texttt{timestamp}(t) + \omega$, and 0 otherwise. Formally, suppose that we wanted to make predictions with the information available at ω time after the tweet t is created. Then, if j is an influencer $\mathbf{RTW}_j(\omega)$ returns the set of m tweets in the timeline of j until time $\texttt{timestamp}(t) + \omega$. The matrix below groups all the vectors associated with the m tweets. Each row t in the matrix serves as input for the model as follows:

$$features_t := \begin{bmatrix} i_{t\,1} & \dots & i_{t\,j} & \dots & i_{t\,n} \end{bmatrix}_t \text{ where } i_{tj} = \begin{cases} 1 \text{ if } t \in \mathbf{RTW}_j(\omega) \\ 0 \qquad \text{otherwise} \end{cases}$$

Note that the content of tweet t is not considered, we only include the information about which of the users in U_I retweeted t. Now, as part of the supervised method, we use the following objective vector, calculated over the training set of tweets. Let $R^\omega(t)$ be a function that returns the number of retweets in U_G for the tweet t until the time $\texttt{timestamp}(t) + \omega$; we define the target vector as follows:

$$classification = \begin{bmatrix} r_1 \\ \dots \\ r_m \end{bmatrix} \text{ where } r_t = \begin{cases} 1 \ R^\omega(t)(s) >= golden \ value \\ 0 \qquad\qquad \text{otherwise} \end{cases}$$

Splitting the Dataset. To evaluate the performance of our models, we divide our dataset of tweets into two parts, one for training and another for evaluation. As usual, these datasets are not overlapping. In other words, the evaluation data is not seen by the training algorithms.

Regardless of the chosen number of influencers for prediction, we want the training and evaluation datasets to remain disjoint. In this sense, as we explained previously in this section, the left diagram in Fig. 1 shows how we split the set $\mathcal{G}$ in two disjoint parts, U_I (influencers) and U_G (common users). For all the other experiments of this paper, U_I is defined as the 25% best-ranked users from $\mathcal{G}$, using the average of centrality and activity to detect influencers.[5]

To determine well-formed training and test sets for tweets, we drop from the **T** dataset the tweets posted by users in U_I named T_I. Besides, it is also necessary to cut from **T** the set T_{SI} used previously in this section to detect influencers. The remaining tweets, i.e. $T_G = \mathbf{T}' - T_I - T_{SI}$ are split again. To do so, T_G is randomly split in training T_G^{train} (75%) and test T_G^{test} (25%) datasets to evaluate prediction models. Now, let $T_G^{train}(\omega)$ and $T_G^{test}(\omega)$ be the corresponding previously defined train and test sets, with the information of the retweet-time-window ω. Next, we show the available retweet information in $T_G^{train}(\omega)$ for different windows ω. In the following list, we show the percentage of retweets available against the total amount of retweets for the T_G^{train} without windows:

1 s	2 s	10 s	30 s	2 m	5 m	15 m	30 m	60 m	90 m	120 m	240 m	540 m
0%	0%	0.04%	0.7%	3%	7.7%	15.1%	21.1%	29.3%	35.7%	40.4%	53.6%	68.5%

Adding Content-Based Features. To achieve an increase in the quality of trending tweet prediction, we apply NLP techniques to extend the purely social model with content-based features, in a similar way as in the previous section.

5.2 Results

Now, we describe how we build our predictive models and the results obtained with and without content analysis for different time-retweet-windows. We will compare our models to a baseline built from a purely social model where users considered influencers are selected randomly instead of using an influencer detection algorithm. With this, we want to show the utility of using an algorithm to detect influencers and the relevant information those provide for learning about the behavior of general users. The experiments were run on two servers for 2×14 core CPU E5-2680 v4 2.40 GHz servers, with 128 Gb of RAM.

Baseline. As a baseline, we use a model that is sufficiently demanding to be compared with our proposals. We decided to use the same kind of features as in the pure social version, but randomly selecting a set of 25% of the users from $\mathcal{G}$ as the set of influencers U_I. To make a fair comparison with our models we

---

[5] Note that we split this dataset to fix the test set when we vary the number of influencers used to make the prediction.

do a new split from the dataset $\mathbf{T}$ to T_I and T_G with the content of users in the random selection of U_I and U_G respectively. In turn, a 75%–25% train-test split is performed on T_G for the training and evaluation of the baseline models under the same conditions as in the social alternative. We keep the datasets disjoint and evaluate over general users with influencer behavior data as input. Following the same pattern as in the other social models, we then proceed to evaluate the social baseline over increasingly large numbers of users from U_I taken as the source of social features. In this case, we do not have a ranking of users to draw the top ones from, so we make these selections randomly as well. In order to calculate the baseline performance, for each value of the number of source influencers (let us call this k), we randomly select k users from U_I, and train and test a model using the train-test split of T_G. To avoid lucky and potentially misleading results, we repeat this process five times for each value of k, reporting the average $F1$-score.

time	Top-10% inf.				Top-15% inf.				Top-20% inf.		
	FT	Base .	Soc.	S+FT.	FT	Base .	Soc.	S+FT.	FT	Base .	Soc.	S+FT.
15m		25.62	46.72	53.06		39.12	52.83	57.32		42.83	58.44	63.95
30 m		32.22	61.54	64.61		39.23	62.91	66		42.15	64.54	67.93
60 m		23.38	64.61	68.98		32.06	65.67	69.47		48.66	67.87	71.21
90 m		32.38	65.17	69.78		32.51	68.68	70.32		47.01	70.77	73.12
120 m	50.71	35.72	69.78	73.18	50.71	39.62	71.66	74.73	50.71	50.08	73.66	75.53
240 m		39.2	73.7	75.99		45.21	74.4	76.32		53.96	76.43	78.45
540 m		43.46	75.25	80.66		51.38	77.51	82.27		56.23	79.93	84.07
n.w.		46.06	77.85	82.69		54.31	80.73	84.72		57.44	82.22	89.17

Fig. 1. Performance in F_1 score for all models, evaluated over U_G, using top 10%, 15% and 20% 1 of users as influencers. Columns: FT = FastText; Model; Base = Baseline; Soc = Social Model; S+FT. = Social and FastText combined model.

Social and Combined Models. Now we show the results obtained from training and evaluating trend prediction models with the features described in Sect. 5.1. We used Support Vector Machine models for classification, more precisely the SVC as in the previous section.

We decided to focus on the experiments considering 10%, 15% and 20% of $\mathcal{G}$ as influencers. We tested models for time-retweet-windows size in minutes $\omega \in \{15, 30, 60, 90, 120, 240\}$ and also without any window (n. w.), that is, with all collected retweets in the dataset. In Table 1, we report the results for all tested models using the F_1 score. The models reported are FastText (**FT**), the baseline described in the previous section (**Base**), social (**Soc.**), and finally, the social combined with FastText (**S+FT.**). In the table we can observe that the results obtained in the previous work [12], with another dataset for the social model with 10% of influencers ($F_1 = 79.2$), is comparable with the results obtained in this work (77.85). In all cases, the social model performs better than the baseline. The results also show that the minimum window to obtain reasonable predictions with the pure social model is around 120 min, taking 10% of users as influencers and this can be reduced 60 min with 20% of influencers.

Now, we combine the social model with the 300-dimensional vector from FastText model described in the previous Sect. 4.2. In Table 1, column **S+FT.**, we can observe that the best results are obtained by combining a 20% of influencers to train the social model with FastText. This combination achieves an F_1 score of 89.17. The results obtained for the combined model shows that, an ω between 30 and 60 min, achieves an F_1 score over 70%.

6   Conclusions and Future Work

As a general conclusion, we confirm that the information about social connections between Twitter users and their first hours of activity on a tweet, can be essential to determine if it is preferred by a particular user or becomes popular among the general audience. In both cases, we obtained a good performance without analyzing the content.

Particularly, for predicting a user's preference with 60 min of information we obtained a performance around 69.08%, and after adding content information, performance grows slightly to 70.05%. We observe that, considering more time of environment behavior, the social model obtained high performance levels that are only barely improved when combining it with FastText content features.

For the popularity prediction problem, considering the top 20% most central and active users as influencers, we need 90 min of their behaviour information to obtain F_1 scores greater than 70%. If we extend the models with content features, these performance levels are achieved earlier, using between 30 and 60 min of information.

In all cases, the results seem to suggest that the source of information has a stronger influence than the actual content when it comes to spreading it across the network. The purely content-based model was far below from the social-based pure model scoring, which reinforces the idea that sometimes our contact lists can provide more information about us than our timeline.

Still, the combined model with content analysis increased the performance significantly, which indicates that content has a level of importance when it is considered within a certain social context, specially early in the lifetime of tweets, when social information about them is still limited. FastText seems particularly well suited for dealing with content from Twitter, mostly because of its ability to obtain representations for unseen or misspelled words.

This research opens many doors to evolve the model. The most relevant to us are described next. One of the upcoming experiments will be to add features that take into account the time elapsed after the original tweet has been published. Another line of research is to try to change to Deep Learning models and replace the SVM models. Additionally, we have the idea to use a Long Short-Term Memory (LSTM) neural network, representing the activity on tweets as a temporal series. For influencers detection, alternatives such as [7] and [1] could be applied to improve the selection of relevant users.

We also propose to research the aggregation formula for sentence embeddings. We have used a simple average of the vectors of the component words, but there are other more sophisticated functions, such as the weighted average by the Inverse Document Frequency (IDF) [11].

Finally, an interesting line of open research is trying to replicate the experiments for other social networks such as Facebook and Instagram, and see to what extent our conclusions apply to those. In particular, the pure social model can be extended to any network of users sharing content, which makes it possible to evaluate it even in image-based networks such as Instagram. However, we are limited by the availability of data to build datasets.

References

1. Azcorra, A., et al.: Unsupervised scalable statistical method for identifying influential users in online social networks. Sci. Rep. **8** (2018). Article number: 6955
2. Celayes, P.G., Domínguez, M.A.: Prediction of user retweets based on social neighborhood information and topic modelling. In: Castro, F., Miranda-Jiménez, S., González-Mendoza, M. (eds.) MICAI 2017. LNCS (LNAI), vol. 10633, pp. 146–157. Springer, Cham (2018). https://doi.org/10.1007/978-3-030-02840-4_12
3. Csardi, G., Nepusz, T.: The igraph software package for complex network research. InterJ. Complex Syst. **1695** (2006). http://igraph.org/python/
4. Grave, E., Mikolov, T., Joulin, A., Bojanowski, P.: Bag of tricks for efficient text classification. In: Proceedings of the 15th Conference of the European Chapter of the Association for Computational Linguistics, EACL 2017, Spain, pp. 427–431 (2017). https://fasttext.cc/
5. Hochreiter, R., Waldhauser, C.: A genetic algorithm to optimize a tweet for retweetability. In: MENDEL, pp. 13–18 (2013)
6. Katz, L.: A new status index derived from sociometric analysis. Psychometrika **18**(1), 39–43 (1953). https://doi.org/10.1007/BF02289026
7. Morone, F., Min, B., Bo, L., Mari, R., Makse, H.A.: Collective influence algorithm to find influencers via optimal percolation in massively large social media. Sci. Rep. **6** (2016). Article number: 30062
8. Nasir, N., Gottron, T., Kunegis, J., Alhadi, A.C.: Bad news travel fast: a content-based analysis of interestingness on Twitter. In: WebSci 2011: Proceedings of the 3rd International Conference on Web Science (2011)
9. Pedregosa, F., et al.: Scikit-learn: machine learning in Python. J. Mach. Learn. Res. **12**, 2825–2830 (2011). http://scikit-learn.org/
10. Pennacchiotti, M., Popescu, A.M.: A machine learning approach to Twitter user classification. In: Proceedings of the Fifth International Conference on Weblogs and Social Media, Barcelona, Catalonia, Spain, vol. 11 (2011)
11. Arora, S., Liang, Y., Ma, T.: A simple but tough-to-beat baseline for sentence embeddings. In: Proceeding of International Conference on Learning Representations, ICLR 2017, Toulon, France, 24–26 April 2017 (2017)
12. Silva, M.G., Domínguez, M.A., Celayes, P.G.: Analyzing the retweeting behavior of influencers to predict popular tweets, with and without considering their content. In: Lossio-Ventura, J.A., Muñante, D., Alatrista-Salas, H. (eds.) SIMBig 2018. CCIS, vol. 898, pp. 75–90. Springer, Cham (2019). https://doi.org/10.1007/978-3-030-11680-4_9. ISBN 978-3-030-11679-8

13. Varol, O., Ferrara, E., Menczer, F., Flammini, A.: Early detection of promoted campaigns on social media. EPJ Data Sci. **6**(1), 1–19 (2017). https://doi.org/10. 1140/epjds/s13688-017-0111-y
14. Vougioukas, M., Androutsopoulos, I., Paliouras, G.: Identifying retweetable tweets with a personalized global classifier. In: Proceedings of the 10th Hellenic Conference on Artificial Intelligence, SETN 2018, Patras, Greece, 09–12 July 2018, pp. 8:1–8:8 (2018). https://doi.org/10.1145/3200947.3201019
15. Zaman, T., Fox, E.B., Bradlow, E.T.: A Bayesian approach for predicting the popularity of tweets. CoRR abs/1304.6777 (2013). http://arxiv.org/abs/1304.6777

Summarization of Twitter Events with Deep Neural Network Pre-trained Models

Kunal Chakma[1](✉)(iD), Amitava Das[2](iD), and Swapan Debbarma[1](iD)

[1] National Institute of Technology Agartala, Agartala 799046, Tripura, India
kchakma.cse@nita.ac.in
[2] Wipro AI Lab, Bangalore, India
https://www.kunalchakma.com

Abstract. Due to the proliferation of online social media services such as Twitter, there is an upsurge in the volume of user-generated textual content. Such voluminous content is difficult to be consumed by users. Therefore, the development of technological solutions to automatically summarise the voluminous texts are essential. The work presented in this paper reports on the development of automatically generating abstractive summaries from a collection of texts from Twitter. Our proposed approach is a two-stage framework which includes: 1) Event detection by clustering and 2) Summarization of the events. We first generated a contextualized vector representation of the tweets and then applied different clustering techniques on the vectors. We evaluated the generated clusters, and based on the evaluation; we chose the best one found suitable for the summarization task. For the summarization task, we used the pre-trained models of two recently developed state-of-the-art deep neural network architectures and evaluated them on the event clusters. Standard measures of ROUGE scores have been used for evaluating the summaries. We obtained best ROUGE-1 score of **46%**, ROUGE-2 score of **30%**, ROUGE-L score of **41%** and ROUGE-SU score of **23%** from our experiments.

Keywords: Abstractive summarization · Twitter · Pointer generator · Transformer · BERT

1 Introduction

Reading large volumes of documents for gathering information is a daunting task for human beings. According to ANSI[1], a summary of a document enables the readers to quickly identify the essential components accurately to determine the document's relevance and its interest to the reader, and thus to decide whether they need to read the documents in its entirety. Manuel and Moreno [1] state that summary generated by humans involves two aspects: understanding the source text and writing a concise and short version of it. Both these

---

[1] http://www.ansi.org.

© Springer Nature Switzerland AG 2021
J. A. Lossio-Ventura et al. (Eds.): SIMBig 2020, CCIS 1410, pp. 45–62, 2021.
https://doi.org/10.1007/978-3-030-76228-5_4

aspects require extra-linguistic skills and knowledge about the document on the part of the human summarizer. Therefore, techniques must be developed for automatically producing summaries from documents. Algorithms and techniques developed for automatic text summarization (ATS) is an approximation of the summaries generated by human summarizers. Therefore, an ATS system is considered good when the generated summaries are as much as similar to the human-generated summaries. ATS is accessible, can be distributed quickly with lower costs concerning time even though human summarizers produce better summaries in terms of readability, content, form and conciseness.

Twitter is a microblogging service that allows the users to post a message which is called a "tweet" within certain character limits. Initially, Twitter was launched in 2006 with a limit of 140 characters for a tweet. The character limitation later increased to 280 characters in late 2017. Twitter users try to express their opinions on a topic or report on the occurrence of an event by covering the maximum information within the limited characters. Therefore, the dissemination of news on Twitter is much faster than conventional media. Now, the question is *"Why summarize tweets?"*. According to Internet Live Stats[2], the number of tweets published on an average is 6000 per second, 350,000 per minute, 500 million per day and around 200 billion per year. It suggests that Twitter generates a massive volume of content, thus making it difficult to be consumed by the users. The entire voluminous content generated from Twitter may or may not be useful to all the users. For example, an organization involved in conducting opinion polls during a political campaign will be interested only in the collection of tweets relevant to the task. It will not be feasible for the organization to go through every tweet to read the opinions. Therefore, an automatically generated summary of the opinions extracted from the collection of tweets will be a much-desired outcome. Similarly, for analyzing the public opinion about a newly launched product, an automatically generated summary from the collection of tweets will be very useful. Hasan et al. [2] describe an event on Twitter as the discussion on a subject matter due to users' interest either shortly after the occurrence or in anticipation of it. Therefore, we can consider tweets as event-driven short texts posted over a particular period. ATS is, therefore, required for generating summaries of such events on Twitter. ATS of a single tweet is not feasible as it is already too short. Therefore, ATS on tweets is instead a multi-document summarization [1] task where the objective is to identify the central topic of discussion from a given collection of tweets. Recently, neural network-based solutions such as Nallapati et al. [3], Chang and Lapata [4], Zhou et al. [5] for ATS from well-formed documents containing texts from books, news articles, web pages have shown groundbreaking results with the development of state-of-the-art solutions. Although studies on ATS from microblogs such as Twitter has been in existence, there are only a few that explored the application of neural networks.

---

[2] https://www.internetlivestats.com/.

This paper reports on the adoption of a pipeline approach for automatic text summarization of tweets using pre-trained models from two state-of-the-art neural network architectures based on *Pointer-generator with coverage mechanism* [6] and *Transformer* [7] based system of Liu and Lapata [8].

The major contribution of our work is:

- Creation of a Twitter corpus on three general topics: *Demonetization*[3], *Me too movement in India*[4] and *US Presidential elections of 2016*[5].
- Segmentation of tweets based on the 5W1H concept
- Identification of events by clustering the tweets after extracting the 5W1H constituents
- Generate abstractive summaries from the event clusters.

The rest of the paper is organized as follows. Section 2 discusses the related works. Section 3 describes the working of the proposed implementation. Section 4 presents our experiments. We discuss our results and analysis in Sect. 5. The paper finally concludes in Sect. 6.

2   Related Works

Earlier, there have been several tweet summarization techniques such as Lexrank [9], LSA [10], Luhn [11], MEAD [12], SumBasic [13], SumDSDR [14], and COWTS [15]. The major limitations of these algorithms are that they consider a single statistical feature to assign a score to each tweet for the summary generation. Inouye et al. [16] introduced two cluster-based approaches to generate multiple summaries of tweets for a Twitter event. In one approach, event relevant posts are clustered into four subtopics by using a hybrid form of k-means++ [17] and bisecting k-means clustering algorithm. The clusters contain the feature vectors of each post in a cluster computed by using Hybrid TF-IDF [16] weighing of words. Tweets with the maximum weights are selected as the most important ones to be included in the summary with a maximum of four tweets. Therefore, the maximum length of the summary is four tweets. In another approach, the hybrid TF-IDF summarization algorithm of Sharifi et al. [18] is modified to produce summaries with up to four posts. A maximum of four tweets is selected by the modified approach instead of the maximum weighted tweets for generating the summary.

The work presented by Beverungen and Kalita [19] normalize the tweet as proposed by Kaufmann [21] and expands tweet terms proposed in Perez et al. [22]. Their approach further optimizes the clustering process by utilizing the gap statistic mechanism of Tibshirani et al. [20].

The evaluation shows that even though the only normalization of posts does not impact the summaries, but optimization of clustering and term expansions

---

[3] https://en.wikipedia.org/wiki/2016_Indian_banknote_demonetisation.

[4] https://en.wikipedia.org/wiki/2016_United_States_presidential_election.

[5] https://en.wikipedia.org/wiki/Me_Too_movement_(India).

significantly improves summaries. The work presented by Shou et al. [23], first performs clustering of tweets, followed by the selection of some representative tweets from each cluster. Then, the arrangement of these tweets is carried out using a graph-based LexRank [9] algorithm.

Another cluster-based approach (SPUR) [29] proposed batch summarization of the stream of tweets by dividing the input stream into clusters based on the time window of one hour. Therefore, the clusters are formed by equal-sized batches of one hour window, which are then compressed by replacing individual words with frequently used phrases. The frequently used phrases are then extracted from the relevant tweets of the event, which are then ranked by their utility values and are finally included in the summary.

"Sumblr" [30] is a summarization framework that summarizes tweet streams with timeline generation. Clusters are generated from the event-related stream of tweets where the clusters hold information by two data structure called tweet cluster vector (TCV) and pyramidal time frame (PTF) [31]. The k-means clustering algorithm is used to generate the initial clusters with small amount of tweets. Then the TCVs are initialized accordingly with the initial cluster statistics. Every incoming new tweet on its arrival either goes to an existing cluster or forms a new cluster based on the cosine similarity of the tweet with the centroid of the cluster. After that, the summary is generated.

OnSes [32] is a pipeline framework that implemented a neural network-based tweet summarization system. They created word vectors using Word2Vec [33] and then clustered the word vectors using the k-means algorithm. The relevance between the tweets in a cluster is then ranked using the BM25 [34] ranking algorithm. They selected the top-ranked tweets within a cluster for generating the summary. Dogan et al. [35] proposed a deep learning-based event summarization system. In this study, the authors created a semantic context using Word2Vec model on the text. They formed a 2-output negative-positive model by training on GRU (Gated Recurrent Unit) neural network. The aim is to generate summary text for the user by gathering comments under a label on Twitter. The model also generated abstract text by associating the notion of sense.

Our work is also based on the pipeline framework of OnSes, which includes: first clustering the tweets and second, generating summaries from each cluster. The earlier studies explored only one clustering technique and did not provide much insight into the effects of choosing a particular clustering technique on the summarization task. In contrast, we explore several clustering techniques, evaluate their outcome, and then select the one with the best possible outcome for our dataset. For the summarization task, we explore two popular neural network architectures: 1) *Pointer Generator with coverage mechanism* [6] and 2) *Bidirectional Encoder Representations from Transformers or BERT* [37] based network of Liu and Lapata [8] and compare the summary generated by them.

3   System Overview

There are two major components of our framework: 1) *event detection* and 2) *event summarization* as shown in Fig. 1. Event detection is done first by segmenting every tweet into the 5W1H (*Who, What, When, Where, Why, How*) semantic components. Based on the semantic similarity of the components, the tweets are then clustered together to represent an event. The generated clusters are then fed to a neural network (pointer or transformer) to generate abstractive summaries. At the initial stage, we segmented the tweets by extracting the 5W1H components *who, what, when, where, why and how* with our [36] deep neural network system implementation that gave an F-1 score of 88.21%. We then manually corrected the errors (11.79%) of the produced results and then converted the 5W1H tagged tweets into a structural vector representation shown in Fig. 2. The structural vector is a contextual embedding of the `verb` with the `subject`, `object` and `modifiers`. Not all the 5W1H components need to be always present in a tweet. Therefore, we replaced the missing components with zeroes. These contextual embeddings are then fed to Bidirectional Encoder Representations from Transformers or BERT [37] network to generate contextual embeddings. The contextual embeddings are obtained by pooling (concatenating) them together on the last axis, resulting in sentence encodes of 1536 dimensions.

3.1 Event Clustering

We group the contextual embeddings generated by BERT into clusters where each cluster corresponds to a possible event. For clustering the contextual embeddings, we applied four clustering techniques such as k-means [38], Hierarchical Density Based Spatial Clustering of Applications with Noise (HDBSCAN) [39], Hierarchical Agglomerative Clustering (HAC) [40] and Affinity Propagation (AP) [41]. k-means requires the number of clusters to be specified before starting the algorithm. We selected the number of clusters k based on quality metrics such as *Silhouette*[6] score for the given dataset. *Silhouette score* is a method of interpretation and validation of consistency within clusters of data. An increase in *Silhouette score* for k represents the suggested number of clusters. For k-means the *Silhouette score* suggested $k = 10$ for the number of clusters. HDBSCAN first computes a *single linkage hierarchy* on the space of transformed distances (i.e., mutual reachability distances) and, then, processes this hierarchy to identify connected components and noise objects at each level. HAC comes under the family of hierarchical clustering algorithms that build nested clusters by merging them successively with a bottom-up approach. The merging could be done by either one of the four approaches: *ward, complete linkage, average linkage* and *single linkage*. Ward minimizes the sum of squared differences within all clusters. Complete linkage minimizes the maximum distance between observations of pairs of clusters. Average linkage minimizes the average of the distances between all observations of pairs of clusters. Single linkage minimizes the distance between the closest observations of pairs of clusters. We used the scikit-learn[7] API for implementing HAC clustering with linkage parameters set to *ward* and *complete linkage*. For *ward*, we set the *affinity* parameter to "euclidean" and for *complete linkage* to "cosine" respectively. We did not observe a significant difference

---

[6] https://bit.ly/33lKpTj.
[7] https://bit.ly/3dVJrQ4.

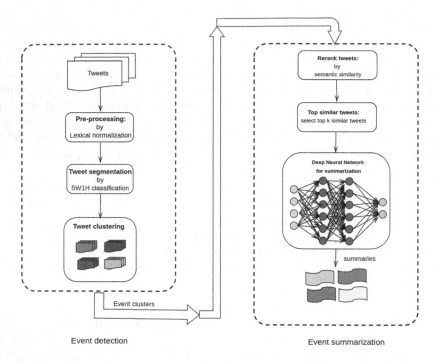

Fig. 1. Framework of the proposed system

in the generated clusters by both the methods. In scikit-learn, HAC requires a threshold value to be set for either one of the two parameters: *n_clusters* which represents the number of clusters to be generated and *distance_threshold* is the linkage distance threshold above which, clusters will not be merged. Selecting a distance threshold is difficult. Therefore, we specified number of clusters k based on two evaluation parameters: *silhouette score* and *dendogram cutoff*. Both *silhouette score* and *dendogram cutoff* suggested $k = 10$ for the given contextual embeddings. In Affinity Propagation, clusters are created by sending messages between pairs of samples until convergence. A concept called "exemplar" is used which are the most representative of other samples in a given dataset. The messages represent the suitability of one sample to be the exemplar of the other. This is then updated based on the values received from the others. This updating process continues iteratively until convergence, and then the final exemplars are chosen, thus giving the final cluster. The messages fall into two categories: a) the accumulated evidence called *responsibility* denoted as $r(i,k)$ such that sample k should be the exemplar for sample i and b) *availability* denoted as $a(i,k)$ which is the accumulated evidence that sample i should choose sample k as its exemplar. The basic idea is that samples choose exemplars if they are 1) similar enough to many samples and 2) chosen by many samples to be representative of

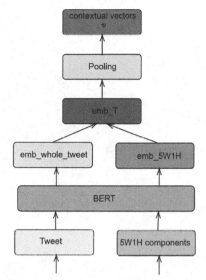

Fig. 2. Contextualized vector generation

themselves. The responsibility of a sample to be the exemplar of the sample is given by:

$$r(i,k) \leftarrow s(i,k) - max\left[a(i,k') + s(i,k') \forall k' \neq k\right] \qquad (1)$$

Where $s(i,k)$ is the similarity between samples i and k. The availability of sample k to be the exemplar of sample i is given by:

$$a(i,k) \leftarrow min\left[0, \ r(k,k) + \sum_{i' \ s.t. \ i' \notin i,k} r(i',k)\right] \qquad (2)$$

Initially, all values for r and a are set to zero, and the calculation of each iterates until convergence. k-means and HAC generated 5 and 10 clusters respectively. HDBSCAN could not cluster 10057 (61.4% of 16,375) tweets and labelled them as "−1". For the remaining 6318 tweets, HDBSCAN generated 2356 clusters with minimum cluster size of 2 and maximum of 23 tweets. AP generated a total of 934 clusters with minimum and maximum cluster size of 2 and 115 respectively. The average size of clusters produced by AP is 17.53. The cluster formation is shown in Fig. 3.

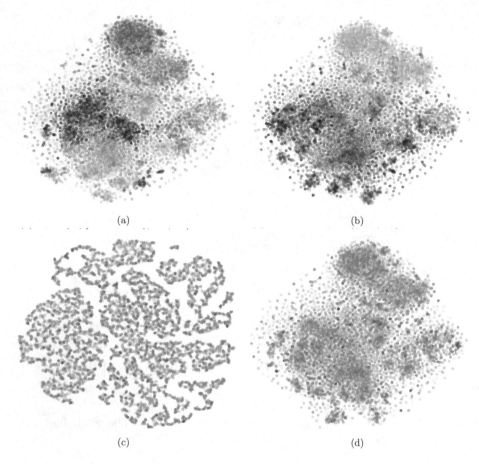

(a)   (b)

(c)   (d)

Fig. 3. Population distribution of clusters by k-means, HAC, AP and HDBSCAN. a) 10 clusters generated by k-means clustering with the distribution of 1466, 2280,1073, 1481, 2073, 834, 1615, 1768, 2117 and 1668 tweets. b) 10 clusters generated by HAC clustering with the distribution of 2267, 2170, 3004, 594, 3928, 1868, 1000, 866, 385 and 293 tweets. c) Total 934 clusters generated by AP with minimum and maximum cluster size of 2 and 115 tweets respectively. d) HDBSCAN failed to cluster 10057 tweets which is 61.4% of the dataset. The remaining 38.6% are clustered into 2356 clusters with length between 2 and 23 tweets.

3.2   Event Summarization

There are two broad categories of text summarization: 1) *extractive* and *abstractive*. Extractive summarization is the task of generating a summary of a document by identifying the most important sentences (or phrases) and then concatenate them without the inclusion of any new words. Abstractive summarization is the task of generating a summary of a document by paraphrasing the sentences (or phrases) to produce newer phrases. For our work, we explore the abstractive summarization approach. Recently, the natural language processing (NLP) domain has observed a significant growth in neural network-based solutions for text summarization task. Encoder-decoder [42] networks are generally used for the summarization task where the encoder could be RNN [43] or Transformer [7] network and the decoder could be either auto-regressive or non-auto-regressive. In the auto-regressive approach, the decoder can make a current prediction with knowledge of previous predictions. For the abstractive summarization task, we explored two neural network architectures : Pointer-generator [44] based network of See et al. [6] (we denote it as P-Gen) and a transformer-based implementation called Presumm by Liu and Lapata [8]. Since neural network-based architectures require dedicated GPU based machines and a large amount of data to produce good results, training from scratch is not a feasible solution for our dataset. We, therefore, used the pre-trained models of P-Gen and Presumm on our dataset and performed several experiments to evaluate the generated summaries.

Pointer-Generator (P-Gen): P-Gen is an encoder-decoder network with LSTM at the encoder side and a pointer-generator network at the decoder side. It is a hybrid of the sequence to sequence [3] attention and pointer network. P-Gen also exploits the concept of coverage [45] mechanism which is added to the pointer-generator network. Here, we reuse the definition of coverage vector and the other parameters defined in P-Gen. Coverage is a vector c^t which is the sum of the attention distributions of all previous decoder time-steps represented as:

$$c^t = \sum_{t'}^{t-1} a^{t'}$$

(3)

The coverage vector is basically a modification of the original attention vector of [46]. The modified attention vector is represented as:

$$e_i^t = v^T tanh \left(W_h h_i + W_s S_t + w_c c_i^t + b_{attn} \right)$$

(4)

where, v^T, $W_h h_i$, $W_s S_t$, $w_c c_i^t$ and b_{attn} are learnable parameters. P-Gen also define *coverage loss* which penalizes the decoder for repeatedly attending to the same locations. The *coverage loss* is represented as:

$$covloss_t = \sum min \left(a_i^t, c_i^t \right)$$

(5)

The final composite loss function in P-Gem is defined as:

$$loss_t = -logP \left(w_t^* \right) + \lambda \sum min \left(a_i^t, c_i^t \right)$$

(6)

where, λ is some hyperparameter.

Presumm: It is an encoder-decoder network with a transformer network both at the encoder and decoder side. Presumm presents a two-stage approach where extractive summarization is done at the first stage and then abstractive summarization at the second stage. The encoder is therefore fine-tuned twice. Since

Presumm is based on the BERT architecture, special tokens [CLS] and [SEP] are inserted between each sentence to generate positional embeddings. Interval segment embeddings are generated to differentiate each sentence. For example, assuming a document D consisting of sentences $[sent_1, sent_2, sent_3, sent_4]$, embeddings can be generated as $[E_A, E_B, E_A, E_B]$. For the extractive summarization, vector t_i of the ith [CLS] token from the top layer is used to represent $sent_i$. Several transformer layers are stacked together to obtain document-level features for extracting summaries:

$$\tilde{h}^l = LN\left(h^{l-1} + MHAtt\left(h^{l-1}\right)\right) \tag{7}$$

$$\tilde{h}^l = LN\left(h^l + FFN\left(h^l\right)\right) \tag{8}$$

where $h^0 = PosEmb(T)$; T denotes the sentence vectors and function $PosEmb$ adds positional embeddings to T. Sigmoid is used at the final output layer which is represented as:

$$\hat{y}_i = \hat{y}_i = \sigma\left(W_o h_i^L + b_o\right) \tag{9}$$

where h_i^L is the vector for $sent_i$ from the top layer (the Lth layer) of the Transformer. For abstractive summarization, **Presumm**, uses the pre-trained encoder of the extractive summarizer and a 6-layered transformer for the decoder.

4   Experiments

In this section, we discuss the various experimentation performed with the pre-trained models of **P-Gen** and **Presumm**.

4.1   Dataset

We collected tweets on three different topics using twitter4j[8] API: *Demonetization* (see footnote 3), *US Elections 2016* (see footnote 4) and *Me Too India Movement* (see footnote 5). For *Demonetization*, a total 14,940 tweets were collected during two different periods, one between 22nd and 23rd November 2016; and the second between 11th and 21st April 2017 (after the beginning of new financial year 2017–18 on 1st April 2017). For *US Elections 2016*, we crawled 38,984 tweets on the day of the elections i.e. 8th November 2016 and on the final declaration of the electoral results on 17th of January 2017. Tweets were collected with hashtags such as "#USElections2016", "#ElectionNight", "#DonaldTrump", "#HillaryClinton", "#DonaldTrumpWins" and "#USElections2016Results". For the *Me Too* topic, a total of 248,160 tweets were collected with queries such as "#MeToo", "#MeTooCampaign", "#MeTooControversy" and "#MeTooIndia" from 11th to 24th October 2018. We performed some preprocessing by lower-casing the tweets, removing Non-English tweets and *retweets*. We observed that approximately 80 to 90% of the collected tweets under each

---

[8] https://github.com/Twitter4J/Twitter4J.

topic contained *retweets* as well as non-English tweets; for which they were not considered for evaluation. Therefore, after pre-processing, we finalized a total of 16,375 tweets: 3484 on *"Demonetization"*, 6558 on *"Me Too India Movement"* and 6333 on *"US Elections 2016"*.

4.2   Cluster Selection

As discussed in Sect. 3.1, based on the suggested *Silhouette score*, we set the number of clusters $k = 10$ for both k-means and HAC. Therefore, these two approaches generated 10 clusters. For k-means we set the following parameters: *n_clusters=best_k, n_jobs=−1* and *random_state=seed*. Parameter *best_k=10* is chosen based on the *Silhouette Score* iterations between 2 and 50. For HDB-SCAN, we set the standard parameter settings: *min_cluster_size=100, prediction_data=True, core_dist_n_jobs=−1 and memory='data'*[9]. For AP clustering, we set the parameters to: *damping=0.5, max_iter=2000, convergence_iter=100, copy=True, preference=10, affinity='euclidean'*. We ignored the clusters generated by HDBSCAN because it did not consider 61.4% of the tweets under any cluster (labelled as −1). For k-means, HAC and AP, we measured the cosine similarity of the tweets under each cluster and compared the lower and upper bounds of the similarity scores. We set the minimum threshold of the similarity score to 70%. If more than 50% of the tweets under a cluster fall below the minimum threshold similarity score of 70%, we did not consider the cluster and the corresponding clustering method (k-means/HAC/AP). Based on the observations, we considered only the clusters from AP with a length of greater than or equal to 10 tweets for the summarization task.

4.3   Reference Summary Creation

As there is no available dataset for abstractive summarization on tweets, we had to build our reference summaries (gold summaries) from our dataset. Since the number of clusters produced by AP is large (449 clusters with length ≥15) as shown in Fig. 3, manually evaluating the clusters for generating reference summaries is a laborious task. We, therefore, adopted a two-step approach for generating reference summaries. In the first step, we applied four extractive summarization techniques such as "Lexrank" [9], "LSA" [10], "Luhn" [11] and "Textrank" [28] to obtain four candidate sets. Then in the second step, we asked two annotators to select the references from the candidate sets based on two criteria. The criteria for selecting the references are: 1) the reference is found in at least two candidate sets; and 2) it is relevant to the event/topic. We measured the similarity of the candidate sets in terms of ROUGE [47] scores and compared Lexrank with the rest. We observed a ROUGE-1 of 61.77%, 60% and 21.64% for Textrank, Luhn and LSA respectively against Lexrank.

---

[9] We experimented with the different values of min_cluster_size but with 100 we got the best clustering.

The relevance of a tweet under a candidate set is measured based on the following procedure. We obtained the top n-grams (unigrams, bigrams and tri-grams) from each candidate set and formulated queries based on the n-grams to re-arrange the tweets. Formally, we can represent this as information retrieval (IR) problem as:

Let q be a query of n-grams given over a set of documents D where the IR task is to rank the documents in D so that the documents most relevant to q appear at the top. In our case, each tweet within a candidate set is a document, and the particular set is the document pool which is represented as:

$$D = \bigcup_{k=1\cdots n} \tau_k \tag{10}$$

where τ_k is the k top tweets retrieved. When $k = n$, all the tweets are retrieved. For obtaining the ranking scores, we used the sentence BERT (SBERT) [48] system, which measures the semantic similarity of the tweets in a given cluster. In SBERT, the cosine similarity between the query and the tweet is measured by computing the cosine of the query vector u with the tweet vector v. Both the vectors u and v are of the same dimensions. To rank the tweets, the *Spearman's Rank Correlation* is computed between the cosine similarity of the query and the tweets, which is defined as:

$$\rho = 1 - \frac{\sum_{i=1}^{n}(u_i - v_i)^2}{n(n^2 - 1)} \tag{11}$$

where u_i and v_i are the corresponding ranks of u and v, for $i = 0, \cdots, n-1$.

For example, in a particular cluster, the top trigram *"mj akbar resigns"* forms the query $q = $ *"mj akbar resigns"*. The query is then issued to SBERT to retrieve the top k tweets from the given cluster. The annotators then pick the tweets from each candidate set based on *informativeness, fluency, and succinctness* of the contents and write the summaries with up to three sentences. We measured the agreement ratio between the annotators with standard ROUGE metrics using *ROUGE-1.5.5* and obtained average F1 ROUGE-1 of 82.8%, ROUGE-2 of 79.5% and ROUGE-L of 82.5%.

P-Gen Setup: For the P-gen setup, we used the pre-trained model *pre-trained_model_tf1.2.1*[10] which is trained on the CNN/Daily Mail dataset. This model uses a vocabulary of 50K words with 21,50,1265 parameters. This model has 256- dimensional hidden states and 128-dimensional word embeddings. Parameters such as max_enc_steps and max_dec_steps are set to 400 and 100 tokens to restrict the length of source text and the summary respectively. For beam search decoding, beam_size is set to 4.

Presumm Setup: From Presumm, we used the *bertext_cnndm_transformer*[11] pre-trained model for the abstractive summarization task. The Transformer

---

[10] shorturl.at/aeOTW.
[11] shorturl.at/crtI4.

decoder has 768 hidden units with hidden size of 2048 for all the feed-forward layers. A beam size of 5 is used during the decoding phase. Presumm uses *Trigram blocking* mechanism to prevent redundancy of phrases/sentences in the generated summary.

5   Results and Analysis

5.1   Cluster Evaluation

On careful analysis, we observed that the clusters generated by k-means and HAC contain tweets that discuss multiple sub-events (or sub-topics) present under the same cluster. For example, cluster1 under k-means contains 2280 tweets mostly containing tweets related to the "Me Too Movement". However, there are latent sub-events such as "Donald Trump mocking the Me Too Movement" and "Resignation of minister M.J. Akbar due to Me Too allegations" which were put under the same cluster by both k-means and HAC. In contrast, AP generated 934 clusters with cluster length between 2 and 115 tweets. Therefore, with AP clustering approach, it was possible to detect the latent sub-events present under the top-level events on our dataset.

To evaluate the quality of the clusters, we measured the semantic similarity of the top 15 tweets (since 15 is the minimum length of a cluster) with SBERT. The similarity score ranges from 0.55 to 0.89, which suggests that the quality of the clusters are non-trivial.

5.2   Summary Evaluation

We evaluated the performances of both P-Gen and Presumm architectures with standard ROUGE-1, ROUGE-2, ROUGE-L and ROUGE-SU scores by using *ROUGE-1.5.5*. The ROUGE scores are shown in Table 1.

Unranked: For the clusters with unranked tweets (clusters with no changes in the ordering of the tweets), both the architectures produced summaries with very low ROUGE scores. The ROUGE-1 F score of P-Gen is 0.07 and that of Presumm is 0.12. As stated earlier, the gold summaries were prepared based on the top-ranked 100 tweets in each cluster. Therefore, the summaries did not match with most of the n-grams of the gold summaries, thus, resulting in very low scores. These observations also suggest that both the architectures perform poorly when the document length is large. The reason for the poor performances is that the summarizers pick the earlier tweets appearing in a cluster.

Ranked: A significant improvement in the ROUGE scores is observed when we rank the tweets within a cluster based on query q. In Table 1, Ranked P-Gen and Ranked Presumm are the ROUGE scores for both the architectures respectively. For the ranked cluster, the pointer-generator with coverage mechanism P-Gen performed slightly better than the transformer-based Presumm. P-Gen beat Presumm by 0.06 ROUGE-1, by 0.01 ROUGE-2 and by 0.04 ROUGE-L scores. These differences are very marginal.

Table 1. ROUGE scores

Summarizer	ROUGE-1			ROUGE-2			ROUGE-L			ROUGE-SU		
	P	R	F	P	R	F	P	R	F	P	R	F
Unranked P-Gen	0.06	0.11	0.07	0.00	0.00	0.00	0.05	0.10	0.07	0.00	0.02	0.01
Unranked Presumm	0.08	0.22	0.12	0.01	0.02	0.01	0.07	0.19	0.10	0.01	0.05	0.01
Ranked P-Gen	0.23	0.51	0.30	0.10	0.22	0.13	0.21	0.45	0.27	0.07	0.26	0.10
Ranked Presumm	0.18	0.42	0.24	0.09	0.22	0.12	0.17	0.41	0.23	0.05	0.26	0.08
Top 15 P-Gen	0.22	0.45	0.27	0.11	0.24	0.14	0.18	0.39	0.18	0.06	0.22	0.06
Top 15 Presumm	0.52	0.49	**0.46**	0.35	0.30	**0.30**	0.48	0.43	**0.41**	0.31	0.28	**0.23**

Table 2. Comparison of summary generated by P-Gen and Presumm. Blue and Red colours indicate the words present in reference summary.

Reference	P-Gen	Presumm
union cabinet minister mj akbar resigns after sexual harassment allegations in the wake of metoo controversy	union minister mj akbar resigns over harassment charges . reports ani #metoo effect; m j akbar has resigned. mj akbar resigns as minister of state for external affairs resigns after being accused of sexual harassment .	mj akbar resigns as minister of state for external affairs mj akbar resigns from minister post after sexual harassment allegation mj akbar resign's as mos external affairs minister in the wake of #metoo controversy
republican candidate donald trump creates history by winning the us presidential elections	trump will elected next president of the united states here is why . @nytopinion has congratulated donald trump for his victory in the us presidential election. donald trump's victory means the era of a palestinian state is over israeli minister.	look back in the wake of donald trump's presidential victory . us election: republican candidate donald trump scores early wins #electionnight. history made as donald trump delivers his victory speech as the president elect of the USA
many think that modi broke the backbone of indian economy by introducing demonetization	demonetization failed to be the next of the indian economy . demonetization akbar has been criticised by the union. he said to burn him if #demonetization turns to be a failure. he lost the backbone of the indian economy.	modi broke the backbone of the indian economy by introducing d by poornachander gourishetty he lost to demonetization !

Top 15 Ranked: We observed a significant improvement in the performance of Presumm when we considered the clusters with the top 15 relevant tweets. A possible reason could be that the gold summaries were prepared based on these top 15 relevant tweets, which resulted in high similarity with the n-grams of the generated summaries. The last two rows of Table 1 show the ROUGE scores for the top 15 ranked tweets in the clusters. ROUGE-1 F score for P-Gen dropped from 0.30 (Ranked P-Gen) to 0.27 (top 15 P-Gen) whereas for Presumm, there is a significant improvement from 0.24 (Ranked Psumm) to 0.46 (top 15 Presumm). Similar are the cases for ROUGE-2, ROUGE-L and ROUGE-SU.

For comparing both the architectures, we show the generated summaries in Table 2. We observe that for abstractive summarization task, in addition to good ROUGE scores, the number of noble n-grams produced by the summarizer are also important. As seen in the summary table, `Presumm` comparatively outperforms `P-Gen` in terms of producing noble n-grams.

6   Conclusion

Studies on ATS from microblogs such as tweets have been in existence for a long time. Earlier approaches are mostly based on constructing graphs, generating clusters where the summarization is based on statistical approaches. There are very few studies on the application of neural networks for the tweet summarization task. In this paper, we presented our framework for generating abstractive summaries from a cluster of tweets. We presented a pipeline based framework that involves clustering in the first phase and then summarization in the second phase. We generated contextual embeddings based on the 5W1H semantic components. We explored several clustering techniques to segregate the contextual embeddings. With empirical analysis, we chose the best clustering technique suitable for our dataset. For the summarization task, we adopted two state-of-the-art neural network architectures and compared them on our dataset. Our experimentation shows that existing neural network architectures do not produce quality summaries when the document size is large. We also observed that better summaries are produced when the tweets are ranked in a cluster. In future, we intend to apply our approach to larger dataset and perform further analysis.

References

1. Manuel, J., Moreno, T.: Automatic Text Summarization. Wiley (2014)
2. Hasan, M., Orgun, M.A., Schwitter, R.: A survey on real-time event detection from the Twitter data stream. Inf. Sci. **44**(4), 443–463 (2017)
3. Nallapati, R. Zhou, B., Santos, C.D., Gulcehre, C., Xiang, B.: Abstractive text summarization using sequence-to-sequence RNNs and beyond. Comput. Nat. Lang. Learn. (2016)
4. Cheng, J., Lapata, M.: Neural summarization by extracting sentences and words. In: Proceedings of the 54th Annual Meeting of the Association for Computational Linguistics, vol. 1, pp. 484–494 (2016)
5. Zhou, Q., Yang, N., Wei, F., Huang, S., Zhou, M., Zhao, T.: Neural document summarization by jointly learning to score and select sentences. In: Proceedings of the 56th Annual Meeting of the Association for Computational Linguistics, vol. 1, pp. 654–663 (2018)
6. See, A., Liu, P.J., Manning, C.D.: Get to the point: summarization with pointer-generator networks. In: Proceedings of the 55th Annual Meeting of the Association for Computational Linguistics, vol. 1, pp. 1073–1083 (2017)
7. Vaswani, A., et al.: Attention is all you need. In: CoRR, (abs/1706.03762) (2017)
8. Liu, Y., Lapata, M.: Text summarization with pretrained encoders. In: Proceedings of the 2019 Conference on Empirical Methods in Natural Language Processing, vol. 1, pp. 3730–3740 (2019)
9. Erkan, G., Radev, D.R.: LexRank: graph-based lexical centrality as salience in text summarization. J. Artif. Intell. **22**, 457–479 (2004)

10. Gong, Y., Liu, X.: Generic text summarization using relevance measure and latent semantic analysis. In: Proceedings 24th Annual International ACM SIGIR Conference Research and Development Information Retrival, September, pp. 19–25 (2001)

11. Luhn, H.P.: The automatic creation of literature abstracts. IBM J. Res. Dev. **2**(2), 159–165 (1958)

12. Radev, D.R., Hovy, E., McKeown, K.: Introduction to the special issue on summarization. Comput. Linguis. **28**(4), 399–408 (2002)

13. Nenkova, A., Vanderwende, L.: The impact of frequency on summarization. Microsoft Res., Redmond, Washington, DC, USA, Technical Report. MSR-TR-2005, vol. 101 (2005)

14. He, Z., et al.: Document summarization based on data reconstruction. In: Proceedings 26th AAAI Conference Artificial Intelligence, July, pp. 620–626 (2012)

15. Rudra, K., Ghosh, S., Ganguly, N., Goyal, P., Ghosh, S.: Extracting situational information from microblogs during disaster events: a classification-summarization approach. In: Proceedings of 24th ACM International Conference Information Knowledge Management, October, pp. 583–592 (2015)

16. Inouye, D.: Multiple Post Microblog Summarization, University of Colorado at Colorado Springs (2010)

17. Arthur, D., Vassilvitskii, S.: k-means++: the advantages of careful seeding. In: Proceedings of the 18th Annual ACM-SIAM Symposium on Discrete Algorithms, New Orleans, LA, pp. 1027–1035 (2007)

18. Sharifi, B., Hutton, M.-A., Kalita, J.: Summarizing microblogs automatically. In: Human Language Technologies: the 2010 Annual Conference of the North American Chapter of the Association for Computational Linguistics, HLT, pp. 685–688 (2010)

19. Beverungen, G., Kalita, J.: Evaluating methods for summarizing Twitter posts. In: Proceedings of the 4th ACM International Conference on Web Search and Data Mining (WSDM), Hong Kong, China, pp. 1–6 (2011)

20. Tibshirani, R., Walther, G., Hastie, T. : Estimating the number of clusters in a data set via the gap statistic. J. Royal Stat. Soc. Ser B (Stat. Methodol.) **63**(2), 411–423 (2001)

21. Kaufmann, M.: Syntactic normalization of Twitter messages. In: Proceedings of International Conference on Natural Language Processing (ICON), Kharagpur, India (2010)

22. Perez-Tellez, F., Pinto, D., Cardiff, J., Rosso, P.: On the difficulty of clustering company tweets. In: Proceedings of the 2nd International Workshop on Search and Mining User-Generated Contents, Toronto, Canada, pp. 92–102 (2010)

23. Shou, L., Wang, Z., Chen, K., Chen, G.: Sumblr: continuous summarization of evolving tweet streams. In: Proceedings 36th Int. ACM SIGIR Conference Research Development Information Retrival, August, pp. 533–542 (2013)

24. Judd, J., Kalita, J.: Better Twitter summaries? In: Proceedings of the Conference of the North American Chapter of the Association for Computational Linguistics: Human Language Technologies, Atlanta, GA, pp. 445–449 (2013)

25. Nichols, J., Mahmud, J., Drews, C.: Summarizing sporting events using Twitter. In: Proceedings of the ACM International Conference on Intelligent User Interfaces, New York, NY, pp. 189–198 (2012)

26. Harabagiu, S., Hickl, A.: Relevance modeling for microblog summarization. In: Proceedings of the 5th International Conference on Weblogs and Social Media (ICWSM), Barcelona, Spain, pp. 514–517 (2011)

27. Garg, N., Favre, B., Reidhammer, K., Hakkani-Tur, D.: ClusterRank: a graph based method for meeting summarization. In: Proceedings of 10th Annual Conference of International Speech Communication, pp. 1499–1502 (2009)
28. Mihalcea, R., Tarau, P.: Textrank: bringing order into texts. In: Proceedings of the Conference on Empirical Methods in Natural Language Processing, Association for Computational Linguistics, pp. 404–411 (2004)
29. Yang, X., Ghoting, A., Ruan, Y., Parthasarathy, S.: A framework for summarizing and analyzing twitter feeds. In: Proceedings of the 18th ACM SIGKDD International Conference on Knowledge Discovery and Data Mining, KDD 2012, pp. 370–378. ACM, New York (2012)
30. Wang, Z., Shou, L., Chen, K., Chen, G., Mehrotra, S.: On summarization and timeline generation for evolutionary tweet streams. IEEE Trans. Knowl. Data Eng. **27**(5), 1301–1315 (2015)
31. Aggarwal, C.C., Han, J., Wang, J., Yu, P.S.: A framework for clustering evolving data streams. In: Proceedings of the 29th International Conference on Very Large Data Bases, Berlin, Germany, pp. 81–92 (2003)
32. Niu, J., Zhao, Q., Chen, H., Atiquzzaman, M., Peng, F. : OnSeS: a novel online short text summarization based on BM25 and neural network. In: IEEE Global Communications Conference (GLOBECOM), Washington, DC, pp. 1–6 (2016)
33. Mikolov, T., Sutskever, I., Chen, K., Corrado, G., Dean, J.: Distributed representations of words and phrases and their compositionality. In: Advances in Neural Information Processing Systems, vol. 26 (2013)
34. Amati, G.: BM25. Encyclopedia of Database Systems, pp. 257–260. Springer, Boston (2009). https://doi.org/10.1007/978-0-387-39940-9
35. Doğan, E., Kaya, B.: Text summarization in social networks by using deep learning. In: 1st International Informatics and Software Engineering Conference (UBMYK), Ankara, Turkey. pp. 1–5 (2019)
36. Chakma, K., Das, A., Debbarma, S.: Deep semantic role labeling for Tweets using 5W1H: who, what, when, where, why and how. Computación y Sistemas **23**(3), 751–763 (2019). https://doi.org/10.13053/CyS-23-3-3253
37. Devlin, J., Chang, M., Lee, K., Toutanova, K.: BERT: pre-training of deep bidirectional transformers for language understanding. arXiv preprint arXiv:1810.04805 (2018)
38. Xin, J., Jiawei, H.: K-means clustering. In: Encyclopedia of Machine Learning and Data Mining, pp. 695–697 (2017)
39. Campello, R.J.G.B., Moulavi, D., Sander, J.: Density-based clustering based on hierarchical density estimates. In: Pei, J., Tseng, V.S., Cao, L., Motoda, H., Xu, G. (eds.) PAKDD 2013. LNCS (LNAI), vol. 7819, pp. 160–172. Springer, Heidelberg (2013). https://doi.org/10.1007/978-3-642-37456-2_14
40. Zepeda-Mendoza, M.L., Resendis-Antonio, O.: Hierarchical agglomerative clustering. In: Dubitzky, W., Wolkenhauer, O., Cho, K.H., Yokota, H. (eds.) Encyclopedia of Systems Biology, Springer, New York (2013). https://doi.org/10.1007/978-1-4419-9863-7
41. Brendan F.J., Delbert, D.: Clustering by passing messages between data points, pp. 972–976 (2007)
42. Sutskever, I., Vinyals, O., Le, Q.V.: Sequence to sequence learning with neural networks. In: Neural Information Processing Systems (2014)
43. Sherstinsky, A.: Fundamentals of recurrent neural network (RNN) and long short-term memory (LSTM) network. In: CoRR, (abs/1808.03314) (2018)
44. Vinyals, O., Fortunato, M., Jaitly, N.: Pointer networks. In: Neural Information Processing Systems (2015)

45. Tu, Z., Lu, Z., Liu, Y., Liu, X., Li, H.: Modeling coverage for neural machine translation. In: Association for Computational Linguistics (2016)
46. Bahdanau, D., Cho, K., Bengio, Y.: Neural machine translation by jointly learning to align and translate. In: Proceedings of the ICLR Conference, San Diego, USA. pp. 1–15 (2015)
47. Lin, C-Y.: ROUGE: a package for automatic evaluation of summaries. In: Proceedings of the Workshop on Text Summarization Branches Out, WAS 2004
48. Nils, R., Iryna, G.: Sentence-BERT: sentence embeddings using Siamese BERT-networks. In: Proceedings of Empirical Methods in Natural Language Processing. Association for Computational Linguistics (2019). http://arxiv.org/abs/1908. 10084

Multi-strategic Approach for Author Name Disambiguation in Bibliography Repositories

Natan de Souza Rodrigues$^{(\boxtimes)}$ ⓘ, Aurelio Ribeiro Costa ⓘ,
Lucas Correa Lemos ⓘ, and Célia Ghedini Ralha ⓘ

Department of Computer Science, University of Brasília, Brasília, DF, Brazil
ghedini@cic.unb.br

Abstract. The problem of author name ambiguity in digital bibliography repositories can compromise the integrity and reliability of data. There are several techniques available in the literature to solve the author name disambiguation problem. In this work, we present a multi-strategic approach for author name disambiguation in bibliography repositories applying comparison of strings with the Jaccard similarity coefficient, Levenshtein distance measure, and social network clustering technique. Information from the DBLP digital bibliography repository is used to compare disambiguation results to SCI-synergy, an online scientific social network analysis artifact. The proposed approach outperforms the baseline with a precision of 0.8867, recall of 1, and F-measure of 0.9399, considering a Brazilian graduate program case.

Keywords: Name ambiguity · Digital bibliographic repository ·
Entity resolution · Social network

1 Introduction

Several digital bibliography repositories provide functionalities that make easy literature research and discovery as well as other features. Such repositories may list millions of bibliographic records becoming an important information source for academic communities, allowing the search for relevant publication in a centralized manner [1]. The Digital Bibliography & Library Project (DBLP)[1] is an example of the computer science area that listed more than 5 million journals, conference, workshop series, and other publications, relating more than 2,4 million authors in July 2020. About 450 thousand new publications have been added to DBLP in 2019 [2].

The analysis of research data in digital repositories is a growing challenge involving different aspects, where author name ambiguity remains an open problem. Many distinct authors may have the same name (homonyms). Also, the same author may use name variants in different repositories (synonyms). If only

---

[1] https://dblp.uni-trier.de/.

J. A. Lossio-Ventura et al. (Eds.): SIMBig 2020, CCIS 1410, pp. 63–76, 2021.
https://doi.org/10.1007/978-3-030-76228-5_5

the implicit bibliographic information is used, with simple string disambiguation to authors identification, the results may lead to misidentification, either by merging identities associated by homonyms or splitting with synonyms [3].

Besides, author name ambiguity may affect significantly the performance of document retrieval through web search engines and obstruct the entity integrity for integrated databases. Efforts to solve this problem is an important research issue, especially in digital bibliography repositories that are becoming more person-centric than document-centric [4]. Several author names disambiguation systems, also known as entity resolution systems, have been developed applying a wide variety of techniques [5–8].

This research aims to contribute to author name disambiguation in digital bibliography repositories, investigating the integration of different techniques, including similarity measures, proximity algorithms, and social network issues. In this direction, we used an online scientific social network artifact called SCI-synergy with DBLP authors' information that is illustrated by a Brazilian graduate program case. SCI-synergy allows analysis of scientific social networks obtaining information from authors, co-author, publications, and institutions relationships [9].

Thus, we propose a multi-strategic approach to author name disambiguation using SCI-synergy with a Brazilian graduate program case as a comparison baseline. The solution is executed in the step of inserting new authorship and co-authorship data during the SCI-synergy workflow. First, a string treatment is performed, then author names and co-authors are compared with the Jaccard similarity coefficient and Levenshtein distance measure. Finally, the social network clustering technique is applied to complete the strategies during the name disambiguation cycle.

An example of a name disambiguation challenge can be illustrated by the author Aletéia Patrícia Favacho de Araújo, which is ambiguous in DBLP, Arnet-Miner, and Microsoft Academic, as presented in this article. The rest of the manuscript includes a literature review in Sect. 2; in Sect. 3 the multi-strategic name disambiguation approach; in Sect. 4 a case study with results to illustrate the disambiguation approach; in Sect. 5 final considerations and future work.

2   Related Work

The continuous growth of scientific publications has made the author name ambiguity problem increasingly harder. Bollen et al. predicted in 2007, a substantial increase in the research articles [10]. Thus, author name disambiguation methods have frequently been proposed.

The CAND system is proposed by [11]. CAND uses an author profile model combined with heuristics, and self-citation, to create less fragmented clusters to improve accuracy. Authors propose a method, called DISC, that uses a graph community detection algorithm, feature vectors, and graph operations to homonym disambiguation [12]. The method includes the following modules: index creator, authors profile builder, data extractor, and comparator. Experiments used the Arnetminer and DBDComp datasets. The results show that the method performance is overall better than the existing state-of-the-art incremental author name disambiguation methods.

To solve the author name disambiguation problem, authors in [13] developed a method based on multi-step clustering using the Chinese literature system. First, the method combines brief characteristics of literature system information with the comparison of co-authors' similarity to perform the initial clustering. The following information is extracted from the papers: title, names of cooperators, work units of authors, publishers, keywords, and publishing time. Then, the authors' information is extracted from the Baidu encyclopedia[2]. Second, the semantic similarity of subordinate units is compared to the basis of identity discrimination. Finally, the extraction of two steps clustering paper keywords in each class cluster is combined into corpus collection through the characteristics of the semantic comparison. Cancellation of indeterminacy results for further adjustment is carried out to complete the multi-step clustering. The experimental data set is from the China National Knowledge Infrastructure (CNKI)[3]. Experimental results show that the hybrid disambiguation framework is feasible and efficient.

LUCID author name disambiguation using graph structural clustering is proposed by [14]. LUCID uses community detection and graph operations defined in different phases. In the first phase, the approach performs pre-processing tasks on the data set and creates blocks of ambiguous authors [4]. In the second phase, the co-authors graph is built, and a structural clustering algorithm for networks is applied to detect hubs, outliers, and clusters of nodes (author communities) [15]. The hub node that intersects with many clusters is considered as a homonym and resolved by splitting across the node. Finally, the synonyms are disambiguated using the proposed hybrid similarity function [16]. Results show that the method performance is better than the baseline methods, achieving 97% in terms of pairwise precision, 74% in recall, and 82% in F1.

In contrast to the related work presented, the novel approach proposed in this article is a multi-strategic one that compares author, co-author, and institutions. The multi-strategic approach integrates the Jaccard similarity coefficient, the Levenshtein distance measure, and the social network clustering technique. The baseline used for comparison the SCI-synergy online scientific social network artifact, which is unique in Brazil [9]. Thus, our approach cannot be compared to [13], since they used the CNKI with Chinese data set to validate their method, which cannot be compared to Brazilian author names. In LUCID [14] work, authors use only two entities to disambiguate: author and co-author, which is not comparable to our approach. Authors in [11] presented an incremental author name disambiguation method, which is evaluated using different metrics than the ones used in this work: ACP (Author Cluster Purity), AAP (Authors Average Purity), and K-metric.

---

[2] https://baike.baidu.com.
[3] http://www.cnki.net/.

3   Social Network Disambiguation Approach

In this section, we initially present some preliminary definitions that are necessary to understand the proposed approach. In the sequence, we present the multi-strategic approach for author name disambiguation including the data extraction and storage (Sect. 3.2), the disambiguation core (Sect. 3.3), and the social network graph creation (Sect. 3.4).

3.1   Preliminaries

The Jaccard similarity coefficient, simply known as intersection over union, is a statistic used for gauging the similarity and diversity of sample sets that are adequate to word similarity computation [17]. Equation 1 presents the coefficient measures similarity between finite sample sets, defined as the size of the intersection divided by the size of the union of the sample sets. If sets A and B are both empty then Jaccard(A,B) = 1, where $0 \leq Jaccard(A, B) \leq 1$.

$$Jaccard(A, B) = \frac{|A \bigcap B|}{|A \bigcup B|} = \frac{|A \bigcap B|}{|A| + |B| - |A \bigcap B|} \tag{1}$$

The Levenshtein distance, also known as edit distance, is a similarity function responsible for determining how similar two references (or groups of references) are [18]. The function returns a number that shows how different two references or strings are, where the higher the number more different are the strings. Informally, the Levenshtein distance between two words is the minimum number of single-character edits (insertions, deletions, or substitutions) required to change one word into the other. Applying the Levenshtein Distance between "magic" and "tragic" results in two edits to transform one string to the other:

- magic - ragic (substitution of "r" for "m"); and
- ragic - tragic (insertion of "t" at the beginning).

Network clustering is a fundamental approach for detecting hidden structures in networks that are receiving increased attention in computer science, physics, and bioinformatics because of many interesting applications [19]. Graph structural clustering is a fundamental graph mining operation that is not only able to find connected clusters, but also identify hub vertices and outliers in the graph. Related to the problem of automatic name disambiguation approaches, there are many in the literature using real-world graphs that apply graph structural clustering techniques [20–22].

3.2   Data Extraction and Storage

To start the data extraction and storage phase, the scientific social network to apply disambiguation has to be defined. Related to this network are the publications, authors, co-authors, and institutions. The authors will initially form the social network *seeds* (*author seeds*). In the graduate programs case, extraction algorithms (or crawlers) have to be used to access the web sites of the institutions and retrieve the researchers' names linked to the graduate programs [23].

After extracting the *author seeds*, it is necessary to retrieve information from the scientific production of each author. In our case, we used the DBLP API[4]. Figure 1 presents the proposed multi-strategic approach architecture that includes the data extraction and storage process in the first phase.

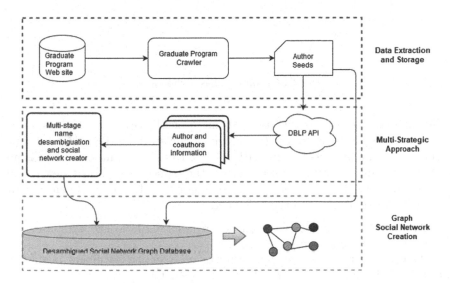

Fig. 1. The multi-strategic proposed approach architecture.

To store the extracted data a NoSQL database is used to deal with the social network information. The graph database was created using Neo4j[5] with the data scheme illustrated in Fig. 2. The Neo4j database allows us to naturally model a real-world network as a graph and persist it. Besides, indexing capabilities simply assure node location [24].

3.3 Multi-strategic Core

In this phase, disambiguation is performed through different steps. The documents with the information of the authors' seeds, co-authors, and their respective publications are processed as shown in Fig. 1. This step starts at Line 2 of Algorithm 1.1. During this process, each author's publication is retrieved extracting the co-authors. This step starts at Line 3 of Algorithm 1.1. In the course of this verification, a multi-strategic sequence is applied to check name ambiguity.

---

[4] https://dblp.org/search/publ/api.

[5] https://neo4j.com/.

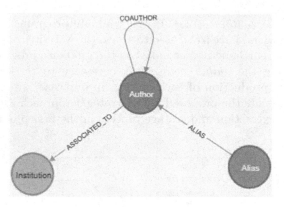

Fig. 2. Graph database schema.

The multi-strategic sequence starts at Line 8 of Algorithm 1.1. If the author's name is detected in the database (using any of the strategies) his *id* is returned and the new name is added as the author *alias*. But, if the author's name is not detected using any disambiguation strategy, the name is stored as a new author in the database as described in Line 23 of Algorithm 1.1. The sequence of the disambiguation strategies are the following:

1. checks whether the name of the author or *alias* exists in the database. This step starts at Line 9 of Algorithm 1.1.
2. checks whether the name of the author or *alias* in the document is abbreviated. This check starts at Line 12 of Algorithm 1.1.
3. verifies whether the name of the author or *alias* in the database is abbreviated. This check starts at Line 14 of Algorithm 1.1.
4. remove author names accentuation and check if the name or *alias* exists in the base. This check starts at Line 16 of Algorithm 1.1.
5. compute the Jaccard coefficient, the Levenshtein distance, and compare the results with authors or *alias* in the database. The Algorithm 1.2 describes this computation at Line 18 of Algorithm 1.1.
6. compute the similarity coefficient of the co-authorship and institution with an author in the network. A similarity function was applied to compare co-authorship, where the clusters of each author's network are checked and then compared. The number of the same co-authors in the authors' clusters is compared. It is checked whether the authors being compared are from the same institution. This procedure starts at Line 20 of Algorithm 1.1.

Experiments were conducted to define empirically the threshold values for the similarity coefficient. For the *Jaccard* coefficient values might be greater than $0,90$, while for the Levenshtein distance the threshold might be less than five. Different values were tested but the results presented bad name disambiguation, and alias-author connections different from reality. The best disambiguation results are greater than four for co-author similarity as presented in the Algorithm 1.1.

```
AD = Author Seeds Documents;

for each document in AD:
    Publications = getPublications(document);

    for each publication in Publications:
        ListOfAuthors = getAuthors(publication);
        #List to process co-authorship of authors of the current
            publication
        ListCoAuthors;

        for each author in ListofAuthors:
            if authors equals from any(author or alias) in database:
                #Get the id Author from database and add to list of co-
                    authors
                ListCoAuthors.add(id.AuthorDB);
            else if abbreviated author name equals from any(author or
                alias) in database:
                ListCoAuthors.add(id.AuthorDB);
            else if authors equals from any(abbreviated author or alias
                name) in database:
                ListCoAuthors.add(id.AuthorDB);
            else if author name without accent is equals from any(author
                or alias) in database:
                ListCoAuthors.add(id.AuthorDB);
            else if JaccardAndLeveshtein(author).Jaccard > 0.90 AND
                JaccardAndLeveshtein(author).Leveshtein < 5:
                ListCoAuthors.add(id.AuthorDB);
            else if Network Clustering Similarity(author) > 4:
                # Similarity of the co-authorship network and
                    institution with an author with a similar first and
                    last name < 4
                ListCoAuthors.add(id.AuthorDB);
            else:
                Add author as new Author in database;
                ListCoAuthors.add(in.newAuthor);

        for each author in ListCoAuthors:
            for i=0, i < ListCoAuthors.length, i=i+1:
                if author <> i:
```

Algorithm 1.1. Multi-strategic algorithm.

```
function JaccardAndLeveshtein(authorA);

    ListAuthors = ListAuthorsAliasEqualFirstName;
    #Get authors list & alias in database  with 1st name equal to the
        author of the function input

    for each authorB in ListAuthors:
        JaccardSimilarity(authorA, authorB);
        LeveshteinDistance(authorA, authorB);

    Jaccard = JaccardSimilarity().max;
    Leveshtein = LeveshteinDistance().min;

    return [Jaccard, Leveshtein]
```

Algorithm 1.2. Function to return Jaccard coefficient and Levenshtein distance.

3.4 Social Network Graph Creation

In this phase, the social network graph is created using the Neo4j database to store information. As presented in Fig. 1, at the end of the data extraction of the *author seeds* are inserted in the database.

After the authors' disambiguation phase of a given publication, the connection of the co-authors of that publication is performed. This step starts at Line 26 in Algorithm 1.1, where the list of co-authors is iterated. In each iteration, a merge transaction is made in the database, as this co-authoring link may or may not have happened in a publication already analyzed.

The previous step is performed in all publications by each *author seed*. In the end, we will have a social network molded in a graph database with the co-authorship links.

4 Case Study

In this section, we present an empirical evaluation of the proposed multi-strategic approach using a Brazilian graduate program case. The SCI-synergy artifact is used as a baseline (Sect. 4.1) and the result analysis is presented in Sect. 4.2.

4.1 Baseline

The multi-strategic approach presented in this work is compared with data from SCI-synergy. SCI-synergy is an online artifact to deal with information regarding research collaboration through the use of scientific social networks [9].

The graduate program case used in SCI-synergy includes five computer science programs of Federal Universities in Brazil located in different states to illustrate the variety of characteristics of the country's research. The universities are the Federal University of Minas Gerais (UFMG), the University of Sao Paulo (USP), the Federal University of Rio Grande do Norte (UFRN), the Federal University of Amazonas (UFAM), and the University of Brasilia (UnB).

The social network includes author and co-authorship relations in publications indexed by the DBLP computer science bibliography repository. Nowadays, data has 180 *author seeds* linked to the five graduate programs, covering 7369 authors and co-authors of 7317 publications such as books, journals, and conference articles.

The name disambiguation method of SCI-synergy uses DBLP, which includes the treatment of homonyms and synonyms. In DBLP different authors with the same name are homonyms. The same name refers exactly to the same (Latin-1) string, taking punctuation (e.g., "O'Shea" and "O-Shea"), diacritics (e.g., "Æleen" and "AEleen"), and case ("Gianluigi" and "GianLuigi") into account to consider different names. At the moment, the splitting of existing DBLP author pages is either triggered by requests of authors or if the DBLP team can prove that there are several persons behind an entry.

Different spelling, misspelling, or mistranslation are causes of author name synonym. In DBLP there are many reasons why several author names are considered to be synonymous for a particular author: name changes, nicknames, sporadic use of middle names, missing or abbreviated name parts, or even pseudonyms. Occasional spelling errors in the publishers' metadata also complicate the matter. When multiple versions of a name are frequently used on publications, these names may be included as aliases to the DBLP data set and we used those in the SCI-synergy artifact. Unfortunately, in many cases, homonyms and synonyms remain undetected needing further investigation.

4.2 Case Results and Analysis

The performance of the multi-strategic disambiguation approach presented in this article is compared with the graduate program case of SCI-synergy, using information from the DBLP repository as described in Sect. 4.1. In our case, 203 authors with the name ambiguity were used. Those authors are linked to three computer science graduate programs - USP, UFRN, and UnB - that together represent 37% of authors in SCI-synergy. Applying the proposed multi-strategic approach, 180 authors were disambiguated and 23 were not, while in SCI-synergy only 44 were disambiguated and 159 were not, as presented in Fig. 3. These three institutions were chosen for better visualization of the network density as presented in Fig. 4.

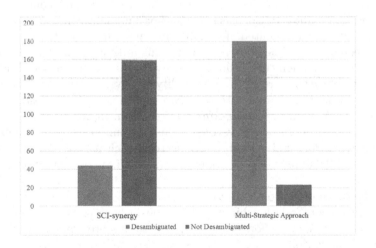

Fig. 3. Comparison between disambiguation approaches.

The ground truth annotations of author disambiguation were done by human checking. Considering the 23 author names unsolved by the multi-strategic approach, we checked them in two different repositories to verify ambiguity. For that, we used ArnetMiner/AMiner, a system to integrate publications from online

Web databases using a probabilistic framework to deal with the name ambiguity problem [25][6]; and Microsoft Academic Search, one of the most popular free citation-based academic search engines, with more than 257 million authors and 242 million publications [26][7]. Table 1 displays seven authors that were not solved by the multi-strategic approach, but even though, they present a smaller number of ambiguous entries compared to other repositories.

Table 1. Number of ambiguous author name entries in different repositories.

Name	AMiner	Microsoft academic	Multi-strategic approach
Alba Cristina Magalhães Alves de Melo	3	4	2
Nina Sumiko Tomita Hirata	3	3	2
Lyrene Fernandes Da Silva	2	3	2
Anarosa Alves Franco Brandão	4	3	2
Priscila Solís Barreto	4	1	3
Aletéia Patrícia Favacho de Araújo	4	3	3
Maria Emília Machado Telles Walter	3	1	2

In some cases, the multi-strategic approach was not able to disambiguate authors with a largely composed name, e.g., when the full name contained more than four middle names. In this case, the author's name was not disambiguated or was partially disambiguated. Partially disambiguated are the cases where there is a decrease in ambiguous records by this author at the base. This case happens more often when the author has many co-authors in the social network. With many publications grows the probability of having many combinations of the author's name. For example, *Maria Clara Machado da Silva Costa Favacho*, *Maria Clara M. S. Costa Favacho*, *Maria Costa Favacho*, *Maria Clara Favacho*. Another problem that has been verified is that the majority of the ambiguous author names in Portuguese contain connectors, such as, *de*, *do*, *da*, *dos* and *das* in the middle names. These connectors sometimes do not appear in the publications.

After the disambiguation techniques were applied, a social network was created with the authors' relationship in publications, where author nodes are represented by points and co-author relationships are represented by lines and arrows. The graph visualization of social networks was created using Neovis.js [27] and presented in the Fig. 4. It is possible to verify that the multi-strategic social network has fewer relationships compared to the SCI-synergy due to the lower number of ambiguous authors.

---

[6] https://web.archive.org/web/20110728092533/http://arnetminer.org/.
[7] https://academic.microsoft.com/home.

Commonly used evaluation methods were applied to evaluate the results with recall rate, precision, and F-measure [28,29]. Precision (Eq. 2) and recall (Eq. 3) are measures used in the information retrieval domain to measure how well an information retrieval system retrieves the relevant documents. The F-measure score is the harmonic mean of the precision and recall with the highest possible value of 1, indicating perfect precision (Eq. 4). Figure 5 presents the results of the multi-strategic approach with a precision of 0.8867, recall of 1, and F-measure of 0.9399.

$$\text{Precision} = \text{TP}/(\text{TP} + \text{FP}) \tag{2}$$

$$\text{Recall} = \text{TP}/(\text{TP} + \text{FN}) \tag{3}$$

$$\text{F-measure} = (2 \times \text{Precision} \times \text{Recall})/(\text{Precision} + \text{Recall}) \tag{4}$$

In Eqs. 2 and 3, true positive (TP) refers to the number of author names correctly disambiguated. False-positive (FP) indicates the number of incorrectly disambiguated names. False-negative (FN) indicates the number of authors that needs to be disambiguated and has not been. When applying the multi-strategic approach, we had the following results: (i) TP1, when the author was correctly disambiguated both in SCI-synergy and in the proposed multi-strategic approach (33 authors corresponding to 16% of the total number of 203 authors), (ii) TP2, when there was the correct disambiguation only on the multi-strategic approach (147 authors, 73%), (iii) FP1, in which multi-strategic approach failed, associating erroneously author of its alias (7 authors, 3%), (iv) FP2, where the multi-strategic approach did not completely disambiguated the author name and did not correctly associate to the alias (16 authors, 8%).

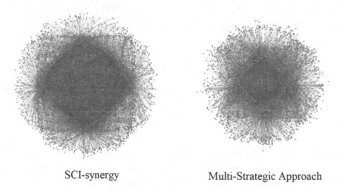

SCI-synergy   Multi-Strategic Approach

Fig. 4. Comparison between social network graphs.

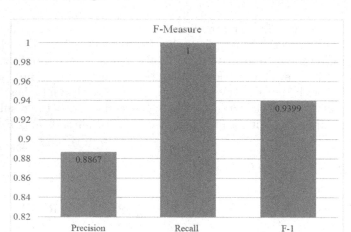

Fig. 5. F-measure of the multi-strategic approach.

5   Conclusion

In this work, we present a novel multi-strategic approach for author name disambiguation in bibliography repositories using co-author names and institutions. The proposal applies the Jaccard similarity coefficient, Levenshtein distance measure, and social network clustering technique that together have not been used in the presented related works.

The presented multi-strategic author name disambiguation approach outperforms the baseline considering commonly used evaluation methods with a precision of 0.8867, recall of 1, and F-measure of 0.9399. In terms of true positive values, the TP2 achieved 73%. The false-positive of FP1 is 3% and FP2 is 8%.

For future work, different bibliography repositories than DBLP can be used to validate the proposed approach. Other similarity measures can be combined with machine learning algorithms that have recently presented promising results. Also, we intend to extend the case study to cover the social network formed by all Brazilian graduate programs.

Acknowledgments. Prof. Célia G. Ralha thanks the support received from the Brazilian National Council for Scientific and Technological Development (CNPq) for the research grant in Computer Science number 311301/2018-5.

References

1. Anderson, A.F., Gonçalves, M.A., Laender, A.H.F.: Automatic disambiguation of author names in bibliographic repositories. Synth. Lect. Inf. Concept. Retrieval Serv. **12**(1), 1–146 (2020). https://doi.org/10.2200/S01011ED1V01Y202005ICR070

2. DBLP: Bibliographies statistics (2020). https://blog.dblp.org/2020/03/26/5-million-publications/
3. Kim, J., Kim, J., Owen-Smith, J.: Generating automatically labeled data for author name disambiguation: an iterative clustering method. Scientometrics **118**(1), 253–280 (2018). https://doi.org/10.1007/s11192-018-2968-3
4. Shin, D., Kim, T., Choi, J., Kim, J.: Author name disambiguation using a graph model with node splitting and merging based on bibliographic information. Scientometrics **100**(1), 15–50 (2014). https://doi.org/10.1007/s11192-014-1289-4
5. Tran, H.N., Huynh, T., Do, T.: Author name disambiguation by using deep neural network. In: Nguyen, N.T., Attachoo, B., Trawiński, B., Somboonviwat, K. (eds.) ACIIDS 2014. LNCS (LNAI), vol. 8397, pp. 123–132. Springer, Cham (2014). https://doi.org/10.1007/978-3-319-05476-6_13
6. Hussain, I., Asghar, S.: A survey of author name disambiguation techniques: 2010–2016. Knowl. Eng. Rev. **32**, (2017). https://doi.org/10.1017/S0269888917000182
7. Saeedi, A., Nentwig, M., Peukert, E., Rahm, E.: Scalable matching and clustering of entities with FAMER. Complex Syst. Inf. Model. Q. **16**, 61 83 (2018). https.//doi.org/10.7250/csimq.2018-16.04
8. Sanyal, D.K., Bhowmick, P.K., Das, P.P.: A review of author name disambiguation techniques for the pubmed bibliographic database. J. Inf. Sci. (2019). https://doi.org/10.1177/0165551519888605
9. InfoKnow Research Group.: SCI-Synergy: Synergy of Science. http://165.227.113.212
10. Bollen, J., Rodriguez, M.A., Van de Sompel, H., Balakireva, L.L., Hagberg, A.: The largest scholarly semantic network...ever. In: Proceedings of the 16th International Conference on World Wide Web, pp. 1247–1248. ACM (2007). https://doi.org/10.1145/1242572.1242789
11. Hussain, I., Asghar, S.: Incremental author name disambiguation using author profile models and self-citations. Turk. J. Electr. Eng. Comput. Sci. **27**, 3665–3681 (2019). https://doi.org/10.3906/elk-1806-132
12. Hussain, I., Asghar, S.: DISC: dsambiguating homonyms using graph structural clustering. J. Inf. Sci. **44**(6), 830–847 (2018). https://doi.org/10.1177/0165551518761011
13. Gu, S., Xu, X., Zhu, J., Ji, L.: Name disambiguation method based on multi-step clustering. In: Shakshuki, E.M. (ed.) The 7th International Conference on Ambient Systems, Networks and Technologies (ANT 2016)/The 6th International Conference on Sustainable Energy Information Technology (SEIT-2016)/Affiliated Workshops, 23–26 May 2016, Madrid, Spain, vol. 83 of Procedia Computer Science, pp. 488–495. Elsevier (2016). https://doi.org/10.1016/j.procs.2016.04.237
14. Hussain, I., Asghar, S.: LUCID: author name disambiguation using graph structural clustering. In: Proceedings of the Intelligent Systems Conference (IntelliSys), pp. 406–413. IEEE (2017). https://doi.org/10.1109/IntelliSys.2017.8324326
15. Shiokawa, H., Fujiwara, Y., Onizuka, I.: SCAN++: eficient algorithm for finding clusters, hubs and outliers on large-scale graphs. Proc. VLDB Endow. **8**(11), 1178–1189 (2015). https://doi.org/10.14778/2809974.2809980
16. Winkler, W.E.: String Comparator Metrics and Enhanced Decision Rules in the Fellegi-Sunter Model of Record Linkage. Distributed by ERIC Clearinghouse, Washington, D.C. (1990). https://eric.ed.gov/?id=ED325505
17. Niwattanakul, S., Singthongchai, J., Naenudorn, E., Wanap, W.E.: Using of Jaccard coefficient for keywords similarity. In: Proceedings of the International MultiConference of Engineers and Computer Scientists (IMECS), vol. 1 (2013)

18. Ferreira, A.A., Gonçalves, M.A., Laender, A.H.F.: A brief survey of automatic methods for author name disambiguation. SIGMOD Rec. **41**(2), 15–26 (2012). https://doi.org/10.1145/2350036.2350040

19. Xu, X., Yuruk, N., Feng, Z., Schweiger, TA.J.: SCAN: a structural clustering algorithm for networks. In: Proceedings of the 13th ACM SIGKDD International Conference on Knowledge Discovery and Data Mining, pp. 824–833. ACM (2007). https://doi.org/10.1145/1281192.1281280

20. Zhang, Y., Zhang, E., Yao, P., Tang, J.: Name disambiguation in aminer: clustering, maintenance, and human in the loop. In: Proceedings of the 24th ACM SIGKDD International Conference on Knowledge Discovery & Data Mining, pp. 1002–1011 (2018)

21. Peng, L., Shen, S., Li, D., Xu, J., Fu, Y., Su, H.: Author disambiguation through adversarial network representation learning. In: 2019 International Joint Conference on Neural Networks (IJCNN), pp. 1–8. IEEE (2019). https://doi.org/10.1109/IJCNN.2019.8852233

22. Xinhua, S.Z.E., Pan. T.: A multi-level author name disambiguation algorithm. IEEE Access **7**, 104250–104257 (2019). https://doi.org/10.1109/ACCESS.2019.2931592

23. Kumar, M., Bhatia, R., Dhavleesh, R.: A survey of web crawlers for information retrieval. WIREs Data Mining Knowl. Discovery **7**(6), (2017). https://doi.org/10.1002/widm.1218

24. WarchaL, L.: Using Neo4j graph database in social network analysis. Stud. Informatica **33**(2A), 271–279 (2012). https://doi.org/10.21936/SI2012_V33.N2A.147

25. Tang, J., Zhang, J., Yao, L., Li, J., Zhang, L., Su, Z.: ArnetMiner: extraction and mining of academic social networks. In: Proceedings of the 14th ACM SIGKDD Int. Conf. on Knowledge Discovery and Data Mining, KDD 2008, pp. 990–998. Association for Computing Machinery, New York (2008). https://doi.org/10.1145/1401890.1402008

26. Wang, K.: A review of Microsoft academic services for science of science studies. Front. Big Data **2**, 45 (2019). https://doi.org/10.3389/fdata.2019.00045

27. Needham, M., Hodler, A.E.: Graph Algorithms: Practical Examples in Apache Spark and Neo4j. O'Reilly Media (2019)

28. Powers, D.M.: Evaluation: from precision, recall and F-measure to ROC, informedness, markedness and correlation. J. Mach. Learn. Technol. **2**, 37–63 (2011). http://www.bioinfo.in/contents.php?id=51

29. Tharwat, A.: Classification assessment methods. Applied Computing and Informatics, ahead-of-print (2020). ISSN: 2634-1964. https://doi.org/10.1016/j.aci.2018.08.003

Machine Learning Techniques for Speech Emotion Classification

Noe Melo Locumber$^{(\boxtimes)}$ and Junior Fabian

Universidad ESAN, Alonso de Molina N° 1652, Lima, Peru
15101369@ue.edu.pe, jfabian@esan.edu.pe
https://www.ue.edu.pe/

Abstract. In this paper we propose and evaluate different models for speech emotion classification through audio signal processing, machine learning and deep learning techniques. For this purpose, we have collected from two databases (RAVDESS and TESS), a total of 5252 audio samples with 8 emotional classes (neutral, calm, happy, sad, angry, fearful, disgust and surprised). We have divided our experiments in 3 main stages. In the first stage, we have used feature engineering to extract relevant features from the time, spectral and cepstral domains. Features like ZCR, energy, spectral centroid, chroma, MFCC etc. were used to train a SVM classifier. The best model obtained an accuracy of 91.1%. In the second stage, we only have considered 40 MFCC coefficients for training several Deep Neural Networks such as CNN, LSTM and MLP were trained, the best model obtained an accuracy of 89.5% with an MLP architecture. Finally, for the third stage we have trained an end-to-end CNN network (SampleCNN) at the sample level. This last approach does not require features engineering, but directly the audio signal. In this stage, we achieve a precision of 81.7%. The experiments show that the results achieved are competitive and some experiments have surpassed in accuracy the related works.

Keywords: Speech emotion classification · Machine learning · Audio processing

1 Introduction

Emotions are part of the human being's existence and are closely linked to rationality. Each person is the sum of their sensations, feelings and experiences, and many times decisions are made based on these ([4] and [5]). This aspect of the human being is so important that disciplines such as psychology have been created in order to study them, thanks to these disciplines concepts such as Emotional Intelligence were born, which according to [12] refers to the human ability to feel, understand, control and modify the emotional states of oneself and also of others. But business-focused sciences such as Digital Marketing were also born, which according to [1], is a science that aims to ensure that a brand

© Springer Nature Switzerland AG 2021
J. A. Lossio-Ventura et al. (Eds.): SIMBig 2020, CCIS 1410, pp. 77–89, 2021.
https://doi.org/10.1007/978-3-030-76228-5_6

has an emotional link with customers, consumers and future customers, so that they feel the brand as their own and need to be part of it.

Emotions have become fundamental in the development of new solutions, whether for health or business, and even more with the growth of technology and information, scientific disciplines such as Machine Learning and Data Science were born, which help to include the analysis of emotions for the development of technological solutions and applications. However, [11] mention that these technologies have focused their efforts on structured data and there is no many studies in multimedia mining with unstructured data.

According to [2], emotions manifest as a reaction or response of the organism to pleasant stimuli or dangerous situations. The reaction of the body can be recorded as information, be it of the face as a photograph or the voice tone in the form of audio waves, and in some other ways. This multimedia information or unstructured data can be processed and analyzed to create technological solutions that can include the emotions that are of great importance.

In this research we propose and analyze different machine learning techniques and digital signal processing techniques for the speech emotions classification. We have found that simple classifiers like the SVM (Support Vector Machine) perform well for this task. We have also found that the first 40 Mel Frequency Cepstral Coefficients (MFCC) are the best audio features for speech emotion classification. In addition, we have found that CNN's end-to-end techniques have performed well in feature extraction of the audio signal.

In Sect. 2, the works related to the classification of speech emotions are described; In Sect. 3, the methodology is presented; Sect. 4 describes the results; finally, in Sect. 5 we discuss the conclusions of the proposed investigation.

2   Related Work

Speech emotion classification has been carried out in several investigations that will be described below. In order to develop a speech emotion classification, several works using machine learning techniques has been applied to solve this problem. Many of them use a well-know classifiers as the SVM which has given good results. In [8] an SVM model has been developed using the audio features: 12 MFCC coefficients and MS (Modulation Spectral), obtaining up to 90.05% accuracy using FS (Feature Selection) with a database of 7 emotional classes. However, in [7] they have used many more audio features such as 13 MFCC coefficients, ZCR (Zero Crossing Rate), Spectral Centroid, 12 Chroma components, etc. With these characteristics, they have trained a SVM model that obtained an average of 80% accuracy with two databases and 4 emotional classes. Another work related to this classifier is [14], where a SVM classifier has been trained with features of the three audio domains: time domain (ZRC, Frame Energy and Frame Entropy), spectral domain (Spectral Centroid, Spectral Entropy, etc.) and cepstral domain (17 MFCC coefficients). Using these features they have obtained up to 80% accuracy with 6 emotional classes. Based on this research, the most common feature is MFCC and it appears to be very good at detecting speech emotions, more so than other audio features.

Works have also been carried out using Deep Learning techniques in the classification of speech emotions. In [8] a model has been developed using a RNN (Recurrent Neural Network) training with some features of the audio (described in the previous paragraph), which obtains an accuracy of 94.01% working with 7 emotional classes. In [3] they applied a CNN (Convolutional Neural Network) model as a feature extractor whose output was used as input to a special recurrent neural network know as LSTM (Long-Short Term Memory) using only 13 MFCC coefficients as the audio feature, obtaining a 80% accuracy, with 7 emotional classes. The research described in this paragraph showed that RNNs appear to be very good at classifying speech emotions and CNNs are a good extractor of audio signal features.

In the feature extraction, the audio information is lost, therefore, another way to train algorithms is using the waveform of the audio signal, as a direct input to the classification algorithms. In [6], 20 ms audio blocks have been entered directly into a 6 convolutional layer of a CNN, using 7×1 and 13×1 filters, obtaining up to 69.55% accuracy in validation with 3 emotional classes. Another investigation [15] used a DBN (Deep Belief Network) as a feature extractor, the output of which was used as input to a Shallow Neural Network, obtaining up to 89% accuracy with 5 emotional classes. These research papers suggest that some neural networks can be used as a feature extractor, without the need to do a feature engineering of the audio signal and avoiding the loss of information. It is worth mentioning that a CNN architecture at the sample level (end-to-end) using the audio waveform as input, was proposed by [9] in 2017, for the classification of 50 musical classes, this architecture had a great result (0.9055 AUC), because it uses very small filters (3×1) in the convolutional layers, extracting more detailed features from the audio.

Considering all the contributions in the state of the art, for this research work we proposed to use the audio features of the three domains (time, spectral and cepstral), but with more emphasis on the MFCC features that have given good results. It has also been considered to use Machine Learning and Deep Learning classifiers such as SVM, CNN, LSTM, etc., which performed well as described in this section. Finally, a focus was made on the use of CNN at the sample level to take advantage of all the possible information.

3   Methodology

The Fig. 1 shows the proposed methodology of this research, which consists of 5 stages:

3.1   Database

In this stage, the database search has been performed. Two databases with similar emotional classes have been found. RAVDESS [10] with 8 emotional classes (neutral, calm, happy, sad, angry, fearful, disgust and surprised), a total of 2452 audio files. TESS [13] with 7 emotional classes (neutral, happy, sad, angry,

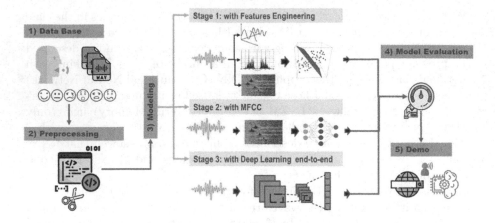

Fig. 1. Solution implementation methodology.

fearful, disgust and surprised), a total of 2800 audio files. These databases were recorded in an anechoic chamber and the emotional phrases were expressed by professional actors (men and women). In order to obtain better results, for this investigation we have joined both datasets as suggested in [14]. Finally, a total of 5252 audio files with 8 emotional classes (neutral, calm, happy, sad, angry, fearful, disgust and surprised) were obtained. The Fig. 2 shows the distribution of emotional classes.

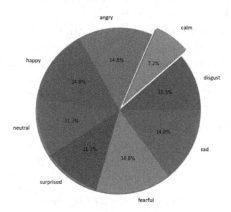

Fig. 2. Percentage distribution of emotional classes RAVDESS + TESS.

3.2   Preprocessing

This section explored the databases found in the previous step. The database has been resampled at 22050 Hz, to be able to work uniformly. The duration of each audio file has been calculated, finding a minimum duration of 1.25 s and maximum duration of approximately 4.5 s. In addition, it has been verified that the database has no noise using waveform plot (Fig. 3).

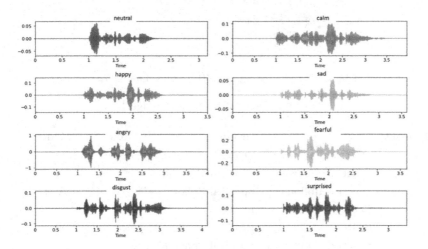

Fig. 3. Waveform plot of emotional classes.

3.3   Modeling

In this part, some classification algorithms have been trained using a database protocol division of 80/20 for training and testing respectively. This part has been divided into 3 stages: Stage 1 with feature engineering, extracting features from the time, spectral and cepstral domains; Stage 2 using only MFCC features; finally, Stage 3 using CNN at the sample level (end-to-end).

Stage 1. Six SVM models have been trained with each group of audio features shown in Table 1. Models have been trained with FS (Feature Selection) and without FS. For this task, we applied the RFE (Recursive Feature Elimination) algorithm with default parameters, which eliminates half of the least important features. All the features have been extracted based on previous works ([7,8] and [14]) in which good results were obtained with the SVM classifier. Additionally, in the training of each model, the best hyper-parameters of the SVM were searched with a 10-fold cross-validation. The training flow for each model can be seen in Fig. 4.

Stage 2. Five Deep Learning models have been trained using only 40 MFCC coefficients as features, because in previous works this features has performed very well in the classification of speech emotions, such as example in [8] and [3]. The first CNN (1D) model with 3 convolutional layers (32, 16, 8 filters of 5×1 respectively). The second CNN model with the same configurations as the previous model, whose output was used as input to a hidden two-layer LSTM network

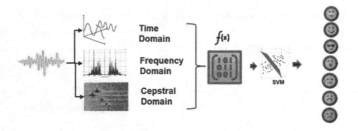

Fig. 4. Stage 1 modeling with feature engineering.

Table 1. Table of features of Stage 1.

Domains	Group 1	Group 2	Group 3	Model
DT	ZCR	ZCR	–	
DS	Spectral Centroid	Spectral Centroid	–	
	Spectral Rolloff	Spectral Rolloff	–	SVM
	Energy	Energy	–	
	RMS	RMS	–	
	Spectral Bandwidth	Spectral Bandwidth	–	
	Spectral Contrast	Spectral Contrast	–	SVM+FS
	Chroma(12)	Chroma(12)	–	
DC	MFCC(13)	MFCC(40)	MFCC(40)	

DT = Dominio Temporal

ST = Dominio Spectral

DC = Dominio Cepstral

RMS = Root-Mean-Square Energy

(50 and 20 nodes respectively). The last three MLP (Multilayer Perceptron) models, the first with 1 hidden layer, the second with 2 hidden layers, and the last with 3 hidden layers, each hidden layer with 500 neurons. The training flow for each model can be seen in Fig. 5.

Stage 3. In the last stage, two sample-level CNN models (end-to-end) were trained, using the audio waveform as a feature to capture all the possible information in the convolutional layers. For this stage, the SampleCNN architecture proposed by [9], which has 11 convolutional layers with 3×1 filters, has been adapted. Because SampleCNN accepts an input of size 59049 (sample length), the first model was trained by dividing the audio into blocks of size 59049, if the block does not reach the required size they were completed with 0, as long as the block size is greater than or equal to half the required size, otherwise they were discarded. The second model was trained trimming the audio into a random block of size 59049, in such a way that many blocks completed with 0 were avoided. The training flow for each model can be seen in Fig. 6.

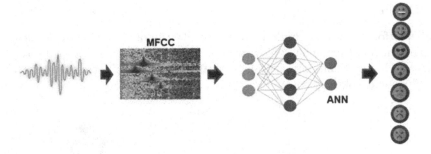

Fig. 5. Stage 2 modeling with MFCC features.

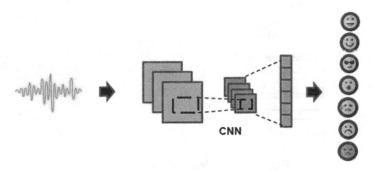

Fig. 6. Stage 3 modeling with CNN end-to-end.

3.4 Model Evaluation

For the evaluation of the trained models, the following indicators have been used: accuracy (Eq. 1), precision (Eq. 2), AUC (area under the curve) (Eq. 3) and confusion matrix. The evaluation has focused more than anything on how good the algorithm is at classifying speech emotions. These metrics have helped us determine if the classification model is capable of differentiating the 8 emotional classes. The results are reported in detail in Sect. 4.

$$Accuracy = \frac{TP + TN}{(TP + TN + FP + FN)} \tag{1}$$

$$Precision = \frac{TP}{(TP + FP)} \tag{2}$$

$$AUC = \int TPR \, d(FPR) \tag{3}$$

where VP: is the number of positives that were correctly classified as positive by the model. VN: is the number of negatives that were correctly classified as negative by the model. FN: is the number of positives that were incorrectly classified as negative. FP: is the number of negatives that were incorrectly classified as positive. TPR: true positive rate. FPR: false positive rate.

3.5   Demo

A web platform has been built to demonstrate the our proposed classification algorithm in real time. The deployment diagram in Fig. 7 and the web interface in Fig. 8. This real time application is available at the following link: https://audioblognoe.herokuapp.com.

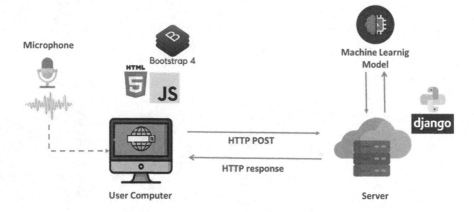

Fig. 7. Demo deployment diagram.

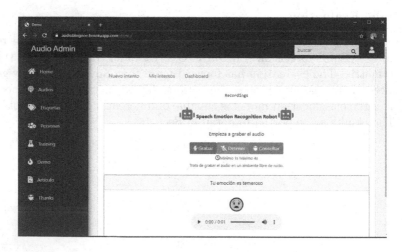

Fig. 8. Demo web interface.

4   Results

In this section the obtained results in each one of the three stages will be reported. Table 2 shows the results of Stage 1. The best SVM model was found using only 40 MFCC coefficients, obtaining an accuracy of 91.1%, precision of 91.1% and AUC of 0.995. In Table 2 it can be seen that trained models that have used features from other domains (time domain and spectral domain), have obtained inferior results despite having trained with many features. Using the cross-validation technique we found that the best SVM model uses the following hyper-parameters: C = 4, Degree = 2, Gamma = 0.12 and Kernel = radial.

Table 2. Comparison of models according to accuracy, precision and AUC of Stage 1.

Model	Feature	Accuracy (avg)	Precision (avg)	AUC (avg)
1. SVM	DT+DS+MFCC(13)	0.886	0.887	0.990
2. SVM	DT+DS+MFCC(13)+FS	0.819	0.817	0.976
3. SVM	DT+DS+MFCC(40)	0.877	0.883	0.992
4. SVM	DT+DS+MFCC(40)+FS	0.792	0.796	0.972
5. SVM	MFCC(40)	**0.911**	**0.911**	**0.995**
6. SVM	MFCC(40)+FS	0.803	0.801	0.972

Table 3 depicts the results of Stage 2. The model with the 3 hidden layers MLP architecture obtained an accuracy of 89.5%, precision of 89.0% and AUC of 0.991. It can be seen that the models using CNN and LSTM networks have obtained the lowest results of this Stage.

Table 3. Comparison of models according to accuracy, precision and AUC of Stage 2.

Model	Feature	Accuracy (avg)	Precision (avg)	ROC AUC (avg)
1. CNN(3)	MFCC(40)	0.834	0.829	0.984
2. CNN(3) + LSTM (2)	MFCC(40)	0.751	0.768	0.968
3. MLP(1)	MFCC(40)	0.882	0.878	0.991
4. MLP(2)	MFCC(40)	0.885	0.879	0.991
5. MLP(3)	MFCC(40)	**0.895**	**0.890**	**0.991**

Table 4 shows the results of Stage 3. The best model was trained with random blocks, with an accuracy of 81.5% and precision of 81.7%.

Table 4. Comparison of models according to accuracy and precision of Stage 3.

Model	Feature	Accuracy (avg)	Precision (avg)
1. SampleCNN	Raw-Form (sequential blocks)	0.771	0.805
2. SampleCNN	Raw-Form (random blocks)	**0.815**	**0.817**

According to this section, the SVM model has obtained the highest accuracy 91.1%, using only 40 MFCC coefficients. A similar result obtained the MLP model with 3 hidden layers using the same characteristics, obtaining an accuracy of 89.5%. On the other hand, with the CNN end-to-end approach at sample level, the best model obtained an accuracy of 81.5%, this result is better than what was obtained in [6], because this architecture use very small filters (3×1), extracting quite small features from the audio signal.

Table 5 shows the report with the accuracy level of the best models at the class level, it can be seen that the SVM model classifies most of the emotional classes better than the other techniques.

Table 5. Class-level accuracy comparison of the best models of Stage 1, 2 and 3.

Stage	Best model	Neutral	Calm	Happy	Sad	Angry	Fearful	Disgust	Surprised
1	SVM	**0.951**	0.882	0.935	**0.873**	**0.947**	**0.919**	**0.900**	0.870
2	MLP(3)	0.921	**0.908**	**0.936**	0.853	0.932	0.839	0.853	**0.921**
3	SampleCNN	0.882	0.791	0.748	0.810	0.889	0.714	0.879	0.826

In the confusion matrix (Fig. 9), it can be seen that the best SVM model has been confused very little when classifying the emotional classes, for example, the fearful emotion was confused in 6 samples by the sad emotion, which is understandable because these emotions even humans can be mistaken for their similarity. In the graph of the ROC curve (Fig. 10) it can be seen that the AUC of each class is very close to 1, this indicates that the model is able to distinguish the classes with a high precision.

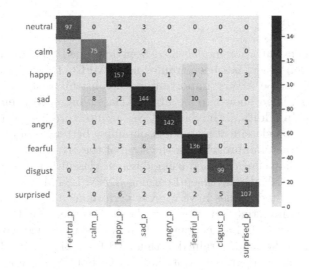

Fig. 9. Confusion matrix of the best SVM model of Stage 1.

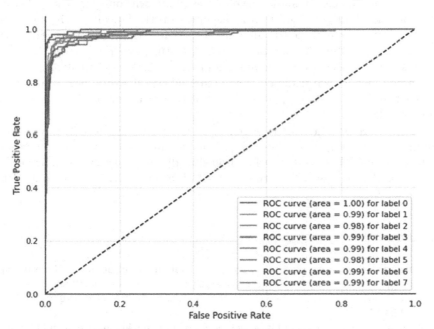

neutral = 0, calm = 1, happy = 2, sad = 3, angry = 4, fearful = 5, disgust = 6, surprised = 7

Fig. 10. ROC curve of the best SVM model of stage 1.

5   Conclusions

Speech emotion classification models have been developed from audio signals. An SVM classification model has been trained using MFCC features. It coefficients has been shown to be a very important feature in this task. A simple MLP network has also been shown to be able of classifying speech emotions with MFCC features. In addition, the SampleCNN architecture has been adapted to train speech emotion classification models, obtaining better results in comparison with others end-to-end approaches of the state of the art.

Many models have been trained using different classification techniques from Machine Learning (SVM) and Deep Learning (DNN, LSTM and CNN). In theory, Deep Learning techniques have a great performance in complicated tasks. However, for this investigation, the best classifier turned out to be the SVM (a simple model) with 91.1% accuracy, which has been trained with 40 MFCC coefficients. While the model trained with an MLP classifier with 3 hidden layers, using the same characteristics of the MFCC, obtained a very close result with 89.9% accuracy. On the other hand, the new technique with Deep Learning CNN end-to-end using the audio waveform as input, without performing feature extraction, also had good results (an accuracy of 81.5%), although not better than the previous mentioned techniques, but better than the state of the art. The difficulty of using the SampleCNN architecture was the size of the audio sample, since this architecture requires an input of 59049 sample length, so the audio samples have been trimmed to the required size. The audio trimming technique that had the best result was the extraction of a random blocks of 59049 sample length.

Finally, we hope that this research can contribute favorably in the analysis of unstructured data, specifically digital audio, in regards to the analysis of speech emotions. This result can be applied to different sectors, such as health, education and business, where the analysis of speech emotions is required for decision making.

References

1. Barragán Codina, J.N., Guerra Rodríguez, P., Villalpando Cadena, P.: La economía de la experiencia y el marketing emocional: estrategias contemporáneas de comercialización. Int. J. Good Conscience (2017). www.spentamexico.org/v12-n2/A9.12(2)159-170.pdf
2. Bisquera, R.: "Cómo educar las emociones" La inteligencia emocional en la infancia y adolescencia. Hospital Sant Joan de Déu, Barcelona (2012)
3. Basu, S., Chakraborty, J., Aftabuddin, M.: Emotion recognition from speech using convolutional neural network with recurrent neural network architecture. In: 2017 2nd International Conference on Communication and Electronics Systems (ICCES) (2017). https://doi.org/10.1109/CESYS.2017.8321292
4. Fernandez-Abascal, E.G., Garcia Rodriguez, B., Jiménez Sánchez, M.P., Martín Diaz, M.D., Dominguez Sanchez, F.J.: Psicología de la emoción, 2nd edn., pp. 18–20. Ramón Aceres, Madrid (2010)

5. Gordillo León, F., Arana Martínez, J.M., Salvador Cruz, J., Mestas Hernández, L.: Emoción y toma de decisiones: teoria y aplicación de IOWA Gambling Task. Revista Electrónica de Psicología Iztacala (2011)
6. Harár, P., Burget, R., Malay Dutta, K.: Speech emotion recognition with deep learning. In: 2017 4th International Conference on Signal Processing and Integrated Networks (SPIN) (2017). https://doi.org/10.1109/SPIN.2017.8049931
7. Iqbal, A., Barua, K.: A real-time emotion recognition from speech using gradient boosting. In: 2019 International Conference on Electrical, Computer and Communication Engineering (ECCE) (2019). https://doi.org/10.1109/ECACE.2019.8679271
8. Kerkeni, L., Serrestou, Y., Mbarki, M., Raoof, K., Mohamed Ali, M., Cleder, C.: Automatic speech emotion recognition using machine learning. Intechopen (2019). https://doi.org/10.5772/intechopen.84856
9. Lee, J., Park, J., Nam, J., Kim, K.L.: End-to-end deep convolutional neural networks using very small filters for music classification. In: 14th Sound and Music Computing Conference (2017). https://arxiv.org/abs/1703.01789
10. Livingstone, S.R., Russo, F.A.: The Ryerson audio-visual database of emotional speech and song (RAVDESS): a dynamic, multimodal set of facial and vocal expressions in North American English. PLoS One (2018). https://doi.org/10.1371/journal.pone.0196391
11. Oviedo Carrascal, E., Oviedo Carrascal, A., Velez Saldarriaga, G.: Minería multimedia: hacia la construcción de una metodología. Sci. Electron. Libr. Online (2016). https://doi.org/10.22395/rium.v16n31a6
12. Platero Ibañez, C.: Aplicaciones de la inteligencia emocional. Revista electrónica de investigación Docencia Creativa (2016). http://hdl.handle.net/10481/27761
13. Pichora-Fuller, M.K., Dupuis, K.: Toronto emotional speech set (TESS). Scholars Portal Dataverse (2010). https://doi.org/10.5683/SP2/E8H2MF
14. Semwal, N., Kumar, A., Narayanan, S.: Automatic speech emotion detection system using multi-domain acoustic feature selection and classification models. In: 2017 IEEE International Conference on Identity, Security and Behavior Analysis (ISBA) (2017). https://doi.org/10.1109/ISBA.2017.7947681
15. Wang, J., Han, Z.: Research on speech emotion recognition technology based on deep and shallow neural network. In: Chinese Control Conference (CCC) (2019). https://doi.org/10.23919/ChiCC.2019.8866568

An Evaluation of Physiological Public Datasets for Emotion Recognition Systems

Alexis Mendoza[1], Alvaro Cuno[1], Nelly Condori-Fernandez[1,2,3(✉)],
and Wilber Ramos Lovón[1(✉)]

[1] Departamento de Ingeniería de Sistemas e Informática,
Universidad Nacional de San Agustín de Arequipa, Arequipa, Peru
{amendoza,acunopa,ocondorif,wramos}@unsa.edu.pe
[2] Universidad de Coruña, A Coruña, Spain
n.condori.fernandez@udc.es
[3] Vrije Universiteit Amsterdam, Amsterdam, The Netherlands
n.condori-fernandez@vu.nl

Abstract. [Background] The performance of emotion recognition systems depends heavily on datasets used in their training, validation, or testing stages. [Aims] This research aims to evaluate the extent to which public available physiological datasets created for emotion recognition systems meet a set of reference requirements. [Method] Firstly, we analyze the applicability of some reference requirements proposed for stress datasets and adjust the corresponding evaluation criteria. Secondly, nine public physiological datasets were identified from a previous survey. [Results] None of the evaluated datasets satisfy all the reference requirements in order to be considered as a reference dataset for being used in the construction of reliable emotion recognition systems. [Conclusion] Although the evaluated datasets do not support the whole reference requirements, they provide a baseline for further development. Also, a greater effort is needed to establish specific reference requirements that can appropriately guide the creation of physiological datasets for emotion recognition systems.

Keywords: Physiological datasets · Reference requirements · Assessment

1 Introduction

In recent years, automatic emotion recognition systems have been undergoing considerable popularity growth because it can be applied in many critical areas such as safe driving [32], health care [19,29] citizen security [21], and so on [1,17,25,33]. In particular, those attracting the most attention are the systems based on physiological signals because of their involuntary nature and the difficulty involved in controlling them. According to Shu et al. [25], in emotion

© Springer Nature Switzerland AG 2021
J. A. Lossio-Ventura et al. (Eds.): SIMBig 2020, CCIS 1410, pp. 90–104, 2021.
https://doi.org/10.1007/978-3-030-76228-5_7

recognition systems, physiological signals (i.e., electroencephalogram, temperature, electrocardiogram, electromyogram, galvanic skin response, respiration, etc.) are having a higher preference than physical signals (i.e., facial expression, speech, gesture, posture, etc.).

Nevertheless, since people's well-being may depend on the reliability of these automatic systems, their performance (i.e., accuracy and error rates) must be optimal. For example, in the case of Self-driving Autonomous Vehicles (SAVs), although manufacturers have tried their best to avoid disasters, yet there have been a few fatal accidents involving SAVs [30].

In building emotion recognition systems, it has been identified that, either in approaches based on Machine Learning or in those based on Deep Learning, one element that has a direct impact on both accuracy and error rates are the datasets used in both training andvalidation stage. If the datasets are not proper, then robust and reliable results could not be expected, particularly when the systems are exposed to new situations, absent in the training datasets. Indeed, Ma et al. [15] have shown that emotions models trained on a dataset of another age group do not generalize well on elders.

Toward improving the performance of emotion recognition systems, in this work, we aim to answer the following research question: *In which extent, public datasets created for emotion recognition systems meet reference requirements?* To answer it, we have used —previous justification— the reference dataset requirements for stress detection proposed by Mahesh et al. [16]. Then, we evaluated the nine emotions datasets identified by Bota et al. [1] against evaluation criteria derived from the requirements. It was found that none of the evaluated datasets satisfy the thirteen established requirements, and of these, only two requirements are met by all datasets and four requirements are not met by any dataset.

The remainder of the article was organized as follows. In the second section, a review of related works is performed. In Sect. 3, we present the selected datasets, reference requirements and our evaluation criteria. Then, Sect. 4 reports our results and discussion is presented in Sect. 5. Finally, the conclusions and future work are discussed.

2   Related Work

To the best of our knowledge, this is the first evaluation of public physiological datasets for emotion recognition systems against reference requirements. Despite that, following, we review some related studies.

Mahesh et al. [16] observed that in order to build robust and reliable stress detection systems, it is necessary to develop, validate and benchmark the different systems on a reference dataset, however, heterogeneity in data collection approaches (stress stimuli, different sensors, multiple signals, etc.) have resulted in inconsistent datasets and the need to have one of reference. For that reason, they proposed five categories of requirements—derived from results and practices of clinical and empirical research—a dataset should fulfill for being qualified as a reference for stress detection systems. Five publicly available stress datasets were evaluated against evaluation criteria defined based on the requirements, and it was found that none of these completely fulfilled them. Therefore, they concluded that efforts should be made to establish a reference dataset to ensure the comparability and reliability of this kind of system.

Another study where the critical role of proper datasets was discussed is the one published by Igual et al. [8]. They performed a comparison of public datasets to determine their influence on the performance of fall detection systems. They showed that (i) detection rates are affected by the specific datasets used to validate the fall detection techniques, (ii) there are significant differences in the generalization capability of a fall detector depending on the dataset used for training, and (iii) the number of training samples also influence the fall detectors performance. In their conclusions, the authors recommended to test algorithms using several datasets (since the results got with them are dissimilar, and they seem to represent different movements) and train them with a dataset and validate them with another (for minimizing the influence of the dataset on the results).

It is also worth noting that some research has been done to consolidate the state-of-the-art of emotion recognition systems. One of them is the work of Bota et al. [1]. They presented a survey of emotion recognition systems based on physiological signals. First, they reviewed theoretical concepts of emotion models, autonomic nervous system, physiological signals, elicitation material, annotation methods, and a benchmark of physiological datasets. Next, they described and analyzed four methods required for the development of a machine learning algorithm for emotion recognition: (i) signal pre-processing, (ii) features representation, (iii) classification techniques, and (iv) validation approaches. After that, an overall analysis of the emotion recognition systems literature was performed. Then, some challenges and opportunities were reported: enhancement of experimental designs for emotion elicitation, validation of elicitation material, development of new emotion dimensions for complex emotions classification, design of person-independent algorithms, use of unsupervised learning algorithms and deep learning in multi-modal settings, and investigate which feature combinations of which physiological signals are the most relevant. Other engaging emotion recognition surveys are those presented by Shu et al. [25], Zhang et al. [33], and Marechal et al. [17].

3   Materials and Method

3.1   The Datasets

There are several physiological datasets for emotion recognition; however, mapping all existing data sets is beyond this paper's scope. Therefore, we decided to use the nine public datasets identified by Bota et al. [1].

Table 1 presents a summary of the main features for each dataset. There, the following acronyms are used: EEG (electroencephalogram), ECG (electrocardiogram), GSR (galvanic skin responses), EDA (electrodermal activity), EMG (electromyography), TEMP (temperature), BVP (blood volume pulse), SCR (skin

Table 1. A summary of the emotion recognition datasets.

Name	Purpose	Age	Gender	Stimuli	Physiological modalities	Annotations	Internal/ External factors
AMIGOS [3]	Research on affect, personality traits and mood on individuals and groups	21–40y (m = 28.3)	27M 13F	short videos (<250 s) and long videos (>14 min)	EEG, ECG and GSR	Basic emotions and arousal, valence, dominance and familiarity. Big five personality traits and PANAS. External annotations of arousal and valence	Age, gender, personality and mood
WESAD [23]	Stress and affect detection	25–35y (m = 27.5, sd = 2.4)	12M 3F	Neutral (sitting/ standing/ reading), 392-s of funny video clips, 5 min of public speech and mental arithmetic calculations and meditation exercises	ECG, EDA, EMG, TEMP and BVP	Baseline, amusement and stress using SAM (valence and arousal), PANAS, SSSQ and STAI	Age, gender, height, weight, dominant hand and prerequisites of what they did on that day about smoking, doing sports, feeling ill and drinking coffee
ASCERTAIN [28]	Emotional and personality recognition	(m = 30)	37M 21F	36 (51– 127 s-long) videos	GSR, EEG, ECG	Seven point scale for valence, arousal, engaging, liking and familiarity and BFMS (big five)	Personality
RWDADW [24]	Assess driver's workload	23–57y (m = 35.60, sd = 9.06)	7M 3F	30 min drives	ECG, SCR, TEMP, HR and HRV	Discrete scale of driver workload	–
DSDRWDT [7]	Assess driver's stress level	–	13	50 min drives	ECG, EMG, GSR and TEMP	Stress scales	–
MAHNOB-HCI [27]	Emotion recognition and implicit tagging	19–40y (m = 26.06, sd = 4.39)	11M 16F	20 film excerpts	EEG, ECG, GSR, RESP and TEMP	9 point scale of arousal, valence, dominance, predictability and emotional labels	Birthday and gender. Nationality and ethnicity
EMDB [2]	Study of affective film clips without auditory	F(m = 21.73, sd = 2.31) M(m = 24.80, sd = 3.90)	16M 16F	52-film clips	HR, SCL	Arousal, valence and dominance	–
8EMOTIONS [18]	Research of unique patterns in emotion set	–	1F	Personal imagery and self-stimuli	BVP, GSR, EMG and RESP	Neutral, anger, hate, grief, joy, platonic love, romantic love, reverence	–
DEAP [10]	Analysis of human affective states	19–37y (m = 26.9)	16M 16F	40 (1 min-long) music videos	EEG, BVP, GSR, EMG, EOG, RESP and TEMP	Self-reports of valence, arousal, dominance, liking and familiarity	Age, gender, education, alcohol, (black/green) tea, tobacco and drug/medication consumption, syndromes, hours of sleep and level of alertness

conductance response), SCL (skin conductance level), HR (heart rate), HRV (heart rate variability), RESP (respiration), and EOG (electrooculogram).

3.2 The Requirements

It is important to highlight that in the past, it was preferred to study stress and emotions separately. However, modern approaches propose to address them together because there is interdependence between the two. According to Lazarus [13], when there is stress, there are also emotions, and the reverse, although not always the case, often applies. In other words, when there are emotions, even positively toned ones, there is often stress too, but by no means always. Although there is an overlap between both, emotion is a superordinate concept because it includes stress.

Hence, since Mahesh et al.'s requirements [16] were established for a reference dataset for stress detection, it was necessary to seek evidence to confirm the relevance of each requirement in datasets for emotion recognition systems. Most of these requirements can be used for emotion datasets without much justification. However, the requirements related to the stimuli and modalities require further attention. Below, we present the justification for each of the thirteen requirements grouped into their five categories.

Category 1: Population

- **REQ-1.1: Sample population should represent the balance of men and women of the target population.** Fischer et al. [5] have been observed that gender can affect the reported emotions in men and women. Also, Kring et al. [12] found that women are more expressive than men, they do not report experiencing more emotion than men, and both differ in their skin conductance reactivity.
- **REQ-1.2: Sample population should represent the age distribution of the target population.** Age has been found to decline emotional capacities to recognize other's emotions [4]. Gross et al. [6] have found that older adults, compared with young, present fewer negative emotional experiences, greater emotional control, and lesser emotional expression.
- **REQ-1.3: Sample population size should be estimated statistically.** Like for stress, sample population size determined based on statistics is useful for emotion studies in order for their outcomes to be generalizable to a majority of the population.

Category 2: Stimuli

- **REQ-2.1: Emotional stimuli should be effective.** Emotions are not random events, but they occur when something happens to us [22]. Emotional stimuli can be objects (visual, verbal, olfactory), acts of nature, the behavior of others, our actions, internal processes (such as imagination or memories of events), hormonal changes, drug effects, and voluntary decisions to experience certain emotions [22]. Nevertheless, not all emotion induction methods are equally effective for all scenarios. According to Siedlecka and Denson [26], experimentally inducing emotions provide the most robust causal evidence of the effects of emotions on psychological and physiological outcomes. They classified these techniques into five specific methods:

- Visual stimuli: It can be static images or videos selected to evoke target emotions (e.g., watching a video where a man is startled by birds).
- Listening to music: It activates affection via specific types of auditory input (e.g., listening to a slow-tempo, minor-key classical composition).
- Autobiographical recall: It involves summoning personal emotional memories to reactivate emotions from the original emotional experience (e.g., asking participants questions about a memory where they were terrified).
- Situational procedures: It involves creating a social situation that elicits the target emotion (e.g., participants receive negative feedback on a personal essay).
- Imagery: It involves participants creating vivid mental representations of novel emotional events (e.g., imagining that "It is your birthday and friends throw you a terrific surprise party").

- **REQ-2.2: Emotional stimuli should be relevant.** The chosen emotion stimuli should be relevant to day-to-day activities or be specific to the use case for which the reference dataset is being collected.

Category 3: Modalities

- **REQ-3.1: Multiple emotion response modalities should be recorded.** Most papers have reported an increase in recognition rate with the increase in the number of data modalities [1]. However, it is necessary to highlight that there is still no clear evidence of which feature combinations of which physiological signals are the most relevant.
- **REQ-3.2: Reliable emotion response modalities should be recorded.** Jang et al. [9] showed that heart rate and skin conductance level/response have higher variability among different emotions. That is consistent with the indices of the Autonomic Nervous System (ANS) activation, namely, electrodermal and cardiovascular signals. ANS activity is viewed as a major component of the emotional response in many recent theories of emotion [11], because it is responsible for the control of the bodily functions that are not consciously directed. Their physiological responses are having a higher preference than others since their involuntary nature and the difficulty involved in controlling them.

Category 4: Self-reported Information

- **REQ-4.1: The emotional state of each participant should be collected.** In order to assess emotion changes after an emotional stimulus, self-reports should be used. Although they are unreliable, subjective, and difficult to verify, they provide useful insights into the psychological response to stimulus [16]. Therefore, it is recommended to collect validated self-reports to assess the emotional state of participants.

- **REQ-4.2: The internal factors of each participant should be collected.** It was found that some internal factors such as age, gender, personality, and medical conditions affect psychophysiological reactions during emotional states [20]. Information about these factors should be collected, from the participants of the experiments.
- **REQ-4.3: The external factors of each participant should be collected.** External factors such as cultural differences, physical activity, food intake, among others may affect how emotions are felt and expressed [14]. Information about these factors should be collected, from the participants of the experiments.

Table 2. Evaluation criteria

Name	Description	Acceptance threshold
Category 1: Population		
CRIT 1.1 Age groups	It tests the presence of different age groups (e.g. children, teens, adults, elderly, etc.)	$Age\ groups > 1$
CRIT 1.2 Gender groups	It tests whether the number of men (M) and number of women (W) in the sample is balanced	$|M - W| \leq 1$
CRIT 1.3 Sample size	It tests whether the sample size was carried out based on statistical analysis	Yes
Category 2: Stimuli		
CRIT 2.1 Effective	It tests whether the stimuli can be categorized into one of the following: visual stimuli, listening to music, autobiographical recall, situational procedures, or imagery	Yes
CRIT 2.2 Relevant	It tests whether the stimuli are relevant to day-to-day activities or specific to the purpose for which the reference dataset is being collected	Yes
Category 3: Modalities		
CRIT 3.1 Multiple	It tests whether more than one physiological signal was collected	$Signals > 1$
CRIT 3.2 Reliable	It tests whether at least both electrodermal activity and cardiovascular physiological signals were collected	Yes
Category 4: Self-reported information		
CRIT 4.1 Annotations	It tests whether the emotional annotations of the participants were collected	Yes
CRIT 4.2 Internal factors	It tests whether internal factors (e.g., age, gender, personality, medical conditions etc.) of the participants were collected	$Internal\ factors > 0$
CRIT 4.3 External factors	It tests whether external factors (e.g., culture of the participants, etc.) of the participants were collected	$External\ factors > 0$
Category 5: Sensors		
CRIT 5.1 Devices	It tests whether the devices used are specified	Yes
CRIT 5.2 Noise	It tests whether the noise characteristics of the used devices are described	Yes
CRIT 5.3 Calibration	It tests whether the sensor calibration details were recorded	Yes

Category 5: Sensors
We consider the requirements related to sensors are technological in essence, consequently they influence emotion recognition, similar just as they do in stress recognition, so it did not need further adaptation or additional justification.

- **REQ-5.1: Clinically validated data acquisition devices should be used.**
- **REQ-5.2: Noise characteristics of the used devices should be specified.**
- **REQ-5.3: Device calibration information should be recorded in a device setup protocol.**

3.3 The Evaluation

In order to perform the evaluation, we derived one evaluation criterion for each requirement, similar to what was done by Mahesh et al. [10]. The evaluation criteria are shown in Table 2, where each one is coded as 'CRIT-' followed by the requirement number from which was derived. The evaluation consisted of inspecting to what extent a dataset fulfills each criterion.

We searched for evidence to evaluate each criterion using all the public information for each dataset. We mainly focus on its research article, its webpage, its metadata, and the dataset data. In Table 3 is presented the information sources used for evaluating each dataset, where in the last row, 'r&g' means access 'requested' and 'granted' for datasets without open access.

Table 3. Sources of inspection for each dataset.

Inspection source	AMIGOS	WESAD	ASCERTAIN	RWDADW	DSDRWDT	MAHNOB-HCI	EMDB	8EMOTIONS	DEAP
Article	Yes	Yes	Yes	Yes	Yes	Yes	Yes	Yes	Yes
Web page	Yes	Yes	Yes	Yes	Yes	Yes	No	Yes	Yes
Dataset metadata	Yes	Yes	Yes	Yes	No	No	No	No	Yes
Dataset data	Yes	Yes	Yes	Yes	Yes	Yes	No	Yes	Yes
Dataset access	r&g	Open	r&g	Open	Open	r&g	r&g	Open	r&g

4 Results

Table 4 shows the evaluation result of the nine datasets against the thirteen criteria presented in Table 2. There, the checked sign (✓) indicates that the dataset meets the acceptance threshold of the evaluation criteria, the cross sign (✗) indicates that it does not meet, and the symbol (**I**) indicates indetermination, i.e., it was not possible to determine whether it meets or does not meet.

Following, we review compliance with each criterion.

Table 4. Results of the evaluation.

Category	Evaluation criteria	AMIGOS	WESAD	ASCERTAIN	RWDADW	DSDRWDT	MAHNOB-HCI	EMDB	8EMOTIONS	DEAP
Population	1.1 Age groups	✗	✗	✗	✗	✗	✗	✗	✗	✗
	1.2 Gender groups	✗	✗	✗	✗	✗	✗	✓	✗	✓
	1.3 Sample size	✗	✗	✗	✗	✗	✗	✗	✗	✗
Stimuli	2.1 Effective	✓	✓	✓	✓	✓	✓	✓	✓	✓
	2.2 Relevant	I	✓	I	✓	✓	I	I	✗	I
Modalities	3.1 Multiple	✓	✓	✓	✓	✓	✓	✓	✓	✓
	3.2 Reliable	✓	✓	✓	✓	✓	✓	✓	✓	✓
Self-reported information	4.1 Annotations	✓	✓	✓	✓	✗	✓	✓	✓	✓
	4.2 Internal factors	✓	✓	✓	✗	✗	✓	✗	✗	✓
	4.3 External factors	✗	✓	✗	✗	✗	✓	✗	✗	✓
Sensors	5.1 Devices	✓	✓	✗	✓	✓	✓	✓	✓	✓
	5.2 Noise	✗	✗	✗	✗	✗	✗	✗	✗	✗
	5.3 Calibration	✗	✗	✗	✗	✗	✗	✗	✗	✗

Category 1: Population

- **CRIT-1.1:** None of the datasets evaluated considered different age groups in their experiments. Moreover, DSDRWDT, 8EMOTIONS, and EMDB do not present information on age groups.
- **CRIT-1.2:** Gender groups were not considered for most of the datasets. DEAP and EMDB were the only ones having an equal proportion of them.
- **CRIT-1.3:** None of the evaluated datasets calculated the number of participants using statistical analysis.

Category 2: Stimuli

- **CRIT-2.1:** All the datasets stimuli can be classified into one of five experimental emotion inductions categories.
- **CRIT-2.2:** Stimuli of WESAD, RWDADW, and DSDRWDT are relevant to day-to-day activities. Because stimuli of AMIGOS, ASCERTAIN, MAHNOB-HCI, EMDB, and DEAP are videos, it is not possible to know whether they are specific to the purpose for which the reference dataset is being collected. So, they were evaluated as indeterminate (**I**). Stimuli of 8EMOTIONS (personal imagery and self-stimuli) were not considered relevant because are not day-to-day activities nor use case specific.

Category 3: Modalities

- **CRIT-3.1:** All the datasets included more than one physiological signal.
- **CRIT-3.2:** As we can see in Table 5, all the datasets included two physiological signals that can be categorized like electrodermal and cardiovascular [11]:

Table 5. Physiological signals for each dataset

Modality	AMIGOS	WESAD	ASCERTAIN	RWDADW	DSDRWDT	MAHNOB-HCI	EMDB	8EMOTIONS	DEAP
Electrodermal	GSR	EDA	GSR	SCR	GSR	GSR	SCL	GSR	GSR
Cardiovascular	ECG	ECG	ECG	ECG	ECG	ECG	HR	RESP	RESP

Category 4: Self-reported Information

- **CRIT-4.1:** All the datasets included their reports except for DSDRWDT, whose questionnaire results were not publicly available.
- **CRIT-4.2:** AMIGOS, WESAD, ASCERTIAN, MAHNOB-HCI, and DEAP included at least one internal factor.
- **CRIT-4.3:** WESAD, MAHNOB-HCI and DEAP included at least one external factor.

Category 5: Sensors

- **CRIT-5.1:** All datasets indicated the devices they used, except for ASCERTAIN, who only mentioned that they used commercial sensors.
- **CRIT-5.2:** None of the datasets discussed the noise characteristics of their devices.
- **CRIT-5.3:** None of the datasets discussed the calibration setup for their experiments.

5   Discussion

As we can see in Table 4, there is not a winner dataset. Overall, most of the datasets' compliance interval is between five and eight requirements, whereas the non-compliance interval is between four and eight requirements (see Table 5). The datasets that meet the most requirements (eight) are WESAD and DEAP. Besides, the datasets that do not meet most of the thirteen requirements (eight) are DSDRWDT and 8EMOTIONS (Table 6).

Table 6. Summary of the evaluation results

Results	AMIGOS	WESAD	ASCERTAIN	RWDADW	DSDRWDT	MAHNOB-HCI	EMDB	8EMOTIONS	DEAP
✗	6	5	7	7	8	7	6	8	4
✓	6	8	5	6	5	5	6	5	8
I	1	0	1	0	0	1	1	0	1

   Also, we found that certain criteria were not satisfied with any dataset. Criteria **CRIT-1.1** (Age groups) and **CRIT-1.3** (Sample size) from the population category were omitted by all datasets, probably due to the difficulty of recruiting experiments participants. Moreover, none of the datasets could satisfy the criteria related to the sensors category: **CRIT-5.2** (Noise) and **CRIT-5.3** (Calibration). This indicates that researchers tend to focus more on checking that the devices used for sensing the physiological datasets are validated than on other aspects such as the device calibration or the specification of noise characteristics. The contrary occurred with the criteria related to the **modalities** category, which were fully satisfied by all datasets. Although all datasets that included more than two modalities (multiple) were also considered as reliable, these results should be interpreted with caution. This is mainly because of the criteria **CRIT-3.2** (Reliable) used for determining the reliability of a dataset. Notice that the threshold of acceptance defined for this criteria is the minimum required to be considered reliable.

5.1   Threats to Validity

There are some threats to validity of this qualitative study [34], which should be considered when interpreting its findings.

– **Construct validity:** It focuses on identifying correct operational measures for the concepts being studied. A possible threat is the use of reference requirements identified for evaluating stress datasets. Given that an emotion is a superordinate concept that includes also stress [13], we decided to use the same reference requirements.

Another threat identified in this study is regarding the acceptance thresholds definition (See Table 2). For some criteria (i.e., CRIT 1.1, CRIT 4.1, CRIT 4.3), we considered the minimum values to satisfy the corresponding criteria. For example, in the CRIT 1.1 (Age groups), we define *age groups* > 1 as the acceptance threshold, which indicates presence of at least two groups. The same applies for CRIT 4.1 and CRIT 4.3, where we verified whether the emotional annotations and external factors were collected respectively. We did not consider the number of factors or annotations. Determining an optimum number is hard since it depends of the study itself.

– **Internal validity:** It seeks to establish a causal relationship, whereby certain conditions are believed to lead to other conditions, as distinguished from spurious relationships. In this study, with the purpose of reducing the subjective quality assessment threat, we have defined an acceptance threshold, which has been discussed among the authors until reach a consensus.

  Another threat is regarding the application of the evaluation criteria. Although most of the criteria could be objectively evaluated by finding evidence in the inspection sources (See Table 3), the criterion CRIT-2.2 could not be directly applied. This is because the stimuli of some datasets are videos whose content are not accessible (it was not possible to know whether their content shown day-to-day activities or were use-case specific).

– **External validity:** It aims to define the domain to which a study's findings can be generalized. As we considered only nine accessible datasets, which were previously surveyed by Bota et al. [1], generalization is not possible. Further research is needed to identify other public datasets.

– **Conclusion validity:** It demonstrates that the operations of a study such as the data collection procedure can be repeated, with the same results. The study has been documented systematically (e.g., the datasets source, the requirements determination, and the evaluation method) so that replicability has been ensured. A researcher should be able to follow the derivation of results and conclusions from this information.

6 Conclusions and Future Work

In this paper, the aim was to assess physiological public data sets for emotion recognition systems. It was found that none of the nine public datasets satisfy all the established requirements in order to be considered as a reference dataset for emotion recognition systems construction. All datasets meet at least five requirements out of thirteen (see Table 5). For example, DSDRWDT and 8EMOTIONS datasets meet only six and five requirements respectively. Also, we found that WESAD and DEAP datasets meet most of the requirements (eight). However, as both datasets fail in addressing relevant requirements related to the population (e.g., sample size), and sensors (e.g., calibration) categories, there is still a necessity for improving the existing datasets to be considered as a reference.

In fact, we found that any dataset does not meet four requirements (i.e., REQ-1.1, REQ-1.3, REQ-5.2, and REQ-5.3) related to these categories. Therefore, we think our work contributes to creating user awareness on the limitations of datasets used, especially whether the purpose is to train any classification technique that requires data or validate general emotion recognition systems. It is also important to remark that requirements related to stimuli and modalities categories were fulfilled by most of the nine datasets. For instance, requirements like REQ-2.1, REQ-3.1 and REQ-3.2 are met by all datasets.

In order to generalize the conclusions, considerably more work will need to be done to systematically identify and evaluate other physiological emotion datasets. It is also interesting to extend the current reference requirements list. For example, in the population and the self-reports categories, some ethnic variables and social environment details could be included respectively. Also, it would be interesting to add a new category of requirements based on the FAIR (findable, accessible, interoperable, and reusable) principles introduced by Wilkinson M. et al. [31]. Finally, we suggest a greater community effort to establish standard requirements for emotion recognition systems that can guide proper datasets development [31].

Acknowledgment. A. Mendoza, A. Cuno, N. Condori-Fernandez and W. Ramos acknowledge financial support from the "Proyecto Concytec - Banco Mundial, Mejoramiento y Ampliación de los Servicios del Sistema Nacional de Ciencia Tecnología e Innovación Tecnológica" 8682-PE, through its executing unit FONDECYT [Contract N° 014-2019-FONDECYT-BM-INC.INV]. Also, this work has been partially supported by Datos 4.0 (TIN2016-78011-C4-1-R) funded by MINECO-AEI/FEDER-UE.

References

1. Bota, P.J., Wang, C., Fred, A.L., Da Silva, H.P.: A review, current challenges, and future possibilities on emotion recognition using machine learning and physiological signals. IEEE Access **7**, 140990–141020 (2019)
2. Carvalho, S., Leite, J., Galdo-Álvarez, S., Gonçalves, Ó.F.: The emotional movie database (EMDB): a self-report and psychophysiological study. Appl. Psychophysiol. Biofeedback **37**(4), 279–294 (2012). https://doi.org/10.1007/s10484-012-9201-6
3. Correa, J.A.M., Abadi, M.K., Sebe, N., Patras, I.: AMIGOS: a dataset for affect, personality and mood research on individuals and groups. IEEE Trans. Affect. Comput. (2018)
4. Ebner, N.C., Fischer, H.: Emotion and aging: evidence from brain and behavior. Front. Psychol. **5**, 996 (2014)
5. Fischer, A.H., Rodriguez Mosquera, P.M., Van Vianen, A.E., Manstead, A.S.: Gender and culture differences in emotion. Emotion **4**(1), 87 (2004)
6. Gross, J.J., Carstensen, L.L., Pasupathi, M., Tsai, J., Götestam Skorpen, C., Hsu, A.Y.: Emotion and aging: experience, expression, and control. Psychol. Aging **12**(4), 590 (1997)
7. Healey, J.A., Picard, R.W.: Detecting stress during real-world driving tasks using physiological sensors. IEEE Trans. Intell. Transp. Syst. **6**(2), 156–166 (2005)

8. Igual, R., Medrano, C., Plaza, I.: A comparison of public datasets for acceleration-based fall detection. Med. Eng. Phys. **37**(9), 870–878 (2015)
9. Jang, E.H., Park, B.J., Park, M.S., Kim, S.H., Sohn, J.H.: Analysis of physiological signals for recognition of boredom, pain, and surprise emotions. J. Physiol. Anthropol. **34**(1), 25 (2015)
10. Koelstra, S., et al.: DEAP: a database for emotion analysis; using physiological signals. IEEE Trans. Affect. Comput. **3**(1), 18–31 (2011)
11. Kreibig, S.D.: Autonomic nervous system activity in emotion: a review. Biol. Psychol. **84**(3), 394–421 (2010)
12. Kring, A.M., Gordon, A.H.: Sex differences in emotion: expression, experience, and physiology. J. Pers. Soc. Psychol. **74**(3), 686 (1998)
13. Lazarus, R.S.: Stress and Emotion: A New Synthesis. Springer, New York (2006)
14. Lim, N.: Cultural differences in emotion: differences in emotional arousal level between the east and the west. Integr. Med. Res. **5**(2), 105–109 (2016)
15. Ma, K., Wang, X., Yang, X., Zhang, M., Girard, J.M., Morency, L.P.: ElderReact: a multimodal dataset for recognizing emotional response in aging adults. In: 2019 International Conference on Multimodal Interaction, ICMI 2019, pp. 349–357. Association for Computing Machinery, New York (2019)
16. Mahesh, B., Prassler, E., Hassan, T., Garbas, J.U.: Requirements for a reference dataset for multimodal human stress detection. In: 2019 IEEE International Conference on Pervasive Computing and Communications Workshops (PerCom Workshops), pp. 492–498. IEEE (2019)
17. Marechal, C., et al.: Survey on AI-based multimodal methods for emotion detection. In: Kołodziej, J., González-Vélez, H. (eds.) High-Performance Modelling and Simulation for Big Data Applications. LNCS, vol. 11400, pp. 307–324. Springer, Cham (2019). https://doi.org/10.1007/978-3-030-16272-6_11
18. Picard, R.W., Vyzas, E., Healey, J.: Toward machine emotional intelligence: analysis of affective physiological state. IEEE Trans. Pattern Anal. Mach. Intell. **23**(10), 1175–1191 (2001)
19. Pujol, F.A., Mora, H., Martínez, A.: Emotion recognition to improve e-healthcare systems in smart cities. In: Visvizi, A., Lytras, M.D. (eds.) RIIFORUM 2019. SPC, pp. 245–254. Springer, Cham (2019). https://doi.org/10.1007/978-3-030-30809-4_23
20. Rukavina, S., Gruss, S., Hoffmann, H., Tan, J.W., Walter, S., Traue, H.C.: Affective computing and the impact of gender and age. PLoS ONE **11**(3), e0150584 (2016)
21. Sajjad, M., Nasir, M., Ullah, F.U.M., Muhammad, K., Sangaiah, A.K., Baik, S.W.: Raspberry Pi assisted facial expression recognition framework for smart security in law-enforcement services. Inf. Sci. **479**, 416–431 (2019)
22. Scherer, K.R., Moors, A.: The emotion process: event appraisal and component differentiation. Ann. Rev. Psychol. **70**, 719–745 (2019)
23. Schmidt, P., Reiss, A., Duerichen, R., Marberger, C., Van Laerhoven, K.: Introducing WESAD, a multimodal dataset for wearable stress and affect detection. In: Proceedings of the 20th ACM International Conference on Multimodal Interaction, pp. 400–408 (2018)
24. Schneegass, S., Pfleging, B., Broy, N., Heinrich, F., Schmidt, A.: A data set of real world driving to assess driver workload. In: Proceedings of the 5th International Conference on Automotive User Interfaces and Interactive Vehicular Applications, pp. 150–157 (2013)
25. Shu, L., et al.: A review of emotion recognition using physiological signals. Sensors **18**(7), 2074 (2018)

26. Siedlecka, E., Denson, T.F.: Experimental methods for inducing basic emotions: a qualitative review. Emot. Rev. **11**(1), 87–97 (2019)
27. Soleymani, M., Lichtenauer, J., Pun, T., Pantic, M.: A multimodal database for affect recognition and implicit tagging. IEEE Trans. Affect. Comput. **3**(1), 42–55 (2011)
28. Subramanian, R., Wache, J., Abadi, M.K., Vieriu, R.L., Winkler, S., Sebe, N.: ASCERTAIN: emotion and personality recognition using commercial sensors. IEEE Trans. Affect. Comput. **9**(2), 147–160 (2016)
29. Suni Lopez, F., Condori-Fernandez, N.: Design of an adaptive persuasive mobile application for stimulating the medication adherence. In: Poppe, R., Meyer, J.-J., Veltkamp, R., Dastani, M. (eds.) INTETAIN 2016 2016. LNICST, vol. 178, pp. 99–105. Springer, Cham (2017). https://doi.org/10.1007/978-3-319-49616-0_9
30. Tahir, Z., Alexander, R.: Coverage based testing for V&V and safety assurance of self-driving autonomous vehicle: a systematic literature review. In: The Second IEEE International Conference on Artificial Intelligence Testing, York (2020)
31. Wilkinson, M.D., et al.: The FAIR guiding principles for scientific data management and stewardship. Sci. Data **3** (2016)
32. Zepf, S., Hernandez, J., Schmitt, A., Minker, W., Picard, R.: Driver emotion recognition for intelligent vehicles: a survey. ACM Comput. Surv. (2020). https://doi.org/10.1145/3388790
33. Zhang, J., Yin, Z., Chen, P., Nichele, S.: Emotion recognition using multi-modal data and machine learning techniques: a tutorial and review. Inf. Fusion **59**, 103–126 (2020)
34. Zhou, X., Jin, Y., Zhang, H., Li, S., Huang, X.: A map of threats to validity of systematic literature reviews in software engineering. In: 2016 23rd Asia-Pacific Software Engineering Conference (APSEC), pp. 153–160 (2016)

Machine Learning

YTTREX: Crowdsourced Analysis of YouTube's Recommender System During COVID-19 Pandemic

Leonardo Sanna[1(✉)], Salvatore Romano[2], Giulia Corona[3], and Claudio Agosti[4]

[1] University of Modena and Reggio Emilia, Modena, Italy
`leonardo.sanna@unimore.it`
[2] University of Padova, Padua, Italy
`salvatore.romano.3@studenti.unipd.it`
[3] University of Milano, Milan, Italy
`giulia.corona1@studenti.unimi.it`
[4] Tracking Exposed, Lazio, Italy
`claudio@tracking.exposed`
`https://tracking.exposed/`

Abstract. Algorithmic personalization is difficult to approach because it entails studying many different user experiences, with a lot of variables outside of our control. Two common biases are frequent in experiments: relying on corporate service API and using synthetic profiles with small regards of regional and individualized profiling and personalization. In this work, we present the result of the first crowdsourced data collections of YouTube's recommended videos via YouTube Tracking Exposed (YTTREX). Our tool collects evidence of algorithmic personalization via an HTML parser, anonymizing the users. In our experiment we used a BBC video about COVID-19, taking into account 5 regional BBC channels in 5 different languages and we saved the recommended videos that were shown during each session. Each user watched the first five second of the videos, while the extension captured the recommended videos. We took into account the top20 recommended videos for each completed session, looking for evidence of algorithmic personalization. Our results showed that the vast majority of videos were recommended only once in our experiment. Moreover, we collected evidence that there is a significant difference between the videos we could retrieve using the official API and what we collected with our extension. These findings show that filter bubbles exist and that they need to be investigated with a crowdsourced approach.

Keywords: Algorithm analysis · Crowdsourced data collections · Network analysis · Official API · COVID-19 · YouTube · Filter bubble

© Springer Nature Switzerland AG 2021
J. A. Lossio-Ventura et al. (Eds.): SIMBig 2020, CCIS 1410, pp. 107–121, 2021.
https://doi.org/10.1007/978-3-030-76228-5_8

1   Introduction

1.1   Algorithmic Personalization

Algorithmic personalization is now part of our lives. In fact, recommendation systems are used for a remarkably high number of tasks, ranging from working to free time. Each time we google something, an algorithm is selecting what is most relevant for us, the same happens when we scroll our Facebook feed and when we use our Netflix or Spotify account. We may say that algorithms are the technological solution to the information overload we live on daily.

However, most of these services are owned by private corporations that use blackbox algorithms to curate the content selection for their users. In the last few years, these platforms have been at the stake of academic research, particularly for what concerns the so called "fake news debacle", with a lot of research focusing on misinformation spreading and on the polarization of the public debate [1–3].

For the sake of clarity, one crucial distinction has to be made about this. Research that considers information spreading, online debate and user engagement is a study on echo chambers. Although not well defined in the literature, echo chambers are social phenomena based on ideological affinity and are relatively accessible for research. Instead, in this paper, we are interested in studying the filter bubble [4], which is the direct effect of algorithmic personalization. To use Zimmer's words [5], echo chambers are created by users, while filter bubbles are made by algorithms.

After the concept became widely discussed in the everyday debate, the academics started questioning the existence of the filter bubble effect, following the ideas proposed by Bruns [6] that claimed that there is no evidence that echo chambers and filter bubbles exist outside the academic theory. Furthermore, studies on filter bubbles and echo chambers focused almost exclusively on the polarization of the debate, overlooking other more critical areas of inquiry such as the lack of tools to account for user personalization. Empirical research on algorithmic personalization is still quite fragmented and we believe that this happens because of the lack of a shared methodology among the researches. The fact that we must take into account user experience is problematic because of the number of uncontrollable variables and also because it requires user collaboration or fabricated profiles.

For its part, YouTube provides information about its algorithm, but just related to the general structure of the recommended system algorithm [7,8]; thus, we cannot state for sure how many variables are used for the personalization process and how. The site also provides an official API, often used by researchers, but this does not include individual personalization, and, as we will show in Sect. 4.2, API data might differ a lot from the actual users' experience.

In the following section, we review the latest methods for algorithmic personalization analysis, then we illustrate our methodology and the YTTREX tool. Finally, we discuss the results of our experiment and the main limitations of our work.

1.2   Methods for Algorithmic Personalization Analysis

There are a number of studies that claim to be focused on filter bubbles. However, the majority of these works is not actually taking into account algorithmic personalization but, instead, it is inquiring ideological preference (echo chambers) with social sciences methods [9,10].

These approaches do not consider the fact that algorithmic personalization is a product of the interaction between users and platforms and it is essentially passive since users have extremely limited or no control of their personalization. Hence, if we approach filter bubbles starting from user behavior, we are not studying filter bubbles but echo chambers. In our opinion, trying to infer conclusions on algorithmic personalization starting from its alleged effects might produce misleading outcomes.

In this work we are proposing a crowdsourced approach, as it was already experimented by Robertson et al. on Google SERP [11]. In their study the authors stated that they found truly little evidence of filter bubble effect. Although we found their methodology robust and well-suited for the study of filter bubbles, we believe that their conclusions should be reconsidered taking into account that:

1. algorithmic personalization is platform-specific, as every platform has its own algorithm
2. Google SERP might not be the best platform to inquiry filter bubble in its original meaning of "informational bubble", as it is produced by an intentional research
3. The "in incognito mode" of the web browser Chrome is not a completely clean navigation, as it keeps a certain level of personalization that is based, for instance, on geographic location.

Regarding point (1), during one of our previous experiments we found evidence of algorithmic personalization on Facebook using synthetic profiles [12]. We used this approach so that we could control all the variables. Regarding point (3) we must recall that controlling the variable is one of the main difficulties while studying algorithmic personalization, also because we have to proceed by trials and errors, since we do not know exactly which variables influence algorithmic decisions. Hence, we propose to investigate specific effects (such as ideological preference) using fabricated profiles and use crowdsourced approach to gain evidence of existence of personalization, namely to account for the fragmentation of content distribution.

Measuring Filter Bubbles on YouTube. We propose a crowdsourced methodology to investigate and measure user personalization within the recommended videos on YouTube (YT). The context of COVID-19 was a unique occasion to test our tool YTTREX, looking at how YouTube distributed its content related to the pandemic. An extensive review on YouTube research has been conducted by Arthurs et al. [13], who highlighted that the platform is vastly understudied. Other studies on YT filter bubbles that propose a crowdsourced approach do not currently exist to the best of our knowledge. Related works use YT API or other methods that are not user-centered, nor they collect empirical data directly from users' browsers [14–17].

2   Tool: YouTube Tracking Exposed

2.1   How It Works

The browser extension (add-on) of Tracking Exposed[1] collects evidence from the metadata that is observable on the web page when the user lands on the homepage, watches a video, or does research on the YouTube website. It creates cryptographic key pairs to ensure the user can access her/his data. It is necessary because the tool does not have an email address, Google profile, or any other authentication method based on personal data. The tool collects separate contributions for each browser with the add-on installed.

The data are collected in three phases:

1. **Collection:** the add-on takes a copy of the HTML when the browser is watching a video. Four buttons appear on the top left of the screen (Fig. 1), when the add-ons is installed and enabled by the popup. The color code represents the different status.

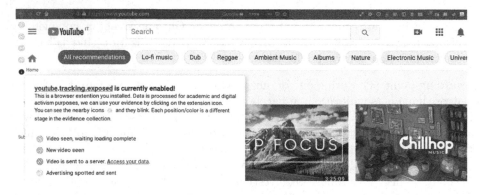

Fig. 1. Screenshot of what the browser extension shows while navigating on YouTube.

2. **Parsing:** server side, the HTML is processed and metadata are extracted. The information is then organized in a dataset. In the HTML there are many different data that might be analyzed to extract metadata. We did not yet extract all possible information, especially we avoided any unique tracker that might become personal data if collected. On the other hand, the YTTREX

---

[1] Site: https://youtube.tracking.exposed, AGPL3 code: https://github.com/tracking-exposed/yttrex/.

Fig. 2. HTML inspection of a recommended video on YouTube and its aria-label.

project still has room for improvement, and we might not have yet mapped 100% of the potentially interesting metadata for YouTube algorithm analysis. We were also able to record the users' interface, detect the language, record related videos, the number of views, and duration. Inspecting the HTML of a recommended video (Fig. 2), you might see the data field named aria-label[2]. This text field is meant for accessibility and contains a compacted, but human formatted, set of information useful for researchers. Because of the localization, YouTube produces aria-label with strings that change accordingly to the user interface Language. For example, the aria-label: "Crise pétrolière : coup de poker sur l'essence—ARTE by ARTE 6 days ago 58 min 213,982 views" is composed by the information shown in Table 1.

Table 1. Aria-label composition.

Title	Crise pétrolière : coup de poker sur l'essence
UX Language dependent stopword	eng
Publisher name	ARTE
Relative human readable publication time	6 days ago
Human readable video length	58 min
Number of views formatted as per UX locale standard	213,982 views

We might externalize this natural language conversion, managed by our aria-label parsing library[3], as an independent library, once we figure out how to maintain the list of fixed terms that scale up proportionally to the language

---

[2] For reference see: https://mzl.la/33dMuRN.

[3] https://github.com/tracking-exposed/yttrex/blob/master/backend/parsers/longlabel.js.

Table 2. Data structure

Field name	Data type	Description
login	Boolean	True if the profile was logged on YT
id	String	Unique identifier for each installed extension
savingTime	ISODate	GMT hour when evidence get saved
clientTime	ISODate	Date on the users' browser
uxLang	ISO 639-1 code	Browser language
recommendedId	String	Unique identifier of the data unit
recommendedVideoId	String	Video unique ID used in YT URL
recommendedAuthor	String	Publisher of the recommended video
recommendedTitle	String	Title of the recommended video
recommendedPubTime	ISODate	Date of recommended video publication
recommendedRelativeS	Number	Sec.between recommended publication and access
recommendedViews	Number	Views at savingTime for the recommended video
recommendedForYou	Boolean	True if YT explicitly says recommended for you
recommendedVerified	Boolean	True if publisher has the blue check
recommendedKind	String	Live streaming or video
recommendedLength	Number	Duration of the video in seconds
recommendedDisplayL	String	Human formatted duration of video
watchedVideoId	String	From YT URL, the Video ID
watchedTitle	String	Publisher of the watched video
watchedChannel	String	Relative URL of YouTube channel
watchedPubTime	ISODate	Publication time of the watched video
watchedViews	Number	Amount of views at savingTime
watchedLike	Number	Amount of thumbs up at savingTime
watchedDislike	Number	Amount of thumbs down at savingTime
sessionId	String	Unique identifier of users' sequence
hoursOffset	Number	Amount of hours after the beginning weTest1
experiment	String	'weTest1', the experiment of this paper
pseudonym	String	A unique pseudonym for each browser plugin
top20	Boolean	True if recommendationOrder <20
isAPItoo	Boolean	True if recommended is also in YT API related
step	String	Human readable language of watched video

supported by YouTube. The sum of session information, video watched, and recommended videos, produces the data unit with the format detailed in Table 2.

3. **Research and data-sharing:** YTTREX was created to support independent analysis and privacy-preserving sharing of the algorithmically powered circulation of videos. Every video observation has a dynamic number of related videos (if the watcher scrolls the video page down, the browser loads 80 or more related videos, but for users who do not scroll down the default is to receive and display only the first 20 related videos). Every related video

becomes a single row, a data record with its own unique ID. Interconnecting these with *metadataId*, the researcher might re-group all the related videos belonging to the same evidence, as they were displayed to the watcher. Certain fields such as logged, pseudo, and *savingTime*, are the same across the same id because they depend on the collection condition. *recommendedVideos*, *recommendedAuthor*, and other *recommended-fields*, changes in each row according to the related video described; *recommendedId* is generated for each row and should be used as guarantee of unique field.

According to the definition provided by Sandvig [18], the tool enables the user to potentially four of the five methods of algorithmic audit: Noninvasive User Audit, Scraping Audit, Sock Puppet Audit, if they have the know-how to use bots, and Crowdsourced or Collaborative Audit, as the experiment presented on this paper.

The database collected for this paper is available on Tracking Exposed website[4] and the code is available on GitHub[5] protected by AGPL v3 license.

3 Experiment

A first test of our methodology was conducted during the Digital Methods Initiative Summer School in 2019[6]. For the first time, we compared the different users' experience in that experiment, manipulating some variables such as logged profile vs unlogged. This experience has been used as a baseline for the experiment design of this study.

3.1 Experiment Design

We made a call for participation on our website to select the participants[7]. Every participant joined the experiment for free and voluntarily. The procedure involved the visualization of five videos about COVID-19 prevention, produced by the BBC channel, one for each of the most spoken languages in the world: Chinese, Spanish, English, Portuguese, Arabic. We picked these videos because we wanted to find a source equally trustworthy in the five languages. Originally the idea of this experiment comes from our doubt that YouTube could not effectively take down conspiracy theory on COVID-19[8], differently to what is claimed. We suspect English language and recommendation might benefit from a better curation, thus by comparing the recommended videos close to equally accurate COVID-19 videos. Still, in different languages, we could neither confirm nor reject the hypothesis.

---

[4] https://youtube.tracking.exposed/data/.
[5] https://github.com/tracking-exposed/youtube.tracking.exposed.
[6] https://wiki.digitalmethods.net/Dmi/SummerSchool2019AlgorithmsExposed.
[7] https://youtube.tracking.exposed/wetest/1.
[8] https://www.nytimes.com/interactive/2020/03/02/technology/youtube-conspiracy-theory.html.

We did not provide additional information about the minimum time that had to be spent watching the videos: loading the page was enough to collect the HTML. Participants could choose to perform the test logged with their personal account or without, the tool records if the user is logged or not, without collecting any data related to the specific account.

3.2 Official API Comparison

The same day of the test, we retrieved via the official YouTube's API the related videos for the five videos included in the methodology.

Since language is an option for the API request, we performed five requests, one for each language. 50 videos were retrieved in each API request. We then stored this information using the metadata isAPItoo (see Table 2) for each of our evidence collected via YTTREX.

4 Findings

4.1 Evidence of Filter Bubbles

The distribution of the recommended videos is clearly skewed as shown in (Fig. 3). We investigated the distribution of recommended videos taking into account the language of the starting video, the browser's language, and considering whether the user was logged or not. No matter of which variable we took into account we always obtained a skewed distribution, as shown in the example of (Fig. 4).

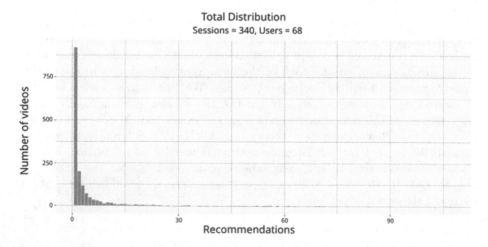

Fig. 3. Frequency distribution of recommended video in our dataset.

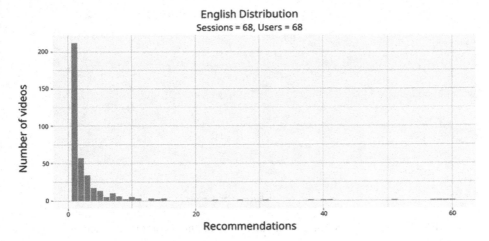

Fig. 4. Frequency distribution of recommended videos starting from the BBC video in English.

Our findings show that the vast majority of videos are recommended very few times (1–3 times), regardless of the variable considered. This distribution is significantly positively skewed according to Fisher's skewness coefficient (>2). Summing up, 57% of the recommended videos have been recommended only once and only around 17% of the videos have been recommended more than 5 times during our experiment.

These results highlight that the filter bubble is real, and that algorithmic personalization produces a high fragmentation of recommended content among YouTube users. Another relevant finding for the study of algorithmic personalization is the huge difference we found using YT API and our tool. For users logged into their Google account only 11% of the recommended videos could be retrieved using the API as showed in the following section, in Fig. 8.

Finally, we calculated Lorenz curve over the distribution of the recommended video, confirming that the inequality in the distribution (Gini >0.5) of the recommended videos.

We also calculated the Gini index for the number of videos selected for each user, since the result shown in (Fig. 5) might be caused by an uneven number of videos selected for each user. However, with a Gini coefficient around 0.2, we have evidence that the algorithm is selecting an equal number of videos for each user, while distributing unevenly the recommendations for each video.

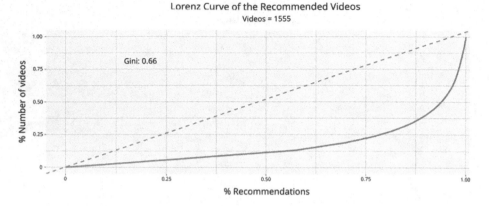

Fig. 5. Lorenz curve and Gini coefficient of the recommended videos

4.2 Network Analysis

We performed a network analysis using Gephi [19] to better understand and visualize how the recommender system creates a filter bubble around users watching the same video the same day. Thanks to the Medialab's tool *Table2net*[9] we extracted a network file from the csv file. We created a bipartite network linking two types of nodes: users' pseudonyms and suggested video's ID.

In the graphs (Fig. 6, 7, 8) we used a circular layout algorithm [20] to dispose of all the users in a circle. We aimed to show all the participants in the same positions, pointing in the same direction, because they were performing the same task: in the examples they are watching the video from the English version of BBC channel "How do I know if I have coronavirus? - BBC News". This representation allowed us to show how, even if they were all watching the same video, they were getting a different configuration of suggested videos.

Then, we performed a Force Atlas 2 Algorithm to place each related video close to the users who received that suggestion by the platform. On the one hand this technique highlights the network centrality of several videos homogeneously suggested across users (the ones in the center of the graph); on the other hand we can clearly see videos suggested to singular users (those who are external to the users' circle, really close to just one pseudonym).

The size of the nodes is based on the degree of each node: in a range between size 15 and size 60, each user and each recommended video is big in relation to the number of links that it has. The videos in the center of the graph are bigger because they have been suggested more than the others. Because of a graphical compromise, the nodes with a degree minor than 15 have the same shape, likewise the nodes with a degree higher than 60 are all the same.

---

[9] https://medialab.github.io/table2net/.

Users by Browser Language

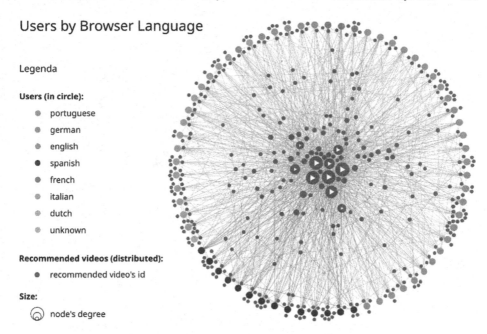

Legenda

Users (in circle):
- portuguese
- german
- english
- spanish
- french
- italian
- dutch
- unknown

Recommended videos (distributed):
- recommended video's id

Size:
- node's degree

Fig. 6. Graph of the videos suggested to the participants while watching the video "How do I know if I have coronavirus? - BBC News"

In Fig. 7 we highlighted how some of the videos recommended appear only to users with English browsers. This shows that the participants in the experiment received personalized suggestions according to their characteristics, despite watching the same video. This type of analysis can demonstrate differences in the users' experiences tracing the most influential features that can generate changes in the platform experiences.

As we already said in the previous section, there is a huge difference between the recommended videos that we retrieved from the API and the actual recommendations (Fig. 8). The majority of the videos retrieved by the Tracking Exposed tool are not present in the database created with YouTube's API. Some of the most suggested videos (biggest nodes in the center of the graph) neither. This is relevant because it is evidence against the usability of official YT's data in academic research. The official API cannot represent the real variance of suggestions present in the actual recommended videos. Many scientific articles

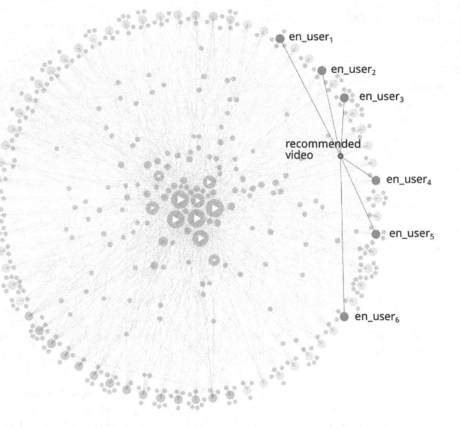

Fig. 7. Zoom of Fig. 6, an example of video suggested only to users with English interface.

[21–24] rely on these data to explain the circulation of videos on the platform, but according to our findings we might say that API data are just a generic representation of an ideal user that is really difficult to find in reality (no one of the users in our experiments gets the same recommendations as in the API).

The official API does not represent the various levels of personalization that occur in relation to the structural users' characteristics and to their past online behaviors. Thus, we cannot use API data to make inferences about personalization, polarization and filter bubbles, because these phenomena presuppose the study of real users in real context.

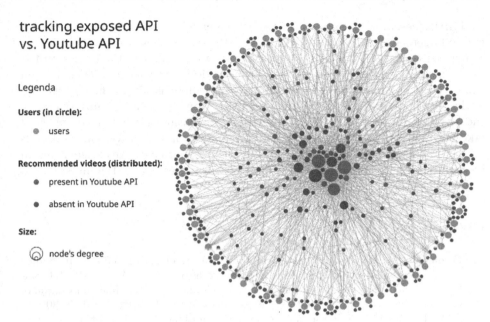

tracking.exposed API vs. Youtube API

Legenda

Users (in circle):

● users

Recommended videos (distributed):

● present in Youtube API

● absent in Youtube API

Size:

◎ node's degree

Fig. 8. Same graph of Fig. 6, here the colors highlight the differences between the videos recorded with Tracking Exposed and the ones retrieved with YouTube official API.

5 Conclusions

This research was intended as a proof of concept work, being the very first crowdsourced experiment carried out with our tool. It is not possible at this stage of our research to further generalize our findings, nor we can go in deep with content analysis, as our sample was quite small (68 users). Nonetheless, we gained evidence of the existence of algorithmic personalization on YouTube, what is also called filter bubble. Our dataset has been collected in a scenario in which we expected a shared common ground among users, since they all started from the same video on how to prevent COVID-19 infections. Instead, our data show a strong fragmentation of content selection, suggesting that there might be a lack of shared information on COVID-19 on YouTube.

We propose to measure the filter bubbles as we did in Sect. 4.1. First of all, it is necessary to investigate the skewness of the distribution of recommended videos; in case it is significantly positively skewed, we have evidence of filter bubbles. Secondly, we argue that it is possibile to measure the filter bubble using the Gini coefficient; a higher value of the Gini index would indicate a stronger filter bubble. Our analysis proves the necessity of further investigation on algorithmic personalization with crowdsourced and independent tools. In fact, our research also showed that official APIs cannot retrieve the majority of videos that are shown to the final users.

Further research on these themes should focus on 1) repeating the experiment with a larger sample 2) qualitatively explore the recommendations 3) study other structural characteristics of the users, better understanding the effects on the recommendations system, as we have already done with visualization time on similar recommender systems 4) investigate the differences in the home page and in the search engine of the platform, as recently done by others groups 5) analyse the levels of curation in different languages, comparing the percent numbers of fake news or conspiracy videos. The distributed approach success also depends on the number of volunteers participating in the experiment. We consider this an issue of outreach, campaigning, and how the promoters frame the investigation to raise interest in key online communities.

References

1. Fernandez, M., Harith, A.: Online misinformation: challenges and future directions. In: Companion Proceedings of the Web Conference 2018, WWW 2018, International World Wide Web Conferences Steering Committee, Republic and Canton of Geneva, CHE, pp. 595–602 (2018). https://doi.org/10.1145/3184558.3188730
2. Zollo, F., Bessi, A., Del Vicario, M., et al.: Debunking in a world of tribes. PLoS One **12**(7) (2017). https://doi.org/10.1371/journal.pone.0181821
3. Del Vicario, M., Vivaldo, G., Bessi, A., et al.: Echo chambers: emotional contagion and group polarization on Facebook. Sci. Rep. **6**, 37825 (2016). https://doi.org/10.1038/srep37825
4. Pariser, E.: The Filter Bubble: What the Internet is Hiding from You. Penguin, London (2011)
5. Zimmer, F., Scheibe, K., Stock, M., et al.: Fake news in social media: bad algorithms or biased users? J. Inf. Sci. Theory Pract. **7**(2), 40–53 (2019). https://doi.org/10.1633/JISTaP.2019.7.2.4
6. Bruns, A.: Filter bubble. Internet Policy Rev. **8**(4). https://doi.org/10.14763/2019.4.1426 (2019)
7. Covington, P., Adams, J., Sargin, E.: Deep neural networks for YouTube recommendations. In: Proceedings of the 10th ACM Conference on Recommender Systems. ACM (2016). https://doi.org/10.1145/2959100.2959190
8. Zhe, Z., Lichan, H., Li, W., Jilin, et al.: Recommending what video to watch next: a multitask ranking system. In: Proceedings of the 13th ACM Conference on Recommender Systems (RecSys 2019), pp. 43–51. Association for Computing Machinery, New York (2019). https://doi.org/10.1145/3298689.3346997
9. Trielli, D., Diakopoulos, N.: Partisan search behavior and Google results in the 2018 U.S. midterm elections. Inf. Commun. Soc. (2020). https://doi.org/10.1080/1369118X.2020.1764605
10. McKay, D., Makri, S., Guiterrez-Lopez, M., et al.: We are the change that we seek: information interactions during a change of viewpoint. In: Proceedings of ACM Conference on Human Information Interaction and Retrieval (CHIIR 2020), p. 10. ACM, New York (2019). https://doi.org/10.1145/1234567890
11. Robertson, R.E., Jiang, S., Joseph, K., et al.: Auditing partisan audience bias within google search. Proc. ACM Hum.-Comput. Interact. **2**(CSCW), 22 (2018). https://doi.org/10.1145/3274417. Article 148

12. Hargreaves, E., Agosti, C., Menasché, D., et al.: Biases in the Facebook news feed: a case study on the Italian elections. In: International Conference on Advances in Social Networks Analysis and Mining, Barcelona, August 2018. arXiv: 1807.08346 (2018)

13. Arthurs, J., Drakopoulou, S., Gandini, A.: Researching YouTube. Convergence **24**(1), 3–15 (2018). https://doi.org/10.1177/1354856517737222

14. Song, M., Yun, J., Anatoliy, G.: Examining sentiments and popularity of pro- and anti-vaccination videos on YouTube. In: Proceedings of the 8th International Conference on Social Media & Society, pp. 1–8 (2017). https://doi.org/10.1145/3097286.3097303

15. Abisheva, A., Garcia, D., Schweitzer, F.: When the filter bubble bursts: collective evaluation dynamics in online communities. In: Proceedings of the 8th ACM Conference on Web Science, pp. 307–308 (2016). https://doi.org/10.1145/2908131.2908180

16. Bishop, S.: Anxiety, panic and self-optimization: inequalities and the YouTube algorithm. Convergence **24**(1), 69–84 (2018). https://doi.org/10.1177/1354856517736978

17. Rieder, B., Matamoros-Fernández, A., Coromina, O.: From ranking algorithms to 'ranking cultures': investigating the modulation of visibility in YouTube search results. Convergence **24**(1), 50–68 (2018). https://doi.org/10.1177/1354856517736982

18. Sandvig, C., Hamilton, K., Karahalios, K., Langbort, C.: Auditing algorithms: research methods for detecting discrimination on internet platforms. In: Data and Discrimination: Converting Critical Concerns into Productive Inquiry, a Preconference at the 64th Annual Meeting of the International Communication Association, 22 May 2014, Seattle, WA, USA (2014)

19. Bastian, M., Heymann, S., Jacomy, M.: Gephi: an open source software for exploring and manipulating networks. In: Third international AAAI Conference on Weblogs and Social Media (2009)

20. Six, J.M., Tollis, I.G.: A framework and algorithms for circular drawings of graphs. J. Discrete Algorithms **4**(1), 25–50 (2006). https://doi.org/10.1016/j.jda.2005.01.009

21. Brbić, M., Rožić, E., Žarko, I.P.: Recommendation of YouTube Videos. In: 2012 Proceedings of the 35th International Convention MIPRO, pp. 1775–1779. IEEE (2012)

22. Ledwich, M., Zaitsev, A.: Algorithmic extremism: examining YouTube's rabbit hole of radicalization. arXiv preprint arXiv:1912.11211 (2019)

23. Marchal, N., Au, H., Howard, P.N.: Coronavirus news and information on YouTube. Health **1**(1), 0–3 (2020). https://doi.org/10.1177/2056305120948158

24. Airoldi, M., Beraldo, D., Gandini, A.: Follow the algorithm: an exploratory investigation of music on YouTube. Poetics **57**, 1–13 (2016). https://doi.org/10.1016/j.poetic.2016.05.001

Parallel Social Spider Optimization Algorithms with Island Model for the Clustering Problem

Edwin Alvarez-Mamani[1]([✉]), Lauro Enciso-Rodas[1], Mauricio Ayala-Rincón[2], and José L. Soncco-Álvarez[1]

[1] Department of Informatics, Universidad Nacional de San Antonio Abad del Cusco, Cusco, Peru
{edwin.alvarez,lauro.enciso,jose.soncco}@unsaac.edu.pe
[2] Departments of Computer Science and Mathematics, Universidade de Brasília, Brasília D.F., Brazil
ayala@unb.br

Abstract. The digital age came with an extraordinary ability to generate data across organizations, people, and devices, data that needs to be analyzed, processed and stored. A well-known technique for analyzing this kind of data is Clustering. Many bio-inspired algorithms were proposed for this problem such as the Social Spider Optimization (SSO). In this work, we propose parallel island models of the SSO algorithm for the Clustering problem, using 24 processors for each parallel algorithm. Such models were implemented using static and dynamic topologies, and datasets from the UCI Machine Learning Repository used for the stage of experiments. The achieved average speedups range from 15 to 28 times faster than the SSO algorithm for large and small datasets, respectively, and a parallel model with static ring topology performs a little bit faster than the other parallel models. The parallel algorithms provide results with similar precision to the ones computed with the SSO algorithm.

Keywords: Bio-inspired algorithm · Social Spider Optimization · Parallel algorithms · Island models · Clustering

1 Introduction

Clustering is one of the most used techniques to analyze data in fields such as: data mining, big data, pattern classification, image recognition, business intelligence, bio-informatics, and outliers detection. The objective of clustering is to group data that share a degree of similarity with each other.

In the literature you can find algorithms such as: Social Spider Optimization (SSO), k-means, Artificial Bee Colony (ABC), Particle Swarm Optimization (PSO), Genetic Algorithms (GA). These optimization algorithms are applied to solve clustering problems of high and low dimensional dataset.

J. A. Lossio-Ventura et al. (Eds.): SIMBig 2020, CCIS 1410, pp. 122–138, 2021.
https://doi.org/10.1007/978-3-030-76228-5_9

Cuevas et al. [1], proposed the SSO algorithm that simulates the behavior and interaction of female and male spiders based on the biological laws of a spider colony. Later, Vera et al. [2] adapted the SSO algorithm for the clustering problem, where the metric for evaluating the clusters is the sum of Euclidean distances. The experiments were performed over five datasets taken from the UCI Machine Learning Repository, and results showed that SSO computes better outputs than both the GA and the k-means algorithm. Afterwards, an algorithm based on the k-means algorithm, EMAX [3], was proposed for a related problem.

Shukla and Nanda [4], proposed a parallel version of the SSO algorithm, where the stage of position update for male and female spiders is performed in parallel. This parallel algorithm showed to be approximately ten times faster than its sequential version for high-dimensional datasets.

In this paper we propose parallel versions of the SSO algorithm, using the island model, where each version has a different topology. The topologies found in the literature can be classified mainly in static (unidirectional ring, tree, 6×4-net, torus and complete graph) [5–11] and dynamic topologies with communication between *similar*, between *good* and *bad* and between randomly selected pairs of islands [6,9–12]. For the experiments, nine datasets from the UCI repository were used. The results show that the parallel models of the SSO algorithm on average are 15 times faster than the SSO algorithm to classify large volumes of data and 28 times faster for small volumes of data. From the performance and precision analyzes, it can be inferred that the island model with static 6×4-net topology is better than the other parallel models.

Organization. Section 2 provides the necessary background, Sect. 3 the parallel SSO algorithms, Sect. 4 the experiments and results, and before concluding in Sect. 6, Sect. 5 presents the discussion.

2 Background

2.1 Clustering

According to Jiawei Han et al. [13] clustering, or simply grouping, is the process of partitioning a set of data objects into subsets or clusters, such that the objects in a cluster are similar to each other, but different from those in other clusters. This work uses the definition of clustering in [14], and given below.

Let $S = \{x_1, x_2, \ldots, x_n\}$ and $C = \{c_1, c_2, \ldots, c_k\}$ be sets of N-dimensional points. The clustering problem in an N-dimensional space $\mathbb{R}^N$ consists in finding a partition of the set S in k clusters based on a similarity measure, where each cluster has as center an element c_i of C.

Assume that $G_i, i = 1, \ldots, k$, represent k clusters, then the following properties hold:

- $G_i \neq \emptyset$, for $i = 1, \ldots, k$
- $\bigcup_{i=1}^{k} G_i = S$
- $C_i \cap C_j = \emptyset$, for $i, j = 1, \ldots, k$ and $i \neq j$;

The metric (similarity measure) used for evaluating a partition is the sum of Euclidean distances. The definition of this metric $\mathcal{M}$ for the k clusters $G_1, G_2 \ldots, G_k$ is the following:

$$\mathcal{M}(G_1, G_2 \ldots, G_k) = \sum_{i=1}^{k} \sum_{x_j \in G_i} ||x_j - c_i|| \tag{1}$$

The algorithms presented in this paper try to find the set of centers $\{c_1, c_2, \ldots, c_k\}$ and also a minimum value for the metric $\mathcal{M}$.

2.2   Social Spider Optimization (SSO) Algorithm

This bio-inspired algorithm was proposed by [1] and adapted by [2] to solve the problem of clustering. The Algorithm 1 presents the SSO Algorithm as implemented by [2].

Algorithm 1: Sequential SSO for clustering

Input: A dataset $D = \{d_1, d_2, \ldots, d_m\}$ of N-dimensional points; a positive
natural k for the number of clusters; *numberGenerations*
Output: Metric $\mathcal{M}$ of the clusters found

1 Read dataset D;
2 **foreach** *spider C in population P* **do**
3 | Choose randomly k points from dataset D and create the array C of
   | clusters centers;

4 Calculate fitness of population P;
5 Calculate weight of population P;
6 **for** $i \leftarrow 2$ **to** *numberGenerations* **do**
7 | Cooperative operator for female spiders;
8 | Cooperative operator for male spiders;
9 | Mating operator;
10 | Replacement of spider in P;
11 | Calculate fitness of population P;
12 | Calculate weight of population P;
13 **return** $\mathcal{M}$

An important operation in Algorithm 1 is calculating the weight w_i of a spider i based on the fitness function, which is done according to [2], with the Eq. 2 below, Where $J(s_i)$ is the fitness value of a spider i, that is, the $\mathcal{M}$ value for the partition that this spider represents.

$$w_i = \frac{worst_s - J(s_i)}{worst_s - best_s}, \text{ where } \begin{cases} best_s = \min_{l \in 1,2,\ldots,N}(J(s_l)) \text{ and} \\ worst_s = \max_{l \in 1,2,\ldots,N}(J(s_l)) \end{cases} \tag{2}$$

2.3   Island Models

In the island models, according to [15], an instance of an algorithm runs in each island, so that many islands execute the algorithm in parallel. A key feature of island models is that the islands have some kind of communication in order to avoid a local stagnation of the population of each island. This communication is performed as a *migration* of individuals between islands according to some parameters. The parameters considered include the mentioned below [10, 15].

- Number of islands: number of instances of an algorithm.
- Migration topology: defines how islands are connected to establish communication. Communication on such topologies may be *static* or *dynamic*.
- Type of emigrants: represents the individuals selected to be sent from a local island to other islands. Emigrants are classified as: *better*, *worse* or *random*.
- Type of immigrants: defines the individuals selected on a local island to be replaced by the immigrants from other islands. These individuals can be *better*, *worse* or *random*.
- Emigration policy: indicates whether emigrants will be *cloned* or *removed*.
- Immigration Policy: indicates if immigrants will *replace* or not individuals from the local island. If the emigration policy *remove* is chosen then the immigrants replace the existing free spaces on the local island. Otherwise, if the emigration policy *clone* is chosen then immigrants replace individuals on the local island according to the type of immigrant individual.
- Number of emigrants/immigrants: refers to the number of individuals that can be sent and received from one population to another.
  Migration interval: defines the migration frequency with which an exchange of individuals between the islands is done, taking into account the emigration and immigration policy.

3   Parallel SSO (P-SSO)

The Algorithm 2 shows the pseudocode of the Parallel SSO algorithm, which was implemented using the MPI Library of the C language. Each island executes an instance of this algorithm, but with a different initial population.

In line 1 the block to be parallelized is initialized; line 2 obtains the identifier of the current process; in line 3 the total number of processes is obtained; command in line 15 blocks all the processes until the communicator has reached this routine; in line 16 the migration process is carried out according to the migration parameters (Table 1); in lines 18 to 19 the process 0 receives the metric $\mathcal{M}$ generated by the rest of the processes and selects the best one to return as a result; then, in line 21 the remaining processes send their best individual metric to the process 0; finally, in line 22 the block to be parallelized is closed.

It is important to note that the overall population is previously generated in a separated file, then is distributed in equal parts among all the islands, where each island read its own part in line 5 of Algorithm 2. Also, the Algorithm 1 uses the overall population.

Algorithms 3 and 4 are required for the exchange of individuals between islands according to the parameters of migration (see Table 1).

Algorithm 2: Parallel SSO (P-SSO)

Input: A dataset N-dimensional points, $D = \{d_1, d_2, \ldots, d_m\}$; number of clusters, $k > 0$; *numberGenerations*; *parameters* of migration

Output: Metric $\mathcal{M}$ of the clusters found

1 MPI_Init;
2 MPI_Comm_rank get process id ($rank$);
3 MPI_Comm_size get the number of processes ($size$);
4 Read dataset D;
5 Read initial population P;
6 Calculate fitness of population P;
7 Calculate weight of population P;
8 **for** $i \leftarrow 2$ **to** *numberGenerations* **do**
9 $\quad$ Cooperative operator for female spiders;
10 $\quad$ Cooperative operator for male spiders;
11 $\quad$ Mating operator;
12 $\quad$ Replacement of spider in P;
13 $\quad$ Calculate fitness of population P;
14 $\quad$ Calculate weight of population P;
15 $\quad$ MPI_Barrier;
16 $\quad$ Run migration according to *parameters*; (See Algorithm 5 as an example)

17 **if** $rank == 0$ **then**
18 $\quad$ **for** $i \leftarrow 1$ **to** $size - 1$ **do**
19 $\quad\quad$ MPI_Recv the metric $\mathcal{M}$ from process i and keep the best one;

20 **else**
21 $\quad$ MPI_Send the best metric $\mathcal{M}$ to process 0;

22 MPI_Finalize;
23 **return** $\mathcal{M}$

3.1 P-SSO with Static Topologies

In this work, the following static topologies are used: unidirectional ring ($\mathcal{P}sso_{ur}$), tree ($\mathcal{P}sso_{tr}$), net-A ($\mathcal{P}sso_{na}$), net-B ($\mathcal{P}sso_{nb}$), torus ($\mathcal{P}sso_{to}$) and complete graph ($\mathcal{P}sso_{cg}$) (see e.g., [5–11]). Except for the unidirectional ring topology, bidirectional communication was applied in all other five topologies.

Figure 1 shows the static topologies, where the nodes of each topology have different degrees: in the unidirectional ring topology the 24 nodes have degree 2; in the tree topology 8 nodes have degree 1, 10 nodes have degree 2 and 6 nodes have degree 3; the net-A topology has 20 nodes with degree 3 and 4 nodes with degree 4; the net-B topology has 16 nodes with degree 3 and 8 nodes with degree 4; in the torus topology the 24 nodes have degree 4; finally, the complete graph topology shows that its 24 nodes have degree 23.

Algorithm 5 shows the pseudocode of migration for the unidirectional ring topology.

Algorithm 3: Function to package individuals for emigration

Input: Spider *population*; array *point* of individuals; migration *parameters*
Output: Array *point* of individuals

1 if *emigration* == *Remove* then
2   for $k \leftarrow 0$ *to* $numberEmiImm - 1$ do
3   Remove selected individuals (Better, Worse or Random) from the current process;
4   Add selected individuals to *point*;
5 else
    // emigration = Clone
6   for $k \leftarrow 0$ *to* $numberEmiImm - 1$ do
7   Clone selected individuals (Better, Worse or Random) from the current process;
8   Add selected individuals to *point*;
9 return *point*

Algorithm 4: Procedure to unpack individuals at immigration

Input: Spider *population*; array *point* of individuals; migration *parameters*
Output: Array *point* of individuals
Output: Replace or restore individuals

1 if *emigration* == *Remove* then
2   for $k \leftarrow 0$ *to* $numberEmiImm - 1$ do
3   Restore individuals (Better, Worse or Random) in the current process;
4 elsc
    // emigration = Clone
5   for $k \leftarrow 0$ *to* $numberEmiImm - 1$ do
6   Replace individuals (Better, Worse or Random) in the current process;

3.2   P-SSO with Dynamic Topologies

In dynamic topologies any island can be dynamically chosen as source or destiny depending on its attractiveness [12]. In this work, islands are classified as *good*, *medium* or *bad* according to their diversity. This classification is also used in works such as [6,9–12]. The islands are classified using a ranking based on the standard deviation and the average of the output (metric) of each island.

The following dynamic topologies were used: communication between similar ($\mathcal{P}sso_{sa}$), communication between good and bad ($\mathcal{P}sso_{gb}$), communication between random ($\mathcal{P}sso_{ra}$) [6,9–12], where each of these topologies have bidirectional communication. The Fig. 2 shows how the topologies are connected. In the so called random case (c), the communication is between good-medium, and bad-bad islands. The selection of the previous configuration is changed after each generation as follows: first chose two groups randomly (from good, medium, or

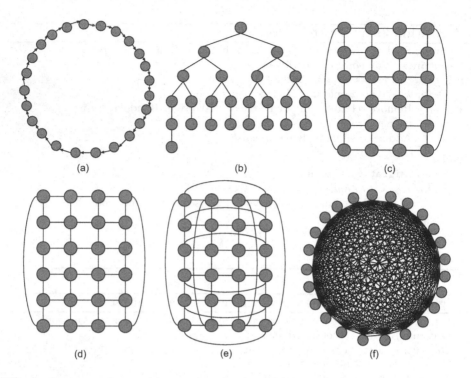

Fig. 1. Static topologies: (a) unidirectional ring, $Psso_{ur}$; (b) tree, $Psso_{tr}$; (c) net-A, $Psso_{na}$; (d) net-B, $Psso_{nb}$; (e) torus, $Psso_{to}$; and (f) complete graph, $Psso_{cg}$

bad) for communication, then the remaining group of islands perform communication between them.

Algorithm 6 shows the pseudocode for generating the ranking of islands used by the algorithms to define the communication of dynamic topologies (see Algorithm 7 as an example). The ranking is an array of islands where the first eight are considered *good*, the following eight *medium*, and the remaining *bad*.

Algorithm 7 shows the pseudocode of migration for the topology between similar islands. This topology considers that pairs of islands in the same group will communicate between them, that is, the process p_0 with p_1, the process p_2 with p_3, and so on (Fig. 2(a)).

4   Experiments and Results

The algorithms presented in Sect. 3 were executed on a computer with 128 GB of RAM memory and two Intel Xeon Gold 6134 s processors, each processor having 8 cores with hyper-threading and a maximum speed clock of 3.7 GHz.

For determining the best parameters of the P-SSO algorithms, each algorithm was executed ten times with each combination of the parameters from Table 1 over twenty datasets: *crude_oil, caesarian, breast_tissue, hayes_roth, iris,*

Algorithm 5: Unidirectional Ring Topology Migration

Input: Spider *population*; array *point* of individuals; migration *parameters*
Output: Array *point* of individuals
Output: Exchange of individuals between islands
1 Package individuals for migration (Alg. 3);
2 MPI_Send *point* to process $P_{(rank+1)\%size}$;
3 MPI_Barrier;
4 MPI_Recv *point* from process $P_{(rank+size-1)\%size}$;
5 Unpack individuals from immigration (Alg. 4);

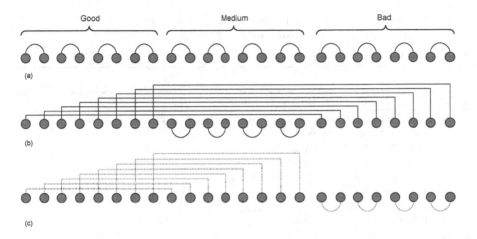

Fig. 2. Dynamic topologies: communication (a) between similar islands, $Psso_{sa}$; (b) between good and bad islands, $Psso_{gb}$; (c) random communication $Psso_{ra}$

tae, wine, glass, statlog_heart, haberman, column_2c, column_3c, ecoli, ilpd, balance_scale, australian_credit, breast_cancer_wisconsin, healthy_older_people, transfusion, and *vehicle_silhouettes*. The results, for each combination of parameters, were normalized using the *min-max* method ranging the data into the interval $[0, 1]$. Subsequently, a ranking of the best configurations of parameters was generated based on the normalized values. The results are shown in Table 2.

The datasets used for these experiments were obtained from the UCI *Machine Learning Repository*, which can be downloaded from the following url: https://archive.ics.uci.edu/ml/datasets.php.

Table 3 shows the datasets used for the experiments, where datasets of size larger that 10 000 are considered as high-volume datasets.

For the experiments, the following configuration was considered: all algorithms were executed fifty times for each dataset; the SSO algorithm has a population of 2400 individuals and the P-SSO algorithms have twenty four islands, where each island has a population of one hundred individuals. Each algorithm has a number of generations equivalent to a given number of execution of the fitness function, for instance, consider k the number of calls to the fitness function,

---

Algorithm 6: Function to generate an ranking of islands

Input: Spider *population*
Output: *ranking* array of islands

1 **if** *rank* == 0 **then**
2   **for** $i \leftarrow 1$ **to** *size* − 1 **do**
3   MPI_Recv *avg* and *stdev* from process P_i;
4   Generate *ranking*;
5   **for** $i \leftarrow 1$ **to** *size* − 1 **do**
6   MPI_Send *ranking* array to P_i;
7 **else**
8   MPI_Send *Avg(population)* and *Stdev(population)* to process P_0;
9   MPI_Recv *ranking* array from process P_0;
10 **return** *ranking*

Algorithm 7: Topology Between Same

Input: Spider *population*; an array of individuals; migration *parameters*
Output: Exchange of individuals between islands

1 Generate island *ranking* (Alg. 6);
2 Get *index* for the current process from *ranking*;
3 Package individuals for migration (Alg. 3);
4 **if** *index*%2 == 0 **then**
5   MPI_Send *point* to process $P_{ranking[index+1]}$;
6   MPI_Recv *point* from process $P_{ranking[index+1]}$;
7 **else**
8   MPI_Send *point* to process $P_{ranking[index-1]}$;
9   MPI_Recv *point* from process $P_{ranking[index-1]}$;
10 Unpack individuals from immigration (Alg. 4);

---

then the SSO algorithm executes a number of generations equivalent to $24 \times k$ calls of the fitness function, and each island of the P-SSO algorithms executes a number of generations equivalent to k calls of the fitness function.

Tables 4 and 5 show the results of the experiments, where the average was calculated over the fifty metrics generated by the execution of each algorithm, in these tables the results highlighted in bold were the best ones among just parallel algorithms.

Table 6 shows the speedups of the parallel algorithms, where the cells in bold represent the best results. For calculating the speedup, the time average of fifty executions was calculated for each algorithm and dataset. The source code of the algorithms and the results of experiments are available at https://github.com/win7/parallel_social_spider_optimization.

Table 1. Estimated values for P-SSO parameters

Parameters	Estimated values
(a) Number of Islands	24
(b) Migration topology	Unidirectional ring, tree, net-A, net-B, torus, complete graph, between similar, between good and bad, between random
(c) Type of migrant individual	Better (0), worse (1), random (2)
(d) Type of immigrant individual	Better (0), worse (1), random (2)
(e) Emigration policy	Clone (0), remove (1)
(f) Immigration policy	Replace (0), restore (1)
(g) Number of emigrants/immigrants	1, 2, 3, 4, 5
(h) Migration interval	1, 2, 4, 6, 8, 10

Table 2. Parameter settings for P-SSO

Parameters	$Psso_{ur}$	$Psso_{tr}$	$Psso_{na}$	$Psso_{nb}$	$Psso_{to}$	$Psso_{cg}$	$Psso_{sa}$	$Psso_{gb}$	$Psso_{ra}$
(c)	0	0	0	0	0	0	0	0	0
(d)	1	2	2	2	2	2	2	2	1
(e)	0	0	0	0	0	0	0	0	0
(f)	0	0	0	0	0	0	0	0	0
(g)	5	5	2	3	1	1	2	4	2
(h)	2	1	1	1	1	2	1	2	1

5   Discussion

From the speedups in Table 6, it can be verified that for the case of high-volume datasets the parallel algorithms are on average 15 times faster than the sequential version. For the remaining datasets, the parallel algorithms are on average 28 times faster. Also, the $Psso_{ur}$ algorithm for the ring topology presented the best speedups in four cases out of nine, which may be explained because of its low degree of connectivity.

From results in Tables 4 and 5 about metrics, it can be observed that the SSO algorithm provides the best metrics in most cases, however, if for each dataset, the average of the absolute differences between the SSO algorithm and each parallel algorithm is calculated, it can be verified that the largest average difference is approximately just 0.15% of the SSO algorithm.

A statistical analysis was performed over the results of parallel algorithms. The procedure, as proposed in [16], is the following: first, the Friedman's test is applied and, second, the Holm's test. Both tests can be found in the software CONTROLTEST package available at https://sci2s.ugr.es/sicidm. These tests are applied with a significance level of $\alpha = 0.05$. Regarding the Friedman's test, the parallel algorithms rejected the null hypothesis for all datasets, except for the

Table 3. Dataset information for experiments

Id	Dataset	Size	Num. classes	Attributes
d1	messidor_features	1151	2	20
d2	website_phishing	1353	3	10
d3	banknote_authentication	1372	2	5
d4	cmc	1473	3	10
d5	yeast	1484	10	9
d6	wifi_localization	2000	4	8
d7	electrical_grind	10 000	2	14
d8	avila_tr	10 430	12	11
d9	firm_teacher	10 800	4	20

Table 4. Average of the metrics for the SSO and P-SSO algorithms. For the dataset d2, the precise values are respectively 2584.82398, 2584.82403, 2584.82406, 2584.82403, 2584.82403, 2584.82422, and 2584.82412.

	Sequential	Parallel static topologies					
Dataset	SSO	$\mathcal{P}sso_{ur}$	$\mathcal{P}sso_{tr}$	$\mathcal{P}sso_{na}$	$\mathcal{P}sso_{nb}$	$\mathcal{P}sso_{to}$	$\mathcal{P}sso_{cg}$
d1	62034.67	62037.93	62037.57	62037.77	**62037.52**	62037.64	62037.62
d2	2584.82	2584.82	2584.82	2584.82	2584.82	2584.82	2584.82
d3	7244.710	7244.747	7244.733	7244.745	**7244.726**	7244.746	7244.743
d4	5541.64	5541.83	5541.72	5541.70	**5541.67**	5541.82	5541.77
d5	205.48	205.87	205.30	**204.88**	204.89	206.70	206.80
d6	20377.77	20379.84	20379.48	20379.27	**20379.01**	20379.68	20379.76
d7	49356.88	49356.94	49356.94	**49356.92**	49356.93	49356.94	49356.94
d8	17626.48	17720.13	17608.66	**17597.48**	17598.78	17704.11	17704.63
d9	20175.29	20219.86	20175.48	20175.32	20175.56	20196.18	20203.76

dataset **d2**. Table 7 shows the results of the Holm's test for small datasets, and Table 8 shows the results of the Holm's test for high-volume datasets. Tables 7 and 8, show that the $\mathcal{P}sso_{nb}$ algorithm appears as the control algorithm in four cases out of eight, and the $\mathcal{P}sso_{na}$ appears as the control algorithm in three cases out of eight. The cells in bold represent those cases where p-value $\leq \alpha/i$, that is, the null hypothesis that a control algorithm and other algorithm (the one in the same raw of the p-value) have the same performance is rejected.

Figure 3 shows the convergence of the SSO algorithm and the P-SSO algorithms, where the parallel algorithms converge slowly and progressively compared to the SSO algorithm. Two small datasets and two high-volume dataset were considered for generating the converge graphics.

Table 5. Average of the metrics for the SSO and P-SSO algorithms. For the dataset d2, the precise values are respectively 2584.82398, 2584.82403, **2584.82401** and **2584.82401**.

	Sequential	Parallel dynamic topologies		
Dataset	SSO	$\mathcal{P}sso_{sa}$	$\mathcal{P}sso_{gb}$	$\mathcal{P}sso_{ra}$
d1	62034.67	62037.56	62037.57	62037.83
d2	2584.82	2584.82	**2584.82**	**2584.82**
d3	7244.710	7244.749	7244.751	7244.749
d4	5541.64	5541.79	5541.79	5541.78
d5	205.48	205.04	205.30	206.11
d6	20377.77	20379.50	20379.52	20379.69
d7	49356.88	49356.93	49356.94	49356.93
d8	17626.48	17604.23	17615.71	17714.60
d9	20175.29	20173.78	**20173.53**	20245.99

Table 6. Speedup of the P-SSO algorithms compared to the SSO algorithm

	Static topologies						Dynamic topologies		
Dataset	$\mathcal{P}sso_{ur}$	$\mathcal{P}sso_{tr}$	$\mathcal{P}sso_{na}$	$\mathcal{P}sso_{nb}$	$\mathcal{P}sso_{to}$	$\mathcal{P}sso_{cg}$	$\mathcal{P}sso_{sa}$	$\mathcal{P}sso_{gb}$	$\mathcal{P}sso_{ra}$
d1	29.55	29.51	29.47	29.37	29.44	29.56	29.35	**29.57**	29.16
d2	**32.26**	32.16	32.17	32.12	32.15	31.97	31.99	32.0	31.81
d3	**18.72**	18.11	18.61	18.09	18.20	18.37	18.69	18.44	18.66
d4	28.51	**28.70**	28.68	28.58	28.58	28.46	28.46	28.55	27.93
d5	33.21	32.65	32.71	32.67	33.0	**33.22**	32.78	32.83	32.76
d6	26.73	**27.08**	27.02	27.06	27.04	27.07	26.93	26.88	26.56
d7	**16.10**	16.08	16.04	16.06	16.06	16.07	16.06	16.07	16.08
d8	**15.17**	15.15	15.15	15.15	15.16	15.14	15.14	15.15	15.16
d9	15.56	15.68	15.81	**15.87**	15.54	15.55	15.58	15.55	15.40

Table 7. Holm test for small dataset

Dataset	Control algorithm	i	Algorithm	Rank	P-Value	α/i
d1	$Psso_{nb}$ (Rank: 4.28)	8	$Psso_{ur}$	6.37	**1.36E−4**	0.00625
		7	$Psso_{ra}$	5.72	0.0086	0.0071
		6	$Psso_{na}$	5.60	0.0159	0.0083
		5	$Psso_{to}$	4.83	0.32	0.01
		4	$Psso_{tr}$	4.60	0.5591	0.0125
		3	$Psso_{gb}$	4.57	0.5965	0.0167
		2	$Psso_{cg}$	4.56	0.609	0.025
		1	$Psso_{sa}$	4.47	0.73	0.05
d3	$Psso_{nb}$ (Rank: 2.66)	8	$Psso_{bg}$	6.07	**4.79E−10**	0.00625
		7	$Psso_{ra}$	5.81	**8.87E−9**	0.0071
		6	$Psso_{sa}$	5.80	**9.88E−9**	0.0083
		5	$Psso_{ur}$	5.53	**1.61E−7**	0.01
		4	$Psso_{to}$	5.36	**8.24E−7**	0.0125
		3	$Psso_{na}$	5.22	**2.96E−6**	0.0167
		2	$Psso_{cg}$	4.91	**3.99E−5**	0.025
		1	$Psso_{tr}$	3.64	0.07	0.05
d4	$Psso_{nb}$ (Rank: 2.41)	8	$Psso_{ur}$	6.85	**5.22E−16**	0.00625
		7	$Psso_{to}$	6.00	**5.591E−11**	0.0071
		6	$Psso_{sa}$	5.93	**1.30E−10**	0.0083
		5	$Psso_{gb}$	5.64	**3.70E−9**	0.01
		4	$Psso_{ra}$	5.52	**1.36E−8**	0.0125
		3	$Psso_{cg}$	5.30	**1.32E−7**	0.0167
		2	$Psso_{tr}$	4.01	**0.003**	0.025
		1	$Psso_{na}$	3.34	0.09	0.05
d5	$Psso_{na}$ (Rank: 1.50)	8	$Psso_{cg}$	8.22	**1.33E−34**	0.00625
		7	$Psso_{to}$	7.96	**4.18E−32**	0.0071
		6	$Psso_{ur}$	6.36	**7.11E−19**	0.0083
		5	$Psso_{ra}$	5.70	**1.75E−14**	0.01
		4	$Psso_{gb}$	5.56	**1.24E−13**	0.0125
		3	$Psso_{tr}$	4.36	**1.77E−7**	0.0167
		2	$Psso_{sa}$	3.68	**6.89E−5**	0.025
		1	$Psso_{nb}$	1.66	0.77	0.05
d6	$Psso_{nb}$ (Rank: 2.20)	8	$Psso_{ur}$	6.62	**7.04E−16**	0.00625
		7	$Psso_{cg}$	6.28	**9.40E−14**	0.0071
		6	$Psso_{ra}$	5.79	**5.59E−11**	0.0083
		5	$Psso_{to}$	5.77	**7.13E−11**	0.01
		4	$Psso_{bg}$	5.05	**1.96E−7**	0.0125
		3	$Psso_{tr}$	4.86	**1.19E−6**	0.0167
		2	$Psso_{sa}$	4.85	**1.31E−6**	0.025
		1	$Psso_{na}$	3.58	**0.01**	0.05

Table 8. Holm test for high-volume dataset

Dataset	Control algorithm	i	Algorithm	Rank	P-Value	α/i
d7	$\mathcal{P}sso_{na}$ (Rank: 2.55)	8	$\mathcal{P}sso_{to}$	7.14	**5.29E−17**	0.00625
		7	$\mathcal{P}sso_{ur}$	6.81	**7.39E−15**	0.0071
		6	$\mathcal{P}sso_{cg}$	6.24	**1.62E−11**	0.0083
		5	$\mathcal{P}sso_{gb}$	6.19	**3.02E−11**	0.01
		4	$\mathcal{P}sso_{tr}$	4.97	**9.95E−6**	0.0125
		3	$\mathcal{P}sso_{ra}$	4.02	**0.0073**	0.0167
		2	$\mathcal{P}sso_{sa}$	3.98	**0.009**	0.025
		1	$\mathcal{P}sso_{nb}$	3.10	0.32	0.05
d8	$\mathcal{P}sso_{na}$ (Rank: 1.48)	8	$\mathcal{P}sso_{ur}$	8.34	**5.48E−36**	0.00625
		7	$\mathcal{P}sso_{ra}$	7.80	**8.42E−31**	0.0071
		6	$\mathcal{P}sso_{cg}$	6.96	**1.45E−23**	0.0083
		5	$\mathcal{P}sso_{to}$	6.90	**4.35E−23**	0.01
		4	$\mathcal{P}sso_{gb}$	4.78	**1.69E−9**	0.0125
		3	$\mathcal{P}sso_{tr}$	3.84	**1.64E−5**	0.0167
		2	$\mathcal{P}sso_{sa}$	3.08	**0.003**	0.025
		1	$\mathcal{P}sso_{nb}$	1.82	0.53	0.05
d9	$\mathcal{P}sso_{gb}$ (Rank: 2.67)	8	$\mathcal{P}sso_{cg}$	7.66	**8.20E−20**	0.00625
		7	$\mathcal{P}sso_{to}$	7.32	**2.07E−17**	0.0071
		6	$\mathcal{P}sso_{ra}$	6.24	**7.13E 11**	0.0083
		5	$\mathcal{P}sso_{ur}$	5.20	**3.85E−6**	0.01
		4	$\mathcal{P}sso_{tr}$	4.54	**6.40E−4**	0.0125
		3	$\mathcal{P}sso_{nb}$	4.41	**0.0015**	0.0167
		2	$\mathcal{P}sso_{na}$	4.05	**0.012**	0.025
		1	$\mathcal{P}sso_{sa}$	2.91	0.66	0.05

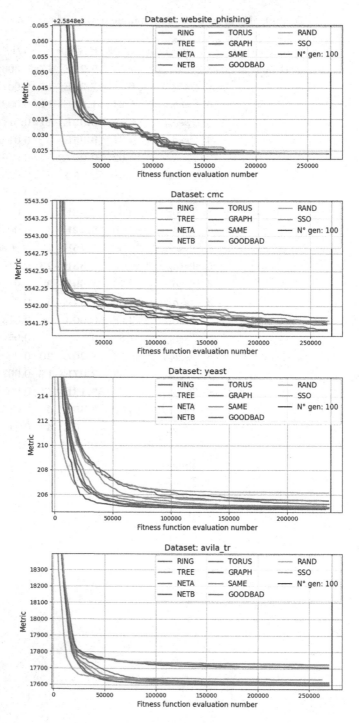

Fig. 3. Convergence of the SSO and P-SSO Algorithms

6   Conclusions and Future Work

This paper proposed several parallel versions of the SSO algorithm for the clustering problem. Each one, implemented as an island model with a different static or dynamic topology, being the main characteristic of each topology the degree of connectivity of its nodes.

Regarding the accuracy of the clustering metric, experiments show that in most cases the best parallel models are $\mathcal{P}sso_{na}$ and $\mathcal{P}sso_{nb}$, both with a static 6×4-net topology. These results were validated by Friedman and Holm tests. Regarding the speedup, the model $\mathcal{P}sso_{ur}$ with the static ring topology showed to have the best speedup in most cases.

As future work, we are planing to explore different topologies of communication such as hypercube, butterfly and pyramid, that offers other degrees of connectivity for each node, this could improve the converge of the P-SSO algorithms. Also, the implementation of a hybrid version of the P-SSO algorithms with a local optimization for the initial population would be of interest.

References

1. Cuevas, E., Cienfuegos, M., Zaldívar, D., Pérez-Cisneros, M.: A swarm optimization algorithm inspired in the behavior of the social-spider. Expert Syst. Appl. **40**(16), 6374–6384 (2013)
2. Vera-Olivera, H., Soncco-Álvarez, J.L., Enciso-Rodas, L.: Social spider algorithm approach for clustering. In: Proceedings of the 3rd Annual International Symposium on Information Management and Big Data (SIMBig), CEUR Workshop Proceedings, vol. 1743, pp. 114–121 (2016)
3. León, J., Chullo-Llave, B., Enciso-Rodas, L., Soncco-Álvarez, J.L.: A multi-objective optimization algorithm for center-based clustering. Electron. Notes Theoret. Comput. Sci. **349**, 49–67 (2020). Proceedings of CLEI 2019, the XLV Latin American Computing Conference
4. Shukla, U.P., Nanda, S.J.: Parallel social spider clustering algorithm for high dimensional datasets. Eng. Appl. Artif. Intel. **56**, 75–90 (2016)
5. da Silveira, L.Â., Soncco-Álvarez, J.L., Ayala-Rincón, M.: Parallel genetic algorithms with sharing of individuals for sorting unsigned genomes by reversals. In: 2017 IEEE Congress on Evolutionary Computation (CEC), pp. 741–748. IEEE (2017)
6. da Silveira, L.Â., Soncco-Álvarez, J.L., de Lima, T.A., Ayala-Rincón, M.: Parallel multi-island genetic algotirth for sorting unsigned genomes by reversals. In: 2018 IEEE Congress on Evolutionary Computation (CEC), pp. 1–8. IEEE (2018)
7. Lynn, N., Ali, M.Z., Suganthan, P.N.: Population topologies for particle swarm optimization and differential evolution. Swarm Evol. Comput. **39**, 24–35 (2018)
8. Andalón-García, I.R., Chavoya, A.: Performance comparison of three topologies of the island model of a parallel genetic algorithm implementation on a cluster platform. In: CONIELECOMP 2012, 22nd International Conference on Electrical Communications and Computers, pp. 1–6. IEEE (2012)
9. da Silveira, L.Â., Soncco-Álvarez, J.L., de Lima, T.A., Ayala-Rincón, M.: Behavior of bioinspired algorithms in parallel island models. In: 2020 IEEE Congress on Evolutionary Computation (CEC). IEEE (2020)

10. da Silveira, L.Â., Soncco-Álvarez, J.L., de Lima, T.A., Ayala-Rincón, M.: Parallel island model genetic algorithms applied in NP-hard problems. In: 2019 IEEE Congress on Evolutionary Computation (CEC), pp. 3262–3269. IEEE (2019)
11. da Silveira, L.Â., Soncco-Álvarez, J.L., de Barros, J., Llanos, C.H., Ayala-Rincón, M.: On the behavior of parallel island models. Universidade de Brasília, Technical report (2019)
12. Duarte, G., Lemonge, A., Goliatt, L.: A dynamic migration policy to the island model. In: 2017 IEEE Congress on Evolutionary Computation (CEC), pp. 1135–1142 (2017)
13. Pei, J., Han, J., Kamber, M.: Data Mining: Concepts and Techniques, 3 edn. Elsevier, Amsterdam (2012)
14. Maulik, U., Bandyopadhyay, S.: Genetic algorithm-based clustering technique. Pattern Recogn. **33**(9), 1455–1465 (2000)
15. Sudholt, D.: Parallel evolutionary algorithms. In: Kacprzyk, J., Pedrycz, W. (eds.) Springer Handbook of Computational Intelligence, pp. 929–959. Springer, Heidelberg (2015). https://doi.org/10.1007/978-3-662-43505-2_46
16. Demšar, J.: Statistical comparisons of classifiers over multiple data sets. J. Mach. Learn. Res. **7**(Jan), 1–30 (2006)

Two-Class Fuzzy Clustering Ensemble Approach Based on a Constraint on Fuzzy Memberships

Omid Aligholipour$^{(\boxtimes)}$ and Mehmet Kuntalp

Dokuz Eylul University, Izmir, Turkey
mehmet.kuntalp@deu.edu.tr

Abstract. In recent years, the motivation to use the hybrid mixture of various methods has been increased. In this regard, the appropriate combination of supervised or unsupervised techniques have been proposed in order to enhances the performance of classification. In this paper, in order to obtain a stable fuzzy cluster scheme, a novel ensemble approach is presented. The proposed model consists of implementations of several Fuzzy C-means (FCM) based algorithms followed by the formation of a co-association matrix in relevant with the probability of each observation belonging to the clusters. The mean of these values is combined with a restriction criterion which have been designed to perceive the exact possibility of assigning observations to clusters. In other words, certain objects receive a reward, and uncertain objects with lower fuzzy coefficient degrees tend to be ineffective. Since partitioning clustering algorithms are commonly used as a consensus function, in this study, achieved row vector is given to K-means and FCM to generate final clusters. Several datasets have been used in order to evaluate the performance of the proposed model in comparison with different methods. Specially in internal validity indices, proposed method fulfills better results than traditional algorithms.

Keywords: Cluster ensemble · Cluster analysis · K-means clustering · Fuzzy C-means clustering

1 Introduction

In the field of machine learning, the ensemble model refers to a system in which it comprises a set of several algorithms. Such algorithms generally run independently but in some cases and according to some rules, they run with interrelation to each other. In this case, their outputs are combined in a particular way in order to find a solution for a specific purpose such as regression, classification or clustering [1]. During recent decades, ensemble methods, in comparison to traditional methods (supervised or unsupervised algorithms) have been increasingly utilized in several applications owing to their effective way of classification [2–4]. Instead of using one classifier, the combination of such methods is used to

© Springer Nature Switzerland AG 2021
J. A. Lossio-Ventura et al. (Eds.): SIMBig 2020, CCIS 1410, pp. 139–153, 2021.
https://doi.org/10.1007/978-3-030-76228-5_10

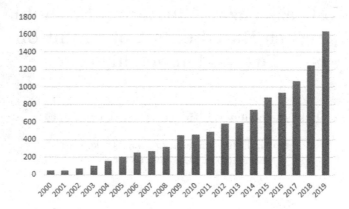

Fig. 1. Comparison of Articles in Ensemble learning topic during last years. (Microsoft database) [5]

take advantage of diverse experts and find the best solution for problems. This integration not only helps to overcome the limitation of some algorithms such as sensitivity to noise and outliers, but also can contribute to the production of much more stable and confident estimations. In ensemble learning, plenty of methods and approaches with a different combination of supervised and unsupervised techniques have been proposed. In Fig. 1, the number of papers in the field of ensemble learning has been shown over recent years, which shows that there has been a significant increase in ensemble topics in recent years.

In clustering ensemble approaches, since each clustering algorithm has its own weakness, the combination of them can diminish the overall errors; therefore, a more accurate and robust clustering model can be created. As depicted in Fig. 2, the main issues in designing cluster ensemble process are as follows:

1. Generation of base clusterings: in the first step, some base clusterings are generated. These partitions are originated by several implementations of one or more algorithms on the whole or subset of data.
2. Consensus Solution: depending on methods used in the previous step, some rules should be considered in order to properly combine decisions that generated by algorithms.

Each step plays a significant role in designing an influential ensemble model. In the first step, if clustering algorithms are not chosen appropriately, weak or possibly meaningless partitions would be generated. Moreover, selection of base clusterings also is an important criterion to alleviate the drawback from low-quality clusterings [6]. On the other hand, even if base clusters are created in the best way but consensus strategy is not formulated properly and effectively, the results will be disappointing. In [7], several consensus techniques were mentioned in terms of application. In [8,9], the capability of combining weak partitions to design a high-quality ensemble approach by appropriate consensus function was

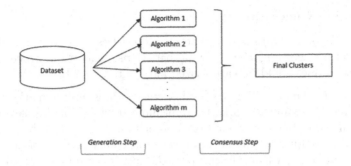

Fig. 2. Simple structure of Cluster Ensemble approaches

introduced. Therefore, a powerful integration could be obtained with respect to clear and right decisions in each step.

It is worth mentioning that the objective of this paper is to focus on ensemble of unsupervised classification methods; thus, cluster ensemble methods have been considered in the literature. Some studies were supposed to employ an algorithm several times. In addition, although considering some mathematical operations on computed co-association matrix based on several implementation of FCM give better results, using statically different methods contributes to a more comprehensive analysis. Our intention is to design a fuzzy based model by analysing distinctive fuzzy values obtained from heterogeneous clusters. In this regard, in generation step, diversity in Fuzzy C-means based algorithms are exploited in order to succeed dissimilar membership values for each observation. In the following, mean of the fuzzy coefficients is investigated via a separator rule. For consensus solution, K-means and FCM are employed on the final vector constructed by separator. Performance of proposed method in comparison with well-known algorithms is assessed based on several experiments. Furthermore, the effect of separator mechanism and quality of final clusters are evaluated. In the following section, fundamental concepts in designing clustering ensemble is discussed in detail.

2 Background

Although there had been a considerable concern on the optimization of clustering methods in the past, nowadays there is intense interest in combining distinctive algorithms [2,3]. As discussed before, cluster ensemble models comprise two steps that have a crucial impact on presenting a powerful and effective approach in clustering.

2.1 Partition Generation

In the clusterings generation step, the characteristics of algorithms should be considered [4]. Regarding the type of partitions generation process, cluster ensemble techniques could be categorized into 3 groups [4,10]:

Homogeneous Ensembles: This method is one of the simplest methods in generative mechanisms, and it works by implementing an algorithm several times with the same or different parameters in order to obtain various base partitions [11,12]. As a consequence, virtually the same base clusterings will be generated by utilizing single algorithm. To improve the quality of clustering, diversity in clustering algorithms and variety in data subset are two crucial points to create the most suitable system for recognizing different patterns in the dataset.

Heterogeneous Ensembles: In contrary to Homogeneous methods, with heterogeneous methods, base partitions will be produced by diverse algorithms that make predictions independently of each other. The idea of diversity, in order to generate ensembles partitions effectively, is an interesting field. Each algorithm inevitably has its own weakness but with the idea of using assortment in algorithms, the overall weaknesses and deficiencies will be diminished. Moreover, each algorithm has its own principle of decisions. Therefore, the integration of different algorithms leads to achieve high quality ensembles in cluster analysis [13–15].

Miscellaneous in a Dataset: A cluster ensemble approach can also be achieved by projecting data into different subsets of generally low dimensions in preprocessing step. This may lead to applying an algorithm to different subsets of data for several times. In this context, data random projection [16,17] and sampling [18,19] methods are the methods commonly used in order to produce new subsets while retaining data attributes. Although obtained feature subspace cannot entirely represent the original data, this strategy is particularly noteworthy when dealing with a high-dimensional dataset.

2.2 Consensus Function

Appropriately combining the decisions of algorithms in previous step is substantial and tricky process that includes evaluation of all results obtained. Depending upon the decisions that taken by algorithms during the generation phase, 3 different information matrix can be formed: label-assignment (which contains labels produced by clusters), co-association matrix (or similarity matrix involves the similarity of objects such as distance between pairs or clusters) and binary cluster association matrix (comprehend the binary representation of decisions (0 or 1) that taken in previous step). Since the information matrix contains the final results of base clusterings, a consensus function analysis the information of this matrix and find solution for cluster analysis. Various algorithms can be utilized depending on the content of the created information matrix, such as: direct approach, co-association based matrix and graph-based algorithms are utilized in many studies [20,21].

One of the simplest and basic concepts in the case of synthesizing information from various sources is voting or direct approach. The voting algorithm attempts to solve the label correspondence problem by permuting the cluster labels. Once base partitions are achieved, the voting algorithm tries to make a decision for each observation and then relabel them based on the frequency of appearing in a similar base cluster [22,23]. Partitional clustering methods are commonly used cause it is easier to apply voting approach on their outputs. However, authors in [24] introduced a new fuzzy voting algorithm which depends on the fuzzy coefficients obtained from FCM. In such algorithm, different partitions, which obtained by several implementations of FCM algorithm, are combined to each other and fuzzy voting applied to find labels and produce final clusters. Khedairia and Kahdir [25] presented an iterative cluster ensemble approach aims to apply ensemble strategy several time at each iteration. In this perspective, base clusters are generated through FCM, EM and DBSCAN algorithms and majority voting mechanism is exploited to find label correspondence.

Co-association Based (CA) methods are another prevalent used technique for finding ensemble solutions because they can represent the occurrence of instances in different clusters over all types of different partitions. The quality of the co-association matrix plays an essential role because the final clusters are achieved by processing the information of this matrix. Berikoy [26] presented an ensemble of fuzzy clusters with implementation of different algorithms and compute the variance of distance of every data object pair to all clusters as weight of base clusterings. Therefore, the weighted co-association matrix is created by the distance of the objects not the similarity of the pair of instances. Hierarchical agglomerative clustering is employed on this weighted co-association matrix. Badelli et al. [14] presented a fuzzy ensemble method by producing fuzzy coefficients matrix based on the combination of several fuzzy clustering algorithms. Final partitions were obtained by applying FCM to the co-association matrix. Authors in [27] introduced a CA-based consensus function which utilizes a new pairwise cluster similarity measure by estimating the correlation between two clusters. Hierarchical clustering algorithm is employed to combine the fuzzy clusters into a predefined number of clusters and final partitions are generated according to mean aggregation. Son and Van Hai [28] exhibited a heterogenous ensemble method that exploits internal validity indices to calculate the weighted co-association matrix, which is the mean of sum of the weighted vectors. Final membership values are achieved by gradient decent method. The application of cluster ensemble in biological gene expression analysis was suggested by Avogadri and Valentini [29]. In proposed method, base partitions are produced by implementing FCM on low dimensional subsets. In each iteration, similarity matrix is generated by multiplication of membership matrix with its transpose. The final similarity matrix is built by averaging all similarity matrices and final clusters are created by applying FCM to the rows of this matrix. In big data clustering, Ye et al. [16] devised an ensemble approach based on the application of FCM on projected data by random projection. Instead of averaging the memberships values, the first left singular vectors of concatenated membership matrices are considered

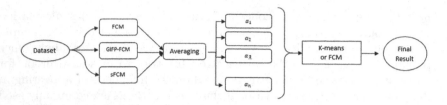

Fig. 3. Proposed Cluster ensemble scheme

as the consensus matrix. Final clusters are obtained by the application of K-means on this vector. Zhong et al. [30] presented a two-level refinement in the co-association matrix followed by spectral clustering to produce final clusters. Moreover, it is worthy to note that computationally expensive is the disadvantage of these methods.

In addition, graph-based algorithms are another consensus strategy commonly used because of their ease of understanding and implementation. A soft version of graph-based algorithms has been introduced that uses Euclidean distance for cluster similarity instead of the Jaccard index [31]. A fuzzy ensemble approach was presented by introducing a fuzzy similarity measure to summarize the ensemble of soft partitions; therefore, the final clusters were obtained by using traditional techniques in order to the partitioning of data that was achieved from the previous step [32].

3   Proposed Ensemble Method

This section provides detail information about the approaches used in generation and consensus schemes. There are two types of clustering methods: soft and hard. K-means [33] and Fuzzy C-means [34] are well-known and popular methods for hard and soft clustering, respectively. As Fig. 3 illustrates, the principle of the proposed method, both algorithms are used for different purposes.

For dataset X in d-dimensional space with a set of instances $X = (x_1, x_2, x_3, \ldots, x_m)$, the objective is to find partitions Z which best depicts the intrinsic structure of X. The decisions of algorithms (Base partitions) on X are represented by $BP = (bp_1, bp_2, bp_3, \ldots, bp_N)$ and $Z = (z_1, z_2, z_3, \ldots, z_k)$ is the final groups with cluster centers $C = (c_1, c_2, c_3, \ldots, c_k)$; k is number of cluster and n is number of base partitions.

Table 1. The contingency table

Thresholds	x_1	x_2	x_3	...	x_M
α_1	μ_{11}	μ_{12}	μ_{13}	$\cdots$	μ_{1M}
α_2	μ_{21}	μ_{22}	μ_{23}	$\cdots$	μ_{2M}
α_3	μ_{31}	μ_{32}	μ_{33}	$\cdots$	μ_{3M}
.	.	.	.	$\cdots$	.
.	.	.	.	$\cdots$	.
α_N	μ_{N1}	μ_{N2}	μ_{N3}	$\cdots$	μ_{NM}
$\sum$	μ_1	μ_2	μ_3	$\cdots$	μ_M

3.1 Generation

In this stage, it is determined how to transform data into a new representation. In this paper, FCMs with different mechanisms are exploited to produce individual (base) partitions. In FCM, objects are allowed to assign several partitions with a degree of similarity (μ) [38]:

$$\mu_{ij} = \frac{1}{\sum_{k-1}^{c} \frac{d_{ij}}{d_{kj}}^{\frac{1}{m-1}}} \tag{1}$$

Where d is the distance and m is the fuzzy exponent. The fuzzy membership value (μ_{ij}) is the probability that instance x_i belongs to the C_j cluster. The idea of finding meaningful information based on the interpretation of membership documents has been discussed in several studies [4].

For better estimation, the intuitive behand this paper is to utilize the algorithms to produce diverse predictions. As a result, membership values are obtained by averaging the coefficients of the algorithms (B). Then, a row vector ($\mu_j = 1/B \sum_{j=1}^{B} \mu_{ij}$) is created which its elements represents the mean of all probabilities for each point obtained by FCMs. Now, a new limitation for computed values is defined for better differentiation of these points:

$$U_j = \begin{cases} \alpha < \mu_j < 1 - \alpha & 0 \\ otherwise & \mu_j \end{cases} \tag{2}$$

$U_j = (\mu_1, \mu_2, \mu_3, \ldots, \mu_j)$ is restricted row vector which exhibits the fact that (according to limitation criteria α) if an object has higher probability to belonging to clusters, it rewards with degree of μ_j, and overlapping objects would give zero value. Threshold value α is chosen from 0.5 to 1. All possible thresholds are implemented on vector U_j and a new $N \times M$ membership matrix (RM) is created in which its rows donate the number of thresholds and columns represent the probability degree of instances (U_j). Finally, by getting averaging of these values vector S is produced:

$$S = \frac{1}{M} \sum_{j=1}^{M} RM_j \tag{3}$$

Table 2. Proposed ensemble algorithm

---

* Input: Dataset, distance measure and membership exponent (m)

* Output: clusters and class labels for each observation

* Generation;

- Run different FCM based algorithms and create co-association matrix

- Find mean value for fuzzy coefficients for each observation

- For threshold values from 0.5 to 1

- Apply Eq. (2) to (μ) to create membership matrix U_j

- Make row vector S through Eq. (3)

* Consensus solution;

- Run K-means or FCM on row vector S

* Evaluate results

---

where $S = (RM_1, RM_2, RM_3, \ldots, RM_j)$ is a row vector which includes the mean of all possibilities for each observation and M is the number of thresholds. This mathematical expression efficiently increases the impact of instances with high membership degrees. The contingency matrix as shown in Table 1 indicates the fundamental principle beyond the threshold criteria. For example, consider two data points with mean of membership degrees are 0.95 and 0.65, respectively. Membership matrix for threshold values between 0.5 to 0.9 will be: $[0.95\ 0.95\ 0.95\ 0.95\ 0.95]$ and $[0.65\ 0.65\ 0\ 0\ 0]$. And final vector $S = [0.95, 0.26]$ represents the mean of possibilities. Deducting observations according to their fuzzy membership values has a great contribution in effectively increasing the weight associated with a particular cluster.

To exploit the complementary information among multiple perspectives, Fuzzy C-means, GIFP-FCM [35] and Suppressed FCM [36] are the algorithms used to obtain distinctive representation of fuzzy coefficients, and accordingly produce a membership matrix. GIFP-FCM and Suppressed FCM (sFCM) have been suggested to suppress data points with lower membership and reward points with higher membership degrees.

3.2   Consensus Scheme

As explained earlier, consensus solution attempts to combine the representation of base clusterings by analysing of them. Since there are no predefined labels in unsupervised classification, correspondence of labels obtained by different partitions would be challenging and complex. Clustering algorithms have generally been used as a consensus function to create final clusters [14, 16, 17]. In this paper, for consensus solution, K-means and FCM are applied to row vector S (obtained from the previous step which encompasses mean of fuzzy membership values). Detailed description of the proposed model is shown in Table 2.

4   Evaluation

4.1   Performance Analysis

In cluster analysis, external and internal validity indices are two approaches that evaluate the quality of obtained partitions. In external methods, the efficiency of the result is evaluated by pre-defined labels. However, distance and position of data points in obtained groups are examined through internal validities [37,38]. For binary classification problems, there are four possible situations: the correct classification of the data point as positive or negative TP and TN, respectively. If a positive data point is selected as negative, it will be FN. Otherwise, this will be FP. According to these responses, the Accuracy parameter is defined [39]:

$$ACC = \frac{TP + TN}{TP + TN + FP + FN} \times 100 \tag{4}$$

In addition to accuracy, commonly used statistical analysis parameters such as AUC, F1 score (or F-score) and Matthews correlation coefficient (MCC) were employed. The area under the ROC (AUROC or AUC) is generally used in classification analysis to evaluate the classifier's final result and can be described by the classifier's degree of detachability [40]. The F1 Score includes both predictive positive rate and sensitivity (proportion of actual positives that are correctly identified). However, MCC depends on all possibilities and can be defined:

$$F1 - Score = \frac{2 \times TN}{2 \times TP + FP + FN} \times 100 \tag{5}$$

$$MCC = \frac{TP \times TN - FP \times FN}{\sqrt{(TP + FP)(TP + FN)(TN + FP)(TN + FN)}} \tag{6}$$

4.2   Experiments and Results

In this section, the performance evaluation of the proposed ensemble cluster model is presented. In order to demonstrate the effectiveness of the proposed method, several datasets with diversity in their number of features and samples have been used, as diversity confirms better results compared to traditional models. Experiments had been performed on existing data from the UCI benchmark repository [41] (including ovarian and breast cancer, ionosphere, speech), Jane [42] and Physionet [43,44] (PAF prediction) databases. The detailed characteristics of the datasets are summarized in Table 3.

Our experiment was performed in MATLAB R2018b environment on a computer with the Windows 10 operating system. For comparison purposes, traditional and well-known algorithms such as K-means, K-median, FCM and an ensemble model based on several implementations of K-means that is followed by majority rule [11]. In our proposed method, the performances of the proposed ensemble scheme with FCM (Proposed1) and K-means (Proposed2) as the consensus functions are evaluated. Each algorithm runs 10 times and the final result is calculated with getting the average of obtained outcomes.

Table 3. Sample datasets used in this study

Dataset	Number of observations	Number of attributes
Speech	756	752
Ionosphere	351	34
Ovarian cancer	216	40000
Breast cancer	569	32
Paroxysmal AF	798	33
Jain	372	2

Table 4 shows the results of the clustering of all datasets. Although the results in all the experiments are close to each other, in terms of accuracy, AUC and F1-score proposed algorithms achieve better performance in the PAF, Ovarian, and Jain datasets than the traditional algorithms. On the other hand, in the breast cancer dataset, traditional algorithms have more satisfactory results.

Although the proposed methods meet the purpose of analysing patterns, in breast cancer, speech, and ovarian cancer, with the K-means algorithm a better clustering rate is obtained. In addition to the mentioned outcomes, it is conspicuous from the Table 4 that using FCM and K-means as consensus function contributes to achieving virtually the same outcomes.

For a better analysis of the results obtained, in the next experiment, the quality of the obtained clusters is compared with fuzzy algorithms. For this purpose, fuzzy validity indices namely: Partition coefficient (PC) [34], Partition Entropy (PE) [45], Modification of PC (MPC) [46] and Xie and Beni Index (XB) [47], are used to evaluate the compactness and separation of final results. Table 5 illustrates the results of performing internal validity indices for fuzzy clustering algorithms. All tests are done through Breast cancer and Jain datasets. In the quality of final generated partitions, the superior performance of the proposed method among other methods is easily noteworthy.

Table 6 shows the impact of the limitation criteria on membership values. In this experiment, the mean values of the three fuzzy-based algorithms are directly given to the FCM (Proposed1) and K-means (Proposed2) for further evaluation without being investigated through the proposed scheme (Eqs. 2 and 3). In this scenario, a $3 \times n$ matrix is generated that contains the membership value of the data points without constraints. For evaluation, two datasets that had previously achieved higher results are considered. The results show that without using the proposed restriction criteria for membership, the clustering performance is significantly reduced.

Table 4. Results of clustering on datasets

		K-means	K-median	FCM	K-means Ensmeble	Proposed1	Proposed2
Speech	MCC	30.22	30.98	30.67	30.22	30.54	30.54
	F1	47.75	52.64	48.47	47.75	48.39	48.39
	AUC	65.02	65.02	65.43	65.02	65.37	65.37
	ACC	73.94	73.94	73.28	73.94	73.19	73.19
Ionosphere	MCC	45.58	36.61	44.74	45.5	45.51	45.51
	F1	64.76	75.36	64.34	36.39	64.6	64.6
	AUC	71.74	71.57	71.4	62.13	71.52	71.52
	ACC	71.16	70.94	70.94	68.06	70.66	70.66
Ovarian cancer	MCC	63.14	39.9	57.99	63.14	63.14	63.14
	F1	74.36	69	73.04	74.36	74.36	74.36
	AUC	74.3	73.25	73.14	74.3	74.3	74.3
	ACC	72.22	71.3	71.3	72.22	72.22	72.22
Breast cancer	MCC	89.18	63.29	89.18	89.18	87.98	87.98
	F1	89.56	75.8	89.56	89.56	88.34	88.34
	AUC	80.52	50.52	80.52	80.52	77.93	77.93
	ACC	85.41	85.41	85.41	85.41	83.48	83.48
PAF	MCC	29.33	34.98	28.41	29.33	34.93	34.93
	F1	71.36	58.94	70.54	72.16	76.43	76.43
	AUC	67.59	65.05	67.24	65.58	67.66	67.66
	ACC	66.79	62.28	66.17	66.49	70.01	70.01
Jain	MCC	44.38	41.35	43.95	36.21	46.75	46.75
	F1	82.15	68.59	81.88	82.64	83.98	83.98
	AUC	84.46	53.9	84.26	76.63	85.07	85.07
	ACC	77.45	76.61	77.15	76.46	79.3	79.3

Table 5. Comparison of cluster validity indices for FCM based algorithm

	Jain dataset				Breast cancer			
	PC	PE	XB1	MPC	PC	PE	XB1	MPC
Proposed1	0.99	0.02	0.003	0.98	0.99	0.013	0.002	0.98
FCM	0.77	0.36	0.07	0.55	0.89	0.18	7.423e–04	0.79
GIFP–FCM	0.88	0.20	0.39	0.77	0.94	0.1154	0.004	0.88
sFCM	0.86	0.23	0.48	0.73	0.94	0.11	0.006	0.88

Table 6. Effect of limitation criteria on performance of proposed ensemble model

	Jain dataset				PAF dataset			
	ACC	AUC	F1	MCC	ACC	AUC	F1	MCC
Proposed1	77.36	84.4	82.06	44.28	66.76	70.24	71.73	29
Proposed2	77.30	84.36	82	33.19	66.78	70.29	71.75	29.02

5   Conclusion

In recent years, cluster ensemble methods are in the center of attention as a solution to overcome the limitations of traditional algorithms. Since in the field of data mining and pattern recognition finding the most appropriate algorithm for clustering depends on the structure of the dataset, there is not any optimal algorithm to use for any purpose. In this paper, an ensemble approach based on the basic principle of combining the features of the algorithms is presented. We first discuss the basic concepts in ensemble methods. In the next step, the proposed method has been shown in detail to represent a simple new strategy for generating membership matrices by applying constraint criteria to membership probability. The average of all values is given to K-means and FCM algorithms for achieving final clustering.

The performance of the proposed method was compared to several algorithms through a number of datasets in the last section. For evaluation, internal and external validity indices are used to examine the performance of the proposed method in terms of the final accuracy and quality of the generated partitions. Regardless of the types of data, with the proposed method, satisfactory and acceptable results are achieved in all experiments although no dominant differences in outcomes were observed. In addition, the constraint criteria has a positive effect in the accuracy measurement due to the application of several thresholds in data points according to membership values.

Finally, in terms of limitations and further work, we want to point out that the proposed method can only be used for two-class clustering, owing to Eq. 2. In addition, although we have benefited from three FCM-based algorithms in partition generation, it is critical to select these algorithms because they affect the final result. Therefore, the future work could be the investigation of the designing an overall threshold criterion for higher number of clusters. Moreover, criteria such as internal validity indices can be used in generation step in order to identify the most appropriate and high-quality partitions.

Conflict of Interest

The authors declare that they have no conflict of interest.

References

1. Wang, W.: Some fundamental issues in ensemble methods. In: 2008 IEEE International Joint Conference on Neural Networks (IEEE World Congress on Computational Intelligence), pp. 2243–2250 (2018)
2. Haixiang, G., Yijing, L., Shang, J., Mingyun, G., Yuanyue, H., Bing, G.: Learning from class-imbalanced data: review of methods and applications. Expert Syst. Appl. **73**, 220–239 (2017)
3. Bolón-Canedo, V., Alonso-Betanzos, A.: Recent Advances in Ensembles for Feature Selection, vol. 147. Springer, Heidelberg (2018)
4. Boongoen, T., Iam-On, N.: Cluster ensembles: a survey of approaches with recent extensions and applications. Comput. Sci. Rev. **28**, 1–25 (2018)
5. Sinha, A., Shen, Z., Song, Y., Ma, H., Eide, D., Hsu, B.J.P., Wang, K.: An overview of Microsoft academic service (mas) and applications. In: Proceedings of the 24th International Conference on World Wide Web, pp. 243–246 (2015)
6. Liang, W., Zhang, Y., Xu, J., Lin, D.: Optimization of basic clustering for ensemble clustering: an information-theoretic perspective. IEEE Access **7**, 179048–179062 (2019)
7. Ghaemi, R., Sulaiman, M.N., Ibrahim, H., Mustapha, N.: A survey: clustering ensembles techniques. World Acad. Sci. Eng. Technol. **5**, 636–645 (2009)
8. Topchy, A., Jain, A.K., Punch, W.: Clustering ensembles: models of consensus and weak partitions. IEEE Trans. Pattern Anal. Mach. Intell. **27**, 1866–1881 (2005)
9. Topchy, A., Jain, A.K., Punch, W.: Combining multiple weak clustering. In: Third IEEE International Conference on Data Mining, IEEE, pp. 331–338 (2003)
10. Alizadeh, H., Minaei-Bidgoli, B., Parvin, H.: Cluster ensemble selection based on a new cluster stability measure. Intell. Data Anal. **18**, 389–408 (2014)
11. Gionis, A., Mannila, H., Tsaparas, P.: Clustering aggregation. ACM Trans. Knowl. Discov. Data (TKDD) **1**, 4 (2007)
12. Gan, Y., Li, N., Zou, G., Xin, Y., Guan, J.: Identification of cancer subtypes from single-cell RNA-seq data using a consensus clustering method. BMC Med. Genomics **11**, 117 (2018)
13. Agrawal, U., et al.: Combining clustering and classification ensembles: a novel pipeline to identify breast cancer profiles. Artif. Intell. Med. **97**, 27–37 (2019)
14. Bedalli, E., Mançellari, E., Asilkan, O.: A heterogeneous cluster ensemble model for improving the stability of fuzzy cluster analysis. Procedia Comput. Sci. **102**, 129–136 (2016)
15. Hadjitodorov, S.T., Kuncheva, L.I., Todorova, L.P.: Moderate diversity for better cluster ensembles. Inform. Fusion **7**, 264–275 (2016)
16. Ye, M., Liu, W., Wei, J., Hu, X.: Fuzzy c -means and cluster ensemble with random projection for big data clustering. Math. Prob. Eng. 1–13 (2016)
17. Popescu, M., Keller, K.M., Bezdek, J.C., Zare, A.: Random projections fuzzy c-means (RPFCM) for big data clustering. In: IEEE International Conference on Fuzzy Systems (FUZZ-IEEE), pp. 1–6 (2015)

18. Wu, X., Ma, T., Cao, J., Tian, Y., Alabdulkarim, A.: A comparative study of clustering ensemble algorithms. Comput. Electr. Eng. **68**, 603–615 (2018)
19. Moazzen, Y., Yalcin, B., Taşdemir, K.: Sampling based approximate spectral clustering ensemble for unsupervised land cover identification. In: 2015 IEEE International Geoscience and Remote Sensing Symposium, pp. 2405–2408 (2015)
20. Strehl, A., Ghosh, J.: Cluster ensembles–a knowledge reuse framework for combining multiple partitions. J. Mach. Learn. Res. **3**, 583–617 (2002)
21. Vega-Pons, S., Ruiz-Shulcloper, J.: A survey of clustering ensemble algorithms. Int. J. Pattern Recognit. Artif. Intell. **25**, 337–372 (2011)
22. Dudoit, S., Fridlyand, J.: Bagging to improve the accuracy of a clustering procedure. Bioinformatics **19**, 1090–1099 (2003)
23. Fred, A.L., Jain, A.K.: Combining multiple clusterings using evidence accumulation. IEEE Trans. Pattern Anal. Mach. Intell. **27**, 835–850 (2005)
24. Li, C.S., Wang, Y., Yang, H.: Combining fuzzy partitions using fuzzy majority vote and KNN. J. Comput. **5**, 791–798 (2010)
25. Khedairia, S., Khadir, M.T.: A multiple clustering combination approach based on iterative voting process. J. King Saud Univ.-Comput. Inform. Sci. (2019)
26. Berikov, V.B.: A probabilistic model of fuzzy clustering ensemble. Pattern Recognit. Image Anal. **28**, 1–10 (2018)
27. Mojarad, M., Nejatian, S., Parvin, H., Mohammadpoor, M.: A fuzzy clustering ensemble based on cluster clustering and iterative fusion of base clusters. Appl. Intell. **49**, 2567–2581 (2019)
28. Son, L.H., Van Hai, P.: A novel multiple fuzzy clustering method based on internal clustering validation measures with gradient descent. Int. J. Fuzzy Syst. **18**(5), 894–903 (2016)
29. Avogadri, R., Valentini, G.: Fuzzy ensemble clustering based on random projections for DNA microarray data analysis. Artif. Intell. Med. **45**, 173–183 (2009)
30. Zhong, C., Yue, X., Zhang, Z., Lei, J.: A clustering ensemble: two-level-refined co-association matrix with path-based transformation. Pattern Recogn. **48**(8), 2699–2709 (2015)
31. Punera, K., Ghosh, J.: Consensus-based ensembles of soft clusterings. Appl. Artif. Intell. **22**, 780–810 (2008)
32. Yang, L., Lv, H., Wang, W.: Soft cluster ensemble based on fuzzy similarity measure. Proc. Multiconf. Comput. Eng. Syst. Appl. **2**, 1994–1997 (2006)
33. MacQueen, K.: Some methods for classification and analysis of multivariate observations. Proc. Fifth Berkeley Symp. Math. Stat. Probab. **1**(14), 281–297 (1967)
34. Bezdek, J.C.: Pattern Recognition with Fuzzy Objective Function, vol. 2981. Plenum Press, New York (1981)
35. Zhu, L., Chung, F.L., Wang, S.: Generalized fuzzy c-means clustering algorithm with improved fuzzy partitions. IEEE Trans. Syst. Man. Cybern. Part B (Cybernetics) **39**(3), 578–591 (2009)
36. Fan, J.L., Zhen, W.Z., Xie, W.X.: Suppressed fuzzy c-means clustering algorithm. Pattern Recogn. Lett. **24**(9–10), 1607–1612 (2003)
37. Halkidi, M., Batistakis, Y., Vazirgiannis, M.: On clustering validation techniques. J. Intell. Inform. Syst. **17**(2–3), 107–145 (2001)
38. Kovács, F., Legány, C., Babos, A.: Cluster validity measurement techniques. In: 6th International Symposium of Hungarian Researchers on Computational Intelligence, p. 35 (2005)
39. Parikh, R., Mathai, A., Parikh, S., Sekhar, G.C., Thomas, R.: Understanding and using sensitivity, specificity and predictive values. Indian J. Ophthalmol. **56**, 45 (2008)

40. Davis, J., Goadrich, M.: The relationship between Precision-Recall and ROC curves. In: Proceedings of the 23rd International Conference on Machine Learning, ACM, pp. 233–240 (2006)
41. Dua, D., Graff, C.: UCI Machine Learning Repository. University of California, School of Information and Computer Science, Irvine, CA (2019). http://archive.ics.uci.edu/ml
42. Jain, A.K., Law, M.H.: Data clustering: a user's dilemma. In: International Conference on Pattern Recognition and Machine Intelligence, pp. 1–10. Springer (2015)
43. Moody, G., Goldberger, A., McClennen, S., Swiryn, S.: Predicting the onset of paroxysmal atrial fibrillation: the Computers in Cardiology Challenge 2001. In Computers in Cardiology 2001, IEEE, 28 (Cat. No. 01CH37287), pp. 113–116 (2001). http://physionet.org/physiobank/database/afpdb
44. Hilavin, I.: Development of a System to Diagnose Paroxysmal Atrial Fibrillation Patients from Arrhythmia Free ECG Records. Ph.D. dissertation, Dokuz Eylul University (2016)
45. Bezdok, J.C.: Cluster validity with fuzzy sets (1973)
46. Dave, R.N.: Validating fuzzy partitions obtained through c-shells clustering. Pattern Recogn. Lett. **17**(6), 613–623 (1996)
47. Xie, X.L., Beni, G.: A validity measure for fuzzy clustering. IEEE Trans. Pattern Anal. Mach. Intell. **8**, 841–847 (1991)

Modeling and Predicting the Lima Stock Exchange General Index with Bayesian Networks and Information from Foreign Markets

Daniel Chapi, Soledad Espezua, Julio Villavicencio, Oscar Miranda,
and Edwin Villanueva[(⊠)]

Pontifical Catholic University of Peru, Lima, Peru
ervillanueva@pucp.edu.pe

Abstract. This paper presents a Bayesian Network approach to model
and forecast the daily return direction of the Lima stock Exchange general index using foreign market's information. Thirteen worldwide stock
market indices were used along with the copper future that is negotiated
in New York.

The proposed approach was compared against popular machine learning methods, including decision tree, SVM, Multilayer Perceptron and
Long short-term memory networks. The results showed competitive
results at classifying both positive and negative classes. The approach
allows graphical representation of the relationships between the markets,
which facilitate the understanding on the target market in the global context. A web application was developed to demonstrate the advantages
of the proposed approach. To the best of our knowledge, this is the first
effort to model the influences of the main stock markets around the world
on the Lima Stock Exchange general index.

Keywords: Stock market index prediction · Bayesian networks ·
S&P/BVL

1 Introduction

Predicting the closing direction of stock market indices is an important task,
since investors could benefit from it to devise strategies for trading the stocks
comprising the index, thereby increasing their potential for future profit. However, predicting the stock index direction is a challenging problem due to the
complex and stochastic nature of the markets. Several machine learning methods have been proposed to address this task, including: Support Vector Machines
[13,14,17,22,29], Tree-based classifiers [2], Fuzzy Inference systems [4–6,15,25],
Artificial Neural Networks (ANN) [1,11,12,26], Neuro-Fuzzy systems [3,24],

Supported by Pontifical Catholic University of Peru.

J. A. Lossio-Ventura et al. (Eds.): SIMBig 2020, CCIS 1410, pp. 154–168, 2021.
https://doi.org/10.1007/978-3-030-76228-5_11

Bayesian networks [18, 26], Hidden Markov models [30] and more recently, Deep Learning models [7, 8, 10, 23, 28].

Despite this considerable amount of research, the focus has been primarily on improving predictive performance by devising new model designs or by searching for new informative variables to incorporate into the models. Regarding the latter, a large proportion of published articles proposes to use predictor variables derived from the same index or from sources of information generated in the same target market, like economic or sentiment indicators. Few works have described models with predictor variables from other markets. One of which came from Sung and So [20], which analyzed various interrelated world stock market indices to extract association rules for predicting daily changes of the Korea Composite Stock Price Index (KOSPI). Their methodology was able to find some unexpected association patterns among global stock market indices that were useful to forecast the target market and understand its behavior in the global context. In addition, following on from this, a recent article from Malagrino et al. [18] described a Bayesian Network (BN) approach to model the conditional dependencies between iBOVESPA index (the main index in the Sao Paulo Stock Exchange) and different stock market indices from around the globe. . The accuracy results were comparable to the obtained by some popular machine learning methods using single market data, but its simplicity was remarkable, since it only used closing directions values from foreign stock market indices.

According to the findings of Malagrino's work, BNs can be a useful tool not just to forecast stock indices, but also to model the interrelationships among the markets. However, the simplifications made in that work by grouping the indices by their home continent limited the understanding whether modeling the indices as individual variables is a worthwhile path. This paper describes a Bayesian Network approach to model and forecast the daily closing direction of the Lima Stock Exchange General Index (S&P/BVL) based on information from 13 foreign market indices. Separately to the work of Malagrino et al. each individual index is modelled as a random variable, thus representing the full joint probability distribution among the different markets. An exhaustive investigation evaluates the appropriate time period for the forecasting task and subsequently compare the results against several popular machine learning models. To the best of our knowledge, this is the first effort trying to model and forecast the S&P/BVL index with information from global markets.

2   Materials and Methods

We collected stock index daily closing prices from Yahoo! Finance's website from 13 representative markets: Dow Jones (USA), S&P 500 (USA), IBEX 35 (Spain), CAC 40 (France), FTSE 100 (UK), DAX (Germany), BSE Sensex (India), Hang Seng (China), Nikkei 225 (Japan), S&P/ASX 200 (Australia), IPC Mexico (Mexico), iBOVESPA (Brasil). We also collected historical Copper Futures prices (that is negotiated in New York Stock Exchange) due to the importance of this commodity in the target market. The period of the collected data was from

03/30/2000 to 03/30/2020, corresponding to a 7306 d. Additionaly, the historical opening and closing prices from the target index S&P/BVL Peru General (Peru) were also collected.

Figure 1 shows the kernel density distribution of each collected index. No index is stationary or follows normal distribution.

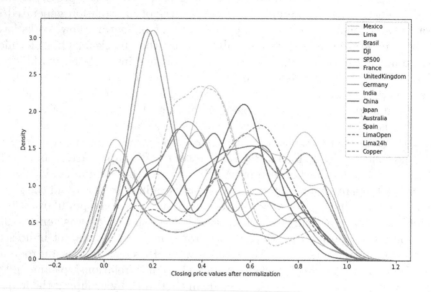

Fig. 1. Kernel density estimate of the different index values

In order to facilitate the modeling with BNs we transformed each index series into a discrete one: values greater than or equal to the previous day are assigned the discrete value "1", otherwise is assigned "0". The resulting discrete dataset was composed by 5205 days (excluding weekends and days where all the markets were closed).

The indices used in this study are from different time zones, which means that the closing time of each stock market may not be the same (Table 1). As our intention is to capture potential relationships from the foreign stock markets with respect to the Lima Stock market in order to predict it, we have constraints in the search of such relationships, which is dictated by the order in which the markets close. Thus, the variables representing the indices are defined and ordered by their closing time relative to the closing time of Lima Stock Exchange. Figure 2 illustrates this, where the longitudinal distance to Lima indicates the difference of a market closing time with respect to that of Lima. Variables in the same longitudinal position represent markets that have the same closing time. For the markets that close at the same time or after Lima, the corresponding variables represent values from the previous day (eg. SP500, DJI, Mexico and Copper). No left-to-right relationships are allowed in the BN structure learning phase in order to respect the flow of information produced by the market closings.

Table 1. Closing times of the modeled stock markets

Index	Stock market	Closing time (GMT+00)
Copper Future	New York Stock Exchange	22:00 h
IPC Mexico	Mexico Stock Exchange	22:00 h
S&P500	New York Stock Exchange	21:00 h
Dow Jones	New York Stock Exchange	21:00 h
iBOVESPA	Brazil Stock Exchange	21:00 h
S&P/BVL Peru General	Lima Stock Exchange	21:00 h
CAC 40	Euronext Paris	16:30 h
DAX	Frankfurt Stock Exchange	16:30 h
IBEX35	Madrid Stock Exchange	16:30 h
FTSE 100	London Stock Exchange	16:30 h
BSE Sensex	Bombay Stock Exchange	10:00 h
Hang Seng	Hong Kong Stock Exchange	08:00 h
Nikkei 225	Tokyo Stock Exchange	06:00 h
S&P/ASX 200	Australian Securities Exchange	06:00 h

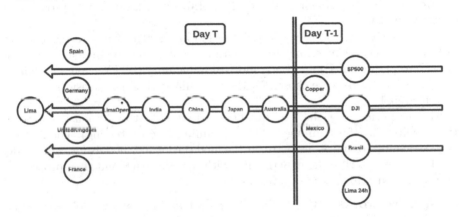

Fig. 2. Temporal order of the indices stock markets closing times

We call the set of variables defined according to Fig. 2 as 24 h set because they all represent indices closed up to 24 h before the Lima stock market. In addition, we generated a 48 h set that include all the variables of 24 h set plus those that represent the closing information of the indices on the previous day (this results in a set of 30 variables and the Lima target variable). In a similar way we generated a 72 h set comprising of 45 variables and the target variable. In Sect. 3 we discuss the results obtained with each set of variables.

For each set of variables we arranged its corresponding dataset. Missing values due to holidays were treated following two different methods. The first corresponds to the removal of all data rows corresponding to the days where some market is on holiday, this resulted in a reduction of the data to a total of 3567 d where all the markets were open. The second method involves imputing the missing value by copying the value from the previous working day. The results with these two methods will later be discussed in Sect. 3.

To learn the structure (acyclic directed graph - DAG) of the BN models we experimented with two algorithms: Hill Climbing and Max-min Hill Climbing [27].

As mentioned before, the learning was constrained to follow the temporal order of the closing times. For this we constructed lists of forbidden edges (blacklists) so the learning algorithms do not consider adding such edges in the structure discovery process. The size of the blacklist was 266 for the 24 h dataset, 1044 for the 48 h dataset and 2332 for the 72 h dataset. After learning the structure of the models, their parameters (conditional probability tables of the variables) are computed by using Maximum Likelihood Estimations from the corresponding dataset.

3   Experiments and Results

Here we describe experiments and results obtained with our BN approach and alternative methods.

As alternative methods we tested the following algorithms: decision trees (DT), support vector machine (SVM) with radial and polynomial kernels, Multilayer Perceptron (MLP) and Long short-term memory (LSTM) neural architectures. These methods were chosen for their popularity and good results reported in the field [9,19].

Prior to performing the experiments we first split the data using a 80:20 ratio (the first 80% for training and the remaining 20% for testing). The 20% set was reserved for comparisons between the final optimized models for each model type. First, we describe the experiments with our approach and then proceed to describe the experiments with alternative models.

Bayesian Networks (BN). With the 80% training data we follow a walkforward validation strategy in order to evaluate the effectiveness of each combination of imputation method, set of variables (time window) and BN structure learning algorithm (12 combinations in total) and identify the optimal one. This consisted of splitting the data in n temporal blocks and iterating from the second one, using all the previous blocks as a training set to induce the BN model and testing it on the iterating block to obtain performance metrics. After doing all n-1 iterations we obtain averaged scores. As performance metrics we register: Accuracy, Precision, Recall, F1-score and G-mean.

Table 2 shows the average G-mean scores obtained in the walk-forward validation of each combination. G-mean is worth observing here since it penalize models that present poor results in any of the classes (we consider that false positives and false negatives are equally important). All configurations presented close scores, ranging from 0.6160 to 0.6344. The best result was obtained with the Hill Climbing learning algorithm, with the dropping-rows-with-nulls as treatment of missing values and using the time window of 24 h. In all time windows the Hill Climbing algorithm presented better results than Max-min Hill Climbing. In relation to the missing values treatment, the dropping-rows-with-nulls strategy tends to present slightly better results than the imputation by duplicating the previous value. This might indicate that adding artificial data adds noise to the model or that the imputation method applied may not be the most appropriate for this problem. The small differences in scores between the configurations (lower than 0.02) suggests that there is not a superior better treatment, learning algorithm or time window for our approach, which can also suggest that the approach is robust to these parameters, according to the G-mean metric.

Table 2. G-mean scores of the bayesian network models

Time window	Missing values treatment	Structure learning algorithm	G-mean
24 h	Duplicating last value	Max-min Hill Climbing	0.6191
24 h	Duplicating last value	Hill Climbing	0.6220
24 h	Dropping rows with null values	Max-min Hill Climbing	0.6246
24 h	Dropping rows with null values	Hill Climbing	**0.6344**
48 h	Duplicating last value	Max-min Hill Climbing	0.6160
48 h	Duplicating last value	Hill Climbing	0.6224
48 h	Dropping rows with null values	Max-min Hill Climbing	0.6279
48 h	Dropping rows with null values	Hill Climbing	0.6309
72 h	Duplicating last value	Max-min Hill Climbing	0.6194
72 h	Duplicating last value	Hill Climbing	0.6268
72 h	Dropping rows with null values	Max-min Hill Climbing	0.6258
72 h	Dropping rows with null values	Hill Climbing	0.6324

Decision Trees (DT). Decision Tree models were induced with the same 80% training datasets used in the BN modeling. In addition, we obtained continuous versions of the datasets to induce DT models with corresponding continuous variables. Also, based on the results obtained in the BN experiments, we hereinafter adopt the dropping-rows-with-nulls strategy to treat the missing values, since it tended to present superior results. The DT learner has a set of hyperparameters that can affect the quality of the resulting models: the max depth of the tree, the minimum samples split and the minimum samples per leaf. We optimized these parameters by using a Bayesian optimization method in order to allow a wide and smart search of the hyperparameter space. The search ranges were: [1, training_data_size] for max depth; [1, 2000] for the minimum samples to split; and [1, 100] for the minimum samples per leaf. The evaluation of each hyperparameter combination followed the walk-forward strategy in the training data with the G-mean as scoring metric (as in BN models). Table 3 shows the G-mean score for the best hyperparameter configuration found in each combination of data type and time window. The results obtained with discrete data are noticeably more accurate than those obtained with continuous data, with almost no difference throughout the different time windows.

Table 3. G-mean results for the best hyperparameters configurations of DT model found by Bayesian optimization in each combination of data type and time window

Data type	Time window	Max depth	Min samples split	Min samples leaf	G-mean
Discrete data	24 h	1	229	1	0.6263
Discrete data	48 h	1	462	1	0.6263
Discrete data	72 h	1	2	1	**0.6265**
Continuous data	24 h	2853	2	1	0.3397
Continuous data	48 h	2852	2	1	0.4084
Continuous data	72 h	2852	2	1	0.3645

Support Vector Machines (SVM). For this kind of model we experimented two common kernels: the radial basis function kernel (RBF) (as in [13]) and the polynomial kernel, as in [19]. Similar to DT models, main SVM hyperparameters were optimized with Bayesian optimization: for RBF kernel models the gamma parameter was optimized in the range [0.01, 100]; for polynomial-kernel models the degree hyperparameter was optimized in the range [1, 5]. In all models the regularization hyperparameter (C) was optimized in the interval [0.01, 100]. Table 4 shows results for the best hyperparameter configuration of RBF-kernel models in each combination of data type and time window. Likewise, Table 5 shows results for SVM model with polynomial kernels. Similar to the DT results, the superiority of the scores obtained with discrete data is noticeable, but minor differences exist along the different time windows in that data type.

Table 4. Results for the best hyperparameter configurations of SVM models with RBF kernels found by Bayesian optimization in each combination of data type and time window.

Data type	Time window	Regularization parameter (C)	Gamma (γ)	G-mean
Discrete data	24 h	13.86	0.01	0.6217
Discrete data	48 h	43.37	0.01	0.6303
Discrete data	72 h	2.01	0.01	**0.6411**
Continuous data	24 h	77.45	31.68	0.4081
Continuous data	48 h	9.52	64.70	0.3860
Continuous data	72 h	41.35	82.31	0.3577

Multilayer Perceptrons (MLP). For this kind of model we experimented 3-layer topologies, as in [16,19,21]. The number of neurons in the input layer is fixed to the size of the set of variables. The number of neurons in the second layer

Table 5. Results for the best hyperparameter configurations of SVM models with polynomial kernels found by Bayesian optimization in each combination of data type and time window.

Data type	Time window	Regularization parameter (C)	Degree (D)	G-mean
Discrete data	24 h	0.03	2	0.6432
Discrete data	48 h	0.12	1	0.6300
Discrete data	72 h	2.52	1	**0.6434**
Continuous data	24 h	83.12	2	0.3132
Continuous data	48 h	100.00	2	0.3622
Continuous data	72 h	43.85	3	0.3273

(hidden layer) is treated as a hyperparameter to be optimized in the range [10, 400]. In the third layer (output layer) there is only one neuron, which delivers the output of the model (the support for positive classification). All neuron units used hyperbolic tangent activation functions (tanh). To adjust weights we used Adam method, which updated the net weights using adaptive momentum in the backpropagation step to avoid local minima. The decay rates for the moments of the exponential moving average of the gradient were set to 0.9 (and 0.999 for the squared gradient) and a penalty term $\alpha = 0.0001$. The maximum number of epochs was set to 1000. The learning rate was treated as another hyperparameter to optimize in the range [0.00001, 0.5]. Table 6 shows results for the best hyperparameter configuration of MLP models in each combination of data type and time window. As with DT and SVM models, the discrete data generated superior Gmean scores but with small differences between the different time windows in that data type.

Table 6. Results for the best hyperparameter configurations of MLP models found by Bayesian optimization in each combination of data type and time window

Data type	Time window	Learning rate	Hidden layer size	G-mean
Discrete data	24 h	0.00291	258	**0.6479**
Discrete data	48 h	0.00020	290	0.6449
Discrete data	72 h	0.00012	400	0.6409
Continuous data	24 h	0.06273	399	0.1459
Continuous data	48 h	0.00001	10	0.2063
Continuous data	72 h	0.00001	14	0.1422

Long Short-Term Memories (LSTM). For this kind of model we used a topology of one input layer, two hidden LSTM layers and a dense output layer with one neuron unit. The two LSTM layers have a dropout rate of 0.2 and

0.1 respectively in order to prevent overfitting in training. As in MLP models, Adam algorithm was used to update the weights in the backpropagation steps. Binary cross entropy was the loss function used for computing error gradients. The maximum number of training epochs was set to 5 due to the large amount of time that this type of model demands on training.

The number of units in the LSTM layers was treated as hyperparameters to be optimized, with the range of [10, 400] for the first layer and [10, 200] for the second layer. The learning rate was also considered as hyperparameter to be optimized, being between 0.00001 and 0.1. Table 7 shows results for the best hyperparameter configuration of LSTM models in each combination of data type and time window. Different from the other kind of models, LSTM models do not show large differences between the results with discrete and continuous data.

Table 7. Results for the best hyperparameter configurations of LSTM models found by Bayesian optimization in each combination of data type and time window

Data type	Time window	Learning rate	Layer 1 size	Layer 2 size	G-mean
Discrete data	24 h	0.09435	10	10	0.6251
Discrete data	48 h	0.04406	10	176	0.6366
Discrete data	72 h	0.08404	10	10	0.6251
Continuous data	24 h	0.03914	89	10	0.6301
Continuous data	48 h	0.03527	58	21	0.6299
Continuous data	72 h	0.04423	10	156	**0.6368**

Model Comparison and Discussion

The previous experiments allowed us to identify the best set of hyperparameters for each combination of model type, data type, and time window. Here we present another set of experiments with hyperparameter-optimized models. The aim with these experiments is to compare the forecasting abilities of the different model-generating methods. The 20% test set is used to perform the model comparison. We performed a 1-day walk forward validation in the test set. This means that we iterate over the days in the test set, each time selecting a new day for testing and using all previous historical data for training the model (with optimized hyperparameters) and asking it to predict the closing price movement of the selected day. After repeating this on every test day we compute the confusion matrix and all associated metrics. For the case of BN model, we used Hill Climbing as a learning algorithm in these experiments. BN models were only evaluated on discrete data.

Table 8 shows the results of all metrics obtained by the different model types and time windows on discrete data. Table 9, shows equivalent results with continuous data.

Table 8. Models accuracy, precision, recall, F1-score and G-mean score with the discrete dataset

Time window	Model	Accuracy	Precision	Recall	F1-score	G-mean
24 h	Decision Tree	0.6275	0.6632	0.6531	0.6581	0.6240
24 h	SVM - RBF kernel	0.6275	0.6632	0.6531	0.6581	0.6240
24 h	SVM - Polynomial kernel	0.6162	0.6705	0.5918	0.6287	0.6183
24 h	Multilayer Perceptron	0.6303	0.6448	0.7270	0.6835	0.6104
24 h	Long short-term memory	0.6176	0.6374	0.7041	0.6691	0.6007
24 h	Bayesian network	0.6232	0.6511	0.6760	0.6633	0.6147
48 h	Decision Tree	0.6275	0.6632	0.6531	0.6581	0.6240
48 h	SVM - RBF kernel	0.6218	0.6412	0.7066	0.6723	0.6054
48 h	SVM - Polynomial kernel	0.6190	0.6546	0.6480	0.6513	0.6151
48 h	Multilayer Perceptron	0.6275	0.6452	0.7143	0.6780	0.6105
48 h	Long short-term memory	0.5560	0.5532	0.9949	0.7110	0.1471
48 h	Bayesian network	0.6261	0.6528	0.6811	0.6667	0.6171
72 h	Decision Tree	0.6269	0.6623	0.6522	0.6572	0.6236
72 h	SVM - RBF kernel	0.6227	0.6533	0.6650	0.6591	0.6164
72 h	SVM - Polynomial kernel	0.6269	0.6623	0.6522	0.6572	0.6236
72 h	Multilayer Perceptron	0.6339	0.6533	0.7084	0.6798	0.6205
72 h	Long short-term memory	0.5372	0.5864	0.5294	0.5565	0.5379
72 h	Bayesian network	0.6255	0.6520	0.6803	0.6658	0.6167

Table 9. Models accuracy, precision, recall, F1-score and G-mean score with the continuous dataset

Time window	Model	Accuracy	Precision	Recall	F1 score	G-mean
24 h	Decision Tree	0.5056	0.5506	0.5408	0.5457	0.5003
24 h	SVM - RBF kernel	0.5224	0.5482	0.7398	0.6298	0.4367
24 h	SVM - Polynomial kernel	0.5392	0.5580	0.7730	0.6481	0.4437
24 h	Multilayer Perceptron	0.5266	0.5482	0.7832	0.6450	0.4097
24 h	Long short-term memory	0.5490	0.5490	1.0000	0.7089	0.0000
48 h	Decision Tree	0.4776	0.5241	0.5281	0.5260	0.4688
48 h	SVM - RBF kernel	0.5224	0.5458	0.7755	0.6407	0.4077
48 h	SVM - Polynomial kernel	0.5378	0.5587	0.7526	0.6413	0.4561
48 h	Multilayer Perceptron	0.5224	0.5636	0.5765	0.5700	0.5130
48 h	Long short-term memory	0.5490	0.5490	1.0000	0.7089	0.0000
72 h	Decision Tree	0.5133	0.5561	0.5575	0.5568	0.5062
72 h	SVM - RBF kernel	0.5456	0.5666	0.7289	0.6376	0.4852
72 h	SVM - Polynomial kernel	0.5288	0.5528	0.7366	0.6316	0.4512
72 h	Multilayer Perceptron	0.5049	0.5403	0.6522	0.5910	0.4612
72 h	Long short-term memory	0.5484	0.5484	1.0000	0.7083	0.0000

From the above results it is clear that the models trained with discrete data tend to achieve better scores in Accuracy, Precision and G-mean. Recall results of LSTM models learnt with continuous data were perfect (value 1), but when inspecting the predictions it was found that such models only predict positive labels (they are totally incapable of predicting the negative class). In the same models the G-mean values were 0, suggesting that this is a better metric to assess the present prediction task.

Models trained with discrete data show close G-mean scores (with the exception of the LSTM models that showed lower results). The scores ranged from 0.6054 (SVM - RBF kernel - 48 h time window) to 0.6240 (Decision Tree - 24 h and 48 h time windows, SVM - RBF kernel - 24 h time window). Figure 3 shows these results in graphical form, where there is no clear difference between models along different time windows. From this graph we can confirm the large advantage of the models induced with discrete data.

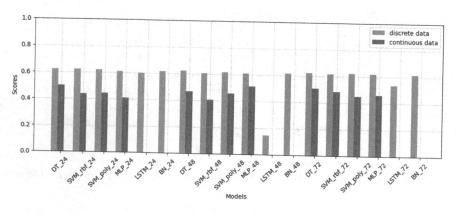

Fig. 3. G-mean scores for the proposed and alternative models experiments using both discrete and continuous datasets and the three time windows

To better understand how the predictive capabilities of the models are balanced in each of the classes, we plot the models in a ROC-fashion plot (True positive rate - TPR vs True negative rate - TNR).

Figures 4 and 5 show such plots for the discrete and continuous cases respectively. Off-diagonal line represents the results of a random predictor and the diagonal line represents the results of a balanced predictor. The perfect predictor is in the top right corner of the plots. With respect to the discrete case (Fig. 4) we note that, even though all the models have close Gmean scores (except the LSTM in 48 h and 72 h that are near to random predictors), the models present some variability in the balance between TPR vs TNR, ranging from 0.65 to 0.73 in the TPR axis and from 0.5 to 0.6 in the TNR axis. It is interesting to note that BN models show values closer to the center in both ranges and a small variability to the time window when compared to the other model types. The increased predictability of the TPR and TNR values in the BN models along with their

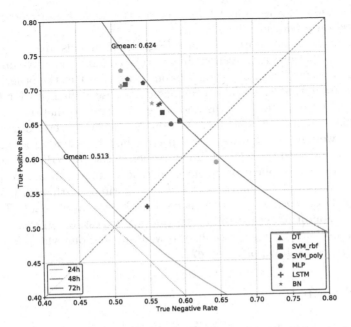

Fig. 4. TPR vs TNR graph for the proposed and alternative models experiments using discrete data and the three time windows

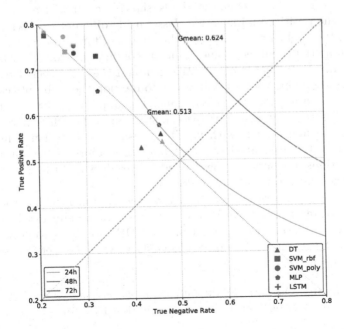

Fig. 5. TPR vs TNR graph for the proposed and alternative models experiments using continuous data and the three time windows

greater robustness to the time windows makes this approach attractive for the closing direction prediction task.

With respect to the continuous case (Fig. 5) the models are mostly near to the random predictions (represented by the off-diagonal). This means that the same quantity of predictability gained in one class is lost in the other.

It is apparent that the raw continuous data pose difficulties for the studied models to learn useful patterns and some data transformation is needed to facilitate this task, as demonstrated with the results in discretized data.

Finally, a web application was developed to show the capabilities of the proposed approach in predicting the closing direction of the S&P/BVL Peru General Index. Each hour the application connects to Yahoo Finance api and retrieves the closing index values of the markets closed at that time. With such information the model makes the prediction and shows it in the web application. The model structure and conditional probability distribution are estimated every 24 h. The model structure can be visualised in the web application, which is hosted at https://chapi-tesis.shinyapps.io/code2/.

4   Conclusion

A Bayesian network approach was proposed to model and forecast the S&P/BVL Peru General index, based on representative stock market indices from four continents. The predictive capabilities of the proposed approach were compared against popular machine learning methods, showing competitive results at classifying both the positive and negative classes using different time windows. One of the advantages of our approach is that it doesn't require all the variables to be known at the prediction time, which is common in stocks markets (some indices may not be available or are still open and therefore their closing direction is unknown). This property allows us to develop the web application that can predict the target market at any time. The approach allows us to specify the temporal flow of information between stock markets, which gives the possibility of generating models with possible causal interpretation. Unlike many existing models that are considered black boxes, our approach graphically represents the relationships between the dependent variables and the target variable, facilitating the understanding of the domain.

As future works we would like to extend the approach to incorporate into the model certain economic variables that investors usually consider in their decisions, such as interest rates, dollar prices, GDP, etc. In the same way, we are planning to extract sentiment indices of market news and tweets to incorporate into our approach.

Acknowledgment. The authors gratefully acknowledge financial support by Pontifical Catholic University of Peru (CAP program, project ID 735).

References

1. Asadi, S., Hadavandi, E., Mehmanpazir, F., Nakhostin, M.M.: Hybridization of evolutionary levenberg-marquardt neural networks and data pre-processing for stock market prediction. Knowl.-Based Syst. **35**, 245–258 (2012)
2. Basak, S., Kar, S., Saha, S., Khaidem, L., Dey, S.R.: Predicting the direction of stock market prices using tree-based classifiers. North Am. J. Econ. Financ. **47**, 552–567 (2019)
3. Boyacioglu, M.A., Avci, D.: An adaptive network-based fuzzy inference system (anfis) for the prediction of stock market return: the case of the istanbul stock exchange. Expert Syst. Appl. **37**(12), 7908–7912 (2010)
4. Chakravarty, S., Dash, P.: A pso based integrated functional link net and interval type-2 fuzzy logic system for predicting stock market indices. Appl. Soft Comput. **12**(2), 931–941 (2012)
5. Chen, M.-Y., Chen, D.-R., Fan, M.-H., Huang, T.-Y.: International transmission of stock market movements: an adaptive neuro-fuzzy inference system for analysis of TAIEX forecasting. Neural Comput. Appl. **23**(1), 369–378 (2013). https://doi.org/10.1007/s00521-013-1461-4
6. Chen, S.M., Chang, Y.C.: Multi-variable fuzzy forecasting based on fuzzy clustering and fuzzy rule interpolation techniques. Inf. Sci. **180**(24), 4772–4783 (2010)
7. Chong, E., Han, C., Park, F.C.: Deep learning networks for stock market analysis and prediction: methodology, data representations, and case studies. Expert Syst. Appl. **83**, 187–205 (2017)
8. Ding, X., Zhang, Y., Liu, T., Duan, J.: Deep learning for event-driven stock prediction. In: Proceedings of the 24th International Conference on Artificial Intelligence. pp. 2327–2333. IJCAI^{TM}15, AAAI Press (2015)
9. Fischer, T., Krauss, C.: Deep learning with long short-term memory networks for financial market predictions. Eur. J. Oper. Res. **270**(2), 654–669 (2018)
10. Gunduz, H., Yaslan, Y., Cataltepe, Z.: Intraday prediction of borsa istanbul using convolutional neural networks and feature correlations. Knowl.-Based Syst. **137**, 138–148 (2017)
11. Hadavandi, E., Shavandi, H., Ghanbari, A.: Integration of genetic fuzzy systems and artificial neural networks for stock price forecasting. Knowl.-Based Syst. **23**(8), 800–808 (2010)
12. Hsieh, T.J., Hsiao, H.F., Yeh, W.C.: Forecasting stock markets using wavelet transforms and recurrent neural networks: an integrated system based on artificial bee colony algorithm. Appl. Soft Comput. **11**(2), 2510–2525 (2011)
13. Huang, W., Nakamori, Y., Wang, S.Y.: Forecasting stock market movement direction with support vector machine. Comput. Oper. Res. **32**(10), 2513–2522 (2005). applications of Neural Networks
14. Ince, H., Trafalis, T.B.: A hybrid forecasting model for stock market prediction. Econom. Comput. Econom. Cybernet. Stud. Res. **51**(3), 263–280 (2017)
15. Jia, J., Zhao, A., Guan, S.: Forecasting based on high-order fuzzy-fluctuation trends and particle swarm optimization machine learning. Symmetry-Basel **9**(7) (2017)
16. Kara, Y., Acar, M., Kaan, Ö.: Expert Systems with applications predicting direction of stock price index movement using artificial neural networks and support vector machines: The sample of the Istanbul Stock Exchange. Expert Syst. Appl. **38**(5), 5311–5319 (2011)
17. Kumar, D., Meghwani, S.S., Thakur, M.: Proximal support vector machine based hybrid prediction models for trend forecasting in financial markets. J. Comput. Sci. **17**, 1–13 (2016)

18. Malagrino, L.S., Roman, N.T., Monteiro, A.M.: Forecasting stock market index daily direction: a Bayesian Network approach. Expert Syst. Appl. **105**, 11–22 (2018)
19. Misra, P., Chaurasia, S.: Data-driven trend forecasting in stock market using machine learning techniques. J. Inform. Technol. Res. **13**(1), 130–149 (2020)
20. Na, S.H., Sohn, S.Y.: Short communication: Forecasting changes in korea composite stock price index (kospi) using association rules. Expert Syst. Appl. **38**(7), 9046–9049 (2011)
21. Patel, J., Shah, S., Thakkar, P., Kotecha, K.: Predicting stock and stock price index movement using trend deterministic data preparation and machine learning techniques. Expert Syst. Appl. **42**(1), 259–268 (2015)
22. Ren, R., Wu, D.D., Liu, T.: Forecasting stock market movement direction using sentiment analysis and support vector machine. IEEE Syst. J. **13**(1), 760–770 (2019)
23. Sezer, O.B., Ozbayoglu, A.M.: Algorithmic financial trading with deep convolutional neural networks: time series to image conversion approach. Appl. Soft Comput. **70**, 525–538 (2018)
24. Singh, P., Borah, B.: High-order fuzzy-neuro expert system for time series forecasting. Know.-Based Syst. **46**, 12–21 (2013)
25. Singh, P., Borah, B.: Forecasting stock index price based on m-factors fuzzy time series and particle swarm optimization. Int. J. Approx. Reasoning **55**(3), 812–833 (2014)
26. Ticknor, J.L.: A bayesian regularized artificial neural network for stock market forecasting. Expert Syst. Appl. **40**(14), 5501–5506 (2013)
27. Tsamardinos, I., Brown, L.E., Aliferis, C.F.: The max-min hill-climbing bayesian network structure learning algorithm. Mach. Learn. **65**(1), 31–78 (2006)
28. Vargas, M.R., de Lima, B.S.L.P., Evsukoff, A.G.: Deep learning for stock market prediction from financial news articles. In: 2017 IEEE International Conference on Computational Intelligence and Virtual Environments for Measurement Systems and Applications (CIVEMSA), pp. 60–65 (2017)
29. Yu, L., Chen, H., Wang, S., Lai, K.K.: Evolving least squares support vector machines for stock market trend mining. IEEE Trans. Evol. Comput. **13**(1), 87–102 (2009)
30. Zhang, M., Jiang, X., Fang, Z., Zeng, Y., Xu, K.: High-order Hidden Markov Model for trend prediction in financial time series. Physica Stat. Mech. Appl. **517**, 1–12 (2019)

Comparative Study of Spatial Prediction Models for Estimating PM$_{2.5}$ Concentration Level in Urban Areas

Irvin Rosendo Vargas-Campos[✉] and Edwin Villanueva

Pontifical Catholic University of Peru, Lima, Peru
{irvin.vargas,ervillanueva}@pucp.edu.pe

Abstract. Having accurate spatial prediction models of air pollutant concentrations can be very helpful to alleviate the shortage of monitoring stations, specially in low-to-middle income countries. However, given the large diversity of model types, both statistical, numerical and machine learning (ML) based, it is not clear which of them are most suitable for this task. In this paper we study the predictive capabilities of common machine learning methods for the spatial prediction of PM$_{2.5}$ concentration level. Three relevant factors were scrutinized: the extent to which meteorological variables impact the prediction performance; the effect of variable normalization by inverse distance weighting (IDW); and the number of neighborhood stations needed to maximize predictive performance. Results in a dataset from Beijing monitoring network show that simple models like Linear Regresors trained on IDW normalized variables can cope with this task. Some knowledge have been derived to guide the construction of competent models for spatial prediction of PM$_{2.5}$ concentrations with ML-based methods.

Keywords: Air quality · Spatial prediction · Machine learning · PM$_{2.5}$

1 Introduction

Air is the most valuable resource on the planet and today it is threatened by high levels of pollution. According to the World Health Organization (WHO), poor air quality causes 1 in 10 deaths globally, 7 million people die each year due to diseases caused by pollution [16]. In addition, it is also a contributing factor to climate change, specifically global warming, due to increased concentrations of greenhouse gases. Among the short-term effects of being exposed to highly polluted environments are: cough, chest pain, headache, nausea, bronchitis, and pneumonia. Long-term effects include lung cancer, cardiovascular and respiratory diseases, and allergies [9].

Having a precise understanding of the distribution of air quality in cities is a necessary step to take actions to reduce air pollution. Governmental and non-governmental entities make great efforts in this regard by deploying air quality monitoring networks. However, such efforts are limited by their high

© Springer Nature Switzerland AG 2021
J. A. Lossio-Ventura et al. (Eds.): SIMBig 2020, CCIS 1410, pp. 169–180, 2021.
https://doi.org/10.1007/978-3-030-76228-5_12

installation and maintenance costs. Spatial prediction methods can be useful in this task, since in principle they could estimate the levels of air pollution at any not measured point, therefore, helping to estimate pollution maps in areas of interest.

There have been many attempts to develop computational models capable of doing spatial and temporal prediction of air pollution concentration levels, specifically the $PM_{2.5}$ level, which is one of the most dangerous air pollutant. $PM_{2.5}$ are particles less than $2.5\,\mu m$ in diameter, and they can penetrate deeply into the lung, irritate and corrode the alveolar wall, and consequently impair lung function [18].

Among those attempts are the work of Liu, B. C. et al. [3], who proposed a model that uses the Support Vector Regression (SVR) algorithm to predict the Air Quality Index (AQI) in three cities; they found that for determining the AQI of the city that has a higher contamination level, it is better not to take into account datasets that have a lower contamination level or are very far apart. Li, X. et al. [4] proposed an extended version of the Long Short Term Memory (LSTME) model, which includes spatial and temporal correlations to achieve a better prediction of $PM_{2.5}$ concentration level; they found that a strong Pearson's correlation (spatial correlation) indicates that only one model was needed for predicting in all their 12 stations, and the higher the lag[1], the less influence it had on the current state. Soh, P. W. et al. [9] proposed to use a model composed by Artifical Neural Network (ANN), Convolutional Neural Network (CNN) and Long Short Term Memory (LSTM) to predict up to 48 h later the $PM_{2.5}$ concentration level; they determined the stations closest to the target station using k-Nearest Neighbor by Euclidean distance for flat terrain, and k-Nearest Neighbor by distance DTW [12,13] for complex terrain, then they use the neural networks to extract the representative features of the air quality in the stations related to the target station, features of the historical data of the target station and features related to the interaction between the terrain and air quality. Wang, J. et al. [10] proposed the assembled spatial-temporal deep learning (STE) model to predict up to 48 h later the $PM_{2.5}$ concentration level; they used Granger causality to determine the stations and areas most correlated with the target station, and LSTM layers to learn the short and long-term dependencies of air quality.

It is observed that the most works are from China, as they have serious air pollution problems, especially with the pollutant $PM_{2.5}$. These articles focus on both spatial and temporal prediction, giving much greater importance to the latter. There has been little effort to study spatial estimation alone, probably due to the large number of air quality stations[2]. This is not the case of low-to-middle income countries like Peru, which has very sparse monitoring network[3].

---

[1] Lag is expressed in units of time (ex: hours) and corresponds to the amount of historical data that we allow the model to be used for prediction.

[2] http://aqicn.org/map/china/.

[3] http://aqicn.org/map/peru/.

Among the meteorological variables frequently used are the climate, temperature, humidity, terrain elevation, wind direction, wind speed, among others.

Despite the large diversity of approaches, both statistical, numerical and machine learning (ML) based, it is not clear which of them are more suitable for the required task. The present paper proposes to study the predictive capabilities of common interpolation and machine learning methods for the spatial prediction of PM$_{2.5}$ concentration level. To do this, the models will be trained and validated with an air quality measurement dataset collected in the city of Beijing, China, which contains information of air pollutant concentrations and meteorological variables.

The paper is composed by four sections. Section 2 describes the data preprocessing pipeline of the Beijing dataset. Then, we describe the data processing pipeline using the dataset previously created, which includes the IDW normalization of air pollutant PM$_{2.5}$ and meteorological variables, and the use of wind direction as a factor to give a weight to each station in the prediction phase, and other techniques. Finally, we describe the model training and validation pipeline using the baseline and machine learning models with the different datasets created. Section 3 shows and discuss the results obtained with the experiments performed. Section 4 summarizes the main findings identified in the work and describes plans of future work.

2 Materials and Methods

For our analysis we used the dataset given in the contest "KDD CUP of Fresh Air"[4]. It has 2 sub-datasets, one of them contains concentrations of various air pollutants such as PM$_{2.5}$, PM$_{10}$, SO$_2$, CO, NO$_2$, O$_3$, and the other contains meteorological variables that are associated with the air quality, such as pressure, temperature, humidity, wind direction and wind speed.

We transformed the air pollution sub-dataset in order to have one column by each air pollution station and pollutant. Also, we focus on analyzing the air pollution information from 2017, since the information from 2018 was incomplete. The resulting dataset contained 7956 records, which had missing records. We follow this procedure to treat such cases in order to improve the data quality.

First, we treat missing values in one station on a given date/time, where the strategy consists in replicating the air pollutant data from the nearest station. That is, if the nearest station has information about the air pollutant, it will be replicated at the target station; otherwise, we will put zero as a value of air pollutant concentration at the target station. Then, we treat missing values in all stations on a given date/time, where the strategy consists in the following: If the totally lost hour is within a period of less than 5 lost hours, it will be completed using a linear interpolation between the two records with information; otherwise, the lost time values will be filled with NaN. We found 791 records of missing values in all stations on a given date/time, where 180 records were imputed and 611 were filled with NaN. The resultant dataset was conformed by 8747 records.

---

[4] https://biendata.com/competition/kdd_2018/.

After that, like the previous case, we transform the meteorology sub-dataset in order to have one column by each air pollution station and meteorological variable. The meteorology stations and air pollution stations are in different places. So, we assign the meteorological variables of the nearest meteorology station to the air pollution stations. Finally, our dataset was conformed by air pollutant and meteorological variables by each station as features, and date/time as index.

In this work we focus on predicting concentration levels of $PM_{2.5}$ with and without the help of meteorological information. From the previous dataset, we extracted the data relative to $PM_{2.5}$ and meteorology.

This study investigates the importance of three factors in the predictor construction, which are frequently observed in air quality modeling. The first factor is the extent to which meteorological variables (temperature, pressure, humidity, wind direction and wind speed) impact the prediction performance. The second factor is the effect that the IDW variable normalization (described below) has on the results. The third factor is the number of nearby stations (k) that we need to observe to maximize prediction performance.

The *Inverse Distance Weighting* normalization [15] consists in transforming the measurements c made by a sensing station according to its distance d to the point where the prediction is to be made. Given a set of k stations, where station i is at distance d_i from the point of prediction , the IDW transformation of this value is given by formula 1.

$$c_{idw} = \frac{\frac{c}{d}}{\sum_{i=1}^{k} \frac{1}{d_i}} \tag{1}$$

In our experiments we tested the IDW normalization on $PM_{2.5}$ variables and the meteorological variables. We also test the application of a transformation on the distance metric (Euclidean, by default) using the wind direction information. Here is the list of the different sets of variables we experimented to build predictors:

- Original $PM_{2.5}$ variables
- IDW normalized $PM_{2.5}$ variables
- Original $PM_{2.5}$ variables + meteorological variables
- IDW normalized $PM_{2.5}$ variables + meteorological variables
- IDW normalized $PM_{2.5}$ variables + IDW normalized meteorological variables
- Original $PM_{2.5}$ variables + meteorological variables (on target point)
- IDW normalized $PM_{2.5}$ variables + meteorological variables (on target point)
- Original $PM_{2.5}$ variables + distances transformed by wind direction
- IDW normalized $PM_{2.5}$ variables + distances transformed by wind direction

The evaluation of the models followed the pipeline of Algorithm 1. For each learning method and set of variables listed above we iterated different numbers of stations (k) closest to the test point ($k = 1$ means that we are going to build a predictor with only variables of the station closest to the test point). In each iteration we selected one of the n stations as testing point and the data of the k nearer stations to that point are used to induce a predictor (see Fig. 1). The induced predictor is asked to predict the PM$_{2.5}$ concentration of the 8747 records of the test point, which are use to calculate the R^2 (coefficient of determination [14])[5] between the predicted and the actual values. The R^2 values are averaged over the different test stations for the same k. Algorithm 2 illustrates this process of training and validation of the models.

Algorithm 1: Data Processing

```
  /* For each value of number of stations closest to the target
     station                                                      */
1 for k do
     /* For each target station                                   */
2     for t-station do
3        Remove target station from dataset;
         /* For each remaining station                            */
4        for r-station do
5           | Create subdataset (k, t-station, r-station);
6        end
7        Concatenate the subdatasets to create the training dataset;
8        Create the test dataset with the same structure, from the latitude and
         longitude of the target station;
9     end
10 end
```

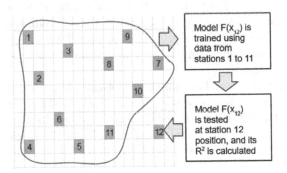

Fig. 1. Illustration of an evaluation iteration ($n = 12, k = 11$) to assess the model performance in predicting PM$_{2.5}$ concentration levels in test points.

---

[5] Statistic that determines the quality of the model to replicate the results, and the proportion of variation of the results that can be explained by the model [14].

Algorithm 2: Training and validation of models

```
   /* For each value of number of stations closest to the target
      station                                                      */
1  for k do
      /* For each target station                                  */
2     for t-estation do
3        Train model with training dataset (k, t-station);
4        Validate model with test dataset (k, t-station);
5        Calculate the metric R²;
6     end
7     Calculate the average of the metrics R²;
8  end
```

As for the model learning method, we tried the following algorithms: *Inverse Distance Weighting (IDW), Nearest Neighbor (k-NN), Linear Regression (LR), Support Vector Regression (SVR), Random Forest (RF), Xtreme Gradient Boosting (XGBoost), Light Gradient Boosting Machine (LightGBM)* and *Feed-Forward Neural Networks (FF-NN)*.

The IDW method [15] builds the predicted value on the target point (c_p) using the IDW formula: $c_p = \sum_{i=1}^{k} \frac{c_i}{d_i} / \sum_{i=1}^{k} \frac{1}{d_i}$, where c_i is the pollutant concentration at station i, k is the number of closest stations, and d_i is the distance from station i to the test point p.

The k-NN method builds the predicted value c_p as the average of the pollutant concentrations of the nearest k stations: $c_p = \sum_{i=1}^{k} c_i / k$.

For the machine learning methods we arranged the training instances in the form *<input, target>* to enable the model training. This is done by selecting one station of the training set as target variable and the variables of the remaining stations as input variables. This process is repeated for each r station of the training set, each time generating a block of training instances (subdataset) as illustrated in Algorithm 1.

The subdataset creation function in Algorithm 1 has some variants corresponding to the various forms of sorting the stations. The Algorithm 3 shows one of the variants. It consists of ordering the stations by Euclidean distance, that is, the PM$_{2.5}$ and the meteorological variables of the station closest to the $r - station$ are be the first attributes of the dataset, and those of the farthest station are the last.

Algorithm 3: Sorting by Euclidian distance

---

1 Calculate the distance between r-station and the other k stations, not including t-station;
2 Create a dataset with the structure: st-1-PM$_{2.5}$, st-1-var, ..., st-k-PM$_{2.5}$, st-k-var; it represents the PM$_{2.5}$ level and meteorological variables of the stations ordered from the closest to the farthest from r-station;

The Algorithm 4 shows another variant of subdataset creation, which is very similar to the previous one. It consists of sorting the stations by Euclidean distance, that is, PM$_{2.5}$ of the station closest to $r - station$ is the first attribute of the dataset, and the one at the farthest station is the last one. As for the meteorological variables, only those of $r - station$ are be taken.

Algorithm 4: Sorting by Euclidian distance, considering only meteorological variables of r-station

1 Calculate the distance between r-station and the other k stations, not including t-station;
2 Create a dataset with the structure: st-1-PM$_{2.5}$, ..., st-k-PM$_{2.5}$; it represents the PM$_{2.5}$ level of the stations ordered from the closest to the farthest from r-station;
3 Add to previous dataset: st-r-var; it represents the meteorological variables of r-station;

Algorithm 5: Sorting by Euclidian distance and wind direction

1 Calculate the distance between r-station and the other k stations, not including t-station;
2 **if** *k-station is not favored by wind* **then**
3 | distance = distance * 1.5;
4 **end**
5 Create a dataset with the structure: st-1-PM$_{2.5}$, ..., st-k-PM$_{2.5}$; it represents the PM$_{2.5}$ level of the stations ordered from the closest to the farthest from r-station, taking into account the wind direction at r-station;

Algorithm 5 shows the last variant of subdataset creation. It consists in ordering the stations by Euclidean distance taking into account the wind direction of $r-station$. The stations are ordered from the closest to the farthest to $r-station$, but also, those stations that are not favored by the wind direction will multiply the distance by a factor of 1.5, so that they have a lesser impact when estimating the PM$_{2.5}$ in the target station. For example, if the wind direction goes from West to East, the stations that are on the East side of $r-station$ would be the ones not favored by the wind, and therefore their distance to $r-station$ would be multiplied by 1.5 since they are less relevant in the test point than the stations located on the west side.

3   Results and Discussions

Figure 2 shows the average R^2 values as a function of k for k-*NN*, *IDW* and *Linear Regression* models using the the IDW normalized PM$_{2.5}$ variables. This variable set were the ones that presented the highest values of R^2 for a given k, although it should be noted that as k increases, the R^2 declines markedly.

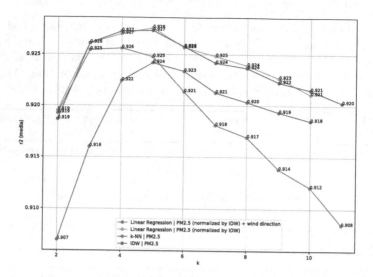

Fig. 2. R^2 average by k of the k-NN, IDW and Linear Regression models

Figure 3 shows a comparison of the performance of the best model (Linear Regression with IDW normalized PM$_{2.5}$ variables) and the *LightGBM* models obtained with the different set of variables tested. It can be noted that the R^2 values, despite being lower than the best model, does not decrease significantly as the k increases.

Figure 4 shows a comparison of the best model (Linear Regression with IDW normalized PM$_{2.5}$ variables) and the *XGBoost* models obtained with the different set of variables tested. The results are slightly better than those of *LightGBM* but lower than those of *Linear Regression* with IDW normalized PM$_{2.5}$ variables. Similar than LightGBM models, the results are more stable with the variations of k.

Table 1 summarize the best R^2 results (along the k parameter) obtained in each model type and variable set performed. Some models were able to overcome the baseline using different approaches by presenting better R^2 values in a given k or by being more robust to the variability of k. In addition, it is seen that in all the experiments the R^2 is quite low when k is equal to 1 or 2, from 3 onward we begin to see improvement in the results. Table 1 shows also comments about the behavior of the R^2 with the k parameter. From a practical perspective, it is desirable to have models with a high R^2 values, but also with acceptable stability against variations of k. The ideal model would be that model that can adapt to the size of the monitoring network without having to make expensive experimentation to fine tune this parameter.

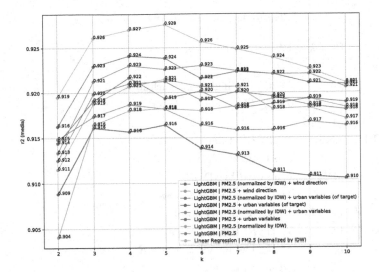

Fig. 3. R^2 average by k of the LightGBM model

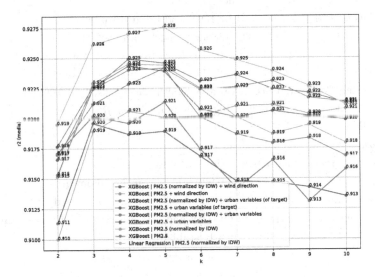

Fig. 4. R^2 average by k of the XGBoost model

Table 1. Best k and R^2 by model

Model	Best k	R^2	Observations
Baseline			
k-NN	4	0.926	The higher k, much lower R^2
IDW	4,5	0.927	The higher k, lower R^2
Models using PM$_{2.5}$			
LightGBM	4,5,6,7	0.923	R^2 stable
XGBoost	4,5	0.924	R^2 stable
Models using PM$_{2.5}$ normalized by IDW			
LR	5	0.928	The higher k, lower R^2
LightGBM	4,5,6,7	0.921	R^2 nearly stable
XGBoost	4,5	0.924	R^2 nearly stable
FF-NN	4,5	0.927	The higher k, lower R^2
Models using PM$_{2.5}$ and urban variables			
LightGBM	4	0.922	$R^2 = 0.919$ stable from $k = 5$ onward
XGBoost	4,5	0.925	R^2 nearly stable
Models using PM$_{2.5}$ normalized by IDW and urban variables			
LR	3	0.921	The higher k, much lower R^2
LightGBM	4	0.919	$R^2 = 0.916$ stable from $k = 6$ onward
XGBoost	5	0.925	$R^2 = 0.917$ stable from $k = 7$ onward
Models using PM$_{2.5}$ and urban variables, both normalized by IDW			
LR	3	0.921	The higher k, much lower R^2
LightGBM	5	0.918	R^2 nearly stable
XGBoost	5	0.923	R^2 nearly stable
Models using PM$_{2.5}$ and urban variables (of target station)			
LightGBM	4,5	0.924	$R^2 = 0.922$ stable from $k = 6$ onward
XGBoost	4,5	0.924	$R^2 = 0.920$ stable from $k = 6$ onward
Models using PM$_{2.5}$ normalized by IDW and urban variables (of target station)			
LightGBM	4,5	0.921	R^2 nearly stable
XGBoost	5	0.924	The higher k, lower R^2
Models using PM$_{2.5}$ and wind direction			
LightGBM	8,9	0.919	R^2 nearly stable
XGBoost	4,7,8,10	0.921	R^2 stable
Models using PM$_{2.5}$ normalized by IDW and wind direction			
LR	5	0.924	The higher k, lower R^2
LightGBM	3,4,5	0.916	The higher k, lower R^2
XGBoost	3	0.920	The higher k, lower R^2

4   Conclusions

Based on the results of our experiments we obtained useful knowledge to guide the construction of spatial prediction models of air quality. *Linear Regression* models using the IDW normalized PM$_{2.5}$ variables tended to present the best predictive performances among all models tested at $k = 5$. The *XGBoost* and *LightGBM* models, despite having a slightly lower predictive performance than Linear Regression, they are more stable to the variations of k, which makes them attractive for practical use without having to fine-tune this parameter. The addition of meteorological variables did not significantly impacted on the model performances. On *Linear Regression* model the effect was negative turning the models very sensitive to the variations of k. The incorporation of wind direction information by distorting the distances according to the wind direction did not have a positive effect on improving model performance. Perhaps the distortion factor of the distances (1.5) was not appropriate. More research is needed in this regard.

As a future work we plan to use the knowledge obtained in this research to build air quality models for Lima (Peru), a city that is known to have poor air quality, but the number of monitoring stations is very sparse. We also plan to investigate ways to incorporate vehicular traffic information in the models. We also intend to investigate new ways to exploit the air quality data to improve predictability, such as causal information derived by Granger causality methods.

Acknowledgment. The authors gratefully acknowledge financial support by Fondo Nacional de Desarrollo Científico, Tecnológico y de Innovación Tecnológica (Fondecyt) - Mundial Bank (Grant: 50-2018-FONDECYT-BM-IADT-MU).

References

1. Baumann, L.M., et al.: Effects of distance from a heavily transited avenue on asthma and atopy in a periurban shantytown in Lima, Peru. J. Aller. Clin. Immunol. **127**(4), 875–882 (2011)
2. Bellinger, C., Jabbar, M.S.M., Zaïane, O., Osornio-Vargas, A.: A systematic review of data mining and machine learning for air pollution epidemiology. BMC Public Health **17**(1), 907 (2017)
3. Liu, B.C., Binaykia, A., Chang, P.C., Tiwari, M.K., Tsao, C.C.: Urban air quality forecasting based on multi-dimensional collaborative support vector regression (SVR): a case study of Beijing-Tianjin-Shijiazhuang. PloS One **12**(7), 1–17 (2017)
4. Li, X., et al.: Long short-term memory neural network for air pollutant concentration predictions: method development and evaluation. Environ. Pollut. **231**, 997–1004 (2017)
5. Xu, Y., Yang, W., Wang, J.: Air quality early-warning system for cities in China. Atmos. Environ. **148**, 239–257 (2017)
6. Freeman, B.S., Taylor, G., Gharabaghi, B., Thé, J.: Forecasting air quality time series using deep learning. J. Air Waste Manage. Assoc. **68**, 1–21 (2018). 1982, p. 301

7. Reátegui-Romero, W., Sánchez-Ccoyllo, O.R., de Fatima Andrade, M., Moya-Alvarez, A.: PM2.5 Estimation with the WRF/Chem model, produced by vehicular flow in the Lima metropolitan area. Open J. Air Pollut. **7**(03), 215 (2018)
8. Sánchez-Ccoyllo, O.R., et al.: Modeling study of the particulate matter in Lima with the WRF-Chem model: case study of April 2016. Int. J. Appl. Eng. Res. **13**(11), 10129–10141 (2018)
9. Soh, P.W., Chang, J.W., Huang, J.W.: Adaptive deep learning-based air quality prediction model using the most relevant spatial-temporal relations. IEEE Access **6**, 38186–38199 (2018)
10. Wang, J., Song, G.: A deep spatial-temporal ensemble model for air quality prediction. Neurocomputing **314**, 198–206 (2018)
11. Wen, C., Liu, S., Yao, X., Peng, L., Li, X., Hu, Y., Chi, T.: A novel spatiotemporal convolutional long short-term neural network for air pollution prediction. Sci. Total Environ. **654**, 1091–1099 (2019)
12. Rakthanmanon, T., et al.: Searching and mining trillions of time series subsequences under dynamic time warping. In: Proceedings of the 18th ACM SIGKDD International Conference on Knowledge Discovery and Data Mining, pp. 262–270. ACM, August, 2012
13. Keogh, E., Ratanamahatana, C.A.: Exact indexing of dynamic time warping. Knowl. Inf. Syst. **7**(3), 358–386 (2004). https://doi.org/10.1007/s10115-004-0154-9
14. Steel, R.G., Torrie, J.H.: Principles and Procedures of Statistics. McGraw-Hill Book Company Inc., New York (1960)
15. Shepard, D.: A two-dimensional interpolation function for irregularly-spaced data. In: Proceedings of the 1968 23rd ACM International Conference, pp. 517–524. ACM, January 1968
16. OMS. Nueve de cada diez personas de todo el mundo respiran aire contaminado. Recuperado de (2018). https://www.who.int/es/news-room/detail/02-05-2018-9-out-of-10-people-worldwide-breathe-polluted-air-but-more-countries-are-taking-action
17. Unidas, N.: La Agenda 2030 y los Objetivos de Desarrollo Sostenible: una oportunidad para América Latina y el Caribe (LC/G.2681-P/Rev. 3), Santiago (2018)
18. Xing, Y.F., Xu, Y.H., Shi, M.H., Lian, Y.X.: The impact of PM2.5 on the human respiratory system. J. Thorac. Dis. **8**(1), 69 (2016)

Prediction of Solar Radiation Using Neural Networks Forecasting

Ponce-Jara Marcos[1], Alvaro Talavera[2(✉)], Carlos Velásquez[1], and David Tonato Peralta[3]

[1] Universidad Laica Eloy Alfaro de Manabí, Av. Circunvalación S/N, Manta, Ecuador
{marcos.ponce,carlos.velasquez}@uleam.edu.ec
[2] Universidad del Pacífico, Av. Salaverry 2020, Lima, Peru
ag.talaveral@up.edu.pe
[3] Instituto Nacional de Meteorología e Hidrología (INAMHI),
Núñez de Vela N36-15 y Corea, Quito, Ecuador
ctonato@inamhi.gob.ec

Abstract. Solar radiation and wind data play an important role in renewable energy projects to produce electricity. In Ecuador, these data are not always available for locations of interest due to absences of meteorological stations. In the scope of this paper, a low-cost automatic meteorological station prototype based on Raspberry technology was developed to measure the aforementioned variables. The objective of this paper is twofold: a) to present a proposal for the design of a low-cost automatic weather station using the Raspberry Pi microcomputer, showing the feasibility of this technology as an alternative for the construction of automatic meteorological station and; b) to use Forecasting with neural networks to predict solar radiation in Manta, Ecuador, based on the historical data collected: solar radiation, wind speed and wind direction. We proved that both technology feasibility and Machine learning has a high potential as a tool to use in this field of study.

Keywords: Weather station · Solar radiation · Wind speed · Neural networks

1 Introduction

Solar radiation and wind speed are one of the most important parameters for research in the renewable energy field focused on the production of electrical energy. Before 1960 Ecuador lacked meteorological stations and the few advances were made in a disparate way [6]. Starting in 1961, through the creation of the National Service of Meteorology and Hydrology (SNMH), current INAMHI, a series of programs aimed at the installation of conventional meteorological stations were carried out for research and development work on both Meteorology and Operational Hydrology [4]. It is estimated that in Ecuador there are approximately more than 250 meteorological stations for synoptic and manual collection,

© Springer Nature Switzerland AG 2021
J. A. Lossio-Ventura et al. (Eds.): SIMBig 2020, CCIS 1410, pp. 181–194, 2021.
https://doi.org/10.1007/978-3-030-76228-5_13

in most of them there is no appropriate maintenance program for the network of stations, so the current status of the stations is unknown. The main variables that measure the different seasons are [11]:

1. Humidity (%)
2. Atmospheric precipitation (mm)
3. Heliofania (hours)
4. Evaporation
5. Wind (direction and speed m/s)
6. Cloudiness (oktas in overcast sky)

Because of the need of having real-time information for Meteorological Surveillance Systems and for Early Warning Systems, in 2003 the first programs for the creation of an automatic meteorology network began. There were 91 automatic meteorological stations by 2013, which had satellite communication and the General Packet Radio Service (GPRS) in real time to link with INAMHI's servers [6]. In general terms, these types of stations are very expensive, which greatly limits their deployment in the country. Figure 1 shows the spatial distribution of automatic meteorological stations in Ecuador.

Fig. 1. Weather station network 2017 [4].

Of these automatic stations, those located in the province of Manabí (where the study is carried out and represent 7% of the country's total), do not measure solar radiation; and in the case of the wind, they measure the instantaneous speed and direction at no more than 10 m above ground level [5]. Currently, Ecuador has a Solar and Wind Atlas made from satellite images [3,9], from which certain areas of interest can be broadly identified where these renewable sources can be exploited. However, the validation of these atmospheric variables with field measurements is of utmost importance due to the different microclimates and variations of these energy resources in the country. In a first instance, according to the Solar and Wind Atlas, the solar resource seems to be one of the most accessible and best distributed in the entire country, while the wind potential is mainly found in the Sierra Region, the Coastal Region does not have great potential; however, it is possible to find locations where mini wind technology can be exploited. The objective of this article is twofold: a) to present a proposal for the design of a low-cost automatic meteorological station using the "Raspberry pi" microcomputer, showing the technical feasibility of this technology as an alternative for the construction of an automatic meteorological station and; b) use the automatic learning method (ML) to predict solar radiation and wind speed in Manta city, Ecuador, based on the historical data collected to date. Section 2 describes the parts that make up the automatic weather station. Section 3 delves into the sensor calibration process and details the results obtained during 3 months of operation. Subsequently, Sect. 4 delves into the prediction analysis through Machine Learning and presents the results obtained. Finally, Sect. 5 presents the findings.

2   Low-Cost Automatic Weather Station

A meteorological station can be defined as a facility that has a series of instruments for the collection and recording of meteorological variables according to their type, be they climatic, synoptic or marine. Within these typologies an automatic meteorological station (EMA) is defined as "a meteorological station in which observations are made and transmitted automatically [10]. Measurements made with an EMA are read and recorded by a central data unit or "datalogger", which can be processed by the device itself or externally. This is one of the most important devices of an EMA and also one of the most expensive devices of such a station.

Some related works discussed various approaches to design a low cost weather station by using different electronic platforms such as Arduino, microcontroller, among others [13,15,17]. For this project, a low-cost datalogger was designed using the "Raspberry Pi" microcomputer, which is in charge of collecting the data from the sensors or measuring instruments, processing them and sending them through the Ethernet network to the server of Universidad Laica Eloy Alfaro de Manabí (ULEAM) and to the server of the National Institute of Meteorology and Hydrology (INAMHI). The data history is displayed, with no cost, on a WEB platform in real time to the university community. On the other hand, the sensors used (Pyranometer, Anemometer and Weather Vane) were calibrated under rigorous processes performed by the National Institute of Meteorology and

Hydrology (INAMHI). In addition, it incorporates a photovoltaic solar system to supply the demand of the meteorological station in the absence of an electrical network. Figures 2 and 3 show the physical and functional design of the meteorological station.

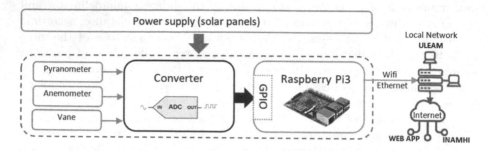

Fig. 2. Global scheme of automatic weather station.

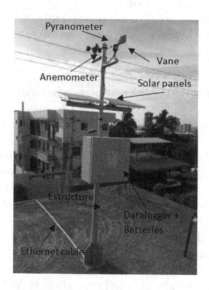

Fig. 3. Prototype – automatic meteorological station.

3   Raspberry Pi and Sensors for Measuring Meteorological Variables

Raspberry Pi. In this project, Raspberry Pi model 3B+ was used to design a low-cost datalogger. This is a small single-board computer that allows algorithms to be performed in different types of languages such as Python, Java, C++, etc. Regarding the hardware characteristics, the most important are:

- Broadcom BCM2837B0, Cortex-A53 (ARMv8) 64-bit SoC @ 1.4 GHz.
- 1 GB LPDDR2 SDRAM.
- 2.4 GHz and 5 GHz IEEE 802.11.b/g/n/ac wireless LAN, Bluetooth 4.2, BLE.
- Gigabit Ethernet over USB 2.0
- Extended 40-pin GPIO header.
- Full-size HDMI.
- 4 USB 2.0 ports.
- CSI camera port for connecting a Raspberry Pi camera.
- DSI display port for connecting a Raspberry Pi touchscreen display.
- 4-pole stereo output and composite video port.
- Micro SD port for loading your operating system and storing data.
- 5 V/2.5 A DC power input
- Power-over-Ethernet (PoE) support (requires separate PoE HAT)

The different sensors were connected to this electronic device to carry out the study of this article. The sensors used to measure solar radiation, wind speed and direction are: CM3 Pyranometer (analog sensor), NRG #40H Anemometer (digital sensor) and Weather Vane NRG #200P (analog sensor). Analog signals are converted to digital using a 16-bit ADS1115A/D converter, and then transmitted to the Raspberry via the I2C communication protocol.

Pyranometer. The pyranometer oversees the measurement of the global incident solar radiation that reaches the earth's surface. The CM3 pyranometer (Fig. 4b) is a thermopile- based sensor that generates a signal in mV (0–50 mV) that can be measured directly on a datalogger without the need for an external power source. The equation used to determine solar radiation (SR) is given by:

$$SR = \frac{V_{out} \times 2000}{0.05} \qquad (1)$$

The pyranometer was calibrated by relating the voltage range (0–50 mV) to the radiation range (0–2000 W/m^2) that this sensor can provide and receive respectively. Fixed voltages of 40 mV, 30 mV, 20 mV, 10 mV and 5 mV were injected into the datalogger using the Fluke 754 Calibrator (Fig. 4a) to ensure that the measurements it receives and converts are correct. Subsequently, the measurements taken with the CM3 pyranometer were compared with the measurements taken by the CMP22 standard sensor.

Anemometer. The anemometer is the sensor that oversees the measurement of the wind speed in m/s. The NRG #40H anemometer, shown in Fig. 5a, is directly connected to one of the digital inputs of the GPIO port of the Raspberry Pi3 and provides a digital signal in the form of train pulses, generating a pulse for each complete turn given by the bowls. The speed that is recorded is

Fig. 4. Left. Calibrator Fluke 754 - Right. Sensor CM3 vs CMP22.

proportional to the number of turns thar occur in a second. The calibration of the anemometer was performed by using a wind tunnel (Fig. 5b). This type of calibration technology is necessary because constant and uniform winds are required to obtain accurate sensor readings; withing the tunnel, samples were taken at different controlled wind speeds at different time intervals to calibrate it. The measurements taken with the NRG #40H sensor were contrasted with the measurements of the KANOMMY 4CH sensor (standard instrument) to establish the compensation coefficients and adjust the measurements of the NRG #40H sensor.

Fig. 5. a. Anemometer NRG #40H - b. Wind tunnel – INAMHI Laboratory.

Wind Direction Vane. The wind direction is registered by the NRG #200P sensor (Fig. 6), which is an analog sensor powered by 5V that provides a voltage proportional to the degrees in which the wind direction vane is located. Th equation that determines the direction (D) is determined by (Table 1):

Table 1. Anemometer calibration.

Tunnel wind speed (m/s)	Pattern sensor Kanommy 4CH (m/s)	Error #1 (%)	Sensor NRC #40H (m/s)	Error #2 (%)
1.61	1.29	19.88	1.45	9.94
3.29	3.1	5.78	3.26	0.91
5.41	5.29	2.22	5.46	−0.92
7.29	7.18	1.51	7.36	−0.96
9.58	9.5	0.84	9.69	−1.15
13.63	13.61	0.15	13.81	−1.32
16.31	16.03	1.72	16.24	0.43
18.53	18.04	2.64	18.26	1.46
	Average	4.34	Average	1.05

$$D = \frac{V_{out} \times 360°}{5V} \tag{2}$$

Fig. 6. Wind direction Vanee NRG #200P.

The wind direction vane calibration was performed considering the voltage levels provided by the instrument (0 to 5 V), relating them to the degrees of rotation (0° to 360°). Table 2 shows the wind direction vane calibration at INAMHI.

4   Forecasting Using Neural Networks

Artificial neural networks ANN are the field of computational intelligence that is inspired by the connection between neurons on the human brain. One kind of neural networks are The Multilayer Perceptron (MLP), an MLP the neurons are usually grouped into layers, one is the input layer, which receives the data from the environment; the other one is the hidden layers that are part of the internal processing of the network and have no direct contact with the external environment and the output layers that provide the response of the network to the input stimulation. In Fig. 7, show this topology.

Table 2. Wind direction vane calibration.

Voltage (V)	Degrees (%)	Direction of wind
0	0	North
1	72	Northeast
2	144	Southeast
3	216	Southwest
4	288	Northwest
5	360	North

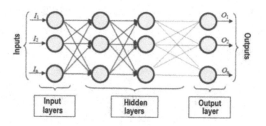

Fig. 7. Multilayer perceptron neural network.

The learning process of an ANN consists update of the weights through learning algorithms, which is a numerical procedure for adjusting weights to minimize the committed error. In this work, the MLP-NN are configured for forecasting, in this sense the topology the inputs data has a delay in t times, similar to nonlinear autoregressive with exogenous (external) input, or NARX. The equation for forecast output (one time ahead) $y(t+1)$ is

$$y(t+h) = f(y(t-1), y(t-2), ..., y(t-d), x(t-1), x(t-2), ..., x(t-d)) \quad (3)$$

where d is a time window size, x is a independent variable, f is the function that represent the MLP-NN and h is the number of values taken as the prediction horizon. Some application of forecasting MLP-NN (FMLP-NN) show in [1,2,7, 8,14]. To measure the prediction accuracy of the forecasting method and to evaluate the performance of the FMLP-NN, we used the mean absolute error (MAE) and the root mean squared error (RMSE).

$$RMSE = \sqrt{\frac{1}{n} \sum_{j=1}^{n} (y_j - \hat{y}_j)^2} \quad (4)$$

$$MAE = \frac{1}{n} \sum_{j=1}^{n} |y_j - \hat{y}_j| \quad (5)$$

A review of machine learning methods for solar radiation forecasting are present in [16], where show a set of methods such as supervised learning and unsupervised learning for forecasting, especially ANN, ARIMA, naive methods to estimate a solar radiation. In [2] predicts the direct solar radiation on a horizontal surface using NARX neural network. In [12], the authors predicted the solar radiation from five stations covering the geography of India using ANN models with different back propagation algorithms. In this sense, this paper, applied a FMLP-NN to predict the solar radiation using the historical data collected minute by minute for three months of an automatic stations in Manta, Ecuador. The data of the station can see in Fig. 8.

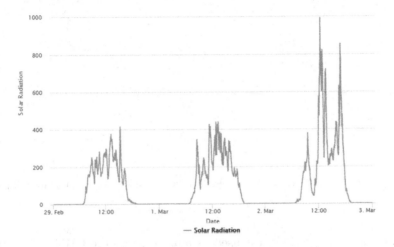

Fig. 8. February 29 to March 02, 2020

For prediction of solar radiation we used a different input-data for the network FMLP-NN such as Solar Radiation (SR), Direction (D) and Wind speed (W). The Table 3 show the result of RMSE and MAE obtained for the prediction of SR on February 29 to March 02, 2020.

Table 3. RMSE and MAE for prediction of SR.

Window size = 10	Step = 3	Horizon = 1	
Attributes	RMSE	MAE	Hidden layer size
SR	12.363	6.678	12
SR, D	19.214	13.838	17
SR, W	18.607	13.173	17
SR, D, W	13.410	8.350	22

where the *step* is the step size between the first values of two consecutive windows. As it can be seen in Table 3, the best prediction of RS is using the same variable time series, that showed the lowest values of RMSE equal to 12.363 and MAE equal to 6.678, see Fig. 9.

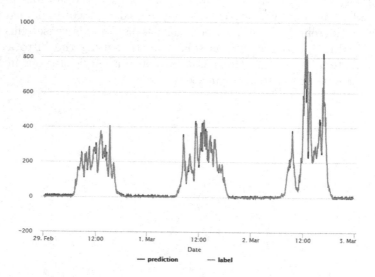

Fig. 9. FMLP-NN for forecast from February 29 to March 02, 2020 using solar radiation.

Finally, the time series SR is used as input data to the FMLP-NN network, we adjust the parameters window size, prediction horizon and step size that is the step size between the first values of two consecutive windows d. The results are shown in the following Table 4 and Table 5.

Table 4. Optimised parameters

Window size = 12	Step = 4	Horizon = 1	
Attributes	RMSE	MAE	Hidden layer size
SR	10.860	5.456	6

In Table 4 the first layer of the neural network has 12 inputs, that is: $SR_{t-1}, SR_{t-12}, ..., SR_{t-12}$. In Table 5 the first layer of the neural network has 32 inputs, that is: $SR_{t-1}, SR_{t-2}, ..., SR_{t-16}, W_{t-1}, W_{t-2}, ..., W_{t-16}$.

The results of Table 4 and Table 5 can be seen in Fig. 10 and Fig. 11 respectively, for forecast from February 29 to March 02, 2020.

Table 5. Optimised parameters

Window size = 16	Step = 4	Horizon = 1	
Attributes	RMSE	MAE	Hidden layer size
SR, W	11.756	5.970	20

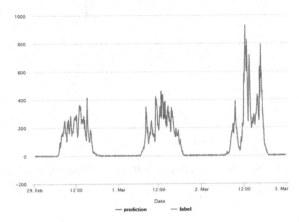

Fig. 10. FMLP-NN for forecast from February 29 to March 02, 2020 using solar radiation.

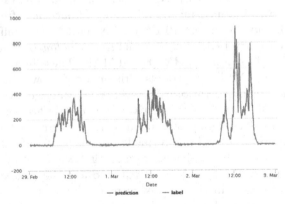

Fig. 11. FMLP-NN for forecast February from 29 to March 02, 2020 using solar radiation and wind speed.

The results of the FMLP-NN presented in Table 4 and Table 5 were better than those shown in the Table 3 (i.e., SR and SR-W as the independent variable). This is because a set of FMLP-NN neural networks with different parameters such as *window sizes* were simulated from 10, 11, ... to 20 and with different *steps* from 1, 2, ... to 5.

Finally, the best FMLP-NN model presented in Table 4 and Table 5 is the network that uses the SR as an independent variable with RMSE equal to 10.86

and MAE equal to 5.45. The model of this network is applied for all the data, that is, from January 08 to April 03, 2020 (see Fig. 12).

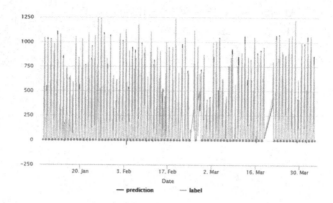

Fig. 12. FMLP-NN for forecast from January 08 to April 03, 2020 using solar radiation and velocity of wind.

5   Conclusion

This paper presents a set of FMLP-NN models for the prediction of solar radiation. Performance was evaluated using minute-by-minute data from February 29 to March 2, 2020, and comparing 19 FMLP-NN models with different independent variable (SR, WS and D), *step time* and *time window* configurations. Good results were obtained in terms of RMSE and MAE. These first results motivate the future work using FMLP-NN models with longer windows and time horizons.

An automatic weather station shows great advantage over conventional weather stations. This can be used in places with little accessibility or in the absence of an electrical network providing meteorological data continuously without human intervention. It has been verified that it is possible to design a reliable and inexpensive automatic weather station using low-cost electronic platforms such as the RasbBerry Pi; This substantially reduces the cost and provides an open platform to be used in the field of meteorology. Once the meteorological data of solar radiation, wind speed and direction has been obtained, it was verified that the interrelation of all these climatic variables has a great influence on the prediction of the evolution of solar radiation. This is because, in order to calculate an atmospheric physical variable, other complementary values must be taken into account. For example, the maximum wind values, which are generated by the movement of the air induced by the geographic thermal differences of the surface, carry in particular different materials that influence the measurement of solar radiation. This is why the three meteorological parameters studied are closely correlated; however, the independent study of each of them will depend on the application for which it is intended and the precision that is needed to validate the influence of the uncertainty that each parameter contributes in the calculation.

References

1. Ansett, M.: Application of neural networking models to predict energy use. ASHRAE Trans. **99**(1), 505–517 (1993). https://ci.nii.ac.jp/naid/80007830543/en/
2. Boussaada, Z., Curea, O., Remaci, A., Camblong, H., Mrabet Bellaaj, N.: A nonlinear autoregressive exogenous (NARX) neural network model for the prediction of the daily direct solar radiation. Energies **11**(3), 620 (2018). https://doi.org/10.3390/en11030620
3. CONELEC: Consejo nacional de electricidad. atlas solar del ecuador. http://www.conelec.gob.ec/archivos_articulo/Atlas.pdf
4. EcuadorUniversitario: Instituto nacional de meteorologia e hidrología cumple 51 años de contribuir al progreso del país. http://ecuadoruniversitario.com/agenda/inamhi-cumple-51-anos-de-contribuir-al-progreso-del-pais/
5. EcuadorUniversitario: Instituto nacional de metorología e hidrología. red de estaciones automaticas hidrometeorológicas 2019. http://186.42.174.236/InamhiEmas/#
6. INAMHI: Instituto nacional de metorología e hidrología 52 años (1961–2013). https://issuu.com/inamhi/docs/inamhi_revista_institucional_2013
7. Luna, A., Nuñez-del-Prado, M., Talavera, A., Holguín, E.S.: Power demand forecasting through social network activity and artificial neural networks. In: 2016 IEEE ANDESCON, pp. 1–4 (2016)
8. Luna, A., Talavera, A., Navarro, H., Cano, L.: Monitoring of air quality with low-cost electrochemical sensors and the use of artificial neural networks for the atmospheric pollutants concentration levels prediction. In: Lossio-Ventura, J.A., Muñante, D., Alatrista Salas, H. (eds.) SIMBig 2018. CCIS, vol. 898, pp. 137–150. Springer, Cham (2019). https://doi.org/10.1007/978-3-030-11680-4_15
9. MEER: Ministerio de electricidad y energías renovable. atlas eólico del ecuador, con fines de generación eléctrica (2013. http://www.energia.gob.ec/biblioteca/
10. OMM: Organización metorológica mundial. guía de instrumentos y métodos de observación meteorológico n°8
11. Peralta, J.M., Casal, C.O., Ángeles López, Tinoco, I.S., Delgado, E., Barriga, A.: Identificación y evaluación del potencial de recursos renovables en el ecuador y su viabilidad de desarrollo local. p. 12. Universidad Tecnologica Nacional - Facultad de Buenos Aires, Tercer Congreso Argentino de Ingeniería Mecánica III CAIM (2012). https://doi.org/10.13140/2.1.1101.9203
12. Premalatha, N., Valan Arasu, A.: Prediction of solar radiation for solar systems by using ANN models with different back propagation algorithms. J. Appl. Res. Technol. **14**(3), 206–214 (2016). https://doi.org/10.1016/j.jart.2016.05.001
13. Rosiek, S., Batlles, F.: A microcontroller-based data-acquisition system for meteorological station monitoring. Energy Convers. Manage. **11**(49), 3746–754 (2008). https://doi.org/10.1016/j.enconman.2008.05.029
14. da Silva, I.N., Hernane Spatti, D., Andrade Flauzino, R., Liboni, L.H.B., dos Reis Alves, S.F.: Artificial Neural Networks. Springer, Cham (2017). https://doi.org/10.1007/978-3-319-43162-8
15. S. Tenzin, Siyang, S., Pobkrut, T., Kerdcharoen, T.: Low cost weather station for climate-smart agriculture. In: 9th International Conference on Knowledge and Smart Technology (KST), pp. 172–177 (2017). https://doi.org/10.1109/KST.2017.7886085

16. Voyant, C., et al.: Machine learning methods for solar radiation forecasting: a review. Renew. Energy **105**, 569–582 (2017). https://doi.org/10.1016/j.renene.2016.12.095
17. Hussein, Z.K., Hadi, H.J., Abdul-Mutaleb, R., Mezaal, Y.S.: Low cost smart weather station using arduino and zigbee. TELKOMNIKA Telecommun. Comput. Electron. Control **18**(1), 282–288 (2020). https://doi.org/10.12928/TELKOMNIKA.v18i1.12784

COVID-19 Infection Prediction and Classification

Souad Taleb Zouggar[1]([⊠]) and Abdelkader Adla[2]

[1] Department of Economics, Oran 2 University, Oran, Algeria
[2] Department of Computer Science, Oran 1 University, Oran, Algeria
adla.abdelkader@univ-oran1.dz

Abstract. Symptoms associated with COVID-19 are very similar to and difficult to distinguish from those of seasonal flu, bronchitis, or pneumonia. The use of tests, expensive and unavailable in most countries, especially developing ones, may be unnecessary in the case of a suspected COVID. This work is carried out in order to decide if a patient is a priori infected and must be tested. Otherwise, the patient will not be screened using a confidence threshold. The data is collected at the emergency department of the EHU of Oran in Algeria. The COVID-19infection classification and prediction are performed by decision trees.

Keywords: Classification · Decision trees · COVID-19 · Prediction · Machine learning · CART · IDT_NIM

1 Introduction

COVID-19, abbreviation of coronavirus disease, is an infectious disease caused by a recently discovered coronavirus. The symptoms are very similar to those of the seasonal flu at the onset of infection namely fever, runny nose, stiffness or pneumonia in somewhat more advanced stages such as a dry cough or breathing difficulties.

COVID-19 was originally discovered in November 2019 in Wuhan in China and since its appearance it has affected all countries over the world and its rapid spread is increasingly worrying.The first reports as of January 15 indicate only 41 cases of COVID 19 detected and after a month the number of cases has increased by more than 1000 cases and keeps increasing very rapidly [1–3]. As a result, quarantine measures have been decided in all countries over the world, starting with China, the country of virus origin. In China, after strict sanitary confinement measures, a drop in cases has been noticed but unfortunately a rapid spread has affected all countries over the world [4].

People infected with COVID-19 have clinical manifestations that look like SARS acute respiratory syndrome but COVID-19 has caused a much higher death rate. The differences lie in the fact that COVID-19 spreads faster and the vast majority of COVID-19 cases are asymptomatic.

In this paper, we propose to use the CART decision trees [5]· and IDT_NIM [6] to detect, a priori, whether a patient presenting symptoms will test positive at COVID-19.

© Springer Nature Switzerland AG 2021
J. A. Lossio-Ventura et al. (Eds.): SIMBig 2020, CCIS 1410, pp. 195–208, 2021.
https://doi.org/10.1007/978-3-030-76228-5_14

The aim is to avoid unnecessary tests for which patients present mild signs, especially for countries which do not have the means to carry out large-scale tests. The use of decision tree-based methods is not arbitrary,by virtue of their intelligibility, they allow subsequent analysis of the rules generated by a human expert.

The remaining part of the paper is organized as follows. First, in Sect. 2 we give a literature review on COVID-19 pandemic. Section 3 is devoted to a background on machine learning and in particular supervised machine learning methods. In Sect. 4 we describe the data of the application domain followed in Sect. 5 by the experiments carried out and the obtained results. Finally, concluding remarks and future work are given in Sect. 6.

2 Literature Review

Several works dealing with the COVID pandemicwere published during this year 2020 [7]. Introduce a new model development concerning the transmission of COVID-19 among the human population. The mathematical model was developed considering several epidemiological parameters which are closely identical to the actual condition. The next step was to perform a sensitivity analysis to determine which parameter is the most dominant in affecting the disease. In the same vein, several other works have opted for the development of a mathematical model to study the transmission of COVID-19 [8–10] or to predict COVID cases in different countries [11,12].

[13] perform data analysis by adopting a statistical model based on a state space combined with the susceptible-infected-recovered (SIR) model, the estimate is made using a Bayesian model. The purpose of the work is to determine the parameters so far unknown that actually affect the process and to predict the future transition including the size and time of the epidemic peak. This issue has also been the subject of the study lead by [12].

[14] propose a heterogeneous model to estimate the number of COVID-19 infections in order to evaluate the different measures that control the risk of infection. The model describesa population which is originally heterogeneous and presents different infection risks. The analyses showed that after integrating this heterogeneity feature in the model, several characteristics of the epidemic are estimated more accurately: the total number of cases and the peak of cases are lower compared to the homogeneous situation. The early growth rate of the number of cases of infection is less affected and the decrease in the number of infections slows down during the late phase of the epidemic.

3 Machine Learning

H. Simon [15] defines learning as "Any change in the system that allows it to perform a task better the second time, when the same task is repeated, or when another task, resulting from the population occurs". Learning involves generalization from experience.

Why do we want a machine to learn to recognize a disease, for example, when so far humans haven't done too badly? There are various reasons for this need. The scarcity of specialists and the impossibility for humans to access hostile or hardly accessible environments are crucial. For example, in some clinical cases, the diagnosis of a disease requires prior surgical intervention; developing an automatic diagnostic system would prevent some patients from being operated wrongly, would allow the community saving health expenditure and would exempt patients from performing unnecessary acts.

3.1 Supervised Machine Learning

In supervised learning, the observations are associated with additional information relating to whether or not they belong to the concept. The goal of a supervised learning algorithm is to correctly classify new examples into the classes defined in the learning phase.

In this type of learning, a sample ΩL contains all the data ω which are used to construct, via a learner (machine), of the hypothesis φ which associates a label $\varphi(\omega)$ with each instance ω. Each instance has a label provided by an expert (or oracle). The learning machine must then find or approximate the target concept; that is, the model allowing to assign the correct label to each example.

A supervised learning problem can be defined according to the interaction of three elements [16]: The prediction model (ranking function) φ is built on a subset of the population, called the learning sample and denoted $\Omega L,2$) An individual belonging to the sample noted ω: 3) Each individual in the sample is described by variables called exogenous variables noted X to predict a class or endogenous variable noted Y taking its values in the set $\{y1,\ldots, ym\}$. X and Y are respectively defined by:

$$Y : \Omega_L \to C \quad X : \Omega_L \to E_j$$

$$\omega \to Y(\omega) \quad \omega \to X_j(\omega)$$

$E_j = \{e_{1j}, e_{2j}, \ldots, e_{pj}\}$: modalities set or values of X_j (Fig. 1).

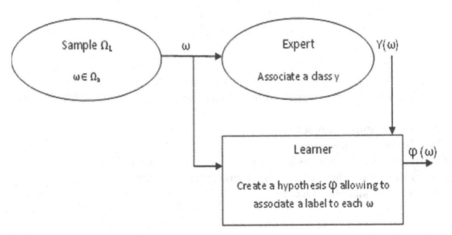

Fig. 1. Machine learning problem elements

3.2 Decision Trees

Decision trees are supervised machine learning methods that generate a tree classification model. CART algorithm [5] is based on the search for uni-varied dichotomous partitions starting from the provided descriptor attributes †. Each node therefore has a simple logical test, based on a single attribute, which leads to two branches corresponding to the positive (true) or negative (false) examples depending on the results of this test. It can be used for both numerical (regression) and qualitative (ranking) target variables.

Constructing a CART tree consists of determining a sequence of nodes:

1. A node is defined by the joint choice of a variable among the explanatory ones and a division which induces a partition into two classes. Implicitly, each node therefore corresponds to a subset of the sample to which a dichotomy is applied.
2. A division is itself defined by a threshold value of the selected quantitative variable or a division into two groups of the categories if the variable is qualitative.
3. The root or initial node corresponds to the entire sample; the procedure is then repeated on each of the subassemblies.

IDT_NIM [6] is a learning method that generates decision trees. It uses the distance measure as a partition criterion. The measure also called FS Segmentation Function is given by the following formulas:

- For the learning sample Ω_L, the value of the function is:

$$FS(\Omega_L) = \sum_{i=1,m} |n_i. - \frac{n}{2}|$$

- For each variable X_j with k modalities $e_{ij}, \ldots, e_{kj}$:

$$FS(X_j) = \left(\sum_{d=1,k} Imp(e_{dj}) + \sigma * LN \right)$$

With:

$\sigma = \{0, +1, -1\}$ is a parameter empirically determined;

LN: the number of leaves generated by segmenting the current node with the variable X_j;

n: Size of the learning sample;

$n_i.$: Number of individuals of the class i,

$n_{.d}$: Number of individuals associated to the modality of the variable X_j,

n_{id}: Number of individuals of the class i having the modality X_j,

m: Number of modalities of a class.

IDT_NIM algorithm is described by the following pseudo code:

Algorithm IDT_NIM (X (Exogenous Variables), Y (Class), Ω_L (Learning sample));
Begin.
Calculate $f(\Omega_a)$;
If $|f(\Omega_a)-n| = 0$ Then «The tree is the root node»;
$D \leftarrow \text{argmax}_{X_j} f(X, \Omega_a)$;
$\{e_{dj(d=1...k)}\}$ set of k modalities associated to X_j;
$\{\Omega_{aj(j=1...k)}\}$ sub sets of Ω_a associated to the values $\{e_{dj(d=1...k)}\}$ of X_j;
If $|Imp(e_{dj})- \Omega_{aj}| \neq 0$ then IDT_NIM(X-D,Y, Ω_{aj});
Output: A tree IDT_NIM;
End.

4 The Learning Data

We have a sample, which we call COVID-EHU, composed of 682 individuals (patients) who presented themselves to the hospital EHU of Oran in Algeria and who were suspected of being infected with COVID-19. Information collected from the patients records are the set of symptoms they showed since the onset of their discomfort. Of all the cases that presented themselves, only 88.85% were tested positive (or 606), the 76 remaining tests are carried unnecessarily.

The learning data is presented in the form of individual/variable table that is adequate to supervised learning. In Fig. 2 below, an excerpt of a sample of the data used for training and testing is shown.

Viewer

Relation: COVID

No	1: Age	2: Sexe	3: Etat	4: EN	5: T	6: F	7: AST	8: A	9: C	10: Dys	11: SDRA	12: E	13: D	14: ANS	15: AGU	16: DD	17: Class
	Nominal	Nominal	Nominal	Nominal	Nominal	Nominal	Nominal	Nominal	Nominal	Nominal	Nominal	Nominal	Nominal	Nominal	Nominal	Nominal	Nominal
1	0	0	N	Y	G	2	N	N	N	N	N	Y	Y	N	N	2	0
2	1	0	N	N	G	2	N	N	N	N	N	Y	Y	N	N	2	0
3	0	1	N	Y	G	1	N	N	N	N	N	Y	Y	N	N	2	0
4	0	1	N	Y	G	2	N	N	N	N	N	Y	Y	N	N	2	0
5	0	1	N	Y	G	2	N	N	N	N	N	Y	Y	N	N	2	0
6	0	1	N	Y	G	2	N	N	N	N	N	Y	Y	N	N	2	0
7	1	0	Y	Y	G	2	Y	N	N	Y	N	Y	Y	N	N	1	0
8	0	0	N	Y	G	2	N	N	N	N	N	Y	Y	N	N	2	0
9	0	0	N	Y	G	2	N	N	N	N	N	Y	Y	N	N	2	0

Fig. 2. An excerpt of COVID-EHU sample

The exogenous variable COV indicates whether the patient has the coronavirus or not. It takes two values: 0 (negative case) or 1 (positive case).

There are 16 endogenous variables:

1- Age: Patient's age = {0: <15, 1: >= 15}, thechildren are rarely and not severely affected (about 2%–6%)

2- Gender = {0: Female, 1: Male}
3- State = = {Yes, No}: Indicates in the case of a female patient, pregnancy or not
4- 4EN: Runny nose = {Yes, No}
5- T: Cough = {Dry (S), Oily (G), No Cough (P)} (59% of COVID-19 patients have a dry cough)
6- F: Fever = {1: >38.5, 2: <38.5}
7- AST: Asthenia = {Yes, No} (70% of COVID-19 patients)
8- A: Anorexia = {Yes, No} (40% of COVID-19 patients)
9- C: Body aches = {Yes, No} (35% of COVID-19 patients)
10- Dys: Dyspnea = {Yes, No} (31% of COVID-19 patients; may appear secondarily between the 5th and 8th day, along with oxygen desaturation of hemoglobin).
11- ARDS: Acute Respiratory Distress Syndrome = {Yes, No} (20% of dyspneic patients).
12- E: Expectoration = {Yes, No} (27% of COVID-19 patients)
13- D: Diarrhea = {Yes, No} (30% of COVID-19 patients)
14- ANOS: Anosmia = {Yes, No}
15- AGU: Ageusia = {Yes, No}
16- DD: D-Dimer = {1: >500, 2: <=500 (normal)}

We note a strong resemblance between the symptoms of COVID-19 and pneumonia with some exceptions, for example dyspnea is more common in a COVID-19 patient, but anosmia and ageusia do not exist for pneumonia. Table 1 summarizes the different variables of the application domain:

Table 1. Variables description, codification, and values

Variable name	Codification	Possible values
COVID	COV	{1: Positive, 0: Negative}
Age	Age	{0: <15, 1: >=15},
Gender	Gender	0: Female; 1: Male
State	State	Yes: Pregnant; No: Not pregnant
Runny Nose	EN	{Yes, No}
Cough	T	{Dry (S), Oily (G), No Cough (P)}
Fever	F	{1: >38.5, 2: <38.5}
Asthenia	AST	{Yes, No}
Anorexia	A	{Yes, No}
Aches	C	{Yes, No}
Dyspnea	Dys	{Yes, No}
Distress Syndrome Acute Respiratory	SDRA	{Yes, No}
Expectoration	E	{Yes, No}
Diarrhea	D	{Yes, No}
Anosmia	ANOS	{Yes, No}
Ageusia	AGU	{Yes, No}
D-Dimer	DD	{1: >500, 2: <=500 (normal)}

4.1 Initial Data Analysis

Based on the collected data, we analyze the behavior by graphs of each of the endogenous variables, one by one, in relation to the exogenous variable or the class. We notice, a priori, that there are variables that have a certain influence on the class; this can be seen on the graphs in the Fig. 3 below generated from the COVID-EHU sample (Figs. 4, 5, 6, 7, 8, 9, 10, 11).

Fig. 3. COV Vs AGU (Axis X: Variable AGU, Axis Y: Variable COV)

Fig. 4. COV Vs ANOS (Axis X: Variable ANOS, Axis Y: Variable COV)

Fig. 5. COV Vs C (Axis X: Variable C, Axis Y: Variable COV)

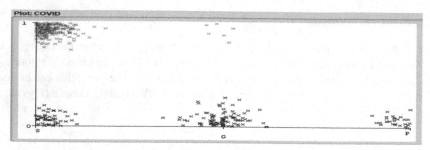

Fig. 6. COV Vs T (Axis X: Variable T, Axis Y: Variable COV)

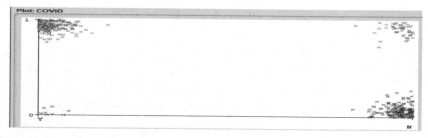

Fig. 7. COV Vs A (Axis X: Variable A, Axis Y: Variable COV)

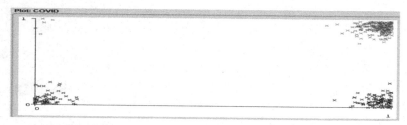

Fig. 8. COV Vs Age (Axis X: Variable Age, Axis Y: Variable COV)

The significant impact of age is also supported by the work of [17–19].

Fig. 9. COV Vs DD (Axis X: Variable DD, Axis Y: Variable COV)

On the other hand, the variables Gender, Expectorations (E) do not have a significant influence on the class, according to the following graphs:

Fig. 10. COV Vs Gender (Axis X: Variable Gender, Axis Y: Variable COV)

Fig. 11. COV Vs Expectoration (E) (Axis X: Variable E, Axis Y: Variable COV)

5 Experimentations

We use Weka platform [20] for the experiments and the 10-folds cross validation method for the generation and the prediction. The CART method (under the name J48) is available within the platform, the IDT_NIM method [6] is combined to all the previous methods (Fig. 12).

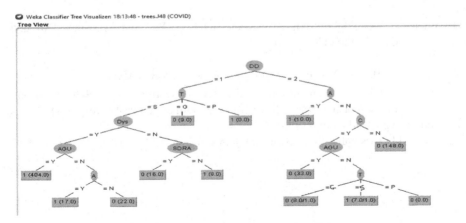

Fig. 12. CART Tree for COVID-EHU.

From the tree, we have the following 13 decision rules:

Rule 1:

If D-Dimer > 500 and Cough = 'Dry' and Dyspnea = 'Yes' and Ageusia = 'Yes' then COV = 1.

Rule 2:

If D-Dimer > 500 and Cough = 'Dry' and Dyspnea = 'Yes' and Ageusia = 'No' and Anorexia = 'Yes' then COV = 1.

Rule 3:

If D-Dimer > 500 and Cough = 'Dry' and Dyspnea = 'Yes' and Ageusia = 'No' and Anorexia = 'No' then COV = 0.

Rule 4:

If D-Dimer > 500 and Cough = 'Dry' and Dyspnea = 'No' and ARDS = Yes'then COV = 0.

Rule 5:

If D-Dimer > 500 and Cough = Dry'and Dyspnea = 'No'and ARDS = No' then COV = 1.

Rule 6:

If D-Dimer > 500 and Cough = 'Fat' then COV = 0.

Rule 7:

If D-Dimer > 500 and Cough = 'No cough' then COV = 1.

Rule 8:

If D-Dimer <= 500 and Anorexia = 'Yes' then COV = 1.

Rule 9:

If D-Dimer <= 500 and Anorexia = 'No' and Aches = 'Yes' and Ageusia = Yes'then COV = 0.

Rule 10:

If D-Dimer <= 500 and Anorexia = 'No' and Aches = 'Yes' and Ageusia = 'No' and Cough ='Fat' then COV = 0.

Rule 11:

If D-Dimer <= 500 and Anorexia = "No" and Aches = "Yes" and Ageusia = "No" and Cough = "Dry" then COV = 1.

Rule 12:

If D-Dimer <= 500 and Anorexia = 'No' and Aches = 'Yes' and Ageusia = 'No' and Cough = 'No Cough' then COV = 0.

Rule 13:

If D-Dimer <= 500 and Anorexia = 'No' and Aches = N then COV = 0.

We note that the variables mentioned in the previous section and which have a strong impact on the class appear in the rules, namely: D-Dimer (DD), Anorexia (A), Aches (C), Ageusia (Agu) and Cough (T).

The 10-fold cross validation results are shown in Fig. 13 below:

```
=== Stratified cross-validation ===
=== Summary ===

Correctly Classified Instances        680                 99.7067 %
Incorrectly Classified Instances       2                   0.2933 %
Kappa statistic                        0.9935
Mean absolute error                    0.0047
Root mean squared error                0.0566
Relative absolute error                1.041  %
Root relative squared error           11.8993 %
Total Number of Instances             682
```

Fig. 13. Cross validation of CART tree

The tree generated by the IDT_NIM method [6] is described by the diagram in Fig. 14:

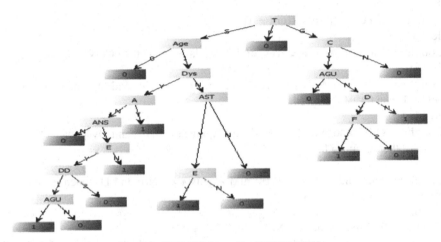

Fig. 14. IDT_NIM tree for COVID-EHU

There are 16 rules:
Rule 1:
If Cough = 'Dry' and Age <= 15 then COV = 0.
Rule 2:
If Cough = 'Dry' and Age > 15 and Dyspnea = 'Yes' Anorexia = 'No' and Anosmia = 'No' then COV = 0.
Rule 3:
If Cough = 'Dry' and Age > 15 and Dyspnea = 'Yes' Anorexia = 'No' and Anosmia = 'Yes' and Sputum = 'Yes' and D-Dimer = 1 and Ageusia = 'Yes' then COV = 1.
Rule 4:
If Cough = 'Dry' and Age > 15 and Dyspnea = "Yes" Anorexia = "No" and Anosmia = "Yes" and Sputum = "Yes" and D-Dimer = 1 and Ageusia = "No" then COV = 0.
Rule 5:
If Cough = 'Dry' and Age > 15 and Dyspnea = 'Yes' Anorexia = Yes'then COV = 1.

Rule 6:
If Cough = 'Dry' and Age > 15 and Dyspnea = 'Yes' Anorexia = 'No' and Anosmia = 'Yes' and Sputum = 'No' then COV = 1.
Rule 7:
If Cough = 'Dry' and Age > 15 and Dyspnea = 'Yes' Anorexia = 'No' and Anosmia = 'Yes' and Sputum = 'Yes' and D-Dimer = 2 then COV = 0.
Rule 8:
If Cough = 'Dry' and Age > 15 and Dyspnea = 'No' Asthenia = 'Yes' and Sputum = 'Yes' then COV = 1.
Rule 9:
If Cough = Dry'and Age > 15 and Dyspnea = 'No'Asthenia = Yes' and Sputum = No'then COV = 0.
Rule 10:
If Cough = 'Dry' and Age > 15 and Dyspnea = 'No' Asthenia = 'No' then COV = 0.
Rule 11:
If Cough = 'No Cough' then COV = 0.
Rule 12:
If Cough = 'Fat' and Aches = 'Yes' and Ageusia = 'Yes' then COV = 0.
Rule 13:
If Cough = 'Oily' and Aches = 'Yes' and Ageusia = 'No' and Dyspnea = 'Yes' and Fever = 1 then COV = 1.
Rule 14:
If Cough = 'Oily' and Aches = 'Yes' and Ageusia = 'No' and Dyspnea = 'Yes' and Fever = 2 then COV = 0.
Rule 15:
If Cough = 'Fat' and Aches = 'Yes' and Ageusia = 'No' and Dyspnea = 'No' then COV = 1.
Rule 16:
If Cough = 'Fat' and Aches = 'No' then COV = 0.

We notice that IDT_NIM brings out more variables, which are much related to the class (see Sect. 4.1). In addition to the variables used for the generation of the CART tree, we still have: Age, Dyspnea (Dys), Asthenia (Ast), Anosmia (Anos), Expectoration (E), D-Dimer (DD).

The 10-fold cross validation results of the IDT_NIM tree are shown in Fig. 15 below:

```
=== Stratified cross-validation ===
=== Summary ===

Correctly Classified Instances        677              99.2669 %
Incorrectly Classified Instances        5               0.7331 %
Kappa statistic                        0.9838
Mean absolute error                    0.0066
Root mean squared error                0.0789
Relative absolute error                1.4573 %
Root relative squared error           16.5941 %
Total Number of Instances              682
```

Fig. 15. Cross validation IDT_NIM

6 Conclusion

This paper presents an approach based on machine learning to predict and classify Covid-19 infection. Covid-19 disease has a very negative impact on all areas of life; social, and economic. The application summarizes the important factors that lead to a correct diagnosis of the disease. We combine two decision tree-based learning methods for classification and prediction: the CART method [5] and the IDT_NIM method [6].

The application of a supervised machine learning based diagnosis system to Covid-19 reduces contact between health personnel and patients to diagnose the disease; the diagnosis can be done remotely by machine; which reduces the risk of contamination. In addition, the machine tool determines whether a patient is affected with COVID-19 or not and thus prevents to take a screening test, which will contribute to save test kits that are unavailable especially in developing countries.

We plan to further evaluate the rules generated by the two methods and select the "most" correct ones in order to develop a knowledge based system for a more efficient use and improvement of the knowledge base by adding new cases.

References

1. Boldog, P., Tekeli, T., Vizi, Z., Dénes, A., Bartha, F.A., Röst, G.: Risk assessment of novel coronavirus COVID-19 outbreaks outside China. J. Clin. Med. **9**(2), 571 (2020)
2. Zheng, R., Xu, Y., Wang, W., Ning, G., Bi, Y.: Spatial transmission of COVID-19 via public and private transportation in China. Travel Med. Infect. Dis. (2020)
3. Zhou, F.: Clinical course and risk factors for mortality of adult inpatients with COVID-19 in Wuhan, China: a retrospective cohort study. Lancet (2020)
4. Heymann, D.L., Shindo, N.: COVID-19: what is next for public health? Lancet **395**(10224), 542–545 (2020)
5. Breiman, L., Friedman, J.H., Olshen, R.A., Stone, C.J.: Classification and Regression Trees. Chapman and Hall (1984)
6. Taleb Zouggar, S., Adla, A.: Proposal for measuring quality of decision trees partition. Int. J. Decis. Supp. Syst. Technol. **9**(4), 16–36 (2017)
7. Resmawan, R., Lailany, Y.: Sensitivity analysis of mathematical model of coronavirus disease (COVID-19) transmission (2020)
8. Tang, B.: Estimation of the transmission risk of the 2019-nCoV and its implication for public health interventions. J. Clin. Med. **9**(2), 462 (2020)
9. Tang, B., Bragazzi, N.L., Li, Q., Tang, S., Xiao, Y., Wu, J.: An updated estimation of the risk of transmission of the novel coronavirus (2019-nCov). Infect. Dis. Model. **5**, 248–255 (2020)
10. Khan, M.A., Atangana, A.: Modeling the dynamics of novel coronavirus (2019-nCov) with fractional derivative. Alexandria Eng. J. **59**(4), 379-2389 (2020)
11. Sun, H., Qiu, Y., Yan, H., Huang, Y., Zhu, Y., Chen, S.X.: Tracking and predicting COVID-19 epidemic in China Mainland (2020)
12. Kuniya, T.: Prediction of the epidemic peak of coronavirus disease in Japan. J. Clin. Med. **9**(3), 789 (2020)
13. Kobayashi, K., Kaki, T., Mizuno, S., Kubo, K., Komiya, N., Otsu, S.: Clinical characteristics of patients with coronavirus disease 2019 in Japan: a single-center case series. J. Infect. Dis. **222**(2), 194–197 (2020)
14. Gerasimov, A., Lebedev, G., Lebedev, M., Semenycheva, I.: COVID-19 dynamics: a heterogeneous model (2020)

15. Simon, H.: Why should machines learn? In machine learning: an artificial intelligence approach, 1 (1983)
16. Cornuéjols, A., Miclet, L.: Apprentissage artificiel: concepts et Algorithmes. Eyrolles (2002)
17. Lee, P.I., Hu, Y.L., Chen, P.Y., Huang, Y.C., Hsueh, P.R.: Are children less susceptible to COVID-19? J. Microbiol. Immunol. Infect. **53**(3), 371–372 (2020)
18. Liu, K., Chen, Y., Lin, R., Han., K.: Clinical features of COVID-19 in elderly patients: A comparison with young and middle-aged patients. J. Infect. **80**(6), e14–e18 (2020)
19. Ruan, Q., Yang, K., Wang, W., Jiang, L., Song, S.: Clinical predictors of mortality due to COVID-19 based on an analysis of data of 150 patients from Wuhan, China. Intens. Med. **46**(5), 846–848 (2020)
20. Witten, I.H., Frank, E.: Data Mining: Practical Machine Learning Tools and Techniques, 2nd edn. Morgan Kaufmann (2005)

Image Processing

Towards a Benchmark for Sedimentary Facies Classification: Applied to the Netherlands F3 Block

Maykol J. Campos Trinidad[1,2]([✉]) [iD], Smith W. Arauco Canchumuni[1,2] [iD], and Marco Aurelio Cavalcanti Pacheco[2] [iD]

[1] National University of Engineering, Lima, Peru
{mcampos,saraucoc}@uni.pe
[2] Pontifical Catholic University of Rio de Janeiro, Rio de Janeiro, Brazil
{saraucoc,marco}@ele.puc-rio.br
https://www.uni.edu.pe/
https://www.puc-rio.br/

Abstract. In this paper, we attempt to provide a new benchmark for image seismic interpretation tasks in a public seismic dataset (Netherlands F3 Block). For this, techniques such as data augmentation together with five different deep network architectures were used, as well as the application of focal loss function. Our experiments achieved an improvement in all evaluation metrics cited at the current benchmark. For instance, we managed to improve in 3.7% the pixel accuracy metric and 5.4% on mean class accuracy for a modified U-Net that uses dilated convolution layers in its bottleneck. In addition to this, the confusion matrices of each model are shown for a better inspection in the classes (sedimentary facies) where the greatest amount of misclassification occurred. The training process of almost all networks took less than one hour to converge. Finally, we applied Conditional Random Fields (CRF) as post-processing in order to obtained smother results. The inferences performed with the best topology, in an inline or section of the test set, is closer to achieving an interpretation at a human level.

Keywords: Seismic data · Seismic interpretation · Semantic segmentation · Reservoir characterization

1 Introduction

In the industry of oil and gas (O&G), one of the most important tasks is to find new possible reserves of hydrocarbon in order to increase the production of barrels. To verify the existence of hydrocarbons, there are various techniques, each day more advanced and precise. Reflection seismic is the most widely used technique. Geophysics provides, in a similar way to ultrasound, a series of virtual images of the subsoil called seismic lines. These images are obtained by emitting low-frequency acoustic signals from the surface. This energy travels at

© Springer Nature Switzerland AG 2021
J. A. Lossio-Ventura et al. (Eds.): SIMBig 2020, CCIS 1410, pp. 211–222, 2021.
https://doi.org/10.1007/978-3-030-76228-5_15

high speeds through the subsoil, being partially reflected towards the surface, where it is detected by a series of receptors and stored for further treatment and processing. The systematic repetition of this emission and reception along a linear path on the surface, together with the measurement of the time elapsed between the acoustic emission and the reception of the reflected energy, will later allow obtaining an image of the subsoil by means of sophisticated mathematical treatments the data acquired. In this way, a seismic line is obtained, which combined with more lines, will allow obtaining maps of the subsoil and identifying the presence of potential hydrocarbon deposits.

Once these images have been obtained, the next process is the interpretation and identification of types of facies, for which a human analysis requires a lot of effort and time due to the large pixel dimensions that should be studied. Therefore, different algorithms have been developed to reduce this problem, from unsupervised to supervised learning methods as Support Vector Machine (SVM) and Artificial Neural Networks (ANN) [31], the latter being the one that is booming, due to the great growth of public data and improved performance in processors.

Over the last decade, facies classification tasks began to be developed using Machine Learning models. For instance, Kim et al. [14] extracted some features to feed his Random Forest model. However, since 2012, when Krizhevsky et al. [16] showed the efficacy of Convolutional Neural Networks (CNN) to extract features from images in a semi-automatic way, this net have been used for different applications. It was not until 2017 that the first papers in seismic were presented, this could be because of the requirement of a large amount of data, being generally private. Waldeland and Solberg [27] used a 3D model to identify the presence of the salt body using $65 \times 65 \times 65$ blocks to classify the pixel in the center. It is important to say that they labeled manually their data. Another interesting contribution was made by Huang et al. [12], who presented a scalable platform for the identification of up to nine classes of facies, which even allowed visualizing the blocks in 3D space.

Other publication in image classification was [10], where Dramsch and Lüthje compared pre-trained known architectures as VGG16 [26] and ResNet [11], in addition to the one presented by Waldeland and Solberg [27]. Li [17] applied a fine-tuning technique using an autoencoder first, then remove the decoder and add a classifier. Finally, Xiong et al. [28] used a custom CNN to identify seismic faults.

The following studies were developed for the task of image segmentation, which means pixel-level classification. Zhao [30] compared the use of patches and 2D sections (inlines and crosslines) as input, and concluded that sections are the best option. Civitarese et al. [8] applied custom architectures, in addition to transfer learning using pre-trained models from classification task. In 2018, a Geophysical Company TGS launched a competition on the Kaggle platform for the segmentation of salt bodies [2], of which we can highlight [4,13] and [21] which use the published dataset.

As of today, few datasets with expertly labeled facies are public [3,25]. This work seeks to improve the benchmark presented by Alaudah et al. [3] and thus motivate more publications on the subject to be developed. In this benchmark was presented two baseline models for facies classification based on convolution/deconvolution architectures. To improve the benchmark, different deep learning models were applied, based on architectures such as ResNet [11], Fully Convolutional Network (FCN) [19], U-Net [23], and others found in related works. Recently, Salvaris et al. [24] launched a repository called DeepSeismic to perform seismic imaging and interpretation on Azure. Within its applications shows results with the same dataset that we use, for which our work delivers better results in less training time.

We divide this work into six sections: in Sect. 2, we describe the public dataset as the pre-processing procedure; Sect. 3 presents the architectures used to train our models; Sect. 4 explains the training parameters and some more details for post-processing; Sect. 5 discusses the experiment results; and finally, Sect. 6 presents the conclusions.

2 Seismic Dataset

The public dataset was presented by Alaudah et al. [3]. It belongs to an area located off the shores of Netherlands, known as the F3 block, whose seismic surveys were published by dGB Earth Sciences. For the construction of the 3D block they used the Petrel software, which had different tools to identify the groups of lithostratigraphic units. They were able to label seven groups, of which two of them (Rijnland and Chalk) were combine since they had problems defining the boundaries between them. The pre-processing code and the dataset are available as a free repository[1].

Furthermore, due to the presence of artifacts, only from inline 100 to 701, crossline from 300 to 1201, and depth from 1005 to 1877 m were used. In Fig. 1, the final block is illustrated with its respective six labels.

Finally, to get a model that generalizes correctly, ranges were defined for split training and testing dataset. Being as follows:

1. Training set: data in the range of inlines [300,700] and crosslines [300,1000].
2. Test set 1: data in the range of inlines [100,299] and crosslines [300,1000].
3. Test set 2: data in the range of inlines [100,700] and crosslines [1001,1200].

Table 1 shows the percentage of pixels for each class for the three dataset to corroborate that we are facing an imbalanced dataset. Also, we can see variations in the distributions of the two test data set, mainly in Scruff group.

2.1 Dataset Preparation

As a result, the final cube for training consists of 401 inlines of size 701 × 255, and 701 crosslines of 401 × 255 pixels. Firstly, to split into training and validation

---

[1] A Machine Learning Benchmark for Facies Classification: https://github.com/yalaudah/facies_classification_benchmark.

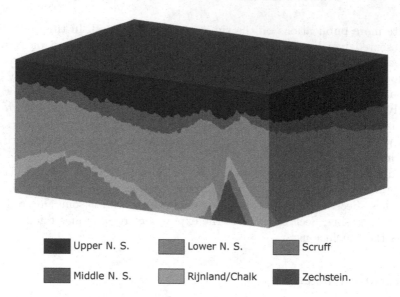

Fig. 1. Final facies seismic cube of the Netherland offshore F3 block in the North Sea, where the six labels are shown.

Table 1. Percentage of pixels from different classes in each dataset

	Zechstein	Scruff	Rijnland/Chalk	Lower N. S.	Middle N. S.	Upper N. S.
Training set	1.50%	3.27%	6.64%	48.59%	11.88%	28.09%
Testing set 1	1.85%	17.08%	6.95%	45.17%	9.72%	19.19%
Testing set 2	2.72%	0.78%	4.99%	57.20%	10.16%	24.13%

sets, it was used the same procedure presented in [8], where the final block is first divided into ten blocks, from which 70% of the slices in each block are chosen for training and the remaining for validation. In this way, both sets are prevented from having a very different pixel ratio of each class.

As in the benchmark [3], it was attempted using 2D patches and sections, giving better results using sections in both inline and crossline directions. The use of both sections is justified in that the test sets are continuations in both axes. The results using patches will be skipped since it does not improve the performance of the benchmark.

Since some of the models used are based on U-Net and ResNet, the 2D sections were resized to measure multiples of 16, in order to avoid sizing problems in pooling layers where dimensions are halved. Thus, there were inlines and crosslines of 688×256 and 400×256 pixels, respectively on training set.

3 Deep Network Architectures

To perform the experiments presented in this paper, we use five different architectures based on FCN for image semantic segmentation task with 2D input. These

FCN allow sharing parameters, that are important due to the high dimension of seismic data. The number of trainable parameters for each architectures is represented in Table 2.

Table 2. Number of trainable parameters.

Model name	U-Net	U-Net+Dil	ResUNet	Danet FCN 3	DeepLabv3+
Millions of parameters	8.6	12.2	4.7	39.2	41.1

3.1 U-Net

It was chosen as the first option due to its good results in image segmentation tasks of gray-scale images. Since the dimensions of our input images were different from those used in the original paper [23], the number of filters used in each layer was reduced following the same structure. So, the decoder consists on four blocks of two convolutional layer of 32, 64, 128 and 256 filters respectively, each one with Batch Normalization and ReLU activation. A similar block is used for the bridge with 512 filters, and the decoder were built to complete the "mirror" scheme, replacing the max-polling layer with the up-convolutional layers. More details from the based on U-Net models in [23].

3.2 U-Net with Dilated Convolutions

The U-Net with Dilated Convolutions (U-Net+Dil) was presented as a solution for a competition on Kaggle platform [1]. Later was used by Piao and Liu [22] for satellite image semantic segmentation task. It consists of the use of several dilated convolution layers described by Chen et al. [5] in bottleneck block. For this, two forms were proposed: in series or cascade, and in parallel. In both cases, the bottleneck output is represented by the sum of the resulting feature maps. The code implementation of this topology was based on [20]. For our task, the parallel mode gave better results.

3.3 Deep Residual U-Net

Deep Residual U-Net (ResUNet) model combines the strengths of both U-Net and ResNet [11], which consists of a series of residual blocks. It was proposed by Zhang et al. [29] in 2018 for the segmentation of the well-known Massachusetts roads dataset. Another difference from U-Net is the use of only three blocks in the encoder as well as the replacement of pooling operations by convolutional layers with a stride of 2. Thanks to this and the use of residual units, the number of trainable parameters are reduced.

3.4   Danet FCN

This architecture was presented by Civitarese et al. [8] for a similar task using also a F3 block based dataset. However, the processing of seismic data as well as the labeling of their classes are their own, for which they had the supervision of two specialists in the area. This architecture also makes use of residual blocks, as well as their "transposed" operation. Although there were three models presented, Danet FCN 3 had the best results, but its training time was longer than the other two.

3.5   DeepLabv3+

The implementation of this architecture is based on what was proposed by Chen et al. [6], which extends DeepLab [5] by employing a encoder-decoder structure. The encoder module encodes multi-scale contextual information by applying dilated convolution at multiple scales (Atrous Spatial Pyramid Pooling) while the decoder module refines the segmentation results. For our purpose, we use the same Xception [7] backbone. The use of bilinear upsampling layers made it difficult to train with different sizes of sections at the same time. Therefore, two alternative approaches were chosen for this model. The first one was the use of fine-tuning where we trained with inlines first and, with these learned weights, we proceeded to train the crossline ones. The second approach was to resize all the sections to the same dimensions, although this meant a great loss of information.

4   Experiments

4.1   Training

To perform the experiments and avoid the class imbalance problem between the majority and minority classes (see Table 1), was set different configurations for data augmentation, but the one that gave the best results was random zoom operation with a maximum scale of 0.75. This can be justified in the fact that there are areas where the classes are very thin, so using a mechanism that allows them to increase in size improves performance.

It was also used the focal loss presented by Lin et al. [18] as loss function, adapted for multi-class cross-entropy loss that penalizes hard-to-classify examples, since it has been shown to improve results for some architectures in image segmentation tasks as Doi and Iwasaki [9] concluded. In the focal loss function, there are two control hyper-parameters, namely, α and γ: (i) The parameter α balances focal loss and (ii) The focusing parameter γ smoothly adjusts the rate at which easy examples are down-weighted. To tune these hyper-parameters different values of α and γ were used for each model ($\gamma = \{0.5, 1, 2\}$ and $\alpha = \{0.25, 0.5, 1\}$). The best configuration of these hyper-parameters for each models are presented in the Table 3.

Table 3. Best focal loss hyper-parameters for the five models.

Hyperparameters	U-Net	U-Net+Dil	ResUNet	DanetFCN3	DeepLabv3+
α	1	1	1	1	1
γ	0.5	2	2	2	1

All models were trained using the well-known Adam optimizer, with a learning rate schedule that begins in $1e-04$ and is halved each time the loss function does not drop in five periods. Besides, the stop criterion is applied when there is no improvement in ten epochs.

We trained the models using Keras framework backend in Tensorflow 1.4, into a GPU Nvidia Volta V100. Almost all of our test do not take more than one hour to converge with exception of DeepLabv3+.

4.2 Post-processing

After careful manual examination of the inferences on an inline, small "inconsistencies" of mispredicted pixels become visible. As part of the search for improvement, it was decided to use a post-processing algorithm to get more smoothed results. For this, we chose Conditional Random Fields (CRF), as it is one of the best known techniques in Image Segmentation. CRF is a method that is used when the class labels for different inputs are not independent. For example, in this case, the class label for one pixel depends on the label of its neighboring pixels. For our application, we use the library `pydensecrf`, which is based on what Krähenbühl and Koltun [15] presented. In addition to this we use parallel processing with 20 CPUs since it is known to be a process that takes time.

5   Results

For the evaluation and comparison of the results, we follow the same procedure presented in the benchmark for the dataset, where the defined metrics are pixel accuracy (PA), class accuracy (CA) for each class (geological facies), mean class accuracy (MCA) and frequency-weighted intersection over union (FWIU). More details of the mathematics formulation of the evaluation metrics are defined on the appendix A of Alaudah et al. [3].

Table 4 shows the performance for each presented model, as well as that of the benchmark and DeepSeismic. As it could be observed, the model with best inference on main metrics was U-Net with dilated convolution, with an improvement of 3.7% on PA and 5.4% on MCA. Something curious that can be rescued is that there is no improvement in the class accuracy on Middle North Sea (M.N.S) group, although it is offset by an increase in the Zechstein (Z) and Scruff (S) groups, which are those with the lowest percentage of pixels as presented in the Table 1. The Upper North Sea (U.N.S) and Lower North Sea (L.N.S) continues with high accuracy class like the reference benchmark.

Table 4. Results of models when tested on both test splits of the dataset

Model	Metric								
	PA	Class Accuracy						MCA	FWIU
		Z	S	R/C	L. N. S.	M. N. S.	U. N. S.		
Benchmark [3]	0.905	0.602	0.674	0.772	0.941	0.938	0.974	0.817	0.832
DeepSeismic [24]	0.928	–	–	–	–	–	–	0.866	0.872
ResUNet	0.931	0.658	0.74	0.809	0.977	0.914	0.979	0.846	0.874
DeepLabv3+	0.933	0.644	0.774	0.813	0.983	0.909	0.962	0.847	0.879
DanetFCN3	0.937	0.693	0.746	0.819	0.993	0.903	0.965	0.853	0.887
U-Net	0.939	0.723	0.817	0.797	0.981	0.916	0.972	0.867	0.891
U-Net+Dil	0.943	0.764	0.82	0.774	0.986	0.902	0.981	0.871	0.895

The most straightforward way to evaluate the performance of classifiers task is based on the confusion matrix analysis. Figure 2 shows a confusion matrix for

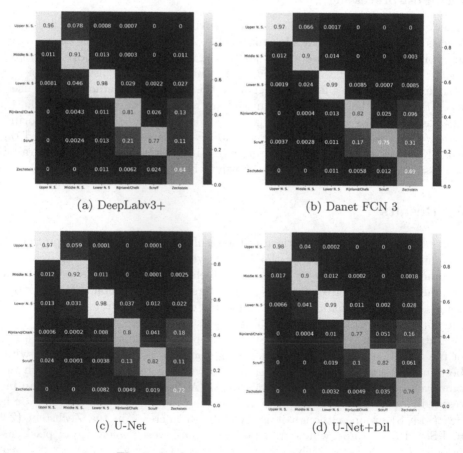

(a) DeepLabv3+   (b) Danet FCN 3

(c) U-Net   (d) U-Net+Dil

Fig. 2. Confusion matrix on both test set.

the multi-class problem having distribution of each model output for each class. From this table, it can be seen how the models that make use of residual units misclassify group Zechstein worse with respect to the Scruff group, but it differs better with respect to the Rijnland/Chalk (R/C) group.

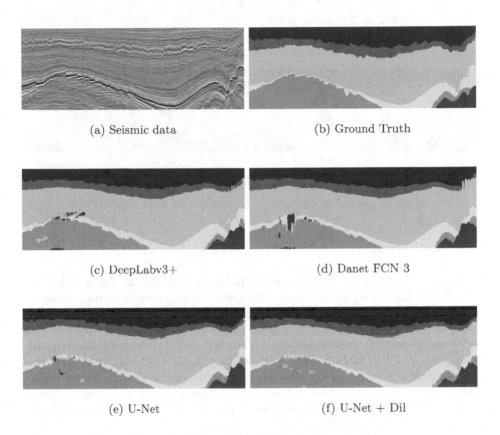

(a) Seismic data   (b) Ground Truth

(c) DeepLabv3+   (d) Danet FCN 3

(e) U-Net   (f) U-Net + Dil

Fig. 3. Results on inline 200 from test set #1.

In general, the three deepest facies have more cases of bad classification, which can be understood by their smaller number of pixels, in addition to a greater complexity in their boundaries. Figure 3 represents a clear example of this in an inline in test set # 1, where the Rijnland/Chalk group is very thin in much of the inline. Hence, the aforementioned inconsistencies can be observed, such as the case where there are misclassified pixels of the L.W.S group within the Scruff group. That is why the CRF was used, whose inferences for the two best models show smoother results. In addition, Table 5 shows the metrics achieved where an increase of almost 0.3% can be distinguished for PA and FWIU. These new inferences are shown in Fig. 4.

Table 5. Results of models when tested on both test splits applying CRF

Model	Metric								
	PA	Class accuracy						MCA	FWIU
		Z	S	R/C	L. N. S.	M. N. S.	U. N. S.		
U-Net	0.942	0.754	0.829	0.792	0.982	0.916	0.973	0.874	0.894
U-Net+Dil	0.945	0.808	0.831	0.765	0.987	0.902	0.981	0.879	0.898

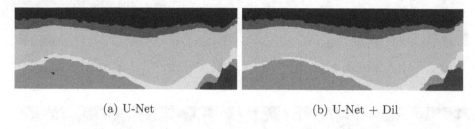

(a) U-Net   (b) U-Net + Dil

Fig. 4. Results on inline 200 from test set #1 applying CRF.

6 Conclusion

In this work, we establish a new benchmark for a public seismic dataset (Netherlands F3 Block), for which we present five deep learning architectures solving the seismic interpretation tasks. Our experiments successfully improved the scores of the current benchmark for the image segmentation task of six different class (sedimentary facies). This demonstrates how the use of different algorithms and techniques, as CRF, in Deep Learning can help in the automation of these processes and thus help the oil and gas industry in future reservoir characterization. In the future, we will continue to focus on the application of combining different levels of deep learning architectures, in addition to making experiments in other seismic datasets with higher levels of complexity.

Acknowledgments. The authors would like to thank at the Applied Computational Intelligence Laboratory (ICA) and Cenpes/Petrobras, partners for 20 years in the research and development of artificial intelligence projects for oil and gas sector.

References

1. Carvana Image Masking Challenge (2017). https://www.kaggle.com/c/carvana-image-masking-challenge
2. TGS Salt Identification Challenge (2018). https://www.kaggle.com/c/tgs-salt-identification-challenge
3. Alaudah, Y., Michałowicz, P., Alfarraj, M., AlRegib, G.: A machine-learning benchmark for facies classification. Interpretation **7**(3), SE175–SE187 (2019). https://doi.org/10.1190/INT-2018-0249.1

4. Babakhin, Y., Sanakoyeu, A., Kitamura, H.: Semi-supervised segmentation of salt bodies in seismic images using an ensemble of convolutional neural networks. In: Fink, G.A., Frintrop, S., Jiang, X. (eds.) DAGM GCPR 2019. LNCS, vol. 11824, pp. 218–231. Springer, Cham (2019). https://doi.org/10.1007/978-3-030-33676-9_15
5. Chen, L.C., Papandreou, G., Kokkinos, I., Murphy, K., Yuille, A.L.: DeepLab: semantic image segmentation with deep convolutional nets, atrous convolution, and fully connected CRFs. IEEE Trans. Pattern Anal. Mach. Intell. **40**(4), 834–848 (2017)
6. Chen, L.-C., Zhu, Y., Papandreou, G., Schroff, F., Adam, H.: Encoder-decoder with atrous separable convolution for semantic image segmentation. In: Ferrari, V., Hebert, M., Sminchisescu, C., Weiss, Y. (eds.) ECCV 2018. LNCS, vol. 11211, pp. 833–851. Springer, Cham (2018). https://doi.org/10.1007/978-3-030-01234-2_49
7. Chollet, F.: Xception: deep learning with depthwise separable convolutions. Proceedings of the IEEE Conference on Computer Vision and Pattern Recognition (CVPR), July 2017. https://doi.org/10.1109/CVPR.2017.195
8. Civitarese, D., Szwarcman, D., Brazil, E.V., Zadrozny, B.: Semantic segmentation of seismic images. arXiv preprint arXiv:1905.04307 (2019)
9. Doi, K., Iwasaki, A.: The effect of focal loss in semantic segmentation of high resolution aerial image. In: IGARSS 2018–2018 IEEE International Geoscience and Remote Sensing Symposium, pp. 6919–6922. IEEE (2018)
10. Dramsch, J.S., Lüthje, M.: Deep-learning seismic facies on state-of-the-art CNN architectures, pp. 2036–2040. Society of Exploration Geophysicists (2018). https://doi.org/10.1190/segam2018-2996783.1. https://library.seg.org/doi/abs/10.1190/segam2018-2996783.1
11. He, K., Zhang, X., Ren, S., Sun, J.: Deep residual learning for image recognition. In: Proceedings of the IEEE Conference on Computer Vision and Pattern Recognition, pp. 770–778 (2016)
12. Huang, L., Dong, X., Clee, T.E.: A scalable deep learning platform for identifying geologic features from seismic attributes. Lead. Edge **36**(3), 249–256 (2017). https://doi.org/10.1190/tle36030249.1
13. ul Islam, M.S.: Using deep learning based methods to classify salt bodies in seismic images. J. Appl. Geophys. **178**, 104054 (2020). https://doi.org/10.1016/j.jappgeo.2020.104054. http://www.sciencedirect.com/science/article/pii/S0926985119307803
14. Kim, Y., Hardisty, R., Torres, E., Marfurt, K.J.: Seismic facies classification using random forest algorithm. In: SEG Technical Program Expanded Abstracts 2018, pp. 2161–2165. Society of Exploration Geophysicists (2018)
15. Krähenbühl, P., Koltun, V.: Efficient inference in fully connected CRFs with gaussian edge potentials. In: Shawe-Taylor, J., Zemel, R.S., Bartlett, P.L., Pereira, F., Weinberger, K.Q. (eds.) Advances in Neural Information Processing Systems, vol. 24, pp. 109–117. Curran Associates, Inc. (2011)
16. Krizhevsky, A., Sutskever, I., Hinton, G.E.: ImageNet classification with deep convolutional neural networks. Commun. ACM **60**(6), 84–90 (2017). https://doi.org/10.1145/3065386
17. Li, W.: Classifying geological structure elements from seismic images using deep learning, pp. 4643–4648. Society of Exploration Geophysicists (2018). https://doi.org/10.1190/segam2018-2998036.1
18. Lin, T.Y., Goyal, P., Girshick, R., He, K., Dollár, P.: Focal loss for dense object detection. In: Proceedings of the IEEE International Conference on Computer Vision, pp. 2980–2988 (2017)

19. Long, J., Shelhamer, E., Darrell, T.: Fully convolutional networks for semantic segmentation. In: Proceedings of the IEEE Conference on Computer Vision and Pattern Recognition (CVPR), June 2015. https://doi.org/10.1109/CVPR.2015. 7298965

20. lyakaap: Kaggle carvana - 3rd place solution (2017). https://github.com/lyakaap/ Kaggle-Carvana-3rd-place-solution/

21. Milosavljević, A.: Identification of salt deposits on seismic images using deep learning method for semantic segmentation. ISPRS Int. J. Geo Inf. 9(1), 24 (2020), https://doi.org/10.3390/ijgi9010024

22. Piao, S., Liu, J.: Accuracy improvement of UNet based on dilated convolution. J. Phys. Conf. Ser. 1345, 052066 (2019). https://doi.org/10.1088/1742-6596/1345/ 5/052066

23. Ronneberger, O., Fischer, P., Brox, T.: U-Net: convolutional networks for biomedical image segmentation. In: Navab, N., Hornegger, J., Wells, W.M., Frangi, A.F. (eds.) MICCAI 2015. LNCS, vol. 9351, pp. 234–241. Springer, Cham (2015). https://doi.org/10.1007/978-3-319-24574-4_28

24. Salvaris, M., et al.: DeepSeismic: a deep learning library for seismic interpretation, vol. 2020, no. 1, pp. 1–5 (2020). https://doi.org/10.3997/2214-4609.202032086

25. Silva, R.M., Baroni, L., Ferreira, R.S., Civitarese, D., Szwarcman, D., Brazil, E.V.: Netherlands dataset: a new public dataset for machine learning in seismic interpretation. arXiv preprint arXiv:1904.00770 (2019)

26. Simonyan, K., Zisserman, A.: Very deep convolutional networks for large-scale image recognition. arXiv preprint arXiv:1409.1556 (2014)

27. Waldeland, A., Solberg, A.: Salt classification using deep learning. In: 79th EAGE Conference and Exhibition 2017, vol. 2017, pp. 1–5. European Association of Geoscientists & Engineers (2017). https://doi.org/10.3997/2214-4609.201700918

28. Xiong, W., et al.: Seismic fault detection with convolutional neural network. Geophysics 83(5), O97–O103 (2018). https://doi.org/10.1190/geo2017-0666.1

29. Zhang, Z., Liu, Q., Wang, Y.: Road extraction by deep residual U-Net. IEEE Geosci. Remote Sens. Lett. 15(5), 749–753 (2018)

30. Zhao, T.: Seismic facies classification using different deep convolutional neural networks, pp. 2046–2050. Society of Exploration Geophysicists (2018). https:// doi.org/10.1190/segam2018-2997085.1

31. Zhao, T., Jayaram, V., Roy, A., Marfurt, K.J.: A comparison of classification techniques for seismic facies recognition. Interpretation 3(4), SAE29-SAE58 (2015). https://doi.org/10.1190/INT-2015-0044.1

Mobile Application for Movement Recognition in the Rehabilitation of the Anterior Cruciate Ligament of the Knee

Iam Contreras-Alcázar(✉) ⓘ, Kreyh Contreras-Alcázar ⓘ,
and Victor Cornejo-Aparicio ⓘ

National University of San Agustin, Arequipa Santa Catalina 117, Arequipa, Peru
{icontrerasa,kcontrerasal,vcornejo}@unsa.edu.pe

Abstract. Anterior cruciate ligament injury is a condition that requires physical rehabilitation therapy. Due to the problems of the COVID-19 pandemic and the patient's mobility problems, it is difficult to attend the rehabilitation sessions. The developed mobile application uses color recognition through the OpenCV library, with which a virtual goniometer can be generated by capturing the specific anatomical points of the lower limb through the camera of the device. It also allows controlling and monitoring the exercises prescribed by a specialist. The exercises performed by the patient are registered by the mobile application which captures the series and repetitions, the flexion and extension movements, and their maximum and minimum angles respectively; Thanks to this, proper performance can be tracked. The results of four test subjects of different ages and sexes were obtained by submitting them to rehabilitation exercises and recording their respective measurements, thus verifying the effectiveness of the mobile application.

Keywords: Rehabilitation · Anterior cruciate ligament · Image recognition · Android OpenCV · Mobile application

1 Introduction

The anterior cruciate ligament injury of the knee is a ligament injury produced during sports activities. The success of your treatment will depend on good medical evaluation, surgical treatment, and the rehabilitation process. Rehabilitation after injury requires physiotherapy which is taught through medical evaluation and trained personnel [1], however, the home exercises proposed by the therapist are not evaluated or supervised, and they are not carried out in an adequate way [1].

There are several reasons why a patient does not attend his rehabilitation center, and even more so in these times when health is saved due to the pandemic caused by COVID-19, so supervision becomes even more difficult and currently there are few verification instruments in our environment that allow us to evaluate the progress of the rehabilitation of the patient at home.

© Springer Nature Switzerland AG 2021
J. A. Lossio-Ventura et al. (Eds.): SIMBig 2020, CCIS 1410, pp. 223–235, 2021.
https://doi.org/10.1007/978-3-030-76228-5_16

Over the years, different technology has been developed to recognize joint movements. In 2013, a software tool kit for physiotherapy was proposed. The software they developed consists of a game where they captured the movement of patients through a Kinect sensor with a Wiimote [2].

In 2016, knee angle analysis was studied by detecting a set of colors using the image processing technique. The software was developed in order to assist patients in their treatment after suffering a knee injury. Detection was performed in real time by means of a video camera using the OpenCV library, the precision of the angle measurement being 96% [3].

In 2020, a joint angle detection system was developed, which observed flexo-extension movements of the upper limb of the elbow through a webcam. The OpenCV and OpenPose libraries were used to estimate the human pose by means of a neural network. Once the points of the human pose were obtained, lines were plotted to obtain a reference to the human skeleton. The purpose was to help the evaluation of physical therapy through the use of artificial vision. The system obtained a level of reliability of 92.60% [1].

By means of the use of a neural network, it learns to detect the position of the human body through an algorithm for estimating human pose through the OpenCV and OpenPose library, once the points of the human pose are obtained, we proceed to graph lines to obtain a human skeleton. With the data obtained, joint angles can be calculated through mathematical formulas that work with the coordinates of the points of the generated skeleton [1].

This work focuses on the recognition of the anatomical structures of the lower limb through the recognition of colors through a smartphone; in this way, the joint movement of the knee is evaluated through a virtual goniometer which measures the flexo-extension angles made by the patient at home; said information is recorded and sent to the treating physician, who can analyze the exercise performed and thus be able to report any error to be amended if it occurs; the progress is stored in the cloud so that both doctor and patient can see the progress of the rehabilitation of the injury.

Using a mobile device, patient resources are optimized. The kinect [4], and a video camera, are devices that not many patients have, while a smartphone is available to most. Please note that this software is exclusive to the Android operating system.

The application performs color recognition through the OpenCV library [1], being necessary to locate three anatomical points in the lower limb [5]. The library recognizes a specific color which is placed by the patient after explanation by the specialist and then proceeds to calculate the coordinates, with this the flexo-extension angles can be calculated and stored in the cloud.

2   Theoretical Framework

2.1   Anterior Cruciate Ligament

It is the weakest ligament of the two cruciate ligaments of the knee, originates in the anterior intercondylar area of the tibia, extends superiorly, posteriorly, and laterally to join the posterior portion of the medial side of the lateral condyle of the femur [6]. This ligament limits the posterior bearing of the condyles of the femur on the superior articular aspect of the tibia during flexion. It also prevents posterior displacement of the femur over the tibia and hyperextension of the knee joint [6].

2.2 Injury of the Anterior Cruciate Ligament

The anterior cruciate ligament injury represents 50% of knee ligament injuries, with 75% occurring during sports activities [7]. Treatment depends on good medical evaluation, surgical treatment, and the rehabilitation process [8].

Patients have damage to anatomical structures and gait involvement [9]. Proprioception and neuromuscular control of the knee are compromised, its kinematics are altered and it probably induces a change in the stimulation and signals of the remaining mechanoreceptors [10]. The muscular hypotrophy that occurs conditions less muscular strength and joint stability [11].

2.3 Rehabilitation and Physiotherapy

The specialist chooses the appropriate exercises for the rehabilitation and respective training of each patient [12]; Rehabilitation protocols have been developed over time [13,14], which have been implementing a variety of exercises and tests [15–18]. Importantly, home strengthening programs are very effective [19].

New modalities have been acquired for the rehabilitation of patients such as: thermotherapy, cryotherapy, electrotherapy, magnetotherapy, kinesitherapy, muscle enhancement, shock waves, laser therapy, etc. [20]. After proper management of a patient, it is possible to regain their lifestyle prior to injury [21], allowing them to return to their sports activities [22].

2.4 Android, OpenCV and RGB

Android is a Linux-based operating system, which uses the Java programming language. This system provides a variety of necessary interfaces, in order to develop different applications [23]. Through the sensors provided by Android, better applications can be made. In 2017, a mobile application focused on the affected wrist with articular mobility disorders was developed. By means of a prototype, it allowed the corresponding measurement and followup to be performed, fulfilling the function of a goniometer [24].

OpenCV is an open-source library which is used for machine learning and artificial vision since its infrastructure allows it. It presents a BSD license; in this way you can modify its source code and use it freely. It allows to identify different objects and to be able to carry out the corresponding monitoring in real time, it works in both 2D and 3D components [1].

RGB is a model that mixes red, green and blue colors, all colors can be created by mixing these three based on their light. The black color is generated by the absence of light in these three colors. The RGB format is used in different multimedia applications and in different systems that use combinations of materials [25].

3   Materials and Methods

3.1   Materials

Previous informed consent, a person who did not present joint pathology was used as a study subject in order to make an adequate measurement of the flexo-extension angles of his knee. For this measurement, three anatomical points were taken into account [5]:

- **Axis:** lateral or external femoral condyle
- **Superior point:** greater trochanter of the femur
- **Lower point:** external malleolus of the fibula

In these reference points, green stickers were placed which served to be recognized by our application.

3.2   Software

Figure 1 shows the development of the software, to carry out a correct development of the application, it was necessary to have the corresponding requirements. Based on these, all the UML diagrams were carried out so that it can be implemented in a more practical way. Finally, tests were carried out to verify the correct operation of the software.

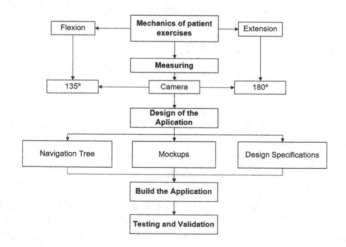

Fig. 1. Software development.

4   Application Development

4.1   Requirements

The requirements were collected from several interviews with different specialists in the area of trauma. Once the information was collected, we proceeded to structure these data into 17 specification tables. For a correct measurement of the angles, it is necessary that the camera of the device points perpendicular to the axis (femoral condyle), it must be taken into account that the distance for recognition ranges from 69 cm to 154 cm in a 1.70 m person, having an average of 111 cm in our case, from that measure; There is a variation of one degree when moving the camera 14.5 cm on the vertical axis and 20 cm on the horizontal axis, with respect to the distance described, this can be seen in Fig. 2 and Fig. 3 respectively.

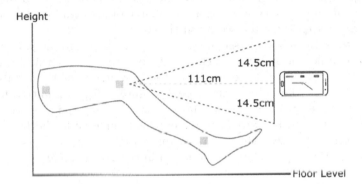

Fig. 2. Lateral view.

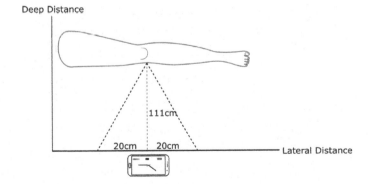

Fig. 3. Frontal view.

A fundamental requirement for the recognition of stickers is an optimal lighting of the environment, it should be noted that the doctor can designate the appropriate distance from the camera, for a specific evaluation of each patient, that distance varies according to the assigned exercise, and the evaluation that the doctor wants to perform.

4.2 Design

For the design, a total of seven diagrams were made based on the requirements previously analyzed: use cases, software architecture, class diagram, collaboration diagram, sequence diagrams, activity diagram, entity-relationship diagram, in this article will only present the most relevant ones.

Figure 4 shows the General Architecture of the mobile rehabilitation application. There are three interfaces based on the type of user. The administrator is in charge of adding the doctors and these to the patients, each doctor can have many patients. The controllers are in charge of managing and treating the information between the interfaces with the server.

The doctor is in charge of assigning a specific treatment to the patient. In the Treatment module, the system is in charge of requesting the information assigned by the doctor and proceeds to calculate the movements of the rehabilitation automatically with the help of the OpenCV library [1], in addition to taking photos so that the specialist can see how he is executing the exercises. All the data is stored and can be consulted in the Results module for both the patient and the doctor, in this way there is a control and the progress can be visualized, the way to use the application can be found in the user manual.

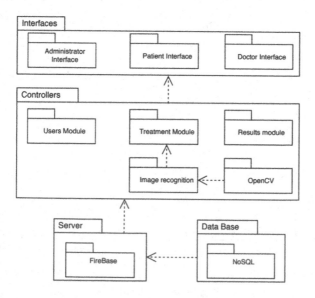

Fig. 4. General architecture.

Figure 5 shows the sequence that the application must follow for the correct reading of the exercises performed by the patient, based on the recognition of the colors of the stickers located in the respective anatomical points. First the patient has to log in correctly; Once validated by the system, you proceed to see the treatment that has been assigned by the doctor.

The patient proceeds to perform the treatment, it is at this time that the application recognizes the color of the stickers, for this, previously the patient had to click on the device screen in a specific color. The software is responsible for calculating the coordinates, once obtained, the flexion and extension angles are calculated.

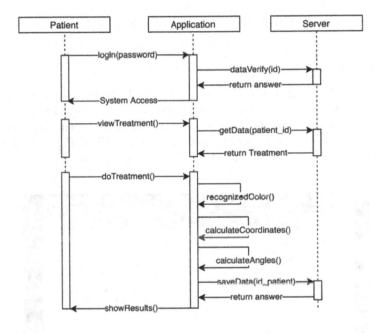

Fig. 5. Image recognition sequence diagram.

The corresponding MockUps were prepared based on the analyzed requirements, Fig. 6 shows the interface that the application must have. In the upper left part, the color assigned by the patient is shown. It has two buttons, the first one is in the center, it is the Play button, which starts the calculation of repetitions and series; the second is the Stop button which serves to stop the recognition in case the patient cannot continue for any reason.

It is necessary to have a helper the first times it is used, in the absence of such help, a voice recognition module could be implemented. The patient says a voice command which will be recognized by the software to start the recognition once the patient has been located to start the exercise routine, the application will start a countdown to indicate to the patient that they can start.

Fig. 6. Reconnaissance view layout.

4.3   Implementation

For the implementation of the prototype, Android Studio 3.5.1 was used with the OpenCV 3.4.1 library. The Treatment module was developed where a doctor can assign the type of exercise, the number of sets and repetitions, and a brief description, in this way the patient can be better guided. Figure 7 shows the view of the treatment window. Labels and EditText were used.

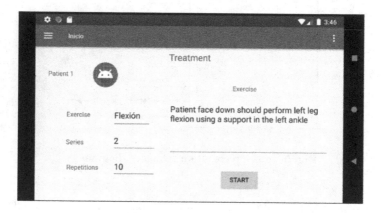

Fig. 7. Treatment window view.

Once the patient clicks on the "Start" button, the system will proceed to load the OpenCV library along with the camera. The calculation of the corresponding angles was performed with the sum of squares formula, since the corresponding coordinates are available. The system is responsible for recognizing repetitions based on a base point calculated prior to movement. Once the restoration is complete, the software stores the information automatically so that it can be viewed in the results view. This view shows the following components:

- Date
- Treatment
- Series
- Repetitions
- Greater Angle
- Minor Angle

In this way, the patient's rehabilitation is correctly monitored. In case the patient cannot continue and stop the recognition with the stop button, the system will save the information obtained up to that moment; with this, the doctor can modify the treatment and adapt it based on the patient's needs.

4.4   Testing

First, animations were developed with the Blender program, three yellow spheres were created, of which two were static and one moved, the purpose was to simulate the basic movement of flexion and extension, the animations, once completed, were tested on a Huawei Y7 2018 smartphone through an LG 21:9 Ultra-Wide monitor.

After completing the tests with animations, we proceeded to test with a subject without knee joint pathology. Figure 8 shows the extension of the right leg of a healthy woman, in it you can see the green color of the stickers with the calculation of the corresponding angle. In the lower left part, the number of repetitions and series assigned by the doctor previously is shown. At the top are the buttons described in Fig. 6.

There is an extra gray square, this is for development purposes to see the base point before making the corresponding movements. This point is calculated at the time of clicking the Play button. A detection margin is assigned, in this way the camera of the device will recognize the moment in which the leg passes again and with this have a counter of the repetitions and based on these, automatically decrease the series.

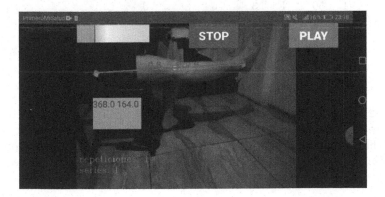

Fig. 8. Test with a subject without pathology. (Color figure online)

5 Results

As seen in the tests, recognition has been feasible, the color of the sticker was recognized correctly. Figure 8 shows the angle of extension which is 179.6° while that of flexion is 0.3°. The number of repetitions and series decreased correctly based on the patient's movements. At the time of clicking the Play button, the software correctly calculated the movement, in case of finishing a series, the system stopped as the patient has to have pauses between repetitions. In order to continue he had to click the Play button again.

In case of clicking the Stop button, the application automatically finishes recognizing the movements and redirects the patient in view of the results obtained up to that moment. The treatment ended and with this the doctor could assign another one based on the results obtained. Four test subjects of different ages and sexes were evaluated to corroborate the proper functioning of the prototype of the mobile application.

The data that identifies the patient serve to better understand the patient and the disease. In this case, the patient's name is not disclosed for ethical reasons. Sex and age orient towards the different pathological possibilities. There is an evident chronological relationship between most diseases and the different periods of life; similarly, sex influences the appearance and development of various pathologies due to the inequality both anatomical, physiological and cultural that each individual present [26].

No test subject has presented anterior cruciate ligament injury to the knee; however female patients (F) were diagnosed with osteoarthritis by a specialist, while male patients (M) were apparently healthy. Table 1 shows the data and exercises assigned to each subject by a specialist from the area.

Table 1. Assigned data and exercises

N°	Years	Sex	Flexion		Extension	
			Series	Repetitions	Series	Repetitions
1	56	F	3	5	3	5
2	78	F	2	5	2	5
3	61	M	3	7	3	7
4	27	M	4	7	4	7

Table 2 shows the results of the flexing exercises in the test subjects based on each series developed and each repetition captured by the mobile device. It can be seen that the application performs the correct recognition of each repetition executed and the data collection of the maximum and minimum angles.

Table 2. Results of flexion exercises in test subjects

N°	Series	Repetitions captured	Flexion	
			Greater angle	Minor angle
1	1	5	135,0	132,6
	2	5	134,3	133,5
	3	5	134,3	133,5
2	1	5	129,5	125,3
	2	5	129,8	127,7
3	1	7	134,6	131,8
	2	7	133,6	131,2
	3	7	134,5	134,2
4	1	7	134,9	134,0
	2	7	135,0	134,1
	3	7	135,1	133,5
	4	7	134,8	133,8

Table 3 shows the results of the extension exercises in the test subjects based on each series developed and each repetition captured by the mobile device. It can be seen that the application performs the correct recognition of each repetition executed and the data collection of the maximum and minimum angles.

Table 3. Results of extension exercises in test subjects

N°	Series	Repetitions captured	Extension	
			Greater angle	Minor angle
1	1	5	180,0	179,1
	2	5	179,8	179,3
	3	5	179,9	179,1
2	1	5	178,2	176,4
	2	5	177,8	175,3
3	1	7	179,4	179,0
	2	7	179,1	178,8
	3	7	179,9	177,8
4	1	7	179,9	179,8
	2	7	180,0	179,6
	3	7	179,8	179,7
	4	7	180,0	179,2

6   Conclusions

The application recognizes the flexion and extension angles; based on a color that stands out from the patient's environment, with which its effectiveness could be verified. Due to the high risk of contagion by COVID-19 in our environment, the application could not be tested in patients with injury in that ligament, however, this application was tested in apparently healthy subjects, and others with osteoarthritis in the knee without having any inconvenience.

The advantage of this application and its color recognition, allows minimizing the costs of any type of physical interface such as the Kinect, in addition, the fact that a smartphone is used, allows the patient's progress to be correctly monitored while they perform their exercises on their home, in this way the treating physician carries out remote supervision, based on the results of the exercises, not having to waste man-hours of a specialist, for each patient who requires to perform the exercises.

The application not only reduces the time required by a specialist to review each exercise performed, thanks to the automatic data collection of this, but also gives the possibility of supervising several patients in a short time, or simultaneously. Finally, it is important to note that strengthening programs at home are very effective for the rehabilitation of a patient; as mentioned in the references.

References

1. Jarrín, C.: Sistema de detección del ángulo articular en los movimientos de miembro superior para evaluación en fisioterapia mediante visión artificial (2020). (Bachelor's thesis)
2. Unnikrishnan, R., Moawad, K., Bhavani, R.: A physiotherapy toolkit using video games and motion tracking technologies. In: IEEE Global Humanitarian Technology Conference: South Asia Satellite, pp. 90–95 (2013)
3. Pramkeaw, P.: The study analysis knee angle of color set detection using image processing technique. In: IEEE 12th International Conference on Signal-Image Technology & Internet-Based Systems, pp. 657–660 (2016)
4. Ruiz-Sarmiento, J., Galindo, C., Gonzalez-Jimenez, J., Blanco, J.: Navegación reactiva de un robot móvil usando kinect. Actas ROBOT (2011)
5. Angulo, C., Álvarez, A.: Biomecánica de la extremidad inferior 3 Exploración de la articulación de la rodilla. Reduca (Enfermería, Fisioterapia y Podología) **1**(3), 26–37 (2016)
6. Moore, K., Dalley, A., Agur, A.: Moore Fundamentos de anatomía con orientación clínica, 6th edn. Wolters Kluwer, España (2019)
7. Gotlin, R., Huie, G.: Anterior cruciate ligament injuries. Operative and rehabilitative options. Phys. Med. Rehabil. Clin. N. Am. **11**(4), 895–928 (2000)
8. Ménétrey, J., Duthon, V., Laumonier, T., Fritschy, D.: "Biological failure" of the anterior cruciate ligament graft. Knee Surg. Sports Traumatol. Arthr. **16**(3), 224–231 (2008)
9. Torry, M., Decker, M., Ellis, H., Shelburne, K., Sterett, W., Steadman, J.: Mechanisms of compensating for anterior cruciate ligament deficiency during gait. Med. Sci. Sports Exerc. **36**(8), 1403–1412 (2004)

10. Hogervorst, T., Brand, R.: Mechanoreceptors in joint function. J. Bone Joint Surg. Am. **80**(9), 1365–1378 (1998)
11. Kai-Nan A.: Muscle force and its role in joint dynamic stability. Clin. Orthop. Relat. Res. (403 Suppl), S37–S42 (2002)
12. Escamilla, R., Fleisig, G., Zheng, N., Barrentine, S., Wilk, K., Andrews, J.: Biomechanics of the knee during closed kinetic chain and open kinetic chain exercises. Med. Sci. Sports Exerc. **30**(4), 556–569 (1998)
13. Shelbourne, K., Nitz, P.: Accelerated rehabilitation after anterior cruciate ligament reconstruction. Am. J. Sports Med. **18**(3), 292–299 (1990)
14. Coronado de la Cruz, J.: Tratamiento fisioterapéutico en lesiones de ligamento cruzado anterior (2017)
15. Thomson, L., Handoll, H., Cunningham, A., Shaw, P.: Physiotherapist-led programmes and interventions for rehabilitation of anterior cruciate ligament medial collateral ligament and meniscal injuries of the knee in adults. Cochrane Database Syst. Rev. **2002**(2), CD001354 (2002)
16. Cascio, B., Culp, L., Cosgarea, A.: Return to play after anterior cruciate ligament reconstruction. Clin. Sports Med. **23**(3), 395–408 (2004)
17. Aagaard, P., Simonsen, E., Magnusson, S., Larsson, B., Dyhre-Poulsen, P.: A new concept for isokinetic hamstring: quadriceps muscle strength ratio. Am. J. Sports Med. **26**(2), 231–237 (1998)
18. Ramos, J., López-Silvarrey, F., Segovia, J., Martínez, H., Legido, J.: Rehabilitación del paciente con lesión del ligamento cruzado anterior de la rodilla (LCA). Revisión. Rev. Int. Med. Cienc Act Fís Deporte **8**(29), 62–92 (2008)
19. Fischer, D., Tewes, D., Boyd, J., Smith, J., Quick, D.: Home based rehabilitation for anterior cruciate ligament reconstruction. Clin. Orthop. Relat. Res. **347**, 194–199 (1998)
20. Mohedo, E.: Manual de fisioterapia en traumatología, 1st edn. Elsevier, España (2015)
21. Orozco, D., Rosero, S., Flores, P.: Tratamiento funcional de la lesión de ligamento cruzado anterior de la rodilla: una revisión. La Ciencia al Servicio de la Salud y la Nutrición **10**(2), 51–59 (2019)
22. Kvist, J.: Rehabilitation following anterior cruciate ligament injury: current recommendations for sports participation. Sports Med. **34**(4), 269–280 (2004)
23. Mallo, J.: Aplicación Android para pacientes de fisioterapia (2015)
24. Cerón, C.: Asistente móvil para la rehabilitación de trastornos de muñeca que presenten limitación en el arco de movilidad articular (2017). (Doctoral dissertation)
25. Chanquín, K.: Diseño de una aplicación web de e-commerce para teléfonos interactivos que permita a los clientes potenciales conocer y adquirir los productos comercializados por las empresas afiliadas al servicio de punto de venta Posfly. Royale Studios. Guatemala, Guatemala (2019). (Doctoral dissertation)
26. Surós, A., Surós, J.: Semiología médica y técnica exploratoria Surós, 8th edn. Elsevier, España (2001)

Semantic Segmentation Using Convolutional Neural Networks for Volume Estimation of Native Potatoes at High Speed

Miguel Chicchón[1]([envelope]) [iD] and Ronny Huerta[2]([envelope]) [iD]

[1] Exponential Technology Group (GITX-ULIMA), Institute of Scientific Research (IDIC), University of Lima, Lima, Peru
mchicchon@pucp.edu.pe
[2] Pontificia Universidad Católica del Perú, Lima, Peru

Abstract. Peru is one of the main producers of a wide variety of native potatoes in the world. Nevertheless, to achieve a competitive export of derived products is necessary to implement automation tasks in the production process. Nowadays, volume measurements of native potatoes are done manually, increasing production costs. To reduce these costs, a deep approach based on convolutional neural networks have been developed, tested, and evaluated, using a portable machine vision system to improve high-speed native potato volume estimations. The system was tested under different conditions and was able to detect volume with up to 90% of accuracy.

Keywords: Semantic segmentation · Convolutional neural network · SegNet · Transfer learning

1 Introduction

The potato (Solanum tuberosum) can grow from sea level up to 4,700 m above sea level; from southern Chile to Greenland and it is produced in over 100 countries worldwide. In the Andean region, there are more than 4,000 varieties of potatoes, representing one of the most important contributions, and collaborating with the strengthening of food security for all Humanity, being one of the most appreciated and consumed food crops [14].

Potatoes are the third most important food crop in the world in terms of human consumption and in the last five years, nearly 60% of global potato production has come from developing countries [11]. At present in Peru, potato is the main crop, since it is produced in 19 of its 24 departments, representing 25% of the agricultural GDP. "Canchan" potato represent 12% of the total cultivated area (260,000 ha/year) with potatoes, and "Amarilla" potato the 10%. Peru currently harvests more than 1 million tons of both annually [4], for these reason, the

J. A. Lossio-Ventura et al. (Eds.): SIMBig 2020, CCIS 1410, pp. 236–249, 2021.
https://doi.org/10.1007/978-3-030-76228-5_17

optimization of processes in sowing, production and harvest monitoring stag-es is required, generating a need for technological advances in the field.

In potato crops, the combination of computer vision with advanced pro-cessing techniques based on artificial intelligence has allowed the automation of tasks, such as: detection of diseases, classification between different degrees of quality, estimation of colors present, productivity monitoring, among others. The purpose is to carried out these tasks quickly, safely and less subjectively. However, the implementation in industrial environments in real time is still a matter of research and improvement.

In this work, we explore the usability of deep neural networks to process RGB images of native potatoes, with the aim of estimating the volume at high speed. Nowadays, estimations are made manually, demanding time and labor force that increases production costs. This work presents a solution to this problem. The article is organized as follows: Sect. 2 presents the data in detail and processing techniques associated with this research. Section 3 shows the experimental results for the estimation of projected area and potato volume. In Sect. 4, there is a comparison between the use of classical techniques and convolutional neural networks in the estimation of native potato. Finally, Sect. 5 shows a summary of most important conclusions of the work.

1.1   Related Work

Potato color is related to its maturity and quality. Research was carried out in the estimation of colors present in potatoes, for example in [22] an artificial vision system was trained to distinguish between good and green potatoes using the HSI color system, finding that the discrimination is not only found in ranges of green nuances but also in non-green nuances. Potatoes have a shiny skin, that it can be removed from images using a relationship between RGB and HSI spaces, improving the results in the process of detecting physiological greening of the skin [7]. Stochastic models are used to explicitly describe the random nature of shape and color texture of normal potatoes, with the in order to classify an unknown object as "acceptable potato" or "unacceptable potato" [8]. There are different classification methods for detection of potatoes defects, for example in [9] an SVM (support vector machines) is used as a size classifier based on color segmentation. The research done in [16], shows a multistage method to recognize external defects in potato color images, first a color-based segmentation, followed by the combination of algorithms IWO (invasive weed optimization) and ANN (artificial neural network) MLP (Multi Layer Perceptron) type for classification.

Potato image segmentation is a previous step in most applications. For exam-ple, in [15] is developed a segmentation based in a combination of a fuzzy rules system, an image threshold based on genetic algorithms (GA) optimization and morphological operators. A segmentation in defective and healthy areas with a c-mean diffuse clustering, Euclidean distance and RGB color space was presented in [3], in order to classify by defects such as: greening, cracking and rotting of potatoes. Also, the work in [5] presents the detection of diseases in potatoes with a system that classifies potatoes according to their defects and external diseases, performing segmentation based on color and projections, next the characteristics HSV and RGB channels of each segmented potato is extracted, and finally perform the classification using the K-NN algorithm optimized with a GA.

Deep learning architectures have been widely used in recent years in different agricultural applications. For example, in [17] a potato disease classification algorithm is developed that use a deep convolutional neural network (CNN) with a robustness in uncontrolled acquisition conditions. In [13], describes the development of a three-stage method, based on CNN, autoencoder, and SVM, that can classify and find blemishes in potatoes, resulting in an overall evaluation of the tuber.

The quantitative aspects such as the estimation of the volume and mass of the potato have been studied in [20]. The research presents the development of a three-dimensional model using image processing algorithms with depth information to estimate the mass and related factors such as: length, width, thickness and volume with high precision compared to area calculation models. However, these the methods based in areas are used in high speed estimation applications. For example, in [23] and [6] show methods based on pixel projected area and a regression model to estimate the mass and potato volume. It is common to consider the shape of the potato as elliptical, although works such as [12] propose a technique to estimate potato volume using polynomial equations obtained from valid limit points in the binary version of the preprocessed image, getting good results even in potatoes with irregular and non-aximetric shapes.

2   Materials and Methods

Based on the work done in [10,12] a workflow is followed considering 3 phases for the artificial vision system algorithm (see Fig. 1). Since the objective is to perform geometric measurements, first a calibration of the system is needed to find the relationships in pixel-to-mm (length) and pixel to mm^2 (area). The phase 1 is the preprocessing of the acquired images. Then, in phase 2 are considered the segmentation and edge extraction processes. Finally, in phase 3 the volume estimation is made.

2.1   Calibration Process

The camera calibration, for experimentation purposes, was performed based on 6 coins of known dimensions (see Fig. 2), the process consists on the segmentation of the coins to calculate the average area of the coin and with the information of 25.5 mm diameter of the coin of Peruvian Sol obtain the ratios of pixel to mm (length) and pixel to mm^2 (area). The relationship between pixel and mm or mm^2 works only for that camera setup (position and distance from the object).

2.2   Approach Based on Classical Methods

In the preprocessing phase, tests were performed on images at maximum acquisition resolution (2248 × 2048) and low resolution (224 × 224) in order to find

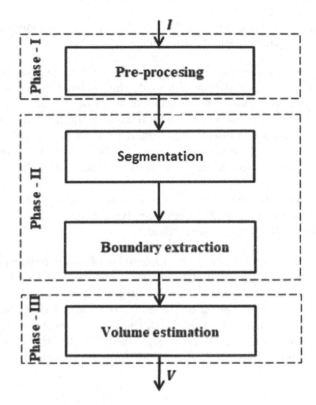

Fig. 1. Workflow of the proposed algorithm for estimating potato volume [12]

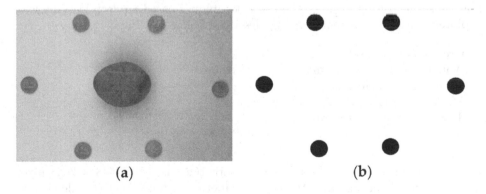

(a)   (b)

Fig. 2. (a) Image used for calibration. (b) Segmented image.

a balance between precision and speed. The better results of the tests were obtained by working in the HSV color space.

In phase II, considering the operation of the system in an environment with controlled visibility, three variants are made:

- In order to obtain the projected area with great accuracy, the maximum resolution of the acquired image is used, then calculate a locally adaptive threshold [2] for the image in the value channel of the HSV color space. A threshold T is selected based on the local average intensity in the vicinity of each pixel, and then the image is converted to a binary image.
- An overall threshold T of the image was calculated to reduce the processing time in the segmentation in the saturation channel of the HSV space, using the Otsu method [18].
- To find a balance between precision and processing time, the input image size was reduced to 224 × 224 before applying the segmentation below the threshold obtained by the Otsu method.

The next step in all variants is the application of morphological erosion and dilatation operations after calculating a disk structure element. The next step is performing a flood fill operation on background pixels of the binary image and then a matrix representation of the image is obtained that contains labels based on at least 8 connected pixels. Next, the largest segmented area (potato) is chosen and a new working image is generated. Finally, the edges are found in points where the image gradient is maximum, using Sobel's approximation derivative [19].

2.3 Deep Learning Approach

For the segmentation process, the use of techniques based on deep learning was explored, following the methodology described below (see Fig. 3):

- Creation of data set.
- Application of data augmentation techniques.
- Creation of a neural network model.
- Model training and validation of results.
- Testing of the selected model.

Data Labeling. The data set was built with 166 images of 2448 × 2048 pixel resolution of "Amarilla" and "Canchan" variety potatoes. Then a scale change was made to reduce the images to 224 × 224 pixels to improve computational capacity. For the development of the approach based on deep learning a supervised method was chosen, for this, it was necessary to label the images. Taking into consideration in deep learning best practices, the data was divided into 100 images for training, 33 for validation, and 33 for testing.

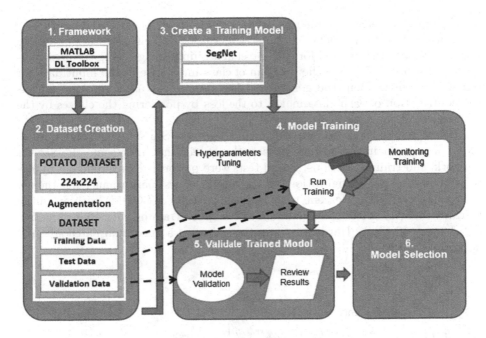

Fig. 3. Process using deep learning technique.

Preprocessing. In general, deep learning methods require a large amount of data, so increasing the amount of original images was done with the following strategies:

- Reflection of images horizontally and vertically.
- 50 pixels of translation in Horizontal and vertical image.
- Image rotation in a range of 10°.
- Scale change of image size in a range from 0.9 to 1.1.
- Shear deformation in a range of −5° to 5°.

Also, the size of the images was reduced to 224 × 224 pixels to have enough computational capacity for testing.

Segmentation Model. SegNet [1] is a deep convolutional neural network architecture for semantic pixel segmentation. It consists of an encoder network, a decoder network followed by a pixel classification layer. The architecture of the encoder network is topologically identical to the convolutional layers of a classifier. The function of the decoder network is to map the low resolution encoder feature maps to the complete input resolution feature maps for pixel classification, this is done by upsampling low resolution input feature maps.

In MatLab, the segnetLayers function allows create uninitialized configured SegNet layers using the input image size, the number of segmentation classes, and the encoder depth as a parameter, selecting an input of 224 × 224 × 3 (height, width, rgb channels), 2 segmentation classes (bottom, potato) and depth of 2 as shown in Fig. 4b. By default, segnetLayers uses a pixelClassificationLayer to predict the categorical label for each pixel in an input image using the loss cross-entropy function. To solve the problem of class imbalance in the input data for semantic segmentation, the generalized loss function is used, since it controls the contribution of each class makes to the loss by pondering the classes by the inverse size of the expected region [21].

TrainNetwork was used to perform the training of SegNet, with input parameters such as an image storage object, the object that represents the SegNet network, and training options. Rapid tests were performed with different hyperparameters and the configuration that achieved the best performance was the use of stochastic gradient descent with moment optimizer (SGDM) with an initial learning rate (lr) of 0.001, a maximum of 100 epoch training with an lr reduction of 0.1 every 50 times. Hardware limitations allowed a maximum batch size of 4 images per iteration.

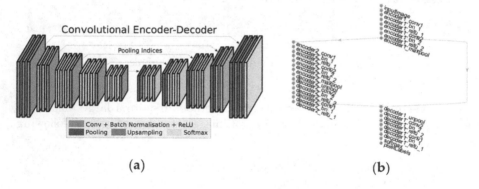

(a)   (b)

Fig. 4. (a) SegNet architecture [1]. (b) Architecture implemented.

Quality Metrics. The Jaccard or Intersection Over Union (IOU) index was used for quality metrics, since it is a regular metric used in the detection of objects and allows to measure the degree of similarity between the predicted image and the mask image, see Eq. 1. Another metric used it is the memory to control the proportion of real positives detected correctly. Furthermore, precision and F1 score were used as complementary metrics to make comparisons with the baseline.

$$IoU\,(A, B) = \frac{|A \bigcap B|}{|A \bigcup B|} \tag{1}$$

2.4   Volume Estimation

Since there is only information in 2 dimensions, it is explored methods of approximations from the state of the art:

- The basic approximation method based on [12], calculates the projected area of the potato, S, in the image and then apply square root and cube, Eq. 2. Although it is not accurate, it allows classify the potatoes by size regardless of shape (irregular potatoes).
- In the case of potatoes with a quasi-spherical shape, the average radius, R, is calculated from the polar coordinates of the potato edges, and the volume of the potato is approximated to the volume of a sphere, Eq. 3.
- In the case of ellipsoidal potatoes, a semi-major axis, b, and semi-minor axis, a, of an ellipse is calculated from a polar coordinate representation of the potato edges and approximates to the volume of an ellipsoid, Eq. 4.
- Based on [12], the main axis of the potato is calculated and the image is aligned horizontally, then dividing the object into two parts along that axis, that is, the top and the bottom. Then 360 pixel samples of the limits are extracted to generate a polynomial equation for each part, yu,yl, using linear interpolation. Finally, the polynomial equation is integrated to estimate the volume (V) using the trapezoidal method. Equations 5–7.

$$V - S^{3/2} \tag{2}$$

$$V = \frac{4}{3}\pi R^3 \tag{3}$$

$$V = \frac{4}{3}\pi ba^2 \tag{4}$$

$$V = \int_{x_1}^{x_m} A_u dx = \frac{\pi}{2} \int_{x_1}^{x_m} y_u^2 dx \tag{5}$$

$$V = \int_{x_1}^{x_m} A_l dx = \frac{\pi}{2} \int_{x_1}^{x_m} y_l^2 dx \tag{6}$$

$$V = V_u + V_l \tag{7}$$

3   Results

3.1   Experimentation Environment

The experimental environment used was Matlab R2020a, running on a computer with an Intel (R) Core 7 @ 2.20 GHz processor with 16 GB of RAM and an NVIDIA GeForce GTX1050 GPU with 4 GB of dedicated memory.

3.2   Qualitative and Quantitative Comparison of Models

A representation of a potato field in the RGB and HSI color spaces is shown in Fig. 5. There are three variants of the classical computational vision and a deep learning-based approach was performed. The results of the segmentation used are shown in Fig. 6, that shows the projected area of the potato in the image plane and the center. The location of the center is important because it will allow finding parameters of approximations to circles or ellipses, average radius or the smaller and larger diagonals, respectively. For approach 2 a SegNet neural network model was used, getting metrics described in Table 1 and 2. From the potato and background segmentation, the procedure is the same in the approaches studied. Figure 7 shows the result of applying the Sobel edge detection method to the images in Fig. 6.

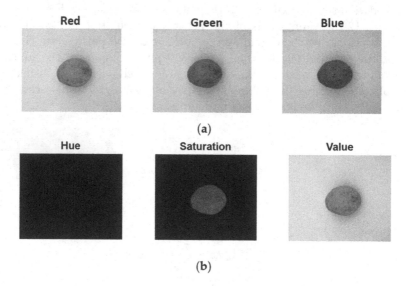

Fig. 5. (a) test image in RGB color space. (b) Test image representation in HSV color space.

Two experiments are performed to validate the volume estimation methods described in Sect. 2.2. In the first experiment, a "Amarilla" variety potato with a manually calculated volume of 74.85 ml is used, and the results using computer vision are described in Table 3. In a second experiment, a "Canchan" variety potato with volume of 180 ml is used, see Table 4. The measurements of the processing time of each of the approaches are shown in Table 5, with respect to the environment described in Sect. 3.1.

Table 1. Global metrics of the trained SegNet model.

Global accuracy	Mean accuracy	Mean IoU	Weighted mean IoU	Mean BFScore
0.9974	0.9912	0.9737	0.9949	0.9871

Table 2. Class metrics of the trained SegNet model.

Class	Accuracy	IoU	BFScore
Potato	0.9842	0.9500	0.9781
Background	0.9981	0.9972	0.9960

Table 3. Results of experimentation on "Amarillas" potatoes

Approach	Area (mm²)	Major axis (mm)	Minor axis (mm)	Volume M1 (ml)	Volume M2 (mL)	Volume M3 (mL)	Volume M4 (mL)
1a	2256.36	55.94	53.45	107.18	80.53	83.67	79.61
1b	2142.52	55.04	52.13	99.17	74.47	78.33	73.66
1c	2116.76	54.80	51.71	97.39	72.83	76.73	71.95
2	2177.95	56.12	52.13	101.64	76.09	79.84	74.80

Table 4. Results of experimentation on "Canchan" potatoes.

Approach	Area (mm²)	Major axis (mm)	Minor axis (mm)	Volume M1 (mL)	Volume M2 (mL)	Volume M3 (mL)	Volume M4 (mL)
1a	4533.42	87.44	68.37	305.23	226.97	214.02	202.52
1b	4431.66	86.03	67.82	295.01	209.33	208.63	195.81
1c	4353.35	85.38	67.07	287.23	213.39	201.11	191.10
2	4362.57	88.19	66.08	287.23	213.39	201.11	189.56

Table 5. Processing time.

Approach	Time (s)
1a – Adaptative Segmentation (2448 × 2048)	21.00
1b – Otsu Segmentation (2248 × 2048)	0.20
1c – Otsu Segmentation (224 × 224)	0.05
2 – SegNet Segmentation (224 × 224)	0.10

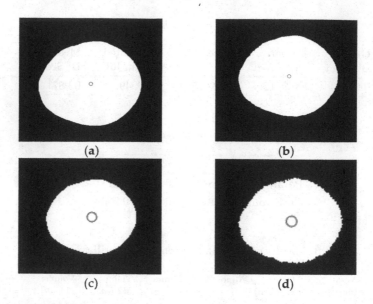

Fig. 6. (a) Adaptive segmentation in approach 1a. (b) Segmentation with Otsu threshold in approach 1b. (c) Segmentation with Otsu threshold in approach 1c. (d) SegNet segmentation in approach 2.

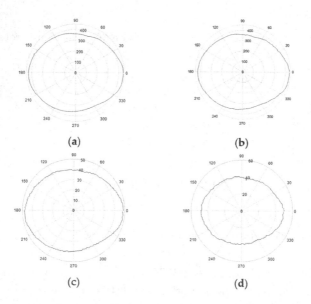

Fig. 7. Edge extraction after segmentation (a) Approach 1a. (b) Approach 1b. (c) Approach 1c. (d) Approach 2.

4 Discussion

The results of the tests of volume estimation methods from 2D images depend on the quality of the segmentation performed to obtain the projected area of the native potato. For these reason, the results will be better with a higher resolution of the input image, however the processing time will be affected, which is a deter-mining factor in high speed application. The adaptive segmentation method has the best results, but with a high processing time. In contrast, the segmentation method using the threshold obtained using the Otsu method allows to obtain better processing time. The disadvantage of these classic approaches is that a previous calibration of parameters is required based on characteristics of the environment such as lighting or of the object itself. For example, in cases where an eye on the outside of the potato falls on the edge of its projected area, in most cases it is segmented as the background. Considering the problems mentioned, the use of deep learning was explored, obtaining good results in the quality of segmentation even under variable conditions, but considering only in the training phase. The processing time results of the two layer deep SegNet architecture shows the feasibility of using it in some high speed applications. The reduction of the processing time of this type of net-work is directly related to techniques typical of the implementation in a deter-mined hardware. Finally, the method based on polynomial approximations achieves the best results for volume estimation. Obtaining an average error of 10% in small potatoes such as the "Amarilla" variety and an error of 20% in the case of large native potatoes such as the "Canchan" potato.

5 Conclusions

This work shows the usability of deep learning strategies, specifically, SegNet, compared to classic threshold-based segmentation methods, in the task of estimating native potato volume at high speed. For testing it was used a sample of 160 images of 50 "Amarilla" and "Canchan" potatoes for the training of the neural network. A total of 40 tests were performed to validate the volume estimation. The results showed an accuracy of up to 99% in segmentation of the projected potato using SegNet and an accuracy of up to 90% in the volume estimation. Processing speed of between 10 and 20 potatoes per second was achieved. Future work will focus on exploring lighter neural architectures for the purpose of reducing processing time without reducing precision.

References

1. Badrinarayanan, V., Kendall, A., Cipolla, R.: SegNet: a deep convolutional encoder-decoder architecture for image segmentation. IEEE Trans. Pattern Anal. Mach. Intell. 39(12), 2481–2495 (2017)
2. Bradley, D., Roth, G.: Adaptive thresholding using the integral image. J. Graph. Tools 12(2), 13–21 (2007)

3. Brar, E.A.S., Singh, K.: Potato defect detection using fuzzy c-mean clustering based segmentation. Indian J. Sci. Technol. 9 (2016). https://doi.org/10.17485/ijst/2016/v9i32/100737
4. Inicio - International Potato Center. https://cipotato.org/es/
5. Dacal-Nieto, A., Vázquez-Fernández, E., Formella, A., Martin, F., Torres-Guijarro, S., González-Jorge, H.: A genetic algorithm approach for feature selection in potatoes classification by computer vision. In: IECON Proceedings (Industrial Electronics Conference), pp. 1955–1960. IEEE Computer Society (2009). https://doi.org/10.1109/IECON.2009.5414871
6. Hofstee, J.W., Molema, G.J.: Machine vision based yield mapping of potatoes. In: 2002 Chicago, IL, 28–31 July 2002. p. 1. American Society of Agricultural and Biological Engineers, St. Joseph, MI, November 2002. https://doi.org/10.13031/2013.9699. http://elibrary.asabe.org/abstract.asp?JID=5&AID=9699&CID=cil2002&T=1
7. Ebrahimi, E., Mollazade, K., Arefi, A.: Detection of greening in potatoes using image processing techniques. J. Am. Sci. **7**(3), 243–247 (2011)
8. Grenander, U., Manbeck, K.M.: A stochastic shape and color model for defect detection in potatoes. J. Comput. Graph. Stat. **2**(2), 131–151 (1993). https://doi.org/10.1080/10618600.1993.10474604
9. Heinemann, P.H., Pathare, N.P., Morrow, C.T.: An automated inspection station for machine-vision grading of potatoes. Mach. Vision Appl. **9**(1), 14–19 (1996). https://doi.org/10.1007/BF01246635
10. Hofstee, J., Molema, G.: Machine vision based yield mapping of potatoes. In: 2002 ASAE Annual Meeting, p. 1. American Society of Agricultural and Biological Engineers (2002)
11. Horton, D.E., Anderson, J.L.: Potato production in the context of the world and farm economy. In: Harris, P.M. (eds.) The Potato Crop, pp. 794–815. Springer, Dordrecht (1992). https://doi.org/10.1007/978-94-011-2340-2_16
12. Jana, S., Parekh, R., Sarkar, B.: Volume estimation of non-axisymmetric fruits and vegetables using image analysis. In: 2019 International Conference on Computing, Power and Communication Technologies (GUCON), pp. 628–633. IEEE (2019)
13. Marino, S., Beauseroy, P., Smolarz, A.: Deep learning-based method for classifying and localizing potato blemishes. In: ICPRAM 2019 - Proceedings of the 8th International Conference on Pattern Recognition Applications and Methods, pp. 107–117. SciTePress, February 2019. https://doi.org/10.5220/0007350101070117. http://www.scitepress.org/DigitalLibrary/Link.aspx?doi=10.5220/0007350101070117
14. Papa. http://minagri.gob.pe/portal/23-sector-agrario/cultivos-de-importancia-nacional/183-papa
15. Moallem, P., Razmjooy, N., Mousavi, B.S.: Robust potato color image segmentation using adaptive fuzzy inference system. Iran. J. Fuzzy Syst. **11**(6), 47–65 (2014). https://doi.org/10.22111/ijfs.2014.1748. https://ijfs.usb.ac.ir/article_1748.html
16. Moallem, P., Razmjooy, N.: A multi layer perceptron neural network trained by invasive weed optimization for potato color image segmentation. Trends Appl. Sci. Res. **7**(6), 445–455 (2012). https://doi.org/10.3923/tasr.2012.445.455
17. Oppenheim, D., Shani, G.: Potato disease classification using convolution neural networks. Adv. Anim. Biosci. **8**(2), 244 (2017)
18. Otsu, N.: A threshold selection method from gray-level histograms. IEEE Trans. Syst. Man Cybern. **9**(1), 62–66 (1979)
19. Patnaik, S., Yang, Y.M.: Soft Computing Techniques in Vision Science, vol. 395. Springer, Heidelberg (2012). https://doi.org/10.1007/978-3-642-25507-6

20. Su, Q., Kondo, N., Li, M., Sun, H., Al Riza, D.F.: Potato feature prediction based on machine vision and 3D model rebuilding. Comput. Electron. Agric. **137**, 41–51 (2017). https://doi.org/10.1016/j.compag.2017.03.020
21. Sudre, Carole H., Li, Wenqi., Vercauteren, Tom., Ourselin, Sebastien, Jorge Cardoso, M.: Generalised dice overlap as a deep learning loss function for highly unbalanced segmentations. In: Cardoso, M.J., et al. (eds.) DLMIA/ML-CDS -2017. LNCS, vol. 10553, pp. 240–248. Springer, Cham (2017). https://doi.org/10.1007/978-3-319-67558-9_28
22. Tao, Y., Heinemann, P.H., Varghese, Z., Morrow, C.T., Sommer, H.J.: Machine vision for color inspection of potatoes and apples. Trans. Am. Soc. Agric. Eng. **38**(5), 1555–1561 (1995). https://doi.org/10.13031/2013.27982
23. Zhou, L., Chalana, V., Kim, Y.: PC-based machine vision system for real-time computer-aided potato inspection. Int. J. Imaging Syst. Technol. **9**(6), 423–433 (1998)

Symbiotic Trackers' Ensemble with Trackers' Re-initialization for Face Tracking

Victor H. Ayma[1]([✉]), Patrick N. Happ[1], Raul Q. Feitosa[1,2],
Gilson A. O. P. Costa[2], and Bruno Feijó[1]

[1] Pontifical Catholic University of Rio de Janeiro, R. Marques de São Vicente, 225,
Rio de Janeiro 22451-900, Brazil
{vhaymaq,patrick,raul}@ele.puc-rio.br, bfeijo@inf.puc-rio.br
[2] Rio de Janeiro State University, R. São Francisco Xavier, 524,
Rio de Janeiro 20550-900, Brazil
gilson.costa@ime.uerj.br

Abstract. Visual object tracking aims to deliver accurate estimates about the state of the target in a sequence of images or video frames. Nevertheless, tracking algorithms are sensitive to different kinds of image perturbations that frequently cause tracking failures. Indeed, tracking failures result from the insertion of imprecise target-related data into the trackers' appearance models, which leads the trackers to lose the target or drift away from it. Here, we propose a tracking fusion approach, which incorporates feedback and re-initialization mechanisms to improve overall tracking performance. Our fusion technique, called SymTE-TR, enhances trackers' overall performance by updating their appearances models with reliable information of the target's states, while resets the imprecise trackers. We evaluated our approach on a facial video dataset, which characterizes a particular challenging tracking application under different imaging conditions. The experimental results indicate that our approach contributes to enhancing individual tracker performances by providing stable results across the video sequences and, consequently, contributes to stable overall tracking fusion performances.

Keywords: Online object tracking · Tracking fusion · Tracking re-initialization · Face tracking

1 Introduction

The proliferation of digital image acquisition devices, such as surveillance cameras and built-in mobile cameras, has led to a generation of large volumes of

This work was supported by CAPES of the Ministry of Education and CNPq of the Ministry of Science, Technology, Innovation and Communication, Brazil.

© Springer Nature Switzerland AG 2021
J. A. Lossio-Ventura et al. (Eds.): SIMBig 2020, CCIS 1410, pp. 250–263, 2021.
https://doi.org/10.1007/978-3-030-76228-5_18

imaging data. In particular, facial imaging data benefits many computer vision-based applications in fields as diverse as security, surveillance, health, sports, and robotics, among others [8]. Nevertheless, most of such applications rely on visual object tracking techniques to fully exploit the increasing wealth of information [15].

The visual object tracking aims to estimate the states of an arbitrary object (henceforth target) across a sequence of images or frames in a video sequence. The state encodes the target's properties, which often correspond to its position and extent within an image or video frame. Traditionally, the target's state inference depends on an appearance model that gathers the possible target appearances experienced during the tracking process. However, such a model is susceptible to internal and external factors that often lead to tracking drifts and interfere with the visual object tracking in real-world scenarios. Some of the tracking restrictive factors include target's deformations, occlusions, illumination variations, and abrupt motion changes [13, 17, 20].

Nowadays, the computer vision community has turned its attention to the development of visual object tracking algorithms built upon deep learning architectures that enable the creation of state-of-the-art trackers, as demonstrated in the last edition of the annual VOT Challenge [10]. However, despite the remarkable results obtained by the deep learning-based trackers, such methods require large-scale datasets to produce potential models able to cope with the target's appearance at the testing stage.

Contrary to the deep learning-based trackers, online tracking algorithms learn the target's appearances on the fly via updating their appearance models. Although there is evidence that Deep Neural Network adaptations can avoid large-scale pre-training [21], online trackers are valuable to cope with real-world scenarios where new data arrives sequentially in a stream. Nevertheless, online trackers are prone to fail and drift away from the target due to the insertion of noisy information into their appearance models.

In an attempt to produce more reliable tracking estimates and solve the tracking problem, several computer vision scientists have designed different kinds of features [6, 7, 22] and implemented sophisticated sample selection schemes [5] for the updating of the tracker's appearance model. Other researchers even have envisaged advantageous interactions between online trackers and object detectors [9] to provide accurate outcomes that serve as input to the appearance model updating process. Moreover, some other scientists have exploited the trackers' strengths to produce reliable unified outcomes trough a fusion process [2, 4, 12, 14, 16, 18] . Others have leveraged the unified outcome to update the trackers' appearances models [1, 3, 23]. Furthermore, a reduced group of researchers has prevented appearance model contamination via a re-initialization scheme [11]. Although previous works have mitigated the drifting issue, the accumulation of error during the target's appearance learning that causes tracking failures remains latent.

In this work, we combine some of the previous ideas to propose a fusion of trackers and re-initialization approach for visual object tracking. The proposed method extends the Symbiotic Tracker Ensemble approach [4], which combines the trackers' outcomes disregarding their designs, but presents limited performance on real-world scenarios. Such performance constraints were mitigated by forwarding the fusion output to the trackers composing the ensemble through a feedback learning process that updates their appearance models [1]. In this paper, we aim to enhance the overall tracking performance by including a re-initialization alternative in the model. In this way, a re-initialization model is proposed to decide if a tracker will be updated or restarted according to current tracker performance. Thus, the main contributions of this work are two-fold: (i) we proposed a tracker re-initialization scheme to improve tracking performance; and (ii) we developed a performance evaluation mechanism to assess the trackers' behaviors at runtime for re-initialization.

Although our method is conceived to operate on the visual tracking of arbitrary objects, we evaluate it in the face tracking scenario, given the uncontrolled intrinsic and extrinsic factors that influence the face appearance in real-world scenarios. Internal factors include deformation, non-rigid deformations, and inherent facial properties, such as age, ethnicity, gender, and facial hair. On the other hand, external factors correspond to the movement of the camera during acquisition, temporal and spatial image resolutions, image noise due to sensor's characteristics, changes in illumination, and occlusions. Such factors represent a challenge for the visual object tracking task and offer representative evaluation conditions.

The rest of this paper is organized as follows: Sect. 2 describes the Symbiotic Tracker Ensemble fusion approach in detail, Sect. 3 introduces the trackers' re-initialization and feedback schemes within the fusion approach, Sect. 4 presents the experimental design to evaluate our proposal, Sect. 5 reports the results obtained from the experimental procedure, and finally, Sect. 6 summarizes our findings and provides directions for future works.

2   Symbiotic Tracker Ensemble

The Symbiotic Tracker Ensemble introduced by Gao et al. [4] is a fusion framework that combines a set of tracking estimates into a unified and expectedly more reliable outcome, i.e., *fusion estimate*. The fusion process, represented in Fig. 1, considers temporal and spatial interactions among the trackers in an ensemble to ponder their contributions to the *fusion estimate*, disregarding their specific designs.

Temporal interactions are obtained through individual trackers' consistency evaluations in the Intra-Tracker Correlation stage. Thus, for every tracker in the ensemble, the Intra-Tracker Correlation stage assesses the smoothness in trajectory to provide an initial weight (*initial credibility*). Its computation relates the tracker's estimates in consecutive frames with the previous *final credibility* coefficient from the Inter-Tracker Correlation stage.

Spatial interactions, on the other hand, are modeled through a collective evaluation of the trackers' behaviors in the Inter-Tracker Correlation stage. It

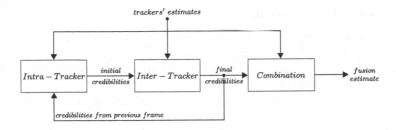

Fig. 1. Symbiotic tracker ensemble.

measures the spatial congruence among the trackers' estimates by performing iterative pair-wise trackers' operations. Thus, for each tracker in the ensemble, the Inter-Tracker Correlation stage assigns a final weight (*credibility*) based on its *initial credibility* coefficient from the Intra-Tracker Correlation stage and its agreement level with other tracking estimates.

In the sequence, the Combination stage computes the *fusion estimate* considering all the trackers' estimates and their respective *final credibilities*.

Next, we describe a set of relationships between tracking estimates used in both Intra-Tracker Correlation and Inter-Tracker Correlation stages, followed by a brief explanation of how to compute both correlations and the *fusion estimate*.

2.1 Relationships Between Tracking Estimates

The Symbiotic Tracker Ensemble objective is to measure the relationships among tracking estimates. To quantify such relationships, Gao et al. introduced two similarity measurements $F(\cdot)$ and $r(\cdot)$. Formally, let two bounding boxes B_1 and B_2, defined by $B = (x, y, width, height)$, represent two tracking estimates, where x and y describe the upper left corner position and *width* and *height* stands for the bounding box extent, then:

- $F(B_1, B_2)$, measures the similarity between B_1 and B_2 as follows:

$$F(B_1, B_2) = \frac{2 \times Pr(B_1, B_2) \times Re(B_1, B_2)}{Pr(B_1, B_2) + Re(B_1, B_2)} \tag{1}$$

where $F(B_1, B_2) \in [0, 1]$, $Pr(B_1, B_2)$ represents the precision and $Re(B_1, B_2)$ stands for the recall.

- $r(B_1, B_2)$, quantifies the congruence between B_1 and B_2 according to:

$$r(B_1, B_2) = exp(-\frac{D^2(B_1, B_2)}{\sigma^2}) \tag{2}$$

where $r(B_1, B_2) \in [0, 1]$, $D(B_1, B_2)$ represents the Euclidean distance between the centers of B_1 and B_2, and σ is a controlling coefficient of the width of the exponential function.

2.2   Intra-tracker Correlation

The first stage of the fusion approach proposed by Gao et al., evaluates a tracker's consistency by assessing the changes in its trajectory. To this end, successive tracking estimates are used to compute a temporal correlation measure, which defines its initial credibility.

In a more formal way, given two consecutive tracking estimates $B_{i,n-1}$ and $B_{i,n}$, corresponding to the i-th tracker in the ensemble at $(n-1)$-th and n-th frames, respectively, the initial credibility $C_{i,n}$ is defined by:

$$C_{i,n} = \xi_i \zeta_i + (1 - \xi_i)\Theta(B_{i,n-1}, B_{i,n})C_{i,n-1}^f \tag{3}$$

where, ζ_i is a tracker's prior credibility defined by the user, $C_{i,n-1}^f$ represents the final credibility coefficient from a previous frame, $\xi_i \in [0,1]$ is a regularization parameter that controls the participation of the tracker's prior credibility, and $\Theta(\cdot)$ is a relation coefficient that assesses the trajectory smoothness of the i-th tracker.

The relation coefficient $\Theta(\cdot)$ can be computed using either $F(\cdot)$ or $r(\cdot)$ similarity metrics, as presented earlier in the previous subsection.

2.3   Inter-tracker Correlation

The second stage of the fusion approach computes a tracker's confidence by assessing its level of congruence with the remaining trackers in the ensemble for a single frame. The individual trackers' credibilities are estimated through an iterative pair-wise correlation procedure among trackers' estimates, as presented in Eq. 4:

$$C_{i,n}^s = \eta_i C_{i,n} + \frac{1 - \eta_i}{I - 1} \sum_{j=1}^{j=I} \Phi(B_{j,n}, B_{i,n})C_{i,n}^{s-1} \quad, \forall i \neq j \tag{4}$$

where, $C_{i,n}^s$ represents the credibility coefficient for the i-th tracker after the s iteration, $\eta_i \in [0,1]$ is a weighting coefficient that controls the importance of the initial credibility $C_{i,n}$, I denotes the total number of trackers, $B_{j,n}$ and $B_{i,n}$ are the tracking estimates at the n-th frame for the i-th and j-th trackers, respectively, and $\Phi(\cdot)$ is a relation coefficient between the i-th and j-th trackers that measures the spatial congruence, which may be computed using either the $F(\cdot)$ or $r(\cdot)$ similarity metrics.

Notice that after convergence the credibility coefficients $C_{i,n}^s$ becomes the final credibility coefficients $C_{i,n}^f$, which will be also used for the Intra-Tracker Correlation at the $n + 1$-th frame.

2.4   Estimates Combination

The last stage in the fusion approach computes the *fusion estimate*, B_{fusion}, through a weighted sum of the trackers' estimates B_i, formally:

$$B_{fusion} = \sum_{i=1}^{I} \pi_i B_i \tag{5}$$

where the weighting coefficient π_i for the i-th tracker is based on the final credibilities coefficients as follows:

$$\pi_i = \frac{C_{i,n}^f}{\sum_{j=1}^{I} C_{j,n}^f} \tag{6}$$

3   SymTE with Trackers Re-initialization

The Symbiotic Tracker Ensemble is a tracking fusion technique, which outcome results from the trackers' interactions that rely solely on the trackers' outputs. Such characteristic permits the participation of any tracker to compose the ensemble; however, the lack of a coupling mechanism connecting the fusion output with the trackers might impair the overall tracking fusion performance.

Indeed, tracking failures in the fusion approach arise from the trackers' updating with imprecise information about the target's state that is often disassociated from the fusion estimate. To overcome this issue, we included a feedback mechanism into the fusion process, which enhances individual trackers by leveraging from the information contained in the fusion estimate [1]; we called this method Symbiotic Tracking Ensemble with Feedback Learning. Nevertheless, despite such an improvement, tracking fusion is still prone to tracking failures.

In this work, we acknowledge that trackers might fail despite having reliable information about the target's state to update their appearances models and that the causes of tracking failures might be a consequence of their internal designs. In such a scenario, tracking failures can only be solved through drastic measures such as trackers' re-initialization. Thus, in this paper, we extend the tracking fusion approach from Gao et al. [4] by implementing a feedback scheme to the trackers in the ensemble [1] and equipping them with a re-initialization mechanism. Our approach assumes that the *fusion estimate* approximates to the real target's state and can be used to either update or re-initialize the trackers composing the ensemble.

Formally, our method comprises a set of I trackers $T = \{T_1, \cdots, T_i, \cdots, T_I\}$ that receive an initial state of the target in the form of a bounding box at the beginning of the tracking process. Then, for each incoming frame, the trackers provide estimates of the target's state B_i, which are combined into the *fusion estimate* by the Symbiotic Tracking Ensemble (SymTE) technique, as depicted in Fig. 2. The *fusion estimate* is later forwarded to the re-initialization component, R_i, within the i-th tracker to decide whether the tracker should be re-initialized or not. Given a tracker's re-initialization command, the tracker erases all the target's registers seen during the tracking and starts over from scratch; otherwise, the tracker uses the *fusion estimate* to update its appearance model and so to infer the next target state.

3.1   Tracker's Re-initialization

A tracker's re-initialization involves erasing its appearance model and starting over from scratch using the latest fusion output as the new initial state

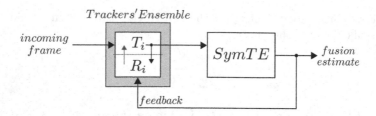

Fig. 2. Symbiotic Tracker Ensemble with Trackers Re-Initialization. Each tracker T_i is associated with a Re-Initialization model R_i that decides if a tracker will be updated or re-initialized.

of the target. To decide whether a tracker should be re-initialized or not, the re-initialization module (R_i) associated with the i-th tracker (T_i) assesses the tracker's performance in the latest processed frame based on the tracker's disagreement level with the fusion estimate. Formally, the i-th tracker's performance (δ_i) can be computed as follows:

$$\delta_i = 1 - F(B_{fusion}, B_i) \tag{7}$$

where, B_{fusion} and B_i correspond to the fusion and the i-th tracker's estimate in the latest video frame, and $F(\cdot)$ represents the measure of similarity defined in Sect. 2.1.

Finally, the tracker's re-initialization module (R_i) will command the i-th tracker re-initialization whenever the performance score δ_i exceeds a pre-defined re-initialization threshold (δ_0).

4   Experimental Settings

We assessed the performance of our method, the Symbiotic Tracker Ensemble with Trackers' Re-initialization (SymTE-TR), using a collection of facial video sequences available for the public. To further validate our proposal, we compared its performance against those obtained by the original fusion tracking approach proposed by Gao et al. (SymTE) [4] and a prior version [1] (SymTE-FL), which considers a feedback mechanism in the SymTE's fusion process.

To evaluate the effect of tracking re-initialization over the tracking fusion and the individual trackers, we varied the re-initialization threshold (δ_0) from 0.0 up to 1.0 in steps of 0.2. Moreover, we commanded the trackers in the ensemble to re-initialize whenever their disagreement levels with the fusion estimate exceeded δ_0. It is worth mentioning that a $\delta_0 = 0$ forces a continuous trackers' re-initialization, whereas a $\delta_0 = 1$ disables re-initialization, forcing the trackers to operate on pure tracking updating mode, which is equivalent to the SymTE-FL variant. Next, we present the experimental settings in detail.

4.1   TB-Face Dataset

Given our interest in assessing our approach's performance in the face tracking task, we conducted a set of experiments in the TB-Face dataset, which is a subset of eleven facial video sequences extracted from the TB-100 object tracking dataset [19]. The targets in the TB-Face dataset undergo severe changes in appearance, resulting from variations in lighting conditions, motion blurriness, in-plane and out-of-plane rotations, and occlusions, among others.

To promote an unbiased comparison among the tracking methods, we manually redefined the facial annotations in the video sequences that compose the TB-Face dataset, as depicted by the white bounding boxes in Fig. 3. We aimed to maintain the facial annotations uniform throughout the dataset, by keeping the bounding boxes centered with the target faces: the superior and inferior edges correspond to the middle forehead and the chin, respectively; whereas the left and right edges correspond to the left and right cheekbones, respectively.

4.2 Evaluation Metrics

In this study, we adopted the Area Under the Curve of the performance plot associated with the F-measure error, $e\left(\cdot\right) \in [0, 1]$, to assess the different tracking techniques. The F-measure error quantifies the disagreement level between a tracking estimate (B_n) and the reference (B_n^{ref}) in the n−th frame. Formally, the F-measure error for the n−th frame is defined as follows:

$$e(B_n, B_n^{ref}) = 1 - F(B_n, B_n^{ref}) \tag{8}$$

where, $F\left(\cdot\right)$ represents the F-measure introduced in Sect. 2.1.

The performance plot summarizes the percentage of frames in which e falls below a set of fixed thresholds, which resulting area under the curve, $AUC(e)$, ranges between 0 and 1.

Fig. 3. TB-Face dataset references annotations. The images correspond to frame samples from different video sequences: FleetFace (top) and Jumping (bottom).

4.3 Trackers

We used five well-known online trackers [17,20] to compose the trackers' ensemble. The trackers, which source code are publicly available, differ in their designs, but were slightly adjusted to fit the operating scheme described in Sect. 3.1: first, the trackers provide the set of target's state estimates; next, the trackers wait for the re-initialization commands to update or re-start their appearance models. Next, we briefly describe the online trackers used in our experiments.

- *Tracking-Learning-Detection* (TLD) [9], is a tracking framework conceived to perform long-term tracking of arbitrary objects via the interaction of a fast tracker and an online object detector. As the name suggests, TLD decomposes the visual object tracking task into three stages: Tracking, which produces an estimate of the target's state in incoming frames; Learning, which produces reliable data for training the online detector; and Detection, which locates the target in the current frame to correct the tracking trajectory after a tracking failure.
- *Kernelized Correlation Filters* (KCF) [7], is an online discriminative tracker of arbitrary objects that exploits what the authors call as a Circulant Matrix to extract thousands of training samples in the frequency domain, and uses a linear ridge regression model to capture the appearances of the object.
- *Structured Output Tracking with Kernels* (STRUCK) [5], is an online discriminative tracking algorithm aiming at predicting the target's state through consecutive frames of a video sequence, while generating high-quality training samples that would enable the correct update of a variant of a Support Vector Machine.
- *Locality Sensitive Histograms* (LSH) [6], LSH is an adaptive tracking algorithm that focuses on handling changes in the target's appearance as a consequence of variations in illumination and occlusions. To this end, the LSH uses a floating-point value histogram that accounts for the influence of every pixel in the image over the regions within the target that describe its appearance.
- *Fast Compressive Tracker* (CT) [22], is a discriminative tracking algorithm that uses an adaptive Naive Bayes binary classifier in a low-dimensional subspace to distinguish the target from the background. The low-dimensional space is chosen at random and contains sufficient information to reconstruct the original pattern.

It is worth mentioning that due to implementation constraints, the STRUCK, LSH, and CT trackers operated on a single scale in our experiments. Moreover, the trackers were set to work with their default parameters.

4.4 Symbiotic Tracker Ensemble Parameters

In this work, we exploited the Symbiotic Tracker Ensemble operational characteristics to combine the set of five tracking estimates into a single outcome. The relation coefficients $\Theta(\cdot)$ and $\Phi(\cdot)$ described in Subsection 2, which measure the temporal and spatial congruence in the intra-tracker and inter-tracker correlation stages, respectively, allow four variants (rr, rF, Fr, and FF), considering the similarity metrics of Eqs. 1 and 2. In our experiments, however, we used the FF variant, which has shown the best fusion results according to the authors' report in visual object tracking tasks. Furthermore, we followed the authors' recommendations to configure the remaining fusion parameters. So, for all the participant trackers, their associated prior credibilities C_i were set to 1.0, and their regularization parameters ξ_i and η_i were set to 0.1 and 0.1, respectively.

5   Results Analysis

In this section, we report and analyze the results obtained from the execution of the experiments described in Sect. 4 regarding the re-initialization of trackers as a mechanism to improve the individual trackers' performances and, consequently, the overall tracking performance via the fusion process.

The boxplots in Fig. 4 show the performance distributions achieved by the tracking fusion techniques in terms of the $AUC(e)$ scores over the video sequences in the TB-Face dataset. The tracking fusion algorithms correspond to the original Symbiotic Tracker Ensemble (SymTE); the Symbiotic Tracker Ensemble with Feedback Learning (SymTE-FL); and the different versions of our approach, the Symbiotic Tracker Ensemble with Trackers' Re-initialization (SymTE-TR), according to the various re-initialization thresholds (δ_0).

A quick inspection of the boxplots shows that the SymTE-FL performed slightly better than the SymTE alone. Indeed, both tracking fusion techniques produced similar median performance scores of about 0.62; however, the SymTE-FL produced smaller overall and interquartile ranges of the $AUC(e)$ score than its original counterpart. The performance distribution plot also indicates that the SymTE-TR tends to improve as the threshold for trackers' re-initialization (δ_0) increases; in fact, the overall and interquartile ranges of the $AUC(e)$ scores get smaller and the median performance score improves as the δ_0 increases up to a value of 0.8.

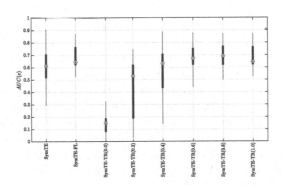

Fig. 4. Overall tracking performance distributions over the TB-Face dataset in terms of the $AUC(e)$ score corresponding to the tracking fusion techniques.

A detailed inspection of the boxplots shows that a continuous trackers' re-initialization ($\delta_0 = 0$) led to a tracking fusion technique with an inferior performance that holds the lowest median performance score (0.15), though with a small interquartile range. On the other hand, the absence of re-initialization ($\delta_0 = 1$) in the trackers led to a tracking fusion technique with the third best performance that provides a median $AUC(e)$ score of about 0.69 and a small interquartile range, but with a marked right-skewed performance distribution.

The results suggest that trackers' re-initialization is beneficial for the fusion, achieving increasingly better performances up to a certain point. Actually, the results seem to indicate that a good trade-off between performance and robustness might be obtained at a $\delta_0 = 0.8$. The results also suggest a positive effect on the trackers composing the ensemble, fundamental in the fusion process.

Figure 5 exhibits the individual trackers' performance distributions in terms of the $AUC(e)$ score grouped by the different tracking fusion techniques. Notice that the trackers in the SymTE operate disregarding the fusion estimate, whereas the trackers in the SymTE-FL and the SymTE-TR employ the fusion estimate to update and update/re-initialize their appearance models, respectively.

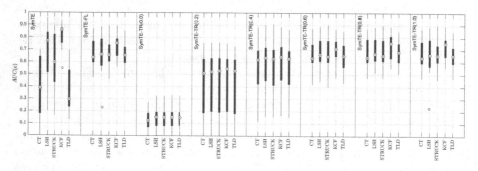

Fig. 5. Trackers' performance distributions in terms of the $AUC(e)$ score over the TB-Face dataset and sorted by the tracking fusion techniques.

The boxplots show that the trackers in the SymTE performed disparately; moreover, except for the KFC, the remaining trackers produced disperse $AUC(e)$ scores with large overall and interquartile ranges. The graphic also shows the trackers in the SymTE-FL scheme produced more stable $AUC(e)$ scores with different interquartile performance ranges. Furthermore, the boxplots show that the re-initialization strategy in the SymTE-TR positively influenced the trackers in the ensemble, originating a standardized behavior among the trackers and consistently improving their tracking performances. Nevertheless, despite such improvements, trackers' median performances across the different δ_0 values are inferior to the LSH and KCF trackers in the SymTE scheme; notice however, the presence of an outlier in the KFC tracker performance.

Figure 6 shows the per sequence tracking performance distributions of the individual trackers and the tracking fusion techniques in terms of the F score. Notice that the exposed SymTE-TR performances correspond to our tracking fusion version with a re-initialization threshold, δ_0, equal to 0.8.

A detailed analysis of the graphics in the figure reveals that the KFC was superior to the remaining trackers in six out of the eleven facial video sequences, producing the highest median F scores, especially in the video sequences in which the face scale variations prevail (David, FleetFace, Freeman1, and Trellis). Such performance results are aligned with the trackers' operation modes, highlighting the KFC ability to handle the target's scale variations. Surprisingly, the TLD tracker produced inferior performances in most of the video sequences despite its adaptation capacity to the target's extent.

On the other hand, the tracking fusion methods remained inferior to the best performing tracker across the video sequences in both the median and interquartile range of the F score. However, they performed similarly in most of the video sequences, showing a slight superiority in the median F score by the SymTE in the David, FaceOcc1, and FaceOcc2 video sequences, but favoring the SymTE-TR in the overall performance range in most of the video sequences. We believe trackers' performances might be improved by considering additional sources about the target states for tracker's re-initialization, such as face detectors. Finally, the results also indicate that the TLD might have a strong influence on the SymTE-TR,

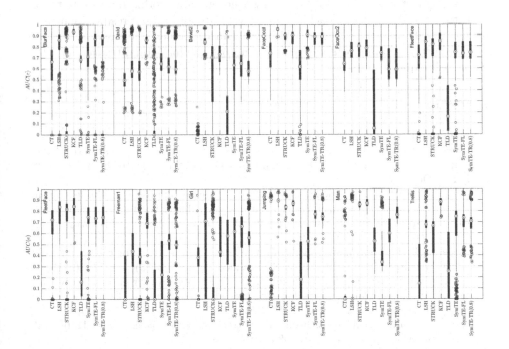

Fig. 6. Per sequence performance plots for the tracking techniques in terms of the F score.

potentiating the tracking fusion performance whenever it performs well (BlurFace, FaceOcc1, Girl, and Man video sequences); nevertheless, additional experiments on this matter should be conducted.

6   Conclusions and Future Works

In this paper, we proposed a tracking fusion technique, the Symbiotic Tracker Ensemble with Trackers' Re-initialization (SymTE-TR), which merges the trackers' outcomes to produce a unified tracking estimate. The SymTE-TR extends previous tracking fusion methodologies [1,4] by equipping the trackers with a re-initialization mechanism.

To evaluate the SymTE-TR, we conducted a set of experiments on the TB-Face dataset, whose video sequences characterize challenging facial imaging conditions, including scale variations and severe occlusions.

The results suggest that the feedback mechanism benefits the tracking fusion process. Moreover, the results showed that the re-initialization positively influenced the trackers in the ensemble and, consequently, the tracking fusion technique, producing more regular tracking performances.

In the experiments, we considered two scale-adaptive trackers (KCF and TLD) and three scale-invariant trackers (LSH, STRUCK, CT). We observed that SymTE-TR performance seems to be strongly affected by KCF and TLD trackers, leading to remarkably good results whenever both produced accurate tracking estimates. We expect to achieve more accurate and robust results by including more scale-adaptive trackers. Also, we plan to include additional sources to provide accurate target states that may improve the individual trackers and the fusion technique.

References

1. Ayma, V.H., Happ, P.N., Costa, G.A.O.P.D., Feitosa, R.Q.: Symbiotic tracker ensemble with feedback learning. In: Proceedings of the 2017 30th SIBGRAPI Conference on Graphics, Patterns and Images (SIBGRAPI 2017), pp. 421–428. IEEE, October 2017
2. Bailer, C., Pagani, A., Stricker, D.: A superior tracking approach: building a strong tracker through fusion. In: Fleet, D., Pajdla, T., Schiele, B., Tuytelaars, T. (eds.) ECCV 2014. LNCS, vol. 8695, pp. 170–185. Springer, Cham (2014). https://doi.org/10.1007/978-3-319-10584-0_12
3. Biresaw, T., Cavallaro, A., Regazzoni, C.: Tracker-level fusion for robust Bayesian visual tracking. IEEE Trans. Circ. Syst. Video Technol. **25**(5), 776–789 (2015)
4. Gao, Y., Ji, R., Zhang, L., Hauptmann, A.: Symbiotic tracker ensemble toward a unified tracking framework trackers-the black boxes approach. IEEE Trans. Circ. Syst. Video Technol. **24**(7), 1122–1131 (2014)
5. Hare, S., et al.: Struck: structured output tracking with kernels. IEEE Trans. Pattern Ana. Mach. Intell. **38**(10), 2096–2109 (2016)
6. He, S., Lau, R.W.H., Yang, Q., Wang, J., Yang, M.: Robust object tracking via locality sensitive histograms. IEEE Trans. Circ. Syst. Video Technol. **27**(5), 1006–1017 (2017)

7. Henriques, J.F., Caseiro, R., Martins, P., Batista, J.: High-speed tracking with kernelized correlation filters. IEEE Trans. Pattern Anal. Mach. Intell. **37**(3), 583–596 (2015)
8. Huang, T., Xiong, Z., Zhang, Z.: Face recognition applications. In: Li, S., Jain, A. (eds.) Handbook of Face Recognition, pp. 617–638. Springer, London (2011). https://doi.org/10.1007/978-0-85729-932-1_24
9. Kalal, Z., Mikolajczyk, K., Matas, J.: Tracking-learning-detection. IEEE Trans. Pattern Anal. Mach. Intell. **34**(7), 1409–1422 (2012)
10. Kristan, M., et al.: The seventh visual object tracking vot2019 challenge results. In: In Proceedings of the 2019 IEEE/CVF International Conference on Computer Vision Workshop (ICCVW), pp. 2206–2241. IEEE, October 2019
11. Leang, I., Herbin, S., Girard, B., Droulez, J.: Robust fusion of trackers using online drift prediction. In: Battiato, S., Blanc-Talon, J., Gallo, G., Philips, W., Popescu, D., Scheunders, P. (eds.) ACIVS 2015. LNCS, vol. 9386, pp. 229–240. Springer, Cham (2015). https://doi.org/10.1007/978-3-319-25903-1_20
12. Leichter, I., Lindenbaum, M., Rivlin, E.: A general framework for combining visual trackers-the black boxes approach. Int. J. Comput. Vis. **67**(3), 343–363 (2006)
13. Li, P., Wang, D., Wang, L., Lu, H.: Deep visual tracking: review and experimental comparison. Pattern Recogn. **76**, 323–338 (2018)
14. Li, Q., Wang, X., Wang, W., Jiang, Y., Zhou, Z.-H., Tu, Z.: Disagreement-based multi-system tracking. In: Park, J.-I., Kim, J. (eds.) ACCV 2012. LNCS, vol. 7729, pp. 320–334. Springer, Heidelberg (2013). https://doi.org/10.1007/978-3-642-37484-5_27
15. Li, S.Z., Jain, A.K.: Introduction. In: Li, S.Z., Jain, A.K. (eds.) Handbook of Face Recognition, pp. 1–15. Springer, London (2011). https://doi.org/10.1007/978-0-85729-932-1_1
16. Shearer, K., Wong, K.D., Venkatesh, S.: Combining multiple tracking algorithms for improved general performance. Pattern Recogn. **34**(6), 1257–1269 (2001)
17. Smeulders, A.W., Chu, D.M., Cucchiara, R., Calderara, S., Dehghan, A., Shah, M.: Visual tracking: an experimental survey. IEEE Trans. Pattern Anal. Mach. Intell. **36**(7), 1442–1468 (2014)
18. Stenger, B., Woodley, T., Cipolla, R.: Learning to track with multiple observers. In: Proceedings of the 2009 IEEE Conference on Computer Vision and Pattern Recognition (CVPR 2009), Miami, FL, USA, pp. 2647–2654, June 2009
19. Wu, Y., Lim, J., Yang, M.: Online object tracking: a benchmark. In: Proceedings of 2013 IEEE Conference on Computer Vision and Pattern Recognition (CVPR 2013), pp. 2411–2418. IEEE, June 2013
20. Wu, Y., Lim, J., Yang, M.: Object tracking benchmark. IEEE Trans. Pattern Anal. Mach. Intell. **37**(9), 1834–1848 (2015)
21. Zhang, J., Zhong, B., Wang, P., Wang, C., Du, J.: Robust feature learning for online discriminative tracking without large-scale pre-training. Front. Comput. Sci. **12**(6), 1160–1172 (2018)
22. Zhang, K., Zhang, L., Yang, M.: Fast compressive tracking. IEEE Trans. Pattern Anal. Mach. Intell. **36**(10), 2002–2015 (2014)
23. Zhong, B., Yao, H., Chen, S., Ji, R., Chin, T., Wang, H.: Visual tracking via weakly supervised learning from multiple imperfect oracles. Pattern Recogn. **47**(2), 1395–1410 (2014)

Multi-class Vehicle Detection and Automatic License Plate Recognition Based on YOLO in Latin American Context

Pedro I. Montenegro-Montori[✉], Jhonatan Camasca-Huamán, and Junior Fabian

Universidad ESAN, Alonso de Molina N° 1652, Lima, Peru
{16100041,15100036}@ue.edu.pe, jfabian@esan.edu.pe
https://www.ue.edu.pe/

Abstract. In Latin America, and many other countries around the globe, serious problems exist regarding the high level of traffic that generates congestion on avenues and streets, with poor road planning being one of the main causes, plus the excess of buses, mini-buses, taxis, and other vehicles that cause obstructions. Therefore, it would be very useful to know the flow of existing vehicles in each area to know and segment which roads certain vehicles should transit, thus generating greater control. This research proposes a methodology for the detection and multi-classification of vehicles in eight classes: cars, buses, trucks, combis (micro-buses), moto-taxis (auto-rickshaws), taxis, motorcycles, and bicycles; to later carry out the detection of the vehicle license plates and do the recognition of the characters on them; using Deep Learning techniques, specifically YOLOv3 and LeNet. The proposed methodology consists of four stages: Vehicle Detection, License Plate Detection, Character Segmentation, and Character Recognition. We also introduce a novel open-access dataset, LAT-VEDA, which contains more than 22 000 images divided into 8 classes. Good results were obtained in each one of the four stages of the system in comparison with the state of the art. Achieving the best mAP of 1.0 in the Vehicle License Plate Detection stage and having the lowest performance in the Vehicle Detection stage with a mAP of 0.68. This approach may be used by the Government to support the management of public transport, giving greater control and information about the flow of vehicles by area, in addition to the fact that the license plate recognition system can help in the management of the control of public policies and regulations.

Keywords: Vehicle detection/classification · License plate detection · ALPR · Deep learning · YOLO

1 Introduction

In Latin America, day by day, vehicular disorder reigns in the streets and avenues, due to poor urban planning and little existing control of vehicle

J. A. Lossio-Ventura et al. (Eds.): SIMBig 2020, CCIS 1410, pp. 264–278, 2021.
https://doi.org/10.1007/978-3-030-76228-5_19

regulations [1,24]. It is a chaotic environment where the authorities that should control it lack the necessary tools to do their jobs effectively. One of these countries is the case of Peru, where illegal means of transport prevail and work without problems due to the low regulation of the authorities [2,3]. In this scenario, the need arises for a control mechanism that supports the Government in monitoring vehicular flow in the cities and compliance with its policies, such as the "Pico y Placa" [5] regulation in Peru. It is important to highlight that this is not only a problem of Latin America but of many countries around the world like India, Russia, Thailand, Turkey, among others [1,23]. Furthermore, this environment not only causes disorder in the streets, but it also affects the health and safety of thousands of citizens, plus generates huge levels of air pollution [4,6]. During the last years, the advance of Deep learning techniques makes possible object detection in real-time with great performance and speed, being able to imbue these methods into CCTV systems, which allows simple monitoring of all kinds of activities, automating formerly manual systems.

In this investigation, we propose a methodology for multi-class vehicle detection and automatic license plate recognition (ALPR) in Latin American Context using deep learning techniques, specifically You Only look Once version 3 (YOLOv3) [19] and LeNet [21]. For this, the vehicles were classified into eight categories: cars, buses, trucks, combis (mini-buses), auto-rickshaws (moto-taxis), taxis, motorcycles, and bicycles. Additionally, in this research, we present a novel open-access dataset of vehicles with these 8 classes called Latin American Vehicle dataset (LAT-VEDA) which is available at [25]. Hence, the ALPR stage consisted in three steps: license plate (LP) detection, license plate character segmentation, and license plate character recognition; for the vehicle detection stage and the two first steps of the ALPR stage YOLOv3 was used, and for the last step of the ALPR stage LeNet-5 was used. This work is structured as follows: Sect. 2 describes Related Works; Sect. 3, Methods; Sect. 4, Results and Discussion; Sect. 5, Conclusions; and, finally, Sect. 6, Future Work.

2   Related Work

Object detection has been one of the most studied topics of the computer vision scientific community [7,8,19,29,30]. One of the objects most studied has been vehicles, specially because of their many applications in different scenarios where its detection is important [7,9–14].

Vehicle Detection
Not all ALPR pipelines include vehicle detection, but it is an important stage to achieve better performance and robust results in License Plate (LP) detection. The YOLO framework has shown really good results in this type of tasks because of its great level of speed and precision [7,9–14,20]. In [7] Fast-YOLO and YOLOv2 were used to obtain high performance with both models, being Fast-YOLO the best of the two with 1.0 recall. Furthermore, Tiny-YOLO has been used to obtain better speed at the cost of performance [20].

LP Detection

Some investigations skip the vehicle detection stage [10,12] and directly apply the LP detection, this is because of the characteristics of their scenario, with input images being of vehicles near and not far behind. In our case, we need a more robust method, that can achieve the detection of LP in vehicles farther away, in different lighting conditions. Like in [7,13,14], where they employed YOLOv2 and Fast-YOLO to achieve this task, obtaining pipelines that are robust, with really good performance and speed, obtaining in the three cases 1.0 accuracy in the test data, and average FPS of 47 and 76 [7,13].

LP Character Segmentation

Jiao et al. in [9], used Optical character recognition (OCR) to segment the LP characters from the plates. Moreover, the OCR module had high recognition accuracy and depended on the correct vehicle detection. On the other hand, Kessentini et al. [12], used YOLOv2 with 30 filters according to the number of classes (plates) and establish the threshold by 0.25 through empirical experimentation with the results of the recall and precision metrics. Furthermore, since there was one car per image, the LP with the largest confidence was cropped for the recognition step. YOLOv2 network is a good model for character segmentation, as proposed in [12,14]. Moreover, for character segmentation, a CNN named CR-NET was used to segment characters from the plates and the input size was changed according to the ratio of the plates.

LP Character Recognition

In Hendry et al. [10], a sliding window single class detector for 36 classes (10 numbers, 25 letters, 1 plate) achieved high recognition accuracy and low loss values. Kessentini et al. [12], implemented two approaches for license plate recognition: the first approach was carried out as a sequence-labeling problem with the implementation of an architecture composed of Convolutional Neural Network (CNN) and recurrent neural network (RNN) with a Bidirectional Long-Short Term Memory network(BiLSTM). This architecture was trained to recognize the sequence features extracted from the LP via CNNs avoiding labeling positions of the characters of the plate and segmentation. The second approach used YOLOv2 with 125 filters to match the 20 classes (20 characters) in the Arabic context. Researchers in [13] implemented a variation of YOLOv2, modifying the input size empirically, reducing the number of max poolings up to 3 to avoid dimensionality reduction, and finally, 4 more convolutional layers were added to improve non-linearity. Another approach [14] suggested training a 2 layer CNN with 36 classes, 64 filters in each layer, and input size of 50×50 achieving a 93.76% accuracy. Laroca et al. [7] employed two CNNs for character recognition to achieve better results: for digit recognition the CR-NET without the last 4 layers and for letter recognition the unmodified CNN. Moreover, the number of filters in the last layers were changed as well, 75 and 155 layers for digit and letter recognition respectively.

YOLO Configuration

For vehicle and plate detection, Laroca et al. [7], changed the number of filters using the following formula: $Filters = (C + 5) \times 5$, being "C" the number of classes. As a result, the filters of the YOLOv2 architecture were 30 and 35 in SSIG and UFLR-ALPR datasets respectively. The threshold used to detect vehicles was 0.25 and for plates 0, because there were some cases that LP was detected with low confidence. Finally, another important aspect is the question of speed, in Putra et al. work [8] YOLOv1 was modified in order to achieve a trade-off between precision and speed. The number of convolution layers was reduced to 7 and the grid size was modified with the following experiments: 7×7, 9×9 and 11×11 grid size. The number of filters was modified as well in order to detect and classify two classes.

3 Methods

The proposed methodology is structured as follows: I) Data collection, II) Data Preparation, III) Data Processing, IV) Vehicle detection, V) Vehicle classification, VI) LP detection, VII) Character segmentation and VIII) Character recognition. The workflow of the methodology of this investigation is depicted in Fig. 1.

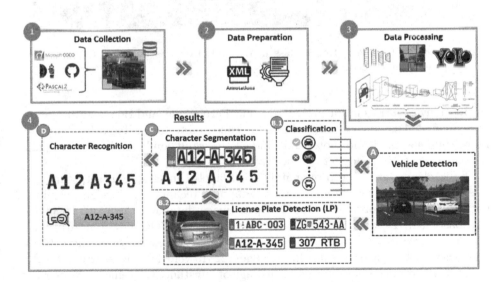

Fig. 1. Proposed methodology in this investigation

3.1 Data Collection

For this investigation, we present a new dataset, LAT-VEDA [25], that contains 8 classes: combis, moto-taxis, taxis, buses, bicycles, trucks, motorcycles, and cars.

To carry out the multi-classification of means of transportation in the Latin American context. A sample of the images of the classes depicted in our dataset is shown in Fig. 2.

Fig. 2. Sample of images of each class in LAT-VEDA dataset used in this research, each row represents a class.

In many countries in Latin America, like Peru, Chile, and Bolivia, mini-buses are called combis, and auto-rickshaws are called moto-taxis. Recently, there are more than 450 thousand moto-taxis and 31 thousand combis in Lima-Peru [22], which causes a great impact on the traffic.

Each class contains approximately 2500 labeled images. This set of images was obtained from these four sources: scrapping techniques, through Selenium with different keywords; the Google Open Image database; the VOC PASCAL database 2007 [15] and 2012 [16] and images from the COCO dataset 2014 [17]. The last three databases provided images of cars, buses, bicycles, motorbikes and trucks. After gathering all these images, 22319 vehicle images were obtained in total, where each one contains an average of 3 instances of vehicles. Moreover, the images were taken from different camera positions, lighting and contained distinct types of vehicles. The distribution of our dataset can be seen in Table 1.

Likewise, three different groups of datasets were used for the LP detection flow: patches of the front and rear of vehicles, images of the segmented plates, and a dataset of already segmented characters extracted from the license plates, some examples are shown in Figure 3. The first group consists of 1,371 patches of car images, focused on the front and rear, where the regions where the license plates

Table 1. Distribution of LAT-VEDA Dataset

Classes	Images
CAR	4000
BUS	3000
BIKE	3000
MOTORBIKE	3000
TRUCK	2750
TAXI	2289
MOTOTAXI	1280
COMBI	3000
Total	**22319**

are located are labeled; the second group consists of 455 license plates already segmented, where each character within the license plate is labeled giving a total of 3185 instances of characters; both of these datasets were extracted from [12]. And the last group consists of 35 classes of characters extracted from license plates, being classes from "A" to "Z" (25 classes) and from 0 to 9 (10 classes), with an average of 1000 images per class, giving an approximate total of 35000 images as suggested in [12].

a) Rear/Front View   b) License Plates   c) Character Patches

Fig. 3. Sample of images used for (a) LP Detection , Character (b) Segmentation and (c) Recognition

3.2   Data Preparation

Four steps were carried out in the preparation stage, which is detailed below. First, images that had been collected by scrapping during the data collection stage were manually labeled. The second thing to do was convert the COCO image annotation format, which was in *json*, to the PASCAL VOC format in *xml*. Later, relevant images were extracted from the dataset(e.g., classes such as a car, bus, bicycle, motorbike, truck). It should be clarified that these first three steps were necessary only for the vehicle dataset, due to its diversity of sources. Finally, in the fourth step, all *xml* labels of images from all datasets were converted to the YOLO annotation format. Additionally, for the evaluation of the performance in terms of FPS of the models in each of the three first stages, two videos of traffic flow in avenues and streets were used [31,32].

3.3   Data Processing, Detection and Classification

Specific CNNs were used for each ALPR stage. Therefore, the parameters were adjusted separately to improve performance for each task. The model used for vehicle and LP detection and character segmentation was YOLOv3. In the case of character recognition, a modified network based on the LeNet convolutional network was used. A CNN was trained for each of these stages: one for vehicle detection in 8 categories and the other for LP detection in the detected vehicle. As suggested by [7], our system first realizes vehicle detection and then LP detection. To use the YOLOv3 model, the number of filters in the last 3 layers must be changed. YOLOv3 uses box widths of size A (we used A = 3) to predict the bounding boxes, that come with the coordinates (x, y, w, h), and their respective class prediction precision. For training in both stages, the learning rate was 0.001, and the number of epochs for the first stage was 16000 and for the second stage, 3000. To determine the number of filters we used the equation suggested in [7,8].

Different images and their respective annotations were used for the training of the Vehicle Detection model. And for the LP detection, images of the front and rear area of the car (since these areas contain LPs) with their respective annotations were used. An example of LP Detections is depicted in Fig. 4.

a) Car's LP detection   **b)** Motorbike' s LP detection

Fig. 4. Results of our LP detection system for (a) Car and (b) Motorbike

By default, YOLOv3 returns detected objects with a confidence of 0.25 or higher. In the validation set the best threshold, 0.25, was evaluated to detect all vehicles with the lowest false positive rate possible. In the case where no vehicle is found, a negative recognition result is given. Since there are classes that are very similar such as car and taxi or motorcycle and moto-taxi, we only maintained the first detection found to avoid that the model miss-classifies it. However, for the LP detection, we used a threshold equal to 0, since there are cases where an LP is detected with low confidence (that is, for example, 0.1). Another case that arises, too, is when two plates are detected, so only the detection with greater confidence is maintained since a car only has one plate. The final result of the integration of these two stages can be seen in Fig. 5.

Fig. 5. Images of the vehicle and LP detection results

3.4 Character Segmentation

Car Front and rear images, and their respective LP Character annotations, were used as input to the YOLOv3 model trained for LP character segmentation. In the configuration of YOLOv3, we used a threshold = 0.1, since some characters have been detected with a low confidence level (0.11). The databases used for this stage had already gone through a data augmentation (4 synthetic images for each real image) process such as vertical flip, horizontal flip, rotation, and zoom. It should be noted that we used the suggested equation in [7,8] to determine the number of filters. The number of epochs used for the training process of the character segmentation model was 10000 and the learning rate was 0.001. Figure 6 shows the Character Segmentation of the LP. The proposed workflow does these classification of characters in the back-end to not generate more labels inside the bounding boxes of the frame and to also reduce the computational cost.

Fig. 6. Results of the LPs character segmentation

3.5 Character Recognition

Once the LP has been detected, we proceed to perform character recognition, we propose a CNN to detect the 35 classes (0–9, A-Z, where the letter O is detected together with the digit 0). Our CNN architecture is inspired in LeCunn et al. [21] LeNet and Dhedhi et al. [14]. Consists of 7 layers: 3 convolution layers, the first has 32 filters of 3 × 3 and the second and third has 64 filters of 3 ×3. Moreover, there are two layers of max pooling, with stride = 1 and filters of 2 × 2 and finally 2 fully-connected layers of 64 and 35 units respectively. The input image size is 100 × 75. The character dataset used had already gone through a data augmentation process by 4 (4 images more per character) with types such as vertical flip, horizontal flip, rotation, and zoom. As in the LP detection step, we used a confidence threshold = 0.1 and only consider the detection with the highest confidence, therefore we ensure that a class is predicted for each character. The number of epochs used for the training process of the character recognition model was 200 and the learning rate was 0.00001 with a momentum equal to 0.9, defined empirically. In Fig. 7 an example of Character Patches recognition can be seen.

Fig. 7. Example of the character recognition stage

3.6 Metrics

The metrics used in the investigation were the Mean Average Precision (mAP), Precision, Recall, F1-score, and Intersection over Union (IoU). They were chosen because they proved to be very useful in [7,8,14] in measuring the performance of detection and classification models. The equations for these indicators were detailed below:

The mAP is represented in Eq. 1, it can be seen that it is the integral over the precision p (r).

$$mAP = \int_0^1 p(r)dr \tag{1}$$

And precision is represented in Eq. 2.

$$Precision = \frac{TP}{(TP + FP)} \tag{2}$$

Where TP refers to the number of true positives and FP to that of false positives. The Recall metric formula is seen in Eq. 3.

$$Recall = \frac{TP}{(TP + FN)} \tag{3}$$

Where, as in the previous case, TP is true positives and FN are false negatives. The F1-score is represented by the following equation.

$$F1 = 2 \cdot \frac{precision \cdot recall}{precision + recall} \tag{4}$$

And finally, the IoU equation:

$$IoU = \frac{Area\,of\,Overlap}{Area\,of\,Union} \tag{5}$$

Where "Area of Overlap" can be understood as the area of intersection between the predicted bounding box and the real annotation, the area they share, and "Area of Union" as the union of these two areas.

4   Results and Discussion

The results regarding the YOLOv3 model for vehicle detection and its classification in each of the 8 classes can be seen in Table 2, where the precision by class obtained by this method is detailed.

Table 2. Comparing results by class of the Vehicle Detection model

Class	Precision (%)
Car	67.46
Bus	77.18
Bike	78.22
Moto	77.94
Truck	52.99
Taxi	81.92
Mototaxi	77.50
Combi	73.64
Total	71.0

In general, the classes have been classified well in comparison to the state of the art, it should be considered that due to the number of classes and their similarity between them, it is normal to achieve these levels of performance for the classes. As in the case of the truck class that obtained 52.99% precision, because most of the time this class was confused with combi or bus. Furthermore, the best-classified class was taxi, 81.92%, this is explained because all the taxi images showed the word "taxi" either on top of the vehicles or on the sides, also the majority of taxi images were of the color yellow, which allowed the detector model to classify these class better.

The corresponding results for the Vehicle detection stage and the three steps of ALPR, that is, of the proposed ALPR system, can be seen in Table 3, where results are shown regarding the metrics mAP, Accuracy, F1-score, Recall and average IoU.

The comparison made with the state of the art has been purely experimental, to give a better understanding of the results obtained. We can see that good results are obtained in each stage, with a mAP of 67.83%, 100%, 97.14% respectively, and accuracy of 97% in the last stage of character recognition, with the LP Detection stage achieving the highest performance. It must be clarified that, in Table 3, the last stage, Character Recognition, doesn't have mAP and IoU

Table 3. Results (%) of the methods used in the proposed workflow

STAGES	mAP	Precision	F1-Score	Recall	IoU
Vehicle Detection	67.83	71.0	64.0	58.0	56.46
LP Detection	100.0	100.0	100.0	100.0	84.61
LP Segmentation	97.14	100.0	100.0	100.0	83.44
Character Recognition	–	98.0	97.0	97.0	–

because, unlike the 3 other models, it's only a CNN classification model. The results of the LP detection and segmentation do not guarantee that the system is perfect and the data used has been accurate under that specific scenario.

Furthermore, the IoU within the stages is good in comparison to the state of the art, with a maximum of 84.61% in the license plate detection stage and a minimum of 56.46% in the vehicle detection stage. It is important to note that the IoU is a good indicator since it shows us how well the predicted bounding boxes are being generated respect the real image annotation, in this case, it corroborates that the vehicle license plates in the image are being correctly detected. In this way, we can verify if the model is robust when making predictions with new data, in videos for example. In the case of the Recall, it has also had good results with the highest values in the stages of Detection and Segmentation of LP with 100% and the lowest value of 58% in the Vehicle Detection stage.

Additionally, we evaluated the performance in terms of average FPS for the three proposed YOLOv3 models for each stage that is shown in Table 4. To evaluate this performance, as said in previous paragraphs, the models were tested on two videos of traffic flow collected from two different avenues of Lima Metropolitana [31,32].

Table 4. Average FPS obtained for each model in each stage

STAGES	Video 01 Avg FPS	Video 02 Avg FPS
Vehicle Detection	19.7	20.1
LP Detection	58.4	59.5
LP Segmentation	17.2	19.3

It is important to highlight that the models achieved great processing times, with a maximum of 59.6 and 58.4 avg. FPS in the LP Detection stage and a minimum of 17.2 and 19.3 avg. FPS in the Vehicle Detection stage in the two videos respectively. The achieved results are at the same level as those obtained in the average of all the ALPR pipeline in [7], 47 FPS, and [14], 76 FPS. This means that our proposed methodology can be used in real-time to analyze surveillance videos (CCTV), which was proposed at the beginning of this investigation.

In this way, it is verified that this system is applicable in a real environment and that it can be executed from the cloud and obtain good results from streaming data.

Moreover, in Fig. 8, the results of the Character Recognition model showed that our CNN achieved a 97.45 % accuracy and a loss of approximately 3% in the validation set. Additionally, the Confusion Matrix shows that our CNN did not struggle to classify correctly most of the classes, except for class 0 and Q.

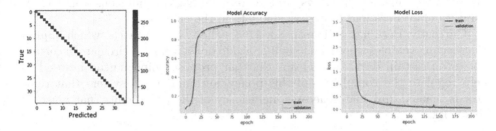

Fig. 8. Confusion matrix (35 classes), accuracy and loss of the character recognition model

5   Conclusions

In this work a methodology was proposed for Multi-class Vehicle detection, where classes from Latin-American context were employed; and an ALPR pipeline. Consequently, a workflow was shown to carry out this process, where very good results were obtained in the stages using YOLOv3, achieving a mAP of 0.68 in Vehicle Detection, a mAP of 1.0 in LP Detection, a mAP of 0.97 in LP Character Segmentation, and a precision of 0.98 using LeNet-5 in LP Character Recognition. The stage that obtained less performance was Vehicle Detection, with a final mAP of 0.68 in test data. This means that due to the nature of the dataset and how some classes are similar, like combis and buses, cars and taxis or motorcycles and moto-taxis, they can get miss-classified easily, that is why it is needed a greater amount of images from these classes.

Regarding the IoU metric, we can highlight that the stages of LP detection and segmentation obtained an optimal result of 0.85 and 0.83, meaning that the generated labels were similar to the real annotations. Furthermore, by looking at the recall we can see that 0.58 of the real vehicles, 1.0 of the real LP, 1.0 of the real characters have been correctly detected and that 0.97 of the characters have been correctly classified.

In the application that is sought in this work, it must be emphasized that it is necessary to have a trade-off between speed and precision, that is why these two metrics must be balanced (since they are correlated) so that FPS is not lost at the cost of precision or vice versa. Furthermore, it is important to note that by increasing the size of the grid, we can detect objects that are farther in a better way, so a greater number of vehicles with their respective license plates can be detected.

As observed with the average FPS obtained between 17.2 and 59.5 during the stages of the pipeline in the test videos in real environments of concurred avenues in Lima Metropolitana, YOLOv3 performs very well in real-time scenarios. This makes it ideal for this type of problematic since it will be able to process streaming data, doing the detection, segmentation, and recognition of the vehicles and LPs in real-time. In other words, it is feasible to implement our proposed pipeline into a system that receives live transmissions from CCTV cameras of avenues and processes this data in the cloud.

Currently, Peru has ordinance No. 2164, called "Pico y Placa" which implies that certain vehicles whose final number is odd or even cannot circulate in certain places on certain days. This means that our proposed pipeline can be used to help regulate the compliance of this policy, automatizing a system that right now is manual and that generates inefficiency of the police units that must do this work.

6 Future Work

In the next advance, we would like to include more license plate datasets, such as UFPR-ALPR [7], Caltech-cars [28], LP Taiwan [26] and EnglishLP [27], for the LP detection and segmentation stages, to make the license plate detection model more robust. Additionally, it would be good to collect more images of the taxi, moto-taxi, and combi classes so that the vehicle detection model can better distinguish each of these classes and have a greater classifying score.

Furthermore, it would be interesting to make a comparison between YOLOv4 and YOLOv5, when their architectures are implemented within the OpenCV library, and see their performance compared to the pipeline presented in this investigation with YOLOv3. Additionally, we would like to implement an own object detection algorithm based in these recent versions, to build an architecture designed especially to obtain better performance in the proposed workflow.

References

1. McCarthy, N.: The World's Worst Cities For Traffic Congestion [Infographic], Forbes, 5 June 2019. https://www.forbes.com/sites/niallmccarthy/2019/06/05/the-worlds-worst-cities-for-traffic-congestion-infographic/#62613e8e12bc
2. Acuña Reyes, J.: La 'industria' ilegal de colectivos invade Lima y va sobre ruedas. Perú 21, 02 November 2019. https://peru21.pe/lima/la-industria-ilegal-de-colectivos-invade-lima-y-va-sobre-ruedas-noticia/
3. Almeida, A.: Congestión vehicular y la autoridad de transporte urbano de Lima y Callao, RPP, 03 December 2018. https://rpp.pe/columnistas/alexandrealmeida/congestion-vehicular-y-la-autoridad-de-transporte-urbano-de-lima-y-callao-noticia-1166651

4. Zhang, K., Batterman, S.: Air pollution and health risks due to vehicle traffic. Sci. Total Environ. **450–451**, 307–316 (2013). https://doi.org/10.1016/j.scitotenv.2013.01.074
5. Municipalidad de Lima: Medida Pico y Placa (2019). https://aplicativos.munlima.gob.pe/pico-y-placa
6. Panamericana. LIMA: TRÁFICO VEHICULAR GENERA ESTRÉS AL 72% DE CIUDADANOS, 22 September 2018. https://panamericana.pe/locales/252432-lima-trafico-vehicular-genera-estres-72-ciudadanos
7. Laroca, R., et al.: A robust real-time automatic license plate recognition based on the YOLO detector.In: 2018 International Joint Conference on Neural Networks (IJCNN), Rio de Janeiro, pp. 1–10 (2018)
8. Putra, M., Yussof, Z., Lim, K., Salim, S.: Convolutional neural network for person and car detection using YOLO framework. J. Telecommun. Electron. Comput. Eng. **10**(1–7), 67–71 (2018)
9. Jiao, Z., Fan, H.: License plate recognition in unconstrained scenarios based on ALPR system. In: Proceedings of the 2019 International Conference on Robotics, Intelligent Control and Artificial Intelligence (RICAI 2019), 540–544. Association for Computing Machinery, New York (2019)
10. Hendry, Chen, R.-C.: A new method for license plate character detection and recognition. In: Proceedings of the 6th International Conference on Information Technology: IoT and Smart City (ICIT 2018), pp. 204–208. Association for Computing Machinery, New York, December 2018
11. Jamtsho, Y., Riyamongkol, P., Waranusast, R.: Real-time Bhutanese license plate localization using YOLO. ICT Express **6**(2), 121–124 (2020)
12. Kessentini, Y., Dhia Besbes, M., Ammar, S., Chabbouh, A.: A two-stage deep neural network for multi-norm license plate detection and recognition. Expert Syst. Appl. **136**, 159–170 (2019)
13. Silva, S.M., Rosito Jung, C.: Real-time license plate detection and recognition using deep convolutional neural networks. J. Vis. Commun. Image Represent. **71**, 10277 (2020)
14. Dhedhi, B., Datar, P., Chiplunkar, A., Jain, K., Rangarajan, A., Kundargi, J.: Automatic license plate recognition using deep learning. In: Akoglu, L., Ferrara, E., Deivamani, M., Baeza-Yates, R., Yogesh, P. (eds.) ICIIT 2018. CCIS, vol. 941, pp. 46–58. Springer, Singapore (2019). https://doi.org/10.1007/978-981-13-3582-2_4
15. The PASCAL Visual Object Classes, "PASCAL VOC 2007 Challenge". http://host.robots.ox.ac.uk/pascal/VOC/voc2007/index.html
16. The PASCAL Visual Object Classes, "PASCAL VOC 2012 Challenge". http://host.robots.ox.ac.uk/pascal/VOC/voc2012/index.html
17. COCO Dataset, "2014 validation data" (2020). https://cocodataset.org/#download
18. Buyssens, T.: License Plate Recognition Dataset (2020). https://github.com/TheophileBuy/LicensePlateRecognition
19. Redmon, J., Farhadi, A.: YOLOv3: An Incremental Improvement. University of Washington, USA (2018). https://pjreddie.com/media/files/papers/YOLOv3.pdf
20. León-Vera, L., Moreno-Vera, F.: Car monitoring system in apartments' garages by small autonomous car using deep learning. In: Lossio-Ventura, J.A., Muñante, D., Alatrista-Salas, H. (eds.) SIMBig 2018. CCIS, vol. 898, pp. 174–181. Springer, Cham (2019). https://doi.org/10.1007/978-3-030-11680-4_18
21. LeCun, Y., Bottou, L., Bengio, Y., Haffner, P.: Gradient-based learning applied to document recognition. Proc. IEEE **86**, 2278–2324 (1998)

22. Más de 31 mil combis y micros saturan las pistas de Lima (2019). https://peru21. pe/lima/31-mil-combis-micros-saturan-pistas-lima-121691-noticia/?ref=p21r

23. Bravo Medina, P.: Estas son las ciudades con peor tráfico; hay 4 latinoamericanas en el top 10, CNN, 14 February 2019. https://cnnespanol.cnn.com/2019/02/14/estas-son-las-ciudades-con-peor-congestion-vehicular-y-movilidad-hay-4-latinoamericanas-en-el-top-10/

24. Barría, C.: Cuál es la ciudad con el peor tráfico vehicular de América Latina (y cómo podría mejorar su problema), BBC, 8 March 2019. https://www.bbc.com/mundo/noticias-47473793

25. Montenegro-Montori, P., Camasca-Huamán, J., Acosta, G., Gave, K.: Latin-American Vehicle Dataset (LAT-VEDA), May 2020. https://bit.ly/2DnuAku

26. Hsu, G.S., Chen, J.C., Chung, Y.Z.: Application-oriented license plate recognition. IEEE Trans. Veh. Technol. 62(2), 552–561 (2013)

27. Srebric, V.: EnglishLP database (2003). http://www.zemris.fer.hr/projects/LicensePlates/english/baza_slika.zip

28. Weber, M.: Caltech Cars dataset (1999). http://www.vision.caltech.edu/Image_Datasets/cars_markus/cars_markus.tar

29. Ren, S., He, K., Girshick, R., Sun, J.: Faster R-CNN: towards real-time object detection with region proposal networks. IEEE Trans. Pattern Anal. Mach. Intell. 39(6), 1137–1149 (2017). https://doi.org/10.1109/TPAMI.2016.2577031

30. Liu, W., et al.: SSD: single shot MultiBox detector. In: Leibe, B., Matas, J., Sebe, N., Welling, M. (eds.) ECCV 2016. LNCS, vol. 9905, pp. 21–37. Springer, Cham (2016). https://doi.org/10.1007/978-3-319-46448-0_2

31. Castillo, R.: Lima, Perú. Combis, colectivos y caos en la Vía de Evitamiento - Lima, 2 June 2012. https://www.youtube.com/watch?v=QLUVVY2FQT8&t=105s. Accessed 18 July 2020

32. ATV Noticias, Perú: Mototaxis formales pueden circular durante cuarentena por COVID-19, 12 May 2020. https://www.youtube.com/watch?v=r1XANkkSDSQ. Accessed 18 July 2020

Static Summarization Using Pearson's Coefficient and Transfer Learning for Anomaly Detection for Surveillance Videos

Steve Willian Chancolla-Neira, César Ernesto Salinas-Lozano,
and Willy Ugarte[✉]

University of Applied Sciences (UPC), Lima, Peru
{u201422771,u201420396}@upc.edu.pe, willy.ugarte@upc.pe

Abstract. Data storage has been a problem as technology advances, there are more devices capable of capturing images, sounds, videos, etc. On the security side, many people choose to use security cameras that are available 24 h a day to capture anomalous events and maintain the security of the area, however, storing all captured videos generates high costs, as well as the prolonged analysis that this type of videos implies. For this reason, we propose a method that allows selecting only the important events captured by a video surveillance camera and then classifying them among the types of most constant criminal acts in Peru.

Keywords: Summarization · Video classification · Convolutional neuronal networks · Image processing · Surveillance videos

1 Introduction

Images and videos have become an important ubiquitous information resource, this due to the facilities provided by current technologies such as the internet, surveillance cameras and mobile devices that are capable of capture this kind of data, which means that over the time they will generate countless amount of data that subsequently will be store.

The main issue of surveillance videos is that most of their parts are irrelevant or redundant, since no major events occur most of the time, given their anomalous behavior. On one hand, storing all this information requires a lot of storage capacity for useless information takes most of the space. On the other hand, analyzing long videos requires a huge effort in concentration and quantity of personnel, thus even implying more costs.

For instance, an investigation carried out by Seagate (one of the major producers of storage devices) indicates that a surveillance camera can store, daily at 30 fps and 1280×1024 resolution, up to 125 GB (thus 1 TB in 8 days)[1]. This

---

[1] Seagate - https://bit.ly/31wPnfn.

© Springer Nature Switzerland AG 2021
J. A. Lossio-Ventura et al. (Eds.): SIMBig 2020, CCIS 1410, pp. 279–290, 2021.
https://doi.org/10.1007/978-3-030-76228-5_20

problem has been tackled by various works that extract relevant information from this kind of videos through search and summarization techniques. For example, Wu *et al.* used a clustering algorithm based on the insights from high density peaks search [19]. Song *et al.* used a disjoint max-coverage algorithm to summarize surveillance videos with maximum coverage of interested events and minimum number of frames [13].

Moreover, the effort and costs involved in a surveillance video analysis led to the development of different methods to classify events in surveillance videos, making video analysis less arduous, for instance, Sultani *et al.* used a multiple instance learning to detect normal and abnormal event [14].

In this paper, we propose a static method for surveillance video summarization with frame checking based on Pearson's coefficient, that check all frames from this kind of videos looking for sudden or substantial changes. Additionally, we develop a surveillance video classification using labeled training videos and Convolutional Neuronal Networks (CNN). Specifically, we aim to detect anomalies such as robbery, shooting and vandalism, feature in the magazine "Lima como Vamos"[2] and reports from INEI[3].

The rest of the paper is organized as follows. Section 2 introduces the notion of summarization and video classification, defining terms highly related to these topics. Section 3 shows our contribution divided in two points, one in the video summarization on the other hand surveillance video classification. Section 4 synthesizes the related works made by other authors. Section 5 describes the experimental study of summarization and video classification, comparing both methods with other ones. Section 6 the results obtained from each applied method are compared and discussed.

2   Background

Now, we will describe the theoretical foundations necessary for the development of our proposal, both in terms of summarization and event classification in surveillance videos.

Definition 1 (Summarization [15]). *It is the mechanism to represent or generate a short video, either through a sequence of still or moving images. In this way, the most important information is concentrated in a short time and the search is optimized if there is an extensive database.*

In [15], the authors group the summarization techniques in two types:

- *Key frame summarization*: this is a summary of still images or a collection of outstanding images extracted from the underlying video source.
- *Skimmed Video Summarization*: consists of a collection of video segments (and their corresponding audio) extracted from a video of greater amplitude.

---

[2] Magazine "Lima como Vamos" - https://bit.ly/394n6i3.
[3] INEI - https://www.inei.gob.pe/.

Definition 2 (Pearson's correlation coefficient [2]**).** *It is the value that measures the trend between two changing variables; that is, it evaluates the relationship between two numerical variables, being able to take values between* -1 *and 1, where 0 indicates no correlation, 1 complete positive correlation and* -1 *complete negative correlation. The correlation coefficient equation is defined by:*

$$r = \frac{\sum_{i=1}^{n} \left(\frac{x_i - \bar{x}}{s_x} \right) \left(\frac{y_i - \bar{y}}{s_y} \right)}{n - 1} \tag{1}$$

Being (x, y) a set of coordinates and r the Pearson's correlation coefficient, which is represented by the sum of the products of standardized deviations.

Deep Learning [8] is defined as the approach to Artificial Intelligence (AI) that allows computers to learn from experience and thus understand a real-world task in terms of a hierarchy of concepts.

Definition 3 (Convolutional Neural Networks (CNN) [8]**).** *It is a type of neural network that allows data processing with a grid-like topology. The term convolutional is because it employs a linear operation called convolution in each of its layers.*

Definition 4 (Transfer Learning [8]**).** *It is the use of a previously defined setting (i.e. P1 distribution) for the improvement of generalization in another setting (i.e. P2 distribution) using less data and training time. In this way, it can be assumed that the distribution being trained will perform two or more different tasks, but that many of the factors that explain the variations in P1 are relevant to the variations that must be captured in P2.*

3 Main Contribution

In this section we describe the two main phases of our work in detail.

3.1 Summarization

An algorithm was developed that has as input a video with .mp4 as a format and output another one with shorter duration without altering the resolution, capturing the important events that occurred in the incoming video. This method is based on the static summary, and consists of iterating each frame of a video, checking the difference between them through Pearson's correlation (see Definition 2).

Our main purpose in choosing this technique is to address the subjectivity in the summary of the videos, not letting any human expert judge during this process, since the frames are chosen under a remarkable difference between them based on a certain threshold. In addition, we achieve a linear temporal complexity by iterating the images (frame by frame at a given speed), so the

---

Algorithm 1: Summarization Algorithm

    Input   : V: input video, ρ: frame rate
    Output: *output*: array of coefficients or keyframe;
1 *firstFrame* ← *false*;
2 f_p ← 0; **// init key frame**
3 $\gamma = \min(r_1, \ldots, r_n) + \left(\frac{mean(r_1,\ldots,r_n) - \min(r_1,\ldots,r_n)}{2} \right)$;
4 *output* ← [ ]; **// output result**
5 **foreach** *frame f in V at ρ rate* **do**
6   **if** *not firstFrame or PearsonCorrelation(f_p.flat, f.flat) < γ* **then**
7 f_p ← f; **// new key frame**
8   *output*.insert(f_p); **// add pivot to the output**
9   **end**
10   *firstFrame* ← *true*;
11 **end**
12 **return** *output*;

---

computational time depends on the length of the video. The method used is divided into two main stages:

Algorithm 1 shows the summarization process of videos by using the Pearson coefficient. The input is the video (as a list of frames), the rate of frames ρ (i.e. the amount of frames that will be extracted per second in the video) and a Pearson threshold γ, for summarizing the video by means of key frames, in case a value is not given it will generate the array of coefficients to generate the threshold using the equation (line 3). In Algorithm 1, it is important to indicate that the threshold γ is needed (line 3) to summarize the video, because when comparing the frames by the Pearson coefficient (line 5), if the value is lower it will take that frame as a key frame and this will be the new frame$_i$ (lines 7–8) which will be compared with the subsequent ones.

3.2 Classification

Usually humans are able to recognize anomalous (human) actions just by directly watching (surveillance) videos. Various methods have been proposed for a surveillance video classification [3,5], in the best of our knowledge, we have noticed that most of the works in the literature make classifications in two ways: i) a multi label case and ii) a binary case. However, most authors related to this approach tend to choose the second one, which motivates us to understand those decisions and to find possible explanations. The proposal begins with the selection and cleaning of the videos of 4 specific classes, then for the binary case three are joined and thus form the normal and abnormal classes. Then they are subdivided into training, testing and validation, finally for both cases, the data passes through the chosen model with its respective configuration to obtain classifications of events in videos,the overview of both approaches are shown in Fig. 1. The process is explained in more detail in Sect. 5.

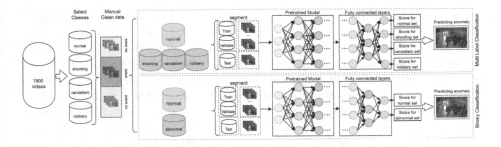

Fig. 1. Surveillance video classification

4   Related Work

Now, we briefly discuss some different techniques for this topic.

4.1   Video Summarization

In one hand, as it was mentioned before, there are many methods to develop a video summarization, for example and one of the most popular technique shown in [19] solves this as a clustering problem inspired in the density peaks, grouping up frames by similar properties but detecting highly relevant frames and generate representatives clustering.

On the other hand, in [6], the authors propose to use clustering to face the problem, but in a different way specifically a graph-based clustering, basically consist in make a feature selection for each frame, then make a dissimilarity measure to compare two frames and group them in clusters according to some found properties and finally with the weights obtained make a hierarchy map in order to partition it and get the key frames.

Another very common technique is CNN [10], mainly used to learn the notion of importance using only video-level annotation, start with performing a forward pass on the video to get scores over the video and finally use a spatio-temporal via back propagation to get the highest score and take that as a key frame.

4.2   Classification of Anomalous Events

In this section we will discuss previous work based on different feature extraction and deep learning algorithms for the detection and classification of abnormal behavior in videos captured by video surveillance cameras. As mentioned in [12,14,21], the detection of abnormalities as one of the most complex challenges within the field of computer vision, this is due to factors such as uneven illumination, object movement, low video resolution and the definition of abnormality, which is mostly vague and context dependent, as described in [12].

We can comment that many of the works analyzed are focused on the detection of anomalies in crowded areas [1,4,9,12,21]. In the case of [9], a combination of a convolutional autoconder and a U-Net with jump connections is applied to design a CNN capable of predicting the optical flow, to determine the association between the appearance of a scene and its movements. While [4], proposes a framework that combines craft movement characteristics and CNN based appearance characteristics for anomaly detection, using a foreground object location strategy and a feature descriptor called SL-MHOF, which describes the statistics of local motion information, and then use a GMM classifier to predict abnormal scores. On the other hand, [21] proposes a neural network specialized in anomaly detection called AnomalyNet based on two subnetworks, the first one consists of a motion fusion block and a feature transfer block, and the second one is an optimization network that achieves scattered representation and dictionary learning using an LSTM network.

Two works using LSTM were also analyzed [18, 20], however, they are focused on the classification of actions, for which they train their model with the UCF101 and HMDB-51 databases. In the case of [18], it applies a method for the recognition of saliences, this way it generates a video that later is entered to a 3D CNN with LSTM, followed by a pooling layer of time series and a Softmax layer to predict activities. While [20], they present a modification of the GoogleLeNet architecture, replacing the convolutional layers with RCNN layers and the fully connected layers with RNN layers, in this way they seek to extract the spatial characteristics of the videos. It is important to note that they use half of the parameters learned from an ImageNet model.

Another work that uses pre-trained data from Imagenet is [1], in this case the authors apply transfer learning in the VGG16 architecture to learn the spatial appearance characteristics, generating a binary classifier. We consider the previous work as one of the bases of our approach, however, we will use a modification of the dataset presented in [14] that consists of 1900 videos with 13 different anomalies that are used as classes, which we believe is widely more challenging, since, non-binary models with weak labels can be trained. It is important to mention that in [14], they train a convolutional neural network with 3-dimensional C3D for the extraction of characteristics that later feeds it with a multiple instance tagging to determine if the video has an anomaly or not.

5   Experiments

Now, the experiments were carried out in two parts: first, *surveillance video summarization* and then *classification events on these surveillance videos*.

5.1   Experimental Protocol

For the first part, the purpose is to fine-tune the input parameters of the summarization and comparing with others methods, therefore generating a dataset. For the second part, the dataset is selected and divided into labeled classes in order to classify the events in the videos. For all experiments, we use Google Colab

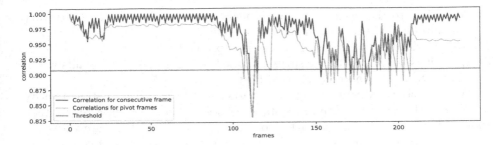

Fig. 2. Summarization technique proposed (Color figure online)

pro, which gives us a cloud server for data preprocessing and model training. This platform gives us a T4 GPU and 25 GB of RAM.

Summarization: Tests were carried out using the VSUMM [7] database which consists of 50 videos. However, in this case we will only use the first 10 videos, which are segments of the videos "The Great Web of Water" and "A New Horizon", these have a total of 240 and 763 s of duration with an average of 2,381 and 2,860 frames, respectively. It is important to mention that the videos have a resolution of 352 × 240 pixels and have 30 frames per second.

Additionally, VSUMM [7] contains 5 manual summarizations per video, these have been made by users in a random order, these summarizations are called ground truth (GT). The comparison with our summarizer is made by varying the frequency of frames per second (i.e. two, one and three frames every second). It is worth mentioning that *useless frames* were not taken into consideration, whether they are transitions, black frames or video errors.

As toy example, we take the first video. In Fig. 2, the blue line is the comparison of consecutive frames for the calculation of the threshold which is represented by the red line. Then, the initial frame is taken as the pivot and it is compared with the subsequent ones until detecting a substantial change, where the Pearson coefficient is less than the threshold, this frame is taken as the new pivot for new comparisons, this process is represented by the green line. Therefore, frames where the blue (resp. green) line are under the red line are the most relevant for summarization according to the consecutive comparison of (resp. pivot) frames.

For further comparison, we implement another clustering-based summarizer inspired by [19], grouping clusters from the histogram of the colors of each frame.

Classification: We use the UCF-Crime dataset[4], but after a cleaning and cutting process, in an effort to reduce useless content and making it more substantial for the training of a model. It is composed of 128 h of video with 13 realistic anomalies including *Abuse, Arrest, Arson, Assault, Road Accident, Burglary, Explosion, Fighting, Robbery, Shooting, Stealing, Shoplifting and Vandalism*. However, we made two subsets of databases from this, first one made for the multi labeled experiment and the second one for a binary experiment.

---

[4] https://www.crcv.ucf.edu/projects/real-world/.

According to the magazine "Lima como Vamos"[5], which is an observatory that monitors and evaluates changes in the quality of life of the inhabitants of Metropolitan Lima and Callao. In this report presents the most serious problems of these cities, according to the surveys carried out with their inhabitants which are robbery, vandalism and armed robbery.

Another source where we got information was INEI[6], it's a national entity of Peru in charge of the country's statistics and information, in a report they show that the main criminal acts from different cities of Peru are the same exposed in the magazine mentioned before. Therefore, we choose 4 classes from the UCF-Dataset Robbery, Vandalism, Shooting and Normal. These are for the first subset that is composed of 280 videos, 70 in each class. And for second one, it's composed of 210 videos of abnormal class and 143 videos for normal class.

The architecture of MobileNet v2 is made up of bottleneck blocks and with expansion rate of 6 represented by the column t, c is the number of inputs and finally s tells us whether the first repetition of a block used a stride of 2 for the down sampling process [11]. We used the transfer learning technique, in order to reduce the training time, we chose to use the MobileNet network pre-trained with the imagenet weights, and we evaluated the performances of each one varying the parameters of the learning rate. This is applied to each subset of the data. We choose 4 metrics to evaluate the results: loss, accuracy, recall and precision.

5.2 Results

Summarization: In Table 1, we see the average precision obtained from the method by cluster and our proposal when summarizing each of the videos and being compared against the ground truth (GT) (3 kinds of frequency for the videos are used). In addition, compared to the GT, we noticed that our method with a configuration of .5, that is 2 frames per second, obtained more matches compared to the number of frames of each GT, as we can see in Fig. 3a.

Finally, when we carried out the summarization with surveillance camera videos we obtained an average of 75.21 % in detection of substantial events compared to the cluster method that obtained 46.42 %. This shows that our method

Table 1. Precision for summarization method using VSUMM dataset

Method		Average Precision
Our proposal	2 frames × second	.6277
	1 frame × second	.6199
	1 frame × 3 s	**.6349**
Clustering-based method [19]		.5925

---

[5] "Lima como Vamos" - https://bit.ly/2BAdj78.
[6] INEI - https://bit.ly/39F7FgD.

achieves better results when detecting a greater variation between frames. In Fig. 3 we observe some frames obtained from our method, we can notice that they represent the video and describe what happened in it in a clear way.

(a) Results of our proposal for the 24th video of VSUMM database.

(b) Result of cluster and proposed method for the 2th surveillance video.

Fig. 3. Sample video summarization results.

Classification: Our first experiment consists in evaluating different models with different parameters in our multilabel dataset. Table 2 shows the results for model accuracy by learn rate and optimizer. In Table 2(a), we can see that average accuracy per model in order from low to high is VGG16, Inception v3 and MobileNet v2. This last getting values above 55% in very case, being the highest 61%, while VGG16 is 52% and Inception v3 56.5% respectively. Additionally, Table 2(b) shows the accuracy using a binary label dataset and MobileNet v2 as pre trained model, getting values above 81%, being the highest 91%.

Table 2. Analysis of accuracy results

Learning Rate	VGG16		Inception v3		MobileNet V2		MobileNet V2	
	Adam	SGD	Adam	SGD	Adam	SGD	Adam	SGD
.001	.51978	.49518	.56577	.56256	.61069	.60748	.81035	.89644
.05	.48342	.52513	.45240	.54866	.55401	.58823	.91391	.90160
.005	.49090	.49839	.54438	.55828	.55080	.61069	.83301	.88220
	(a) Multilabel Dataset						(b) Binary Dataset	

Values are much higher for binary labels, enforcing our remark that most of works [6,9,10,12,14,19] treat binary datasets, furthermore multilabel datasets do not focus in any of the classes, unlike binary labels that can be seen as one class against the other ones. Finally, Fig. 4 and 5 show the precision, recall and loss in each one for each learn rate tested with SGD optimizer. Precision (.97) and Recall (.98) have high values for 100 epochs, while loss is reduced (.03).

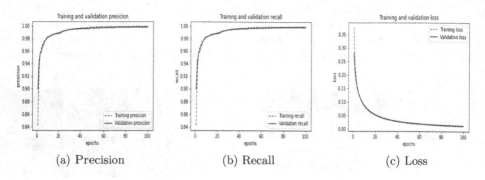

(a) Precision   (b) Recall   (c) Loss

Fig. 4. Results of MobileNet v2 with binary Dataset and learn rate .001

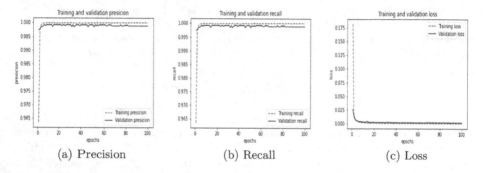

(a) Precision   (b) Recall   (c) Loss

Fig. 5. Results of MobileNet v2 with binary Dataset and learn rate .005

6   Conclusion

In this work we propose a method to summarize videos, showing better performance than other methods, mainly we do not require various parameters (e.g., a number of clusters as in the case of clustering-based method). Experiments with real surveillance videos showed that we obtained essential frames of the events that the other method (see Fig. 3). Also, we conclude that it is easier for a model to differentiate a video as normal or abnormal as opposed to many classes, because the differences in the actions captured by surveillance cameras are not very noticeable. Compared to a classification of animals, flowers, fruits and others, there are defined and notable features, in addition an abnormal event detection by class must be learned from the environment and situation in which the event occurs to categorize it completely, making this a harder and complex job, therefore grouping the events in two are less difficult to categorize correctly and this is evidenced in the results obtained. Furthermore, it might be possible to use softness into the threshold choice [16, 17].

References

1. Bansod, S.D., Nandedkar, A.V.: Transfer learning for video anomaly detection. J. Intell. Fuzzy Syst. **36**, 1967–1975 (2019)
2. Boslaugh, S., Watters, P.A.: Statistics in a Nutshell. O'Reilly, Farnham (2008)
3. Chen, X., Xu, X., Yang, Y., Wu, H., Tang, J., Zhao, J.: Augmented ship tracking under occlusion conditions from maritime surveillance videos. IEEE Access **8**, 42884–42897 (2020)
4. Chen, Z., Li, W., Fei, C., Liu, B., Yu, N.: Robust anomaly detection via fusion of appearance and motion features. In: VCIP (2018)
5. Cheng, Y., et al.: An anomaly comprehension neural network for surveillance videos on terminal devices. In: DATE (2020)
6. dos Santos Belo, L., Caetano Jr., C.A., Gonçalves do Patrocínio Jr., Z.K., Ferzoli Guimarães, S.J.: Summarizing video sequence using a graph-based hierarchical approach. Neurocomputing. **173**, 1001–1016 (2016)
7. Fontes de Avila, S.E., Brandão Lopes, A.P., da Luz Jr., A., de Albuquerque Araújo, A.: VSUMM: a mechanism designed to produce static video summaries and a novel evaluation method. Pattern Recognit. Lett. **32**, 56–68 (2011)
8. Goodfellow, I.J., Bengio, Y., Courville, A.C.: Deep Learning. Adaptive Computation and Machine Learning, MIT Press, Cambridge (2016)
9. Nguyen, T., Meunier, J.: Anomaly detection in video sequence with appearance-motion correspondence. In: ICCV (2019)
10. Panda, R., Das, A., Wu, Z., Ernst, J., Roy-Chowdhury, A.K.: Weakly supervised summarization of web videos. In: ICCV (2017)
11. Sandler, M., Howard, A.G., Zhu, M., Zhmoginov, A., Chen, L.: MobileNetV2: inverted residuals and linear bottlenecks. In: CVPR (2018)
12. Singh, K., Rajora, S., Vishwakarma, D.K., Tripathi, G., Kumar, S., Walia, G.S.: Crowd anomaly detection using aggregation of ensembles of fine-tuned convnets. Neurocomputing **371**, 188–198 (2020)
13. Song, X., Sun, L., Lei, J., Tao, D., Yuan, G., Song, M.: Event-based large scale surveillance video summarization. Neurocomputing **187**, 66–74 (2016)
14. Sultani, W., Chen, C., Shah, M.: Real-world anomaly detection in surveillance videos. In: CVPR (2018)
15. Truong, B.T., Venkatesh, S.: Video abstraction: a systematic review and classification. ACM Trans. Multimedia Comput. Commu. Appl. **3**, 3 (2007)
16. Ugarte, W., Boizumault, P., Loudni, S., Crémilleux, B.: Soft threshold constraints for pattern mining. In: Ganascia, J.-G., Lenca, P., Petit, J.-M. (eds.) DS 2012. LNCS (LNAI), vol. 7569, pp. 313–327. Springer, Heidelberg (2012). https://doi.org/10.1007/978-3-642-33492-4_25
17. Ugarte, W., Boizumault, P., Loudni, S., Crémilleux, B., Lepailleur, A.: Soft constraints for pattern mining. J. Intell. Inf. Syst. **44**(2), 193–221 (2015). https://doi.org/10.1007/s10844-013-0281-4
18. Wang, X., Gao, L., Song, J., Shen, H.T.: Beyond frame-level CNN: saliency-aware 3-D CNN with LSTM for video action recognition. IEEE Signal Process. Lett. **24**, 510–514 (2017)

19. Wu, J., Zhong, S., Jiang, J., Yang, Y.: A novel clustering method for static video summarization. Multimedia Tools Appl. **76**, 9625–9641 (2017)
20. Xu, Z., Hu, J., Deng, W.: Recurrent convolutional neural network for video classification. In: ICME (2016)
21. Zhou, J.T., Du, J., Zhu, H., Peng, X., Liu, Y., Goh, R.S.M.: AnomalyNet: an anomaly detection network for video surveillance. IEEE Trans. Inf. Forensics Secur. **14**, 2537–2550 (2019)

Humpback Whale's Flukes Segmentation Algorithms

Andrea Castro Cabanillas[✉] and Victor H. Ayma

Universidad de Lima, Santiago de Surco, Lima, Peru
20160315@aloe.ulima.edu.pe, vayma@ulima.edu.pe

Abstract. Photo-identification consists of the analysis of photographs to identify cetacean individuals based on unique characteristics that each specimen of the same species exhibits. The use of this tool allows us to carry out studies about the size of its population and migratory routes by comparing catalogues. However, the number of images that make up these catalogues is large, so the manual execution of photo-identification takes considerable time. On the other hand, many of the methods proposed for the automation of this task coincide in proposing a segmentation phase to ensure that the identification algorithm takes into account only the characteristics of the cetacean and not the background. Thus, in this work, we compared four segmentation techniques from the image processing and computer vision fields to isolate whales' flukes. We evaluated the Otsu (OTSU), Chan Vese (CV), Fully Convolutional Networks (FCN), and Pyramid Scene Parsing Network (PSP) algorithms in a subset of images from the Humpback Whale Identification Challenge dataset. The experimental results show that the FCN and PSP algorithms performed similarly and were superior to the OTSU and CV segmentation techniques.

Keywords: Artificial intelligence · Image segmentation · Computer vision · Cetology · Photo-identification

1 Introduction

Photo-identification refers to the analysis of the photographs for recognizing cetacean individuals. It focuses on the comparison of unique visual characteristics on the cetacean individuals, such as the pigmentation, scars, and notches of its dorsal fins or flukes, or the different patterns of callosities on its heads. For marine biologists, photo-identification is an important tool that contributes to wildlife studies, for example, it assists in the estimation of the size of a cetacean population by counting the unique individuals sighted in an area during different seasons (Barlow et al. 2011; Felix et al. 2011); it is also essential for assessing the migration patterns of cetacean populations, which can be determined by identifying cetacean individuals seen in different locations (Titova et al. 2018); finally, using photo-identification, marine biologists can keep a record of the population group structure, as well as the fidelity to a geographical point (Ballance 2018).

© Springer Nature Switzerland AG 2021
J. A. Lossio-Ventura et al. (Eds.): SIMBig 2020, CCIS 1410, pp. 291–303, 2021.
https://doi.org/10.1007/978-3-030-76228-5_21

Among the species of cetaceans that frequent peruvian seas is the humpback whale. These marine mammals can reach a length of 16 m and weigh 30 tons. They are known for making the most extensive migration with distances of between 6 and 8 thousand kilometers (Ruiz 2016) and for delighting with their acrobatics in the air during their journey; which contribute to the economy of northern Peru. According to Barrientos (2019), 45000 tourists arrived to participate in the humpback whale watching activity by the end of 2019. Therefore, there are a large number of studies based on photo-identification on a group of humpback whales that arrive in Peru called Stock G (Felix et al. 2011; Ruiz 2016); this studies have determined that this population arrives during the winter to the north of Peru, to reproduce and give birth to their calves, and leaves from Antarctica where they feed during the summer (Ruiz 2016); furthermore, it has been estimated that Stock G is composed of 6504 individuals (Felix et al. 2011); however, it has been estimated a low population growth rate of 2.31% per year in a subgroup of the Stock G (Monnahan et al. 2019), raising the concerns on monitoring the Stock G population.

Traditionally, photo-identification is done manually; however, this manual process demands considerable effort as it involves the review of extensive image catalogues (Weideman et al. 2017; Maglietta et al. 2018), which gets affected by the mammals' poses, the variant viewpoints and the partial occlusions caused by sea factors (Bouma et al. 2018). These problems have motivated the proposal of a variety of methods aiming at the automation of photo-identification in different cetacean species (Weideman et al. 2017; Hsu et al. 2018), but with limited results.

However, recent studies have shown that sea-related information removal might improve photo-identification performance. For example, Reno et al. (2018) is aimed at constructing a method able to identify Risso's dolphins. They proposed the use of the Otsu image processing algorithm to segment the fins before executing an Speeded Up Robust Features (SURF) based identification algorithm; finally, Reno et al. (2018) reached 89% of accuracy in the identification. Similarly, Maglietta et al. (2018) proposed to combine Otsu's algorithm with morphological filters to enable the extraction of distinctive characteristics from the Risso's dolphin; then, they used Scale Invariant Feature Transform (SIFT) and RUSBoost algorithms to classify individuals, achieving 84% of accuracy in this identification.

Meanwhile, Weideman et al. (2017) used a Fully Convolutional Neural Network (FCN) to segment and extract the fin edge of humpback whales and dolphins, aiming at compare individuals, this method obtained a 89% of accuracy in the identification. Hsu et al. (2018) constructed a hybrid segmentation algorithm based on four prominence methods for segmenting dolphin dorsal fins; this algorithm reached a F1-score of 0.81 in the segmentation. Most recently, Pollicelli et al. (2020) conducted a comparison between multifractal spectrum with Support Vector Machine and Mask R-CNN to detect the region of interest (RoI) in dolphin fins images for photo-identification, the last method obtained a better performance with a mean IoU of 0.79.

Motivated by the previous studies, we propose to compare the performance of four different segmentation techniques in the task of segmentation of humpback whale's flukes so we can use the algorithm with the best results as a previous phase of photo-identification in the future.

The remaining of this paper is organized as follows: Sect. 2 will describe four segmentation techniques to be evaluated; Sect. 3 presents the methodology followed to carry out the evaluation, as well as details regarding the implementation of each algorithm; finally, Sect. 4 explains the results obtained and Sect. 5 shows our conclusions.

2   Background

According to Gonzales and Woods (2018) segmentation is a process where an image is partitioned into regions or objects. For the segmentation to be complete, each pixel must belong to a region; furthermore, the regions must be connected but not overlapping each other; finally, each region must contain pixels that have characteristics in common.

The field of image processing proposes different techniques that manipulate the original image with the purpose of producing an alternative representation. Segmentation methods in this field may be based on discontinuity, when it uses edge detection, or similarity, where the image is partitioned into regions that are similar according to certain criteria (Gonzales and Woods, 2018). On the other hand, computer vision sees segmentation as a pixel level classification task called semantic segmentation (Li et al. 2018), these algorithms aim to predict a tag for each pixel that corresponds to the class of the object it belongs to.

In this section, we explain four image segmentation algorithms for their comparison in the task of humpback whale's flukes segmentation. Formally, we will describe the Otsu and Chan Vese segmentation techniques, which belong to the image processing field, as well as the Fully Convolutional Neural Network (FCN) and Pyramid Scene Parsing Network (PSPNet) that belong to the computer vision field.

2.1   Otsu

Otsu (Otsu 1979) is a similarity-based segmentation technique, in which the main idea is to find a threshold value, in the range of [0, 255], that will create a binary image, separating the object of interest from the background. To this end, Otsu's algorithm seeks to find the threshold value (t) that minimizes the sum of intra-class weighted variances, while maximizing the inter-class variance, wrapping the image segmentation task as an optimization problem.

Formally, given a histogram of the image pixels intensities, the Otsu's objective function can be defined as follows:

$$\sigma^2 = \sigma_w^2(t) + q_1(t)[1 - q_1(t)][\mu_1(t) - \mu_2(t)]^2 \tag{1}$$

where, the first term, $\sigma_w^2(t)$, is the weighted intra-class variance and the second term, $q_1(t)[1 - q_1(t)][\mu_1(t) - \mu_2(t)]^2$, represents the weighted inter-class variance, whereas $q_1(t)$ is the total probability that each pixel belongs to class 1, and $\mu_1(t)$ and $\mu_2(t)$ correspond to the mean of the pixel intensity values in classes 1 and 2, respectively.

2.2   Chan Vese

The Chan Vese algorithm (Chan and Vese 1999) is a discontinuity-based segmentation algorithm that uses active contours curves evolutionary techniques to find a curve that encompasses the object even when its boundaries do not have well-defined gradients; that is, when its edges do not necessarily constitute sudden changes in pixel intensity. To this end, Chan & Vese proposed to find the values of the constants c_1 and c_2 that minimizes the energy function $F(\cdot)$ in the inside and the outside of the curve C in a iterative process, formally:

$$F(C, c1, c2) = \mu.length(C) + v.area(insideC)$$

$$\lambda_1 \int_{inside(C)} (u_0 - c_1)^2 dxdy + \lambda_2 \int_{outside(C)} (u_0 - c_2)^2 dxdy \qquad (2)$$

where the μ and v are regularization parameters that control the length and direction of the fitting curve towards the object, respectively; whereas μ_0 represent the average pixels' intensities in the image and λ_i is a weight parameter for pixels belonging to class i, the class with lower weight will have larger range of pixel values than the other.

The authors recommend the set the values of v equal to 0 and to establish $\lambda_1 = \lambda_2$ because the range of pixel intensity values can be shared between both classes.

2.3   Fully Convolutional Neural Network

The Fully Convolutional Network (FCN), proposed by Long et al. (2015), attempts to make a pixel-wise prediction. It replaces the last dense layer of the convolutional network with another convolutional layer, so that a map of features is returned. Then, a deconvolution layer with stride of 32 is used to expand the output to the size of the input image.

Long et al. (2015) comments that one of the main problems in transforming a CNN architecture into a FCN is that the deeper the network becomes, the more semantic information is obtained, but spatial information is lost, which is essential for segmentation. For this reason, FCN propose to combine the spatial information of the first layers with the semantic information learned by the last layers through skip connections in order to make more accurate predictions. FCN-32s, FCN-16s and FCN-8s are constructed upsampling and fusing the results of several pooling layers as Fig. 1 shows.

This author transforms the AlexNet, VGG16, GoogLeNet architectures into FCN-32s, FCN-16s and FCN-8s and tests them in the PASCAL VOC 2012

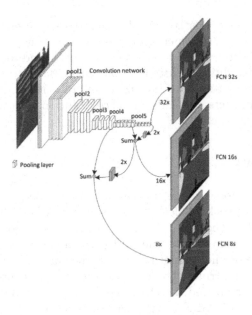

Fig. 1. Fully Convolutional Neural Network' architecture. (Liu et al. 2018)

dataset. The FCN-8s with VGG16 obtains the best results with an average IoU of 62.2%

2.4   Pyramid Scene Parsing Network

The Pyramid Scene Parsing Network (PSP), introduced by Zhao et al. (2017), is a semantic segmentation algorithm that aims to solve the loss of spatial information from convolution operation in common convolutional network architectures, such as the FCN (Fig. 2).

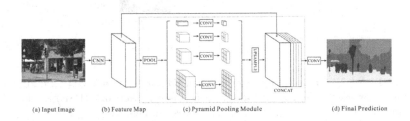

Fig. 2. Architecture of Pyramid Scene Parsing Network (PSP) (Zhao et al. 2017)

Given an input image, the PSPNet extracts a map of features using a convolutional network, such as ResNet; however, it modifies the last layers by adding dilated convolutions. Dilated convolutions are similar to traditional convolutions, but they add zeros every other kernel value, in order to preserve the spatial information required for better segmentation results. Later, it performs the average pooling operation for the whole initial feature matrix and for each 2×2, 3×3 and 6×6 matrix; in addition, it uses a deconvolution layer to enlarge the feature matrix and the pooling results to the size of the real image. Finally, it concatenates all these components and adds a final convolution layer which will produce the final pixel-level prediction.

3   Methodology

In this paper, we compare the performance of four different algorithms in the segmentation of humpback whales' flukes: Otsu, Chan Vese, FCN and PSPNet. We cover this problem because it is an important process for the identification of individuals and we aim to use the best performing segmentation algorithm as a previous phase of photo-identification in the future. We started manually constructing the ground truth, then we divided the dataset into training, validation and test sets. We applied the Otsu and Chan Vese techniques; in addition, we trained the FCN and PSPNet architectures using the training and validation sets. Finally, each method was compared using the test images, by calculating the Intersection over Union (IoU) metric of its predictions against the ground truth (Fig. 3).

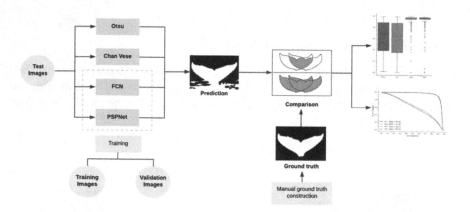

Fig. 3. Methodology for the comparison of Otsu (OTSU), Chan Vese (CV), Fully Convolutional Network (FCN) and Pyramid Scene Parsing Network (PSP) segmentation algorithms in the task of humpback whales' flukes segmentation.

Next, we detail the experimental setting adopted in our work to perform the segmentation algorithms comparison.

3.1   Dataset

In our experiments, we have worked with the publicly available "Humpback Whale Identification Challenge" dataset, published in the photo-identification competition held by the Kaggle in 2019 (Kaggle 2019). The dataset comprises 25000 images containing the flukes of humpback whales; the images belong to real catalogs collected on different dates and in different parts of the world, resulting in images with variable illumination and contrast conditions, as well as different image resolutions and different color space representations (RGB and grayscale images).

Despite the large amounts of humpback whales' flukes images, the dataset lack annotated references for the flukes, which prohibits the comparison of the segmentation algorithms. To overcome such an issue, we randomly selected a subset of 4000 images to build the ground truth, where each pixel within the flukes regions received a label of 1, whereas the pixels in the background got a label of 0. The annotation process was carried out using the MatLab R2019a Image Labeler application. We are planning to make the dataset available for other researchers to conduct investigations on the related photo-identification tasks of humpback whales.

We randomly divided this dataset into training, validation and test sets; composed of 2400, 800 and 800 images, respectively.

3.2   Algorithms Implementations Details

Given our interest in assessing the segmentation algorithms performances in the task of segmenting the humpback whale's caudal fin, we have compared four general purposes segmentation algorithms, namely, the Otsu (Otsu 1979), the Chan Vese (Chan and Vese 1999), the Fully Convolutional Network (Long et al. 2015) and the Pyramid Scene Parsing Network (Zhao et al. 2017). In our experiments, we have used publicly available implementations of such algorithms, which were deployed on the Google Collaboraty programming environment using Keras, skimage, NumPy, pandas, and matplotlib libraries.

Next, we detail the parameter settings used in the algorithms.

- *Otsu* (OTSU)[1], here, we have first transformed the color images to their grayscale versions and normalized the resulting pixel intensities to belong in the range of $[0, 1]$. Moreover, we have empirically proven that noise removal and image smoothing improved the Otsu's segmentation results; thus, we have applied a gaussian filter with a sigma value of 5 and a kernel size of 3×3 pixels before executing the Otsu algorithm.
- *Chan Vese* (CV)[2], seeks to find a bounding curve that encompasses the object even though there are no sudden changes between the pixels' values regarding

---

[1] Available in: https://scikit-image.org/docs/stable/auto_examples/applications/ plot_thresholding.html Last accessed: April 13, 2020.

[2] Available in: https://scikit-image.org/docs/stable/auto_examples/segmentation/ plot_chan_vese.html Last accessed: June 12, 2020.

the background, which usually happens when the humpback whale's flukes are light-colored and blended with the background of the image. Therefore, we pre-processed the images similar the Otsu algorithm. Moreover, we set the μ parameter to 0.25, enforcing a relatively precise curved to the caudal fins; we also initialized the curve fitting in checkerboard mode, which evolves several reduced size curves across the image to fit the object more precisely; finally, we set the remaining parameters as recommended by the author: v equal to 0 and $\lambda_1 = \lambda_2$.

- *Fully Convolutional Network* (FCN), here, we used the FCN-8s with VGG16 version in the Image Segmentation Keras repository[3] to implement the FCN algorithm since it performed superior to other segmentation algorithms on the PASCAL VOC 2012 dataset (Long et al. 2015). However, before executing the FCN, we first transformed the images and their corresponding references to their color version on the RGB color space by concatenating the layers. Moreover, we exploited the VGG16 weights information in the ImageNet dataset for training the FCN, we also choose the best performing model among those trained in 60 epochs using Categorical Cross-entropy loss function and Adam optimizer with a learning rate of 0.001. Furthermore, we established a batch size of 10 images along with 120 steps per epoch on the training set and 80 steps on the validation set.
- *Pyramid Scene Parsing Networks* (PSP), here, we used the ResNet101 network (See footnote 3) with its weights initialization corresponding to the PAS-CAL VOC 2012 dataset trained version. It is worth mentioning that PSP uses more computer resources during its training, thus we reduced the batch size to 2 images. Similar to the FCN algorithm, we trained the PSP on 60 epochs with 600 and 400 steps in the training and validations sets, respectively using Categorical Cross-entropy loss function and Adam optimizer with a learning rate of 0.001.

It is worth mentioning that we have applied a morphological filler filter over the outputs of the OTSU, CV, FCN and PSP segmentation algorithms to detect and fill the holes in the flukes' masks and improve the segmentation results.

3.3   Evaluation Metrics

Given our interest in evaluating the segmentation algorithms, we used the Intersection over Union (IoU) metric as a basic performance measure to calculate how similar a segmentation outcome is regarding an expected image (reference). Thus, given a reference image and a segmentation outcome image, the IoU score is obtained by dividing the number of pixels that constitute both images intersection area by the number of pixels of their union. Notice that a perfect correspondence between the reference and segmentation outcome images occurs when the IoU metric equals 1; otherwise, the IoU denotes errors as it approximates to 0.

---

[3] Available in: https://github.com/divamgupta/image-segmentation-keras. Last accessed: April 13, 2020.

4   Results Analysis

In this section, we report the experimental results obtained from the execution of the experimental design described in Sect. 3, which aim is to compare four algorithms for segmenting the humpback whales' flukes from digital whale images. The algorithms correspond to Otsu (OTSU), Chan Vese (CV), Fully Convolutional Networks (FCN), and Pyramid Scene Parsing Network (PSP) segmentation techniques. It is worth mentioning that we performed a parameter tunning procedure of the OTSU and CV algorithms using the training set, whereas, we trained the FCN and PSP algorithms with the training and validation sets. Moreover, the models of the FCN and PSP algorithms used in our experiments correspond to the 47th and 14th epochs-models of their training, respectively.

Figure 4 exhibits the performance distributions of the four segmentation algorithms in terms of the Intersection over Union (IoU) score over the testing set, which consist of a subset of humpback whales' flukes images from the "Humpback Whale Identification Challenge" dataset[4]. The graphic shows that the FCN and PSP algorithms outperformed both the OTSU and CV techniques. Indeed, the FCN and PSP obtained similar mean IoU scores of about 0.94 and small overall and interquartile ranges, which correspond to 0.07 and 0.09 standard deviations, respectively; whereby the OTSU and CV produced disperse performances with a mean IoU and standard deviation values of approximately 0.62 and 0.28 for the OTSU algorithm, and 0.60 and 0.29 for the CV technique.

Figure 5 shows the success plots associated with the segmentation algorithms. A success plot visually expresses the proportion of images where a segmentation algorithm complies with an IoU score greater than or equal to a threshold in the range of $[0, 1]$, for a set of predefined thresholds. An ideal scenario would occur whenever a segmentation algorithm complies with the condition 100% of the times across the threshold values, producing a rectangle-wise plot, which area under the curve (AUC) equals 1.0. Figure 5 shows that the OTSU and CV success plots decreased as the IoU threshold increased, obtaining an AUC score of 0.62 and 0.60, respectively. On the other hand, the graphic shows that the PSP and FCN produced almost perfect success plots, whose AUC scores correspond to 0.94 for both algorithms.

The similar results of the FCN and PSP in Fig. 4 and Fig. 5 suggest that both segmentation algorithms can be used in the isolation of humpback whales' flukes for photo-identification purposes.

Figure 6 shows the segmentation outcomes for a subset of 10 challenging humpback whale's fluke images in the testing set. A visual inspection of the OTSU results indicates that the algorithm provides good segmentation outcomes on images having good contrast, especially on the images containing dark whale flukes that differentiate from the background sea, refer to images in the rows A, B, and C in the Fig. 6. On the other hand, the results in the fourth column

---

[4] Available in: https://www.kaggle.com/c/humpback-whale-identification   Last accessed: April 1, 2020.

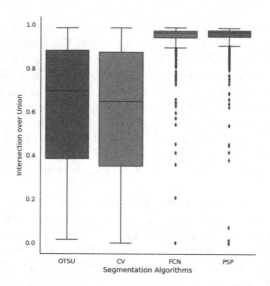

Fig. 4. Performance distribution boxplots in terms of the Intersection over Union (IoU) score for the Otsu (OTSU), Chan Vese (CV), Fully Convoluational Network (FCN) and Pyramid Scene Network (PSP) segmentation algorithms.

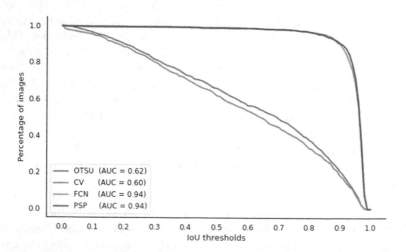

Fig. 5. Success plot for Otsu (OTSU), Chan Vese (CV), Fully Convolutional Network (FCN) and Pyramid Scene Parsing Network (PSP) segmentation algorithms in terms of the Intersection over Union score.

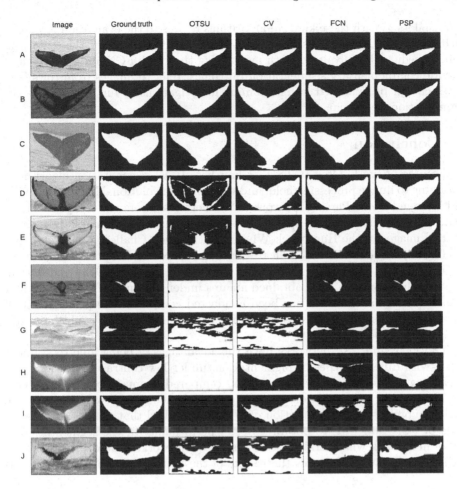

Fig. 6. Visual comparison of humpback whales' flukes segmentation outcomes. From left to right the image samples correspond to the original humpback whales' flukes images and their references, as well as the Otsu (OTSU), Chan Vese (CV), Fully Convolutional Network (FCN), and Pyramid Scene Parsing Network (PSP) segmentation outcomes.

of Fig. 6, indicate that the CV algorithm corrects OTSU weaknesses, producing more accurate segmentation masks of the whales' flukes having large white areas, as can be observed in row images D, E, H, and I. Nevertheless, it encounters troubles to isolate the flukes that are similar to the background sea, considering the surrounding sea waves as part of the whales' flukes (refer to images in rows E, F, G, and J).

Further examination on Fig. 6 reveals that deep neural network-based approaches, FCN and PSP, provided more accurate results, removing the background sea information from the segmented outcomes. Such results are in correspondence with the previous analysis in Fig. 4 and Fig. 5. Nevertheless, one potential issue with these kinds of algorithms relates to the evaluation of images with low resolution, which seem to provide little information for the segmentation procedure. Finally, it is worth mentioning that both FCN and PSP seem to provide complementary segmentation outcomes, refer to images from rows F to J, which can be exploited in forthcoming investigations to further improve the segmentation performance.

5   Conclusion

In the present work, Otsu (OTSU), Chan Vese (CV) segmentation algorithms, belonging to image processing field, and the Fully Convolutional Networks (FCN) and Pyramid Scene Parsing Network (PSP) networks, from the computer vision field, were implemented and applied to isolate the humpback whales' flukes from a set of images in the Humpback Whale Identification Challenge dataset.

The experimental results indicates that the FCN and PSP networks achieve the best results, scoring an Intersection over Union value of 0.9434 and 0.9433, respectively; moreover, they obtained an area under the curve of the success plot of 0.94. So far, no research has been conducted comparing the performance of these techniques on the species of our interest; therefore, this would be a first work of this type.

The FCN and PSP networks have the advantages of being able to segment flukes with different types of pigmentation, under low contrast conditions and discarding sea foam in the segmentation compared to image processing methods. Sometimes, the predictions of both are complementary; therefore, as a future work, we propose the construction of a hybrid method that merges the predictions of FCN and PSP to obtain a better performance in the segmentation of fins of humpback whales. Likewise, in a subsequent work, it is expected to verify if this segmentation improves the results of the identification algorithm in this species.

References

Ballance, L.: Contributions of photographs to cetacean science. Aquat. Mamm. **44**(6), 668–682 (2018). https://doi.org/10.1578/AM.44.6.2018.668

Barrientos, Y.: El avistamiento de ballenas jorobadas espera atraer a 45,000 turistas. El Correo, 16 July 2019. https://diariocorreo.pe/edicion/piura/el-avistamiento-de-ballenas-jorobadas-espera-atraer-45000-turistas-898801/

Barlow, J., et al.: Humpback whale abundance in the North Pacific estimated by photographic capture-recapture with bias correction from simulation studies. Mar. Mamm. Sci. **27**(4), 793–818 (2011)

Bouma, S., Pawley, M.D., Hupman, K., Gilman, A: Individual common dolphin identification via metric embedding learning. In: 2018 International Conference on Image and Vision Computing New Zealand (IVCNZ), Auckland, New Zealand (2018). https://doi.org/10.1109/IVCNZ.2018.8634778

Chan, T., Vese, L.: An active contour model without edges. In: Nielsen, M., Johansen, P., Olsen, O.F., Weickert, J. (eds.) Scale-Space 1999. LNCS, vol. 1682, pp. 141–151. Springer, Heidelberg (1999). https://doi.org/10.1007/3-540-48236-9_13

Félix, F., Castro, C., Laake, J., Hasse, B., Scheidat, M.: Abundance and survival estimates of the Southeastern Pacific humpback whale stock from surveys in Ecuador. J. Cetecean Res. Manag. **3**, 301–307 (2011)

Gonzalez, R., Woods, R.: Digital Image Processing (4th ed.), Pearson (2018)

Hsu, H., Lee, Y., Ding, J., Chang, R.: Dolphin recognition with adaptive hybrid saliency detection for deep learning based on DenseNet recognition. In: 2018 IEEE Asia Pacific Conference on Circuits and Systems (APCCAS), Chengdu, China (2018). https://doi.org/10.1109/apccas.2018.8605718

Kaggle: Humpback Whale Identification Challenge (2019). https://www.kaggle.com/c/humpback-whale-identification. Accessed 1 Apr 2020

Li, B., Shi, Y., Qi, Z., Chen, Z.: A survey on semantic segmentation. In: 2018 IEEE International Conference on Data Mining Workshops (ICDMW), pp. 1233–1240 (2018). https://doi.org/10.1109/ICDMW.2018.00176

Liu, X., Deng, Z., Yang, Y.: Recent progress in semantic image segmentation. Artif. Intell. Rev. **52**, 1089–1106 (2019). https://doi.org/10.1007/s10462-018-9641-3

Long, J., Shelhamer, E., Darrell, T.: Fully convolutional networks for semantic segmentation. IEEE Trans. Pattern Anal. Mach. Intell. **39**(4), 640–651 (2015). https://doi.org/10.1109/cvpr.2015.7298965

Maglietta, R., et al.: The promise of machine learning in the Risso's dolphin Grampus griseus photo-identification. In: 2018 IEEE International Workshop on Metrology for the Sea; Learning to Measure Sea Health Parameters (MetroSea), pp. 183–187 (2018). https://doi.org/10.1109/metrosea.2018.8657839

Monnahan, C., Acevedo, J., Noble Hendrix, A., Gende, S., Aguayo-Lobo, A., Martinez, F.: Population trends for humpback whales (Megaptera novaeangliae) foraging in the Francisco Coloane Coastal-marine protected area, Magellan Strait. Chile. Mar. Mamm. Sci. **35**, 1212–1231 (2019). https://doi.org/10.1111/mms.12582

Otsu, N.: A threshold selection method from gray-level histograms. IEEE Trans. Syst. Man Cybern. **0**, 62–66 (1979). https://doi.org/10.1109/TSMC.1979.4310076

Pollicelli, D., Coscarella, M., Delrieux, C.: RoI detection and segmentation algorithms for marine mammals photo-identification. Ecol. Inform. **56**, 101038 (2020). https://doi.org/10.1016/j.ecoinf.2019.101038

Reno, V., et al.: Exploiting species-distinctive visual cues towards the automated photo-identification of the Risso's dolphin Grampus griseus. In: 2018 IEEE International Workshop on Metrology for the Sea; Learning to Measure Sea Health Parameters (MetroSea), pp. 125–128 (2018). https://doi.org/10.1109/MetroSea.2018.8657861

Ruiz, M.: Ballenas en el norte del Perú. Fondo Editorial Universidad Científica del Sur, Lima (2016)

Titova, O., et al.: Photo-identification matches of humpback whales (Megaptera novaeangliae) from feeding areas in Russian Far East seas and breeding grounds in the North Pacific. Mar. Mamm. Sci. **34**(1), 100–112 (2018). https://doi.org/10.1111/mms.12444

Weideman, H., et al.: Integral curvature representation and matching algorithms for identification of dolphins and whales. In: 2017 IEEE International Conference on Computer Vision Workshop (ICCVW), pp. 2831–2839 (2017). https://doi.org/10.1109/iccvw.2017.334

Zhao, H., Shi, J., Qi, X., Wang, X., Jia, J.: Pyramid scene parsing network. In: 2017 IEEE Conference on Computer Vision and Pattern Recognition (CVPR), pp. 6230–6239 (2017). https://doi.org/10.1109/cvpr.2017.660

Improving Context-Aware Music Recommender Systems with a Dual Recurrent Neural Network

Igor André Pegoraro Santana and Marcos Aurélio Domingues[(⊠)]

Department of Informatics, State University of Maringá, Maringá, Brazil
{pg400816,madomingues}@uem.br

Abstract. Day by day, online content delivery services suppliers grow the volume of data on the internet. Music streaming services are one of those services that increase the number of users every day, as well as the number of songs in their catalog. To help the users to find songs that fit their interests, music recommender systems can be used to filter a large number of songs according to the preference of the user. However, the context in which the users listen to songs must be taken into account, which justifies the usage of context-aware recommender systems. The goal of this work is to use a Dual Recurrent Neural Network to acquire contextual information (represented by embeddings) for each song, given the sequence of songs that each user has listened to. We evaluated the embeddings by using four context-aware music recommender systems in two datasets. The results showed that the embeddings (i.e. the contextual information) obtained by our proposed method are able to improve context-aware music recommender systems.

Keywords: Recurrent Neural Networks · Context-aware recommender systems · Music recommendation · Embeddings · Context acquisition.

1 Introduction

With the growing of music streaming services nowadays, the abundance of available songs for the users grows as well. Spotify[1], as an example, has 50 million songs available in its directory. Users can not handle so much data, making it necessary for the system to implement a tool that assists users in finding songs that are fit for their preferences.

The usage of smartphones with music streaming services changed how people listen to music. A user can be texting a friend, browsing through its social networks or answering e-mails, while listening to music in the background. In this way, a user is inserted in a broader context while listening to a song. Also, as seen in [10], people look for songs based on occasions, events and emotions, which suggests that listening to songs is not an isolated event.

---

[1] https://www.spotify.com.

© Springer Nature Switzerland AG 2021
J. A. Lossio-Ventura et al. (Eds.): SIMBig 2020, CCIS 1410, pp. 304–314, 2021.
https://doi.org/10.1007/978-3-030-76228-5_22

A useful tool to deal with this information overload is a recommender system, which can recommend songs to users based on their preferences. Several works propose and review music recommender systems [1–3,11], however, knowing that users usually listen to songs given a context, we can replace it by context-aware recommender systems, which can include this kind of information in their model. The work of [9] reviews some context-aware music recommender systems.

Although there are some works about context-aware music recommender systems, there is a lack of automatic techniques for extracting contextual information. To obtain such information, we proposed a Dual Recurrent Neural Network model that uses Long Short-Term Memory (LSTM) networks to analyze the sequence of songs that the users listened to and to produce an embedding vector (i.e. a contextual information) for each song. Embedding is a method to represent items using a real values vector that is obtained by using a neural network trained to understand the context of the items. LSTM is a kind of Recurrent Neural Network (RNN) that was proposed with the intent to solve problems with long term dependencies [7]. The embedding vector contains the contextual information that encircle the songs for each user.

We evaluated our proposal by using four context-aware recommender systems in two music datasets that include the listening history of thousands of users. As a baseline, to compare our proposal against to, we used the model proposed by [19]. That model was based on the Skip-Gram architecture [13], a state-of-the-art embedding model. The results showed that, in both datasets, our proposed model outperformed the baseline, indicating that it can capture better contextual information through the embedding vector.

The remaining of this paper is organized as follows: In Sect. 2, we describe some works that use embedding vectors and context-aware music recommender systems. Section 3 contains our proposed model. Section 4 describes the empirical evaluation, i.e. the datasets, the recommender systems, the evaluation setup, and the results. Finally, in Sect. 5, we present our conclusions and future directions.

2 Related Work

Context-aware music recommender systems have gained notoriety in recent years, with several researches being published in this area. To the best of our knowledge, most of the works [12,13,19,20] that tried to recommend songs to a user, using contextual information, obtained such information by analyzing the sessions from the user, which are the sequence of songs that the user has listened to. Only one work did not use sessions to infer the contextual information [5]. That previous work uses emotions as contextual information, in which the emotions obtained from the user's tweets were encoded in fixed-sized tweets, using an adaptation of the bag-of-words method.

A common and effective approach to extract contextual information from sequences of data is the Skip-Gram model [13]. In [20], the authors included additional information about songs (metadata) in the Skip-Gram model. In [19], the authors proposed a Skip-Gram based model that produces embeddings based on the general preferences from the user, and embeddings based on the preferences that come from the sessions (i.e. contextual preferences).

In [18], an AutoEncoder model was proposed to obtain embeddings to the next song recommendation task. The work does not only encode the songs using the AutoEncoder, but also encode the playlists to estimate the most similar songs to the playlists.

3 Proposed Work

Inspired by the word2vec model proposed in [13], Wang et al. introduced a model to obtain the embedding vectors from songs [19]. The model is based on the Skip-Gram architecture and consists of two methods: music2vec and session-music2vec. The methods obtain embeddings from songs with different goals: one goal is to obtain the general preference from the user (music2vec) and another one is to obtain the contextual preference from the user (session-music2vec). The user's general preference can be inferred by its complete listening history and refers to the user's specific preferences for music. The contextual preference for songs indicates the recent preferences of the user in the current session. Here, we used the work proposed in [19] as the baseline.

As already stated, embedding is a method to represent items using a real values vector that is obtained by using a neural network trained to understand the context of the items. Instead of using traditional neural networks to obtain the embeddings, as proposed in [19], our model captures the context of the songs by using a Recurrent Neural Network (RNN).

In our work, we propose a Dual Recurrent Neural Network that is able to learn the general and contextual preferences in a same model, generating embeddings (i.e. contextual information) for the songs that can be used in context-aware music recommenders. Similar to the Context Bag-of-Words model (CBOW) proposed by [13], the goal of our model is to predict the center song in the contextual window given its neighborhood songs. Figure 1 contains an overview of the proposed model and its most important layers. However, in contrast to the CBOW model, as we use a Recurrent Neural Network (i.e. LSTM layers) to analyze the contextual windows, the order in which the songs are in the window matter.

Long Short-Term Memory (LSTM) is a kind of Recurrent Neural Networks that was proposed with the intent to solve problems with long term dependencies [7]. It uses gated cells that are capable to forget information that will no longer be useful, and keep information that can be used later on the sequence [6]. There are three gates in the LSTM cell: forget gate, input gate, and output gate. Through those gates, the LSTM cell learns which information is useful in a sequence and passes that information to make predictions through the output gate, and the cell state containing the relevant information that is passed to the next timestamp.

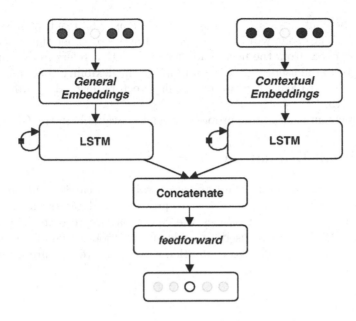

Fig. 1. Overview of the proposed model.

As defined by [19], let $U = \{u_1, u_2, \ldots, u_{|U|}\}$ be the set of users and $M = \{m_1, m_2, \ldots, m_{|M|}\}$ be the set of songs, in which $|U|$ e $|M|$ are the total number of unique users and songs, respectively. For each user u, their listening history are the songs that were listened to by the user with its respective date and time, defined as $H^u = \{m_1^u, m_2^u, \ldots, m_{|H^u|}^u\}$.

According to how much time has passed between two songs, the user's listening history can be divided into sessions $S^u = \{S_1^u, S_2^u, \ldots, S_{|S^u|}^u\}$. A session n from user u is defined as $S_n^u = \{m_{n,1}^u, m_{n,2}^u, \ldots, m_{n,|s_n'|}^u\}$, in which $m_{n,j}^u \in M$.

As seen in Fig. 1, our model receives streams of data: the left one, which has as input the sliding window of a song m_i^u, taking into the complete listening history of a user H^u, for all users. The right stream has as input the sliding window of the same song $m_{n,i}^u$, taking into account the session which the song is, instead of the whole listening history.

Those sliding windows are passed to the LSTM layers, that are responsible to analyze the hidden relationships between the sequences of songs in the windows of both streams of data. Then, the cell state of the last timestamp of both LSTMs are concatened in a single vector. Finally, this vector is used as input by a fully connected feedforward layer, that tries to predict the song that is in the center of both sliding windows, using as input the concatenated vector.

Each part of the model has its own embedding matrix that is initialized with all the songs in the dataset and, as the model learns through the forward and back-propagation process, this matrix gets updated. These embeddings will later be used in the context-aware recommender systems. The result of this training process is that each song will have two embedding vectors: one that refers to the general preferences from the users and another one that refers to the contextual preferences from the users. Thus, we can explore the flexibility of neural networks in a single model to learn the two embedding vectors, instead of two models as proposed in [19].

The implementation of our proposed model is available in the GitHub[2].

4   Empirical Evaluation

In this section, we describe the empirical evaluation carried out to evaluate our proposed model. In Subsect. 4.1, we present the datasets and their main statistics. Subsection 4.2 introduces the context-aware recommender systems proposed by [19] that were used to evaluate our model against the baseline. In Subsect. 4.3, we present the evaluation setup. The results are discussed in Subsect. 4.4.

4.1   Datasets

The two datasets used in the empirical evaluation contain the listening history for each user as well as the timestamp for each listening event, without any information about sessions. So, to generate the sessions, we decided to split songs that were listened 30 min apart from each other. The first dataset was proposed by [19] and was built using a web crawler on the application Xiami Music[3], referred here as Xiami[4]. The dataset has 361,899 songs; and 4,284 users with 1,000 listened songs in its listening history, with an average of 370 unique songs per user. The second dataset, called Music4All[5] [16], was created by obtaining the listening history of random users from the last.fm[6] application through its official API. The dataset has many more users (15,602), but there are fewer songs per user, with an average of 361 songs per user, and 184 unique songs per user. The total number of song in this dataset is 109,269.

4.2   Context-Aware Recommender Systems

To evaluate the embeddings (i.e. contextual information) from our proposed model against the ones from the baseline, we used the four context-aware recommender systems proposed by [19]. The recommenders make use of a general preference and a contextual preference for each user, which are built based on the learned embeddings. The general preference for a user u can be learned from its entire listening history $H^u = \left\{ m_1^u, m_2^u, \ldots, m_{|H^u|}^u \right\}$ and is defined as:

---

[2] https://github.com/igorsantana/rnn-embeddings.
[3] https://www.xiami.com.
[4] https://1drv.ms/f/s!ApojZBGe9UzXgaI6x8pBf8JgN4PfZg.
[5] https://sites.google.com/view/contact4music4all.
[6] https://www.last.fm.

$$\mathbf{p}_g^u = \frac{1}{|H^u|} \sum_{m_i^u \in H^u} \mathbf{v}_{m_i^u}^{g2v}, \tag{1}$$

where $\mathbf{v}_{m_i^u}^{g2v}$ is defined as the general embedding vector. The contextual preference for the user u, given their current session $S_n^u = \left\{ m_{n,1}^u, m_{n,2}^u, \ldots, m_{n,|S_i^u|}^u \right\}$ can be defined as:

$$\mathbf{p}_c^u = \frac{1}{|S_n^u|} \sum_{m_{n,i}^u \in S_n^u} \mathbf{v}_{m_{n,i}^u}^{c2v}, \tag{2}$$

where $\mathbf{v}_{m_{n,i}^u}^{c2v}$ corresponds to the contextual embedding vector for the song. As we can see in Eq. 1, the general preference is defined as an average of all the general embedding vectors of the songs in the user's listening history. On the other hand, the contextual preference, defined in Eq. 2, is the average of all the contextual embedding vectors of the songs in the user's current session. Given the general and contextual embedding vectors as well as the preferences for each user, four context-aware recommender systems were defined in [19]: Music2vec-TopN (M-TN), Session-Music2vec-TopN (SM-TN), Context-Session-Music2vec-TopN (CSM-TN) and Context-Session-Music2vec-UserKNN (CSM-UK).

Of all the context-aware recommender systems, the M-TN is the only one that uses only the general preference (i.e. the general embedding vector) to recommend songs to the users. Given a user u and their general preference $\mathbf{p}_g^u$ for songs, the recommender system measures the cosine similarity between $\mathbf{p}_g^u$ and the general embedding vector of all the songs in the set of songs M. The top-N songs with the highest value of cosine similarity are recommended to the user. Formally, the predicted preference of the user u to the song m can be defined as:

$$pp_{M-TN}(u, m) = \cos\left(\mathbf{p}_g^u, \mathbf{v}_m^{g2v}\right). \tag{3}$$

The SM-TN recommender system is similar to M-TN, but it uses contextual information instead of the general information. Given a user u and their contextual preference $\mathbf{p}_c^u$, the SM-TN measures the cosine similarity between the contextual embedding vector $\mathbf{v}_{m_{n,i}^u}^{c2v}$ of the songs and the contextual preference of the user. The top-N songs with the highest cosine similarity are then recommended to the user. Formally, the preference can be defined as:

$$pp_{SM-TN}(u, m) = \cos\left(\mathbf{p}_c^u, \mathbf{v}_m^{c2v}\right). \tag{4}$$

The CSM-TN recommender system is a combination of the previous recommender systems: M-TN and SM-TN. After the similarity of each recommender is calculated for each song, they are summed to obtain the most similar songs according to both the contextual and general preferences of the user. Formally, the preference is defined as:

$$\mathrm{PP}_{CSM-TN}(u,m) = \cos\left(\mathbf{p}_g^u, \mathbf{v}_m^{g2v}\right) + \cos\left(\mathbf{p}_c^u, \mathbf{v}_m^{c2v}\right). \tag{5}$$

The last recommender system, CSM-UK, proposes a combination of the traditional recommender system, UserKNN [15], with the learned embedding vectors. The UserKNN recommender system needs a similarity function to build a neighborhood of similar users. In [19], the similarity function between two users, u and v is defined as follows:

$$\mathrm{sim}(u,v) = \sum_{m \in M_u \cap M_v} \frac{1}{\sqrt{|M_u| \times |M_v|} + \cos\left(\mathbf{p}_g^u, \mathbf{p}_g^v\right)}, \tag{6}$$

where M_u e M_v are the set of songs listened by the users u and v, respectively. With the similarity function, the CSM-UK system recommends the top-N most similar songs for each user, given the user contextual preference and their most similar users. The predicted preference for the target user u to a song m can be defined as:

$$pp_{CSM-UK}(u,m) = \left(\sum_{v \in U_{u,K} \cap U_m} \frac{\mathrm{sim}(u,v)}{|U_{u,k} \cap U_m|}\right) + \cos\left(\mathbf{p}_c^u, \mathbf{v}_m^{c2v}\right), \tag{7}$$

where $U_{u,K}$ is the set with the K users more similar to u, and U_m is the set of users who have listened to song m.

4.3   Evaluation Setup

In order to evaluate the recommendations generated by using our proposed model against the ones generated by using the baseline, we used a 5-fold cross-validation, and computed five evaluation metrics. We computed the well known Precision, Recall, and F-measure [17], and also computed two ranking metrics, Normalized Discounted Cumulative Gain (NDCG) [8] and Mean Average Precision (MAP), which try to determine if the order of the items recommended by the systems matches the list of test items [17]. Here, we follow the k-fold cross-validation presented in [19]. Users who are in the training partitions use all of their songs to build their general and contextual preferences, in contrast to the users who are in the testing partitions, that use only half of the songs in their sessions to build their preferences, with the second half of the session being used as the testing songs for computing the metrics.

To optimize our model, we tested several parameters values by using Python and Keras. The best values for the Xiami dataset consisted of 256 LSTM units and embedding vector of size 256. For the Music4All dataset, we used 512 LSTM units and embedding vector of size 1024. For both datasets, the Dropout was setup to 0.2, the Activation Function adopted was *tahn*, and the Window Size was setup to 3. As we can see, although there are fewer songs in the Music4All dataset, the model needed more LSTM units and a much bigger embedding vector to capture the relevant information about songs that can be used effectively in context-aware recommendations.

Finally, to compare two context-aware recommender systems, we applied the two sided paired t-test with a 95% confidence level [14].

4.4   Results

In this subsection, we present the results for the top-5 recommendations generated by the recommender systems. As we can see in Figs. 3 and 2, and in Tables 2 and 1, our proposed model was able to outperform the baseline in both datasets for all context-aware recommender systems. The metric that shows the best improvement over the baseline was MAP, with an improvement of over 25% for the CSM-TN recommender system in the Xiami dataset.

In the Music4All dataset, the contextual embedding vector obtained by our model showed small improvement in comparison to the baseline, as we can see in the metrics of the SM-TN recommender systems, which uses only the contextual embeddings. Although there was not a big improvement in the contextual embedding vector, the general embeddings exhibited great improvements over the embeddings obtained by the baseline. The M-TN recommender system, for example, showed an improvement of $6,56\%$ in F-measure and $7,14\%$ in Recall. The mean and standard deviation for all metrics are presented in details in Table 1.

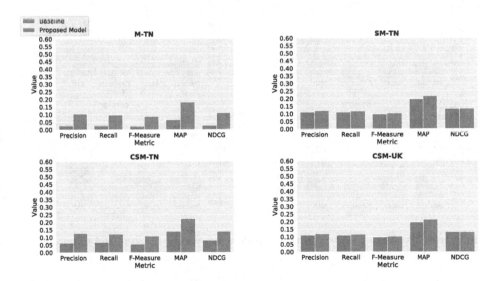

Fig. 2. Results obtained by using the embeddings from the baseline and the proposed model on the Music4All dataset.

Table 1. Results obtained by using the embeddings from the baseline and the proposed model on the Music4All dataset.

Models	Recommenders	Precision	Recall	F-Measure	MAP	NDCG
Baseline	M-TN	0.025 ± 0.001	0.024 ± 0.001	0.021 ± 0.001	0.064 ± 0.007	0.026 ± 0.001
Proposed model	M-TN	0.104 ± 0.001	0.095 ± 0.001	0.086 ± 0.001	0.179 ± 0.005	0.109 ± 0.001
Baseline	SM-TN	0.110 ± 0.003	0.109 ± 0.002	0.097 ± 0.002	0.196 ± 0.005	0.132 ± 0.002
Proposed model	SM-TN	0.120 ± 0.003	0.116 ± 0.002	0.103 ± 0.002	0.216 ± 0.003	0.133 ± 0.002
Baseline	CSM-TN	0.062 ± 0.001	0.067 ± 0.001	0.055 ± 0.001	0.139 ± 0.006	0.079 ± 0.002
Proposed model	CSM-TN	0.126 ± 0.003	0.121 ± 0.002	0.108 ± 0.002	0.223 ± 0.005	0.138 ± 0.002
Baseline	CSM-UK	0.110 ± 0.003	0.109 ± 0.002	0.097 ± 0.002	0.196 ± 0.005	0.131 ± 0.002
Proposed model	CSM-UK	0.119 ± 0.003	0.115 ± 0.002	0.102 ± 0.002	0.214 ± 0.004	0.132 ± 0.002

For the Xiami dataset, there was an improvement for both general and contextual embedding vectors in all metrics. The improvement for the CSM-UK algorithm is similar to the improvement observed in the SM-TN, which might indicates that the relationship between users are not interfering in the final results. The most significant improvement in the Xiami dataset, for the F-measure metric, is in the CSM-TN, which combines both embeddings (contextual and general), with an improvement of 7, 26%. In Table 2, we present the mean and standard deviation for all metrics.

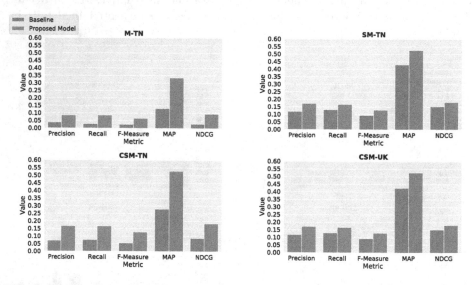

Fig. 3. Results obtained by using the embeddings from the baseline and the proposed model on the Xiami dataset.

Table 2. Results obtained by using the embeddings from the baseline and the proposed model on the Xiami dataset.

Models	Recommenders	Precision	Recall	F-Measure	MAP	NDCG
Baseline	M-TN	0.038 ± 0.003	0.028 ± 0.002	0.026 ± 0.002	0.130 ± 0.009	0.029 ± 0.002
Proposed model	M-TN	0.080 ± 0.001	0.087 ± 0.004	0.066 ± 0.001	0.335 ± 0.021	0.096 ± 0.004
Baseline	SM-TN	0.119 ± 0.002	0.132 ± 0.005	0.095 ± 0.002	0.431 ± 0.021	0.153 ± 0.006
Proposed model	SM-TN	0.017 ± 0.004	0.167 ± 0.007	0.129 ± 0.004	0.527 ± 0.027	0.182 ± 0.008
Baseline	CSM-TN	0.071 ± 0.002	0.077 ± 0.003	0.055 ± 0.002	0.278 ± 0.015	0.087 ± 0.003
Proposed model	CSM-TN	0.167 ± 0.004	0.167 ± 0.007	0.128 ± 0.004	0.529 ± 0.029	0.184 ± 0.008
Baseline	CSM-UK	0.117 ± 0.002	0.131 ± 0.005	0.094 ± 0.002	0.426 ± 0.023	0.152 ± 0.006
Proposed model	CSM-UK	0.172 ± 0.004	0.167 ± 0.007	0.129 ± 0.004	0.526 ± 0.027	0.182 ± 0.008

5   Conclusion and Future Work

In this work, we proposed a model that uses LSTM units in a Dual Recurrent Neural Network to learn both general and contextual embeddings for songs that can be used in context-aware music recommender systems.

The results obtained by our model in two datasets, that contain the listening history of users, showed that our model outperformed the baseline in both datasets and for the four context-aware recommenders, using metrics that measured how good the recommendations are for the user and if the recommendations are ranked accordingly. This shows that a Recurrent Neural Network can be used effectively in capturing the intrinsic relationship between the sequence of songs that the user has listened to and generating contextual information for context-aware recommender systems.

For future work, we plan to use different Recurrent Neural Networks such as Gated Recurrent Units (GRU) [4], which has fewer parameters as LSTM and can be used to decrease the training time and memory consumption. Another possibility to improve our model is to try different methods of initializing the embedding matrices of the model.

Acknowledgments. To CNPq/Brazil (grant #403648/2016-5) for financial support and NVIDIA Corporation for donation of a Titan V GPU used in this work. This work was also supported by grant 2019/25010-5, Sao Paulo Research Foundation (FAPESP).

References

1. Bu, J., Tan, S., Chen, C., Wang, C., Wu, H., Zhang, L., He, X.: Music recommendation by unified hypergraph. In: Proceedings of the International Conference on Multimedia, p. 391. ACM Press, New York (2010)
2. Celma, O.: Music recommendation. In: Music Recommendation and Discovery, pp. 43–85. Springer, Heidelberg (2010). https://doi.org/10.1007/978-3-642-13287-2_3
3. Chen, H.C., Chen, A.L.P.: A music recommendation system based on music data grouping and user interests. In: Proceedings of the 10th International Conference on Information and Knowledge Management, pp. 231–238. ACM, New York (2001)

4. Cho, K., et al.: Learning phrase representations using RNN encoder-decoder for statistical machine translation. In: Proceedings of the 2014 Conference on Empirical Methods in Natural Language Processing (EMNLP), Doha, Qatar, pp. 1724–1734. Association for Computational Linguistics, October 2014
5. Deng, S., Wang, D., Li, X., Xu, G.: Exploring user emotion in microblogs for music recommendation. Expert Syst. Appl. **42**, 9284–9293 (2015)
6. Goodfellow, I., Bengio, Y., Courville, A.: Deep Learning. The MIT Press, Cambridge (2016)
7. Hochreiter, S., Schmidhuber, J.: Long short-term memory. Neural Comput. (1997)
8. Järvelin, K., Kekäläinen, J.: Cumulated gain-based evaluation of IR techniques. ACM Trans. Inf. Syst. **20**(4), 422–446 (2002)
9. Kaminskas, M., Ricci, F.: Contextual music information retrieval and recommendation: state of the art and challenges. Comput. Sci. Rev. **6**(2–3), 89–119 (5 2012)
10. Kim, J.-Y., Belkin, N.J.: Categories of music description and search terms and phrases used by non-music experts. In: Proceedings of the Third International Conference on Music Information Retrieval, p. 327. Paris (2002)
11. Koenigstein, N., Dror, G., Koren, Y.: Yahoo! Music recommendations: modeling music ratings with temporal dynamics and item taxonomy. In: Proceedings of the 5th ACM Conference on Recommender Systems, pp. 165–172. ACM, New York (2011)
12. Mayerl, M., Vötter, M., Zangerle, E., Specht, G.: Language models for next-track music recommendation. In: 31st GI-Workshop on Foundations of Databases (Grundlagen von Daten-banken) (2019)
13. Mikolov, T., Chen, K., Corrado, G., Dean, J.: Efficient estimation of word representations in vector space. In: 1st International Conference on Learning Representations, ICLR 2013 - Workshop Track Proceedings (2013)
14. Fernandes de Mello, R., Antonelli Ponti, M.: A brief introduction on kernels. In: Machine Learning, pp. 325–362. Springer, Cham (2018). https://doi.org/10.1007/978-3-319-94989-5_6
15. Resnick, P., Iacovou, N., Suchak, M., Bergstrom, P., Riedl, J.: GroupLens: an open architecture for collaborative filtering of netnews. In: Proceedings of the 1994 ACM Conference on Computer Supported Cooperative Work, CSCW 1994 (1994)
16. Santana, I.A.P., et al.: Music4All: a new music database and its applications. In: Proceedings of the 27th International Conference on Systems, Signals and Image Processing (IWSSIP 2020) (2020)
17. Shani, G., Gunawardana, A.: Evaluating recommendation systems. In: Ricci, F., Rokach, L., Shapira, B., Kantor, P.B. (eds.) Recommender Systems Handbook, pp. 257–297. Springer, Boston, MA (2011). https://doi.org/10.1007/978-0-387-85820-3_8
18. Vötter, M., Zangerle, E., Mayerl, M., Specht, G.: Autoencoders for next-track-recommendation. In: 31st GI-Workshop on Foundations of Databases (Grundlagen von Daten-banken) (2019)
19. Wang, D., Deng, S., Xu, G.: Sequence-based context-aware music recommendation. Inf. Retrieval J. 230–252 (2017). https://doi.org/10.1007/s10791-017-9317-7
20. Wang, D., Deng, S., Zhang, X., Xu, G.: Learning music embedding with metadata for context aware recommendation. In: ICMR 2016 - Proceedings of the 2016 ACM International Conference on Multimedia Retrieval (2016)

Social Networks

Classification of Cybercrime Indicators in Open Social Data

Ihsan Ullah[1,2] , Caoilfhionn Lane[2] , Teodora Sandra Buda[3] ,
Brett Drury[1] , Marc Mellotte[2] , Haytham Assem[3] ,
and Michael G. Madden[1,2(✉)]

[1] Computer Science, National University of Ireland Galway, Galway, Ireland
michael.madden@nuigalway.ie
[2] Insight Center for Data Analytics, National University of Ireland Galway,
Galway, Ireland
[3] Cognitive Computing Group, Innovation Exchange, IBM, Dublin, Ireland

Abstract. Posting information on social media platforms is a popular activity through which personal and confidential information can leak into the public domain. Consequently, social media can contain information that provides an indication that an organization has been compromised or suffered a data breach. This paper describes a technique for inferring if an organization has been compromised from information posted on social media. The proposed strategy forms the basis of an alarm system which generates an alert for possible unreported cybercrime incidents. The proposed strategy used two social media cybercrime related datasets that were collected from the Irish and New York regions from financial organizations' Twitter accounts. The Tweets are labelled as either containing cybercrime indicators or not, and then the cybercrime Tweets were labelled further into crime categories. A deep dense pyramidal Neural Network model is used to classify the Tweets. This approach achieves an AUC of 0.85 ± 0.03 which outperforms the baseline of deep convolutional neural networks.

Keywords: Data breaches · Cybercrime classification · Pyramidal deep learning model · Open social data

1 Introduction

In recent times, the frequency of cyber-attacks on well-known organizations has increased dramatically. Data theft and financial theft are both particularly harmful, as clients, as well as the organization, can suffer financial loss. The financial loss suffered by clients can cause reputational damage. Reputational damage may cause an immediate and future loss of business as clients lose trust in the organization. The potential for reputational damage may incentive organizations to hide

This project is funded by IBM and Science Foundation Ireland (SFI) under Grant Number SFI/12/RC/2289.

J. A. Lossio-Ventura et al. (Eds.): SIMBig 2020, CCIS 1410, pp. 317–332, 2021.
https://doi.org/10.1007/978-3-030-76228-5_23

such events [21,23]. Consequently, traditional crime statistics may underestimate the true nature of cybercrime. When a cybercrime directly affects customers, even if the organizations do not disclose it in a timely fashion, information about it can leak onto social media through indirect communication to the clients or from the customers themselves. The posting of an informal question or commentary about a potential cybercrime on open social media can be easily done via mobile devices. A big advantage of using open social media is that it is often immediate, and can have indications of the nature of a crime such as (1) named entities, for example, Bitcoin or PayPal; (2) geocoding information; and (3) the affected persons [29]. Such signalling of incidents is arguably a better indicator of the extent and effect of cybercrime than traditional reporting methods. These indicators can be identified through text classification and NLP techniques. While we do not know of any system that monitors social media for indicators of the types of cybercrime described in this paper, there are other social media monitoring tools available to researchers. As an example, the Cardiff Online Social Media Observatory (COSMOS) [5] is a platform which allows researchers to mine social media data and provides analysis tools to interpret the data. For instance, the platform can monitor indicators of tension in online communities, which combined with other information such as location, may be useful for gathering online indicators of social unrest that is likely to escalate [6]. The platform also links to the UK Police API, which provides monthly crime data by district. This paper presents a system for identifying indicators of cybercrime in social media posts. We propose three types of pyramidal deep neural network model: a dense network and two types of convolutional neural network (CNN). We have compared these against each other and against a baseline random forest model. If correctly classified, these indicators can be used in generating an alarm in a cybercrime alarm forecasting/generating system. Our models are designed in such a way that it can be utilized in such a real-time system.

2   Related Work

The use of social media to detect or infer events, in general, is a relatively popular area of research. The most frequently used social media platform is Twitter because of its large number of users and its free availability for academic research [6]. The detection of indicators of cybercrime on social media is a new area of research, with a limited number of previous papers specifically on this topic. There are, however, a number of papers in areas related to cybercrime that use Twitter as an information source. For example, Twitter was used to predict and report other types of crime. Common areas of investigation include traffic alerts [32] and cyber hate [6]. This review of related work will concentrate upon topics directly related to cybercrime, including phishing, fraud, and spam. Recently, a forecasting/detection approach has been introduced to identify/detect cyberattacks (e.g., distributed denial of service (DDoS) attacks, data breaches, and account hijacking) in a weakly supervised manner [14]. It uses a small number of keywords related to events that trigger detections. This model does not require labelled training data; it works more like an event identification or topic modelling technique, based on a burst of Tweets within a short time span. Phishing is a technique through which attackers can gather personal information to enter financial systems and make fraudulent transactions. The original attack vector was the use of bulk emails to potential victims [3,18]. However, social media platforms are also used to phish unsuspecting users, using similar techniques to the bulk email approach. Phishing posts and the associated websites have a number of indicators that denote that they are for the purposes of phishing. The most common phishing indicators are shortened URLs (using Bitly), trending '#' tags, indiscriminate use of '@' tags and URL 'typo-domains' [1,24]. These indicators can be used as features for classifiers such as Random Forests and Naive Bayes. The classification approach was followed by PhishStorm [22] which is a real-time system for automatic detection of phishing sites. An alternate approach to the classification of posts is to identify the redirect chains of URLs [20]. Spam email is often a precursor to cybercrime as it is used to gather personal financial details from unsuspecting individuals. A common approach to detection of spam is to classify it based on the content of the email, or the account/server it was sent from. Social media can also be used to propagate spam content. The indicators of spam accounts, posts and emails are the length of the profile name, the ratio of followers to followed accounts; the age of the account; and features of the post itself, such as the number of words and the use of hashtags and exclamation marks [19,31]. Twitter has been used as a source of intelligence for law enforcement, such as providing information about the planning of riots and incitement of violence [26]. The precursors of violence and public disorder have also been identified through information on Twitter [5]. Incitement of violence is a crime of intent where a conviction may be based upon the content of a social media post alone. The same is true for hate speech, which in many European jurisdictions is a crime. A strategy was proposed in [27] where standard text classification techniques were used to detect hate speech in social media posts. The usage of Natural Language Processing (NLP) techniques for hate speech detection was surveyed in [2]. It was noted that the best-performing features are uni-gram and n-gram with BOW, word generalization (word or paragraph embedding, clustering techniques such as Brown clustering or LDA), sentiment analysis (SentiStrength), lexical resources (specific negative or hate-related words on the web), linguistic features (deeper syntactic and dependency related features), knowledge-based features (concept that are connected by relations to form assertions), meta-information (information about an utterance), and multi-modal information (include text, image, and video). That paper also reviewed the classifiers used for hate speech and reported that the most successful approaches were based on support vector machines (SVMs) and recurrent neural networks (RNNs). Levi et al. [21] defined cyberfraud as a fraud with an online dimension, and examined the role of cyberfraud for financial gain. One of the main characteristics of cyberfraud is that it is borderless. The pervasive use of smartphones, the rise of botnets, and the growth in volumes of electronic transactions create challenges for cyber-security teams in financial organizations.

In particular, they are concerned with the protection of their online systems and prevention of data leakage. The challenge becomes harder to tackle because there is a lack of accurate reported or known data and lack of mechanisms for the measurement of the nature, scale, and impact of cyber attacks and cyber frauds. The SWIFT fraud [12,29] provides recent example of cyberfraud. Despite the lack of previous work in the detection/identification of indicators of data breaches and other cybercrimes on social media, there is a relatively large research literature on complementary areas that use Twitter to detect or infer crime. The approaches use standard NLP techniques to identify indicators of crime within social media posts. The research literature provides support to the hypothesis of this paper, that indicators of financial data breaches/theft can be detected through social media posts.

3   Proposed System

This section presents the proposed system that identifies linguistic features in Tweets to infer the occurrence of a data breach or related cybercrime. The hypotheses underpinning the system described in this paper are: indicators of unreported data breaches will leak onto social media; a classifier can be trained to identify these indicators, and the use of the synthetic data can improve the performance of the aforementioned classifier.

The indicators will take the form of customers posting details about anomalies that have affected their account or communication they have received from the compromised organization.

3.1   System Overview

The system's objective is to classify Tweets into two classes: Cybercrime Indicator (CC) and Non-Cybercrime Indicators (NCC). The system has three phases: (1) data collection & labelling; (2) preprocessing, and (3) classification. Each of these will be discussed in detail in following subsections.

3.2   Data Collection and Labeling

The first step is to collect data. Twitter supplies two APIs, the Twitter Stream API and the Twitter Search API, which allows the gathering of Tweets. We used two sets of data collected from Twitter i.e. a small set of data from financial institutions in Ireland (FII-dataset) and one year of data from New York, USA (NYK-dataset). The first set of data will be used to train a model and the second set of data is used to validate the performance of the deep model trained over the Irish dataset.

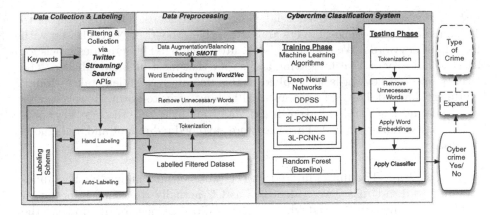

Fig. 1. Proposed system

FII-Dataset. As the authors are based in Ireland, Tweets were gathered from Irish financial institutions. The Tweets were initially filtered into the aforementioned CC and NCC categories by using keywords, such as: 'fraudulent', 'scam', 'fraud' and 'hacked'. The keywords were selected by a domain expert.

A schema is required for a human or algorithmic labeller to label the Tweets correctly. If the questions are not properly organized, the literature review shows that the labeller faces difficulty in labelling, as well and it affects the performance of the subsequent machine learning algorithm in classification. In [33], rumour analysis was done using Twitter data. [33] mentioned that Tweets containing the first-hand perspective are most interesting for machine learning classification. As an example, the organization statement may provide us the time that an incident is made public.

The inspiration from [33] helped us in proposing two questions that will be asked form each hand labellers or in the labelling mechanism system. The questions are:

– Q1: Does this Tweet refer to an unlawful online activity such as fraud, phishing, hacking or ransomware? Please select the type of cybercrime referred to, select 'No cybercrime' if no unlawful online activity is discussed, or 'None of the previously stated' if some other type of cybercrime is discussed.
  The possible values options are:
  Not cybercrime; Fraud; Hacking; Phishing; Ransomware; DDoS; Other

– Q2: What type of information does this Tweet provide?
  First Hand Perspective; Indirect Experience; Confirmation; News Report; Organisation Statement; Supplementary Data; None Of Above.

The answer to the first question will provide information that a machine learning classifier can use for classification (whether a CC occurred or not, and of which type). The second question will provide information about the source of information, that can help in authentication of the tweeter and time.

Auto Labeling. Our schema for labelling has two steps. The first step is to filter and narrow down the Tweets and assign them to CC or NCC classes, with the help of keywords. We refer to this as auto-labelling. This provides labels for the vast majority of Tweets, leaving a minority that must be hand-labelled. The initially selected keywords we applied in this domain are: stolen, taken, fraud, fraudulent, hacked, DDoS, Ransomware, Phishing, website-down. However, later we have found that 'stolen, taken, fraud, and fraudulent' are the best keywords for FII-dataset (Irish banks). These keywords avoided redundant and ambiguous Tweets.

Hand Labeling. The initial filtered Tweets were verified manually. The annotator had to decide if a Tweet identified as CC actually contained information about cybercrime and if it did which category did it belong to. In addition, the labeller had to decide if the Tweet was from one of the following perspectives: first-hand perspective; a description of another person's or organization's experience; a news report or statement from a financial institution (either the original or re-tweeted report, or a discussion of a news report).

Collected Data. Tweets that were gathered covered two discrete time periods: 2nd September 2017 to 12nd September 2017 and 16th November 2017 to 2nd January 2018. In the aforementioned time periods, finally after applying our schema and labelling each Tweet first with Auto labelling followed by Manual labelling, 5137 (in the first period) and 8545 (in the second period) Tweets were gathered. The datasets are very imbalanced between the CC and NCC classes with 16 positive Tweets in the first time period and 127 in the second time period. This represented a CC class membership of 0.31% and 1.5%, respectively. Examples of CC Tweets can be found in Table 1 (As noted previously, the Tweets listed are modified anonymised versions of the actual Tweets).

The majority of the keywords were not helpful in querying the dataset/Tweets because in that time no incident related to Data Breach, DDoS, or Ransomware happened in Ireland. Second, the population of Tweets in Ireland is very small compared to other jurisdictions such as New York or London. Hence, the majority of the Tweets mentioned fraud or being referred to the fraud department for further actions. The imbalanced data prevents the construction of a classifier that can perform well. Consequently, it is necessary to balance the data.

Table 1. Example Tweets

@BankAccountName i had 500e in my account last tuesday, I checked now they are %200e less than before did somebone took my money ???? is it a fraud?
@BankAccountName i have an new issue - I think a possibly fraudulent transaction %in my account, marked as "university fee"; what should i do, who do I talk to?

NYK-Dataset. This data set is used to analyse the trained model over an year of Twitter data from New York. The data is collected since 1st July 2016 until 15th July 2017. However, it is missing data between 14–20th July 2016 and 7–26th June 2017. It consists of 31323569 Tweets. Similar to FII-dataset, we first filtered the Tweets based on the names of 16 top financial institutions of New York, USA and than auto-labelled and hand-labelled those as being explained in Sect. 3.2. While filtering, we analysed that there were 153194 retweets that we removed. Out of the original Tweets (31170961), there were 31163393 off-topic Tweets that were not related to cybercrime and only 427 Tweets that are related to fraud.

Fleiss Kappa Statistics: The Tweets were hard to be considered related to cybercrime or not a cybercrime. To tackle the complexity and confusion in understanding, we used three independent labellers who have domain knowledge of cybercrime and are working in the area of machine learning. We calculated the Fleiss Kappa statistics for the manual labelling of the Tweets. Kappa value between 0 (no agreement) and 1 (perfect agreement) shows the agreement on a label among the labellers. We achieved a kappa value of 0.65 that shows a substantial or good agreement among the labellers on a Tweet and can be considered a good kappa value.

3.3 Preprocessing

The second module in our system performs data preprocessing. It consists of tokenization, removing unnecessary words, word-embedding, and data augmentation. The original Tweets include several unnecessary words, symbols, punctuation, stopwords, characters, etc. To remove them, we used tokenization with libraries such as natural language toolkit (NLTK) and regular expressions (RE). In addition, we removed account usernames, symbols like '@', '#', and URLs. These all would affect the overall performance of the system negatively.

Word-Embedding Through Word2Vec: We adopted word-embedding for two reasons. Firstly, it allows us to capture the similarities between words by extracting the semantic relation between the words in a corpus [25]. Each word is represented by an n-dimensional embedding (n = 200). This will identify/select words which are semantically similar to the cybercrime related keywords. Secondly, it allows us to augment the data. With text, the data cannot be directly augmented using approaches that work for images, which can be cropped, rotated, have colours adjusted, or noise can be added to individual pixels. With text, we cannot simply apply fractional changes to words while maintaining semantics and meaning. However, if we convert the words to a vector form using word2vec, and combine all vectors to form one vector for the Tweet using Averaged TF-IDF, we then can apply the SMOTE algorithm to generate synthetic data. Overall, therefore, word2vec provides an effective approach for using word embeddings to learn semantic relations, while also allowing us to generate synthetic data in a sophisticated way to improve the balance between classes in the dataset.

Data Augmentation/Balancing Through SMOTE: The collected dataset was very imbalanced with the minority class containing about 1% of the total Tweets. Severely imbalanced datasets often create weak models. A common technique to mitigate the effects of imbalanced data is to balance the classes by equalizing the numbers of members of each class. Frequently used balancing strategies are random undersampling of the majority class, and random oversampling of the minority class. In this case, these techniques are not advisable to use because of the very limited numbers of CC Tweets. A third option is synthetic data generation. Synthetic data generation has shown to aid imbalanced text classification problems [8].

There are a small number of synthetic data generation techniques, such as SMOTE [7] and adaptive synthetic sampling approach for imbalanced learning (ADASYN) [9]. The proposed technique used SMOTE, which generates synthetic nearest neighbours for training instances in the minority class. We adopted the balancing strategy that increased the number of minority class training instances to 40.00% of the number of training instances in the majority classes. The balanced class numbers can be found in Table 2. This augmentation not only helped in balancing the dataset but also increasing the number of training samples for the model.

Table 2. Dataset before and after augmentation through SMOTE

Name	Before SMOTE			After SMOTE		
	+ive	−ive	Total	+ive	−ive	Total
Training	95	9014	9109	3605	9014	12619
Testing	48	4507	4555	48	4507	4555
Total	143	13521	**13664**	3653	13521	**17174**

4   Experimental Setup

This section discusses the machine learning classifiers that were used to classify test instances into the aforementioned CC or NCC categories. The classifiers were: Random Forest (RF), the baseline classifier, and the deep neural networks with pyramidal structure classifiers: Deep Dense Model with Pyramid Structure and SELU (DDPSS), and two variation of 1DCNN i.e. 1DCNN with ReLu and Batch Normalization (2L-PCNN-BN) and 1DCNN with SELU and DropOut (3L-PCNN-S).

4.1   Random Forest (RF)

RF is an ensemble learning method for supervised classification [4]. It operates by constructing a multitude of decision trees at training time and outputting the mode of the class of the individual trees. A forest consists of a large number of deep trees, where each tree is trained on bagged data using random selection of features. A number of iterations were made to identify the best number of trees. The number of trees were: 350, 300, 250, 200, 150, 100, 90, 80, 70, 60, 50, 40, 30, 20, and 10. At each interval level the RF was trained for 10 epochs with batch-size of 5000.

4.2   Deep Neural Networks with Pyramid Structure

In the past 5 years, Deep Neural Networks (DNN) such as CNN, RNN, etc. have demonstrated results in various areas such as vision, NLP, and robotics. These models are becoming deeper and wider eventually resulting in a large number of parameters to train. The millions of parameters in the trained model take a large amount of memory on disk, e.g. AlexNet model with 8 layers require 238 MB on space [17]. Recent deeper models require even more memory on disk. This memory requirement becomes a problem in various scenarios where the systems require regular updates/up-gradation e.g. Tesla Cars. More specifically, it requires a large amount of labelled data for training and providing optimal performance. In the application area where we have limited data, literature review suggests that besides data augmentation, another possible solution is to use a small network or a network with less number of trainable parameters. One way to have fewer trainable parameters is to use a pyramid structure in the network that helps in the refinement of features as the network goes deeper. Therefore, taking inspiration from [30], we designed three types of models with a pyramid structure that produces fewer parameters with equal or better performance than non-pyramid structures. Pyramidal models can help the systems at deployment time in two ways: 1. due to the small size of the trained pyramidal models, it does not require large bandwidth to update the deployed systems, hence less overhead, and 2. it requires small disk space, hence these are feasible for FGPAs and deployed systems with small storage. The initial neural network (NN) we used is a deep dense/fully-connected network that is designed in a pyramid structure. The remaining NNs are *CNN* based models. The models are explored with a varying number of kernels, kernel size, epochs, and learning rate. The number of kernels/neurons in each layer are reduced with a constant rate to form a pyramid structure.

Deep Dense Model with Pyramid Structure and SELU (DDPSS). Generally, dense models over-fits quickly due to a large number of parameters. However, if designed in a proper way they can perform efficiently despite a limited amount of data. This model consists of three types of layers: dense D, activation layer AL, and Dropout DO. The first layer $D1$ is followed by an AL that uses a recently introduced scaled exponential linear units ($SELU$) function [15]. $SELU$ perform activation as well as normalization in zero mean unit variance, hence resulting in smooth training and achieving good results. It is followed by two sets of D, $SELU$, and DO layers i.e. (*D2-SELU2-DO1* and *D3-SELU3-DO2*).

The *DO1* and *DO2* drops 30% and 60% of neurons, respectively. The output of *DO2* is used to calculate the resultant output at *D4* which is followed by an *AL* having sigmoid (*Sig*) activation function. We used 1200 - 100 neurons in each layer where each following layers have 100 fewer neurons in the previous layer to maintain the pyramid structure. It provides refinement of features at each layer and reduces any ambiguity that might exist in features.

The model uses regularization with L1 as 1e−9 and L2 as 0.0001, Adam optimizer, and binary cross-entropy. The models are trained from 30–2000 epochs.

Two Layered 1DCNN with ReLu & Batch Normalization (2L-PCNN-BN). CNN has several variations, however, we want to explore and find the best model for classification of CC vs. NCC Tweets. This CNN model (*2L-PCNN-BN*) consists of convolution layers (*C*), batch-normalization (BN) layers [10], and ReLu6 [16] activation layers. ReLu6 helps in quickly learning the sparse features. Beside normalizing the input data at the start, we adopted BN to normalize the output feature maps at each layer before passing it through AL (ReLu6). This per layer BN helps in fast learning despite saturating nonlinearities. Further, BN avoids the use of dropout and regularization. However, from our experience with this imbalanced dataset, we used dropout to avoid over-fitting.

The size of the kernel is 5 in *C1* and 4 in *C2*. The *C* layers are followed by *ALs* 1 and 2 having *Relu6*. *AL2* is followed by a dense layer (*D1*) with 80 neurons, an AL having (*ReLu6*), *DO* with 50%, and *D2* layer with 2 neurons. Finally, a softmax is used at output layer. A softmax layer is used in the end to find the output class. The batch size is 50, learning rate (*LR*) of 1e−7, and the model is trained with Adam optimizer and cross-entropy loss function. Each model is trained for 39 to 594 epochs. The number of kernels in each layer is: $C1 \in \{102, 94, 86, 80, 72, 64, 56, 48, 32, 24, 16\}$ $C2 \in \{94, 86, 80, 72, 64, 56, 48, 32, 24, 16, 8\}$

Three Layered 1DCNN with SELU (3L-PCNN-S). Using a BN makes the model slower. Therefore, the motivation behind this model is to reduce training time without affecting the performance. Therefore, we avoided BN after each layer by introducing *SELU*. This can provide both activation as well as normalization. This model consists of three sets of 1D convolution and *AL* having *SELU* i.e. (*C1-AL1-C2-AL2-C3-AL3*) layers. *AL3* is followed by two fully connected layers and *ALs* i.e. *D1* having 80 neurons and *AL4* with *SELU*. *DO1* layer drops 30% of neurons. Whereas, *D2* is having 1 neuron that is activated by *Sig* function. The model is trained with Adam optimizer, binary cross-entropy loss function, and regularization *L1* and *L2* values as in previous section. We also examined its performance with 5, 4, and 3 kernel size.

4.3   Evaluation Metrics

The experiments used a 1 × 3 cross validation. A number of evaluation measures were used. They were: *AUC*, balanced accuracy (*B-Acc*), average of per class F1-Score (*F1score*), and Matthews correlation coefficient (*MCC*) [11,13]. The data is highly imbalanced. In this scenario, accuracy cannot be considered as the correct metric due to the reason that the classifier most of the time learn and predict negative class correctly, resulting in high overall accuracy. An alternative is to calculate balanced accuracy. In the identification of cybercrime indicators, classifying the true positive was the selected option. Consequently we selected the maximum area under the ROC curve It can provide the maximum correct true positives that we can achieve. A recent review [28] concluded that the most widely used and recommended performance measure in case of imbalanced data is AUC. In [28], F1Score is shown as being used less often than AUC. The value of MCC is between -1 and 1. A classifier having MCC value greater than 0 is considered a good classifier.

5   Results

The results for the optimal configurations of each classifier is shown in Table 3. It is clear from the experiments that synthetic data played a positive role in learning. The CC class had so few training instances that it was not possible to build models without synthetic data. The following subsections present some observations about the performance of each classifier.

Table 3. Best models Epochs, Time, Parameters, B-Acc, AUC, F1-Score, and MCC

Model	Epochs	Time	Parameters	B-Acc	AUC	F1Score	MCC
DDPSS-1	**50**	22.13	1463101	**0.6463**	**0.85 ± 0.03**	0.9733	**0.1695**
DDPSS-2	55	**15.63**	**140701**	0.6138	0.85 + 0.02	0.9733	0.1432
3L-PCNN-S-1	100	31.05	197683	0.5885	0.82 ± 0.03	**0.0767**	0.1319
3L-PCNN-S-2	**50**	30.716	152835	0.6450	0.82 ± 0.02	0.9600	0.1310
2L-PCNN-BN-1	356	1810.7	1678069	0.6139	0.83 ± 0.01	0.9733	0.1445
2L-PCNN-BN-2	594	1730.9	746648	0.6285	0.82 ± 0.03	0.9700	0.1469

5.1   Random Forest

The objective is to emphasize the importance and provide a baseline for future research. It achieved lower AUC for trees less than 200 and more than 250. RF with 200 (*RF-200*) up to 250 trees achieved a stable AUC of 0.83 ± 0.01. RF with 200 trees (*RF-200*) and 250 (RF-250) achieved highest F1-Score of 0.98. On the contrary, these two achieved lowest *B-Acc* of 0.5151 and 0.5182, respectively. Similarly, they achieved lowest *MCC* of 0.0723 and 0.0370. RF is faster in terms of learning the model as compared to most of the DNN. However, DNNs are faster at test time and shows higher accuracy than RF. Further, some of the DNN models, if efficiently designed, can provide better fast training and testing on GPU.

5.2 2L-PCNN-BN

In this case, the best model (*2L-PCNN-BN-1*) in-terms of highest AUC have 110 and 102 kernels in *C1* and *C2* layer, respectively. It achieved AUC of 0.83 ± 0.01. This model results in 2084968 parameters and achieved optimal performance in 394 epochs that took 1810.7 s. In terms of overall performance, the best model in *2L-PCNN-BN* is *2L-PCNN-BN-2* having 54 and 46 kernels at *C1* and *C2* layer, respectively. It achieved AUC of 0.82 ± 0.02 with 746648 parameters in 1730.9 s. Although BN gives an opportunity to use higher LR and avoid DO layers, still we were unable to completely avoid it. Without DO and using higher LR, the models did not learn or show over-fitting. Similarly, it takes more time to learn and achieve optimal performance.

5.3 3L-PCNN-S

We learned from *2L-PCNN-BN* models that due to excess amount of parameters and limited data, the networks over-fits and show lower performance. In this group, the best model is *3L-PCNN-S-1* which have 102, 94, and 86 kernels in C1, C2, and C3, respectively. This model have kernel size of 5, dropout rate of 50%, and batch size of 5000. It achieved AUC of 0.82 ± 0.03 balanced accuracy of 0.589, and weighted F1-Score of 0.977. This model has 197683 parameters that took 31.19 s to train and test. Table 3 shows all the best models, having highest AUC and fewer number of parameters. We have learned that smaller batch sizes does not show good results. Over-fitting is observed if the models is trained for more than 50 epochs.

Table 4. Comparison of overall best case models with Baseline Random Forest

Model	Epochs	Time	Param	B-Acc	AUC	F1 Score	MCC
DDPSS-2	55	**15.63**	**140701**	0.6138	**0.85 $\pm$ 0.02**	0.9733	0.1432
3L-PCNN-S-2	**50**	30.716	152835	**0.6450**	0.82 $\pm$ 0.02	0.9600	0.1310
2L-PCNN-BN-2	594	1730.9	746648	0.6285	0.82 $\pm$ 0.03	0.9700	0.1469
RF-200	–	139.2	–	0.5151	0.83 $\pm$ 0.01	**0.9800**	0.0723

5.4 Comparison

Table 3 shows AUC, $B\text{-}Acc$, $F1Score$, MCC, number of parameters the model have (Param), and time each model took to train and test the same dataset. We evaluated the models in two ways. Section 4.3 highlighted that the recommended/widely used approach to evaluate a model in imbalanced dataset scenario is based on maximum AUC. Therefore, we will select the first best model for solely AUC. Whereas, the second best model is selected based on the good performance in majority of the metrics (AUC, less training Time, fewer/reasonable parameters, $B\text{-}ACC$, $F1Score$, and MCC). All the models are greatly affected by the noise in Twitter data. The preprocessing has a great impact on the performance of the models. Word2Vec model helps us in two ways, providing embedding based on the surrounding context of the collected Twitter Corpus as well as a mean (vectors) to generate synthetic data using SMOTE. The configuration of Word2Vec and SMOTE are the same for all experiments. If we don't use synthetic data in training, none of the models learns due to the limited amount of samples in CC class. *RF-200* has shown good *AUC*, as compared to *3L-PCNN-S*. In the case of *B-Acc* and *MCC*, it shows lower results than all the other three models. In terms of speed, it is slower as compared to *DDPSS-2* & *3L-PCNN-S* trained on GPU i.e. 139.2 vs. 15.63 s. Whereas, when we trained *DDPSS-1* on CPU, it was slower than RF by 79 s for training and testing the same dataset. In addition, it was 13x faster than *2L-PCNN-BN-2*. However, at test time the deep models are faster as compared to RF.

Table 3 shows that based on the first type of evaluation, the best *AUC* of 0.85 ± 0.03 is given by *DDPSS-1* (D1:900, D2:800, & D3:700). However, this model has large number of parameters as compared to *DDPSS-2*. Similarly, Table 4 shows that *DDPSS-2* (D1:300, D2:200, & D3:100) is second overall best model due to speed, fewer parameters, higher *AUC*, and second best *F1Score* and *MCC*. It shows that if a dense network is properly designed, it can achieve good results in imbalanced datasets. *2L-PCNN-BN-2* showed optimal *B-Acc* and *MCC* but due to the number of parameters and time it takes to train the model, it can be considered the worst for real-time applications.

Regularization with *L1* as 1e−9 and *L2* as 0.0001 has shown positive impact on overall performance. In addition, SELU as compared to ReLu and other activation functions has shown better performance.

5.5   Analysis over NYK-dataset

Based on the analysis in the previous section, we chose DDPSS-2 as an optimal model (DDPSS-2) by considering its speed, fewer parameters, higher AUC, and comparable F1Score and MCC. To analyze its generalization, we evaluated its performance over the NYK-dataset. From the confusion matrix in Table 5, we achieved a balanced accuracy of 65.75% with a sensitivity of 0.4826 and specificity of 0.8324. Although the accuracy and sensitivity of our model are not optimal, this could be due to several reasons e.g. trained on a small data, the regional specific tone in the Tweets compares to New York where people with different ethnicity around the world lives together. However, the higher B-Acc (by 4.37% compare to *DDPSS-2* and by 1.25% compare to *3L-PCNN-S-2* which are trained and tested on the same model) shows that the model if trained on a large dataset can further help in enhancing the performance. This highlights, that if a model is well trained, it can be used in any country to find indicators of cybercrime. In addition, high specificity value indicates that the system is capable of avoiding false alarms in the majority of cases. This is a good sign because around 99% of Tweets are normally not-cybercrime. This shows that a well-trained model can be used in an alarm generating system that will find indicators of cybercrime and avoid false alarms. In future, we would like to enhance the sensitivity by enhancing the model by training it with more related data either collected from Twitter or generated synthetic data.

Table 5. Confusion Matrix for testing NYK-dataset on the DDPSS-2 model

	Cybercrime	Not-Cybercrime
Cybercrime	83	91
Not-Cybercrime	89	452

6 Conclusion

We have highlighted a new application area that will be of interest to governmental or cybersecurity agencies to identify cybercrime vs. non-cybercrime Tweets in open social data related to financial organizations. The work consists of data collection & proposed labelling scheme, preprocessing, augmentation with sophisticated techniques, learning and classifying through deep pyramidal structured networks. We discussed that successful identification of indicators of cybercrime can lead us in designing an automatic alarm generation system. We proposed three pyramidal DNN that have fewer parameters to train, hence showed better speed and performance as compared to baseline RF. The model is suitable for real-world application due to the reason that the trained model is smaller in size and easy to deploy. Further, we highlighted the challenges due to an imbalanced dataset that have rare positive Tweets. In the future, we would like to extend and make available the collected dataset for future research. We will utilize GLoVe and ADASYN techniques instead of Word2Vec and SMOTE for generation of synthetic data. In addition, we will extend the system for generating alarms in near real-time by predicting cybercrime event.

References

1. Aggarwal, A., Rajadesingan, A., Kumaraguru, P.: PhishAri: automatic realtime phishing detection on twitter. In: eCrime Researchers Summit, eCrime, pp. 1–12 (2012)
2. Alsaedi, N., Burnap, P.: Feature extraction and analysis for identifying disruptive events from social media. In: Proceeding of the IEEE/ACM International Conference on Advances in Social Networks Analysis and Mining, pp. 1495–1502. ACM Press (2015)
3. Anti Phishing Working Group (APWG): Phishing Activity Trends Report Q4 2016. Tech. Rep. December, APWG (2016). http://docs.apwg.org/reports/apwg_trends_report_q4_2016.pdf
4. Breiman, L.: Random forests. Mach. Learn. **45**(1), 5–32 (2001). https://doi.org/10.1023/A:1010933404324
5. Burnap, P., et al.: Detecting tension in online communities with computational Twitter analysis. Technol. Forecast. Soc. Change **95**, 96–108 (2015). https://doi.org/10.1016/j.techfore.2013.04.013
6. Burnap, P., Williams, M.L.: Us and them: identifying cyber hate on Twitter across multiple protected characteristics. EPJ Data Sci. **5**(1), 1–15 (2016). https://doi.org/10.1140/epjds/s13688-016-0072-6

7. Chawla, N.V., Bowyer, K.W., Hall, L.O., Kegelmeyer, W.P.: SMOTE: synthetic minority over-sampling technique. J. Artif. Intell. Res. **16**, 321–357 (2002)
8. Drury, B.M., Lopes, A.D.A., et al.: A comparison of the effect of feature selection and balancing strategies upon the sentiment classification of Portuguese news stories. In: Brazilian Conference on Intelligent Systems, 3th; Encontro Nacional de Inteligência Artificial e Computacional, 11th (2014)
9. He, H., Bai, Y., Garcia, E.A., Li, S.: ADASYN: adaptive synthetic sampling approach for imbalanced learning. In: International Joint Conference on Neural Networks, pp. 1322–1328 (2008)
10. He, K., Zhang, X., Ren, S., Sun, J.: Deep residual learning for image recognition. In: IEEE Conference on CVPR, pp. 770–778. IEEE, June 2016
11. Indola, R.P., Ebecken, N.F.F.: On extending f-measure and g-mean metrics to multi-class problems. In: 6th International Conference on Data Mining, Text Mining and Their Business Applications, UK, vol. 35, pp. 25–34 (2005)
12. Institute, I.: New wave of cyber-attacks on banks (2016). http://resources. infosecinstitute.com/new-wave-of-cyber-attacks-on-banks/#gref
13. Jurman, G., Riccadonna, S., Furlanello, C.: A comparison of MCC and CEN error measures in multi-class prediction. PLoS ONE **7**(8), 1–8 (2012)
14. Khandpur, R.P., Ji, T., Jan, S., Wang, G., Lu, C.T., Ramakrishnan, N.: Crowdsourcing cybersecurity: cyber attack detection using social media. In: Proceeding of the ACM Conference on Information and Knowledge Management, pp. 1049–1057 (2017)
15. Klambauer, G., Unterthiner, T., Mayr, A., Hochreiter, S.: Self-normalizing neural networks. In: Advances in Neural Information Processing Systems, pp. 971–980 (2017)
16. Krizhevsky, A., Hinton, G.: Convolutional deep belief networks on cifar-10. Unpublished Manuscript **40**(7), 1–9 (2010)
17. Krizhevsky, A., Sutskever, I., Hinton, G.E.: ImageNet classification with deep convolutional neural networks. In: Advances in NIPS, pp. 1097–1105 (2012)
18. Lee, J.K., Moon, S.Y., Park, J.H.: CloudRPS: a cloud analysis based enhanced ransomware prevention system. J. Supercomput. **73**(7), 1–20 (2016)
19. Lee, K., Eoff, B.D., Caverlee, J.: Seven months with the devils: a long-term study of content polluters on twitter. Icwsm **2011**, 185–192 (2006)
20. Lee, S., Kim, J.: Warning bird: a near real-time detection system for suspicious URLs in twitter stream. IEEE Trans. Dependable Secure Comput. **10**(3), 183–195 (2013)
21. Levi, M., Doig, A., Gundur, R., Wall, D., Williams, M.: Cyberfraud and the implications for effective risk-based responses: themes from UK research. Crime Law Soc. Change **67**(1), 77–96 (2017). https://doi.org/10.1007/s10611-016-9648-0
22. Marchal, S., Francois, J., State, R., Engel, T.: Phish storm: detecting phishing with streaming analytics. IEEE Trans. Netw. Serv. Manage. **11**(4), 458–471 (2014)
23. Randazzo, M.R., Keeney, M., Kowalski, E.: Insider threat study: illicit cyber activity in the banking and finance sector. Tech. rep., 2018 (2005)
24. Maurer, M.-E., Höfer, L.: Sophisticated phishers make more spelling mistakes: using URL similarity against phishing. In: Xiang, Y., Lopez, J., Kuo, C.-C.J., Zhou, W. (eds.) CSS 2012. LNCS, vol. 7672, pp. 414–426. Springer, Heidelberg (2012). https://doi.org/10.1007/978-3-642-35362-8_31
25. Mikolov, T., Sutskever, I., Chen, K., Corrado, G.S., Dean, J.: Distributed representations of words and phrases and their compositionality. In: Advances in Neural Information Processing Systems, pp. 3111–3119 (2013)

26. Procter, R., Vis, F., Voss, A.: Reading the riots on Twitter: methodological innovation for the analysis of big data. Int. J. Soc. Res. Methodol. **16**(3), 197–214 (2013). http://www.tandfonline.com/doi/abs/10.1080/13645579.2013.774172

27. Schmidt, A., Wiegand, M.: A survey on hate speech detection using natural language processing. In: Proceedings of the Fifth International Workshop on Natural Language Processing for Social Media, pp. 1–10 (2012)

28. Shang, J.: Learning from class-imbalanced data: review of methods and applications. Expert Syst. Appl. **73**(January), 220–239 (2017). https://doi.org/10.1016/j.eswa.2016.12.035

29. Ullah, I., Lane, C., Drury, B., Mellotte, M., Madden, M.: Open social data crime analytics. In: International Workshop on Artificial Intelligence in Security, At IJCAI, Melbourne, Australia, pp. 86–87 (2017)

30. Ullah, I., Petrosino, A.: About pyramid structure in convolutional neural networks. In: Proceeding of the International Joint Conference on Neural Networks, pp. 1318–1324 (2016)

31. Wang, B., Zubiaga, A., Liakata, M., Procter, R.: Making the most of tweet-inherent features for social spam detection on twitter. CEUR Workshop Proc. **1395**, 10–16 (2015)

32. Wang, X., Gerber, M.S., Brown, D.E.: Automatic crime prediction using events extracted from twitter posts. In: Yang, S.J., Greenberg, A.M., Endsley, M. (eds.) SBP 2012. LNCS, vol. 7227, pp. 231–238. Springer, Heidelberg (2012). https://doi.org/10.1007/978-3-642-29047-3_28

33. Zubiaga, A., Liakata, M., Procter, R., Wong, G., Tolmie, P.: Analysing how people orient to and spread rumours in social media by looking at conversational threads. PLoS ONE **11**(3), 1–16 (2016)

StrCoBSP: Relationship Strength-Aware Community-Based Social Profiling

Asma Chader$^{(\boxtimes)}$ ⓘ, Hamid Haddadou ⓘ, Leila Hamdad ⓘ,
and Walid-Khaled Hidouci ⓘ

Laboratoire de la Communication dans les Systèmes Informatiques (LCSI),
Ecole Nationale Supérieure d'Informatique (ESI), BP 68M,
16309 Oued-Smar Algiers, Algeria
{aa_chader,h_haddadou,l_hamdad,w_hidouci}@esi.dz

Abstract. User interest inference in social media is an important research topic with great value in modern personalization and advertisement systems. Using relationships characteristics such as strength may allow more refined inference. Indeed, due to influence and homophily phenomena, people maintaining strongest relationships tend to be and become more similar. Accordingly, we present StrCoBSP a Strength-aware Community-Based Social Profiling process that combines community structure and relationship strength to predict user's interests in his egocentric network. We present empirical evaluation of StrCoBSP performed on real world co-authorship networks (DBLP/ResearchGate). The performances of the proposed approach are superior to the ones achieved by the existing strength-agnostic process with lifts of up to 18,46% and 18,15% in terms of precision and recall at top 15 returned interests.

Keywords: Social profile · Relationship strength · Ego networks · Weighted social networks · Weighted ego networks

1 Introduction

In the era of web 2.0, online social networks (OSNs) have become an integral part of daily life for millions of people who constantly maintain social relationships to connect with one another, share thoughts and opinions, consume news or entertain themselves. Analyzing social generated content have received much attention in last decade [20]. Several models aiming at better understanding users' behaviors were proposed for a myriad of applications. Amongst them, one fundamental task is social profiling which aims to derive attributes that characterize various aspects of a user such as demographics, educational background, political affiliation, location or personal interests; Information that represent a key input for modern personalization and advertisement systems. Nevertheless, in many situations data are inaccurate or missing especially with the rise of passive use of OSNs (users do not generate any content but only consume

© Springer Nature Switzerland AG 2021
J. A. Lossio-Ventura et al. (Eds.): SIMBig 2020, CCIS 1410, pp. 333–347, 2021.
https://doi.org/10.1007/978-3-030-76228-5_24

information) and the increasing awareness of privacy among users [20]. Addressing this, researchers identified phenomenon like *homophily* and *social influence* stating that people tend to be linked to others that are similar in some sense (homophily) and influence each other to become more similar over time (social influence) [10].

In this context, different profiling techniques are discussed in the literature [20]. Some of them are designed to operate on a full social graph while others focus on direct neighborhood of the user, aka. Egocentric (or simply ego) network [12,13,16–18,23]. Ego networks are models that represent social relations from a user's point of view. They consist of a focal node, called ego, his direct friends, known as alters, and the existing relationships among them. Several relationships' properties in ego networks were explored; we mention for instance, link type [12,13], community structure [16–18,23]. and relationship's dynamics [17,18]. In our research team, we are working on approaches that explore the influence of other relationship characteristics to enhance social profile prediction, in particular tie strength [1,2], this paper presents one of them in more details. The study that motivated this work [23] proposed a community based process, named CoBSP (Community-Based Social Profile), to infer user's attributes in egocentric network. Authors estimate that social circles or groups around the user are more significant to describe him and report satisfactory results on real social networks such as Facebook and DBLP. However, they assumed the network to be binary, i.e. all friends are equally related to ego user as well as to each other. Accordingly, we present StrCoBSP: a strength-aware Community-Based Social Profiling process that leverages both community structure and relationship strength to infer social profiles.

Tie strength was introduced by Mark Granovetter in his landmark paper [6] and defined as "*a (probably linear) combination of the amount of time, the emotional intensity, the intimacy (mutual confiding), and the reciprocal services which characterize the tie*" [6]. The study of tie strength speculates also that "*the stronger the tie connecting two individuals, the more similar they are*" [6]. Against this background, close friends (in generic social networks) or frequent collaborations (in co-authorship or professional networks) reflect in most cases individuals shared interests; such relations are more likely to provide relevant information about the profiled user than acquaintances or occasional collaborations (weak links). Besides, integrating tie strength in CoBSP allows to fully exploit alters relationships. While ego-alter ties are directly related to homophily and users' similarity, alter-alter ones enable to correctly depict the community structure of the ego network. In fact, previous studies [5,15] have shown that communities extracted on binary representation of social connections are different and less accurate than those extracted by including tie strength. To illustrate this, Fig. 1 shows an example of detected communities on a weighted network and its binary representation using *greedy optimization of modularity* method [3], where we can see different structures (four communities detected on weighted network versus only three on binary one). We can also see that some nodes such as d,c or a,o showing greater strength are assigned to the same community in weighted version (which makes sense since they reflect close relationships), but are not correctly depicted on binary network. Note that edge's width reflects strength of relationship between extremity nodes and red edges represent inter-community ties.

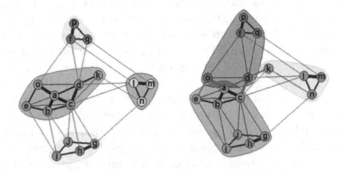

Fig. 1. Communities detected on weighted (left) and binary representation (right) of the network (Color figure online)

To sum up, the value of integrating relationship strength is two-fold, inferring interests from most relevant people, i.e. those having strongest relationship and thus greater similarity with ego (this involves ego-alter connections' strength) and depicting the most realistic community structure of the ego network; which is enabled through alter-alter connections' strength.

The remainder of the paper is organized as follows: the next section presents the related work. Section 3 describes our approach to extend the CoBSP process to operate on weighted egocentric networks. In section four, we present experiments conducted on DBLP bibliography network and the obtained results. Finally, Sect. 5 concludes the paper and presents future works.

2   Related Work

We briefly overview studies most related to this research. Social profiling literature outlines several approaches using direct neighborhood of a user to infer his attributes [12,13,16–18,20,23]. Many studies were conducted on twitter and only consider ego-alter connections [20]. We reviews in this section works that include connections among friends too. Different relationship information and social graph characteristics were explored in social profiling such as link type [12,13], community structure [16–18,23]. and relationship's dynamics [17,18]. For instance, Li et al. [12] attempt to learn profile by capturing the correlation between attributes (e.g., employer) and social connections type (e.g., colleague) in an ego network and proposed a new co-profiling approach to jointly infer users' attributes and relationship type. Similarly, [13] attempts to learn profile via a social-aware semi-supervised topic model that relies on latent reasons behind social connections and refined the profiling results by a novel label propagation strategy. Exploring another aspect of social graphs, works in [16–18,23]. describe a community-based algorithm to infer attributes via user-groups affinities. In the first, on which our approach is based, Tchuente et al. [23] represent each user profile with a personal and social dimensions and propose a three-step process, called CoBSP, to derive the social dimension: community extraction, community profiling (aggregating community's members interests) and finally social profile derivation combining all found interests; a process that achieved very satisfactory performance compared to individual based models. The others extend CoBSP process in different aspects, [16] attempted to address the sparse network problem by adding distance-2 neighbors (friends of a friend) while [17,18] studied network dynamics; they integrate temporal criteria and consider evolution of both relationships and shared information in the network.

As for relationship strength, several research studies were conducted, some discussed the quantitative measurement of strength [7] while others were interested at applications that could benefit from its computation, notably in decision support systems such as recommendation and location prediction [14]. In this later, McGee et al. developed a network-based model to infer user's locations by leveraging the strength between users on twitter [14]. To the best of the author's knowledge, this is the only study that directly investigates tie strength in attribute profiling. However, their model is specific to location prediction. Conversely, the community-based process proposed in [23] is designed to be generic but assumed the network to be binary. This motivates us to investigate tie strength contribution over such model to infer more relevant social profile.

3   Proposition: Strength-Aware Method to Construct Social Profiles

3.1   Notation

For a given user u (so called ego), let $G(V, E, E', U)$ be the graph describing his egocentric network, where V is the set of individuals directly connected to u (alters) and E, E' the sets of alter-alter and ego-alter weighted edges. E' records strength of relationships with the ego user, for each alter $v \in V, E'(v) = Sv$ denotes his strength to u. E is an adjacency matrix, where $E(v, v') = Svv', v, v' \in V$ is the edge weight from user v to user v'. In this study, we discuss undirected graphs (matrix E is symmetric) and assume that strengths can take on only positive values. The set U, for its part, describes alters' profiles, $U = \{P(v), v \in V\}$. In this study, we discuss profiles with respect to user's interests. For each user (ego and alters), a vector (see Eq. 1) of weighted interests is used to describe his profile. The weight of each interest $i \in I$, denoted $w(i, v)$, indicates its importance with respect to the user.

$$P(v) = \{(i, w(i, v)), \ i \in I, \ v \in V\} \tag{1}$$

where I denotes the set of interests, and V denotes the set of users.

Each profile is represented by two dimensions [23] a *user dimension*, $U(v)$, which represents his real interests (provided by the user or computed based on his own activities such as shared information, tweets, etc.) and a *social dimension* $S(v) = P(G)$ where interests are learned from user's social relations.

In the following, we will first give an overview of the existing CoBSP process, and then present our proposal that leverages relationship strength and community structure to build social profile from user's egocentric network while highlighting at each stage of the process the main differences with CoBSP process.

3.2   CoBSP: Community-Based Social Profile Process

Operating on a binary egocentric network, the CoBSP process considers the sub graph $G(V, E, U)$ where all the $Svv' \in E$ values equal to 1 (which means a relationship exists between v and v'). The set E' is not used as all the users are related (without any associated strength) to the ego. Further details about this process can be found in [23].

The CoBSP process starts with overlapping (where nodes can simultaneously belong to several groups) community detection in the user's egocentric network, followed by a community profiling step where interests of each community are computed using information of its members. Following ideas of the well-known TF-IDF measure, each interest is assigned a score according to its frequency in profiles of the community members as well as to its presence in other communities' profiles. The third step consists in computing the final weight of interests in communities' profiles. The weight of each interest i in the community c called $w(i, c)$ is a combination of structural score of the community (centrality measure) and semantic score (calculated in previous step) as in Eq. 2:

$$w(i, c) = Combination(Struct_{score}(c), Semantic_{score}(i, c), \alpha) \qquad (2)$$

This combination is a linear function: $combination(X, Y, a) = a \times X + (1-a) \times Y$, where $a \in [0, 1]$ is a tuning parameter to relativize the importance of semantic and structural scores.

Finally, the social dimension $S(u)$ of the user's profile is derived by combining the weights calculated in the previous phase for each interest.

3.3   StrCoBSP: Strength-Aware Community-Based Social Profile Process

We present in this section our strength-aware process, called StrCoBSP, which leverages the strength of both ego-alter and alter-alter relationships to infer user's interests. The alter-alter tie strength takes part in the first three stages relating to communities' processing (community detection, profiling and structural score calculation) whereas ego-alter strength is considered in the last stage to derive the user's social profile.

Community Detection. Community extraction is well-studied in literature and various solutions were proposed. In OSNs, users usually belong to multiple groups at once and network structure evolves continuously. Thus, to extract communities from the weighted egocentric network, we use the OSLOM algorithm [9]; which considers the link weights, and handles both overlapping communities and network dynamics. We note $C = \{C1, C2, C3...\}$ the set of extracted communities. For simplicity we refer to c_j as c if there is no confusion. Note that this first stage involves exclusively alter-alter tie strength.

Community Profiling. In this phase, we compute the profile of each community $c \in C$ as a set of weighted interests denoted $I(c)$. We assume that the profiles of all alters (the set $U(v), v \in V$) are already calculated and properly represented. Each interest i in $I(c)$ is weighted according to two scores: its semantic score in the community c and the structural score of c. The semantic score is computed using Eq. 3.

$$Semantic_{score}(i, c) = Sif(i, c) \times Sicf(i, c) \qquad (3)$$

where Sif and $Sicf$ represent respectively the weighted frequency of interest i in community c members' profiles and the relevance of interest i for the community.

The Sif score, standing for *Semantic Interest Frequency*, allows identifying the members' shared interests; the more frequent (and important) an interest is among the members of a community, the more this interest characterizes it. The Sif score is computed as follows (Eq. 4):

$$SIf(i, c) = \frac{\sum_{v_c=1}^{m} W(i, U(v_c))}{m} \; , \; W(i, U(v_c)) = \begin{cases} w(i, v_c) \; if(i, w(i, v_c)) \in U(v_c) \\ 0 \quad otherwise \end{cases}$$
$$(4)$$

where $U(v_c)$ is the *user dimension* of the node $v_c \in c$, $w(i, v_c)$ represents the weight of the interest i in $U(v_c)$ and m is the number of users in community c.

The $Sicf$ score, for *Semantic Inverse Community Frequency* (Eq. 5), is analogous to the IDF used in Information Retrieval [21]. Herein, it is about finding out what differentiates each community from other ones. The rarer an interest is, the more representative of the intrinsic affinity between members of the community, it will be.

$$Sicf(i, c) = \log \frac{|C|}{|\{c \in C : i \in I(c)\}|} \qquad (5)$$

where $|C|$ is the total number of communities in the egocentric network and $|\{c \in C : i \in I(C)\}|$ is the number of communities having the interest i in their profiles.

The structural score, for its part, relies only on network topology to characterize the communities. This score (Eq. 6) applied to an interest $i \in I(c)$ is the centrality value of c compared to other communities in the egocentric network. In this work, we consider the degree centrality which is regarded as one of the most important tools to explore actor roles in social networks [23].

Other centrality measures (such as betweenness, or proximity) can also be applied and will be considered in our future work.

In our context, two different aspects must be considered to compute the structural score. On the one hand, the degree centrality at a group level (since we deal with communities instead of individuals); and on the other hand, the strength of relationships. Based on a combination of extensions proposed in literature: the group centrality degree [4] and the weighted degree centrality [19], we formally define the weighted degree centrality for a community $c \in C$ as follows:

$$StrStructural_{score}(c) = \frac{|N(c)|^{(1-\beta)} \times W(c)^{\beta}}{|V| - |c|}, \quad W(c) = \sum_{v \in c, v' \in (V \setminus c)} S_{vv'} \quad (6)$$

where $|N(c)|$ denotes the number of people outside the group that are connected to at least one c member (the group extended degree centrality) and $W(c)$ denotes the group extended strength centrality similarly computed; normalized by the number of people that are not in c, $|V| - |c|$. For both group degree and strength, multiple connections to the same member of c community are only counted once.

This score combines both number of ties that a community has, and the average weight of these ties (strength) using a tuning parameter (β in Eq. 6) to set the relative importance between them. Setting β above 1 decreases the value of the degree in favor of a greater concentration of node strength whereas a value of β between 0 and 1 allows us to consider both number and strength of links. If the parameter is set to 0, the outcomes of the measures are solely based on the number of ties and conversely, if it equals to 1, the measure is based on ties strength only and the number of ties is disregarded.

Interest Weight Calculation. At this stage, each interest i in a community c's profile is assigned a score computed as in the original CoBSP process by an adjusted combination of the semantic and structural scores as in Eq. 7 below:

$$w(i, c) = \alpha \times StrStructural_{score}(c) + (1 - \alpha) \times Semantic_{score}(i, c) \quad (7)$$

where $\alpha \in [0,1]$ is a tuning parameter to evaluate the impact of structural score compared to semantic one.

Social Dimension Derivation. This step consists on deriving the social dimension of the user from communities' profiles by computing the final score of each interest $i \in S(u)$. Since communities are treated separately in previous stages, an interest i may appear in several profiles with different scores that should be combined in one single score, which will represent the weight of i in $S(u)$, called $W(i, S(u))$.

To do so, we adapt the linear function LIN-CombMNZ [8] used in Information Retrieval (IR) to merge results of different search engines. By analogy to IR systems, users' interests are seen as document and communities as search engines [23]. We consider the relationship strength of each community (treated as a whole) with the ego user as an importance weight attached to the search engine.

In the LIN-CombMNZ function, each score given by a search engine to the document is multiplied by a coefficient that relativizes its contribution in the final score. This coefficient varies between 1 and the number of merged systems and privileges systems having the highest score for the document.

To compute $W(i, S(u))$ by considering tie strength, communities are ordered increasingly ($StrCj < StrCj - 1$) according to their strength value with ego user. Like LIN-CombMNZ does for documents with highest score, we privilege the communities having strongest relationship with the profiled user. Thus, with n communities in the user's egocentric network, the community which has the highest strength with the ego is privileged and its score for the interest is multiplied by n ($j = n$ in Eq. 8), the second score is multiplied by $n - 1$, etc., the weakest relationship is not privileged and its score is multiplied by 1. Then, these adjusted scores are summed to obtain the final score of the interest. Formally, for each interest, its combined weight $W(i, S(u))$ is calculated as:

$$W(i, S(u)) = \overset{Str_{Cj-1} < Str_{Cj}}{\underset{j=1}{\overset{N}{\sum}}} W(i, Cj) \times j \qquad (8)$$

where $W(i, Cj)$ is the score for the interest i in Cj's profile as in Eq. 7 and $StrCj$ is the strength of community Cj in the user's egocentric network (Eq. 9). Note that communities are denoted Cj because this stage implicates several communities at once (those concerning the interest i).

We focus now on how to formulate the strength of a community $c \in C$ with the profiled user from relationship strength of all its members. We propose to compute Str_C, by a combination between the number of links the community has with ego (size of the community, denoted $|c|$) and the sum of those links strength, denoted $W(c)$. Each of them normalized by whether the total number of links or the total strength of all users in the egocentric network, see Eq. 9 below. This definition results from an analogy we did with the degree centrality in weighted networks [4]. We deem that the presence of many ties might also be considered to measure the involvement of the community in the user's egocentric network. Hence, for each community $c \in C$, we define its strength as:

$$Str_c = \left(\frac{|c|}{|E'|}\right)^{(1-\gamma)} \times \left(\frac{W(c)}{W_T}\right)^{\gamma}, \quad W(c) = \sum_{v \in c} S_v, \quad W_T = \sum_{v \in V} S_v \quad (9)$$

where $Sv \in E'$ denotes the tie strength between ego and node v and γ is a damping factor to relativize the importance of community size or strength as for β parameter used in communities' structural score . We describe in Sect. 4 the parametric study that enabled us to identify the fittest values of γ.

4 Experiment

In this section, we empirically evaluate the performance of our strength-aware approach. The experiments are conducted on the DBLP co-authorship network where an author's egocentric network is composed of his co-authors and the set of the weighted relationships between them. The DBLP database provides a comprehensive list of research papers with several metadata (publication date, venue, authors...) [11]. Authors' profiles can be easily built by analyzing keywords (considered as interests) from the titles of their publications [22,23] whereas authors' links can be weighted by a measure of strength of their collaboration; for instance frequency of co authorship, duration of relationship, etc.

4.1 Relationship Strength Calculation

We propose to compute the strength of co-authorship link between two nodes u and v in the egocentric network (denoted W_{uv}) based on two factors: the frequency of co-authorship (higher strength to frequent collaborations) and the total number of authored articles (exclusivity of co-authorship relation), formally:

$$W_{uv} = \frac{2 \times N_{uv}}{N_u + N_v} \tag{10}$$

where N_{uv} is the number of co-authored papers, and N_u, N_v represent the total number of author's u and v publications respectively.

4.2 Evaluation

To evaluate the performance of our strength-aware approach, we consider the users real profiles from ReasearchGate as a ground truth and determine which of CoBSP and StrCoBSP provides the most relevant social profiles (i.e. the closest to the users' real profiles). The real profiles of ego users are built from a different network in order to avoid identical data sources (publication titles). We consider the explicit interests indicated in user's ResearchGate profile. Figure 2 gives an example of an author's profile in the ResearchGate social network where can be seen his function, affiliation as well as the explicit list of interests that he filled in his profile (we use this latter to construct the real profile). In this experiment, we retain authors with at least 50 co-authors (to get consistent data for community extraction) and that have more than six interests in their ResearchGate profile. The identification of these authors is conducted manually. A set of 75 egocentric networks was collected [1]. The studied authors have an average of 95 co-authors (min = 50, max = 214) and an average of 19 interests indicated in their ResearchGate profiles.

To fairly compare our approach against the existing CoBSP, the same community detection algorithm (OSLOM algorithm [9]) is applied for both approaches. This allows us to exclude any effect from external processing to profiling process.

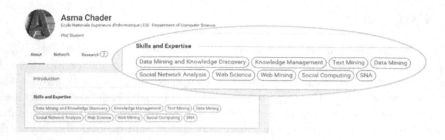

Fig. 2. An author's explicit interests from his profile on ResearchGate

Results are evaluated using the precision, recall and F-measure metrics as commonly done in related work [13, 16–18, 23]. The precision represents the proportion of relevant found interests and the total number of found interests; the recall represents the proportion of relevant found interests compared to the total number of real interests (user real profile) and the F-measure is the harmonic mean of precision and recall. As the number of interests computed in the social dimension can be too large, we only consider the top N interests from the social dimension.

$$Precision = \frac{N(I_{su})}{N(I_s)} \qquad Recall = \frac{N(I_{su})}{N(I_u)}$$

$$F - measure = 2 \times \frac{Precision \times Recall}{Precision + Recall} \qquad (11)$$

where $N(I_{su})$ is the number of relevant interests in the social dimension (present in the real user's profile), $N(I_s)$ is the total number of interests in the social dimension and $N(I_u)$ is the total number of interests in the user dimension(real profile).

4.3   Results and Discussion

This section presents the results of our evaluation. We perform a lot of experiments with different values of N and α, β, γ parameters (to infer their fittest values). Results are presented by the average of metrics for all 75 egos.

Figure 3 shows the overall performance comparison in terms of best precision and F-measure when varying the top N returned interests, $N \in \{5, 10, 15, 20, 30\}$ with $\beta = 0.3$ and $\gamma = 0.7$ for StrCoBSP process. From this figure, we can see that on both metrics and over all values of N, our proposed approach significantly outperforms the existing CoBSP. The best precision results are achieved at the top 5 returned interest while the best F-measure values are observed when $N > 15$. Regarding improvement, we can observe that the best results of the proposed StrCoBSP process outperforms those obtained by CoBSP of 3.73 and 2.95% in terms of mean precision (P@10) and F-measure (F@20) representing relative improvements of 19.58% and 19.80% respectively. This improvement shows the effectiveness of our proposition and confirms our premise that strongest relationships play an important role in social profiling.

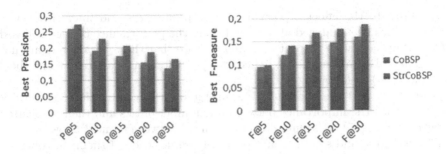

Fig. 3. Comparison of the best results of StrCoBSP and CoBSP approacheswhen varying top returned interests

Results presented hereafter are computed at the top 15 returned interests. This value ($N = 15$) offers a good compromise between precision and recall and ensures significant values of these metrics (users have an average of 19 interests indicated in their real profiles). In following, we first compare our approach against the existing CoBSP and then investigate StrCoBSP specifically through parametric study. Figure 4 depicts results of each process by the average precision, recall and F-measure according to α values for all users.

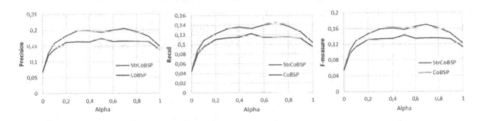

Fig. 4. Comparison of average precision, recall and F-measure according to α for all users ($\beta = 0.3$, $\gamma = 0.7$ for StrCoBSP)

For all values of α, the proposed StrCoBSP outperforms the CoBSP process. The highest results are obtained when $\alpha \in [0.6, 0.8]$ in which interval we observe an average gain of 0.1066, 0.078 and 0.091 in terms of precision, recall and F-measure; representing improvements of 20.51, 21.39 and 20.94% respectively. For the CoBSP approach, the best precision (0.173) and recall (0.122) are observed when $\alpha = 0.5$. In comparison, our StrCoBSP approach achieves its best precision and recall of 0.205 and 0.144 respectively when (α, β, γ) equals to (0.7, 0.3, 0.7) with up to 18,46% and 18,15% improvement over CoBSP. It is worth noting that unlike conclusions from [23], best results of both approaches are recorded with greater α values ($\alpha \in [0.05, 0.2]$ in [23] against $\alpha > 0.5$ in our study) which can be explained by the size/density of egocentric networks or else keywords extracted from publication titles. We leave a detailed study of these latter to future work.

To illustrate the effect of varying tuning parameters and infer their most accurate values, we analyzed at a second stage the performance of the proposed StrCoBSP process with respect to β and γ. Note that these parameters are not involved in CoBSP calculations; hence its representation as a straight line (best result recorded) in following graphs.

We first studied the effect of β parameter used in communities' structural score to control the importance between the number of ties and their associated strengths (see Fig. 5). We remind that ranging β between 0 and 1 allows to consider both degree and strength and positively values each of them; In contrast, a value of β above than 1 negatively values the number of links. We are not interested at this latter case in our study since we deem important to leverage both number and strength of links. Yet, we are still testing the value $\beta = 1.5$ only as confirmation. Figure 5 presents results of StrCoBSP process in terms of average precision and recall when β varies (horizontal axis) and $\alpha \in [0.5, 0.8]$ (different curves) by fixing γ to 0.7 (Results according to other values of γ parameter are also comparable). We observe that the curves follow roughly the same distribution. The optimal results are always achieved when both links number and strength are taken into account. The best results are obtained when $\beta \in [0.2, 0.4]$ with a substantial improvement upon the worst observed results (for $\beta > 1$) which means that number of ties is relatively more important. This supports our hypothesis that number of ties (the presence of many ties) as well as ties with greater strength have a part to play in quantifying the involvement of communities in the egocentric network. Moreover, and as expected, the performance decreases significantly when the number of links is not considered (i.e. when $\beta = 1$) and attains its worst rates if this latter is negatively valued (i.e. $\beta = 1.5$).

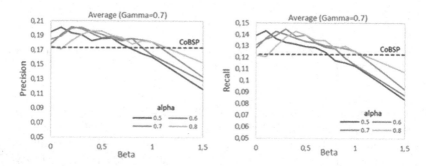

Fig. 5. Comparison of the average precision (left) and average recall (right) of StrCoBSP according to β variation for $\alpha \in [0.5, 0.8]$, $\gamma = 0.7$

Similarly, the variations of StrCoBSP results were studied according to γ (as shown in Fig. 6). The γ parameter controls the importance between the number of ties and associated strengths when computing the strength of communities to ego user (Eq. 9). Note that in this experiment, we are not studying the relevance of community-ego connections but the contribution of number of links and their strengths to characterize these connections. We observe that the curves are almost flat over the range of γ values. This suggests that variation of γ, compared to β, has relatively low impact on the effectiveness of our strength-aware process. However, the best results are reported for high γ values ($\gamma > 0.7$) when both number and strength are considered (with a higher contribution from links strength). This demonstrates the promising ability of strength to correctly characterize the ego-community connections.

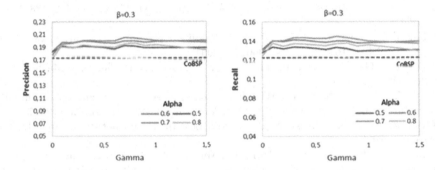

Fig. 6. Comparison of the average precision (left) and average recall (right) of StrCoBSP according to γ variation for $\alpha \subset [0.5, 0.8]$, $\beta = 0.3$

Based on the above results, we can globally conclude that both ego-alter and alter-alter connections' strength holds valuable information to characterize communities in the user's egocentric network. This empirical evaluation amply demonstrates the potential of StrCoBSP to accurately infer user's interests in his egocentric network.

5   Conclusions

In this paper we study the problem of social profiling. We investigate the ability of tie strength along with community structure to accurately infer users' interests on their egocentric networks. Our proposed approach leveraging both ego-alter (that allows to select most relevant people around the user from whom to infer interests) and alter-alter (which allows to depict the most realistic community structure around the user) strengths substantially improved the existing strength-agnostic process with lifts of up to 18.28% for F-measure@15, demonstrating the relevance of our premises. As our future work, our short-term perspective is to evaluate the contribution of alter-alter and ego-alter connections separately as well as to explore other ways to integrate them to the profiling process. We would like further to evaluate our approach in a large dataset and to different social networks presenting distinct characteristics (e.g., Facebook or

LinkedIn). Finally, with the popularity of different social platforms, users nowa-days tend to have multiple accounts across them. It will be interesting as a long term perspective to explore this direction for cross-system social profiling.

References

1. Chader, A., Haddadou, H., Hamdad, L., Hidouci, W.K.: The strength of consider-ing tie strength in social interest profiling. J. Web Eng. **19**(3–4), 457–502 (2020)
2. Chader, A., Haddadou, H., Hidouci, W.K.: All friends are not equal: weight-aware egocentric network-based user profiling. In: 2017 IEEE/ACS 14th International Conference on Computer Systems and Applications (AICCSA), pp. 482–488. IEEE (2017)
3. Clauset, A., Newman, M.E., Moore, C.: Finding community structure in very large networks. Phys. Rev. E **70**(6), 066111 (2004)
4. Everett, M.G., Borgatti, S.P.: The centrality of groups and classes. J. Math. Sociol. **23**(3), 181–201 (1999)
5. Fan, Y., Li, M., Zhang, P., Wu, J., Di, Z.: The effect of weight on community structure of networks. Physica A: Stat. Mech. Appl. **378**(2), 583–590 (2007)
6. Granovetter, M.S.: The strength of weak ties. In: Social networks, pp. 347–367. Elsevier (1977)
7. Gupta, J.P., Kärkkäinen, H., Torro, O., Mukkamala, R.R.: Revisiting social media tie strength in the era of data access restrictions. In: Proceedings of the 11th International Joint Conference on Knowledge Discovery, Knowledge Engineer-ing and Knowledge Management (IC3K 2019): Volume 3: KMIS, pp. 187–194. SCITEPRESS Digital Library (2019)
8. Hubert, G., Loiseau, Y., Mothe, J.: Etude de différentes fonctions de fusion de systèmes de recherche d'information. Le document numérique dans le monde de la science et de la recherche (CIDE 2010), pp. 199–207 (2007)
9. Lancichinetti, A., Radicchi, F., Ramasco, J.J., Fortunato, S.: Finding statistically significant communities in networks. PLoS ONE **6**(4), e18961 (2011)
10. Lee, S.Y.: Homophily and social influence among online casual game players. Telematics Inf. **32**(4), 656–666 (2015)
11. Ley, M.: DBLP: some lessons learned. Proc. VLDB Endowment **2**(2), 1493–1500 (2009)
12. Li, R., Wang, C., Chang, K.C.C.: User profiling in an ego network: co-profiling attributes and relationships. In: Proceedings of the 23rd International Conference on World Wide Web, pp. 819–830. ACM (2014)
13. Ma, C., Zhu, C., Fu, Y., Zhu, H., Liu, G., Chen, E.: Social user profiling: a social-aware topic modeling perspective. In: Candan, S., Chen, L., Pedersen, T.B., Chang, L., Hua, W. (eds.) DASFAA 2017. LNCS, vol. 10178, pp. 610–622. Springer, Cham (2017). https://doi.org/10.1007/978-3-319-55699-4_38
14. McGee, J., Caverlee, J., Cheng, Z.: Location prediction in social media based on tie strength. In: Proceedings of the 22nd ACM International Conference on Infor-mation & Knowledge Management, pp. 459–468 (2013)
15. Newman, M.E.: Analysis of weighted networks. Phys. Rev. E **70**(5), 056131 (2004)
16. On-At, S., Canut, M.F., Péninou, A., Sèdes, F.: Deriving user's profile from sparse egocentric networks: using snowball sampling and link prediction. In: Ninth Inter-national Conference on Digital Information Management (ICDIM 2014), pp. 80–85. IEEE (2014)

17. On-At, S., Quirin, A., Péninou, A., Baptiste-Jessel, N., Canut, M.F., Sèdes, F.: Taking into account the evolution of users social profile: Experiments on twitter and some learned lessons. In: 2016 IEEE Tenth International Conference on Research Challenges in Information Science (RCIS), pp. 1–12. IEEE (2016)
18. On-at, S., Quirin, A., Péninou, A., Baptiste-Jessel, N., Canut, M.-F., Sèdes, F.: A parametric study to construct time-aware social profiles. In: Missaoui, R., Abdessalem, T., Latapy, M. (eds.) Trends in Social Network Analysis. LNSN, pp. 21–50. Springer, Cham (2017). https://doi.org/10.1007/978-3-319-53420-6_2
19. Opsahl, T., Agneessens, F., Skvoretz, J.: Node centrality in weighted networks: Generalizing degree and shortest paths. Soc. Netw. **32**(3), 245–251 (2010)
20. Piao, Guangyuan, Breslin, John G.: Inferring user interests in microblogging social networks: a survey. User Model. User-Adapted Interact. 1–53 (2018). https://doi.org/10.1007/s11257-018-9207-8
21. Salton, G., Waldstein, R.K.: Term relevance weights in on-line information retrieval. Inf. Process. Manage. **14**(1), 29–35 (1978)
22. Shubankar, K., Singh, A., Pudi, V.: A frequent keyword-set based algorithm for topic modeling and clustering of research papers. In: 2011 3rd Conference on Data Mining and Optimization (DMO), pp. 96–102. IEEE (2011)
23. Tchuente, D., Canut, M.F., Jessel, N., Péninou, A., Sèdes, F.: A community-based algorithm for deriving users' profiles from egocentrics networks: experiment on Facebook and DBLP. Soc. Netw. Anal. Min. **3**(3), 667–683 (2013)

Identifying Differentiating Factors for Cyberbullying in Vine and Instagram

Rahat Ibn Rafiq[1]([✉]), Homa Hosseinmardi[2], Richard Han[1], Qin Lv[1],
and Shivakant Mishra[1]

[1] University of Colorado Boulder, Boulder, USA
{rahat.rafiq,richard.han,qin.lv,shivakaht.mishra}@colorado.edu
[2] University of Southern California, Los Angeles, CA, USA
homahoss@isi.edu

Abstract. A multitude of online social networks (OSNs) of varying types has been introduced in the past decade. Because of their enormous popularity and constant availability, the threat of cyberbullying launched via these OSNs has reached an unprecedented level. Victims of cyberbullying are now more vulnerable than ever before to the predators, perpetrators, and stalkers. In this work, we perform a detailed analysis of user postings on Vine and Instagram social networks by making use of two labeled datasets. These postings include threads of media posts and user comments that were labeled for being cyberbullying instances or not. Our analysis has revealed several important differentiating factors between cyberbullying and non-cyberbullying instances in these social networks. In particular, cyberbullying and non-cyberbullying instances differ in (i) the number of unique negative commenters, (ii) temporal distribution of positive and negative sentiment comments, and (iii) textual content of media captions and subsequent comments. The results of these analyses can be used to build highly accurate classifiers for identifying cyberbullying instances.

Keywords: Cyberbullying · Social computing · Social network analysis

1 Introduction

The past decade has seen an unprecedented growth of Online Social Networks (OSNs). Unfortunately, this rise has also paved the way for online predators, stalkers and cyberbullying to wreak havoc on the psyche of potential victims. Cyberbullying has the potential to be more damaging than real-life bullying since it follows children and teens even outside of their schools, e.g. in their homes where they were safe earlier. The constant threat of cyberbullying in online social networks has led to devastating psychological effects in victims such as nervous breakdowns, low self-esteem, self-harm, clinical depression and in some extreme cases, suicides [5, 28].

© Springer Nature Switzerland AG 2021
J. A. Lossio-Ventura et al. (Eds.): SIMBig 2020, CCIS 1410, pp. 348–361, 2021.
https://doi.org/10.1007/978-3-030-76228-5_25

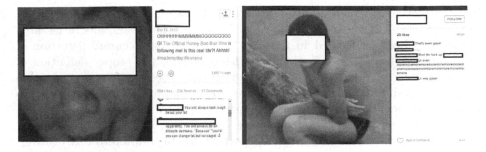

Fig. 1. Examples of cyberbullying in the (L) Vine and (R) Instagram online social networks.

In this work, we focus on the analysis of cyberbullying on Instagram and Vine, which are especially popular with the current youth. We acknowledge that, even though Vine has been discontinued by Twitter [11], similar short video social networks are still available, such as Byte [15] and TikTok [23]. We argue that thus, the analysis of user behaviors on Vine will not be much different from the other OSNs similar to it. Cyberbullying in Instagram and Vine can happen in different ways, including sharing a humiliating/insulting/edited image/video of a victim, posting mean and hateful comments on victim's profile, including aggressive captions on shared media or hashtags, or even creating fake profiles pretending to be someone else [27]. Figure 1 provides an illustration where the profile owner is victimized by hurtful and aggressive comments posted by others in Vine and Instagram respectively. In the context of OSNs, cyber-aggression is defined as a type of behavior in an electronic context that is meant to harm another person (e.g., verbal abuse from an anonymous user online). Cyberbullying is cyber-aggression that is carried out repeatedly, against a person who cannot easily defend himself or herself, and where the bully has power over the victim [14,22]. Previous works on Instagram [7] and Vine [25] have reported that not all media sessions (shared media + associated comments) that exhibit cyber-aggression are necessarily instances of cyberbullying. In this paper, we go deeper to identify distinguishing features that differentiate cyberbullying postings from non-cyberbullying postings by conducting the following.

- Investigation of number of (i) unique commenters, (ii) unique positive sentiment commenters, and (iii) unique negative sentiment commenters
- Temporal analysis of comments belonging to the shared media
- Text-content analysis of the media captions and comments associated with the media sessions

2 Related Work

The majority of the earliest works on cyberbullying did not differentiate between instances of cyberbullying and cyber aggression [3,4,12,13,17,19,24,26,30].

This distinction is crucial since the imbalance of power in favor of the bully magnifies the effects of cyber aggression [14]. In the last few years, lots of research works have been performed in the area of efficient and accurate detection of cyberbullying using datasets that were labeled using the proper definition of cyberbullying [1,2,8,25,29,32]. Although works have been performed to develop machine learning algorithms and features, very few works have been done to understand these features' temporal properties across a media session.

Previous research on comment analysis was mostly based on analyzing and labeling the text-content of the comments [1,12,26]. In addition to text features, the number of sent and received comments [20] and graph properties [10] were also considered to detect instances of cyberbullying. Analysis of profanity of the comments [4,6,17,19] and sentiments [18,31] in many social networks have also been explored extensively. To the best of our knowledge, none of these works explored the influence of profanity or sentiments of different parts of the comment thread (profile owner comments, media caption, etc.) across a media session's temporal frame.

3   Data Set

We use labeled data from Instagram [16] and Vine [25], which label each media session (shared media + associated comments) as an instance of cyberbullying, cyber-aggression, both, or neither. The data was originally collected using snowball sampling and labeled using the crowdsourcing work platform Crowd-Flower (See [25] for the detailed methodology for data collection and labeling). To improve the quality of our analysis, we filter the data-set to include only media sessions with a high confidence score of being correct. For each media session, each judgment is given a trust score that incorporates the overall trust score of a labeler with the score that the labeler got while answering the test questions given on the survey (administered during the labeling process). This trust value is, in turn, incorporated with the majority voting method to assign a confidence score to the label given to a particular media session. In addition to the comment-texts and confidence score of each label, the data-sets also contain the profile owner-id, media caption, and time stamp of the shared media, timestamps of the comments, and id of the commenters belonging to the media session. For our analysis, we only use media sessions with a confidence score of 90% or higher. For Vine, this filtering reduced 983 media sessions to 42 cyberbullying media sessions and 213 non-cyberbullying media sessions. For Instagram, this filtering reduced 2216 media sessions to 239 cyberbullying media sessions and 769 non-cyberbullying media sessions. Using a high confidence score meant that the labelers were unanimous in their labeling of a particular media session.

4   Analysis of Unique Commenters

We first investigate whether the number of unique commenters has any possible influence when it comes to making a media session an instance of cyberbullying. Here, the number of unique commenters means the number of distinct

Table 1. CCDF of number of (unique, unique positive, unique negative) commenters vs percentage of total (cyberbullying, non-cyberbullying) media sessions for Vine and Instagram

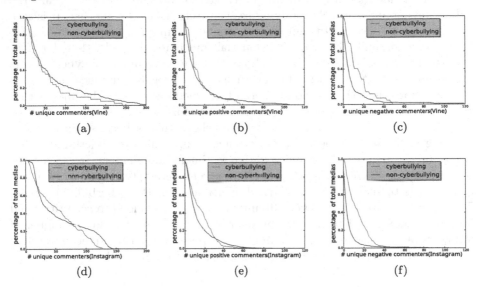

(a)   (b)   (c)

(d)   (e)   (f)

users who comment on a media session. We consider the total number of unique commenters, the total number of unique positive sentiment commenters, and the total number of unique negative sentiment commenters. For this purpose, we take the comments associated with the labeled media sessions for both Vine and Instagram and perform sentiment analysis of all the comments using Python's NLTK library [21]. NLTK computes polarity for each comment that shows how negative or positive a particular comment's sentiment is. After getting all the comments and getting their corresponding sentiments, we generate CCDF (Complementary Cumulative Distribution Function) of the number of unique commenters (Table 1a, 1d), number of unique positive sentiment commenters (Table 1b, 1e) and the number of unique negative sentiment commenters (Table 1c, 1f) vs the percentage of total cyberbullying (non-cyberbullying) media sessions for Vine and Instagram, respectively.

In Table 1a and 1d, the red and blue plots stand for the cyberbullying and non-cyberbullying media sessions respectively. The X-axis denotes the number of unique commenters and the Y-axis denotes the percentage of cyberbullying (non-cyberbullying) media sessions out of total cyberbullying (non-cyberbullying) media sessions having at least that many numbers of unique commenters. It is evident from the figure that for both Vine and Instagram, the number of unique commenters tends to have the same pattern for cyberbullying and non-cyberbullying. The same indistinguishable trend for both labels is also seen for the total number of unique positive sentiment commenters from Table 1b and 1e. This means that *for both Vine and Instagram, cyberbullying, and non-cyberbullying media sessions tend to have the same trend when it comes to the number of unique commenters and the number of unique positive sentiment commenters.*

However, for the number of unique negative commenters (Table 1c and 1f), cyberbullying and non-cyberbullying sessions differ from one another. It is seen that, for both Vine and Instagram, the number of unique negative commenters trend for cyberbullying media sessions fall much more slowly than for non-cyberbullying sessions. The figure shows that the percentage of cyberbullying media sessions that have at least a certain number of negative unique commenters is much more than that of non-cyberbullying media sessions. This means that *cyberbullying media sessions are likely to have more unique negative sentiment commenters for Vine and Instagram.* We believe this is because, in a cyberbullying media session, perpetrators often gang up against the victim and thus spikes up the number of unique negative sentiment commenters. It can also be seen that after 40 unique negative sentiment commenters, the non-cyberbullying trend starts to show a long tail, which is not seen for the cyberbullying trend. This is because some non-cyberbullying media sessions belong to celebrities and famous brands that have a large number of comments from a large number of followers, and sometimes the commenters express awe with expletives and/or swear words in those media sessions, thus contributing to the long tail.

5   Temporal Analysis of Negative and Positive Sentiment Comments

Now we turn our attention to the temporal analysis of comments on a particular media session since the media session is shared. We perform the analysis on all negative and positive sentiment comments where the sentiment was determined by using Python's NLTK library [21]. We do the temporal analysis for both negative and positive sentiment comments because we think media sessions that are tagged as cyberbullying are more likely to have a higher concentration of negative sentiment comments and a lower concentration of positive comments, thus resulting in the imbalance of power as per the definition of cyberbullying.

Figures in Table 2 show the temporal comment polarity for all negative sentiment comments for a particular cyberbullying (not cyberbullying) media session since the sharing of the media session for Vine and Instagram respectively. It is evident from the figures that the negative sentiment comments are much more spread up across the temporal frame of each media session in the case of cyberbullying sessions than for the non-cyberbullying sessions. The cyberbullying media sessions have a constant flow of high negative sentiment comments pouring in, even after a considerable amount of time since the sharing of the media. On the contrary, the same cannot be said for the non-cyberbullying sessions as the number of negative sentiment comments tend to go down as time moves on. We believe this is a very important factor that can differentiate a cyberbullying media session from a non-cyberbullying one. This shows that *in the cyberbullying media sessions, the negative sentiment comments persist even after a long time since the sharing of the media, which confirms the factor of repetition of aggression in the definition of cyberbullying.*

Table 2. Polarity of negative sentiment comments as time moves on since the media session has been posted for cyberbullying and non-cyberbullying media sessions in Vine and Instagram

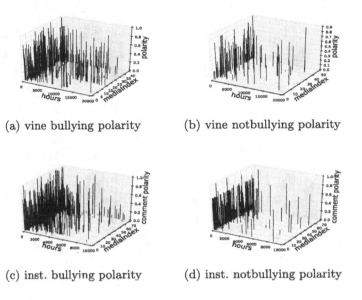

(a) vine bullying polarity   (b) vine notbullying polarity

(c) inst. bullying polarity   (d) inst. notbullying polarity

Table 3. Subjectivity of negative sentiment comments as time moves on since the media session has been posted for cyberbullying and non-cyberbullying media sessions in Vine and Instagram

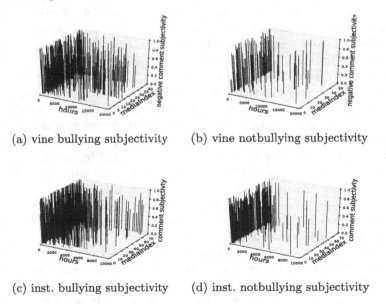

(a) vine bullying subjectivity   (b) vine notbullying subjectivity

(c) inst. bullying subjectivity   (d) inst. notbullying subjectivity

Table 4. Polarity of positive sentiment comments as time moves on since the media session has been posted for cyberbullying and non-cyberbullying media sessions in Vine and Instagram

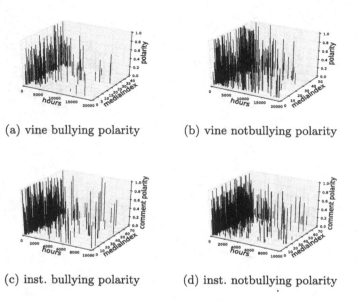

(a) vine bullying polarity   (b) vine notbullying polarity

(c) inst. bullying polarity   (d) inst. notbullying polarity

Next, we conduct the same kind of temporal analysis to investigate the subjectivity of the negative sentiment comments for cyberbullying and non-cyberbullying media sessions for both Vine and Instagram. Subjectivity determines how severe a negative sentiment comment is [21]. The intuition is that the cyberbullying media sessions should have more negative sentiment comments with comparatively higher subjectivity, thus being more aggressive which in turn results in cyberbullying. Figures in Table 3 show the subjectivity values of all the negative sentiment comments posted for the cyberbullying and non-cyberbullying media sessions since the sharing of the media sessions for both Vine and Instagram. It is apparent from the figures that the cyberbullying media sessions for both Vine and Instagram keep having negative sentiment comments with very high subjectivity spread across the temporal frame since the sharing of the media session. This results in the denser concentration of high bars for the cyberbullying sessions. *So not only the cyberbullying media sessions keep getting more negative sentiment comments even after a long time since the media session is posted, but also the negative sentiment comments tend to have more subjectivity than non-cyberbullying media sessions.*

Now, we conduct a temporal analysis of the polarity of all the positive sentiment comments for cyberbullying and non-cyberbullying media sessions for both Vine and Instagram. The expectation is that the cyberbullying sessions should have a less concentrated positive sentiment comments, thus rendering the effect of the imbalance of power as delineated in the definition of cyberbullying. Figures in Table 4 show the temporal comment polarity for all positive sentiment comments for a particular media session since the moment the media session has been posted for Vine and Instagram respectively. From the figures, it is seen that the *density of positive comments coming in for cyberbullying media sessions for both Vine and Instagram is much less than the non-cyberbullying media sessions*. This lesser concentration of positive sentiment comments coupled with the denser concentration of negative sentiment comments with high subjectivity spread across the temporal frame instigates the effect of the imbalance of power and repeated aggression, thus rendering the media session a cyberbullying one.

6 Analysis of Comments

Table 5. Frequency distribution and top idf valued distribution of words used for the cyberbullying and non-cyberbullying media sessions' comments in Vine and Instagram.

(a) vine bullying words   (b) vine not bullying words   (c) insta. bullying words

(d) insta. notbullying words   (e) vine bullying idf   (f) vine notbullying idf

(g) insta. bullying idf   (h) insta. notbullying idf

Next, we perform a text-content analysis for the comments associated with a media session for both Vine and Instagram. We consider the comments associated with a media session from part of a discussion thread, and our goal is to determine the differences between a discussion thread of a cyberbullying session and a discussion thread of a non-cyberbullying thread.

First, we devise a word frequency cloud for the cyberbullying and non-cyberbullying media sessions for both the social networks to get an idea of the words that occur frequently. Figures in Table 5a, 5b, 5c, 5d show the frequency distribution of words of all the media sessions' comments belonging to cyberbullying and non-cyberbullying media sessions for Vine and Instagram respectively. It can be seen from these figures that *negative sentiment words are much more frequent in the discussion comment threads of cyberbullying sessions.*

Next, we do an IDF (Inverse Document Frequency) analysis of the media sessions' comments that measures how common a word is across all media session comment discussions for cyberbullying and non-cyberbullying sessions. The difference between the frequency analysis and IDF analysis is that frequency analysis only takes into account the number of times a word appears in a discussion thread whereas IDF analysis gives us words that are common across all cyberbullying and non-cyberbullying comment discussion threads. Thus, a word that appears 10 times in 10 different documents will have lower IDF than a word that appears 10 times in a single document. Figures in Table 5e, 5f, 5g and 5h show the commonly appearing words for cyberbullying and non-cyberbullying media session comment threads for both Vine and Instagram respectively across all the corresponding media session comment threads. The bigger a word is in the word cloud, the more common it is across all the media session comment threads belonging to either cyberbullying or non-cyberbullying label. It is evident that, as it was seen also from the previous paragraph, *a cyberbullying media session comment discussion thread is much more likely to have negative sentiment words.*

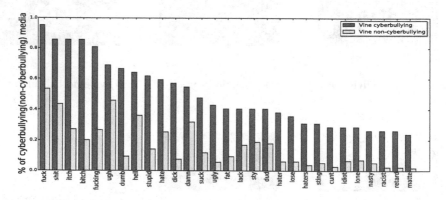

Fig. 2. Negative sentiment words vs percentage of cyberbullying (non-cyberbullying) media sessions out of total cyberbullying (non-cyberbullying) media sessions' comment threads containing that word in Vine.

To further confirm the aforementioned claim, we use the negative sentiment word list [9] and find out the percentage of cyberbullying (non-cyberbullying)

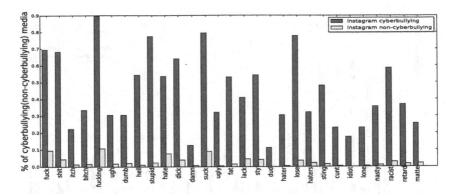

Fig. 3. Negative sentiment words vs percentage of cyberbullying (non-cyberbullying) media sessions out of total cyberbullying (non-cyberbullying) media sessions' comment threads containing that word in Instagram.

media sessions out of total cyberbullying (non-cyberbullying) media sessions whose comment threads contain those negative sentiment words. We intuit that negative sentiment words appear more in the cyberbullying media sessions than the non-cyberbullying media sessions for both the social networks, thus forming a differentiating factor for cyberbullying. We can see from Figures 2 and 3, negative sentiment words are much more likely to appear in a cyberbullying media session's associated comments than the non-cyberbullying media sessions, thus further confirming our claim: *a cyberbullying media session comment discussion thread is much more likely to have negative sentiment words.*

7   Analysis of Media Captions

In this section, we analyze the captions that the profile owners put for each media-sessions when they share the media in Vine and Instagram. We intuit that these media captions set the topic of the discussion that comes after the media is shared and thus setting precedent for the oncoming comment threads. We do this analysis to check if there are any differentiating topics, words, or subjects when it comes to cyberbullying and not-cyberbullying media sessions for both Vine and Instagram.

For this analysis, we use the negative sentiment word list [9] and find out the percentage of cyberbullying and not-cyberbullying media sessions out of total cyberbullying and not-cyberbullying media sessions respectively whose captions contain those negative sentiment words. Our intuition is that negative sentiment words appear more in the cyberbullying media sessions' captions than the not-cyberbullying media sessions' captions, thus forming a differentiating factor for cyberbullying. Surely enough, as it can be seen from Fig. 4, negative sentiment words are much more likely to appear in a cyberbullying media session's associated caption than the not-cyberbullying media session's captions, thereby further supporting our claim: *a cyberbullying media session caption is much more likely to have negative sentiment words.*

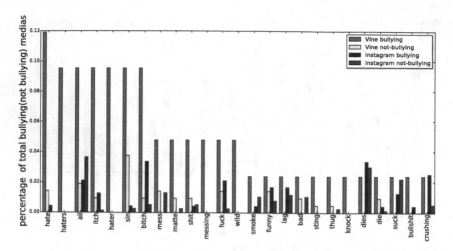

Fig. 4. Negative sentiment words vs percentage of bullying (not bullying) media sessions out of total cyberbullying (not-cyberbullying) media sessions' captions containing that word in Vine and Instagram

8 Conclusions

To the best of our knowledge, this is the first paper to investigate factors that differentiate a cyberbullying session from a non-cyberbullying one for both Vine and Instagram, two media-based online social networks leveraging labeled data that used appropriate definition of cyberbullying. We analyze the number of unique commenters, unique positive sentiment commenters, and unique negative sentiment commenters. We then perform a temporal analysis of all comments for both social networks. Finally, we conduct a content analysis of the comment threads and media-captions belonging to the labeled cyberbullying and non-cyberbullying media sessions.

The key findings of this research are as follows. First, for both Vine and Instagram, cyberbullying media sessions are more likely to have more unique negative sentiment commenters. Second, in the cyberbullying media sessions, negative sentiment comments persist with higher subjectivity even after a long time since the media has been posted, which is not the case for non-cyberbullying media sessions. Third, the density of positive comments coming in for cyberbullying media sessions for both Vine and Instagram is much less than that for the non-cyberbullying media sessions across the temporal frame. Fourth, the comment discussion threads across time units belonging to cyberbullying media sessions show a high level of negative sentiment polarity than those belonging to non-cyberbullying sessions. Fifth, while for non-cyberbullying media sessions, negative sentiment discussions tend to fizzle out as time moves on, that is not the case for cyberbullying media sessions in Vine and Instagram. Sixth, a cyberbullying media session's media caption is more likely to have negative sentiment words. Seventh, a cyberbullying media session comment thread is much more likely to have negative sentiment words than a non-cyberbullying media session. In future, we plan to leverage these insights to build a highly accurate cyberbullying classifier for both Vine and Instagram.

Acknowledgement. This work was supported by the US National Science Foundation (NSF) through grant CNS 1528138.

References

1. Arslan, P., Corazza, M., Cabrio, E., Villata, S.: Overwhelmed by negative emotions? Maybe you are being cyber-bullied! In: Proceedings of the 34th ACM/SIGAPP Symposium on Applied Computing, SAC 2019, pp. 1061–1063. Association for Computing Machinery, New York (2019). https://doi.org/10.1145/3297280.3297573
2. Cheng, L., Li, J., Silva, Y.N., Hall, D.L., Liu, H.: XBully: cyberbullying detection within a multi-modal context. In: Proceedings of the Twelfth ACM International Conference on Web Search and Data Mining, pp. 339–347. WSDM 2019. Association for Computing Machinery, New York (2019). https://doi.org/10.1145/3289600.3291037
3. Dadvar, M., de Jong, F.M.G., Ordelman, R.J.F., Trieschnigg, R.B.: Improved cyberbullying detection using gender information. In: Twelfth Dutch-Belgian Information Retrieval Workshop, DIR, pp. 23–25. University of Ghent (2012)
4. Dinakar, K., Reichart, R., Lieberman, H.: Modeling the detection of textual cyberbullying (2011)
5. Goldman, R.: Teens indicted after allegedly taunting girl who hanged herself, bbc news (2010). http://abcnews.go.com/Technology/TheLaw/teens-charged-bullying-mass-girl-kill/story?id=10231357. Accessed 14 Jan 2014
6. Hosseinmardi, H., Ghasemianlangroodi, A., Han, R., Lv, Q., Mishra, S.: Towards understanding cyberbullying behavior in a semi-anonymous social network. In: IEEE/ACM International Conference on Advances in Social Networks Analysis and Mining (ASONAM), Beijing, China, pp. 244–252. IEEE (2014)
7. Hosseinmardi, H., Rafiq, R.I., Han, R., Lv, Q., Mishra, S.: Prediction of cyberbullying incidents in a media-based social network. In: Proceedings of the 2016 IEEE/ACM International Conference on Advances in Social Networks Analysis and Mining, San Francisco, CA, USA. IEEE (2016)
8. Hosseinmardi, H., Rafiq, R.I., Han, R., Lv, Q., Mishra, S.: Prediction of cyberbullying incidents in a media-based social network. In: 2016 IEEE/ACM International Conference on Advances in Social Networks Analysis and Mining (ASONAM), pp. 186–192. IEEE (2016)
9. Hu, M., Liu, B.: Mining and summarizing customer reviews. In: Proceedings of the Tenth ACM SIGKDD International Conference on Knowledge Discovery and Data Mining, pp. 168–177. ACM (2004)
10. Huang, Q., Singh, V.K., Atrey, P.K.: Cyber bullying detection using social and textual analysis. In: Proceedings of the 3rd International Workshop on Socially-Aware Multimedia, pp. 3–6. ACM, New York (2014). https://doi.org/10.1145/2661126.2661133. http://doi.acm.org/10.1145/2661126.2661133
11. Huddleston, T.: Twitter is officially shutting down vine today (2017). https://fortune.com/2017/01/17/twitter-shut-down-vine-tuesday/. Accessed 28 July 2020

12. Reynolds, K., Kontostathis, A., Edwards, L.: Using machine learning to detect cyberbullying. In: Proceedings of the 2011 10th International Conference on Machine Learning and Applications and Workshops, vol. 2, pp. 241–244 (2011). http://doi.ieeecomputersociety.org/10.1109/ICMLA.2011.152

13. Kontostathis, A., Reynolds, K., Garron, A., Edwards, L.: Detecting cyberbullying: query terms and techniques. In: Proceedings of the 5th Annual ACM Web Science Conference, pp. 195–204. ACM (2013)

14. Kowalski, R.M., Limber, S., Limber, S.P., Agatston, P.W.: Cyberbullying: Bullying in the Digital Age. Wiley, Reading (2012)

15. Law, T.: Vine has a new successor: the 6-second video app byte (2020). https://time.com/5771854/vine-byte-app-launch/. Accessed 28 July 2020

16. Li, H.H.S., Yang, Z., Lv, Q., Han, R.I.R.R., Mishra, S.: A comparison of common users across Instagram and ask.fm to better understand cyberbullying. In: 2014 IEEE Fourth International Conference on Big Data and Cloud Computing, Sydney, Australia, pp. 355–362. IEEE, December 2014. https://doi.org/10.1109/BDCloud.2014.87

17. Nahar, V., Li, X., Pang, C.: An effective approach for cyberbullying detection (2013)

18. Nahar, V., Unankard, S., Li, X., Pang, C.: Sentiment analysis for effective detection of cyber bullying. In: Sheng, Q.Z., Wang, G., Jensen, C.S., Xu, G. (eds.) APWeb 2012. LNCS, vol. 7235, pp. 767–774. Springer, Heidelberg (2012). https://doi.org/10.1007/978-3-642-29253-8_75

19. Nahar, V., Al-Maskari, S., Li, X., Pang, C.: Semi-supervised learning for cyberbullying detection in social networks. In: Wang, H., Sharaf, M.A. (eds.) ADC 2014. LNCS, vol. 8506, pp. 160–171. Springer, Cham (2014). https://doi.org/10.1007/978-3-319-08608-8_14

20. Nalini, K., Sheela, L.J.: Classification of tweets using text classifier to detect cyber bullying. In: Emerging ICT for Bridging the Future-Proceedings of the 49th Annual Convention of the Computer Society of India CSI, vol. 2, pp. 637–645. Springer (2015)

21. NLTK: Python nltk library (2020). https://www.nltk.org/. Accessed 30 Mar 2020

22. Patchin, J.W., Hinduja, S.: An update and synthesis of the research. Cyberbullying Prevention and Response: Expert Perspectives, p. 13 (2012)

23. Perez, S.: It's time to pay serious attention to Tiktok (2019). https://techcrunch.com/2019/01/29/its-time-to-pay-serious-attention-to-tiktok/. Accessed 28 July 2020

24. Ptaszynski, M., et al.: In the service of online order tackling cyberbullying with machine learning and affect analysis. Int. J. Comput. Linguist. Res. 1(3), 135–154 (2010)

25. Rafiq, R.I., Hosseinmardi, H., Han, R., Lv, Q., Mishra, S., Mattson, S.A.: Careful what you share in six seconds: detecting cyberbullying instances in vine. In: Proceedings of the 2015 IEEE/ACM International Conference on Advances in Social Networks Analysis and Mining 2015, Paris, France, pp. 617–622. ACM (2015)

26. Sanchez, H., Kumar, S.: Twitter bullying detection. In: NSDI, pp. 15–15. USENIX Association, Berkeley, CA, USA (2012)

27. Silva, T.H., de Melo, P.O.S.V., Almeida, J.M., Salles, J., Loureiro, A.A.F.: A picture of Instagram is worth more than a thousand words: Workload characterization and application. In: 2013 IEEE International Conference on Distributed Computing in Sensor Systems (DCOSS), pp. 123–132. IEEE (2013)

28. Smith-Spark, L.: Hanna smith suicide fuels calls for action on ask.fm cyber-bullying, CNN (2013). http://www.cnn.com/2013/08/07/world/europe/uk-social-media-bullying/. Accessed 14 Jan 2014

29. Soni, D., Singh, V.K.: See no evil, hear no evil: Audio-visual-textual cyberbullying detection. Proc. ACM Hum.-Comput. Interact. 2(CSCW), November 2018. https://doi.org/10.1145/3274433

30. Xu, J.M., Jun, K.S., Zhu, X., Bellmore, A.: Learning from bullying traces in social media. In: NAACL HLT, pp. 656–666. Association for Computational Linguistics (2012)

31. Xu, J.M., Jun, K.S., Zhu, X., Bellmore, A.: Learning from bullying traces in social media. In: Proceedings of the 2012 Conference of the North American Chapter of the Association for Computational Linguistics: Human Language Technologies, pp. 656–666. NAACL HLT 2012, Association for Computational Linguistics, USA (2012)

32. Yao, M., Chelmis, C., Zois, D.: Cyberbullying ends here: towards robust detection of cyberbullying in social media. In: The World Wide Web Conference, WWW 2019, pp. 3427–3433. Association for Computing Machinery, New York (2019). https://doi.org/10.1145/3308558.3313462

Effect of Social Algorithms on Media Source Publishers in Social Media Ecosystems

Ittipon Rassameeroj[1(✉)] and S. Felix Wu[2]

[1] Faculty of ICT, Mahidol University, Nakhon Pathom, Thailand
ittipon.ras@mahidol.edu
[2] Department of Computer Science, UC Davis, Davis, USA
sfwu@ucdavis.edu

Abstract. Social media systems have become a primary platform to consume and exchange information nowadays. The systems usually have three main components: media sources, content distributors (social media services), and content consumers, which we call social media content delivery ecosystem. A content distributor has social algorithms, as a black box, that were designed and trained to pick up, filter, and rank the most relevant and desired content to be delivered to each individual one of us. However, these modern social algorithms were typically complicated, so we do not really know how these social algorithms work such that we are unsure about the quality of the delivered content. Most researchers have worried about user side and investigated how fair of the contents that were delivered from social algorithms to users. On the other hand, no one focuses on impact of social algorithms on publisher side. Thus, the main purpose of this paper is to understand how social algorithms have an impact on content publishers in social media ecosystem. From our SINCERE data, we firstly illustrate time series of all posts in each of global and local news media Facebook pages, including CNN, Fox News, The New York Times, and The Sacramento Bee, which were plotted in timeline during 2008 to early 2018 to see how they changed in terms of publishing times. We found that global news media changed their publish time. Our hypothesis was that they changed because social algorithms were changed. If they got better user reaction after changing publishing time somehow, we could assume social algorithms might deliver more contents to users at that time. We evaluated user reactions by the number of participants and user response time. We found that content most publishers got better reactions from users after changing publishing time. Therefore, we conclude that news media changed their time periods to published their post in order to make their content be more visible to users because social algorithms were changed.

Keywords: Social algorithms · Social media ecosystem · Time series · News media · Digital journalism · Facebook pages

© Springer Nature Switzerland AG 2021
J. A. Lossio-Ventura et al. (Eds.): SIMBig 2020, CCIS 1410, pp. 362–375, 2021.
https://doi.org/10.1007/978-3-030-76228-5_26

1   Introduction

We nowadays have a huge amount of online contents on the Internet. In the past, we mostly used online search engines as an interface to search and bring us to desired contents. However, our information consumption behavior has been changed. In addition to search engines, many people have currently used social media to consume information. Social media systems normally provide us with online socialization, information dissemination and consumption, and content creation. In particular, we have enabled social media to push us content instead of searching and going to information sources.

Social media systems have some mechanisms to select and rank a bunch of different contents for each user based on personalization, which we call *social algorithms*. Basic techniques of social algorithms are based on users social network data (such as relationship), personalization, and online activities. Unfortunately, we do not really know how social algorithms actually work, which is like a black box. Also, we do not have any formal or standard methodology for content delivery algorithms in social media systems, and there is no existing work about that so far, especially for Facebook pages and communities. Thus, it is really challenging to evaluate whether contents filtered from the systems are the most desired and suitable for us.

In social media content delivery ecosystem, there are three main components–content publishers or media source (such as news media), content distributors (such as Facebook), and information consumer. Two kinds of content are created in the system. The first one is from content publisher that could be a post from news media. On Facebook, we can see those posts on our news feed. The second kind is user-created contents that could be user comments in original posts. All kinds of content are delivered to users through social algorithms that are in content distributors in the system, so social algorithms control content delivery. Our previous work [13] examined how user-created contents (or user comments) were delivered among online participants by reverse engineering of social algorithms based on participant activities. However, no existing work explores behavior of content publishers in a long period of time in the ecosystem. Also, if their behavior has been changed, our next research question is that do social algorithm have impact on their changed behavior?

In this work, we explored media source or content publisher of local and global news media on Facebook pages: CNN, Fox News, The New York Times, and The Sacramento Bee, from 2008 to early 2018 to see how they changed in terms of publishing date and time. If they changed, we assumed they changed because social algorithms might change at that time. For example, if our assumption was correct, when content publishers changed time to publish contents, they should get some good response from online participants. Thus, we investigated user reaction for each content to make sure that our assumption is correct. We used the number of participants and user response time as the measurement of user reactions. If the user reactions look good, we may assume when social algorithms were changed, publishers probably needed to change some of their strategies to publish contents so as to deliver content to user more efficiently.

The remainder of this paper is organized as follows. We further motivated our study with additional related work and backgrounds in Sect. 2. In Sect. 3, we presented social media content delivery ecosystem with its related technical backgrounds, definitions, and an overview of this work. In addition, in Sect. 4, we introduced our SINCERE data and the data set we used in this paper. In Sect. 5, we presented time series of all posts of local and global news media Facebook pages since 2008 to early 2018. Then, we examined the number of participants and grouped them for each post in Sect. 6. In Sect. 7, another measurement of user reaction, response time, was investigated for each post. Finally, we summarize all of this paper in Sect. 8.

2   Related Work

As we investigate social algorithms, let us start with social algorithm concepts. Lazer [10] has presented some ideas, overview, and brief definition of social algorithms. The author has also given some examples to show how social algorithm has an impact on choosing and ranking all content on the Internet for users. On the other hand, Yang [14] has presented social algorithms in terms of computational algorithms, which is a special class of algorithms for solving optimization problems. The author has shown the algorithms that does not focus on only social media systems, but they could be applied for general context, mainly nature-inspired, population-based algorithm for optimization.

Social media systems have become one of the main channels to diffuse information rapidly. Basic techniques that have been used for their content delivery algorithms include personalization, interests, and online activities. In addition, the strength of weak ties theory [9] is the most popular technique applied to content delivery algorithm in most of social media services. Gilbert and Karahalios [8] have presented a predictive model that maps social media data to tie strength in online social networks. For example, contents that are created from friends whom we frequently interact with should be picked and shown first. Bakshy et al. [2] have presented how strong and weak ties are influent in terms of information propagation in social networks.

We receive contents filtered by social algorithms as a black box, but how do we know whether a received content is the most desired we want to get? There are existing researches investigating bias in social algorithms. Pariser has presented *filter bubble*, which personalization makes people see different viewpoint of content [12]. [11] is the first paper to measure the filter bubble effect by exploring content diversity of a filter-based recommender system, MovieLens. In addition, since we all do not really know how social algorithms work, there are some concerns about bias of algorithmically selected content. Notwithstanding, Bozdag [4] has presented another side of those processes. The author has shown that online services that filter information are not only algorithms, but humans can also manually influence the filtering process. Furthermore, ideological diverse issue is another concern. Flaxman et al. [7] have pointed out that both search engines and social media may use ideological distance as a factor to pick a content up and push to users. Also, these tools are associated with an increase in the mean ideological distance between individuals. Bakshy et al. [1] have studied impact of social algorithms on Facebook by exploring whether personalized news feed on Facebook hide some content to prevent users from accessing posts contained conflicting political views. Flaxman et al. have explored an impact of polarizing channels on news consumption for ideological segregation in [6]. Bernstein et al. [3] have done reverse-engineer to estimate invisible audiences on Facebook. What they have done is to survey active users to ask them to estimate their audience size, then they have compared their estimates to their actual audience size from server logs. However, apart from News Feed algorithm, no one explores social algorithms of content in Facebook pages or communities.

3 Social Media Content Delivery Ecosystem

Social Media Ecosystem typically has three main components: media source or content publisher, content distributor (or social media services, e.g. Facebook and Twitter), and online content consumers. We presented social media ecosystem in Fig. 1. It shows how we consume information via Facebook nowadays. Media sources could be news publishers (e.g., Fox News in the figure), journalists, online content creators, etc. They use a social media like a channel to publish or push their contents to groups of people or members who are interested in that contents. The content from media source is an original post on a Facebook page in this case. Then, social media systems will spread the contents to users.

Social media systems have some mechanisms to choose and rank a bunch of contents to each of different individual users, which we call *social algorithms*. However, as a black box, we do not really know how social algorithms work. When users get contents, they can participate with original content or other people that also react with the content as the orange arrow in Fig. 1, which we call user-created contents. For instance, users interact by liking the content or write a comment under the post. After users have reactions or participation on contents, some properties of contents are changed, and social media systems will take those reactions and participation to adjust social algorithms for those users or future users. Hence, social algorithms need to deal with both original contents from publishers and user-created contents (e.g. user comments). On Facebook, social algorithms have to first choose and rank posts from publishers and display on our news feed. Also, if we click to see other user comments in a particular post, the social algorithms will choose and rank a couple relevant comments to us. In this work, we focused on relationship between original contents from media source and social algorithms only.

4 Data Set

We used our social interactive networking and conversation entropy ranking engine (SINCERE) data [5]. It has been crawled via Facebook API from the public interactions data on many Facebook pages and public communities from

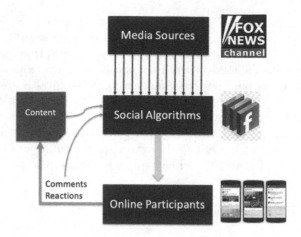

Fig. 1. Social media content delivery ecosystem

2008 to early 2018. The SINCERE data is composed of almost all posts, comments, likes, Facebook reactions (love, haha, wow, anger, sad), and shares. In this work, we focused on a couple global and local news media Facebook pages, including CNN, Fox News, The New York Times, and The Sacramento Bee. We considered CNN and Fox News as global news media; The Sacramento Bee as a local news media, and The New York Times as both local and global news media. From the SINCERE data, we totally had 34,365 posts from CNN, 46,121 posts from Fox News, 71,688 posts from The New York Times, and 31,874 posts from The Sacramento Bee. We used date and time of all original post contents that were created by their own content publishers on those news media Facebook pages and their user interactions (such as likes and comments) with the post on the pages to understand their behaviors and social algorithm impacts. The timestamp on the data set is Coordinated Universal Time (UTC) time zone.

5   Time Series of Publishing Contents

Initially, we focused on only dates and times when all original posts that were created in news media Facebook pages. We firstly would like to see a big picture of how posting times have been changed in last 10 years approximately in each news page. Figure 2–5 presents all posts on The Sacramento Bee, CNN, Fox News, and The New York Times pages from the SINCERE data respectively. Each dot represents a post created at a particular date on x-axis starting from midnight (from the bottom to top) and time on y-axis. Let us note that we had some technical problems for collecting and crawling data. There were some missing posts data in those news media Facebook pages, so some parts of time duration (e.g. some of the whole days or months) for the result were missed. For example, in The Sacramento Bee in Fig. 2, posts after June 2016 were missed. For CNN page in Fig. 3, data from August 2013 to May 2014 and from March 2016 to November 2017 were missed.

From those figures, we could see overview and evolution of media source in common. After mid 2013 approximately, all news media have used social media to publish contents a lot, and many content were posted per day. Figure 2 shows all posting time in The Sacramento Bee Facebook page, which is the local news channel mostly for local northern California people around Sacramento and Yolo countries. It is very obvious that the publishing times in The Sacramento Bee are mostly around the same time because of local online times and sleep times typically. On the contrary, CNN, Fox News, and The New York Times, in Fig. 3–5, are mostly global news media, which participants are from around the world. They posted contents during a single period of time at the beginning, their posting times were generally spread around the whole day in recent years. Let us note that please ignore colors of each dot for categorization in Fig. 3 for CNN at this moment. We will discuss about that shortly.

For those global news media pages, we can notice their posting times had been changed in some periods of time. To illustrate, For Fox News page in Fig. 4, they mostly posted around 4 AM–4 PM in 2008–2011, but they changed to the opposite time range around the end of 2011. Also, CNN and The New York Times pages are similar to Fox News page. CNN page had changed between 2009–2011 and 2012. The New York Times had also changed between and after August 2012.

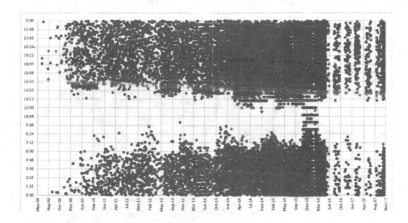

Fig. 2. All posts in The Sacramento Bee Facebook page

That is very explicit most pages changed the posting time around the same time, in 2012 approximately. As we have earlier mentioned, the main goals of news media side after creating and publishing contents are to make their content to be more accessible and popular. As a result, we believed if publishers change some publishing behavior, they should do that because they wanted to reach the goals. However, accessibility and popularity of contents are controlled by the social algorithms, so we could summarize social algorithms in the ecosystem were changed around August 2012 approximately. However, we still needed to investigate more in detail whether their contents would get more popular or accessible after they changed the publish time shortly.

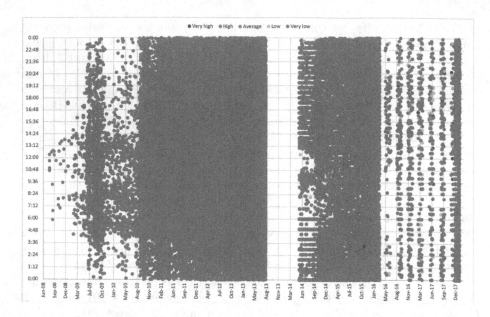

Fig. 3. All posts in CNN page categorized by the number of participants

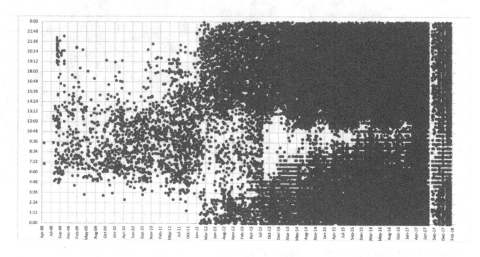

Fig. 4. All posts were created in Fox News Facebook page

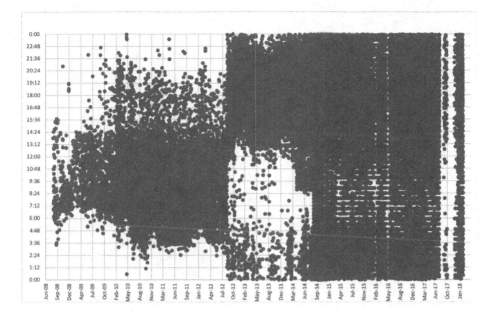

Fig. 5. All posts in The New York Time Facebook page

6 The Number of Participants

We considered the number of participants to measure popularity and accessibility. Thus, from the figures we just presented, we could represent and classify each post (each dot) by the number of participants in different levels, which is popularity and accessibility measurements. For The Sacramento Bee, we did not see any different in overview in terms of the number of participants because that page is for the local people, and the number of user interactions was not much. For CNN page, Fig. 3 shows all posts categorized by very high, high, average, low, and very low number of participants, which is hard to categorize, so we took all posts with "very low" comments out, that is shown in Fig. 6. Even we could not see a big difference when changing times, we could notice that the time when posts got more participants was in the changing time after August 2012 if we simply focused on only posts with "high" and "very high" participants.

One main problem that we might not be able to find a significant change was that we missed a lot of post data in CNN pages. In Fox News page, the first time change in the page was around the end of 2011. We scaled the number of participants to be very high, high, average, low, and very low. Figure 7 shows all post as dots representing and categorized by the participant levels as we just mentioned in different colors in Fox News page. In order to see which time duration had many participants, we presented only the high and very high number of participants in Fig. 8. By comparing Fig. 7 and 8, we could see contents that were posted after 1 PM would get more participants than other times. Thus, this may be one reason why Fox News changed their posting times, which was an impact of social algorithms.

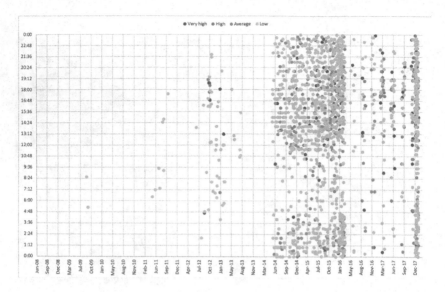

Fig. 6. All posts without "very low" number of participants in CNN page

7   Response Time

When we carefully took a look at the post contents, we found that the number of participants may not be a good measurement for a few reasons. First, different people are interested in different post topics and contents. Also, different topics get the different volume of interactions. For instance, political posts usually have very high volume of participation. Second, some users see posts on their news feed, but they do not like to react or make any comments on the contents. Third, participation activities depend on their online or active time.

All content publishers not only want their contents to be popular, but also they want their content to be quickly delivered to online users. Accordingly, in addition to the number of participants, we would like to see how fast users got the original contents that were just published by media sources, which is also a good way to evaluate how social algorithms is efficient for publisher side in the ecosystem. Thus, we used the number of comments in first five minutes to measure user response time. On the data set, we scaled the number of comments in first five minutes after posts were created in different ranges (different colors in the graphs) for CNN, Fox News, and The New York Times pages in Fig. 9, 10 respectively.

For CNN page in Fig. 9, we could not see significant changes because they usually posted all the time. However, from May 2014, we could notice users got contents very fast around after noon because of many dark blue, orange, and gray dots during that time.

For Fox News page in Fig. 10, it is very obvious there were significant changes before and after early 2012. They completely changed range time to publish

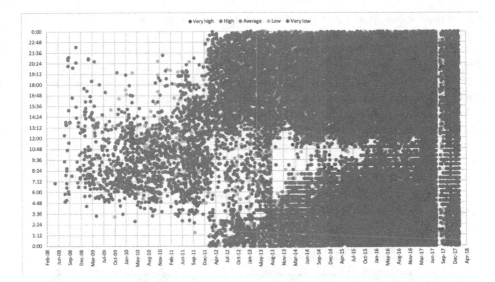

Fig. 7. All posts in Fox News page categorized by the number of participants

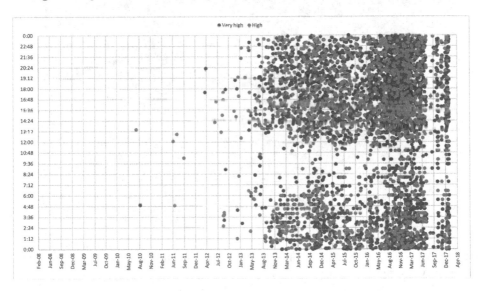

Fig. 8. Posts with only very high and high number of participants in Fox News page

contents from mostly morning time to afternoon time. After changed, it is very obvious that users earlier responded as we could see a lot of orange and gray dots during afternoon. Even they started to post their content all the time since early 2014, posts that were published in afternoon time were quickly delivered to user due to a lot of comments in first five minutes. In addition. After July 2016, it is very obvious Fox News got much more early comments from user because of blue and orange dots in Fig. 10.

The graph of The New York Times page in Fig. 11 looks very similar to Fox News page (Fig. 10) in terms of both publishing times and user behavior. From 2008 to late 2012, they mostly published from early morning to early afternoon. However, during that time, there are many blue dots (earliest user interaction) in late afternoon. After late 2012, they mostly changed to another time range, which they started publishing from early afternoon to night time. After they changed, it is clear that more people interacted very quickly as many dark blue and orange dots in mid 2012 to mid 2013. Even, since mid 2014, they published contents most of the time, we still could notice early interaction starting from early afternoon (gray, orange, and dark blue dots). In mid 2016 to mid 2017 especially, they got huge early user interaction.

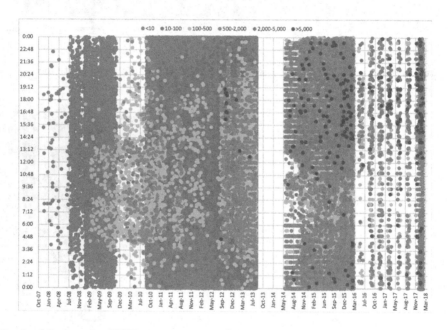

Fig. 9. All posts in CNN page categorized by the number of comments in first five minutes (Color figure online)

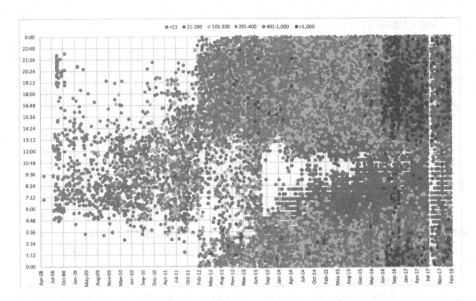

Fig. 10. All posts in Fox News page categorized by the number of comments in first five minutes (Color figure online)

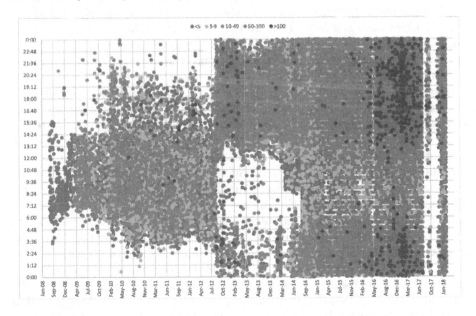

Fig. 11. All posts in The New York Times page categorized by the number of comments in first five minutes (Color figure online)

8   Conclusion

Our main purpose of this paper is to understand how social algorithms have an impact on content publishers in social media content delivery ecosystem. From our SINCERE data, we firstly illustrate overview of all posts in each of global and local news media, including CNN, Fox News, The New York Times, and The Sacramento Bee, which were plotted in timeline during 2008 to early 2018 to see how they changed in terms of publishing times. We found that The Sacramento Bee, which we considered as local news media, did not change their posting time in overall. On the other hand, the other global news media (CNN, Fox News, and The New York Times) changed their publishing time in an opposite way during a period of time, especially Fox News and The New York Times. Our hypothesis was that they changed because social algorithms might be changed around that time. If they got better user reaction after changing publishing time somehow, we could assume social algorithms might deliver more contents to users at that time.

Thus, we evaluated user reactions by the number of participants and user response time. For the user response time, we measured by the number of comments in five minutes. We categorized both measurements in a few levels (e.g. high, medium, low) and plotted to see how better user reaction each publisher got after changing the time. For the number of participants, we did not find any significant except in Fox News that we found they got higher number of participants after changing. For user response time, it was very obvious Fox News and The New York Times got faster response time from user after changing their publishing time.

Hence, two big news publishers, Fox News and The New York Times (Fig. 10 and 11), changed publishing time so that they could get more early interaction from users. Getting early interactions means their contents can be delivered to user very quickly. Also, we could assume that social algorithms have tried to push contents from publishers to users a lot during that time. In addition, when users interacted with a post, their friend might see that they reacted or made comments on the post, for instance. Thus, if publisher could make many users interact with contents, more other users, not only users who subscribe for that page, could probably see those contents as well. Moreover, when users could get very fresh contents from publishers, they might feel they were very up to date to the world. Therefore, from these figure, we summarized social algorithms have impact not only on users to see desired content, but also on content publishers to make their contents be more visible as fast as possible and more popular. Finally, we could see how social algorithms have been changed for such a long period of time, around 10 years. We could also assume social algorithms indirectly force publishers from the media sources to change publishing strategies or behavior.

References

1. Bakshy, E., Messing, S., Adamic, L.A.: Exposure to ideologically diverse news and opinion on facebook. Science **348**(6239), 1130–1132 (2015). https://doi.org/10.1126/science.aaa1160, http://science.sciencemag.org/content/348/6239/1130
2. Bakshy, E., Rosenn, I., Marlow, C., Adamic, L.: The role of social networks in information diffusion. In: Proceedings of the 21st International Conference on World Wide Web, New York, pp. 519–528. WWW 2012, ACM (2012). https://doi.org/10.1145/2187836.2187907
3. Bernstein, M.S., Bakshy, E., Burke, M., Karrer, B.: Quantifying the invisible audience in social networks. In: Proceedings of the SIGCHI Conference on Human Factors in Computing Systems, New York, pp. 21–30. CHI 2013. ACM (2013). https://doi.org/10.1145/2470654.2470658
4. Bozdag, E.: Bias in algorithmic filtering and personalization. Ethics Inf. Technol. **15**(3), 209–227 (2013). https://doi.org/10.1007/s10676-013-9321-6
5. Erlandsson, F., Nia, R., Boldt, M., Johnson, H., Wu, S.F.: Crawling online social networks. In: 2015 Second European Network Intelligence Conference, pp. 9–16 (2015). https://doi.org/10.1109/ENIC.2015.10
6. Flaxman, S.R., Goel, S., Rao, J.M.: Ideological segregation and the effects of social media on news consumption (2014)
7. Flaxman, S., Goel, S., Rao, J.M.: Filter bubbles, echo chambers, and online news consumption. Public Opin. Q. **80**(S1), 298–320 (2016). https://doi.org/10.1093/poq/nfw006
8. Gilbert, E., Karahalios, K.: Predicting tie strength with social media. In: Proceedings of the SIGCHI Conference on Human Factors in Computing Systems, New York, pp. 211–220. CHI 2009, ACM (2009). https://doi.org/10.1145/1518701.1518736
9. Granovetter, M.S.: The strength of weak ties. Am. J. Soc. **78**(6), 1360–1380 (1973). https://doi.org/10.1086/225469
10. Lazer, D.: The rise of the social algorithm. Science **348**(6239), 1090–1091 (2015). https://doi.org/10.1126/science.aab1422, http://science.sciencemag.org/content/348/6239/1090
11. Nguyen, T.T., Hui, P.M., Harper, F.M., Terveen, L., Konstan, J.A.: Exploring the filter bubble: the effect of using recommender systems on content diversity. In: Proceedings of the 23rd International Conference on World Wide Web, New York, pp. 677–686. WWW 2014. ACM (2014). https://doi.org/10.1145/2566486.2568012
12. Pariser, E.: The Filter Bubble: What the Internet Is Hiding from You. The Penguin Group (2011)
13. Rassameeroj, I., Wu, S.F.: Reverse engineering of content delivery algorithms for social media systems. In: 2019 Sixth International Conference on Social Networks Analysis, Management and Security (SNAMS), pp. 196–203 (2019). https://doi.org/10.1109/SNAMS.2019.8931859
14. Yang, X.S.: Social algorithms. In: Adamatzky, A. (ed.) Unconventional Computing. ECSSS, pp. 1–15. Springer, New York (2017). https://doi.org/10.1007/978-3-642-27737-5_678-1

The Identification of Framing Language in Business Leaders' Speech from the Mass Media

Brett Drury[1](✉)(iD) and Samuel Morais Drury[2]

[1] LIAAD-INESC-TEC, Porto, Portugal
[2] Colégio Puríssimo, Rio Claro, SP, Brazil

Abstract. The value of a company can soar and plunge upon the utterances of its leaders. Organisation leaders are aware of the power of their words to influence their employees, customers and the financial markets, consequently, they use rhetorical tricks such as framing to present statements that contain little or no useful information as containing positive material. These types of statements are not suitable for traditional sentiment analysis which can be used to predict the prospects of a company. On occasion, business leaders are forced to make objective statements which contain useful information that could be used to predict the future share price or profit levels using sentiment analysis. This paper presents a technique that uses sentimental low information words in quotes from business leaders to identify framing words. The identification of framing words allows the ranking of quotes from business leaders by framing likelihood, which can be used for further analysis.

1 Introduction

The value of a company or organisation can soar and plunge upon the utterances of their leaders and associates. An unguarded or honest reported comment can send an organisation on the path to bankruptcy. The most famous example was that of Gerald Ratner who famously stated: "People say, How can you sell this for such a low price?, I say, because it's total crap." [10]. Immediately after the comment made its way into the British Press, the value of his company (Ratners Jewellers) plunged [10]. The company was forced to change its name to Signet to avoid what the British press dubbed: "The Ratner effect" [10].

The content of speech from business leaders can contain information that may be a predictor of future company performance. Therefore business leaders' speech can be used as part of a trading strategy. However, business leaders are aware of the Ratner effect and use rhetorical tricks such as framing language to present the company or organisation in a positive light to the markets, customers and employees, even when there is no information to communicate. For example, "We are *thrilled* to welcome Michael who is a *world-class* executive.", is typical. The italicised text demonstrates the positive orientation of the selected words.

© Springer Nature Switzerland AG 2021
J. A. Lossio-Ventura et al. (Eds.): SIMBig 2020, CCIS 1410, pp. 376–383, 2021.
https://doi.org/10.1007/978-3-030-76228-5_27

The quote, however, contains no actionable information and is useless for trading. Consequently, trading techniques that rely upon traditional text analysis such as sentiment analysis are unlikely to be successful. The majority of reported business leaders speech is of this type. On occasion, business leaders are forced to communicate in an unambiguous and objective manner, for example when announcing profits or redundancies. This objective language can often contain information from which the future prospects of the organisation can be inferred, consequently, trading strategies will want to have access to this type of language.

The technique proposed by this paper presents a method by which objective and rhetorical speech can be separated through the identification of framing words. Framing words are low information words that shape a reader's perspective of the remaining information in the quote. The technique allows the ranking of quotes in order of estimated rhetorical content. This ranking will allow researchers to concentrate their labelling efforts in areas that will have a high concentration of either objective or rhetorical quotes

The remainder of this paper will adhere to the following structure: related work, proposed technique, evaluation and conclusion.

2   Related Work

There are relatively few linguistic resources for business leaders' reported speech. The major corpus located in the literature review for this paper was the Minho Quotation Resource [4]. The resource has approximately 500,000 quotations, each quotation has a speaker, job role and the quote itself.

Although there are relatively few linguistic resources for business leaders' reported speech, the area of business rhetoric is relatively well-studied [1,2,7]. Conger [2] identified the practice in business speech of rhetorical framing, where words are framed to communicate the grander purpose of an organisation. An example given by Conger contrasts the following quotes: "I want us to build X number of products by this year and return so much on our assets" and "I want us to revolutionise the way people see and act in the world through the use of our products" [2]. The second quote uses framing to project the values of the company. Conger identified a number of techniques that are used in framing such as belief and value amplification. In addition, Conger claimed that business leaders heavily rely upon "metaphors, analogies, and organisational Stories" [2].

These rhetorical tricks impede the ability of traditional text analysis techniques such as sentiment analysis to identify trading signals in the reported speech from business leaders. Therefore there are relatively few papers that have attempted to classify business leaders' quotes into sentiment categories. The main paper in this area is a technique described by [5]. The technique relied upon matching quotes from objective sources with objective speech from non-objective sources (CEOs). The shared vocabulary then can be used to build classifiers that separate objective speech from rhetorical. The drawback of this technique is that relies upon knowing the job title of the speaker in the training phase.

There is some related work to polarity classification of quotes, but these techniques ignored the motivation of the speaker. A typical example is provided by [9] who identified and classified different types of Indonesian quotes published on Twitter. The types of quotes that were classified are "Love, Life, Motivation, Education, and Religion"[9]. The technique used linguistic features and a Naive Bayes classifier. Another example of polarity classification was described by [12]. They used linguistic features to discover literary quotes, their polarity and their author.

The literature review identified a limited number of techniques that can be used to separate business leaders quotes into objective and rhetorical categories. There are at present no unsupervised techniques for this task in the research literature.

3   Proposed Technique

The hypothesis of this paper is that rhetorical speech used by business leaders will contain low information framing words. These framing words will have high entropy because they will be repeated frequently by different business leaders. Additionally, the framing words will have the highest entropy in the reported quote because the event that they are framing will occur less often in business speech than the framing words themselves. Consequently, the analysis of the lowest information words in a quote will allow the deduction of whether the remainder of the quote is either: rhetorical or objective. Also framing words will have a positive sentiment because the intention of the speaker is to portray the subject matter in the most appealing manner possible. The proposed technique has four steps: Preprocessing, Entropy computation,Sentiment Computation and Quote Ranking.

The preprocessing step simply removes stop words[1] from all of the candidate quotes. Stop words will have high entropy because they will appear in every quote. Consequently, the proposed technique will not be able to rank quotes with stop words because all quotes are likely to score similar entropy scores.

The entropy calculation is intended to provide an information score for each non stop word in a quote. High entropy indicates that a word is evenly distributed throughout the corpus, and therefore does not communicate any information unique to the quote. The entropy calculation computes an entropy score [11] as per Eq. 1 for each non stop word in a quote.

$$entropy(W) = -P(W = 0)log_2 P(W = 0) - P(W = 1)log_2 P(W = 1) \qquad (1)$$

where W is a word, and $W = 0$ indicates the number of sentences where the word is not present, and $W = 1$ is the number of sentences where the word is present.

---

[1] Stop words from NLTK were used. A full list of NLTK stop words can be found here.

The sentiment computation step identifies the word-sense of each word using the Lesk algorithm [8] and retrieves the sentiment score from Sentiwordnet [6] using the identified Synset. An overall sentiment score is determined by subtracting the negative score from the positive. A final score for each word is the product of each word with the sentiment score as shown in Eq. 2.

$$score(W) = (entropy(W)).(pos\_score(w) - neg\_score(w)) \tag{2}$$

The words are ranked in order of the score calculated in Eq. 2, and the sum of the n words with the highest entropy and positive sentiment, where n is a pre-set constant, is taken. If $n = 1$ then entropy of the word with the highest entropy is taken.

The ranking step ranks the reported speech by the total score of the n highest scoring words. The quotes are ranked from highest to lowest. The quotes with the lowest score are likely to be objective, whereas high scoring sentences are likely to have framing words, and contain no useful information. The overall technique is described in Algorithm 1.

Data: Pass in a : List of Quotes (QUOTES), Numb of Words (n)
Result: Returned Ranked List of Quotes
1: $results \leftarrow list()$ Declare Empty List
2: **foreach** $quote \in QUOTES$ **do**
3: $\quad quote \leftarrow removeStopword(quote)$ 'Remove stop-words from quote'
4: $\quad scores \leftarrow entropyAndSentiment(quote, n)$ 'Score: sent . entropy'
5: $\quad scores \leftarrow Sort(scores)$ 'Sort in descending order '
6: $\quad results \leftarrow addquote(results, quote, scores)$
   end
7: $results \leftarrow Sort(results)$ 'Sort in descending order of Sent . Entropy'
8: $return\ (results)$
Algorithm 1: Description of Proposed Technique

4   Evaluation

The evaluation for this paper was designed to demonstrate:

1. The relationship between high entropy positive words and their framing properties.
2. The ability of the technique to separate rhetorical from objective quotes.
3. The accuracy difference between the Proposed Technique, and the baselines of Entropy only, Positive Sentiment only and Random Selection.

The evaluation ranks quotes by framing properties. It samples the ranked list at intervals of ten documents up to a maximum of sixty. At each document interval an accuracy which is computed $accuracy = \frac{RQ}{TOTAL}$, where RQ is the number of quotes manually labelled as rhetorical and returned by the technique, for the interval. This evaluation technique is referred to as precision at k [13].

The Entropy baseline computes the entropy of each word and sorts the entropy words by descending order of value. A quote is scored by summing n words with the highest entropy. The quotes are then ranked by total entropy score.

The Positive Sentiment baseline computes the score of the quote by computing the sentiment of each word using the aforementioned Lesk algorithm and Sentiwordnet and sorts the words in a quote by descending order of sentiment. A quote is scored by summing n words with the highest positive sentiment. The quotes are then ranked by total positive sentiment.

The Random Baseline chooses labels at random and chooses quotes at random for each interval. This process is repeated 1000 times and an average score is taken. The process is repeated to ensure that very good or poor scores obtained by chance are mitigated.

The evaluation created a hand labelled gold standard of English language quotes from the Minho Quotation Resource [4]. Framing language is more likely to be present in quotes made by CEOs, because Chief Executive Officers are compelled to manipulate: Employees, Customers and Financial Markets [3]. Consequently, a random selection of 384 quotes made by Chief Executive Officers (CEOs) was selected from the Minho Quotation Resource. This represents a confidence interval of 5.00 at a confidence level of 95% of the total Minho Quotation Resource, and 4.88 of the CEO quotes. The 384 quotes were labelled by three domain experts. The annotators decided if each quote in the sample was rhetorical or objective. A majority vote decided the label of the quote. There were 158 objective quotes and 226 rhetorical quotes, with a Fleiss Kappa of 0.20 which suggests a high level of a disagreement between the annotators.

4.1   Results

The results of the experiment are shown in Table 1. Each of the scores has a plus/minus of 0.05 which is derived from the aforementioned confidence interval. It is clear from the results that the proposed technique produces the superior results at each interval as well as at each word interval.

Table 1. Precision at K evaluation results, where *Numb. of Words* Represent the Number of Words Used in the Framing Calculation.

Numb. of Words:	1	2	3	1	2	3	1	2	3
Doc. Interval	Random	Proposed			Entropy			Sentiment	
10	0.60	0.80	0.90	0.80	0.80	0.60	0.50	0.80	0.70	0.50
20	0.60	0.85	0.75	0.90	0.65	0.60	0.70	0.80	0.70	0.55
30	0.57	0.73	0.73	0.83	0.63	0.70	0.67	0.73	0.63	0.60
40	0.55	0.70	0.75	0.78	0.63	0.68	0.68	0.73	0.65	0.70
50	0.50	0.70	0.76	0.76	0.68	0.68	0.72	0.70	0.68	0.68
60	0.53	0.70	0.73	0.73	0.63	0.68	0.73	0.67	0.72	0.71

It is possible that using fixed number of words to calculate the framing score is not sufficient because the number of words which have framing properties may vary quote by quote. Therefore in Table 2 the mean of the techniques is shown. This evaluation technique is referred to as Mean Average Precision (MAP).

It is clear from the results that the proposed technique outperforms the baselines, and at intervals ten to thirty documents the proposed technique gains scores higher than the baselines when allowing for the sample error. At intervals forty to sixty documents the baseline techniques are superior to the baselines, but within the sample error.

Table 2. Mean average precision evaluation results

Doc. Interval	Random	Proposed	Entropy	Sentiment
10	0.60 ± 0.05	0.83 ± 0.05	0.63 ± 0.05	0.66 ± 0.05
20	0.60 ± 0.05	0.83 ± 0.05	0.65 ± 0.05	0.68 ± 0.05
30	0.57 ± 0.05	0.76 ± 0.05	0.66 ± 0.05	0.65 ± 0.05
40	0.55 ± 0.05	0.74 ± 0.05	0.66 ± 0.05	0.69 ± 0.05
50	0.50 ± 0.05	0.74 ± 0.05	0.69 ± 0.05	0.68 ± 0.05
60	0.53 ± 0.05	0.72 ± 0.05	0.68 ± 0.05	0.70 ± 0.05

4.2 Ranked Quotes

To illustrate the results returned by the proposed technique and a baseline (Sentiment only), Table 3, shows the quotes the highest ranked quote by each number of words configuration. It is clear from the Proposed Technique is that all three quotes are rhetorical, and have a positive sentiment orientation. The positive sentiment baseline demonstrates the role of entropy because the quote returned by lines two and three are objective. The quotes returned by the Proposed Technique are not useful for trading or prediction of the fortunes of an organisation.

Table 3. Examples of Rhetorical Quotes Returned by Candidate Techniques

Numb. words	Proposed technique	Sentiment only
1	Working together with our partners, our overriding aim is to make XING even more valuable for our business community.; With this goal in mind, ...	Watson SCS has led large complex security projects from initiation to implementation while maintaining excellent customer satisfaction .....
2	We are delighted to contribute to the safety of service men and women around the world; This contract award highlights the best-in-class	As the Pre-Paid Debit Reloadable market continues to enjoy favorable growth the demand for Pre-Paid Instant Issue Gift Cards is enjoying ....
3	To win this award based on client satisfaction is proof of our staff's passion and skills to solve our advertisers' challenges in the media industry every	As the Pre-Paid Debit Reloadable market continues to enjoy favorable growth the demand for Pre-Paid Instant Issue Gift Cards is enjoying ....

5   Reproducibility

To support the replication of the work described a Jupyter Notebook with the code for the described experiments can be found here and the annotated data can be found here.

6   Conclusion

The proposed strategy demonstrates that it is possible to identify rhetorical speech made by business leaders. Framing words are low information positive words and are embedded into manipulative statements made by business leaders. It is clear from the experiments is that not all positive words are farming words, and not all high entropy words are framing words. And the number of framing words varies depending upon the speaker.

Future work will concentrate upon identifying other indicators of rhetorical indicators such as quote length, similes, metaphors and risk averse language. It is hoped that with a greater understanding of CEO language it will be possible to predict the financial prospects of their organisation.

References

1. Bono, J.E., Ilies, R.: Charisma, positive emotions and mood contagion. Leadership Q. **17**(4), 317–334 (2006)
2. Conger, J.A.: Inspiring others: the language of leadership. Executive **5**(1), 31–45 (1991)

3. Drury, B.: Text Mining System for Evaluating the Stock Market's Response To News. PhD thesis, University of Porto (2013)
4. Drury, B., Almeida, J.J.: The minho quotation resource. In: LREC, pp. 2280–2285 (2012)
5. Drury, B., Dias, G., Torgo, L.: A contextual classification strategy for polarity analysis of direct quotations from financial news. In: Proceedings of the International Conference Recent Advances in Natural Language Processing, vol. 2011, pp. 434–440 (2011)
6. Esuli, A., Sebastiani, F.: SentiwordNet: a publicly available lexical resource for opinion mining. LREC **6**, 417–422 (2006)
7. Knapp, M.L.: Business rhetoric: opportunity for research in speech. South. J. Commun. **35**(3), 244–255 (1970)
8. Lesk, M.: Automatic sense disambiguation using machine readable dictionaries: how to tell a pine cone from an ice cream cone. In: Proceedings of the 5th Annual International Conference on Systems Documentation, pp. 24–26 (1986)
9. Rachmadany, A., Pranoto, Y.M., Multazam, M.T., Nandiyanto, A.B.D., Abdullah, A.G., Widiaty, I., et al.: Classification of Indonesian quote on twitter using naïve bayes. In: IOP Conference Series: Materials Science and Engineering, vol. 288, pp. 012162. IOP Publishing (2018)
10. Ratner, G.: The Rise and Fall...and Rise Again. Capstone Publishing, The Atrium Southern Gate Chichester West Sussex, UK (2008)
11. Shannon, C.E.: Prediction and entropy of printed English. Bell Labs Tech. J. **30**(1), 50–64 (1951)
12. Søgaard, A.: Mining wisdom. In: Proceedings of the NAACL-HLT 2012 Workshop on Computational Linguistics for Literature, pp. 54–58 (2012)
13. Zuva, K., Zuva, T.: Evaluation of information retrieval systems. Int. J. Comput. Sci. Inf. Technol. **4**(3), 35 (2012)

Clustering Analysis of Website Usage on Twitter During the COVID-19 Pandemic

Iain J. Cruickshank$^{(\boxtimes)}$ and Kathleen M. Carley

Center for Computational Analysis of Social and Organizational Systems,
Carnegie Mellon University, Pittsburgh, PA 15213, USA
icruicks@andrew.cmu.edu, kathleen.carley@cs.cmu.edu

Abstract. In this study we analyzed patterns of external website usage on Twitter during the COVID-19 pandemic. We used a multi-view clustering technique, which is able to incorporate multiple views of the data, to cluster the websites' URLs based on their usage patterns and tweet text that occurs with the URLs. The results of the multi-view clustering of URLs used during the COVID-19 pandemic, from 29 January to 22 June 2020, revealed three, main clusters of URL usage. These three clusters differed significantly in terms of using information from different politically-biased, fake news, and conspiracy theory websites. Our results suggest that there are political biases in how information, to include misinformation, about the COVID-19 pandemic is used on Twitter.

Keywords: Clustering · COVID-19 · Multi-view data

1 Introduction

The COVID-19 pandemic, which is caused by the SARS-CoV-2 virus, has caused immense societal and economic disruption across the world. The disruption caused by the pandemic has spread to nearly every facet of human social behavior to include how humans are interacting with information through mediums like social media [1,18]. Thus far, much of the work with COVID-19 social media data has focused on the prevalence and spread of COVID-19 misinformation. There has been less work on understanding holistically what information social media users are interacting with and if there are any patterns in these interactions. In particular, a key source of information for social media users are external websites which often publish material that is shared through social media. This sharing of information from external websites, through the use of Uniform Resource Locators, or URLs, is often an important behavior not only for propagating useful information that individuals can use to help combat the pandemic, but also propagating conspiracy theories or fake news which can harm individuals and exacerbate the effects of the pandemic. Thus, it is important to understand if there are distinct patterns of usage of URLs on social media sites to better understand what information is being propagated and give insight into what communities are using which information sources.

© Springer Nature Switzerland AG 2021
J. A. Lossio-Ventura et al. (Eds.): SIMBig 2020, CCIS 1410, pp. 384–399, 2021.
https://doi.org/10.1007/978-3-030-76228-5_28

One means of discerning patterns from digital data is clustering. In this work, we propose the use of multi-view clustering to discern different patterns of URL usage on Twitter. Many naturally-occurring, social phenomena give rise to multiple types and views of data [9]. So, using a clustering method that can exploit information from all of those views results in a better clustering of the phenomena that gave rise to all of the data. To date and the best of the authors' knowledge, most clustering of social media data is not clustered by multi-view clustering. So, in this work, we use of multi-view clustering in order to better understand the usage patterns of URLs on social media during the COVID-19 pandemic. The main contributions of this work are summarized as follows:

- The first use of a multi-view clustering technique and approach to understand clusters of website usage on social media.
- Characterization of patterns of usage of all websites on Twitter, not just those related to misinformation, during the COVID-19 pandemic. The results show that politically-biased websites and those associated with fake news and conspiracy theories have different patterns of usage then those related to science or other content.

2   Related Research

Current studies into online social behavior during the COVID-19 pandemic have largely focused on how misinformation spreads during a pandemic. This is because good information is a key enabler to combat the effects of the pandemic whereas misinformation can exacerbate its effects [14, 18]. Recent studies into the prevalence and persistence of misinformation have shown that misinformation on the COVID-19 pandemic has been especially persistent and spreads through online social networks quickly [1, 6, 30]. The spread of COVID-19 misinformation has become so problematic and widespread that many researchers are referring to it as an 'Infodemic' [1, 8, 14]. The Infodemic is characterized by a virus-like spread of misinformation across many different communication mediums, most notably online social networks. Additionally, other researchers have identified important mechanisms by which the misinformation propagates in social media. Recent research has identified the importance of bots in the spread of misinformation [11]. Other research has highlighted the role of alternative news sources and user characteristics like political beliefs in the spread of COVID-19 misinformation [6, 16]. Finally, some recent research has found that low-credibility information about the COVID-19 pandemic tends to be frequently used and have a high persistence on Twitter [30].

One of the common artifacts used for the determination of information veracity on social media sites are the URLs cited for that information. Recent research has shown social-media users use external websites for information relating to the COVID-19 pandemic [6, 30]. In fact, it is the use of these external websites which can allow for researchers to assess the spread of things like misinformation during the pandemic [8, 14]. Despite the utility of external websites in assessing things like misinformation spread, there has not been a holistic look at the usage of websites on social media during the COVID-19 pandemic. It is unclear if there are different usage patterns or clusters of websites that exist during a pandemic, beyond those explicitly related to misinformation.

An increasingly used means of finding patterns or clusters within data is multi-view clustering. Multi-view clustering techniques are techniques designed to handle clustering of objects which can be described by more than one data source. Many different real-world, social phenomena give rise to 'views' of data which are often different types of data that can be used to describe the same set of actors. For example, social media users can post content, which could give rise to a text view, and have interactions with each other, which can give rise to network views. So, multi-view clustering aims to fuse the information from these different views of the data to produce one clustering of the objects that created the data [3, 4,31,32]. There has been a surge of new techniques developed in multi-view clustering for handling genetic data [17,34], image data [2,31], and more recently human, social-based data [9]. In particular, recent research with hashtags on Twitter during the COVID-19 pandemic has found multi-view clustering to be an effective means of characterizing topical discussion groups [10]. So, multi-view clustering can be used as a means of finding richer clusters from real-world data, than just clustering any particular view of then data by itself.

3   Methodology

Since there are different data modalities, or views, of how URLs are used on Twitter (i.e. how the URL is spread in Tweets, how the URL is described by the verbiage of the Tweets, etc.), we have adopted a multi-view clustering framework for clustering URLs in the COVID-19 Twitter data. By using a multi-view clustering, we can use all of the views of URL usage that previous research has identified as being important to their usage in one cohesive clustering. So, in this section we detail the methods used to obtain the multi-view clusters of the URLs. The first subsection describes the multi-view clustering technique used to produce the clusters. The second subsection describes the data statistics and processing done to obtain the views of the data used in the clustering.

3.1   Multi-view Clustering of URLs

In order to cluster the URLs, we adopted the multi-view clustering technique of Multi-view Modularity Clustering (MVMC). MVMC is a technique designed to work with multiple views, of any data type, of the same underlying social-based phenomena to produce one set of clusters [9,10]. The technique works in two main steps. First, a graph is learned for every view of the data, then an iterative procedure clusters all of the view graphs by optimizing the following modularity function:

$$\sum_{v=1}^{m} w^v \sum_{ij \in E^v} [A_{ij}^v - \gamma^v \frac{deg(i)^v \times deg(j)^v}{2 \sum A^v}] \delta(C_i, C_j) \tag{1}$$

where v is a particular view, m is the total number of views, A^v is the adjacency matrix for the graph of the vth view, $deg(i)^v$ is the degree of the object i in view, v, and $\delta(.,.)$ is the delta function which returns one if the two items are the same and 0 otherwise. The parameters that are used in the optimization are w^v which is the weight assigned to the vth view, which controls how much impact upon the clustering solution the vth view should have, γ^v which is the resolution parameter for the vth view, which controls for the resolution limit inherent in the modularity function [13,20,27], and C_i which is the cluster assignment for object i. In order to optimize the cluster assignments as well as the weights and resolutions for each view, an iterative procedure is used. In the first step, the view graphs are clustered using a modularity optimization technique (i.e. Louvain [5] or Leiden [28]) with the current view weights and resolutions to produce provisional cluster assignments. Then, in the second step, the view weights and resolutions are updated by the provisional cluster assignments. This procedure is repeated until the view weights and resolutions no longer change. The pseudocode for the MVMC procedure is displayed in Algorithm 1[1].

Algorithm 1. Multi-view Modularity Clustering (MVMC)

---

input:
- Adjacency for each view: A^v
- Max number of iterations: $max\_iter = 20$
- Starting resolutions: $\gamma_1^v = 1$, $\forall v \in m$
- Starting weights: $w_1^v = 1$, $\forall v \in m$
- Convergence tolerance: $tol = 0.01$

output: Cluster assignments

$clustering^* \leftarrow None$

$modularity^* \leftarrow -\infty$

for $i = 1 : max\_iter$ **do**

    $clustering_i \leftarrow cluster(A, w_i, \gamma_i)$

    $modularity_i \leftarrow RBmodularity(A, clustering_i, w_i, \gamma_i)$

    $\theta_{in}, \theta_{out} \leftarrow calculate\_thetas(A, clustering_i)$

    $\gamma_{i+1}^v \leftarrow \frac{\theta_{in}^v - \theta_{out}^v}{\log\theta_{in}^v - \log\theta_{out}^v}$, $\forall v \in m$

    $w_{i+1}^v \leftarrow \frac{\log\theta_{in}^v - \log\theta_{out}^v}{<\log\theta_{in}^v - \log\theta_{out}^v>_v}$, $\forall v \in m$

    if $abs(\gamma_{i+1} - \gamma_i) < tol$ AND $abs(weights_{i+1} - weights_i) < tol$ **then**

        $clustering^* \leftarrow clustering_i$

        $modularity^* \leftarrow modularity_i$

        BREAK

    end if

    if $iter >= max\_iter$ **then**

        $best\_iteration \leftarrow argmax(modularity)$

        $clustering^* \leftarrow clustering[best\_iteration]$

        $modularity^* \leftarrow modularity[best\_iteration]$

    end if

end for

return $clustering^*$

---

[1] A Python implementation of this algorithm is available on the lead author's GitHub page: https://github.com/ijcruic/Multi-view-Clustering-of-Social-Based-Data.

The algorithm begins by initializing all the resolution parameters, γ_1^v, and weight parameters, w_1^v to one (or whatever the user may specify). The algorithm then goes on to cluster the view graphs, A^v, by a modularity maximization technique (i.e. Louvain, Leiden), $cluster()$, with the current resolution and weight settings. The output of this is then used to determine the propensities for internal edge formation θ_{in}^v, and external edge formation, θ_{out}^v for each view. These values are then used to update the resolution, γ^v, and weight parameters, w^v, for each of the views. If the new weight and resolution parameters are the same as the previous ones (within tolerance), the algorithm then exits and returns the final clustering. If the algorithm fails to converge to stable resolution and weight parameters, within the maximum number of iterations allowed, then the algorithm returns whichever clustering produced the highest modularity.

One of the important elements in the aforementioned algorithm, Algorithm 1, is the computation of the edge propensities, θ. In order to calculate these edge propensities, we follow the guidance outlined in previous works and assume edges form by a degree-corrected model [24, 25]. The following pseudocode, Algorithm 2, details the procedure for calculating these edge propensities:

Algorithm 2. Calculation of Edge Propensities

---

input:
  – Adjacency for each view: A^v
  – clustering: C
output: Internal and external edge propensities ($\theta_{in}, \theta_{o}ut$)
for v = 1:m **do**
  $e_{in} = 0$
  $\kappa^2 = []$
  for c = 1:—C— **do**
    $e_c = \sum E_c^v$
    $e_{in} + = e_c$
    $\kappa^2.append((\sum_{i \in V_c^v} deg(i))^2)$
  end for
  if $e_{in} = 0$ **then**
    $\theta_{in}^v \leftarrow \frac{1}{|E^v|}$
  else
    $\theta_{in}^v \leftarrow \frac{e_{in}}{\sum \frac{\kappa^2}{4 \sum E^v}}$
  end if
  if $e_{in} == \sum E^v$ **then**
    $\theta_{out}^v \leftarrow \frac{1}{|E^v|}$
  else
    $\theta_{out}^v \leftarrow \frac{\sum E^v - e_{in}}{\sum E^v - \sum \frac{\kappa^2}{4 \sum E^v}}$
  end if
end for
return $\theta_{in}, \theta_{out}$

The algorithm goes through each graph to calculate the propensities for each graph separately. For each graph, the algorithm begins by calculating the number of internal edges and the degree-corrected, null-model terms (i.e. κ^2) for each of the clusters [24]. Then, the algorithm checks as to whether the graph is directed or undirected and whether there are no internal or external edges and then calculates the final propensities for that view graph: θ_{in}^v and θ_{out}^v. Once the propensities have been calculated for all of the view graphs, these are then returned.

3.2   Data Processing and View Graph Creation

The data for this analysis comes from Twitter's streaming API[2]. The data was collected using a list of keywords including "coronavirus", "wuhan virus", "wuhanvirus", "2019nCoV", "NCoV", "NCoV2019" [16]. The collected data spans the time period from 29 January 2020 to 22 June 2020 and consists of just over 500 million tweets that have, on average, 120,000 unique URLs per day. The data was first processed by grouping all tweets into daily collections, and then filtering for only those tweets with an English-language tag. Then, each of the URLs was processed in order to remove any query terms, so that all that is left is the base URL itself. Finally, for the clustering, only the top 50,000 most tweeted URLs across the entire time period were used.

The following figure, Fig. 1 depicts the daily statistics concerning the use of URLs within the data set.

There are some distinct temporal regions in URL usage in the data. In the first place, both the number of daily unique URLs along with the daily count of unique users starts small in the end of January and then surges around the end of February and beginning of March with the onset of lock-downs in many countries [19]. From there, the number of unique users and URLs slowly declines. In terms of the usage rates for URLs, they are both generally high for users and within tweets, with 47% of users using at least one URL on any given day and 42% of tweets containing a one URL. The usage ratios do, however, vary over the time-span of the data with there being low periods in URL usage at the end of January and again at the beginning of March. So, there are distinct temporal shifts in URL usage which generally mirrors patterns surrounding Twitter usage during the pandemic more broadly [7,9].

In order to multi-view cluster the URLs, three views were created to describe the URLs. The first view was the text view, which consist of all of the text that co-occurs with a URL in all of the tweets that mention a URL. Tweet text has been commonly used to cluster social media devices, like hashtags [12,29]. The next two views derive from the users that tweet the URLs. Since it has been noted in other works that retweeting behavior can differ from other tweeting behavior on Twitter [23], we broke the users into two views: those who retweet the URL versus those that tweet the URL.

---

[2] https://developer.Twitter.com/en/docs/tweets/filter-realtime/guides/basic-stream-parameters.

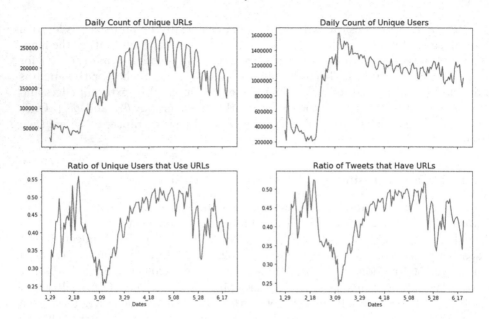

Fig. 1. Daily Statistics of the COVID-19 Twitter Data from 29 January 2020 to 22 June 2020. Use of URLs remains high both within tweets and by users, but does see a precipitous low-period of usage in the beginning of March, when many of the shutdowns were going into effect.

Now, the first step of the MVMC procedure is to create graphs of each of the views. For each view, a similarity graph was created. So, for each view graph, an edge represents how similar two objects are with respect to that view. For the users view, the similarity graphs were created by multiplying the URLs-by-users matrices by their transpose (i.e. $A = XX^T$) to produce a URLs-to-URLs shared users graph. To produce the text view graph, the text was broken down into terms by a bag-of-words model and Term Frequency-Inverse Document Frequency (tf-idf) was applied to the URL-by-term matrix. We then used a symmetric k-Nearest Neighbor Graph (k-NN) with the number of nearest neighbors as $k = \sqrt{n}$, where n is the number of objects being clustered, and cosine similarity was used to measure the similarity between the different URLs [21,22]. To symmetrize the k-NN, the average strategy, $A' = \frac{1}{2}A + A^T$, which is common in spectral clustering methods [26,33], was used to produce the final view graph. With that, we then had three different views of URL usage that were transformed to view graphs for clustering by MVMC.

4   Results

In this section, we describe the results of the multi-view clustering. In the first subsection we describe the cluster statistics. In the second subsection we compare the clusters to some additional labels from the domains that the URLs originate from. And, finally, in the third section, we analyze the content present within the most important of the clusters.

For clustering the COVID-19 URLs data, the following parameters for MVMC were used based on the parameter settings used in previous analyses using COVID-19 Twitter data [10]: The initial weights and resolutions were all set to one. The convergence tolerance for the resolutions was set to 0.01 and for the weights to 0.01, and the procedure was allowed to run for a maximum of 20 iterations.

4.1   Multi-view Clustering Statistics

We begin the analysis of the multi-view clustering by looking at the clustering statistics. The procedure produced 71 clusters with an average membership of $704.7 \pm 3,361.8$ URLs. In terms of the cluster sizes, there are three main clusters of URLs, and several smaller clusters. 98.8% of the URLs fall within the first three clusters which are of sizes 18,987, 15,859, and 14,636 URLs respectively. Of the smaller clusters, they had URLs that were generally from common news sources such as the *New York Times* or *Washington Post*. The formation of these small clusters was generally a result of a lack of overlap in user bases in both the non-retweet and retweet user views, which is likely a result of the data being collected from the streaming API, meaning it is only a sample of the data available. So, the clustering produced a collection of small, outlier clusters, and three main URL usage clusters.

From the MVMC algorithm we also obtained some insight into the nature of the clusters. First, the algorithm converged in three iterations. Typically a faster convergence (i.e. less than 20 iterations) is linked to a stronger cluster structure being present in the data [9]. Also, the learned weights of the different views, w^v, were 1.036, 1.27, and 0.698 for the retweet users, non-retweet users, and tweet text views respectively. These weights indicate that the non-retweet users which tweet a URL were the most important view to the cluster structure followed by those users that retweet a tweet containing a URL. So, from the performance of the MVMC algorithm, there is a strong cluster structure present in the data and the users who tweet a given URL form the most important view of that cluster structure.

4.2   Comparison of Clusters to Domain Labels

In order to understand the clusters produced by the URLs' different usage, we analyzed the domains of the URLs present in each of the three clusters. We compiled three different sets of labels for some of the commonly used domains of the URLs in the data. The first set of domain labels, which were compiled from various previously published articles on fake news and conspiracy theory domains, are color-based labels that relate to a domain's propensity to produce fake news articles [15,16,30]. For example, The 'black' domains contain websites which published exclusively fabricated stories while the 'red' list is a set of websites spreading falsehoods with a flawed editorial process, and the 'green' list

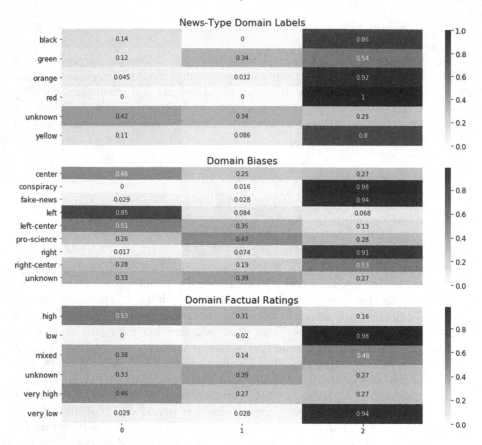

Fig. 2. Confusion matrices of three primary clusters of URLs and domain labels. The third cluster contains most of the URLs that come from domain labels that have been identified with producing fake news (i.e. 'black', 'red') as well as those domains with a US, politically right bias.

are websites that follow full editorial processes in their news publications and are not known to produce fabricated content. We also compiled a set of domain labels based on biases of the domain and factual ratings of the domain which were compiled using several fact checking and bias checking websites[3]. The following figure, Fig. 2, displays the breakdown of the various domain labels across the three main clusters of URLs.

The domain labels are not evenly distributed across the three main clusters of URLs. The first cluster contains the predominance of US, politically-left leaning

---

[3] These bias and fact checking websites are: https://mediabiasfactcheck.com/, http://www.fakenewscodex.com/, and https://www.snopes.com/. For transparency, these labels along with the associated URLs are available in a public repository: https://figshare.com/articles/conference_contribution/Clustering_Analysis_of_Website_Usage_on_Twitter_during_the_COVID-19_Pandemic/13079657.

domains as well as those that are evaluated to produce information that is rated as being high or very high in factual content. The second cluster tends to have most of the domains associated with a pro-science bias in their information. The third cluster, in contrast to the other two, contains most of the domains associated with various types of news websites, especially those that produce fabricated content, websites that promulgate conspiracy theories, as well as those websites that tend to have a US politically right or right-center bias. So, the clusters of usage have different political and factual biases of the URLs present within the clusters. In particular, websites with high factual ratings and left-leaning biases tend to have different usage patterns than those websites with low-factual ratings and a right-leaning bias. It is also interesting to observe that the various color-based labels for news sites tend to congregate in the same cluster indicating that usage patterns of fake news can be similar to usage patterns of more legitimate news on Twitter.

4.3   Content of Clusters of Interest

In order to get a better sense of the differences between the three main clusters found by multi-view clustering we then analyzed the clusters' content. In particular, we looked at the commonly occurring verbiage that occurs with tweets that contain the various URLs in each cluster and any hashtags that tend to co-occur with the URLs. In order to analyze the verbiage that occurs in tweets with the URLs, we first removed any common English stop words along with commonly used terms for this data like 'COVID-19', emojis, URLs, hashtags, and Twitter specific text (i.e. 'RT' for retweet) from all of the tweets. The text was then combined across all URLs for each cluster. The following figure, Fig. 3, displays a word map of the commonly used verbiage with URLs from the first cluster.

Much of the verbiage co-occurring in tweets with URLs from the first cluster centers around the US White House and President along with positive tests for the Coronavirus itself. Some of the hashtags which commonly occur with these URLs and their counts are: '#Trump': 62,102, '#TrumpVirus': 35,109, and '#MOG': 29,061. As was noted in the previous analysis section, this cluster tends to have the most domains related to a left-leaning bias. This bias is again seen somewhat in the hashtags that co-occur with URLs in this cluster. And, from the verbiage that occur with this cluster, much of the URL usage centers on President Trump and his administration. So, the first cluster of URLs seems to be URLs used as means of criticizing President Trump and his administration's response to the COVID-19 pandemic.

The next figure, Fig. 4, displays a word map of the commonly occurring verbiage with the URLs from the second cluster.

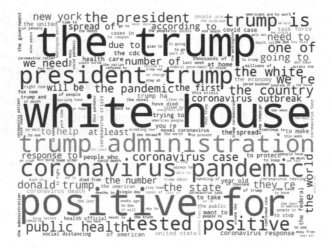

Fig. 3. Commonly used terms and phrases from the first cluster of URLs (label 0).

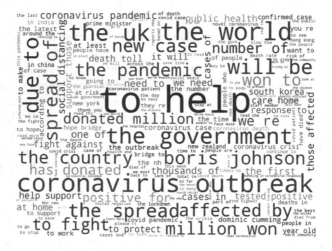

Fig. 4. Commonly used terms and phrases from the second cluster of URLs (label 1).

The verbiage co-occurring with the second cluster's URLs does not have as prominent of a dominant theme as the other clusters. There is verbiage related to the UK government as well as efforts related to fighting the spread of the COVID-19 pandemic, such as social-distancing. Some of the hashtags which commonly occur with these URLs and their counts are: '#IndiaFightsCorona': 127,747, '#TogetherAtHome': 82,962, '#lockdown': 43,151, and '#StayHome': 42,899. From the previous section, this particular cluster was not particularly high in any of the domain labels except for having the most URLs from pro-science biased domains. So, it would seem based on the verbiage and commonly occurring hashtags within this cluster that the URLs usage is generally meant to inform about actions taken to fight the COVID-19 pandemic.

Finally, the next figure, Fig. 5, displays a word map of the commonly occurring verbiage with the URLs from the third cluster.

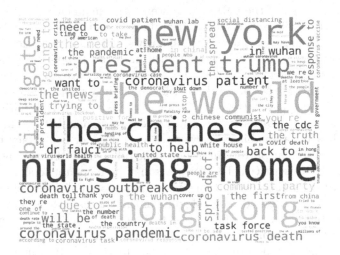

Fig. 5. Commonly used terms and phrases from the third cluster of URLs (label 2).

The verbiage from the third cluster centers around a couple of different topics. The prominent topics include verbiage around restrictions or impacts to nursing homes by the Coronavirus, criticisms of certain locations and their governments (i.e. China, Hong Kong, New York), and discussion around certain prominent individuals like Bill Gates, Dr. Anthony Fauci, or President Donald Trump. Some of the hashtags which commonly occur with these URLs and their counts are: '#FoxNews': 66,955, '#Wuhan': 62,760, '#QAnon': 47,237, and '#MAGA': 42,610. Much of the verbiage along with some of the hashtags relate to conspiracy theories surrounding the Pandemic as well as politically right leaning news websites. Thus, this cluster seems to contain both politically right biased news along with things like conspiracy theories, which would indicate both of these types of websites see similar usage patterns on Twitter.

5   Discussion

In this work we analyzed the usage patterns of websites on Twitter during the COVID-19 pandemic. We used multi-view clustering to do a clustering analysis on the 50,000 most used URLs on Twitter during the COVID-19 pandemic. The novel use of multi-view clustering allowed for then incorporation of multiple different views which could be used to describe how URLs are used in Twitter. In order to perform the multi-view clustering, we used three different views of usage of URLs on Twitter: the text the co-occurs in the tweets with the URLs, the users who retweet tweets of the URLs and the users who normally tweet the URLs. From the performance of the multi-view clustering algorithm, MVMC, we observed that the users who tweet a URL are the most important view for finding cluster structures in the usage patterns of URLs in the data. From the multi-view clustering of the URLs, there were three main clusters of URL usage.

These clusters differed in composition largely along political biases and by their having domains associated with fake news and conspiracy theories. In particular, one of the clusters, which contained most of the politically right-biased domains also contained nearly all of the domains that have been associated with fake news, conspiracy theories and other low-reliability information sources. This is to say that the usage patterns in terms of the text that occurs with particular URLs and the users that tweet and retweet particular URLs tend to be the same for politically right biased news sites as it does for conspiracy theories or fake news. This similar pattern in usage of the different URLs may indicate that more politically conservative Twitter users may be more apt to share and interact with conspiracy theories and fake news than more politically liberal leaning users. Furthermore, these ideological splits in the clusters also implies that users who share content from one political bias tend not to share, either through tweeting or retweeting, content of other political biases. So, for a major world event which is not inherently political in nature, like the COVID-19 pandemic, Twitter users still engage in discussion about the world event with political overtones, especially with regards to the external content that they share. So the findings of this study could have implications in terms of how best to craft important medical information about the COVID-19 pandemic in order to reach a populace through social media. In order to reach a wider audience with good health information through a social-media site like Twitter, it may be necessary to craft multiple messages along political lines in order reach a large number of users.

There are some limitations and directions for future research presented by this study. First, the Twitter data used in this study was collected through Twitter's streaming API and so it is not all of the data that occurred on Twitter during the time period of investigation. So, while we used a large sample of the available Twitter data and the Tweets follow patterns observed by other studies, it is still important to note that the data used in this study was a sample of all of the available data. Additionally, it is also important to note that the domain bias and factual rating labels come from professional bias and domain rating websites, which can themselves be subject to biases when labeling domains. This is in many ways an unavoidable problem, but we have used labellings from industry-standard bias and fact-checking sources as the best means to mitigate the possible bias within the labels. Also, given the prevalence in bot activity, especially on Twitter, its not clear how much the tweeting activity of COIVD-19 information along political lines is manufactured by bots or genuine, real-life user behavior. Finally, it is unclear if the same usage patterns of URLs—namely similar usage in terms of content and interactions for fake news and conspiracy theories as right-leaning news media—holds on other social media platforms. So, for future research, we intend to investigate website usage on other social media sites to see if there are similar patterns of website usage as was observed in this study. We also intend to conduct a more focused clustering analysis of those websites associated with conspiracy theories to see if there are different patterns of usage of different conspiracy theories during the COIVD-19 Pandemic.

Acknowledgement. This work is supported in part by the Office of Naval Research under the Multidisciplinary University Research Initiatives (MURI) Program award number N000141712675, Near Real Time Assessment of Emergent Complex Systems of Confederates, the Minerva program under grant number N000141512797, Dynamic Statistical Network Informatics, a National Science Foundation Graduate Research Fellowship (DGE 1745016), and by the center for Computational Analysis of Social and Organizational Systems (CASOS). The views and conclusions contained in this document are those of the authors and should not be interpreted as representing the official policies, either expressed or implied, of the ONR or the U.S. government.

References

1. Article 19: Viral lies: Misinformation and the coronavirus. Technical report, March 2020.   https://www.article19.org/wp-content/uploads/2020/03/Coronavirus-briefing.pdf
2. Bai, S., Sun, S., Bai, X., Zhang, Z., Tian, Q.: Improving context-sensitive similarity via smooth neighborhood for object retrieval. Pattern Recogn. **83**, 353–364 (2018). https://doi.org/10.1016/j.patcog.2018.06.001. http://www.sciencedirect.com/science/article/pii/S0031320318302115
3. Baltrusaitis, T., Ahuja, C., Morency, L.: Multimodal machine learning: a survey and taxonomy. CoRR abs/1705.09406 (2017). http://arxiv.org/abs/1705.09406
4. Baltrušaitis, T., Ahuja, C., Morency, L.: Multimodal machine learning: a survey and taxonomy. IEEE Trans. Pattern Anal. Mach. Intell. **41**(2), 423–443 (2019). https://doi.org/10.1109/TPAMI.2018.2798607
5. Blondel, V.D., Guillaume, J.L., Lambiotte, R., Lefebvre, E.: Fast unfolding of communities in large networks. J. Stat. Mech: Theory Exp. **2008**(10), 10008 (2008). https://doi.org/10.1088/1742-5468/2008/10/P10008
6. Boberg, S., Quandt, T., Schatto-Eckrodt, T., Frischlich, L.: Pandemic populism: Facebook pages of alternative news media and the corona crisis - a computational content analysis. arXiv e-prints arXiv:2004.02566, April 2020
7. Chen, E., Lerman, K., Ferrara, E.: COVID-19: the first public coronavirus Twitter dataset. arXiv e-prints arXiv:2003.07372, March 2020
8. Cinelli, M., et al.: The COVID-19 social media infodemic. arXiv e-prints arXiv:2003.05004, March 2020
9. Cruickshank, I.J.: Multi-view clustering of social-based data. Ph.D. thesis, Carnegie Mellon University, July 2020
10. Cruickshank, I.J., Carley, K.M.: Characterizing communities of hashtag usage on Twitter during the 2020 COVID-19 pandemic by multi-view clustering. Appl. Netw. Sci. **5**(66) (2020). https://doi.org/10.1007/s41109-020-00317-8. https://appliednetsci.springeropen.com/articles/10.1007/s41109-020-00317-8
11. Ferrara, E.: #COVID-19 on Twitter: bots, conspiracies, and social media activism. arXiv e-prints arXiv:2004.09531, April 2020

12. Figueiredo, F., Jorge, A.: Identifying topic relevant hashtags in Twitter streams. Inf. Sci. **505**, 65–83 (2019). https://doi.org/10.1016/j.ins.2019.07.062. http://www.sciencedirect.com/science/article/pii/S0020025519306668
13. Fortunato, S., Barthelemy, M.: Resolution limit in community detection. Proc. Natl. Acad. Sci. **104**(1), 36–41 (2007). https://doi.org/10.1073/pnas.0605965104
14. Gallotti, R., Valle, F., Castaldo, N., Sacco, P., De Domenico, M.: Assessing the risks of "infodemics" in response to COVID-19 epidemics. arXiv e-prints arXiv:2004.03997, April 2020
15. Grinberg, N., Joseph, K., Friedland, L., Swire-Thompson, B., Lazer, D.: Fake news on Twitter during the 2016 U.S. presidential election. Science **363** (2019). https://doi.org/10.1126/science.aau2706. https://pubmed.ncbi.nlm.nih.gov/30679368/
16. Huang, B.: Learning user latent attributes on social media. Ph.D. thesis, Carnegie Mellon University, May 2020
17. Huang, S., Chaudhary, K., Garmire, L.X.: More is better: recent progress in multi-omics data integration methods. Front. Genet. **8**, 84 (2017). https://doi.org/10.3389/fgene.2017.00084. https://www.frontiersin.org/article/10.3389/fgene.2017.00084
18. Hussain, W.: Role of social media in COVID-19 pandemic **4** (2020). https://doi.org/10.37978/tijfs.v4i2.144. http://publie.frontierscienceassociates.com/index.php/tijfs/article/view/144
19. Kantis, C., Kiernan, S., Bardi, J.: Timeline of the coronavirus: think global health. https://www.thinkglobalhealth.org/article/updated-timeline-coronavirus
20. Lancichinetti, A., Fortunato, S.: Limits of modularity maximization in community detection **84**, 066122 (2011). https://doi.org/10.1103/PhysRevE.84.066122
21. Maier, M., Hein, M., von Luxburg, U.: Optimal construction of k-nearest neighbor graphs for identifying noisy clusters. arXiv e-prints arXiv:0912.3408, December 2009
22. Maier, M., von Luxburg, U., Hein, M.: How the result of graph clustering methods depends on the construction of the graph. arXiv e-prints arXiv:1102.2075, February 2011
23. Majmundar, A., Allem, J.P., Boley Cruz, T., Unger, J.B.: The why we retweet scale. PLoS ONE **13**(10), 1–12 (2018). https://doi.org/10.1371/journal.pone.0206076
24. Newman, M.E.J.: Community detection in networks: modularity optimization and maximum likelihood are equivalent. arXiv e-prints arXiv:1606.02319, June 2016
25. Pamfil, A.R., Howison, S.D., Lambiotte, R., Porter, M.A.: Relating modularity maximization and stochastic block models in multilayer networks. CoRR abs/1804.01964 (2018). http://arxiv.org/abs/1804.01964
26. Qiao, L., Zhang, L., Chen, S., Shen, D.: Data-driven graph construction and graph learning: a review. Neurocomputing **312**, 336–351 (2018). https://doi.org/10.1016/j.neucom.2018.05.084. http://www.sciencedirect.com/science/article/pii/S0925231218306696
27. Reichardt, J., Bornholdt, S.: Statistical mechanics of community detection. Phys. Rev. E **74**, 016110 (2006). https://doi.org/10.1103/PhysRevE.74.016110
28. Traag, V.A., Waltman, L., van Eck, N.J.: From Louvain to Leiden: guaranteeing well-connected communities. Nat. Sci. Rep. **9** (2019). https://doi.org/10.1038/s41598-019-41695-z. https://www.nature.com/articles/s41598-019-41695-z
29. Vicient, C., Moreno, A.: Unsupervised topic discovery in micro-blogging networks. Expert Syst. Appl. **42**(17), 6472–6485 (2015). https://doi.org/10.1016/j.eswa.2015.04.014. http://www.sciencedirect.com/science/article/pii/S0957417415002444

30. Yang, K.C., Torres-Lugo, C., Menczer, F.: Prevalence of low-credibility information on Twitter during the COVID-19 outbreak. arXiv e-prints arXiv:2004.14484, April 2020
31. Yang, Y., Wang, H.: Multi-view clustering: a survey. Big Data Min. Anal. **1**(2), 83–107 (2018)
32. Ye, F., Chen, Z., Qian, H., Li, R., Chen, C., Zheng, Z.: New approaches in multi-view clustering. In: Recent Applications in Data Clustering (2018). https://doi.org/10.5772/intechopen.75598. https://www.intechopen.com/books/recent-applications-in-data-clustering/new-approaches-in-multi-view-clustering
33. Zhu, X., Loy, C.C., Gong, S.: Constructing robust affinity graphs for spectral clustering. In: 2014 IEEE Conference on Computer Vision and Pattern Recognition, pp. 1450–1457, June 2014. https://doi.org/10.1109/CVPR.2014.188
34. Zitnik, M., Nguyen, F., Wang, B., Leskovec, J., Goldenberg, A., Hoffman, M.M.: Machine learning for integrating data in biology and medicine: principles, practice, and opportunities. arXiv e-prints arXiv:1807.00123, June 2018

Data-Driven Software Engineering

Calibrated Viewability Prediction for Premium Inventory Expansion

Jonathan Schler[1][(✉)] and Allon Hammer[2]

[1] Holon Institute of Technology, Holon, Israel
schler@hit.ac.il
[2] Browsi Ltd., Tel Aviv, Israel
alonha@gobrowsi.com

Abstract. Billions of ads are displayed on a daily basis, making it a multi-billion industry. Most of web pages contain multiple ads, which are largely served in real time using a bidding process where buyers (advertisers) offer a price tag to the seller (publishers) for each given possible ad on the page. There are multiple factors that impact an ad price, one of the primary ones is the ad-location's viewability likelihood. Due to the length of many web pages, certain ad locations are invisible to the visiting user, as he may not scroll far enough on the page to where the ads are placed. According to recent industry metrics, less than 60% of ads are viewable. This poses a challenge to both: buyers and sellers. Buyers want to optimize the likelihood they buy an ad that will be viewed, while sellers want to maximize ad prices (by setting higher floor prices) by providing as many possible ad placements with high viewability probability. This paper addresses the viewability prediction from the publisher's side, and proposes a novel algorithm based on cascading gradient boosting. The algorithm enables sellers to predict an accurate viewability probability for ad impressions, which is optimized to match the actual viewability rate that will be measured for the served ads. Unlike other algorithms that optimize these problems to an average minimal difference from a central mean error, we propose an algorithm that increases the amount of extreme cases - which are the most valuable ones, thus expanding the premium ad inventory. We evaluate the algorithm on two datasets with a total of over 500 million impressions. We found that the algorithm outperforms other viewability prediction algorithms, works well for publishers while providing a measurable fairness metric to advertisers.

Keywords: Machine learning · Advertising technology · Viewability prediction · Cascading gradient boosting

1 Introduction

Online advertisement has two main players: publishers and advertisers. Publishers are the creators and owners of web-pages. One of their primary goals is to provide information of interest to users, traditionally measured by the number

© Springer Nature Switzerland AG 2021
J. A. Lossio-Ventura et al. (Eds.): SIMBig 2020, CCIS 1410, pp. 403–418, 2021.
https://doi.org/10.1007/978-3-030-76228-5_29

of users that visit their pages. The more visits a web page (or web site) has, the more valuable it is. In addition to the information or content that is provided on web pages, many pages contain (pre-defined) locations for placing ads. Those locations are called ad units (or ad placements). While those locations are on fixed places on the page and are defined to host the ads, they can display different ads for different users. In many cases, two different users that visit the same web page, will see different ads on the same ad placement. Each user visit to a given web page is called – "page view", and every display of a specific ad at a specific location in any given page view is called "ad impression".

Different advertisers may have interest in presenting an ad to a given user on a specific web page. Their interest depends on one hand on the subject of the specific ad (advertiser related parameters) and on the other hand, on the content type of the web page, the information that is available about the audience of that page or site, and possible information about the given user. Usually, advertisers look for a match in terms of content and profile, to the subject of their ad. Traditionally, the price is set according to the advertiser's level of interest, the higher the interest, the higher the price. In some cases, this is referred as the process of matching supply and demand.

But not only the match of content and users matters, also the potential exposure of the ad to the user. The longer the potential ad exposure the higher the price. Hence, ads that are placed towards the top of the page, and at a centralized location, are priced higher than others. Contrary to this, ads that are placed towards the end of the page, are not being seen by a large portion of users (especially on long pages), thus result in lower prices for those locations. A recent indsustry benchmark shows[1], that at least 40% of ads were placed at non-viewable locations. As a result, during the last years, the "Interactive Advertising Bureau" (IAB) introduced a new pricing method, in which advertisers pay only for viewable impressions. There are various methods in place, which measure on the advertiser's behalf, if the ad was in a viewable state by the user.

IAB defined a viewable impression as an impression which at least 50% of the ad is shown in the user's screen for at least one second [7]. Figure 1 shows an illustration of 3 ads appearing on a user's screen (screen marked as dotted square), the top 2 ads are viewable (as more than 50% of the ad is viewed for more than 1 s), the ad at the bottom is a non-viewable ad.

Over the last years, more than 80% of the ad inventory is sold using a real time auction system (called RTB = Real Time Bidding) [3]. In this environment, before a page view request is fulfilled by the publisher, an auction process takes place, in which advertisers place bids (for all relevant placements on that page) of how much they are willing to pay to serve an ad to this specific user at the specific location. The highest advertising bid wins, and its ad is displayed on the publishers page. Both parties, publishers and advertisers, try to optimize their yield as much as possible. During this process, advertisers try to optimize their bidding strategy to assure they pay only for premium, highly viewable inventory. Publishers, on the other hand try to increase their income by promoting high quality inventory

---

[1] As shown in [6].

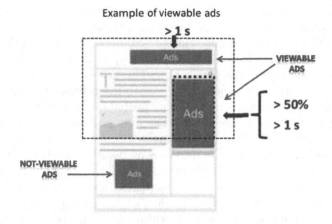

Fig. 1. Illustration of ad viewability definition

and sell it at higher prices. One specific quality metric is viewability likelihood - in which the higher the viewability likelihood of an ad is, the higher its value, hence advertisers would pay more, yielding higher profit to the publisher.

A common KPI (Key Performance Indicator) that is used to asses inventory's viewability quality is based on the percentage of ads that were viewed, out of the total amount of ad impressions. The actual metric is given by the formula:

$$viewability = \frac{viewable\_impressions}{impressions} \qquad (1)$$

Advertisers own the ad that is served, therefore, they can get impression level data on viewability of the specific ad and combine it with other performance metrics to predict ad impression viewability in real time. This combination of powerful data allows advertisers to determine the value of a given inventory and bid for it at the **ad impression granularity**. On the contrary, due to the absence of impression level data for publishers (as they control only the location but not the ad itself), they have to rely on historical data at the **placement (ad unit) granularity**. Using historical data to determine future behavior is common. This simply means looking at past viewability of a single ad unit in a specific article, and assuming the future viewability rate on the same unit will be the same. This method, yet simple works, but is not very optimal, as it is not able to assign fine grained probability at the user level, but rather provides a single score to all impressions for the given placement.

In order to enable publishers to predict with more accuracy on each impression, they must do it at the user level. This requires the creation of machine-learning models that in addition to historical data, use also real-time engagement data to predict viewability. This combination generates a unique prediction for each impression, per user engagement on the page.

Viewability prediction at the ad-impression granularity provides several advantages to the publisher as it provides them more flexibility and increases the amount of impressions that can be sold. This problem can be seen as a standard probabilistic binary classification problem. The output of such a prediction would be the probability of a single impression to be viewed. Aggregating these predictions should give us the viewability rate as in Eq. 1. Since advertisers' bids rely heavily on viewability rate, and expect to see this criteria met in their campaigns, publishers will benefit most from correct viewability rate prediction. Simply predicting a binary result is not sufficient, and probability calibration is key to this matter. If predicting viewability at the ad impression granularity is the first challenge, doing so with calibrated predictions is the second. Publishers would also like to mark as many premium impressions as possible (without compromising prediction accuracy), this ensures them unique campaigns with higher payoffs[2].

Therefore, shifting predicted values to the extreme (0 or 1) while maintaining accuracy and calibration will yield the publisher even better results. However, as traditional machine learning algorithms are built, they optimize towards minimizing the average deviation from the prediction, which typically yields in providing a prediction closer to the average and hence less of extreme values predictions. As mentioned at the beginning of this paragraph, this is less favorable for the publisher. As a result, publisher would benefit from a shifted-calibrated probabilistic classification model. Such a model also requires to define adequate evaluation methods, since regular methods (e.g. F1 score, log-loss, accuracy) fail to capture all aspects of the problem from a Publisher's perspective. Building an algorithm that addresses these 4 challenges (accurate viewability prediction at the ad impression level, calibration, shifting to the extreme thus providing more premium inventory and relevant evaluation) is the scope of this paper. An additional contribution (upon acceptance of this paper) is the release of a large public dataset for viewability prediction (first of its kind).

The remainder of the paper is organized as follows. In Sect. 2 we review the existing work on viewability prediction. We follow this, in Sect. 3, with the introduction of the Cascading Gradient Boosting algorithm which will tackle the shifted-calibrated viewability prediction challenge. We then (Sect. 4) apply the algorithm on a large scale industry dataset, evaluate its performance against baseline methods and discuss the results. Finally, in Sect. 5, we conclude with directions for future research.

2   Related Work

In general, limited research has been done on viewability prediction [1,14]. Callejo et al. [1] showed that predicting the probability of a single display ad to be viewed is challenging. Different user behaviours, sparse interactions between users and web pages and volatile and noisy patterns all contribute to the difficulty. Wang et al. [14] used a Probabilistic Latent Class (PLC) model to predict the maximum

---

[2] Predicting very low probability is also useful for some publishers, for example by using it for campaigns that are based on pay per impression (and are not interested in clicks). These campaigns are for example about brand awareness and do not require high viewability, therefore the total ad inventory could be better utilized.

scroll depth of a user in a certain web-page (as a viewability estimate). These models assume a prior distribution for a user to belong to a latent user class, and a web-page to belong to a latent web-page class, and calculate the joint distribution of a single user in a single web-page to scroll to a specific depth in the page. The joint probability is updated using the EM (Expectation Maximization) algorithm. In turn, viewability could be inferred by the prediction of max scroll depth. Performance of those models was measured using precision, recall, F1-score and RMSE. Precision, recall and F1-score, convert the viewability prediction to 0 or 1, i.e., if it is greater or equal to 0.5 then the impression is considered viewable, otherwise, it is not viewable. RMSE measures the difference between the viewability values predicted by the model and the actual observed value. RMSE penalizes large errors more. For example given a positive label (marked as 1), a prediction of 0.05 will be penalized more than a prediction of 0.15 as shown: $(1-0.05)^2 - (1-0.15)^2 = 0.18$, this is regardless of both being wrong predictions. On the other hand given the same label, a prediction of 0.95 compared to 0.85 suffers from diminishing returns $(1 - 0.85)^2 - (1 - 0.95)^2 = 0.02$. This intuitive explanation, shows why RMSE will converge towards more subtle values and not favor extreme predictions.

Other studies by Wang et al. [13] predicted web-page depth dwell time using Deep Sequential Neural Networks. Every time-stamp in the input is comprised of information about the user, the page, the depth, and the dwell time sequence and page meta-data. That problem is different than the viewability problem. The viewability case enforces the publisher to determine the price of a single ad before it is fetched (before the RTB auction occurs). This process should be quick, ideally a couple hundreds of milliseconds, to avoid latency on the page and bad user experience. Therefore, predictions must be emitted before the user has started interacting with the page. To this matter, dwell-time sequence is not available to us at real time.

Gradient boosting is a machine learning technique for regression and classification problems, based on an ensemble of many weak prediction models, typically decision trees [4]. It builds the model in a stage-wise fashion like other boosting methods do, and it generalizes them by allowing optimization of an arbitrary differentiable loss function. Ensemble models and Gradient Boosting in particular are very efficient in classification and regression tasks [8,17].

Gradient boosting decision trees usually yield superior performance in metrics such as precision, recall, area under ROC curve and accuracy [10]. However, from a probabilistic perspective, these algorithms provide poorly calibrated predictions and relatively poor cross entropy score compared to other classification models (such as Naive Bayes, SVM, Random Forest and more) [5]. Friedman et al. showed [5] that gradient boosting can be viewed as an additive logistic regression model. As a result, each tree tries to fit the logit of the true probabilities (not the true probabilities themselves). In order to obtain large margin on cases close to the decision surface, the Gradient boosted classifier will sacrifice the margin of the easier cases. As a result the predicted values are shifted away from 0 and 1 in favor of more accurate predictions in the harder cases, thus hurting calibration [12]. To address this [9] tried to convert the boosted model to have well calibrated predictions using methods such as Platt Scaling [11] and Isotonic Regression [16].

As mentioned in Sect. 1, we want to provide viewability predictions that are both calibrated and shifted towards the extreme. Calibrated predictions ensure that our predictions represent the expected viewability (e.g. out of 50 impression that got viewability prediction of 0.1, a total of 5 will indeed be viewable). Shifted predictions will ensure that more impressions will receive the higher (or lower) probable predictions (i.e., closer to 0 and 1) making it easier to mark premium inventory and price it accordingly. Shifting predictions while maintaining calibration is a challenging task, which to our best knowledge has not been addressed so far. The novelty this paper suggests is using a Cascading architecture for this purpose.

3   Cascading Gradient Boosting Trees

Traditional prediction algorithms are optimized to have the majority of predictions in the central range (i.e. between 35%–65%), and smaller number of predictions on the extremes (similar to a Gaussian distribution). Our goal, is to identify predictions that fall in the "central range" and push them towards one of the extremes - by getting a better and more accurate prediction on their probability. In order to push predictions towards 1, we need to penalize False Negatives severely, whereas in order to push predictions towards 0 we to penalize False Positives severely. The two terms are contradictory, therefore we will have to train separate models for these tasks and relying on their accumulated predictions to give us improvement in both tasks.

In order to build the cascading gradient boosting learner, we need to define its loss function. Traditionally, the standard log-loss function is defined as:

$$L = y \cdot \log p(y) + (1 - y) \log(1 - p(y)) \tag{2}$$

where p denotes the probability of this impression to be viewed (due to the binary nature of the problem, the probability of this impression to not be viewed is $1 - p$). The first term $y \cdot \log p$ penalizes False Negatives. Since $y \in \{0, 1\}$, only positive labels that were predicted as negative will be calculated. The second term $(1 - y) \log(1 - p)$ penalizes False Positives. Only negative labels that were predicted as positive will be calculated. We will define three models:

1. **Base model**, predicts the probability of the impression to be viewed. This model is based on the standard loss function as defined by Eq. (2) and is optimized as described in the previous Section.
2. **Zero model**, "pushes" predictions towards 0. This model is based on the loss function:

$$L = y \cdot \log p + (1 - y) \log(1 - p) \cdot \beta \quad ; \beta > 1 \tag{3}$$

β is the factor to increase the penalty for false positives.

3. **One model**, "pushes" predictions towards 1. This model is based on the loss function:

$$L = y \cdot \log p \cdot \alpha + (1 - y) \log(1 - p) \quad ; \alpha > 1 \tag{4}$$

α is the factor to increase the penalty for false negatives.

One may note that the Zero model puts more emphasis on the F1 score of the negative labels, and the One model puts more emphasis on the F1 score of the positive labels.

The process first trains the Base model (optimizing "regular" log-loss), then creates a new input vector by concatenating the original input vector with the output from the Base model. Finally two models (Zero, One) are trained simultaneously on the new input (thus creating the cascading model). For readability purposes we skip here the full derivation process. The formal training algorithm is defined in Algorithm 1 below:

Algorithm 1. Cascading Gradient Boosting Training Algorithm

Train Base model $F_{base}(\boldsymbol{x})$
$\boldsymbol{x}' = [\boldsymbol{x}, \hat{\boldsymbol{y}}]$
Train Zero and One models simultaneously $F_{zero}(\boldsymbol{x}'), F_{one}(\boldsymbol{x}')$

Tuning the tree hyper-parameters (depth, leaf regularization) and Boosting hyper-parameters (number of trees, learning rate) is performed using a grid search on the Base Model (maximizing log loss). Hyper-parameters α and β are tuned separately on the Zero model and One model correspondingly (maximizing the F_β score, which is the weighted harmonic mean of precision and recall, recall gets 0.5 times less weight than precision).

The inference algorithm calculates the final prediction based on different scenarios. When both models agree on the label (positive or negative) and their predictions are more certain[3] than the base model - the final prediction is more certain as well. When both models give contradictory but less certain predictions than the base model - the final prediction equals to the base prediction. When both models give contradictory but more certain predictions- the final prediction uses a smoothing function.

$$\zeta(\hat{y}_b, \hat{y}_0, \hat{y}_1) = (1 + 2(\hat{y}_b - 0.5))((\hat{y}_0 + \hat{y}_1)/2) \tag{5}$$

To obtain a single prediction from the aforementioned cascading architecture we follow the following algorithm

---

[3] Closer to zero in case of a negative label, and closer to one when the label is positive.

Algorithm 2. Cascading Gradient Boosting Inference Algorithm

Obtain prediction from Base model on x, mark as $\hat{y}_b$ and construct x'

Obtain prediction from Zero model on x' mark as $\hat{y}_0$

Obtain prediction from One model on x' mark as $\hat{y}_1$

Mark $\hat{y_{0pred}} = \begin{cases} 1 & \hat{y}_0 > 0.5 \\ 0 & \text{otherwise} \end{cases}$

Mark $\hat{y_{1pred}} = \begin{cases} 1 & \hat{y}_1 > 0.5 \\ 0 & \text{otherwise} \end{cases}$

return

$$y_{\hat{final}} = \begin{cases} \hat{y}_b & \hat{y_{0pred}} = 1, \hat{y_{1pred}} = 0 \\ \max(\hat{y}_0, \hat{y}_1) & \hat{y_{0pred}} = 1, \hat{y_{1pred}} = 1, \hat{y}_b < \hat{y}_1 \\ \min(\hat{y}_0, \hat{y}_1) & \hat{y_{0pred}} = 0, \hat{y_{1pred}} = 0, \hat{y}_0 < \hat{y}_b \\ \zeta(\hat{y}_b, \hat{y}_0, \hat{y}_1) & \hat{y_{0pred}} = 0, \hat{y_{1pred}} = 1 \\ \hat{y}_b & \text{otherwise} \end{cases}$$

---

4   Evaluation and Results

In order to evaluate the Cascading Gradient Boosting algorithm we used two data sets. The first dataset consists of 20 million impressions from 10 different publishers (5 mobile sites and 5 desktop sites). Part of this dataset was used for training, and the other part for detailed evaluation of the results. We then applied the same model to a larger dataset (the second dataset) with over 500 million impressions and used it for aggregated result analysis with additional dimension of pricing.

The baseline viewability rate for the datasets was 65% for mobile sites and 60% for desktop sites, thus showing a fairly balanced data set[4]. No balancing methods took place in the experiment.

We selected a random set of sites across several domains (such as: news, sports, entertainment, forums) and covering several counties according to impression distribution (majority of traffic from United States and Israel as shown in Fig. 2).

The layouts of these sites varies greatly, and usually differs by the number of words, paragraphs, images, videos, social widgets, comment sections, content recommendations and other 3rd party ads. Sites also vary in their response and interaction time, most likely due to different implementations of web-developers such as AJAX and dynamic content solutions. All of the ads in the data-set are display ads, with varying sizes from different providers (ad sources). All of the ads in the data-set are inline (ads that appear inline with other content in the web-page). Other ad types such as sticky ads and interstitial ads have been filtered out. The majority of the ads (>80%) are within the main-content of the page. Nevertheless, the location of the ads within the web-pages (and within the main-content in particular) varies greatly. Figure 3 shows that the distribution of ad location in relation to the length of the page (in %) is very

---

[4] A two-proportion-z-test was conducted (p-value > 0.05) to show that the proportions are indeed comparable to IAB [7] accredited viewability measures on those sites.

broad. Both desktop and mobile ads are distributed across the page (top, bottom and middle).

Sessions from Bot users and ad-blockers were filtered out, using 3rd party tools. The feature spec in the data set is vast. It includes real time aggregated and static features at the user and web-page levels. User data is collected using cookies (more than 50% of desktop users and 60% of mobile users are identified as returning users). Examples for aggregated user features are: historic scrolling patterns (velocity, lingering time, latency), session history, clicks, views, RTB bidding history, referrers, recent visits to similar articles and more. Static user features are: country, device, OS, browser, hour, day and more. Web-page features include the page layout (location of images, paragraphs and other items described in this section), the location of the ad on the page, the topic and author of the article and more. Since the model is user-based it induces the cold-start problem. This problem is dealt with using several methods: separate models for new users and returning users, filling missing values with mean values, and fall-back to web-page aggregations.

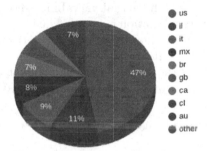

Fig. 2. Ad distribution by Geo

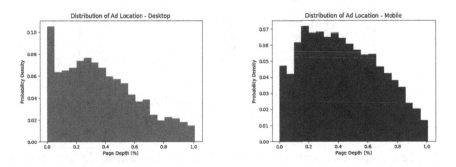

Fig. 3. Ad location distribution by depth on page (desktop and mobile)

For the first dataset, we selected and random set of 20 million impressions from 10 publishers. We split the data into four parts (partitioned by timestamp):[5]

1. Train set (35%)- Base model is trained on this data
2. Validation I (25%)- Base model is evaluated on this data, and Zero and One models are trained on this data
3. Validation II (25%)- Zero and One models are evaluated on this data
4. Test (15%)- This is a hold-out set. The full algorithm is evaluated on this data.

As mentioned in Sect. 2 classical evaluation metrics are less suitable for this matter. Therefore, we will use metrics of SSE (Sum of Squared Errors) and RMSE (Root Mean Square Errors) which were widely used for viewability prediction [1, 13, 14].

In order to provide a broader picture of the viewability predictions we want to introduce the tiered prediction rate table. The table contains several rows that present viewability prediction tiers. In an ideal world, given n predictions with an average prediction of 0.8 , the actual viewability should be 80% as well. In order to measure this, every prediction is rounded down to a 1 decimal prediction probability, creating 10 different possible values, called tiers. In the table each tier contains the number of ad impressions that were assigned the given probability. The other column contains the actual number of viewable impressions in that tier. For each tier the viewability rate is calculated based on Eq. (1) as seen in Table 1.

Table 1. Calculating SSE for each tier

Tier	Impressions	Viewed impressions	Viewability	SSE
0	1000	50	0.05	2.5
0.1	2000	300	0.15	5
0.2	5000	1200	0.24	8
0.3	10000	3200	0.32	4
0.4	10000	4600	0.46	36
0.5	10000	5200	0.52	4
0.6	10000	6600	0.66	36
0.7	5000	3800	0.76	18
0.8	2000	1680	0.84	3.2
0.9	1000	940	0.94	1.6
Total	56000	27570		118.3

The SSE (sum of squared error) for each tier measures the gap between the predicted viewability (noted in the "tier" column) of the impressions in

---

[5] Since some of the features are real-time aggregated features, splitting by time-stamp is used to avoid information leakage. **These results were reproduced with different cutoffs to avoid time-based bias.** Using K-fold cross validation is not suitable for this matter.

Table 2. Low $RMSE_{agg}$ for tier Prediction but no dispersion

Tier	Impressions	Viewed impressions	Viewability	SSE
0	20	0	0	0
0.1	100	15	0.15	0.25
0.2	1000	270	0.27	4.9
0.3	2000	620	0,31	0.2
0.4	10000	4100	0.41	1
0.5	10000	5000	0.5	0
0.6	2000	1250	0.625	1.25
0.7	1000	730	0.73	0.9
0.8	100	84	0.84	0.16
0.9	20	19	0.95	0.05
Total	**26240**	**12088**		**8.71**

the bucket to the actual viewability rate of those impressions (noted in the "Viewability" column). SSE is defined as

$$SSE = impressions * (viewability - tier)^2 \qquad (6)$$

According to the formula, the SSE of the first tier (tier is 0, it contains 1000 impressions, and viewability of 0.05) is $1000 * (0.05 - 0)^2 = 2.5$.

$RMSE_{agg}$ (Root Mean Square Error) is a measure for the accuracy of the predictions. It measures the aggregated differences between the values predicted by the model, and the values that were actually observed for each of the tiers. The lower the $RMSE_{agg}$ score is, the better is the prediction. The $RMSE_{agg}$ score is defined as:

$$RMSE_{agg} = \sqrt{\frac{\sum_{t \in tiers} SSE_t}{\sum_{t \in tiers} Impressions_t}} \qquad (7)$$

Therefore the $RMSE_{agg}$ score for the data in Table 1 is $\sqrt{\frac{118.3}{56000}} = 0.046$. While RMSE can be used to calculate the minimal error, it doesn't measure the dispersion of predictions. An illustrative example can be found in Table 2:

As can be seen Table 2 yields a very low error thus much lower than $RMSE_{agg}$ found in Table 1. $RMSE_{agg} = \sqrt{26240/8.71} = 0.018$ but on the other hand fails to deliver a good dispersion of predictions (very few predictions on the extreme tiers and most in the center, much worse than the dispersion of results in Table 1). Therefore, three additional metrics for dispersion are introduced.

The first metric is Certain Predictions Percentile (marked as CPP) and given by:

$$CPP = \frac{\sum_{t \in 0,0.9} Impressions_t}{\sum Impressions} \qquad (8)$$

The second metric is Uncertain Predictions Percentile (marked as $UCPP$) and given by:

$$UCPP = \frac{\sum_{t \in 0.3..0.6} Impressions_t}{\sum Impressions} \qquad (9)$$

The third metric is Premium Predictions Percentile (marked as PPP) and given by:

$$PPP = \frac{\sum_{t \geq =0.7} Impressions_t}{\sum Impressions} \qquad (10)$$

Essentially, CPP measures the amount of predictions in the extreme tiers ,$UCPP$ measures the amount of predictions in the middle tiers and PPP measures the amount of Premium predictions (defined as 70% or higher - according to industry standards). The ideal is to maximize CPP and PPP while minimizing $UCPP$ and $RMSE_{agg}$.

These results were compared to a baseline model - a single Gradient Boosting model with no cascading. This is equivalent to using only the base model (without the Zero and One models). In most cases, the baseline model outperforms other classic classification algorithms (XGboost, Random Forest, Logistic Regression, SVM, DNN). However, in order to enable comparison to the work done by [14], we added the following algorithms.[6]

1. Logistic Regression (LR)
2. Singular Value Decomposition (SVD)
3. Feed-forward Deep Neural Network (DNN)
4. Deterministic model, according to historical viewability per ad-unit (DET) (see Sect. 1)

Tables 5 and 6 in Appendix 1, contain the results of the four classic algorithms. Analysis of those metrics shows some interesting findings. While the simplest algorithm, based on historical data (DET) provides the lowest (i.e. best) $RMSE_{agg}$ for both desktop and mobile sites, it has also the lowest CPP and PPP scores (i.e. worst). This demonstrates again one of the main motivations of this work: the optimization of the viewability prediction rate table is different from optimal viewability prediction. In fact, DET seems to be the best viewability predictor (among base algorithms - according to the $RMSE_{agg}$), but is the worst on the tiered prediction.

The best tiered viewability predictors among the base algorithms are LR and DNN. As can be seen, the proposed baseline algorithm (gradient boosting trees) outperformed LR and DNN on both types of sites (desktop and mobile), in all four metrics.

Table 3 in Appendix 1 contains the comparison of the Cascading Gradient Boosting (CGB) algorithms to the baseline algorithm. It lists the $RMSE, CPP, UCPP$ and PPP scores for each of the 5 desktop sites it was tested on. One can see that CGB outperformed the baseline algorithm, on all 3 metrics of:

---

[6] The Probabilistic Latent Class (PLC) model presented in [14] was not added to the comparison, since it does not suit to our problem. Main reason is that our data consists of many first time users (without history) and hence can't build a user level prior.

$CPP, UCPP$ and PPP. There is a an average increase of 13% in CPP (even with excluding site F), and of 6.8% in PPP, as well as an average decrease of 13.4% in $UCPP$ (we prefer lower $UCPP$ scores). One can also note, that the $RMSE_{agg}$ is only slightly higher by less than 1%[7] on average, meaning we managed to improve the dispersion without significant harm to the accuracy of the model.

Comparing benchmark results to the CGB ones, on mobile sites shows similar findings (Table 4 in Appendix 1). We observed a significant improvement of over 33% on average in CPP score. An increase of 2% in PPP and decrease of 6.6% in $UCPP$.

As mentioned before, we applied the above this model to a larger set, of about 500 million random impressions from 500 mobile sites and 300 desktop during a period of a month. In such scale the detailed analysis done before is impossible, but we can see the overall statistics at much larger scale. In addition, we analyzed the correlation of those results to the pricing a publisher sees. Table (Table 7 in Appendix 1) summarizes the performance results. We can see a significant improvement in prediction quality. There is an average improvement of 8% in CPP, and 4% in PPP as well as an average decrease of 10% in $UCPP$. $RMSE_{agg}$ is barley affected.

Finally, Table 8 in Appendix 1 shows the median CPM (revenue per 1000 impressions) for each tier. It is evident that for both desktop and mobile sites, higher predictions for viewability are correlated with higher payoffs (Pearson correlation coefficient between predictions and cpm is greater than 0.75 for both desktop and mobile). It can also be inferred that an uplift in CPP and PPP (given fixed $RMSE_{agg}$) yield a significant uplift in CPM.

5   Discussion and Future Work

As mentioned above, publishers achieve significant gains to their inventory given a correct and robust pricing per single impression. We proposed a model to address the unique problem of tier prediction. The Cascading Gradient Boosting Decision Trees framework managed to yield accurate results and uplift dispersion at the extreme and more valuable tiers, thus expanding premium inventory for publishers.

Interestingly, at first glance the cascading models might seem contradictory, but their mutual predictive power succeeded in predicting difficult cases, where a single classifier might yield an uncertain prediction.

Additional hyper-parameter tuning (such as the parameters in Eq. 5) accompanied by an appropriate optimization method (such as Bayesian Optimization [15]) could be conducted as future work. In addition, we plan to use the the algorithmic framework presented in this paper for other use-cases in the ad-tech industry. Such application could be ad click prediction, completion rate prediction and many more.

---

[7] A Diebold-Mariano [2] test for statistical significance was conducted on $RMSE_{agg}$ of the Baseline compared to CGB. The test yielded $P_{value} > 0.05$ suggesting no significant difference in the $RMSE_{agg}$ between the Baseline and CGB.

1   Appendix 1 - Additional Tables and Graphs

Table 3. Results-Desktop Sites

Site	Baseline (Base model only)				Cascading Gradient Boosting			
	$RMSE_{agg}$	CPP	UCPP	PPP	$RMSE_{agg}$	CPP	UCPP	PPP
A	0.042	0.97%	69.37%	7.75%	0.042	5.87%	45.00%	9.93%
B	0.046	46.76%	8.76%	89.67%	0.043	50.51%	8.33%	89.86%
C	0.052	28.22%	52.00%	44.24%	0.051	31.11%	50.88%	44.95%
D	0.032	11.97%	57.92%	31.44%	0.037	14.20%	52.16%	32.05%
E	0.057	6.26%	12.17%	55.17%	0.055	7.03%	10.36%	56.41%

Table 4. Results-Mobile Sites

Site	Baseline (Base model only)				Cascading Gradient Boosting			
	$RMSE_{agg}$	CPP	UCPP	PPP	$RMSE_{agg}$	CPP	UCPP	PPP
F	0.054	8.25%	41.93%	48.22%	0.051	15.45%	38.41%	49.74%
G	0.052	10.99%	35.29%	53.58%	0.051	13.15%	33.46%	54.46%
H	0.047	8.96%	41.26%	35.71%	0.050	10.14%	39.26%	36.17%
I	0.041	10.35%	29.53%	61.42%	0.040	14.11%	27.30%	62.66%
J	0.048	3.44%	32.30%	61.71%	0.055	3.76%	29.99%	61.93%

Table 5. Benchmark Results-Desktop Sites

Site	LR				SVD				DET				DNN			
	$RMSE_{agg}$	CPP	UCPP	PPP	$RMSE_{agg}$	CPP	UCPP	PPP	$RMSE_{agg}$	CPP	UCPP	PPP	$RMSE_{agg}$	CPP	UCPP	PPP
A	0.058	0.91%	75.50%	7.29%	0.066	0.82%	92.45%	6.13%	0.047	0.26%	99.39%	5.55%	0.052	0.91%	73.35%	7.65%
B	0.064	44.06%	9.47%	85.68%	0.073	38.98%	11.65%	70.95%	0.051	12.25%	12.46%	64.12%	0.057	43.85%	9.25%	87.84%
C	0.071	26.56%	56.32%	42.24%	0.083	23.91%	69.47%	35.54%	0.058	7.66%	73.98%	31.57%	0.065	26.60%	54.80%	43.65%
D	0.031	11.31%	62.53%	30.17%	0.035	9.96%	77.12%	24.89%	0.024	3.33%	83.00%	22.48%	0.027	11.35%	61.12%	30.63%
E	0.079	5.93%	13.16%	52.33%	0.090	5.30%	16.10%	44.67%	0.063	1.71%	17.46%	39.31%	0.070	5.89%	12.87%	53.92%

Table 6. Benchmark Results-Mobile Sites

	LR			SVD			DET			DNN		
Site	$RMSE_{agg}$	CPP	UCPP	PPP	$RMSE_{agg}$	CPP	UCPP	PPP	$RMSE_{agg}$	CPP	UCPP	PPP	$RMSE_{agg}$	CPP	UCPP	PPP
F	0.078	7.70%	45.60%	45.51%	0.094	6.19%	56.16%	34.60%	0.063	1.06%	65.28%	31.74%	0.069	7.72%	44.56%	46.31%
G	0.076	10.43%	38.24%	50.44%	0.090	8.30%	47.24%	38.75%	0.061	1.38%	54.98%	35.48%	0.067	10.18%	37.71%	51.98%
H	0.068	8.38%	44.43%	33.66%	0.081	6.88%	54.70%	26.03%	0.055	1.18%	63.73%	23.28%	0.060	8.30%	43.98%	34.53%
I	0.060	9.70%	32.04%	58.90%	0.071	7.79%	39.53%	44.31%	0.048	1.31%	45.63%	40.09%	0.053	9.62%	31.11%	60.15%
J	0.070	3.24%	34.95%	58.49%	0.084	2.60%	42.96%	44.47%	0.056	0.44%	49.97%	40.97%	0.062	3.17%	34.03%	59.75%

Table 7. Results-500 million impressions

Site	Baseline (Base model only)				Cascading Gradient Boosting			
	$RMSE_{agg}$	CPP	UCPP	PPP	$RMSE_{agg}$	CPP	UCPP	PPP
Desktop	0.072	13.52%	51.44%	23.45%	0.071	21.16%	41.62%	27.83%
Mobile	0.067	17.11%	42.55%	42.17%	0.068	26.46%	31.13%	46.11%

Table 8. Median CPM by Tier

DESKTOP		MOBILE	
Tier	Median CPM	Tier	Median CPM
0	0.022	0	0.076
0.1	0.187	0.1	0.085
0.2	0.298	0.2	0.121
0.3	0.335	0.3	0.130
0.4	0.379	0.4	0.156
0.5	0.371	0.5	0.172
0.6	0.366	0.6	0.180
0.7	0.377	0.7	0.200
0.8	0.491	0.8	0.215
0.9	0.525	0.9	0.268

References

1. Callejo, P., Pastor, A., Cuevas, R., Cuevas, Á.: Q-tag: a transparent solution to measure ads viewability rate in online advertising campaigns, pp. 151–157 (2019). https://doi.org/10.1145/3359989.3365434
2. Diebold, F., Mariano, R.: Comparing predictive accuracy. J. Bus. Econ. Stat. **20**, 134–44 (2002). https://doi.org/10.1080/07350015.1995.10524599
3. Fisher: https://www.emarketer.com/content/us-programmatic-digital-display-ad-spending
4. Friedman, J.: Greedy function approximation: a gradient boosting machine. Ann. Stat. **29**, 1189–1232 (2001). https://doi.org/10.2307/2699986
5. Friedman, J., Hastie, T., Tibshirani, R.: Additive logistic regression: a statistical view of boosting. Ann. Stat. **28**, 337–407 (2000). https://doi.org/10.1214/aos/1016218223
6. GmbH, M.: https://www.meetrics.com/wp-content/uploads/sites/2/2020/01/Meetrics-Benchmark-Report_Q4_2019_1.pdf

7. IAB: Internet advertising bureau-viewability guidelines (2014). http://www.iab. net/viewability
8. Ke, G., et al.: Lightgbm: a highly efficient gradient boosting decision tree. In: Guyon, I., et al. (eds.) Advances in Neural Information Processing Systems 30. pp. 3146–3154. Curran Associates, Inc. (2017). http://papers.nips.cc/paper/6907-lightgbm-a-highly-efficient-gradient-boosting-decision-tree.pdf
9. Niculescu-Mizil, A., Caruana, R.: Obtaining calibrated probabilities from boosting. CoRR ArXiv:abs/1207.1403 (2012). http://arxiv.org/abs/1207.1403
10. Nielsen, D.: Tree boosting with XGBoost-why does xgboost win "every" machine learning competition? Master's thesis, NTNU (2016)
11. Platt, J.: Probabilistic outputs for support vector machines and comparisons to regularized likelihood methods. Adv. Large Margin Classif. **10** (2000)
12. Schapire, R., Freund, Y., Bartlett, P., Lee, W.: Boosting the margin: a new explanation for the effectiveness of voting methods. Ann. Stat. **26**, (2001). https://doi.org/10.1214/aos/1024691352
13. Wang, C., Kalra, A., Borcea, C., Chen, Y.: Webpage depth-level dwell time prediction. In: Proceedings of the 25th ACM International on Conference on Information and Knowledge Management (CIKM'16), pp. 1937–1940. Association for Computing Machinery, New York, NY, USA (2016). https://doi.org/10.1145/2983323.2983878
14. Wang, C., Kalra, A., Zhou, L., Borcea, C., Chen, Y.: Probabilistic models for ad viewability prediction on the web. IEEE Trans. Knowl. Data Eng. **29**(9), 1 (2017). https://doi.org/10.1109/TKDE.2017.2705688
15. Xia, Y., Liu, C., Li, Y., Liu, N.: A boosted decision tree approach using bayesian hyper-parameter optimization for credit scoring. Expert Syst. Appl. 78 (2017). https://doi.org/10.1016/j.eswa.2017.02.017
16. Zadrozny, B., Elkan, C.: Transforming classifier scores into accurate multiclass probability estimates. iN: Proceedings of the ACM SIGKDD International Conference on Knowledge Discovery and Data Mining (2002). https://doi.org/10.1145/775047.775151
17. Zhang, Y., Haghani, A.: A gradient boosting method to improve travel time prediction. Transp. Res. Part C Emerg. Technol,. **58** (2015). https://doi.org/10.1016/j.trc.2015.02.019

Data Driven Policy Making: The Peruvian Water Resources Observatory

Giuliana Barnuevo, Elsa Galarza, Maria Paz Herrera, Juan G. Lazo Lazo,
Miguel Nunez-del-Prado[(✉)], and José Luis Ruiz

Universidad Del Pacifico, Lima, Peru
{g.barnuevoreategui,galarza_ep,m.herreraquiroz,jg.lazol,
m.nunezdelpradoc,ruiz_jl}@up.edu.pe

Abstract. Nowadays, Big Data holds vast potential for improving decision-making in public policy due to the different methodologies for working with complex heterogeneous big data, which allows proposing policies based on real and measurable key performance indicators. This article aims to describe the water resource observatory of the Public Management School of Universidad del Pacífico. The idea behind the observatory is to handle data extracted from non-traditional sources to enhance efficient and responsive government solutions through evidence-based public policies for water regulation. We used Elastic Search stack to centralize and visualize data from different sources, which was standardized using river basins as basic units. Finally, we show a use case of the data gathered to optimize the water supply in new urban zones in Lima's periphery.

Keywords: Public policy · Data-driven decision · Big data · Water management

1 Introduction

The amount of data being generated in the world is increasing as citizens become more digital. Therefore, citizens generate digital traces, which led to new possibilities of data gathering, storage, and processing. This amount of data enables governments to use new forms of data analysis to understand the citizen's behavior, needs, and demands [18]. Therefore, Data Science and Big Data offer a great potential in the public sector to transform the traditional policy-decisions making [10], often supported by traditional forms of policy analysis, including methods as cost-benefit analysis, among others. Thus, few governments have already managed a systemic use of data [7] to produce relevant, high-quality, and timely evidence to underpin and guide decisions. This process is well known as data-driven decision making [16]. To cite some international examples of this kind of platform, the Kenyan national government [20] uses a mapping platform to show areas where educational resources are lacking. Another example is HealthMap [20], a platform that automatically tracks and analyzes multiple data-feeds in 15 languages to produce an online visualization of disease trends.

© Springer Nature Switzerland AG 2021
J. A. Lossio-Ventura et al. (Eds.): SIMBig 2020, CCIS 1410, pp. 419–431, 2021.
https://doi.org/10.1007/978-3-030-76228-5_30

In the Peruvian context, there is an opportunity to use Key Performance Indicators (*i.e.*, KPIs) issued from public and private datasets to manage natural resources like water. Besides, it is a complex resource owing to is considered as a resource as well as a service. Its regulation is also intricate due to the multisectoral nature, multiple uses, and diverse actors who have their interests and must build a shared vision about water usage. Thus, obtaining geo-referenced datasets from diverse traditional and non-traditional sources serves to have a holistic view of water usage instead of a limited sectorial view. Therefore, the novelty of this paper is to propose a platform to gather datasets from different sources in an integrated water management tool to enhance better information for policy-making in the Peruvian reality.

The present work is organized as follows. Section 2 presents the related works in state of the art. Section 3 introduces water resource management, while Sect. 4 introduces the water resource observatory platform. Then, Sect. 5 describes an optimization water supply problem using our proposed tool. Finally, Sect. 6 concludes the paper and presents new research avenues.

2 Related Works

In recent years, the managing water supply systems have been considering a more sustainable and broader vision of water resources. Furthermore, the sustainable use of water, flood control, diminishing freshwater resources, continuously increasing demand, water losses within the systems themselves, the potential for interruption of the primary sources of supply, the effects of climate on the renewal of these resources and security of water supply, among other aspects of an ecological and eco-systemic nature, must be taken into account. In order to make decisions or establish public policies on water resources considering all these new aspects, it is necessary to count and analyze all information related to these variables. In this sense, it is necessary to implement continuous and massive data collection systems using sensors and the Internet of Things (IoT) throughout the water supply infrastructure and consumer use in the United States, using Wireless Sensor Network (WSN). With the help of Big Data, a technological solution can be implemented for monitoring, evaluation, and rapid intervention to maintain the state of the infrastructure before the failure. Besides, thanks to this system, it is possible to solve problems such as deterioration modeling, pressure and flow, and leakage and loss detection. This allows to improve the performance of the system by minimizing water cuts, water leaks, identifying vulnerable areas in the infrastructure, optimizing the performance of the system, including pressure, flow and water use [13]. Yonsoo et al. [12] discusses the application of big data and cloud computing for efficient water resources management in South Korea to monitor the quantity, variety, speed, and consumption of water. The authors highlight how big data and cloud computing can improve the information value for water resource management, disaster prevention, and the protection of life and property. Wu et al. [21] presents another work showing the relevance of Big Data and the challenges when building green applications addressing. In this work, the authors summarize and discuss several works developed on Big Data for different green applications in different areas, such as the environment, energy efficiency, and sustainability.

In [2] discusses how the use of Big Data presents great promise for solving water-related problems and applications, ranging from planning optimal water systems, detecting changes in the ecosystem, to through a big remote monitoring network and a geographic information system, predicting or detecting natural and artificial disasters, scheduling irrigation, mitigating environmental pollution, as well as studying the impacts of climate change, among others. The article reviews essential information about Big Data, presents a literature review of Big Data applications in studies related to water resources engineering, discussing the advantages and disadvantages of Big Data in the area. On the other hand, in [17] discusses the need to understand the water systems of cities more profoundly and the need for sustainable solutions for water supply. They used for this purpose computer models based on mathematical equations and rules that mimic the system's actual behavior and management decisions. Furthermore, with the advancement of sensor technology, it is possible to monitor many places in real-time with little supervision. It is possible to store this large volume of data while also updating the models in real-time to automate the entire process. For this, they propose a generic framework for the processing of large-size data, the collection of information, and the use of data to improve computer models of water to have intelligent management of water resources, considering the process of integrating Big Data with models and discuss benefits along with challenges. In [6] a study is presented about the characteristics of the Big Data system architectures proposed in the literature for the improvement in the management of water resources, highlighting the components, technologies, and tools used in the implementation of the Big Data.

Li et al. [14] present a system for water resources management and planning based on genetic algorithms and its application to a specific case in China. The objective of the system is the rational use of groundwater using a non-linear programming model, which considers as objective function the ideal number of wells in the study area and the pumping capacity of each well. Thus, the decision variables, namely economic benefit, risk of penalties, and continuity of supply, also consider the demand for water resources, the reduction of the water level, and groundwater depth, having as restrictions structural safety and technical feasibility.

In [19] an intelligent water network based on IoT technology, artificial intelligence, Big Data analysis, and cloud processing is proposed. The aim of the system optimizes the operational performance of the water supply network, the rupture of pipes, leaks, and waste of water, as well as water auditing and pressure management. In [9] a Systematic Literature Review (SLR) of articles related to Big Data and water resources is carried out in the scientific database: ACM Digital Library, IEEE, Scopus, MDPI, Elsevier, ScienceDirect, SciencePG and Taylor, and Francis, to which uses Meta-analysis techniques, finding 74 articles divided into three topics related to water/big data Analytics, water/big data tools, and water/cloud computing containing the works of [1, 3, 5, 12, 22]; the last three propose architectures with big data analytic to problematic of water resources management. Despite the importance of the subject and the work done so far, there are few works related to water resources management monitoring using systems for integrating multiple variables, information, and data from various sources and Big Data Analytic Architecture, as proposed in present article.

Based in the aforementioned works, we present our platform in the next section.

3   Background

To understand the complexity of water regulation, we need to explain the Integrated Water Resources Management (IWRM) process. This process aims to promote the development and coordinated management of the water system's components to maximize economic and social well-being, without compromising the sustainability of ecosystems in the future [11]. IWRM takes into account any positive or negative impact of any intervention on the different components of the system in the territory.

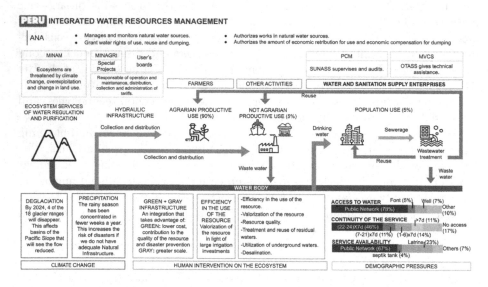

Fig. 1. Integrated water resource management

Figure 1 describes the institutions and actors of the water system. The former ones are composed of the *Water National Authority* (*ANA* for the acronym in Spanish) that regulates water usage. In rural zones, the *Ministry of Environment* (*MINAM* for the acronym in Spanish) whose responsibility is to protect water sources and glaciers; and the *Minister of Agriculture* (*MINAGRI*), which main task is to develop water infrastructure for agricultural activities through special investments projects. Regarding water supply in cities, the *National Superintendence of Sanitation Services* (*SUNASS* for the acronym in Spanish) that belongs to the *Presidency of the Council of Ministers* (*PCM*) regulates and supervises the development of the market for drinking water and sanitation services. The *Technical Organism of the Sanitation Services Administration* (*OTASS* for the acronym in Spanish,) in charge of the Ministry of Housing, Construction and Sanitation (*MVCS* for the acronym in Spanish), promotes and executes the policy of the Governing Body in matters of management and administration of the provision of sanitation services. The latter are the farmers that use water for agricultural production; the non-agricultural activities, namely transformation industries, mining, among others, employ water as part of the production and transformation processes, respectively. Finally, citizens living in urban areas consume water in their daily basis activities.

In addition to the complex regulatory schema, it is essential to consider the interaction between actors before it is described. For instance, highlands are inhabited by a population dedicated to agriculture and livestock farming, sometimes next to mining operations. Actors from the private sector and local population interact in this territory and share the use of water. Another interaction to be considered is due to the rivers' flow from the mountains (source) to the Pacific coast, where diverse uses and actors met. Thus, farming and water energy production in arid coastal areas generate the need to develop infrastructure to guarantee resource availability in the lower part of the basin. Therefore, the development of this infrastructure is in charge of the respective sectoral ministries, namely MINAGRI, MVCS, and *Ministry of Energy and Mines* (*MINEM*). Finally, it is important to mention that the system has permanent pressure due to constant demand increment as the population grows.

Furthermore, beyond the complexity of the water regulation, it is crucial to have a geographical spatial administrative unit. Therefore, the international experience recognizes the basin as the most suitable territorial unit for integrated water resources management. Besides, the OECD Principle of Water Governance number 2 establishes the importance of appropriate scale governance systems to reflect local conditions and foster coordination between the different scales [4]. Nevertheless, the local governance of the geographic delimitation and the actors' characterization should not be considered only in hydrological terms, but rather in economic, social, and environmental systems. In some cases, the resource influence area is not delimited by the hydrographic basin. Instead, it is possible to consider the users' location or the social organization to consume the resource. For instance, a basin supplies electricity to different users in an interconnected system in a completely different place. Another example is the growth of coastal cities, initially located within a particular basin, to inter-basins arid lands that require common sanitation services management.

In the present section, we presented the complexity of the Peruvian IWRM. Therefore, the IWRM implementation requires global vision articulating the actors on a local scale and the elements at the basin level. In the next section, we detail our Water Resources Observatory platform to support IWRM in Peru with functionalities such as visualization, aggregation, selection, updating of data from different social, economic and political indicators of Peru, all at the basin level. In addition, the system must allow the aforementioned functionalities in a friendly way with the end user.

4   Water Resources Observatory Platform

In the present section, we detail the Water Resources Observatory platform components and data gathering process. As described in the previous section, to support the complex interactions between institutions and actors, the first step is to establish a scale. Following the international experiences, we decided to standardize all datasets at the basin scale. Thus, the big data coming from different national public and private entities should be processed at the basin scale. In the following paragraphs, we describe the components of the proposed platform.

The Water Resources Observatory platform is composed of three blocks, namely data extraction, data processing, and data visualization, as depicted in Fig. 2. The *data extraction* block handles the data acquisition from different public and private institutions such ANA, PCM, SUNASS, Minister of Health (*MINSA* for their acronym in Spanish). The data have been collected between October 2019 until February 2020. The data extracted are provided by the Presidency of the Council of Ministers and are continuously updated. For each institution we collect geo-referenced datasets D_i. Therefore, to start working with these spatial datasets, it is necessary to consider the data type file, the data extraction source, and the cleaning procedure,which included an exhaustive review of the characteristics of each entity and comparing them to avoid redundancies. It should be noted that before processing the data to store them, a Database model was developed that allowed a second review of redundancy and other problems that may be generated by working with large volumes of data. On the other hand, when inconsistencies were found in the databases, decisions were made based on what the experts on these topics could recommend. The principle is to have clean, scaled data to become a layer. Thus, each information layer would contain important data of the Peruvian reality. In this way, each layer will be scaled at the basin level. To implement this collection, cleaning and scaling process we rely on Python[1] scripts and QGIS[2] tool, which allows organizing spatial data. It is worth noting that we implement a different script S_i to gather and digest the dataset D_i' to be stored for each institution. Once the dataset D_i' is cleaned and standardized at the basin level, the *data processing* block takes this dataset as input. Thus, we rely on Logstash[3] tool to dynamically parse the dataset D_i' for shipping it to the Elasticsearch[4] NoSql database, where we store the layer for queries or operations. Finally, the *data visualization* component

---

[1] Python: https://www.python.org.
[2] QGIS: https://www.qgis.org/es/site/.
[3] Logstash: https://www.elastic.co.
[4] Elasticsearch: https://www.elastic.co/logstash.

of our platform deal with the visualization. Therefore, to integrate visualization over the Elasticsearch stack, we rely on Kibana[5], which is a cross-platform visualization tool that enables the functionality to perform queries through the Kibana graphical user interface.

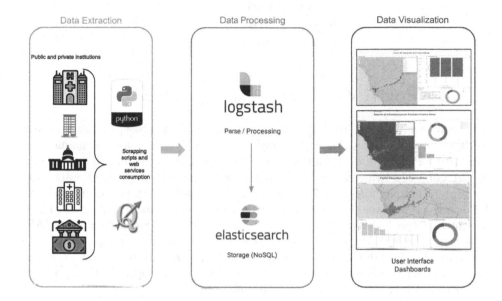

Fig. 2. Water Resources Observatory platform architecture.

It is important to note that our platform is already collecting datasets from different sources, namely Peruvian Spatial Data Infrastructure (*GEOIDEP*[6]), ANA[7], MINSA[8], and SUNASS[9] as summaries in Table 1.

The collected information ranges from airports, tanker trucks, forest carbon, populated center, concessions, basins, hydraulic excavator, educational factor, health infrastructure, snow mountains, environmental-mining liabilities, tolls, bridges, ports, medium voltage power grids, river gorges, rural sanitation forest harvesting, trash dumping, volcanoes, number of individuals infected with SarsCoV-2, water collection point, to water non-supplied points. The data gathered in our platform could be used to tackle critical problems linked to water consumption. Thus, in the next section, we present a Study case perform with SUNASS to optimize the number of tanker trucks to supply drinkable water to undeserved peripheral areas of Lima city.

---

[5] Kibana: https://www.elastic.co/kibana.

[6] GEOIDEP: https://www.geoidep.gob.pe/.

[7] ANA: https://www.ana.gob.pe/.

[8] MINSA: https://www.gob.pe/minsa/.

[9] SUNASS: https://www.sunass.gob.pe/websunass/.

Table 1. Dataset registers

Institution	# Dataset registers
GeoIdep	292248
ANA	15290
MINSA	9000
SUNASS	4302
Total	320840

5   Case Study: Water Distribution in Lima

In the present section, we examine the water supply problem in Lima's areas with no drinking water. More precisely, Lima is the political and economic capital city of Peru. It has around 9.5 million inhabitants, a third of the country in an area of 2 672 Km^2. Nevertheless, peripheral zones in Lima are extending due to a migration phenomenon. Therefore, the water supply infrastructure needs to be developed to these new human settlements that represent a total of 183 Km^2. Meanwhile, the *National Superintendence of Services and Sanitation (SUNASS)* supervises the drinking water supply through tanker trucks by the public-private company *Lima Water and Sewer Service (SEDAPAL* for the acronym in Spanish). Thus, in the following paragraphs, we describe the optimization problem to provide drinkable water from supply points to unserved areas.

To pose the optimization problem, we use population density, water demand (unserved area, location), water supply (supply point and location) from the Water Resources Observatory platform combined with a graph representing real traffic conditions in Lima city-issued from *Open Street Maps* (OSM) and *Waze Route Calculator*[10]. Figure 3 depicts the architecture of the proof of concept using the Water Resources Observatory platform with additional information. In the first block, we extract supply points and unserved areas data from the Elasticsearch NoSql database. Then, the *data modeling* block constructs the graph of Lima's streets weighted with the congestion level from OSM and Waze Route Calculator, respectively. It is essential to know that we built six different graphs taking into account different traffic jams' scenarios, such as Monday to Thursday and Friday between 8AM and 10AM, 12M and 2PM, and 6PM and 8PM.

Thus, the objective of this case study is to optimize the tanker trucks travels to supply drinking water using a variation of the Simplex method [8]. This method integrates the algebraic simplex algorithm, which transforms by repetitive steps a starting solution to an optimum solution if a solution exists. We rely on the Simplex implementation in the Solving Constraint Integer Programs[11]

---

[10] Waze Route Calculator: https://github.com/kovacsbalu/WazeRouteCalculator.
[11] SCIP: www.scipopt.org/.

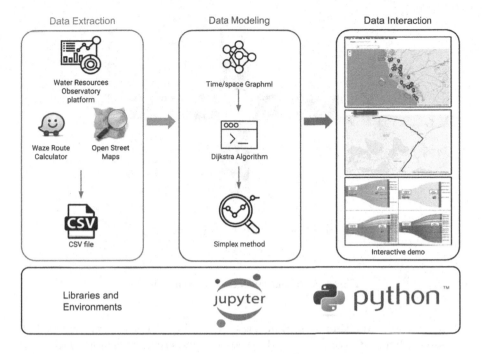

Fig. 3. Route optimization architecture.

library implemented in Python PySCIPOpt[12] [15]. The algorithm takes as input the transportation cost matrix, the capacity vector corresponding to the 22 supply points, and the demand vector corresponding to the 4280 unserved areas. We assume that each supply point has 15 tanker trucks able to transport 10000 L, eight times a day, and each person demands 20 L of water.

The next step is to obtain the costs which must be minimized subject to demand and maximum capacity. The costs can be associated with the minimum distances to be covered or the elapsed time under traffic conditions. This allows us to form the cost matrix based on distance and time. Thus, concerning time cost matrix, we generate 7 different scenarios. One relies on distance and 6 rely on time, namely Monday to Thursday from 8AM to 10AM, Monday to Thursday from 12M to 2PM, Monday to Thursday from 6PM to 8PM, Friday from 8AM to 10AM, Friday from 12M to 2PM, and Friday from 6PM to 8PM. To show the difference between the aforementioned scenarios, Fig. 4 depicts the Euclidean distance between normalized cost matrix of each scenario. We observe that scenario of Monday to Thursday from 6PM to 8PM is distinct from other scenarios. In the contrary, the other scenarios are slightly similar.

---

[12] PySCIPOpt: https://github.com/SCIP-Interfaces/PySCIPOpt.

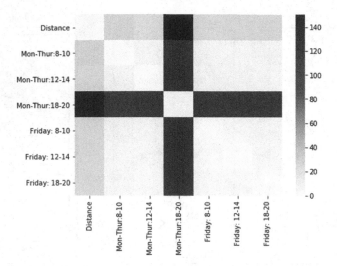

Fig. 4. Cost matrix scenarios comparison.

The objective function to minimize is shown in Eq. 1. The cost matrix could be expressed either in Km or hours, and $x_{i,j}$ are the liters to be transported from supply points j to unserved areas i. Thus, the optimization has the following restrictions: the number of liters transported should not exceed the water capacity of the supply points (Eq. 2), and the demand served may eventually be less than the quantity of water required by the population in the unserved area (Eq. 3).

$$\min \sum_{i \in Demand} \sum_{j \in Capacity} Cost_{i,j} x_{i,j} \tag{1}$$

$$\text{s.t} \sum_{i \in Demand} x_{i,j} = Capacity_j, \forall j \in Capacity \tag{2}$$

$$\sum_{j \in Capacity} x_{i,j} \leq Demand_i, \forall j \in Demand, \tag{3}$$

The result of the optimization process is depicted in Fig. 5. On the one hand, Fig. 5(A) illustrates the optimal number of Km. to be covered. On the other hand, Fig. 5(B) depicts the optimal amount of hours that trucks will need to distribute water. We remark that the scenario of Monday to Thursday from 8AM to 10AM needs more time for distributing water. Thus, the best scenario to supply water is from Monday to Thursday from 12M to 2PM, and Friday from 8AM to 10AM. In those two scenarios, the trucks spend less fuel spent saving money. Besides, a sample of this result is shown in the Fig. 6, where, for example, *supply points 0* distributes to different homes the corresponding number of liters to certain unserved areas around Lima.

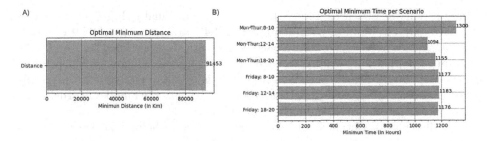

Fig. 5. Optimization results.

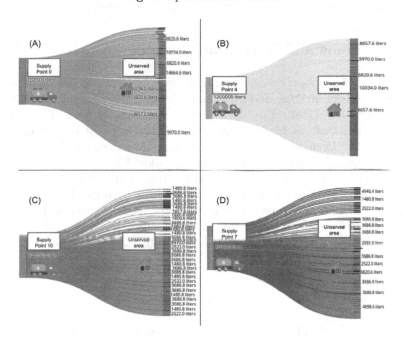

Fig. 6. Sankey diagram matrix

Another significant result is the visualization depicted in Fig. 6, which illustrates the amount of water to be transported between supply points and unserved areas. It is worth noting that we show only 4 of the 22 supply points, randomly chosen. This information allows policymakers to manage water capacity in supply points, the number of trucks to deliver water, etc. For instance, Fig. 6(A) illustrates the supply point $i = 0$ with a capacity of 1.2 millions liters of water (we assume a homogeneous capacity for all supply points), which furnishes water to different unserved areas with heterogeneous demands, namely 6820.6 L, 14664.6 L, etc. Figure 6(B) shows the transport of water to different areas with established demands of 8657 L, 10034 L, etc. Another example is Fig. 6(C), which transports water to several families, more than the other supply points, with different demands such as 1480.8 L, 3686.8 L, etc. Finally, Fig. 6(D), provides water to different families with demands of 4940.9 L, 1480.8 L, 2522.0 L, etc. It is important to note that the difference in demands to be satisfied is given by the amount of population grouped in each unsupplied area, which varies depending on the population density. For this reason, it is essential to monitor the supply points to better allocate the available resources, such as the number of trucks, the number of trips per trunk, and other variables.

Finally, what is obtained in this subsection is very helpful for various applications such as planning and projection of water demand for Lima, investment of capacity for distribution. All this is part of the initial premise of data-driven decisions to solve public issues and the need for new techniques to support it.

6   Conclusions and Recommendations

In the present effort, we show the significant impact that Big Data can have on government decision-making and how the use of emerging technologies can allow greater efficiency in creating public policies based on real data. The Peruvian Governmental Indicators Map evidences the importance of having the whole panorama of the Peruvian reality. Thus, as the case study of Water Distribution in Lima, propose different measures that allow for an improvement in the management of public resources. It is essential to highlight that the paradigm shift must also be supported by public servants, who need to adapt to new technologies to focus on proposing policies that are more aligned and generate a more significant impact on the citizen. Finally, this opens a path of opportunities for many other, more complex and integrated, Big Data applications to be implemented in the platform.

References

1. Abdullah, M., Zulkifli, h., Ibrahim, M.: Big data technology implementation in managing water related disaster: Nahrim's experience. In: Learning from the Past for the Future (2017)
2. Adamala, S.: An overview of big data applications in water resources engineering. Mach. Learn. Res. **2**(1), 10–18 (2017)
3. Ai, P., Yue, Z.X.: A framework for processing water resources big data and application. In: Computer and Information Technology. Applied Mechanics and Materials, vol. 519, pp. 3–8. Trans Tech Publications Ltd. (2014). https://doi.org/10.4028/www.scientific.net/AMM.519-520.3
4. Akhmouch, A., Correia, F.N.: The 12 OECD principles on water governance-when science meets policy. Utilities policy **43**, 14–20 (2016)
5. Chalh, R., Bakkoury, Z., Ouazar, D., Hasnaoui, M.D.: Big data open platform for water resources management. In: 2015 International Conference on Cloud Technologies and Applications (CloudTech), pp. 1–8 (2015)
6. Cravero, A., Saldana, O., Espinosa, R., Antileo, C.: Big data architecture for water resources management: a systematic mapping study. IEEE Latin Am. Trans. **16**(3), 902–918 (2018). https://doi.org/10.1109/TLA.2018.8358672

7. Daniell, K.A., Morton, A., Insua, D.R.: Policy analysis and policy analytics. Annal. Oper. Res. **236**(1), 1–13 (2016)
8. De Wolf, D., Smeers, Y.: The gas transmission problem solved by an extension of the simplex algorithm. Manag. Sci. **46**(11), 1454–1465 (2000)
9. Elhassan, J., Aniss, M., Jamal, C.: Big data analytic architecture for water resources management: A systematic review. In: Proceedings of the 4th Edition of International Conference on Geo-IT and Water Resources 2020, Geo-IT and Water Resources 2020, pp. 1–5 (2020)
10. Engin, Z., Treleaven, P.: Algorithmic government: automating public services and supporting civil servants in using data science technologies. Comput. J. **62**(3), 448–460 (2019)
11. Jønch-Clausen, T.: Integrated water resources management (IWRM) and water efficiency plans by 2005: Why, what, and how?, pp. 5–4 (2004)
12. Kim, Y., Kang, N., Jung, J., Kim, H.S.: A review on the management of water resources information based on big data and cloud computing. J. Wetlands Res. **18**(1), 100–112 (2016)
13. Koo, D., Piratla, K., Matthews, C.J.: Towards sustainable water supply: schematic development of big data collection using internet of things (IoT). Procedia Eng. **118**, 489–497 (2015)
14. Li, M., Zhang, J., Cheng, X., Bao, Y.: Application of the genetic algorithm in water resource management. In: Advances in Intelligent Systems and Computing 1117 AISC, pp. 1681–1686 (2020)
15. Maher, S., Miltenberger, M., Pedroso, J.P., Rehfeldt, D., Schwarz, R., Serrano, F.: PySCIPOpt: mathematical programming in python with the SCIP optimization suite. In: Greuel, G.-M., Koch, T., Paule, P., Sommese, A. (eds.) ICMS 2016. LNCS, vol. 9725, pp. 301–307. Springer, Cham (2016). https://doi.org/10.1007/978-3-319-42432-3_37
16. Rodríguez, P., Palomino, N., Mondaca, J.: Using big data and its analytical techniques for public policy design America and the Caribbean (2017). Accessed 31 July 2020
17. Shafiee, M.E., Barker, Z., Rasekh, A.: Enhancing water system models by integrating big data. Sustain. Cities Soc. **37**, 485–491 (2018). https://doi.org/10.1016/j.scs.2017.11.042, http://www.sciencedirect.com/science/article/pii/S2210670717303840
18. Studinka, J., Guenduez, A.A.: The use of big data in the public policy process-paving the way for evidence-based governance (2018). Accessed 31 July 2020
19. Sánchez, A., Oliveira-Esquerre, K., dos Reis Nogueira, I., de Jong, P., Filho, A.: Water loss management through smart water systems. In: Smart Village Technology. Modeling and Optimization in Science and Technologies, vol. 17, pp. 233–266 (2020)
20. World Bank: BIG DATA in ACTION for GOVERNMENT: Big Data Innovation in Public Services, Policy and Engagement(2017). http://documents1.worldbank.org/curated/en/176511491287380986/pdf/114011-BRI-3-4-2017-11-49-44-WGSBigDataGovernmentFinal.pdf. Accessed 2 July 2020
21. Wu, J., Guo, S., Li, J., Zeng, D.: Big data meet green challenges: Big data toward green applications. IEEE Syst. J. **10**(3), 888–900 (2016). https://ieeexplore.ieee.org/abstract/document/7473815
22. Zhao, Y., An, R.: Big data analytics for water resources sustainability evaluation. Commun. Comput. Inf. Sci. **913**, 29–38 (2019)

Graph Mining

Complex Networks to Differentiate Elderly and Young People

Aruane M. Pineda$^{(\boxtimes)}$ (ID) and Francisco A. Rodrigues (ID)

Institute of Mathematical and Computer Sciences (ICMC),
University of Sao Paulo (USP), Sao Carlos, Sao Paulo, Brazil
aruane.pineda@usp.br

Abstract. Cardiovascular disease (CVD) is a general term that describes different heart problems. There are several heart diseases, which still lead thousands of people to sudden death. Among them are high blood pressure, ischemia, variation in cardiac rhythms, and pericardial effusion. Studies about these diseases are usually made through the analysis of electrocardiogram (ECG) signals, which presents valuable information on the development of the heart's status. Recent papers have posited the creation of quantile graphs (QG) using data from ECG. In this method, based on transition probabilities, these quantile graphs are a result of a time series mapped into a network. This so-called QG method can be employed to differentiate between young and elderly patients using their ECG signals. The primary goal of our paper is to show how variations in ECG signals are mirrored in the respective QGs' topology. Our analyses were centered on three metrics: mean jump length, betweenness centrality and clustering coefficient. The results indicate that the QG method is a reliable tool for differentiating ECG exams regarding the age of the patients.

Keywords: Electrocardiogram · Time series · Network measures · Complex networks · Machine learning · Statistical tests

1 Introduction

Aging is a process of organic and functional decrease, not caused by disease, that inevitably happens over time. Aging includes physical and psychological changes that reduce the ability of the elderly to adapt to society, being the greatest risk factor for cardiovascular diseases. The electrocardiogram (ECG) is a simple exam and a valuable asset that can diagnose 90% of various heart diseases. It is a low-cost and highly versatile test, which provides fast results and can be performed by doctors of different specialities. According to a survey by the WHO (World Health Organization), approximately 140,000 people die annually due to heart diseases [1]. Some of those deaths could be avoided with diagnoses from a simple electrocardiogram, followed by proper treatment. Therefore, the study of techniques to assist professionals in the diagnosis of ECG exams is extremely relevant.

© Springer Nature Switzerland AG 2021
J. A. Lossio-Ventura et al. (Eds.): SIMBig 2020, CCIS 1410, pp. 435–444, 2021.
https://doi.org/10.1007/978-3-030-76228-5_31

1.1   Methods for Comparing Time Series

Currently, there is a great number of techniques for analysing time series, from time-frequency methods, such as Fourier and Wavelet transforms [21,25], artificial neural networks [29], and non-linear methods, including phase space reconstruction, correlation dimension, the Lyapunov exponent, and Lempel-Ziv entropies and complexities [2,20,33,34]. Such techniques allow researchers to summarize the characteristics of a time series and, thusly, determine the underlying dynamic of a system or predict how it will evolve with time. These techniques are widely utilized in the analysis of stationary time series, producing satisfying results. From a statistical viewpoint, to produce trustworthy results, the aforementioned techniques employ a great number of samples (realizations) from each series, which hampers the analysis of many experimental time series, since, generally, they are nonstationary and created from experiments with a reduced number of samples [13]. Fourier transforms are quicker when compared to different available methods. However, it doesn't allow for the analysis of nonstationary signals. In addition, this technique cannot be utilised to analyze short signals and has a high sensitivity to noise [3]. Wavelet transform was presented as a solution in the analysis of nonstationary signals. However, the performance of this technique is conditioned to the choice of the mother wavelet when decomposing the signal in different scales of frequency and time [6]. Neural networks are capable of identifying patterns in time series and divide them into classes according to a set criterion. Nonetheless, to ensure that the results are statistically precise, it is necessary to use a large number of samples to be tested and trained [10,36]. Nonlinear methods enable the analysis of long and stationary signals, but are highly sensitive to noise and to the choice of a variety of parameters, such as time delay and dimension of immersion [34]. The characterization of time series dynamics is a constant challenge. Consequently, new methods have been proposed in the scientific literature to capture additional information or to quantify time series in new ways [22,37]. One of these advancements came from the application of complex network theory to the analysis of time series dynamics [9,15,38]. This new technique, called quantile graph (QG) method, is capable of mapping a time series into a complex network. It was recently posited by Campanharo *et al.* [9], and it does not have any restrictions of use. Therefore, it can be applied to both stationary and nonstationary, long and short time series. Furthermore, the characteristics of a variety of experimental series can be analyzed based on a reduced number of samples, through the lens of complex network theory. The proposed mapping for the analysis of time series has but one parameter, the number of Q quantiles.

This mapping was applied in a set of synthetic time series with periodic, pseudoperiodic, random, and fractal features [7,9]. It was observed that time series with different dynamics were mapped into complex networks with distinct topologies, which attests the efficiency of the proposed mapping. Additionally, the mapping was utilized to classify EEG data from healthy and epileptic individuals [4,6], as well as from epileptic patients during the ictal period. Different analyses have shown that the aforementioned mapping was able not only to tell sick patients from healthy ones, but also, to distinguish different stages of an epileptic crisis. Furthermore, this method can also be applied to differentiate healthy patients from patients with Alzheimer's disease [28]. These results show the efficiency of the method employed in distinguishing structures in physiologic data. Here, we inquire whether the suggested method can be utilized as a tool for differentiating elderly patients from young ones.

This paper is organized as follows. In the next section, the quantile graph (QG) method for creating networks from time series is described. Section 3 presents the network measures to characterize, analyse, and discriminate complex networks. The data set explored within this study is described in Sect. 4. Sections 5 and 6 are dedicated to the presentation of our results and conclusions, respectively.

2   Techniques

Campanharo et al. [8] proposed a map from a time series to a complex network that allows analyzing the dynamics of a time series through an extensive set of topological properties of the associated complex network. Given a time series, the Q quantiles are identified, and then, each quantile q_i is associated with a vertex $n_i \in N$ in the corresponding network. Two vertices n_i and n_j are connected by the edge $(n_i, n_j, w_{ij}^k) \in L$, where the weight w_{ij}^k is given by the number of times that a given point x_t in the quantile q_i is followed by a point x_{t+k} in the quantile q_j, for $t = 1, 2, ...T-k$ and $k = 1, ...k_{max} < T$. The resulting complex network has weight, direction, $Q \approx 2T^{1/3}$ [24] vertices and is connected, that is, it does not contain isolated vertices [6]. Figure 1 illustrates the application of this map for a series with $T = 20$ points, $Q = 5$ quantiles and the two choices $k = 1$ and $k = 2$, mapped in two networks containing five vertices each. The quantile intervals are given by $[x(0), x(4)[, [x(4), x(8)[, [x(8), x(12)[, [x(12), x(16)[$ and $[x(16), x(20)]$. Each quantile is associated with a vertex in the corresponding network. The weight of each edge w_{ij}^k represents the number of transitions between the quantiles q_i and q_j for a given value of k.

3   Network Measure

Studies demonstrate the usefulness of mathematical metrics for quantifying different characteristics of complex networks. The following network measures are used in this work: mean jump length (Δ), betweenness centrality (B) and clustering coefficient (C). These same measures were used in [27,28].

3.1   Mean Jump Length

With W_k we are able to execute a random walk on the quantile graph g, and the mean jump length can be calculated in this manner:

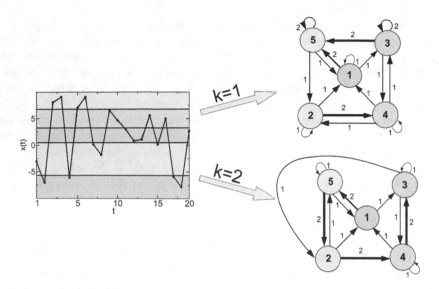

Fig. 1. Exemplification of the method applied here for a time series X with $T = 20$ time points, $Q = 5$ quantiles and $k = 1$ and $k = 2$. Note that, regardless of the chosen k value, this map produces connected networks with weight and direction. Figure adapted from [27].

$$\Delta(k) = \frac{1}{S} \sum_{s=1} \delta_{s,k}(i,j), \qquad (1)$$

where $s = S$ is the total number of jumps, and the length $\delta_{s,k}(i,j) = |i - j|$, with $i, j = 1, ..., Q$ being the node indices, as defined by W_k. Previous work has provided an approach that is less time consuming for the calculation of the mean jump length $\Delta(k)$, which is given by [5]:

$$\Delta(k) = \frac{1}{Q} tr(PW_k^T), \qquad (2)$$

where W_k^T is the transpose of W_k. P is a $Q \times Q$ matrix with elements $p_{i,j} = |i-j|$, and tr is the trace operation.

3.2   Betweenness Centrality

The betweenness centrality of a given node n_k is given by:

$$B_n = \sum_{i,j} \frac{\phi(n_i, n_k, n_j)}{\phi(n_i, n_j)} \qquad (3)$$

where $\phi(n_i, n_k, n_j)$ is the number of shortest paths between nodes n_i and n_j that pass through node n_k, $\phi(n_i, n_j)$ is the total number of shortest paths between n_i and n_j, and the sum is calculated over all pairs n_i, n_j of distinct nodes [12,14]. The value of B is given by the average of the local betweenness centralities of all the nodes.

3.3   Clustering Coefficient

The clustering coefficient measures the degree wherein the nodes of a network tend to cluster. For a weighted directed adjacency matrix and a node n_i, C_i is defined as [32]:

$$C_i = \frac{1}{s_i(k_i - 1)} \frac{\sum_{j,k}(w_{ij} + w_{ik})}{2}(a_{ij}a_{jk}a_{ik}) \tag{4}$$

where w_{ij} is the element from weighted matrix W and $a_{ij} = 1$ if there is an edge between i and j, and 0 otherwise, k_i is the total degree of node n_i, and s_i is the strength of connectivity of node n_i.

4   Database Information

In this work, we consider an artifact-free ECG database [16,19]. The database contains 5 young (21–34 years old) and 5 elderly (68–85 years old) rigorously-screened healthy subjects who underwent 120 min of continuous resting in the supine position, while connected to an electrocardiograph. All subjects remained resting in sinus rhythm while watching the movie Fantasia (Disney 1940) to maintain wakefulness. The continuous ECG for breathing was digitized 250 Hz. Each heartbeat was registered using an automated arrhythmia detection algorithm, and each beat recorded was verified by visual inspection. Each record includes ECG (with heartbeat annotations) and breathing. Sample data on the ECG signal of an elderly patient and a young patient are shown in Fig. 2. This database is limited and only provides five patients from each age group (elderly and young). We do not have data on patients from different age groups (for instance, adults from 34 to 68). Therefore, our results only pertain to young and elderly patients, since variables such as age, sex, biotype, and weight can influence ECG signals [23,30].

5   Results

We apply the aforementioned QG method to the problem of differentiating elderly patients and young patients. All time series are of equal length, $T = 4,000$, we used $Q = 2(4,000)^{\frac{1}{3}} \approx 30$ and $k = 1, 2, 3..., 20$ in all computations. We calculate $\Delta(k)$ with the Eq. 2, $B(k)$ with the Eq. 3, and $C(k)$ with the Eq. 4. It is noticeable in all cases that the curves for elderly patients (E) and young patients (Y) form two distinct clusters at approximately $k = 6$ for $\Delta(k)$, $k = 1$ for $B(k)$, and $k = 1$ for $C(k)$ (Figs. 3, 4 and 5), respectively. For all metrics, for $k > 20$, as correlations between QG nodes vanish, all curves tend to merge into one. To confirm the results, we use three different classifiers: a support vector machine (SVM) [11,26], the K-Nearest Neighbors algorithm (KNN) [11,18], and the Naive Bayes classifier [11,31], which is a supervised machine for two-class classification problems (in our case, elderly and young patients). These analyses were based on the values of $\Delta(k)$, $B(k)$ and $C(k)$, of 5 elderly patients

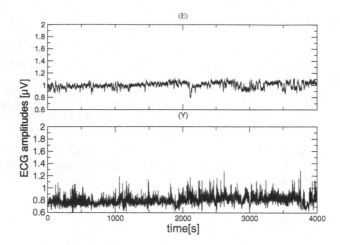

Fig. 2. ECG signals from each of the two sets. From top to bottom: set E (elderly patient) and Y (younger patient).

(group E) and 5 young patients (group Y). We use the holdout strategy and normalized the data with *MinMaxScaler* in *Python*. We considered 33% the test set and the rest for training. The confusion matrix (CM) is the same for the three classifiers (SVM, KNN, and Naive Bayes) and shows their performance. The main diagonal of the confusion matrix shows the correct results, which is, when the predicted value was positive (being elderly) and the actual value was also positive (being elderly); and when the predicted value was negative (being young) and the actual value was also negative (being young). This demonstrates that the classifiers got all the data right. These prelimiary results are promising. Nonetheless, more data is needed for precise conclusions. Therefore, to confirm these results, we use two statistical tests; namely, the Student's t-test and the Receiver Operating Characteristic (ROC). We execute a t-test [35] analysis to quantify the sample mean differences found in the two groups in studies. Table 1 shows a 95% confidence interval and a p-value of less than 0.05 among the sample means of the network measures Δ, B and C for the groups E and Y. Besides, we determine a Receiver Operating Characteristic [17] analysis to quantify the accuracy of the QG method in discriminating subjects from different age groups. Table 2 shows the areas under the ROC curves of the network metrics Δ, B and C, for elderly patients and young patients. In all cases, our tests showed that the QG method is a reliable technique for differentiating elderly patients (E) from young patients (Y).

$$CM = \begin{bmatrix} 2 & 0 \\ 0 & 2 \end{bmatrix}$$

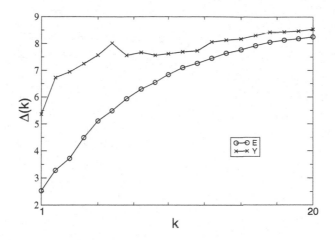

Fig. 3. $\Delta(k)$ in function of k, which was calculated with Eqs. 2. With $Q = 30$, $T = 4,000$ and $k = 1, 2, \ldots, 20$ for sets E (elderly patients) and Y (younger patients).

Table 1. Statistical comparison (95% confidence interval, $p < 0.05$) between the sample means of the network measures Δ, B and C for the sets E (elderly patients) and Y (younger patients), through t-test.

	Δ	B	C
CI_{EY}^1	$[-3.6568; -1.3986]$	$[0.0004; 0.0232]$	$[-0.0584; -0.0115]$
$p - valor$	0.0009	0.0437	0.0104

[1] E-elderly; Y-young.

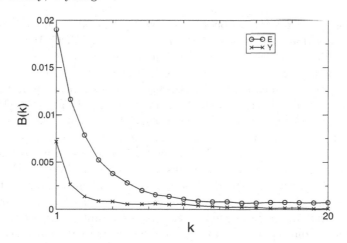

Fig. 4. $B(k)$ in function of k, which was calculated with Eq. (3), $Q = 30$, $T = 4,000$ and $k = 1, 2, \ldots, 20$ for sets E (elderly patients) and Y (younger patients).

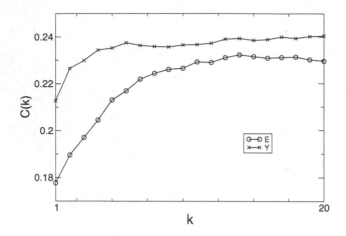

Fig. 5. $C(k)$ in function of k, which was calculated with Eq. (4), $Q = 30$, $T = 4,000$ and $k = 1, 2, \ldots, 20$ for sets E (elderly patients) and Y (younger patients).

Table 2. AUCs (areas under the ROC curves) of the network metrics $\Delta(k)$, $B(k)$ and $C(k)$, between participants in sets E and Y for $k = 6$, $k = 1$ and $k = 1$, respectively.

	Δ	B	C
AUC_{EY}	1.00	0.96	0.96

6 Conclusions

Heart diseases affect millions of people worldwide. A powerful, non-invasive automatic method of diagnosis based on the investigation of ECG data would likely have a large utilization. Here, we presented an unique approach based on the data of quantile graphs for the classification of ECG signals. The network topological classifiers utilized (mean jump length, betweenness centrality and clustering coefficient) demonstrated that the QG technique is useful to discern elderly participants from young ones through the values of different k parameters. This differentiation is based on the natural aging process. The complex networks obtained are directly linked to ECG. If the ECG belongs to a false positive (a young smoker, for instance), the networks are also able to indicate that. Results are significant and prove the QG method is a convenient assessment for the analysis of complex, nonlinear data like those originated from ECGs from participants. We intend to expand our database in future works. Additionally, we aim to study ECGs from sick young patients (obese, smokers, sedentary, or stressed patients, for instance), generate networks from these patients' data, and compare it with the networks from healthy elderly patients, to verify how the sick young patients are already being affected by their illnesses. Furthermore, these networks can be explored and compared to discuss habits that are harmful to the health of the heart, since cardiovascular diseases are becoming an increasingly common threat to human health and well-being.

References

1. Who. www (2019). https://www.who.int/news-room/
2. Adeli, H., Ghosh-Dastidar, S., Dadmehr, N.: Alzheimer's disease: models of computation and analysis of EEGs. Clin. EEG NeuroSci. **36**(3), 131–140 (2005)
3. Al-Fahoum, A.S., Al-Fraihat, A.A.: Methods of EEG signal features extraction using linear analysis in frequency and time-frequency domains. ISRN Neurosci. **2014**, 730218 (2014)
4. Rojas, I., Joya, G., Catala, A. (eds.): Advances in Computational Intelligence. IWANN 2017. LNCS, vol. 10306. Springer, Cham (2017)
5. Campanharo, A.S.L.O., Doescher, E., Ramos, F.M.: Automated EEG signals analysis using quantile graphs. In: Rojas, I., Joya, G., Catala, A. (eds.) International Work-Conference on Artificial Neural Networks. Lecture Notes in Computer Science, vol. 10306, pp. 95–103. Springer, Cham (2017). https://doi.org/10.1007/978-3-319-59147-6_9
6. Campanharo, A.S.L.O., Doescher, E., Ramos, F.M.: Application of quantile graphs to the automated analysis of EEG signals. Neural Process. Lett. **52**, 5–20 (2018). https://doi.org/10.1007/s11063-018-9936-z
7. Campanharo, A.S.L.O., Ramos, F.M.: Hurst exponent estimation of self-affine time series using quantile graphs. Phys. A: Stat. Mech. Appl. **444**, 43–48 (2016)
8. Campanharo, A.S.L.O., Ramos, F.M.: Hurst exponent estimation of self-affine time series using quantile graphs. Phys. A: Stat. Mech. Appl. **444**, 43–48 (2016)
9. Campanharo, A.S.L.O., Sirer, M.I., Malmgren, R.D., Ramos, F.M., Amaral, L.A.N.: Duality between time series and networks. PLoS ONE **6**(8), e23378 (2011)
10. Cannady, J.: Artificial neural networks for misuse detection. In: National Information Systems Security Conference, vol. 26. Baltimore (1998)
11. Cerri, R., de Leon Ferreira, A.C.P., et al.: Aprendizado de máquina: breve introdução e aplicações. Cadernos de Ciência & Tecnol. **34**(3), 297 313 (2019)
12. Costa, L.F., Rodrigues, F.A., Travieso, G., Villas, P.R.: Characterization of complex networks. Adv. Phys. **56**(1), 167–242 (2007)
13. Eckmann, J.P., Ruelle, D.: Fundamental limitations for estimating dimensions and Lyapunov exponents in dynamical systems. Phys. D **56**, 185–187 (1992)
14. Freeman, L.C.: A set of measures of centrality based on betweenness. Sociometry **40**(1), 35–41 (1977)
15. Gao, Z., Jin, N.: Complex network from time series based on phase space reconstruction. Chaos **19**, 033137 (2009). https://doi.org/10.1063/1.3227736
16. Goldberger, A.L., et al.: Physiobank, physiotoolkit, and physionet: components of a new research resource for complex physiologic signals. Circulation **101**(23), e215–e220 (2000)
17. Hajian-Tilaki, K.: Receiver operating characteristic (ROC) curve analysis for medical diagnostic test evaluation. Caspian J. Intern. Med. **4**(2), 627 (2013)
18. Horton, P., Nakai, K.: Better prediction of protein cellular localization sites with the it k nearest neighbors classifier. Proc. Int. Conf. Intell. Syst. Mol. Biol. (ISMB) **5**, 147–152 (1997)
19. Iyengar, N., Peng, C., Morin, R., Goldberger, A.L., Lipsitz, L.A.: Age-related alterations in the fractal scaling of cardiac interbeat interval dynamics. Am. J. Physiol.-Regul. Integr. Comp. Physiol. **271**(4), R1078–R1084 (1996)
20. Kantz, H., Schreiber, T.: Nonlinear Time Series Analysis. Cambridge University Press, Cambridge (2003). https://doi.org/10.1017/CBO9780511755798
21. Korner, T.W.: Fourier Analysis. Cambridge University Press, Cambridge (1988)

22. Lai, C., Chung, P., Tseng, V.S.: A novel two-level clustering method for time series data analysis. Expert Syst. Appl. **37**(9), 6319–6326 (2010). https://doi.org/10.1016/j.eswa.2010.02.089
23. Macfarlane, P.W.: The influence of age and sex on the electrocardiogram. In: Kerkhof, P., Miller, V. (eds.) Sex-Specific Analysis of Cardiovascular Function. Experimental Medicine and Biology, vol. 1065, pp. 93–106. Springer, Cham (2018). https://doi.org/10.1007/978-3-319-77932-4_6
24. Morris, A.S., Langari, R.: Measurement and Instrumentation: Theory and Application, 2nd edn. Academic Press, Cambridge (2012)
25. Percival, D.B., Walden, A.T.: Wavelet Methods for Time Series Analysis. Cambridge University Press, Cambridge (2000)
26. Pereira, F., Mitchell, T., Botvinick, M.: Machine learning classifiers and fMRI: a tutorial overview. Neuroimage **45**(1), S199–S209 (2009)
27. Pineda, A.M., Ramos, F.M., Betting, L.E., Campanharo, A.S.: Use of complex networks for the automatic detection and the diagnosis of Alzheimer's disease. In: Rojas, I., Joya, G., Catala, A. (eds.) International Work-Conference on Artificial Neural Networks. Lecture Notes in Computer Science, vol. 11506, pp. 115–126. Springer, Cham (2019). https://doi.org/10.1007/978-3-030-20521-8_10
28. Pineda, A.M., Ramos, F.M., Betting, L.E., Campanharo, A.S.: Quantile graphs for EEG-based diagnosis Alzheimer's disease. PloS ONE **15**(6), e0231169 (2020)
29. Pritchard, W.S., et al.: EEG-based, neural-net predictive classification of alzheimer's disease versus control subjects is augmented by non-linear EEG measures. Electroencephalogr. Clin. Neurophysiol. **91**(2), 118–130 (1994). https://doi.org/10.1016/0013-4694(94)90033-7
30. Perez Riera, A.R., Barros, R.B.: Hypertrophic cardiomyopathy: value of electrocardiogram for the diagnosis of different types and for differential diagnosis with athlete's heart. Revista De La Federacion Argentina De Cardiologia **44**(1), 12–24 (2015)
31. Rish, I., et al.: An empirical study of the naive bayes classifier. In: IJCAI 2001 Workshop on Empirical Methods in Artificial Intelligence, vol. 3, pp. 41–46 (2001)
32. Saramäki, J., Kivelä, M., Onnela, J.P., Kaski, K., Kertesz, J.: Generalizations of the clustering coefficient to weighted complex networks. Phys. Rev. E **75**(2), 027105 (2007)
33. Stam, C., Jelles, B., Achtereekte, H., Van Birgelen, J., Slaets, J.: Diagnostic usefulness of linear and nonlinear quantitative EEG analysis in Alzheimer's disease. Clin. Electroencephalogr. **27**(2), 69–77 (1996)
34. Strogatz, S.H.: Nonlinear Dynamics and Chaos. Westview Press, Boulder (1994)
35. Supe, A., et al.: A study of stress in medical students at seth GS medical college. J. Postgrad. Med. **44**(1), 1 (1998)
36. Tu, J.V.: Advantages and disadvantages of using artificial neural networks versus logistic regression for predicting medical outcomes. J. Clin. Epidemiol. **49**(11), 1225–1231 (1996)
37. Zhang, J., Luo, X., Small, M.: Detecting chaos in pseudoperiodic time series without embedding. Phys. Rev. E **73**, 016216 (2006)
38. Zhang, J., Small, M.: Complex network from pseudoperiodic time series. Phys. Rev. Lett. **96**(23), 238701 (2006)

Analysis of the Health Network of Metropolitan Lima Against Large-Scale Earthquakes

Miguel Nunez-del-Prado[(✉)] [iD] and John Barrera

Universidad del Pacífico, Lima, Peru
m.nunezdelpradoc@up.edu.pe

Abstract. Peru is a highly seismic country located in the Ring of Fire, making it vulnerable to earthquakes and tsunamis. In the present work, we examined Lima's health system capacity from three different and complementary points of view. We first analyze the Hospital Treatment Capacity (HTC) of 41 hospitals of II and III categories from EsSalud and MINSA in Lima, Peru. Second, we computed the hospitals' coverage area and their citizens' health demand as the aftermath of an earthquake of 8 Mw magnitude. Finally, an accessibility simulation to reach the hospitals was performed, taking into account real traffic jams conditions and street degradation. This document aims to provide elements for the strengthening of the Peruvian fragile health system.

Keywords: Health network · Earthquakes · Graph theory · Optimization

1 Introduction

Peru is a highly seismic country, located in the so-called fire belt between the Nazca plates and the South American plate, where the Geophysical Institute of Peru (*i.e.* IGP) identified 33 different sources of earthquakes [7]. Mainly, Lima is within the source number 24 of earthquakes, namely *Region 24*. Besides, the study of Pulido *et al.* confirms this source of earthquakes with observations suggesting an aftershock of the Lima earthquake of 1746 [18].

The Ministry of Housing, Construction, and Sanitation of Peru consider that the m^2 of housing construction is valued at $580 US Dollars [23] in Lima. Based on the coefficients determined in [7], the cost of building a square meter of a hospital in the Lima region would be around $870 US Dollars for the 2019–2020 fiscal period. Additionally, literature studies agree that the Peruvian hospital system is fragile due to its age and lack of investment in decades [3,10,13,19]. To this, we add the allocation of hospital demand by political divisions (*i.e.*, districts) that unrealistically capture hospitals' demand. Moreover, in a context like Peru, where we are close to the queue in terms of public health investment in Latin America, the health system is not prepared to receive a large number of

© Springer Nature Switzerland AG 2021
J. A. Lossio-Ventura et al. (Eds.): SIMBig 2020, CCIS 1410, pp. 445–459, 2021.
https://doi.org/10.1007/978-3-030-76228-5_32

expected cases due to the magnitude of the earthquake. Therefore, it is relevant to analyze the state of the health system.

In this study, we propose to analyze hospitals' demand under the hypothesis that after an earthquake of 8 Mw of magnitude, only twenty hospitals will be operational. In a second stage, we will proceed to analyze the resistance of the access roads to the hospitals against the degradation they may suffer due to an earthquake of such magnitude. Thus, this evaluation will take into account the time of traffic that a vehicle may encounter when transiting through Lima on a Friday between noon and two o'clock in the afternoon. Finally, this document is organized as follows. Section 2 describes the works found in the literature. Section 3 details both the hospital demand and route degradation estimation, while Sect. 4 presents the results found. Finally, Sect. 5 concludes this study and presents new avenues of research to be explored.

2   Related Works

In this section, we describe the different studies on demand for hospitals after an earthquake and hospital capacity evaluation. For example, Bambarén *et al.* [3] proposes a probabilistic model to determine the demand for hospital care after a significant earthquake in metropolitan Lima. The authors consider the demand for hospital care, time of arrival at the hospitals, type of medical treatment; reason for hospital admission; and the need for specialized care such as hemodialysis, blood transfusions, and surgical procedures. The authors estimated that between 23 328 and 178 387 wounded would go to hospitals, of which between 4 666 y 121 303 would require hospital care, while between 18 662 and 57 084 could be treated as outpatients. It was estimated that there would be an average of 8 768 cases of crush syndrome and 54 217 cases of other health problems. Enough blood would be needed to 8 761 injuries in the first 24 h. Also, it was expected that there would be a shortage of hospital beds and operating theatres due to high demand. Unfortunately, the authors do not detail the mathematical model used to obtain these values.

Liguori *et al.* [13], propose a model to estimate the capacity of a hospital in metropolitan Lima after a seismic event. To achieve this objective, they evaluated hospitals' seismic response capacity considering variables such as seismic risk, hospital integrity, supplies, hospital treatment capacity, and resources for emergency response coordination. This study determined that structural damage due to the hospital's age conditions the hospital's proper functioning in the event of an earthquake. Also, the priority hospitals would not be able to handle the estimated between 4 666 and 121 303.

In the evaluation of hospitals raised in [14], a five-step qualitative methodology is presented. The first step characterizes the Health Network in provinces. In the second step, the different phenomena that could occur in the evaluated territory are evaluated. In the third step, they determine the magnitudes or severities of the different phenomena evaluated in the previous step. In the fourth step, the vulnerability of that health network to the phenomena and levels determined is analyzed. Finally, the level of risk is determined in a double-entry matrix to characterize it in terms of danger and vulnerability, depending on low, medium, and very high. However, one of the limitations of this evaluation is the lack of a quantitative model. According to the Hospital Safety Index guide (*ISH*) [16], this measure helps to quantify how robust a hospital is in the face of an adverse situation such as a natural disaster.

Liguori *et al.* [11] do a study on the losses, safety and functionality of 41 hospitals in metropolitan Lima using the *Comprehensive Approach for Probabilistic Risk Assessment* (CAPRA) [5]. The CAPRA methodology evaluates physical and human economic losses by analyzing hazards, exposure, and vulnerability. This work showed that for earthquakes with a return period of 500 and 1000 years, only 14% and 18% of the analyzed infrastructure would be operational, respectively. Based on this work. Liguori *et al.* [10] proposes a quantitative methodology to assess the care capacity of a hospital HTC in an earthquake scenario. The adapted model of [12] contemplates for the Peruvian case an efficiency factor α, human component β, number of operating environments in normal conditions γ, the average time for a surgery t, the operational probability of the physical component δ, and operational autonomy k.

Santa-Cruz *et al.* [17,20] presents the seismic risk assessment of hospitals in the city of Lima. This work aims to evaluate the seismic risk of Lima's health system on a metropolitan scale. The seismic risk analysis was carried out using a comprehensive approach for the Probabilistic Risk Assessment Methodology (CAPRA). A total of 41 hospitals were evaluated to obtain risk indicators in terms of economic losses. The results show that after an earthquake of magnitude 8.2 Mw with an epicenter on the coast of Lima, 85% of the hospital buildings have more than 10% of structural damage. This study seeks to understand and evaluate hospitals' seismic risk at the municipal level to define measures, priorities, and actions for the future development of Lima's health system.

Mulyasari *et al.* [15] assesses how well hospitals in the Tohoku and Nankai regions are prepared for earthquakes. The authors use a questionnaire survey consisting of six parameters and 21 indicators of the "four pillars of hospital preparedness," including structural, non-structural, functional, and human resources. The results show that most hospitals surveyed comply with functional preparedness, which is useful during the emergency period of a disaster, while the other three pillars (structural, non-structural, and human resources) need to be strengthened. This study helps assess the state of disaster preparedness and the gaps for these hospitals, drawing lessons from the Great Earthquake and Tsunami in eastern Japan's Tohoku area. The gaps found are used as a starting point to indicate how to improve preparedness and resilience to future disaster risks.

The work of Carrasco et al. [6] computes travel times for different cities in Peru to primary, secondary, and tertiary health service. Authors use satellite images to build a 500 × 500 grid to compute the time to travel in each grid. For computing travel time, authors rely on Google Earth Engine finding travel times ranging from 39, 152, and 448 min.

The following section details the proposed methodology for determining hospital capacity, demand for care, and post-seismic care facility accessibility assessment.

3 Methodology

In this section, we detail the methodology to be followed, which consists of three phases.

1) Scenario Generation.- For the scenario generation, we use the data collected in the literature [11,14,17,20] to calculate the HTC of the 41 MINSA and EsSalud for both category II and category III public hospitals considered in this study. Taking the model proposed in [11], which we extended to include the number of wards the hospital has δ and operating time k autonomous after an earthquake (*c.f.*, Eq. 1).

$$HTC(\delta, k) = \alpha\beta\frac{\gamma\delta}{t}k \tag{1}$$

Where the emergency plan efficiency α, and the preparedness of health care professionals, β, are set at 0.8 in a range of 0–1. With regard to operational autonomy, different scenarios were considered in hours $k = \{12, 24, 48, 72, 120\}$, while γ was determined using the performance point assessment [1,8] to obtain an estimate of 23%. In our case, we will take different scenarios considering the number of buildings δ essential E, and some essential buildings plus operational wards ER (*i.e.*, $E \geq ER$), to determine the number of people who can attend, with different times of autonomy. As for the average duration of surgical intervention. As for the average duration of a surgical intervention t, they decided two hours on average based on Lupoi's study *et al.* [12]. In the case of other types of care that are not surgeries (*i.e.* operaciones), it was estimated that the average time is $t = 1.5h$. This time was found based on telephone interviews with doctors working at the Rebagliati Hospital, the Collique Hospital, and the Cusco Regional Hospital in Peru. Finally, based on the different scenarios, we generated different hospital care capacity (HTC) rankings to obtain the top 20 categories II and III hospitals that will attend in that scenario.

2) Estimating Demand for Medical Care.- Regarding the demand for hospital services after an earthquake of grade 8 Mw, we collected information from the literature summarized in Table 1. This table shows the minimum, maximum and average for different types of hospital services, such as: *surgeries, medical care, outpatient care, crush syndrome* and *others* types of hospital care. Traditionally, demand estimation is performed by districts in a static way [3]. However, the before-mentioned assumption is unrealistic. Thus, after an earthquake, affected individuals try to reach the nearest hospital, whether it is in the same district of residence.

Table 1. Summary of estimated demand for the number of surgical procedures (*surgeries*), (*medical care*), (*outpatient care*), or (*crush syndrome*) and other types of care *others* after an 8 Mw earthquake.

Demand	Min	Average	Max
Surgeries [10]	2 481	33 499	64 515
Medical care [3]	4 666	62 985	121 303
Outpatient care [3]	18 662	37 873	57 084
Crush syndrome [3]			8 768
Others [3]			54 217
Total			305 887

To determine the demand, we took as input the top 20 hospitals' locations with the highest HTC to determine their coverage area using Voronoi diagrams [2]. Thus a coverage area can comprise fractions of different districts. Finally, to estimate the demand by km^2, we only consider the areas of the districts delimited by the streets. For this we built the Lima street network, extracted from the Open Street Maps API[1] (*OSM*). This graph $G(E, V)$ models in its vertices (V) the intersections of streets and its edges (E) the city's streets.

To formalize this approximation, we take the Eq. 2. Where D_x represents the sum of the demand for $x = \{$surgeries, medical care, outpatient care, crush syndrome, others$\}$, for each district fraction d within the hospital's area of influence D_v for all district fractions N_v. It is essential to notice that the sum of each area fraction is taken in Km^2 by the factor calculated $fact_x$. This factor corresponds to the proportion of the population treated within 12, 24, 48 and 72 h after the earthquake.

$$D_x = \sum_{d \in D_v}^{N_v} (d \times fact_x) \tag{2}$$

Finally, the total demand for a hospital is given by the vector: $DT_v = [D_{Surgeries}, D_{Medicalcare}, D_{Outpatientcare}, D_{Crushsyndrome}, D_{Others}]$.

3) Hospital accessibility estimation.- For the calculation of the roads' accessibility, we take the subgraph $G_v(V, E) \subset G(V, E)$ corresponding to a hospital's area of influence. Based on $G_v(V, E)$, we compute the time it takes to get from an extreme point in the region of influence to the hospital using the Dijkstra [9] algorithm. It is important to note that the edges of the network used are weighted by the time it takes to drive in the street in question. This information was taken from Waze's SDK[2],[3]. For measuring access time to hospitals,

---

[1] OSM API: https://wiki.openstreetmap.org/wiki/API_v0.6.

[2] SDK Waze: https://www.waze.com/es-419/sdk.

[3] Waze API https://github.com/kovacsbalu/WazeRouteCalculator/blob/.

road degradation was simulated by randomly removing up to 30% of the edges (*i.e.*streets), as formalized in the Eq. 3.

$$R_c = \frac{1}{|P|} \sum_{p \in P}^{|P|} (dijkstra(p, H)) \tag{3}$$

Where R is the average time with a c% degraded roads, p is a node in the P set of the outermost nodes, and H is the node where the hospital is in the area of influence.

Finally, when we measure the access time to hospitals and if it is indeed possible to reach them, we can estimate the number of people who die because they cannot reach the hospital in less than an hour. We focus on the second peak of trauma after instantaneous deaths, which occurs within minutes to several hours after the injury. Deaths in this period are usually due to epidural and subdural hematomas, hemopneumothorax, ruptured spleen, liver lacerations, pelvic fractures, or multiple other injuries associated with significant blood loss. **The golden hour** of post-injury care is characterized by the need for rapid assessment and resuscitation, which are the fundamental principles of advanced trauma life support [22]. It is important to emphasize that in the present study, we make the hypothesis that the distribution of the density of injured is uniform. The third peak, which occurs days after the initial injury, is often due to sepsis and multi-organ dysfunction. The care provided during each of the previous periods affects the results during this stage.

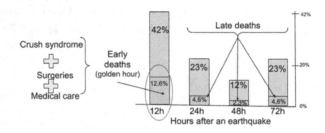

Fig. 1. Distribution of the percentages of need for hospital care according to the hours after the earthquake and the percentage of care within the golden hour.

Depending on the various traumas distribution, 30% correspond to those that must be treated in less than an hour [4,21]. Thus, the Fig. 1 outlines the percentage of people with crushing, trauma, and need for surgical procedures of the total (*i.e.* 42%) of the total demand for hospital care within the first hours after the earthquake, need to be attended to in less than one hour (*i.e.* 12.6%). In this sense, the estimated deaths are proportional to the trips reaching the hospital despite road access degradation. As for the third peak, the amount of severe trauma represents 20% of the need for hospital care after 12 h of the earthquake. This represents 4.6%, .3%, and 4.6% of the demand to be met after

24, 48 and 72 h respectively (*c.f.*, Fig. 1). In the following section, we describe
the results obtained by applying the methodology described in this chapter.

4 Results

In this section, we describe the obtained results for different HTC hospital rankings and autonomy attention hours. It is worth noting that we take the HTC and
the reinforced HTC, which considers the surgical procedures buildings plus the
capacity for medical care and outpatient care, among others. Thus, we have the
hospital care capacity scenario after 12 h. (*E12*), which considers only the supply of surgical procedures and another that also considers the supply of medical
care, outpatient care, and others (*E12R*).

In the Table 2, we detail the index of each of the hospitals that would intervene in the different scenarios. We can see that depending on the HTC different
hospitals are selected in each scenario. For example, if we take scenarios E12
and E12R with capacities *HTC12* and *HTC12R*, the hospitals in common are
the ones that have indexes *1, 2, 3, 4, 5, 9, 10, 20, 21, 22, 23, 25, 35, 36,* and
41. We also note that hospitals that are unique in *E12* are *8, 13, 24, 29,* and
33; and the only ones in *E12R* are *15, 16, 19, 38,* and *40*.

Table 2. Hospital facilities code in different scenarios.

Scenario	Hospital facilities code
E12	22, 23, 35, 4, 5, 21, 36, 41, 9, 1, 20, 10, 24, 25, 2, 3, 29, 33, 8, 13
E12R	23, 9, 5, 4, 10, 21, 35, 1, 22, 2, 3, 20, 38, 41, 36, 40, 15, 25, 19, 16
E24	23, 22, 4, 35, 5, 21, 41, 36, 9, 1, 25, 10, 20, 3, 29, 7, 16, 40, 6, 19
E24R	23, 9, 5, 4, 10, 1, 35, 21, 22, 3, 20, 38, 41, 36, 40, 25, 19, 12, 16, 7
E48	23, 4, 35, 21, 36, 41, 1, 20, 10, 25, 3, 16, 7, 6, 12, 26, 38, 27
E48R	23, 4, 10, 1, 35, 21, 3, 20, 38, 41, 36, 25, 12, 16, 7, 14, 27, 26, 6, 11
E72	35, 41, 36, 1, 25, 20, 16, 26, 12, 38, 27
E72R	1, 35, 20, 38, 41, 36, 25, 12, 16, 27, 26

Now that the scenarios have been defined, we will calculate the demand for
hospital care by each hospital in the established scenario. One of the problems
with the works found in the literature is that they calculate the demand according to the political division *i.e.*, districts. However, after an earthquake, people
do not necessarily think about going to their district hospital because it may
be geographically farther away or because it may be inoperable after the earthquake. In that sense, we assume that people go to the nearest open hospital.

This way, we take the hospitals in each scenario, and from the 20 hospitals
that offer the most *HTC*. So, we calculated the area of influence using Voronoi
diagrams. The Figs. 2A, 2B, 2C, 2D, 2E, 2F, 2G, and 2H shows the area of influence of hospitals in scenarios E12, E12R, E24, E24R, E48, E48R, E72, and E72R,

respectively. These areas of influence intersected with the Lima graph allow us to find the areas of influence in Km^2 to find the demand for the number of surgeries, hospital care, outpatient care, people with crush syndrome, and other care. Note that the demand for hospital care also has minimum and maximum levels (*c.f.*, Chart 1). For this reason, we decided to additionally include an optimistic estimate of the demand for hospital care following an 8 Mw magnitude earthquake.

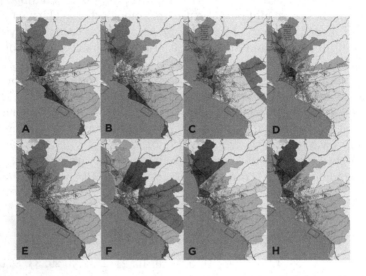

Fig. 2. Voronoi diagrams intersected with districts for the scenarios (A) E12, (B) E12R, (C) E24, (D) E24R, (E) E48, (B) E48R, (C) E72, and (D) E72R.

Table 3 summarizes the demands for hospital care measured in numbers of people for all scenarios and also shows the different capacities of hospital care in numbers of people that can be served. It should be noted that the demands for hospital care do not vary practically between the simple hospital care capacity scenarios (E) and reinforced (ER) when we compare the Operations columns against the hospital care capacity in Table 3. We observe that an average of 15% of the demand for operations is covered in the optimistic scenario (*i.e.* EO) at different times. In this sense, if we consider the total demand and contrast it with the reinforced hospital care capacity (*i.e.* HTCR), the coverage drops to 1% of the demand for care. This situation becomes critical when we take into account the pessimistic scenario (*i.e.* EP) for different hours. For such a scenario, the hedge falls to 0.63% and 0.32%. That is, less than 1% of the demand for hospital care is met.

As far as hospital accessibility analysis is concerned. First, we take the network corresponding to a region of influence. Over this region, we choose the most external nodes to the network so that, through the Dijkstra algorithm, we measure the time of arrival at the hospital from a certain point. Now for each graph,

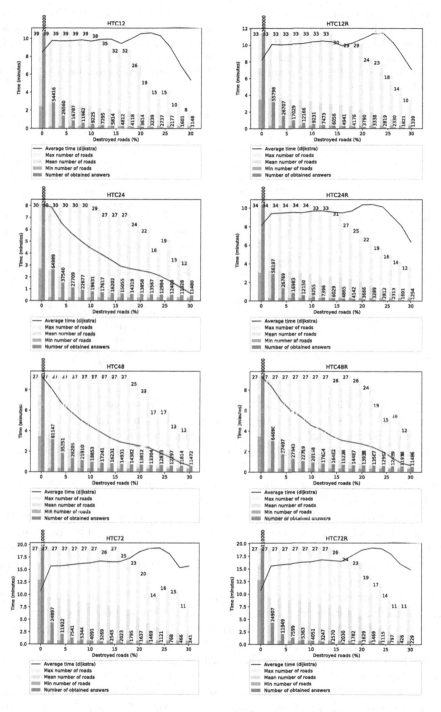

Fig. 3. Summary of the simulation of accessibility times for hospitals corresponding to all HTC scenarios.

Table 3. Summary of hospital care demands in number of people for the optimistic (OE) and pessimistic (PE) scenarios of 12, 24, 48 and 72 h after an 8 Mw magnitude earthquake. Where R, corresponds to the reinforced scenario (which takes into account infrastructure for outpatient care, hospitalization, crushing and others). The column 'Total accumulated demand' reports the need for accumulated care for the 12, 24, 48 and 72 h elapsed.

Scenario	Demand	Operations	Hospitable	Ambulatory	Flattening	Others	Total demand acum	HTC	HTCR
EO12	41%	1107	2079	8071	3755	23230	38242	150	318
EO24	65%	1714	3217	12489	5807	35946	59173	284	644
EO48	77%	2028	3811	14586	6881	42581	69887	424	1025
EO72	100%	2634	4949	18603	8933	55298	90417	321	798
EO12R	41%	1107	2079	8072	3753	23229	38240	143	346
EO24R	65%	1714	3218	12091	5804	35946	58773	281	672
EO48R	77%	2027	3811	14189	6876	42578	69481	424	1067
EO72R	100%	2633	4949	18206	8928	55295	90011	321	798
EP12	41%	27638	51969	24460	3752	23230	131049	150	318
EP24	65%	42778	80431	37851	5804	35946	202810	284	644
EP48	77%	50678	95282	44838	6876	42581	240255	424	1025
EP72	100%	65819	123743	58229	8928	55298	312017	321	798
EP12R	41%	27638	51969	24460	3752	23230	131049	143	346
EP24R	65%	42779	80430	37851	5804	35947	202811	281	672
EP48R	77%	50679	95281	44838	6876	42582	240256	424	1067
EP72R	100%	65820	123742	58229	8928	55299	312018	321	798

we degrade the roads by removing 2% to 30% from the streets. Thus for each level of degradation, 10 000 simulations were performed by the Monte Carlo method to measure the average time of arrival between the external points to the hospital. We measured the degradation level of the roads and the probability distribution of arrival times at the hospital for all scenarios from these simulations.

On the one hand, Fig. 3 shows a blue line indicating the average time - in minutes - it takes to reach the hospital from outside the hospital's region of influence as a function of the percentage of roads destroyed. However, we see that the curve falls when the percentage of destruction is higher. This phenomenon can be explained by looking at the orange and green bars. Thus, the orange bars measure the number of available routes and the green ones the number of trips that reach the hospital.

On the other hand, concerning the distribution of the probability of arrival times at the hospital, for each of the trips, we make that return a positive value, i.e., a route is found, we show the distribution of the probability of arrival times at the hospital. As can be observed in Fig. 4, the distribution of arrival times shows a form of decreasing. Thus, we record the ratio of p of successful trips about the number of expected simulations, the mean, median, and standard deviation for each level of degradation. We can observe that the distribution shifts to the right as the destruction increases. However, from 16% of destruction, we see that

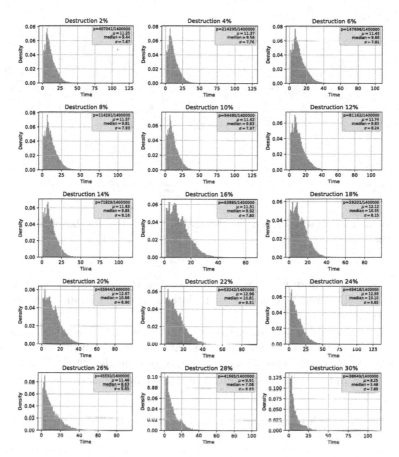

Fig. 4. Distribution of accessibility times to hospitals in different scenarios. (Color figure online)

the mean falls as the p ratio becomes smaller due to isolated nodes without being able to reach the hospital. Only the closest external nodes remain accessible.

Based on the results of accessibility times (*c.f.*, Fig. 3), it is possible to estimate the percentage of trips that do not reach the hospital due to the percentage of roads degradation. Thus, taking into account the total demand for hospital care composed of surgical interventions, hospital care, and crushing syndromes, we have a total 194 586 of people who needed care. Of this total, 42% will need attention in the first twelve hours, and of that total 30% is considered early death. That is, they need to be attended to in less than an hour. Thus, 24 518 people who needed attention in the first hour after the earthquake. Then, we calculated the percentage that does not arrive due to the road's degradation. Figure 5 illustrates the percentage of deaths according to the level of destruction of access to the hospital for different scenarios. The results range from 16 189 people passed away in the scenario with less destruction, which is 2% until 24 467

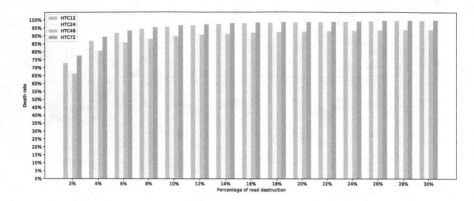

Fig. 5. Number of deaths caused by the inability to reach the hospital within the golden hour.

people passed away than when access degradation reaches 30% of the hospital's influence area. This must be added to the late deaths, that is, after the first 12 h of the earthquake.

In that sense, Table 4 summarizes the final demands after the considered deaths. It is essential to consider that we position ourselves in the worst scenario where 30% of the roads were destroyed. Thus practically 100% of people who need help both in the golden hour and after twelve hours in the late death phase

Table 4. Summary of hospital care demands expressed in the number of people for the optimistic (EO) and pessimistic (PE) scenarios for 12, 24, 48, and 72 h after an 8 MW earthquake. where R corresponds to a reinforced scenario (which takes into account infrastructure for outpatient care, hospitalizations, crushing, and others).

Scenario	Demand	Operations	Hospitable	Ambulatory	Flattening	Others	Total demand acum	Deaths	Deaths acum	Final demand	HTC	HTCR
EO12	41%	1107	2079	8071	3755	23230	38242	2082	2082	36160	150	318
EO24	65%	1714	3217	12489	5807	35946	59173	971	3053	56120	284	644
EO48	77%	2028	3811	14586	6881	42581	69887	249	3302	66585	424	1025
EO72	100%	2634	4949	18603	8933	55298	90417	953	4255	86162	321	798
EO12R	41%	1107	2079	8072	3753	23230	38240	2082	10014	28226	143	346
EO24R	65%	1714	3218	12091	5804	23514	58773	497	10511	48262	281	672
EO48R	77%	2027	3811	14189	6876	23938	69481	476	10987	58494	424	1067
EO72R	100%	2633	4949	18206	8928	24259	90011	1904	12892	77119	321	798
EP12	41%	27638	51969	24460	3752	23230	131049	25008	29898	101151	150	318
EP24	65%	42778	80431	37851	5804	35946	202810	3330	33227	169583	284	644
EP48	77%	50678	95282	44838	6876	42581	240255	869	34096	206159	424	1025
EP72	100%	65819	123743	58229	8928	55298	312017	3330	37426	274591	321	798
EP12R	41%	27638	51969	24460	3752	23230	131049	25008	29898	101151	143	346
EP24R	65%	42779	80430	37851	5804	35947	202811	3330	33227	169584	281	672
EP48R	77%	50679	95281	44838	6876	42582	240256	869	34096	206160	424	1067
EP72R	100%	65820	123742	58229	8928	55299	312018	3330	37426	274592	321	798

cannot reach the nearest hospital. The column *Demanda* shows the percentage of care that must be carried out. In this way, we cumulatively represent the need for care according to how time passes at 12, 24, 48, and 72 h after the earthquake with the different hospitals changing according to the optimistic scenario (OS) or pessimistic scenario (PS). The evolution of the scenario after the magnitude 8 Mw earthquake is alarming since, in the best of the EO48R scenarios and discounting deaths due to not reaching the hospitals, barely 2% of the demand for care is covered more catastrophic scenarios of 0.3% care coverage. These figures reflect the fragility of the Peruvian system.

5   Conclusions

This paper analyzes the hospital system in metropolitan Lima in the face of an 8 MW magnitude earthquake scenario to assess the gaps between the need for hospital care and the capacity of hospital care. For this analysis, we took 41 category II and III hospitals from the health network of MINSA and EsSalud, where we calculated the hospital care capacity (HTC). Thus, we took the 20 hospitals with the best care capacity for four different scenarios based on the number of hours after the earthquake. At this point, we found that hospitals significantly vary when considering the time of autonomy they have. This means that not all hospitals are prepared to provide care for 12, 24, 48, or 72 h autonomously after an earthquake.

Depending on the hospitals for different scenarios, we build the hospitals' influence zone to determine the number of people who need care. We then measure whether the hospital's care capacity (HTC) meets the minimum and maximum demand for hospital care. The results corroborate what we found in the literature, where the fragility of the health system in metropolitan Lima is evident. Thus, we simulated the hospitals' accessibility according to road degradation using the hospital's areas of influence. By simulating the degradation of the accessibility of the outermost points of the zones of influence to the hospital, we observe that several points in the zones of influence remain isolated and cannot reach the hospital because of the destroyed roads. This allowed us to observe that only the closest external points can access the hospital, with the degradation of 16%.

Finally, road degradation allowed us to quantify the number of deaths within the first twelve hours (early deaths) and after 24 h (late deaths) due to road degradation. Thus, we found that for degradation of 30% almost 100% of people do not reach the hospital and if they still do, the capacity of hospital care does not cover the large number of people who would reach the hospitals, since hospitals cover between 1% and 15% of the demand for hospital care depending on the scenario.

It would be interesting to integrate population density dynamics in the hospitals' demand estimation using Call Detail Records data for changes as a function of day and time due to population mobility. Also, modeling the queues for the same care services would provide a more accurate picture of actual care capacity.

Acknowledgment. We would like to thank our colleagues Gabriel Aguirre Martens and Hugo Alatrista-Salas for the discussion, review and suggestions that enrich the present work.

References

1. ATC, S: Evaluation and retrofit of concrete buildings, rep. ATC-40, Applied Technology Council, Redwood City, California (1996)
2. Aurenhammer, F., Klein, R.: Voronoi diagrams. Handb. Comput. Geometry **5**(10), 201–290 (2000)
3. Bambarén, C., Uyen, A., Rodriguez, M.: Estimation of the demand for hospital care after a possible high-magnitude earthquake in the city of Lima, Peru. Prehospital Disast. Med. **32**(1), 106–111 (2017)
4. Bartholdson, S., von Schreeb, J.: Natural disasters and injuries: what does a surgeon need to know? Current trauma reports **4**(2), 103–108 (2018)
5. Cardona, O., Ordaz, M., Reinoso, E., Yamín, L., Barbat, A.: Comprehensive approach to probabilistic risk assessment: international initiative for risk management effectiveness-capra. In: 15th World Conference on Earthquake Engineering (2012)
6. Carrasco-Escobar, G., Manrique, E., Tello-Lizarraga, K., Miranda, J.J.: Travel time to health facilities as a marker of geographical accessibility across heterogeneous land coverage in Peru. MedRxiv p. 19007856 (2019)
7. CIRNA-PUCP, C.: Perfil de riesgo sísmico a nivel nacional de los bienes inmuebles de propiedad del estado y viviendas. Technical Report, Banco Interamericano de Desarrollo (2014)
8. (FEMA), F.E.M.A: Hazus MR4 multi-hazard loss estimation methodology (2003)
9. Johnson, D.B.: A note on Dijkstra's shortest path algorithm. J. ACM (JACM) **20**(3), 385–388 (1973)
10. Liguori, N., Tarque, N., Bambarén, C., Spacone, E., Viveen, W., de Filippo, G.: Hospital treatment capacity in case of seismic scenario in the lima metropolitan area, Peru. Int. J. Disast. Risk Reduction **38** (2019)
11. Liguori, N., Tarque, N., Santa-Cruz, S., Spacone, E.: Losses, safety, and functionality of the hospitals in lima in case of an earthquake, pp. 55–64 (2017)
12. Lupoi, G., Franchin, P., Lupoi, A., Pinto, P., Calvi, G.: Probabilistic Seismic Assessment for Hospitals and Complex-social Systems, Pavia, p. 635. IUSS Press (2008)
13. Minaya-Robles, J., Rodríguez-Ramos, A., Rospigliosi-Monteagudo, L., Uchazara-Rivera, B.: Capacidad de respuesta del personal, pacientes y familiares antes un simulacro en caso de sismo del servicio de emergencia de un hospitalnacional (2017)
14. MINSA and ESSALUD: Guía para la evaluación de riesgos en el sector salud. Technical Report, Ministerio de Salud (2014)
15. Mulyasari, F., et al.: Disaster preparedness: looking through the lens of hospitals in Japan. Int. J. Disaster Risk Sci. **4**(2), 89–100 (2013)
16. OMS: índice de seguridad hospitalaria. guía para evaluadores. Technical Report Organización Mundial de Salud (2017)
17. Palomino Bendezú, J.S., Ly, T., Eduardo, R.: Evaluación probabilista del riesgo sísmico de hospitales en lima con plataforma capra (2016)
18. Pulido, N., et al.: Scenario source models and strong ground motion for future mega-earthquakes: Application to Lima, central Peru. Bull. Seismol. Soc. Am. **105**(1), 368–386 (2015)

19. Ríos, J., et al.: Estudios de vulnerabilidad sísmica: estructural, no estructural y funcional en catorce (14) establecimientos de salud de la provincia de lima hospital nacional dos de mayo, el cercado de lima. Technical Report, Instituto Nacional de Defensa Civil (2017)
20. Santa-Cruz, S., Palomino, J., Liguori, N., Vona, M., Tamayo, R.: Seismic risk assessment of hospitals in Lima city using GIS tools. In: ICCSA 2017. LNCS, vol. 10406, pp. 354–367. Springer, Cham (2017). https://doi.org/10.1007/978-3-319-62398-6_25
21. Sobrino, J., Shafi, S.: Timing and causes of death after injuries. In: Baylor University Medical Center Proceedings, vol. 26, pp. 120–123. Taylor & Francis (2013)
22. on Trauma American College of Surgeons, T.C.: Advanced trauma life support. The Committee on Trauma - American College of Surgeons (2018). Accessed 29 Jan 2014
23. Wendorff, R.Y.: Resolución ministerial 351 2019 vivienda. Technical Report, Ministerio de Vivienda (2019)

Quasiquadratic Time Algorithms
for Square and Pentagon Counting
in Real-World Networks

Grover E. C. Guzman[1] and Jared León[1,2]

[1] Institute of Mathematics and Statistics, University of São Paulo, São Paulo, Brazil
grover@ime.usp.br
[2] Department of Informatics, Universidad Nacional de San Antonio Abad del Cusco,
Cusco, Peru

Abstract. Counting structures in graphs (triangles, cliques, graphlets, etc.) is an important task when analyzing real-world networks given its usefulness to make link prediction, community discovery, graph classification, etc. Among many structures in graphs, triangle counting (cycles of length 3) has been a hot research topic in recent years. As a result of that, a number of algorithms have been developed for counting triangles and many closely related structures. However, square and pentagon counting (cycles of length 4 and 5 respectively) have received less attention despite its importance when analyzing real-world bipartite graphs and its influence on the graph spectrum. In this work, we propose quasiquadratic time algorithms for approximately counting the number of squares and pentagons in a simple graph as a whole, and also obtain such counts per vertices.

Keywords: Square counting · Pentagon counting · Counting cycles in graphs

1 Introduction

Some important and also interesting tasks when analyzing large scale real networks can sometimes include counting defined special structures on graphs such as triangles, cliques, graphlets, etc. The count of some of these structures can be used in a number of tasks including link prediction, community discovery, centrality analysis, graph classification, etc. Among these structures, triangle counting has received a lot of attention due to its importance for analyzing real-world networks. For this reason, a number of algorithms have been developed to obtain the exact and approximate number of triangles in a given graph. However, less attention has been given to cycles of greater length, such as squares and pentagons. Squares, also called rectangles, are elementary substructures of bipartite graphs [8]. Hence, square counting is important to obtain metrics like clustering coefficient and rectangle-based connectivity; it is also used for estimating larger cycles in order to analyze bipartite real-world networks (author-paper,

© Springer Nature Switzerland AG 2021
J. A. Lossio-Ventura et al. (Eds.): SIMBig 2020, CCIS 1410, pp. 460–470, 2021.
https://doi.org/10.1007/978-3-030-76228-5_33

user-product, actor-movie, etc.). As for pentagons; it has recently been found that they have a direct influence on the graph spectrum and the spectral radius of networks [6,10]. Despite these applications, square and pentagon counting is a significantly less studied topic than triangle counting [2].

The naive brute force algorithms for counting squares and pentagons have $\mathcal{O}(n^4)$ and $\mathcal{O}(n^5)$ time complexity respectively. However, if fast matrix multiplication is used, each one can be obtained in $\mathcal{O}(n^{2.376})$ time [3]. Recently, two algorithms for exact and approximate square counts were proposed [9,11,14], whose time complexity is $\mathcal{O}(\sum_{v \in V(G)} d(v)^2)$ (where $d(v)$ stands for the degree of vertex v). However, those algorithms only attain that complexity for bipartite graphs or only return the global count when sometimes we are interested in the local count. Pentagon counting is an even less studied topic [9,15]; however, the mentioned papers only give the global count. Furthermore, those methods have a high running time complexity of $\mathcal{O}(n^4)$ when the graph is dense. Thus, it is clear the necessity to develop faster methods for counting the number of squares and pentagons both globally and locally in large-scale real-world networks.

In this work, we propose an $\mathcal{O}(\alpha n^2)$ time algorithm to approximately counting the local and global number of squares and pentagons by using spectral graph theory [12,13]. In the time complexity above, the factor α can be both fixed or seen as a function of n and a precision parameter $1/\varepsilon$, which is $o(n/\varepsilon)$. We consider an undirected graph $G = (V, E)$ with adjacency matrix $\mathbf{A}$. A *closed walk* (i.e. a walk that starts and end in the same vertex) of length k is denoted by k-walk. We denominate k–gons to cycles (closed walks with no repeated vertex except for the first and last) of length k. By using this notation, squares and pentagons are 4-gons and 5-gons respectively. We also use $|G_{C_4}|$ and $|G_{C_5}|$ to denote the number of different squares and pentagons in a graph respectively. Recall that two cycles C_1 and C_2 are considered different if G induced by each of them are not isomorphic.

The paper is organized as follows: In Sect. 2, two algorithms are proposed. The first one is the EIGEN-K-WALKS algorithm, which is used to approximately counting the number of k–walks present in a given graph. The second one is the EIGEN-LOCAL-K-WALKS algorithm that counts the number of k–walks that contain a given vertex. In Sect. 3, the number of squares and pentagons for any graph are expressed in terms of the number of k–walks on the graph (for every vertex and the total number), where k varies depending on the situation. These formulas are then used to derive the algorithms to approximately counting the structures of interest. In Sect. 4 we perform some experiments with 3 real-world networks. The conclusions are then presented in Sect. 5.

2   Proposed Method

In order to obtain an efficient method for counting squares and pentagons on a graph G with adjacency matrix $\mathbf{A}$, we make use of the following property:

$$\text{Tr}(\mathbf{A}^k) = \sum_{i=1}^{n} \lambda_i^k \tag{1}$$

Where $\lambda_1, \lambda_2, \ldots, \lambda_n$ are the eigenvalues of the adjacency matrix $\mathbf{A}$. Note that $\mathrm{Tr}(\mathbf{A}^k)$ is the total number of k–walks in the graph G. This fact was used in [12] to efficiently count triangles in a graph. In this work, we use it to extend the methods proposed in [12] and develop algorithms for counting squares and pentagons globally.

We also developed an efficient method to count the approximate number of squares and pentagons by vertex. To accomplish such tasks we used the following property:

$$\mathbf{A}^k = \sum_{i=1}^{n} \lambda_i^k \mathbf{u}_i^\top \mathbf{u}_i \tag{2}$$

Where $\mathbf{u}_i$ is the eigenvector corresponding to the i-th eigenvalue λ_i of $\mathbf{A}$. Notice that the i-th entry of the diagonal of the matrix $\mathbf{A}^k$ contains the total number of k-walks which start and end in vertex i. This property was also used in [12] to obtain the approximate number of triangles per vertex, and we use it to approximate the number of squares and pentagons for each vertex.

2.1   Proposed Algorithms

We first propose a generalization of the triangle counting and local triangle counting proposed in [12] to count the number of k–walks in a graph G; namely, the EIGEN-K-WALKS and EIGEN-LOCAL-K-WALKS algorithms.

Algorithm 1: The EIGEN-K-WALKS algorithm

Require: Graph G
Require: Integer k
Require: Precision ε
Output: $\Delta_k'(G)$ global k–walks estimation
Let $\mathbf{A}$ be the adjacency matrix of G
$\lambda_1 \leftarrow LanczosMethod(\mathbf{A}, 1)$
$\vec{\Lambda} \leftarrow [\lambda_1]$
$i \leftarrow 2$
do
$\quad \Big| \quad \lambda_i \leftarrow LanczosMethod(\mathbf{A}, i)$
$\quad \Big| \quad \vec{\Lambda} \leftarrow [\vec{\Lambda}\ \lambda_i]$
$\quad \Big| \quad i \leftarrow i + 1$
until $0 \leq \dfrac{|\lambda_i^k|}{sum_{j=1}^{i} \lambda_j^k} \leq \varepsilon$
$\Delta_k'(G) \leftarrow \sum_{j=1}^{i} \lambda_j^k$
return $\Delta_k'(G)$

As observed, the algorithm first receives a simple graph G, an integer k, and a precision parameter ϵ as input. It then uses the well known Lanczos Method to find the "most useful" eigenvalues [12] (the concept is made by using the ε

parameter). It then returns the sum of the k-th powers of the found eigenvalues as an estimate of the number of k-walks in G.

We now state the second algorithm:

Algorithm 2: The EIGEN-LOCAL-K-WALKS algorithm

Require: Graph G
Require: Integer k
Require: Tolerance ε
Output: $\vec{\Delta}'_k(G)$ per vertex k–walk estimation
Let $\mathbf{A}$ be the adjacency matrix of G
$\langle \lambda_1, \vec{u}_1 \rangle \leftarrow LanczosMethod(\mathbf{A}, 1)$
$\vec{\Lambda} \leftarrow [\lambda_1]$
$\mathbf{U} \leftarrow [\vec{u}_1]$
$i \leftarrow 2$
do
$\quad \langle \lambda_i, \vec{u}_i \rangle \leftarrow LanczosMethod(\mathbf{A}, i)$
$\quad \vec{\Lambda} \leftarrow [\vec{\Lambda} \ \lambda_i]$
$\quad \mathbf{U} \leftarrow [\mathbf{U} \ \vec{u}_I]$
$\quad i \leftarrow i + 1$
until $0 \leq \dfrac{|\lambda_i^k|}{\sum_{j=1}^{i} \lambda_j^k} \leq \epsilon$
for $j = 1$ *to* n **do**
$\quad \Delta'_j \leftarrow \sum_{r=1}^{i} \lambda_r^k u_{jr}^2$
end
$\vec{\Delta}'_k(G) \leftarrow [\Delta'_1, \ldots, \Delta'_n]$
return $\vec{\Delta}_k^{\,\prime}(G)$

As in the previous case, the algorithm receives a simple graph G, an integer k, and a tolerance parameter ϵ as input.

We can efficiently obtain the i-th eigenpair (eigenvalue and eigenvector) of $\mathbf{A}$ the subroutine $LanczosMethod$ as in [12]. Notice that we could use the power iteration method [7] instead of the Lanczos method to obtain the i-th eigenpair of the matrix. However, the Lanczos method is well suited for large matrices and has minimal memory requirements [4].

The efficiency of our method is based on the fact that eigenvalues of real-world networks follow a power law property [1,12]. The computational complexity to obtain the i-th eigenpair with the Lanczos method is $\mathcal{O}(n^2)$, where n is the number of vertices of graph G. So, if α eigenpairs are needed for a fixed tolerance of ε, then the total running time of our proposed method is $O(\alpha n^2)$.

In the following sections, we use both the EIGEN-K-WALKS and EIGEN-LOCAL-K-WALKS algorithms to obtain the approximate number of squares and pentagons in a graph.

3   Counting Squares and Pentagons

3.1   Squares

In order to count the number of squares on G, we take the number of 4–walks on it and subtract the number of those that do not form a square from it. Since the maximum number of traversed edges in a 4–walk is 4, we can construct every possible substructure of G with at most 4 edges searching for those that can be formed by a 4–walk. For each of these substructures that are present on G, we subtract the number of 4–walks that form the substructure. There are two substructures that can be formed by 4–walks but that are not squares. The first one is the raw edge since starting from a vertex, we can traverse it 4 times and reach the same vertex.

The number of 4–walks that form the structure on the left is:

$$\text{Tr}\begin{bmatrix}0 & 1\\1 & 0\end{bmatrix}^{4} = \text{Tr}\begin{bmatrix}1 & 0\\0 & 1\end{bmatrix} = 2.$$

For every present edge, it is necessary to remove the number of 4–walks on it, i.e., discount $2|E|$ from the total.

The second structure that can be formed by a 4–walk is:

The number of 4–walks that form the structure on the left is:

$$\text{Tr}\begin{bmatrix}0 & 1 & 0\\1 & 0 & 1\\0 & 1 & 0\end{bmatrix}^{4} = \text{Tr}\begin{bmatrix}2 & 0 & 2\\0 & 4 & 0\\2 & 0 & 2\end{bmatrix} = 8.$$

To prevent over-counting (we have already considered the edges separately), we discount 2 units for every edge of the structure. That gives 4 possible 4–walks that form the structure. To count the number of occurrences of this structure in the graph, it is sufficient to look at the degree of every vertex. If some vertex v has a degree of at least 2, that means that it can be considered the "middle point" of the searched structure. More precisely, a vertex v is the central point of $\binom{d(v)}{2}$ of these structures. Hence, we discount $4 \times \binom{d(v)}{2}$ from the total so far for every vertex v of G.

It is trivial to show that there is no structure with three edges that can be formed by a 4–walk. The only possible structure with four edges formed by a 4–walk is the square [2,5]. The last thing to consider is that every square can be formed by many 4-walks considering starting vertex and direction (8 in total). For this reason, we divide the remaining number by the total number of possibilities. With this information, the number of squares on any graph G is:

$$|G_{C_4}| = \frac{1}{8} \left(\mathrm{Tr}A^4 - 2|E| - \sum_{v \in V(G)} 4 \times \binom{d(v)}{2} \right)$$

$$= \frac{1}{8} \left(\mathrm{Tr}A^4 - 2|E| - 2 \sum_{v \in V(G)} d(v)\,(d(v) - 1) \right). \tag{3}$$

The correctness of this result follows from the previous discussion.

We then propose the EIGEN-SQUARES and EIGEN-LOCAL-SQUARES algorithms to count the total number of squares in a graph and the number of squares per-vertex respectively.

Algorithm 3: The EIGEN-SQUARES algorithm

Require: Graph G
Require: Precision ε
Output: $\Delta'_S(G)$ global square count estimation
$\Delta'_4(G) \leftarrow$ EIGEN-K-WALKS$(G, 4, \varepsilon)$
$\Delta'_S(G) \leftarrow \left(\Delta'_4(G) - 2|E| - 2\sum_{v \in V(G)} d(v) \times (d(v) - 1) \right) / 8$
return $\Delta'_S(G)$

Algorithm 4: The EIGEN-LOCAL-SQUARES algorithm

Require: Graph G
Require: Precision ε
Output: $\vec{\Delta}'_{squares}(G)$ squares per vertex estimation
$\vec{\Delta}'_4(G) \leftarrow$ EIGEN-LOCAL-K-WALKS$(G, 4, \varepsilon)$
for $j = 1$ *to* n **do**
$\quad \Delta'_{S,j} \leftarrow \left(\vec{\Delta}'_{4,j}(G) - d(j) * (d(j) - 1) \sum_{v \in |} (d(v) - 1) \right) / 2$
end
$\vec{\Delta}'_S(G) \leftarrow [\Delta'_1, \ldots, \Delta'_n]$
return $\vec{\Delta}'_S(G)$

3.2   Pentagons

As in the previous case, to count the number of pentagons in G, we can consider all 5–walks present on G and subtract those that do not form a pentagon. There are again two possible substructures that can be formed by a 5–walk that is not a pentagon. The first one is the triangle. Let $|G_{C_3}|$ be the number of triangles in G.

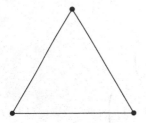

The number of 5–walks that form a triangle is:

$$\mathrm{Tr}\begin{bmatrix}0\ 1\ 1\\1\ 0\ 1\\1\ 1\ 0\end{bmatrix}^5 = \mathrm{Tr}\begin{bmatrix}10\ 11\ 11\\11\ 10\ 11\\11\ 11\ 10\end{bmatrix} = 30.$$

For every triangle, we discount the number of 5–walks that form it (i.e., 30) from the total. Since the number of triangles in G is $\mathrm{Tr}A^3/6$, we discount a total of $5\mathrm{Tr}A^3$ for this structure.

The second structure that can be formed by 5–walks is:

The number of 5-walks that form the structure in the left is:

$$\mathrm{Tr}\begin{bmatrix}0\ 1\ 0\ 0\\1\ 0\ 1\ 1\\0\ 1\ 0\ 1\\0\ 1\ 1\ 0\end{bmatrix}^5 = \mathrm{Tr}\begin{bmatrix}2\ 11\ 6\ 6\\11\ 14\ 17\ 17\\6\ 17\ 12\ 13\\6\ 17\ 13\ 12\end{bmatrix} = 40.$$

However, since this structure contains one triangle, and 5-walks involving just triangles are being considered separately; we ignore those from the calculation, getting 10 5-walks that form the structure. Notice for this case that the central vertex, i.e. the one with degree 3, has two useful properties: first, it always belongs to some triangle; and second, every 5–walk that forms the structure visits it at least once. This fact means that any vertex v that is part of a triangle and having a degree greater than 2 is the central vertex of at least one structure identical to the shown above (in fact, it is the central point of exactly $d(v) - 2$ of them for each triangle to which vertex v belongs to). So, for every vertex v, we discount $10 \times \mathrm{nt}(v) \times (d(v) - 2)$ from the total answer, where $\mathrm{nt}(v)$ is the number of triangles in which the vertex v is part.

It can be easily shown that these are the only structures that can be formed by 5-walks other than pentagons [2,5]. As in the previous case, every pentagon can be formed by many 5-walks considering starting vertex and direction. Therefore, we divide the remaining number by the number of these possibilities. This is enough to calculate the number of pentagons present in G:

$$|G_{C_5}| = \frac{1}{10}\left(\mathrm{Tr}A^5 - 30|G_{C_3}| - \sum_{v \in K_3 \subseteq G} 10 \times (d(v) - 2)\right)$$

$$= \frac{1}{10}\left(\mathrm{Tr}A^5 - 5\mathrm{Tr}A^3 - 10\sum_{v \in G_{K_3} \subseteq G}(d(v) - 2)\right). \tag{4}$$

$$= \frac{1}{10} \left(\mathrm{Tr} A^5 - 5\mathrm{Tr} A^3 - 5 \sum_{v \in G_{W_3} \subseteq G} (d(v) - 2) \right) \tag{5}$$

where G_{K_3} denotes the set of all triangles in G, and G_{W_3} denotes the set of all 3-walks in G.

The correctness of the result follows from the previous discussion. Note that $|G_{K_3}| = |G_{W_3}|/2$ since starting from a vertex, a triangle can be constructed from 2 3-walks: one going clockwise, and the other going counterclockwise.

We then propose the EIGEN-PENTAGONS algorithm to count the total number of pentagons in a graph and the EIGEN-LOCAL-PENTAGONS algorithms to count the number of pentagons per vertex.

Algorithm 5: The EIGEN-PENTAGONS algorithm

Require: Graph G
Require: Tolerance ε
Output: $\Delta'_P(G)$ global pentagon count estimation
$\Delta'_5(G) \leftarrow$ EIGEN-K-WALKS$(G, 5, \varepsilon)$
$\Delta'_3(G) \leftarrow$ EIGEN-K-WALKS$(G, 3, \varepsilon)$
$\vec{\Delta}'_3(G) \leftarrow$ EIGEN-K-LOCAL-WALKS$(G, 3, \varepsilon)$
$\Delta'_P(G) \leftarrow \left(\Delta'_5(G) - 5\Delta'_3(G) - 5\sum_{v \in V(G)} \vec{\Delta}'_{3,v}(G)(d(v) - 2) \right) / 10$
return $\Delta'_P(G)$

Algorithm 6: The EIGEN-LOCAL-PENTAGONS algorithm

Require: Graph G
Require: Tolerance ε
Output: $\vec{\Delta}'_P(G)$ pentagons per vertex estimation
$\vec{\Delta}'_5(G) \leftarrow$ EIGEN-K-LOCAL-WALKS$(G, 5, \varepsilon)$
$\vec{\Delta}'_3(G) \leftarrow$ EIGEN-K-LOCAL-WALKS$(G, 3, \varepsilon)$
for $j = 1$ *to* n **do**
$\quad \Delta'_{pentagons,j} \leftarrow [\vec{\Delta}'_{5,j}(G) - 10\Delta'_{3,j}(G) - 4\vec{\Delta}'_{3,j}(G)(d(j) - 2) -$
$\quad 2\sum_{u,v \in \mathcal{N}(j)} ((d(u) + d(v) - 4))\delta(u, v)] / 2$
end
$\vec{\Delta}'_P(G) \leftarrow [\Delta'_1, \ldots, \Delta'_n]$
return $\vec{\Delta}_P{}'(G)$

Where $\delta(u, v) = 1$ if $(u, v) \in G$ and zero otherwise.

4 Experiments

In order to show the accuracy of the estimates for the proposed method. We executed it in 3 real-world networks obtained from https://snap.stanford.edu/data/:

- **Facebook ego network:** This network represents a small subset of the friendship relationship from Facebook. It consists of $4,093$ vertices and $88,234$ edges. Each vertex represents a user and each edge represents the connection between its endpoints (friendship).
- **Enron Email exchange network:** This network represents e-mail exchanges between different e-mail users. It consists of 36692 vertices and $183,831$ edges.
- **Condensed Matter collaboration network of Arxiv:** This network represents the scientific collaborations between authors of papers submitted to the Condense Matter category of Arxiv. It consists of $4,093$ vertices and $88,234$ edges (Table 1 and 2).

Table 1. Signed percent error, the runtime in second of the exact and approximate method, and the number of eigenvalues required to achieve the tolerance 10^{-6} obtained for three real-world networks counting the number of squares.

	$|V|$	$|E|$	Percent error	Exact time	Approx. time	Eigenvalues
Facebook	4039	88234	−1.28	0.94	0.33	19
Condensed matter	23133	186936	−31.48	132.97	25.14	196
Email Enron	36692	367662	−11.41	701.40	3.11	60

Table 2. Signed percent error, the runtime in second of the exact and approximate method, and the number of eigenvalues required to achieve the tolerance 10^{-3} obtained for three real-world networks counting the number of pentagons.

	$|V|$	$|E|$	Percent error	Exact time	Approx. time	Eigenvalues
Facebook	4039	88234	−0.46	1.72	0.33	10
Condensed matter	23133	186936	−8.71	318.47	1.41	129
Email Enron	36692	367662	−1.22	1568.12	1.42	128

To make all the experiments we used a computer with 12 Intel(R) Core(TM) i7-3960X CPU @ 3.30 GHz processors and 48 GB of RAM. We obtained the exact and approximate number of squares and pentagons of the three real-world networks. In all cases, the tolerance values ε were fixed to 10^{-3}. We also report the number of eigenvalues that were necessary to achieve the ε tolerance.

Notice that in both cases, the number of eigenvalues required to attain the tolerance is much lower than the number of vertices of the graphs. This indicates that we were able to estimate the number of squares and pentagons of large graphs in quasiquadratic time. Notice also that the approximations obtained by our proposed algorithm are very close to the exact values (for the given ε value). This indicates that for these kinds of networks, the number of relevant eigenvalues to consider to get a good approximation is significantly small. The downside of this method is the memory it required. For instance, the largest graph already occupied 23 GB of memory during the execution. Thus, larger networks would require significantly larger amounts of memory.

5 Conclusions

In this work, we proposed a method to approximate the global and local number of squares and pentagons in a network in $\mathcal{O}(\alpha n^2)$ time, where $\alpha = o(n)$. We also showed experimentally how our method is capable to efficiently compute good approximations for the counts by using 3 real-world networks. It was observed that the number of eigenpairs that the proposed algorithms need (i.e., the value α) is, in practice, sublinear in n and in $1/\varepsilon$.

As future works, we plan to extend the experiments for even larger networks and to implement parallel versions of the proposed algorithms. An interesting path is also to explore trace of function matrices in order to count some other short-cycles. Given that the main drawback of the presented method is the memory needed for its execution, it is also an interesting option to develop faster methods to count the number of squares and pentagons by exploiting the graph sparsity, hence saving on memory.

References

1. Al Hasan, M., Dave, V.S.: Triangle counting in large networks: a review. Wiley Interdisciplinary Rev. Data Min. Knowl. Dis. **8**(2) (2018)
2. Alon, N., Yuster, R., Zwick, U.: Finding and counting given length cycles. Algorithmica **17**(3), 209–223 (1997). https://doi.org/10.1007/BF02523189
3. Coppersmith, D., Winograd, S.: Matrix multiplication via arithmetic progressions. J. Symb. Comput. **9**(3), 251–280 (1990)
4. Cullum, J.K., Willoughby, R.A.: Lanczos Algorithms for Large Symmetric Eigenvalue Computations: Volume 1 Theory, vol. 41. SIAM (2002)
5. Harary, F., Manvel, B.: On the number of cycles in a graph. Matematický časopis **21**(1), 55–63 (1971)
6. Liu, Q., Dong, Z., Wang, E.: Moment-based spectral analysis of large-scale generalized random graphs. IEEE Access **5**, 9453–9463 (2017)
7. Mises, R., Pollaczek-Geiringer, H.: Praktische verfahren der gleichungsauflösung. ZAMM-J. Appl. Math. Mech./Zeitschrift für Angewandte Mathematik und Mechanik **9**(2), 152–164 (1929)
8. Newman, M.: Networks. Oxford University Press, Oxford (2018)
9. Paranjape, A., Benson, A.R., Leskovec, J.: Motifs in temporal networks. In: Proceedings of the Tenth ACM International Conference on Web Search and Data Mining, pp. 601–610 (2017)
10. Preciado, V.M., Jadbabaie, A.: Moment-based spectral analysis of large-scale networks using local structural information. IEEE/ACM Trans. Networking (TON) **21**(2), 373–382 (2013)
11. Sanei-Mehri, S.V., Sariyuce, A.E., Tirthapura, S.: Butterfly counting in bipartite networks. In: Proceedings of the 24th ACM SIGKDD International Conference on Knowledge Discovery and Data Mining, pp. 2150–2159. ACM (2018)

12. Tsourakakis, C.E.: Fast counting of triangles in large real networks: Algorithms and laws. cis. temple. edu, pp. 608–617 (2008)
13. Van Mieghem, P.: Graph Spectra for Complex Networks. Cambridge University Press, Cambridge (2010)
14. Wang, J., Fu, A.W.C., Cheng, J.: Rectangle counting in large bipartite graphs. In: 2014 IEEE International Congress on Big Data, pp. 17–24. IEEE (2014)
15. Wang, P., et al.: MOSS-5: a fast method of approximating counts of 5-node graphlets in large graphs. IEEE Trans. Knowl. Data Eng. **30**(1), 73–86 (2017)

Identifying Covid-19 Impact on Peruvian Mental Health During Lockdown Using Social Network

Josimar E. Chire Saire[1]([✉]) [iD] and Jimy Frank Oblitas Cruz[2] [iD]

[1] Institute of Mathematics and Computer Science (ICMC), University of São Paulo
(USP), São Carlos, SP, Brazil
jecs89@usp.br
[2] Facultad de Ingeniería, Universidad Privada del Norte, Trujillo, Peru
jimy.oblitas@upn.edu.pe

Abstract. The actual outbreak generated by SARS-CoV-2, presented a challenge to the governments because PublicS Health, Economy, and Society are different in every country so actions must fit considering these previous conditions. South America is a region with developing countries, limitations, problems and the pandemic highlighted them. Peru is a country with good initial policies to contain the pandemic, a lockdown started on March 15 and lasted more than 100 days. By consequence, people were forced to change daily activities and of course, social and mental problems started to grow. The actual study wants to identify the covid-19 impact on the Social Network, Twitter filtering posts related to the topic. The initial findings present a high interest in the topic during the first week and a decreasing pattern in the last weeks.

Keywords: Natural language processing · Text mining · Social network · Twitter · People behaviour · Coronavirus · Covid-19 · Pandemic · Peru · South America · Latin America

1 Introduction

Until June 14 2020, around 7.840.408 COVID-19 cases and 431.236 deaths have been reported [1]. Some countries have a significant overflow of their national health systems, while others have mitigated the crisis impact by implementing diverse policies to contain the spread of the virus: school closures, physical distancing, cancellation of mass events, restriction on the movement of individuals, and border closures, among others [2]. However, all these measures and the generalized pandemic situation itself are causing a great impact on people's mental health around the world. Regarding this, the forceful emergency calling made by diverse international organizations on the need to make greater efforts to assist people's mental health and, particularly, the most vulnerable people are not by chance [3].

© Springer Nature Switzerland AG 2021
J. A. Lossio-Ventura et al. (Eds.): SIMBig 2020, CCIS 1410, pp. 471–483, 2021.
https://doi.org/10.1007/978-3-030-76228-5_34

Fear, worry, and stress are normal responses to perceived or real threats, so it is normal and understandable that people are experiencing fear in the context of the COVID-19 pandemic. In Peru, mental health issues have also been reported in health care workers, especially among female professionals, nurses, and those who work directly with suspected or confirmed cases of COVID-19.

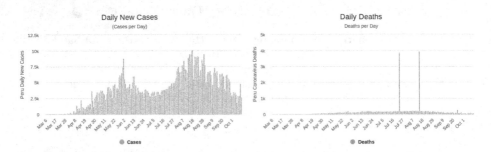

Fig. 1. Covid-19 daily cases and death - Peru, image generated from available tool of https://virusncov.com/covid-statistics/peru

The outlook of mental health has suffered dramatic changes during the last two decades, but the research on mental health is still in its initial period with substantial knowledge gaps and the lack of an accurate diagnosis. Currently, big data and artificial intelligence offer new opportunities to detect and predict mental problems [4].

About 80 percent of Internet users have searched for online health information [5]. During the pandemic lockdown and under the strict social distancing restrictions, people are more reliant on the Internet than ever before and therefore are likely to instigate increased Internet search if they undergo mental health issues.

In order to help public health and to make better decisions regarding Public Health and to help with their monitoring, Twitter has demonstrated to be an important information source related to health on the Internet, due to the volume of information shared by citizens and official sources. Twitter provides researchers an information source on public health, in real time and globally. Thus, it could be very important for public health research [6].

Within the context of COVID 19, users from all over the world may use it to identify quickly the main thoughts, attitudes, feelings, and matters in their minds regarding this pandemic. This may help those in charge to make policies, health professionals, and citizens to identify the main problems that concern everybody and deal with them more properly [7].

Data in Peru also show preliminary symptoms in targeted populations, such as police officers, where the presence of symptoms that could deteriorate their mental health is shown [8]. This, along with other social groups, such as education and commerce, could have effects on their mental health. In addition, none of the institutions was prepared to deal with the mental health problems experienced by its members due to the COVID-19 pandemic.

According to the Peruvian Ministry of Health, an average of 70 Peruvians have been affected in their mental health. These initial studies report high values in concepts of anxiety. Also, this institution developed strategies, such as call centers to address these cases that Peruvians relate to stress due to COVID 19. Likewise, the study states that these symptoms are caused by uncertainty. Along with this, the World Health Organization (WHO) warned that COVID-19 Pandemic will have consequences for mental health in the future [9], with a possible increase in suicides and disorders, and urged governments not to neglect psychological care.

The advantages of detection and communication technologies allow to detect and collect subtle signs and to offer data on a large scale for digital preliminary exploration on mental health. This research is aimed to determine the level of impact of social isolation due to COVID-19 by using digital information.

The remainder of the paper follows. Section 2 presents related works regarding the retrieval of infectious diseases information from social media. In Sect. 3, the data collection methodology for extracting relevant information of Covid-19 from Twitter is presented. Section 4 describes experimental findings and a discussion related to the analysis. Finally, conclusions and future work are described in Sect. 5.

2   Related Work

Surveillance pretends to observe what happens over one population, region, or city to support on Politics Decisions. Cost and time are advantages because usually surveys have two components: collection and processing, both can spend many days, even months.

Sinnenberg [10] performs a study about Twitter as a tool for Research on Public Health, is necessary to highlight researchers uses traditional databases for studies and Twitter can provide useful data from people. From 137 papers for the review, research fields as Public health (31), infectious disease (28).

Breland [11] express in Social Media people create content, exchange information, and use this tool for communication. A four benefits from the use: a) disseminate Research on the Public Health field, b) fight against misinformation, c) influence policies, d) aid Public Health Research, and e) enhance professional development. And Yepes [12] can support the affirmation: Twitter is a source from useful data for surveillance, considering relevant terms and geographical locations.

More applications using Twitter and Natural Language Processing are found: monitor H1N1 flu [13], Dengue in Brazil [14], covid-19 symptomatology in Colombia [15], covid-19 infoveillance in South America countries [16] and monitor City of Mexico [17]

Finally, Ear [18] found, Peruvian Internal Agencies have overlapping functions so this can limit collaboration, there is not enough technical capacity and resources outside the capital, Lima. Besides, cultural diversity and geographical issues can present challenges to fight against one disease infection. Therefore, the use of an infoveillance tool based on Text Mining can provide support to the government and the creation of public policies

3   Methodology

The data collection and processing procedures were conducted to support an analysis process of the situation in Peru. In particular, we carried out the following steps:

- Select the relevant terms related to covid-19 pandemic
- Set the parameters to collect related posts
- Pre-processing
- Visualization

To see the sequence of steps, Fig. 2 is presented.

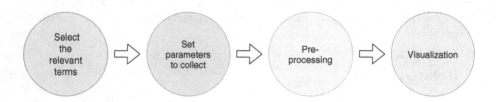

Fig. 2. Methodology used for the present study

The next subsections explain in detail each step of the methodology.

3.1   Select Relevant Terms

The main topic of the study is about covid-19 pandemic. Then, the source to obtain data to conduct the study is Twitter, because this Social Network provides affordable access to posts' users.

Therefore to collect tweets, terms related to coronavirus are useful to select posts related to the pandemic. After a preliminary search, the next finding was verified: users do not follow good writing and exist many variations. For the previous reason, the selected terms are:

- 'coronavirus', 'corona_virus', '#coronavirus', '@coronavirus'
- 'covid19', 'covid-19', '#covid-19', '@covid19', '@covid_19'

3.2   Build the Query and Collect Data

Twitter has access to tweets/posts through an Application programming interface (API), then to do a query a set of parameters are necessary. For this application, the next setting is used:

- date: 03-08-2020 to 30-06-2020
- terms: the chosen words mentioned in previous Subsect. 3.1
- geolocalization: -12.05, -77.050000, Lima (capital of Peru)
- language: Spanish
- radius: around 50 km

The official language in Peru is Spanish, then most of the population uses this language for daily communication. The chosen radius was selected using the proposed radius in a study focused on South American capitals [16].

3.3   Preprocessing Data

Users do not follow good writing suggestions/recommendations then there are many variations of how they write, using emoticons, special characters, and more. The preprocessing cleans the text for the next step, where filtering operators are used to support analysis.

  Clean urls/links, using regulars expression this text can be removed, i.e. $https? : \backslash S+$
- Clean emoticons, special characters, and numbers. Considering letters and number has a related Unicode format. It is possible to clean them using regular expressions.
- Convert uppercase to lowercase, i.e. Peru to peru, Lima to lima
- Remove stopwords, i.e. articles: el (the), la (the) and pronouns: el (he), ella (she)

3.4   Visualization

The study wants to identify what people were talking about during the pandemic. Considering terms related to Mental Health. Then a filtering step is performed using these terms: ansiedad (anxiety), miedo (fear), muerte (death), salud mental (mental health), estres (stress), familia (family).

Besides, a division of weeks is done to have the evolution weekly from March to June, see Table 1. The previous consideration is used to create a bar plot graphic which is presented in the next Sect. 4. This graphic is generated using the ranges and counting the number of posts with the related terms of study.

4   Results and Discussion

This section presents the results of the experiments performed in the collected data and the discussion of them is introduced.

Table 1. Weeks and range

Week	Range
1	2020-03-08', '2020-03-14'
2	2020-03-15', '2020-03-21'
3	2020-03-22', '2020-03-28'
4	2020-03-29', '2020-04-04'
5	2020-04-05', '2020-04-11'
6	2020-04-12', '2020-04-18'
7	2020-04-19', '2020-04-25'
8	2020-04-26', '2020-05-02'
9	2020-05-03', '2020-05-09'
10	2020-05-10', '2020-05-16'
11	2020-05-17', '2020-05-23'
12	2020-05-24', '2020-05-30'
13	2020-05-31', '2020-06-06'
14	2020-06-07', '2020-06-13'
15	2020-06-14', '2020-06-20'
16	2020-06-21', '2020-06-27'
17	2020-06-28', '2020-06-30'

4.1   Dataset Description

The Fig. 3 is presented to show the number of publications during the period of study. The collected data have the next features:

- Number of tweets: 4,268,057
- Number of unique users: 284,620
- Fields: date (YYYY-MM-DD-HH-MM-SS), text, user_name
- Range date: 08 March to 30 June
- Language: Spanish

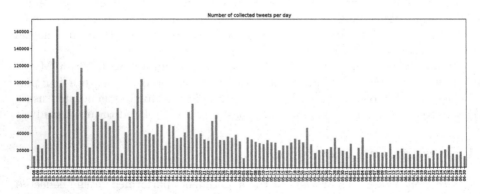

Fig. 3. Number of collected tweets daily

4.2   What Is the Covid-19 Impact on Peruvian Mental Health?

The question is an actual concern because after being during many weeks at home. This was a consequence of severe lockdown established by the Peruvian government. The objective was to reduce the flow of people and decrease the rate of infections. The lockdown started after the second week of March and continue during the next four months. This isolation can produce different behaviors, feelings in the citizens. Therefore considering this previous scenario, the paper aims to know how Peruvian users reacted to this topic.

The filtering step is performed to select the content related to mental health, the terms were mentioned in Visualization subsection previously. And a division of time using the week ranges presented in the subsection of Visualization above.

The findings reported in Fig. 5 show words such as "anxiety", "fear" , "death", "stress", and a great fear of the family future. Precisely, this agrees with researches made until now where stress, anxiety, depression, sleep disorders, fear, negation, distress, and anger are the most outstanding symptoms of this pandemic [19].

As the graph shows the terms related to anxiety, fear, death, and family are more strongly present in the first 6 weeks of the study, which are related to news trends that the state of the health emergency would continue and an economic impact seen in the rate of unemployment. In the following weeks, there is a process of presence decrease on Twitter that is related to news trends, such as the appearance of vaccines and announcements related to Reactiva Peru. Helping the visualization from Monday to Sunday during the last seventeen weeks, a cloud of words is presented in Fig. 4.

Most tools for assessing mental health were developed in approaches that did not assess situations, such as a pandemic, and those that were conducted at this stage may not be sensitive enough to assess different mental health problems during this stage [20]. On the other hand, the scales were validated on the targeted population, who are not necessarily the most vulnerable.

This kind of study with text-mining tools is focused on the use of Twitter where users have an age range between 35 to 49 years [21]. Although they are the ones who generate communication that can be used, it is also necessary to look for instruments focused on populations of children and adolescents. We know of the difficulties in evaluating children, but it is relevant how little consideration is given to adolescents [22].

Therefore, studies in different techniques are needed to obtain measures with properties that are more appropriate and sensitive to various interventions. This has made many countries establish diverse policies of attention to the people's psychological crisis, especially focusing on people infected by COVID-19, front-line health workers and people who could be infected [23].

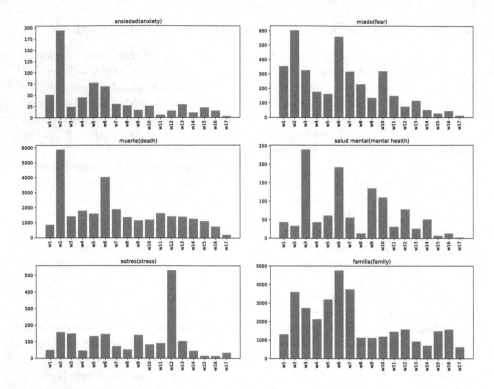

Fig. 4. Evolution of tweets frequency during seventeen weeks, from March - June

Such early determinations using data mining become powerful social sensors in a situation like the Pandemic we live in today, considering that there are many different social groups with different behaviors and reactions. The Peruvian Ministry of Health shows a curve of social adaptation that involves a process of rebellion, generating the perception of a fragmented, individualistic society with a high selfish sense, which aggravates the feeling of anxiety in Peruvians.

Liang [24] shows this kind of information tools to measure the level of presence of certain thinking have constantly increased for topics related to mental health, showing the studies forming information technologies on mental health to offer more efficient, precise, automated methods for psychiatric evaluation and help, were drawing the attention of psychiatric researchers, information professionals, and engineers.

Besides, we can see this kind of tools may be effective to determine alerts in mental health situations. In Latin America, there are no tools to measure this problem [25], even more if a wide scope of measurement is required. The bibliography shows that only the Scale for the measurement of fear perception and magnitude of the issue has been developed in the Latin American context, but it is not easily applicable [19]. This must draw attention to psychometric research in the region, so that this field of health science may widen and include tools, such as Text Mining, for diagnosis and early alerts.

Among the strengths of using this tool can be mentioned the ease of administration and rating [26]. This makes it possible to develop studies on a large scale and in clinical contexts where time is limited. The dynamism of the pandemic confronts us with the need to have systematic, rapid, and consistent epidemiological data, and, for this purpose, this kind of instrument is presented as an excellent resource, especially for the elaboration of public policies on mental health [27]. However, it should be noted that they alone cannot exclusively guide decision-making on mental health.

Stressful life events, such as those instigated by the coronavirus pandemic, have a significant influence on an individual's psychological functioning and wellbeing and can be a catalyst for psychological problems including anxiety, confusion, social withdrawal, and depression [28]. In this situation of COVID 19, the World Health Organization has indicated the infection epicenter is in Latin America [29]. Thus, it is not clear how it could affect the evolution of the disease nor how mitigation measures will be carried out, but, anyway, a significant repercussion on mental health is foreseen. Besides, it is necessary to take into account that many countries of the region have taken diverse strong and early measures of strict quarantine, which also implies variability in terms of psychosocial affectation.

The COVID-19 pandemic is having monumental effects on the mental health and wellbeing of populations worldwide. With seemingly low capacity to respond, it is unclear how the world will deal with this looming mental health crisis. To minimize the impact of the pandemic, we must also address the substantial unmet mental health needs, with a focus on the most vulnerable.

The methodology used and the data generated in this study are clear points that must be taken into account by government institutions, since there is a part of the Peruvian population that requires information encouraging their capacity to trust and they can analyze, avoiding problems in Peruvian mental health.

It has been seen in many works that the use of data mining is suitable tools to measure topics related to the mental health approach linked to covid-19. Recent research shows that it is evident from the results that negative feelings are dominating tweets posted by people during this pandemic [30]. Therefore, it is feasible to implement a system based on text-mining to assess the general state of the feelings of Internet users and, therefore, monitor public health problems.

Fig. 5. Cloud of Word using bigrams (two terms)

5   Conclusions

In conclusion, text mining showed it reached the same preliminary conclusions on topics related to mental health as the instruments used in psychometrics. Even if both of them have advantages and disadvantages, text mining is showed as a fast option to make decisions on crisis times like the one we are living, and, at the same time, it represents a significant help for evaluating people's mental health during the development of COVID-19 pandemics. However, it is important to take into account this is an initial measure and programs and policies derived from these results should not be conditioned at all. Even if this kind of instruments allow an efficient and brief evaluation, it will be important to combine actions and policies with other supplies and diagnosis of the different study situations.

6   Future Work

Increasing the number of terms related to Mental Health and considering the evolution day by day and do a correlation with events that happened in Lima, can help to the analysis of the reaction of people in front of good news/bad news. Besides, it is possible to the analysis for women/men because people have different responses struggling with difficulties. Besides, the addition of data to create artificial data, i.e. social-economic can improve how deep the study is. And the inclusion of Google trends to compare how were the searches of Peruvian users around Mental Health terms, i.e. anxiety, fear, stress.

References

1. WHO: WHO Coronavirus Disease (COVID-19) Dashboard. https://covid19.who. int. Accessed 14 June 2020
2. Brouwer, E.D., Raimondi, D., Moreau, Y.: Modeling the COVID-19 outbreaks and the effectiveness of the containment measures adopted across countries. medRxiv, p. 2020.04.02.20046375, April 2020. https://doi.org/10.1101/2020.04.02.20046375, https://www.medrxiv.org/content/10.1101/2020.04.02.20046375v3
3. Chong Ng Kee Kwong, K., Mehta, P.R., Shukla, G., Mehta, A.R.: COVID-19, SARS and MERS: a neurological perspective. J. Clin. Neurosci. May 2020. https://doi.org/10.1016/j.jocn.2020.04.124, http://www.sciencedirect.com/science/article/pii/S0967586820311851
4. Feng, L.S., et al.: Psychological distress in the shadow of the COVID-19 pandemic: preliminary development of an assessment scale. Psychiatry Res. **291**, 113202, September 2020. https://doi.org/10.1016/j.psychres.2020.113202, http://www.sciencedirect.com/science/article/pii/S016517812031595X
5. Drias, H.H., Drias, Y.: Mining twitter data on covid-19 for sentiment analysis and frequent patterns discovery. medRxiv (2020). https://doi.org/10.1101/2020.05.08.20090464, https://www.medrxiv.org/content/early/2020/05/18/2020.05.08.20090464
6. Jordan, S.E., Hovet, S.E., Fung, I.C.H., Liang, H., Fu, K.W., Tse, Z.T.H.: Using Twitter for public health surveillance from monitoring and prediction to public response. Data **4**(1), 6 (2019). https://doi.org/10.3390/data4010006, https://www.mdpi.com/2306-5729/4/1/6
7. Abd-Alrazaq, A., Alhuwail, D., Househ, M., Hamdi, M., Shah, Z.: Top concerns of tweeters during the covid-19 pandemic: infoveillance study. J. Med. Internet Res. **22**(4), e19061 (2020). https://doi.org/10.2196/19016
8. Caycho-Rodriguez, T., Carbajal-Leon, C., Vilca, L.W., Heredia-Mongrut, J., Gallegos, M.: COVID-19 y salud mental en policías peruanos: resultados preliminares. ACTA MEDICA PERUANA **37**(3), October 2020. https://doi.org/10.35663/amp.2020.373.1503, https://amp.cmp.org.pe/index.php/AMP/article/view/1503
9. Diseases, T.L.I.: The intersection of COVID-19 and mental health. Lancet Infect. Dis. 0(0), October 2020. https://doi.org/10.1016/S1473-3099(20)30797-0, https://www.thelancet.com/journals/laninf/article/PIIS1473-3099(20)30797-0/abstract
10. Sinnenberg, L., Buttenheim, A.M., Padrez, K., Mancheno, C., Ungar, L., Merchant, R.M.: Twitter as a tool for health research: a systematic review. Am. J. Public Health **107**(1), e1–e8 (2017)

11. Breland, J.Y., Quintiliani, L.M., Schneider, K.L., May, C.N., Pagoto, S.: Social media as a tool to increase the impact of public health research. Am. J. Public Health **107**(12), 1890 (2017)

12. Yepes, A.J., MacKinlay, A., Han, B.: Investigating public health surveillance using twitter. Proc. BioNLP **15**, 164–170 (2015)

13. Chew, C., Eysenbach, G.: Pandemics in the age of twitter: content analysis of tweets during the 2009 H1N1 outbreak. PLoS ONE **5**(11), p14118 (2010)

14. Saire, J.E.C.: Building intelligent indicators to detect dengue epidemics in brazil using social networks. In: 2019 IEEE Colombian Conference on Applications in Computational Intelligence (ColCACI), pp. 1–5. IEEE (2019)

15. Saire, J.E.C., Navarro, R.C.: What is the people posting about symptoms related to coronavirus in bogota, colombia? arXiv preprint arXiv:2003.11159 (2020)

16. Chire Saire, J.E.: Infoveillance based on social sensors to analyze the impact of covid19 in South American population (2020). https://doi.org/10.1101/2020.04. 06.20055749

17. Chire Saire, J.E., Pineda-Briseno, A.: Text mining approach to analyze coronavirus impact: Mexico city as case of study. medRxiv (2020). https://doi.org/10. 1101/2020.05.07.20094466, https://www.medrxiv.org/content/early/2020/05/12/ 2020.05.07.20094466

18. Ear, S.: Towards effective emerging infectious diseases surveillance: evidence from Kenya, Peru, Thailand, and the U.S.-Mexico (2012). https:// siepr.stanford.edu/research/publications/towards-effective-emerging-infectious-diseases-surveillanceevidence-kenya-peru

19. Huarcaya-Victoria, J.: Consideraciones sobre la salud mental en la pandemia de COVID-19. Revista Peruana de Medicina Experimental y Salud Pública **37**(2), 327–34, April 2020. https://doi.org/10.17843/rpmesp.2020.372.5419, https:// rpmesp.ins.gob.pe/index.php/rpmesp/article/view/5419

20. Lee, S.A.: Coronavirus anxiety scale: a brief mental health screener for COVID-19 related anxiety. Death Stud. **44**(7), 393–401 (2020). https://doi.org/10.1080/ 07481187.2020.1748481

21. Singh, P., Dwivedi, Y.K., Kahlon, K.S., Sawhney, R.S., Alalwan, A.A., Rana, N.P.: Smart monitoring and controlling of government policies using social media and cloud computing. Inf. Syst. Front. **22**(2), 315–337 (2020). https://doi.org/10.1007/ s10796-019-09916-y

22. Ayyoubzadeh, S.M., Ayyoubzadeh, S.M., Zahedi, H., Ahmadi, M., Kalhori, S.R.N.: Predicting COVID-19 incidence through analysis of google trends data in Iran: data mining and deep learning pilot study. JMIR Public Health Surv. 6(2), e18828 (2020). https://doi.org/10.2196/18828, https://publichealth.jmir.org/ 2020/2/e18828/, company: JMIR Public Health and Surveillance Distributor: JMIR Public Health and Surveillance Institution: JMIR Public Health and Surveillance Label: JMIR Public Health and Surveillance Publisher: JMIR Publications Inc., Toronto, Canada

23. Rajkumar, R.P.: COVID-19 and mental health: a review of the existing literature. Asian J. Psychiatry **52**, 102066, August 2020. https://doi.org/10.1016/j.ajp.2020. 102066, http://www.sciencedirect.com/science/article/pii/S1876201820301775

24. Liang, Y., Zheng, X., Zeng, D.D.: A survey on big data-driven digital phenotyping of mental health. Inf. Fusion **52**, 290–307, December 2019. https://doi.org/10.1016/j.inffus.2019.04.001, http://www.sciencedirect. com/science/article/pii/S1566253518305244

25. Mejia, C.R., et al.: The media and their informative role in the face of the coronavirus disease 2019 (COVID-19): validation of fear perception and magnitude of the issue (MED-COVID-19). Electron. J. General Med. **17**(6), em239, April 2020. https://doi.org/10.29333/ejgm/7946, https://www.ejgm.co.uk/article/the-media-and-their-informative-role-in-the-face-of-the-coronavirus-disease-2019-covid-19-validation-7946

26. de Melo, T., Figueiredo, C.M.S.: A first public dataset from Brazilian twitter and news on COVID-19 in Portuguese. Data Brief **32**, 106179, October 2020. https://doi.org/10.1016/j.dib.2020.106179, http://www.sciencedirect.com/science/article/pii/S2352340920310738

27. Zhang, T.: Data mining can play a critical role in COVID-19 linked mental health studies. Asian J. Psychiatry **54**, 102399, December 2020. https://doi.org/10.1016/j.ajp.2020.102399, http://www.sciencedirect.com/science/article/pii/S1876201820305128

28. Arslan, G., Yıldırım, M., Tanhan, A., Buluş, M., Allen, K.A.: Coronavirus stress, optimism-pessimism, psychological inflexibility, and psychological health: psychometric properties of the coronavirus stress measure. Int. J. Mental Health Addict. (2020). https://doi.org/10.1007/s11469-020-00337-6

29. Benítez, M.A., Velasco, C., Sequeira, A.R., Henríquez, J., Menezes, F.M., Paolucci, F.: Responses to COVID-19 in five Latin American countries. Health Policy Technol. August 2020. https://doi.org/10.1016/j.hlpt.2020.08.014, http://www.sciencedirect.com/science/article/pii/S2211883720300861

30. Singh, P., Singh, S., Sohal, M., Dwivedi, Y.K., Kahlon, K.S., Sawhney, R.S.: Psychological fear and anxiety caused by COVID-19: insights from Twitter analytics. Asian J. Psychiatry **54**, 102280, December 2020. https://doi.org/10.1016/j.ajp.2020.102280, https://covid19.elsevierpure.com/en/publications/psychological-fear-and-anxiety-caused-by-covid-19-insights-from-t

Diagnosis of SARS-CoV-2 Based on Patient Symptoms and Fuzzy Classifiers

Fray L. Becerra-Suarez[1,2(✉)] ⓘ, Heber I. Mejia-Cabrera[1] ⓘ,
Víctor A. Tuesta-Monteza[1] ⓘ, and Manuel G. Forero[3] ⓘ

[1] Laboratorio de Investigación en Sistemas Inteligentes y Seguridad Informática,
Universidad Señor de Sipán, Chiclayo, Perú
{bsuarezf,hmejiac,vtuesta}@crece.uss.edu.pe
[2] Universidad Privada Antenor Orrego, Trujillo, Peru
[3] Facultad de Ingeniería, Universidad de Ibagué, Ibagué, Colombia
manuel.forero@unibague.edu.co

Abstract. The contention, mitigation and prevention measures that governments have implemented around the world do not appear to be sufficient to prevent the spread of SARS-CoV-2. The number of infected and dead continues to rise every day, putting a strain on the capacity and infrastructure of hospitals and medical centers. Therefore, it is necessary to develop new diagnostic methods based on patients' symptoms that allow the generation of early warnings for appropriate treatment. This paper presents a new method in development for the diagnosis of SARS-CoV-2, based on patient symptoms and the use of fuzzy classifiers. Eleven (11) variables were fuzzified. Then, knowledge rules were established and finally, the center of mass method was used to generate the diagnostic results. The method was tested with a database of clinical records of symptomatic and asymptomatic SARS-CoV-2 patients. By testing the proposed model with data from symptomatic patients, we obtained 100% sensitivity and 100% specificity. Patients according to their symptoms are classified into two classes, allowing for the detection of patients requiring immediate attention from those with milder symptoms.

Keywords: SARS-CoV-2 · Covid-19 · Coronavirus · Fuzzy classifier · Diagnosis

1 Introduction

One of the major public health problems worldwide is caused by SARS-CoV-2 [1, 2]. First cases were reported in Wuhan, China, in December 2019 [3]. Since then, the number of infected and dead people has increased despite rigorous efforts at containment and prevention worldwide [4]. According to the report provided by the Center for Science and Systems Engineering at Johns Hopkins University, the number of SARS-CoV-2 infections and deaths worldwide as of 25th September, 2020 was 32.284.038 and 983.952 cases respectively [5]. Numbers that continue to rise.

© Springer Nature Switzerland AG 2021
J. A. Lossio-Ventura et al. (Eds.): SIMBig 2020, CCIS 1410, pp. 484–494, 2021.
https://doi.org/10.1007/978-3-030-76228-5_35

The mechanism of propagation of the virus among humans is mainly due to close contact, through secretion droplets emitted when sneezing, coughing or speaking at a distance lower than two meters [6, 7]. The viral load present in an infected person lasts for up to two weeks after recovery from illness symptoms [8].

The standard technique for detecting SARS-CoV-2 is the World Health Organization (WHO) approved real-time reverse transcription polymerase chain reaction (RT-PCR) due to its high specificity and sensitivity. However, this technique is expensive, presents a high degree of complexity, requires sophisticated equipment and the processing time takes between 5 and 6 h [9]. In addition, a new technique based on the response of the antibodies to the patient's infection has been developed, called rapid serology test, which is more economical and whose results are generated in 15 min. However, this technique is deficient in the sense that the presence of antibodies depends on the host and, therefore, it is not useful in an acute disease context [10]. Other methods developed for the clinical diagnosis of SARS-CoV-2, combine chest CT scan, patient's clinical signs and symptoms, as well as contacts and travel history, using mobile device sensors to collect patient information. The collected data is then used for disease diagnosis using deep learning techniques [11–14].

The most common clinical symptoms of SARS-CoV-2 disease include: dry cough, fever, sputum production, dyspnea, myalgia, headache, and diarrhea [2, 4, 15–17]. In some cases, sore throat and rhinorrhea appear as additional symptoms [18–22].

In general, clinical diagnosis is based on a deductive process, in which the physician, based on the symptoms, determines a patient's disease, so these medical concepts could be modeled using fuzzy classifiers [23]. Taking as a main basis the clinical diagnosis that a person presents after contracting SARS-CoV-2 disease, and other variables, analyzed in Sect. 3, a model based on fuzzy classifiers is developed, which consists of a set of fuzzy rules, using the approach proposed by Mamdani, to carry out the fuzzification and defuzzification process to make an early diagnosis of this disease.

2   Materials and Method

In this study we used a database with the symptoms of 19 symptomatic and 3 asymptomatic patients diagnosed with SARS-CoV-2, and 14 subjects with negative diagnosis from a public hospital in Chiclayo (Peru) and 14 patients surveyed from Chiclayo and Ibague.

The proposed model was implemented on a computer Intel Core i3-2310 M processor (R) CPU 2.10 GHz with 4 GB of RAM, running on Microsoft Windows 7. The method was developed using the XFuzzy 3.5 application.

The developed model is based on the theory of fuzzy logic, particularly on the linguistic information provided by experts in the medical field for the diagnosis of the disease [24]. This information can be represented by means of fuzzy rules and inference methods [25].

2.1   Fuzziness Interface

Also known as "blurring", it converts the input data into linguistic values that are the labels of the belonging functions or fuzzy sets [26].

Input and Output Variables

A total of eleven linguistic variables were defined as classifier entries; of which two correspond to the age and sex of the patients, seven variables represent the most common signs and symptoms, which were selected according to their frequency. For this purpose, clinical histories published in nine articles [2, 15–22] were taken and the symptoms that appeared at least five times were selected, that is, in half plus one of the publications. In addition, other symptoms mentioned by WHO or used by other technological tools [27–29] were considered as important factors to be considered in the diagnosis of SARS-CoV-2. These are external contact with an ill patient and if general malaise has occurred in recent days (Table 1).

Table 1. Analysis of the most common clinical symptoms presented by patients after contracting coronavirus disease, covid-19.

	Fever	Cough	Dyspnea	Phlegm production	Myalgia	Headache	Diarrhea	Rhinorrhoea	Throat pain
(Huang et al. 2020) [2]	x	x	x	x	x	x	x	–	–
(Li et al. 2020) [15]	x	x	x	–	x	x	–	–	–
(Huang et al. 2020) [16]	x	x	x	x	x	x	–	–	–
(Tian et al. 2020) [17]	x	x	x	–	x	x	–	–	–
(Chen et al. 2020) [18]	x	x	x	–	x	x	x	x	x
(Wang et al. 2020) [19]	x	x	x	x	x	x	x	–	x
(Liu et al. 2020) [20]	x	x	x	x	x	x	x	–	x
(Guan et al. 2020) [21]	x	x	x	x	x	x	x	–	x
(Rodriguez et al. 2020) [22]	x	x	x	x	x	x	x		x
Symptom frequency	*9*	*9*	*9*	*6*	*9*	*9*	*6*	*1*	*5*

In summary, the input variables used are: general malaise, external contact, age, sex, fever, cough, dyspnea, phlegm production, myalgia, headache and diarrhea. The classifier has as its output the diagnosis of the patient, identifying it as infected or not with covid-19.

Membership Functions

The fuzzification process is performed by introducing membership functions, which represent the degree of belonging of a variable to a given fuzzy set.

The input variables: general malaise, external contact, fever, cough, dyspnea, phlegm production, myalgia, headache and diarrhea, whose linguistic values are "YES" and "NO", where "YES" is represented as 1 and "NO" as 0 (Table 2), a triangular function was taken as a membership function (Fig. 1). Each of these variables has a speech universe of [0, 1].

Table 2. Linguistic representation of input variables with linguistic values are only Yes or No

Membership function	Type	Parameters
Yes	Triangular	[0 1 2]
No	Triangular	[−1 0 1]

Fig. 1. Representation of the triangular membership function of the input variables general malaise, external contact, fever, cough, dyspnea, phlegm production, myalgia, headache and diarrhea

In the case of the input variable Gender, there are two types of linguistic values: "Man" and "Female", where the former is represented as 1 and the latter as 0 (Table 3). The membership function of each set was also represented as a triangular one. This variable has a speech universe of [0, 1] (Fig. 2).

Table 3. Linguistic representation of the gender input variable.

Membership function	Type	Parameters
Man	Triangular	[0 1 2]
Female	Triangular	[−1 0 1]

Fig. 2. Representation of the triangular membership function of the gender input.

As for the variable Age, we used the same linguistic values published in three previous works "Young", "Young adult", "Old" and "Very old" [25, 30, 31], shown in Table 4. We chose trapezoidal functions as membership functions of the sets "Young" and "Very old" and triangular ones as membership functions of the sets "Young adult" and "Old" (Fig. 3). This variable has a speech universe of [0 100].

Table 4. Linguistic representation of the age input.

Membership function	Type	Parameters
Young	Trapezoidal	[−20 0 25 38]
Young adult	Triangular	[32 40 45]
Old	Triangular	[40 50 60]
Very old	Trapezoidal	[50 60 100 120]

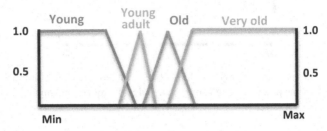

Fig. 3. Representation of the trapezoidal and triangular membership functions of the Age variable.

Finally, the classifier output corresponding to the patient's diagnosis was divided into four sets, corresponding to the linguistic values: "Very Low", "Low", "Medium", and "High", shown in Table 5. Trapezoidal functions were chosen as the membership functions of the "Very Low" and "High" sets, while triangular ones were used for the "Low" and "Medium" sets, as shown in Fig. 4. This variable has a speech universe of [−1, 5].

Table 5. Linguistic representation of the output variable diagnosis.

Membership function	Type	Parameters
Very low	Trapezoidal	[−2 −1 0.5 1]
Low	Triangular	[0.5 1.5 2.5]
Medium	Triangular	[2 3 4]
High	Trapezoidal	[3.5 4 5 6]

2.2 Knowledge Rules

The rules of knowledge, also known as fuzzy rules, are considered one of the most important parts of the fuzzy classifier and their interpretation of the rules decides the accuracy of the system [31, 32]. The inference mechanism used to calculate the overall fuzzy value of the system corresponds to Mamdani, who represents each rule as a set of

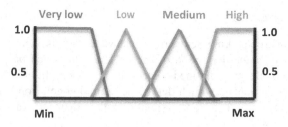

Fig. 4. Representation of the trapezoidal and triangular membership functions of the output variable diagnosis.

IF-THEN statements.

Rule i : If X is A, Y is B, then Z is Ci

where X is known as antecedent and A is known as consequent, which is formed by means of conjunctions (AND). The rules were empirically adjusted, having built a total of 4096, validated with data from the medical records of 36 patients and by the Director of the Professional School of Human Medicine of the Universidad Señor de Sipán. Table 6 shows some of the rules built.

Table 6. Fuzzy rules if- then

1.	IF (GM = NO & EC = NO & SEX = MAN & AGE = YOUNG & FEVER = NO & COUGH = NO & DYSPNEA = NO & FLEMA = NO & MYALGIA = NO & HA = NO & DIARRHEA = NO) → DIAGNOSIS = VERY_LOW;
2.	IF (GM = NO & EC = NO & SEX = MAN & AGE = YOUNG & FEVER = NO & COUGH = NO & DYSPNEA = NO & FLEMA = NO & MYALGIA = YES & HA = YES & DIARRHEA = YES) → DIAGNOSIS = LOW;
3.	IF (GM = NO & EC = NO & SEX = MAN & AGE = YOUNG & FEVER = NO & COUGH = NO & DYSPNEA = NO & FLEMA = YES & MYALGIA = NO & HA = YES & DIARRHEA = YES) → DIAGNOSIS = LOW;
:	:
4094	IF (GM = YES & EC = YES & SEX = FEMALE & AGE = VERY_OLD & FEVER = YES & COUGH = YES & DYSPNEA = YES & FLEMA = NO & MYALGIA = NO & HA = NO & DIARRHEA = NO) → DIAGNOSIS = HIGH;
4095	IF (GM = YES & EC = YES & SEX = FEMALE & AGE = VERY_OLD & FEVER = YES & COUGH = YES & DYSPNEA = YES & FLEMA = YES & MYALGIA = YES & HA = YES & DIARRHEA = NO) → DIAGNOSIS = HIGH;
4096	IF (GM = YES & EC = YES & SEX = FEMALE & AGE = VERY_OLD & FEVER = YES & COUGH = YES & DYSPNEA = YES & FLEMA = YES & MYALGIA = YES & HA = YES & DIARRHEA = YES) → DIAGNOSIS = HIGH;

Legend: GM: General malaise; EC: external contact; HA: Headache.

2.3   Fuzzy Inference Engine

From the set of constructed knowledge rules, known as premises, the fuzzy logic inference rules preside over the deduction of each of the established propositions. In this case, the fuzzy logic inference engine is represented by the traditional fuzzy logic inference known as modus ponens, which determines a final conclusion from the premises $p_i = [p_i^-, p_i^+]$, in general, an approximation rather than an exact consequence of $\{[p_i^-, p_i^+] | i \in Z_+\}$ [33].

2.4   Defuzzification Interface

Defuzziness is the process of selecting an output value to its corresponding discourse universe [26]. In this work, the centre of gravity or centre of mass, presented in the following equation, was chosen to perform the defuzzification, which allows the equilibrium value of a property to be found [34].

$$z = \frac{\sum_{i=1}^{n} z_i C(z_i)}{\sum_{i=1}^{n} C(z_i)} z = [z_1 \ldots z_n], C = \bigcup_{k=1}^{N} C_k$$

Where N is the number of rules.

3   Results

The proposed model obtained an identical diagnosis to that given by the specialist, correctly identifying all symptomatic patients and identifying asymptomatic patients as negative. This is because the different input/output variables and the creation of the fuzzy classifier knowledge base was the product of a thorough study of the effects of the different input variables on the output variable, which classifies the subject into four possible classes, depending on the degree of class membership. A subject is identified as positive if assigned to the medium or high classes. The output generated by the model for the two test data sets is shown in Table 7, in the columns "Fuzzy value" and "Fuzzy diagnosis".

The data in Table 7 were used to construct the confusion matrix to analyze the results obtained with the proposed model, which consists of four parameters known as Real Positive (RP), False Positive (FP), False Negative (FN) and Real Negative (RN), as shown in Table 8. Where the rows represent the actual instances of the classes presenting the data, while the columns represent the result produced by the model. From these data it is found that the model obtains 100% accuracy and 100% sensitivity for the detection of symptomatic patients.

As mentioned above, the model allows for the correct identification of all positive symptomatic cases, classifying them into two classes, which makes it possible to determine those that may require urgent attention. As can be seen, since the model was not based on the description of the characteristics of the asymptomatic patients, it fails to identify them. Therefore, it is necessary to study new variables that may be determinant in detecting them, which is still a challenge for these systems.

Table 7. Clinical data of symptomatic and asymptomatic patients diagnosed with SARS-CoV-2 and the diagnosis produced by the proposed model.

	GM	EC	S	FV	T	D	PP	M	HA	DA	E	Medical diagnosis	Fuzzy value	Diagnosis fuzzy
1.	N	Y	F	N	N	N	N	N	N	N	35	Positive	3.00	Medium
2.	N	Y	F	N	N	Y	N	Y	N	N	34	Positive	3.00	Medium
3.	Y	N	M	Y	Y	Y	Y	Y	N	N	73	Positive	3.00	Medium
4.	Y	N	M	Y	Y	Y	Y	Y	N	Y	60	Positive	4.52	High
5.	Y	N	M	Y	Y	Y	Y	Y	N	Y	69	Positive	4.52	High
6.	Y	N	F	Y	Y	Y	Y	Y	N	N	60	Positive	3.00	Medium
7.	Y	N	M	Y	Y	Y	Y	Y	N	Y	69	Positive	4.52	High
8.	Y	N	M	Y	Y	Y	N	N	N	N	41	Positive	1.52	Low
9.	Y	N	M	N	N	Y	N	Y	N	N	32	Positive	−0.33	Very low
10.	Y	N	M	Y	Y	Y	Y	Y	N	Y	31	Positive	4.43	High
11.	Y	N	F	N	N	Y	N	Y	N	N	26	Positive	1.52	Low
12.	Y	N	M	Y	Y	Y	Y	Y	N	Y	59	Positive	4.51	High
13.	Y	N	M	Y	Y	Y	N	Y	N	N	57	Positive	3.00	Medium
14.	Y	Y	F	N	Y	Y	N	Y	N	N	33	Positive	3.00	Medium
15.	Y	N	F	Y	Y	Y	N	Y	N	N	50	Positive	3.00	Medium
16.	Y	N	M	Y	Y	Y	Y	Y	N	N	30	Positive	3.00	Medium
17.	Y	N	M	Y	Y	Y	N	Y	N	Y	56	Positive	3.00	Medium
18.	Y	N	M	Y	Y	Y	N	Y	N	N	68	Positive	3.00	Medium
19.	Y	N	M	Y	Y	Y	Y	Y	N	N	80	Positive	3.00	Medium
20.	Y	Y	M	Y	Y	Y	Y	Y	N	Y	17	Positive	4.52	High
21.	Y	Y	M	Y	Y	N	Y	Y	N	N	41	Positive	3.00	Medium
22.	Y	N	M	Y	Y	Y	Y	Y	N	N	47	Positive	3.00	Medium
23.	Y	Y	F	Y	Y	N	N	Y	Y	N	26	Positive	4.51	High
24.	Y	Y	F	Y	Y	Y	Y	Y	Y	N	68	Positive	4.52	High
25.	Y	Y	M	Y	Y	Y	N	Y	Y	N	47	Positive	4.47	High
26.	Y	N	F	Y	Y	Y	Y	Y	Y	N	23	Positive	4.52	High
27.	Y	N	F	Y	Y	N	Y	Y	Y	N	33	Positive	4.36	High
28.	Y	N	F	Y	Y	Y	Y	N	Y	N	28	Positive	4.49	High
29.	N	Y	M	N	N	Y	Y	N	N	N	90	Positive	3.0	Medium
30.	Y	Y	F	N	Y	N	Y	N	N	N	11	Positive	3.0	Medium
31.	N	Y	F	N	Y	N	Y	N	N	N	30	Positive	3.0	Medium

(*continued*)

Table 7. (*continued*)

	GM	EC	S	FV	T	D	PP	M	HA	DA	E	Medical diagnosis	Fuzzy value	Diagnosis fuzzy
32.	Y	Y	F	N	N	N	Y	N	N	Y	34	Positive	3.0	Medium
33.	Y	Y	M	Y	Y	Y	N	N	N	N	73	Positive	4.52	High
34.	N	Y	F	N	Y	N	N	N	N	N	67	Positive	3.0	High
35.	N	Y	F	Y	Y	N	Y	N	N	N	67	Positive	3.0	Medium
36.	Y	Y	F	Y	Y	Y	N	N	N	N	42	Positive	4.45	High
37.	N	N	F	N	Y	Y	Y	Y	N	N	39	Negative	1.52	Low
38.	N	N	F	Y	Y	Y	N	N	N	N	29	Negative	1.49	Low
39.	N	N	M	N	Y	N	Y	N	N	N	39	Negative	−0.33	Very low
40.	N	N	M	Y	Y	N	N	N	N	N	11	Negative	−0.33	Very low
41.	N	N	F	N	Y	N	Y	Y	N	N	47	Negative	1.50	Low
42.	N	N	M	Y	Y	Y	N	Y	N	N	43	Negative	1.51	Low
43.	N	N	M	N	Y	N	Y	N	N	N	37	Negative	−0.33	Very low
44.	N	N	M	N	Y	N	Y	Y	N	N	27	Negative	1.52	Very low
45.	N	N	F	N	Y	Y	Y	N	N	N	23	Negative	1.52	Low
46.	N	N	F	N	Y	N	N	Y	N	N	38	Negative	−0.33	Very low
47.	Y	N	M	N	Y	N	Y	N	N	N	59	Negative	−0.33	Very low
48.	Y	N	F	N	Y	N	Y	N	N	N	59	Negative	−0.33	Very low
49.	Y	N	M	N	N	Y	N	Y	N	N	53	Negative	−0.33	Very low
50.	Y	N	F	N	Y	N	N	N	N	N	37	Negative	−0.33	Very low

Legend: MG: general malaise, EC: external contact, S: sex, FV: fever, T: cough, D: dyspnea, FP: phlegm production, M: myalgia, DC: headache, DA: diarrhea, E: age, F: female, M: male, Y: Yes, N: No.

Table 8. Confusion matrix of the fuzzy model proposed for the diagnosis of SARS-CoV-2 of symptomatic and asymptomatic patients.

		Result classification	
		SARS-CoV-2 (+)	SARS-CoV-2 (−)
Real instances	SARS-CoV-2 (+)	33	3
	SARS-CoV-2 (−)	0	14

4   Conclusions

Since the SARS-CoV-2 virus spread around the world, it has forced governments to take very drastic prevention and containment measures in order to control the pandemic that has caused millions of infections and deaths. To diagnose this disease, the antibody test has been developed, which determines whether or not the immune system has the virus. However, the antibodies could react in a period of 9 to 28 days, so this process is considered very slow, and therefore, the person can easily spread the disease if not properly isolated. RT-PCR tests take about 5 to 6 h to determine whether or not you have the disease. Despite the short period of time this test is used, it faces a constraint such as the cost of importing the chemicals and other items used.

Automatic learning is playing a very important role in the field of medicine, which has allowed the development of other methods that combine the application of neural networks and chest CT to diagnose SARS-CoV-2. The response time of these systems is less than five (5) s. However, the limiting factor of these methods, require specialized equipment of high quality to take samples and obtain reliable results.

The proposed method allows to overcome these limitations, as it is non-invasive, does not require specialized equipment and only the symptoms of the patient are needed as inputs. The model allows the correct identification of all positive symptomatic cases, classifying them into two classes, helping to determine those that may require urgent attention.

References

1. Chih-Cheng, L., et al.: Severe acute respiratory syndrome coronavirus 2 (SARS-CoV-2) and coronavirus disease-2019 (COVID-19): the epidemic and the challenges. Int. J. Antimicrobial. Agents **55**, 105924 (2020)
2. Huang, C., et al.: Clinical features of patients infected with 2019 novel coronavirus in Wuhan, China. Lancet **395**, 497–506 (2020)
3. Lu, H., Stratton, C.W., Yi-Wei. T.: Outbreak of pneumonia of unknown etiology in Wuhan, China: the mystery and the miracle. J. Med. Virol. **92**, 401–402 (2020)
4. Sohrabi, C., et al.: World Health Organization declares global emergency: a review of the 2019 novel coronavirus (COVID-19). Int. J. Surg. **76**, 71–76 (2020)
5. Hopkins, J.: COVID-19 Dashboard by the Center for Systems Science and Engineering (CSSE) at Johns Hopkins University (JHU) (2020). https://www.arcgis.com/apps/opsdashbo ard/index.html#/bda7594740fd40299423467b48e9ecf6
6. Ministerio de Sanidad: España: Información científica-técnica. Enfermedad por coronavirus, COVID-19, 02 June (2020). https://www.mscbs.gob.es/profesionales/saludPublica/
7. Centers for Disease Control and Prevention: Coronavirus Disease 2019 (COVID-19) (2020). https://www.cdc.gov/coronavirus/2019-ncov/about/transmission.html
8. Ortiz-Prado, E., et al.: Clinical, molecular and epidemiological characterization of the SARS-CoV2 virus and the Coronavirus disease 2019 (COVID-19), a comprehensive literature review. Diagn. Microbiol. Infect. Dis. **98**, 115094 (2020)
9. Cassaniti, I., et al.: Performance of VivaDiag COVID-19 IgM/IgG Rapid Test is inadequate for diagnosis of COVID-19 in acute patients referring to emergency room department. J. Med. Virol. **92**, 1724–1727 (2020)
10. Al-Muharraqi, M.: Testing recommendation for COVID-19 (SARS-CoV-2) in patients planned for surgery - continuing the service and 'suppressing' the pandemic. Br. J. Oral Maxillofac. Surg. **58**, 503–505 (2020)
11. Zheng, C., et al.: Deep learning-based detection for COVID-19 from chest CT using weak label. MedRxiv (2020)

12. Maghdid, H.S., et al.: A novel AI-enabled framework to diagnose coronavirus COVID 19 using smartphone embedded sensors: design study (2020)
13. Ophir, G. et al.: Rapid AI development cycle for the Coronavirus (COVID-19) pandemic: initial results for automated detection & patient monitoring using deep learning CT image analysis (2020)
14. Panwar, H., et al.: Application of deep learning for fast detection of COVID-19 in X-rays using nCOVnet (2020)
15. Li, R., et al.: Identification of a novel coronavirus causing severe pneumonia in human: a descriptive study. Chin. Med. J. **9**, 1015–1024 (2020)
16. Huang, C., et al.: Clinical features of patients infected with 2019 novel coronavirus in Wuhan, China. Lancet **395**, 497–506 (2020)
17. Tian, S., et al.: Characteristics of COVID-19 infection in Beijing. J. Infect. **80**, 401–406 (2020)
18. Chen, N., et al.: Epidemiological and clinical characteristics of 99 cases of 2019 novel coronavirus pneumonia in Wuhan, China: a descriptive study. Lancet **395**, 507–513 (2020)
19. Wang, D., et al.: Clinical characteristics of 138 hospitalized patients with 2019 novel coronavirus–infected pneumonia in Wuhan. China JAMA Netw. **323**, 1061–1069 (2020)
20. Liu, J., et al.: Neutrophil-to-lymphocyte ratio predicts severe illness patients with 2019 novel coronavirus in the early stage. MedRxiv (2020)
21. Guan, W., et al.: Clinical characteristics of 2019 novel coronavirus infection in China. MedRxiv (2020)
22. Rodriguez, A., et al.: Clinical, laboratory and imaging features of COVID-19: a systematic review and meta-analysis. Travel Med. Infect. Dis. **34**, 101623 (2020)
23. Ahmed, S., et al.: Diagnosis of kidney disease. In: The 8th International Conference on Software, Knowledge, Information Management and Applications (SKIMA 2014), pp. 1–8 (2014)
24. Allahverdi, N., Akcan, T.: A fuzzy expert system design for diagnosis of periodontal dental disease. In: International Conference on Application of Information and Communication Technologies (AICT) (2011)
25. Kahtan, H., et al.: Heart disease diagnosis system using fuzzy logic In: International Conference on Software and Computer Applications, pp. 297–301 (2018)
26. Ponce, P.: Inteligencia artificial con aplicaciones a la ingeniería. Alfaomega Grupo Editor S.A., México (2010)
27. OMI: Organizador Médico Informático (2020). https://omi.app/covid-19/welcome.
28. Comunidad de Madrid: Haz tu autoevaluación del Covid-19 (2020). https://coronavirus.com unidad.madrid/
29. Apple: Herramienta de la evaluación de COVID-19 (2020). https://www.apple.com/covid19.
30. Diusenbayeva, A., et al.: Using Fuzzy logic concepts in creating the decision making expert system for cardio—vascular diseases (CVD). In: International Conference on Application of Information and Communication Technologies (AICT) (2016)
31. Kasbe, T., Singh, R.: Design of heart disease diagnosis system using fuzzy logic. In: International Conference on Energy, Communication, Data Analytics and Soft Computing, pp. 3183–3187 (2017)
32. Reshmalakshmi, C., Sasikumar, M.: Fuzzy inference system for osteoporosis detection. In: Global Humanitarian Technology Conference, pp. 675–681 (2016)
33. García Infante, J.C., et al.: Sistemas con lógica difusa, México (2009)
34. Silva, C., Ribeiro, B.: Aprendizagem Computacional em Engenharia (2020)

Semantic Web, Repositories,
and Visualization

Distributed Identity Management for Semantic Entities

Falko Schönteich[1]([⊠]), Andreas Kasten[2], and Ansgar Scherp[3]

[1] Christian-Albrechts-Universität, Kiel, Germany
`falko.schoenteich@stu.uni-kiel.de`
[2] Debeka, Koblenz, Germany
`andreas.kasten@debeka.de`
[3] Ulm University, Ulm, Germany
`ansgar.scherp@uni-ulm.de`

Abstract. We propose semDIM, a novel approach for Semantic Distributed Identity Management based on a Semantic Web architecture. For the first time, semDIM provides a framework for a distributed definition and management of entities such as persons being part of an organization, groups, and roles across namespaces. It is suitable for informal, i.e., social networks, as well as for professional networks such as cross-organizational collaborations. Beyond the capabilities of existing Identity Management solutions, we allow distributed identifiers and management of groups (consisting of agents and sub-groups) and roles. semDIM uses `owl:sameAs` as a central property to represent and verify distributed identities via formal reasoning. This concept enables novel functionalities for Distributed Identity Management, as these entities can be referred to, related to each other, as well as be managed across namespaces. Our semDIM approach consists of a modular software architecture, a process model, as well as a set of state-of-the-art DUL-based OWL ontology patterns. We demonstrate our approach by an example implementation that evaluates its functional fitness.

Keywords: Distributed systems · Identity management · Semantic web · Semantic reasoning · OWL · Ontology patterns · DOLCE+DnS Ultralite

1 Introduction

Organizations regularly fail to securely and reliably manage identities, roles, and groups across namespaces, be it corporations, departments, institutes, or any other organization form. Often times, no Identity Management (IM) solutions are in use at all. Existing approaches for Identity Management typically focus on a single organization and thus centrally organized systems. Solutions addressing distribution often focus only on managing identities of persons. Neither do they support distributed groups nor distributed roles for a Distributed Identity Management setting. In this context, groups are sets of agents representing persons

© Springer Nature Switzerland AG 2021
J. A. Lossio-Ventura et al. (Eds.): SIMBig 2020, CCIS 1410, pp. 497–512, 2021.
https://doi.org/10.1007/978-3-030-76228-5_36

and/or other groups. Group members may act as representatives of their collective, e.g., "system admins" or "member of accounting department", and execute tasks related to roles. Roles are sets of permissions.

Classic Identity Management approaches are designed for a single organization or authority. However, in multi-organizational collaborations, a Distributed Identity Management (DIM) including agents, groups, and roles is needed, as integrating multiple namespaces most often imply multiple identifiers for each entity or at least multiple bodies of authorities being responsible for different kinds of relations of entities. Such inefficiencies in identity management cause significant operational costs for organizations as well as security risks in the sensitive topic of permission management. For example, if a reliable Distributed Identity Management is not provided, changes, such as removal of access rights for a group, must be managed in each affected local Identity Management system instead of having a consistent process. Therefore, the risk related to misconfigurations, privilege creep, man-in-the-middle attacks, and similar threats may increase. The system landscape of most organizations is increasingly complex with diverse components from multiple providers, software developers, and hardware manufacturers each exhibiting their own functional and non-functional requirements, interfaces, and protocols. Some interfaces and protocols may even be proprietary and hard to be integrated in other frameworks. As Identity Management must be integrated with many components of multiple organizations' system landscapes, they must offer a way to manage identities, groups, roles, permissions, etc. across multiple namespaces independent from—yet integrateable with—data models specific to various software applications.

Despite best efforts to provide Distributed Identity Management, existing approaches are limited to centralized solutions that are not interoperable or do not offer management of all relevant entities across namespaces. For example, it is not supported to associate an identity a-1 in group g-1 with an identity b-1 in g-2, where both identities refer to the same real-world person but each identity having different group memberships and roles. Approaches like DID [26] or WebIDs [25] (formerly FOAF+SSL) address different forms of decentralization or federation of identity provision and authentication, but do not offer group and role management. The Semantic Web approach dgFOAF [19] supports distributed authorities for managing groups, which is useful for scenarios like emergency response. However, the fact that within a single organization users have multiple identities due to the use of different IT systems is ignored, not to mention that users will have different identities in cross-organizational collaborations and need to access information systems outside their organization. Similarly, SOLID [11] addresses parts of DIM in the context of social web applications, but does not address the management of multiple identities and their groups. Overall, there is no solution for a secure distributed definition and management of identities, groups, and roles across different namespaces, i.e., organizations and/or IT systems.

To address these challenges, we propose Semantic Distributed Identity Management (semDIM). It is a framework that for the first time supports the distributed definition and management of identities, groups, and roles. Motivated by the foundational ontology DOLCE+DnS Ultralight (DUL) [4], we understand an entity as any kind of object. Particularly, in our scenario of organizations collaborating on projects, we model identities for persons, groups, and roles. As discussed above, the distributed definition and management of groups and roles is novel as it is not yet supported by existing systems. Our approach consists of (1) a modular server-client architecture, (2) a process-model for graph-based client and server requests, (3) a semantic reasoner for validating these requests as well as (4) ontology patterns for semantically formalizing the data as well as the processes. We evaluate our approach by implementing a prototype and examining its fitness in regard to the functional requirements for DIM.

The remainder of the paper is organized as follows: First, we discuss the related work in Sect. 2. Then, we present a scenario addressing the challenges of DIM in Sect. 3. Based on this, Sect. 4 deducts requirements for a DIM solution. In Sect. 5, we elaborate on our solution semDIM. Section 6 discusses knowledge representation in DIM. An evaluation of our solution against the requirements follows in Sect. 7, before we conclude.

2   Related Work

We discuss the literature in Identity Management and their features. We cluster the papers based on the DIM features they support. The clusters are: a) Identity Management *without* referencing across namespaces, i.e., they do not consider uniquely referring of entities across namespaces. b) Identity Management *with* unique identifiers, i.e., they uniquely refer to entities across namespaces, but not offering connecting and managing distributed entities. c) Identity Management addressing distributed groups. These approaches support all features of a) and b) and additionally address the problem of group definitions being distributed over multiple sources of authority.

Regarding a) Identity Management without referencing across namespaces, Gai et al. [3] propose an attribute-based approach to group management, but the approach is not considering connecting distributed entities. Obrst et al. [13] propose a combination of OWL, Prolog, and a bit-level Java Class to optimize reasoning on platform-independent access rules. As they are using a semantic basis and unique identifiers, their approach supports referring entities across namespaces. However, the connection of such entities, i.e., equality of instances and other relations between entities, is not considered. Therefore, it belongs to category b). Another approach in this category is the Semantic Access Control Policy Language by Hu et al. [5] based on the eXtensible Access Control Markup Language (XACML) [12] and OWL. XACML is a commonly used standard for attribute-based access control (ABAC), defining an access control policy language as well as an architecture and a processing model for access requests. Hu et al. focus on the syntax and semantics of their language. However, they do not consider how the language can be used in a distributed environment to manage distributed entities. Many more approaches for identity and access management exist [2,9,14,21,22], which do offer the use of unique identifiers, but are not considering distributed entities and distributed identifiers. Kirrane et al. give an overview of many of these approaches in their survey [10].

Regarding category c) Identity Management with support for distributed groups, the approach closest to ours is dgFOAF [19] based on the wide-spread FOAF ontology [1]. By extending FOAF with a Datalog-based reasoning engine, dgFOAF allows to define and reason on group policies integrated in FOAF-profiles. However, dgFOAF does not support full distributed management of all relevant entites. First, dgFOAF does not allow connecting distributed identities. This feature could technically be added. However, adding support for distributed group identifiers and distributed role identifiers to dgFOAF is not possible without significant changes to the approach, as it is incompatible with the fundamental principles of dgFOAF: groups are equivalent if and only if they have identical group policies (including default members, especially in context of admin groups) and identical labels defined in each namespace they are used in (see [19] for details). This limitation of dgFOAF does not allow entities to be defined and managed across namespaces, e.g., remotely managing an admin group defined in a different FOAF-profile. Similarly, SOLID [11] addresses parts of DIM in context of social web applications with a focus on social network settings. However, it does not address the management of multiple identities and their groups.

Table 1 shows an overview of the related work and compares it against the functional features of the categories a) to c). Category a) is not fit for DIM, as it does not support any distribution features. In contrast, category b) supports uniquely identifiable entities and therefore takes a large step into the direction of DIM. However, this category still misses significant functional features regarding distributed roles and groups. Category c) is very promising, but nonetheless, falls short when applied in context of real life multi-party collaboration, as not all entities can be defined, referenced, and managed in a distributed way. Only our approach semDIM supports all features required for a Distributed Identity Management, i.e., support for a distributed definition of identities, groups, and roles.

There is some further relevant literature that does not directly fit into the categories above. We discuss this literature in the following: WebID (formerly FOAF+SSL) is an authentication protocol based on FOAF-profiles [25]. It offers only authentication but not any other aspect of Distributed Identity Management, such as distributed identities, i.e., connecting multiple different identities of the same person, groups, and roles. Any approach for Distributed Identity Management relying on certificate-based authentication and signatures could use WebID for authentication as a subcomponent, as implemented by SOLID. However, WebID itself does not address the key challenges of DIM involving Identity Management, group management, and policy management. Self-Sovereign Identities (SSI) is a concept which allows individuals to provide and manage their identities, e.g., as used in the W3C standard of Decentralized Identifiers (DID) v1.0 [26]. Thus, SSI addresses only a focused aspect of DIM, which is about coining, providing, and resolving URI identifiers. We take up the idea of using URIs for distributed identifiers. However, unlike DID, we explicitly model the parameters of identifiers in an ontology pattern and do not encode this into a single URI as done by DID. This gives more stability to the URIs, as they do not depend on the specific methods used for coining them. Another related research area are policy languages. Yet again, the literature about this area covers policy related parts of DIM but does not address the whole spectrum of DIM. We refer to [7,8], and [6] for a more detailed discussion on policy languages.

Table 1. Literature comparison against functional features of Distributed Identity Management (n = no, y = yes, p = partial)

Identity Management with …	Unique identifiers	Distributed identifiers	Distributed groups	Distributed roles
a) Standard features [3]	n	n	n	n
b) Unique identifiers [2, 5,9,13,14,21,22]	y	n	n	n
c) Distributed groups [11,19]	y	n	p	n
d) *Our approach* semDIM	*y*	*y*	*y*	*y*

3   Distributed Industrial Engineering and Manufacturing Scenario: The *LEGO Train* Project

A common problem in high-tech engineering and manufacturing industries is that the products consist of tens of thousand to millions of parts that are distributively designed, manufactured, and assembled to result in the end product. For example, a passenger car consists of around 30,000 individual parts.[1] An airline plane even has approximately six million parts.[2] Handling the various information objects as well as physical products and its parts over time is a key challenge of Product Lifecycle Management (PLM) [18].

Our scenario is derived from a real industrial use case, in which one of the author's employer is involved. It is based on an international joint-venture project in the high-tech engineering and manufacturing industries. We altered some aspects of the scenario, i.e., fictional products and organizational structures, due to confidentiality and didactic reasons. However, the challenges directly relate to the ones observable in the above mentioned real life setting. The scenario also

---

[1] http://www.toyota.co.jp/en/kids/faq/d/01/04/, last accessed: 2020-09-14.
[2] https://web.archive.org/web/20191214095113/http://magazin.lufthansa.com/xx/ en/fleet/boeing-747-8-en/one-plane-six-million-parts/, last accessed: 2020-09-14.

matches with other similar projects and presents repeating patterns in a compressed form. Below, we first describe the general problem that arises in such distributed organizational collaborations at the example of the collaboration of two companies A and B. Without loss of generalizability, we reduce the problem to two companies, which can be easily extended to an arbitrary number of collaborators. Subsequently, we introduce the specific project of the LEGO Train model, where the two companies A and B collaboratively design and build a train.

Challenges of IM in Distributed Engineering and Manufacturing. To illustrate the challenge addressed by Distributed Identity Management, we describe two companies A and B collaborating on a joint project where they are developing, manufacturing, and distributing a complex industrial product. As any larger organization, company A and company B are organized in different organizational units, e.g., divisions and departments. In order to not overload the scenario, we do not present full organizational charts at this point, but only describe a simplified version with some key employees, groups, and roles. Each company manages its own organizational structure as well as, e.g., identities, groups, and roles themselves. Therefore, we introduce a root identity for each company. This is basically a technical identity representing the root of authority in that organization. It does not need to belong to a real person (such as a super-administrator, a CEO, or any other person of authority), but it could also simply belong to a technical agent, e.g., if only used once during the very first setup of an Identity Management system.[3] It is not feasible to expect from the companies, to agree on a shared company structure implemented by both companies. Even during the project, the company structures change. Figure 1 depicts a simplified overview of identities and groups available in the two companies.

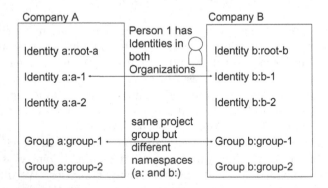

Fig. 1. Identity Management scenario with two companies A and B (with the corresponding namespaces a: and b:)

---

[3] In a real life setting, the chain of command may be more complex than simply having one root authority, e.g., multiple founders all having equal rights, but for the sake of brevity, we discuss the compact situation of one root authority per company.

As depicted in the figure, relations between entities even across organizational borders exist. For example, separate identities in different namespaces may exist which refer to the same person (see `a:a-1` and `b:b-1` for Person 1 in Fig. 1).

In our context, a namespace defines a prefix of identifiers. It can relate, e.g., to an organization, a part of an organization, or an information system. Usually, every organization has its own namespace, e.g., `a:` or `b:`, and may have several sub namespaces, e.g. for departments or projects.

While technically `a:group-1` and `b:group-1` are two separate groups, defined with different namespaces of their companies, they both describe the same group here. In our scenario, this group is a project group consisting of employees of both companies. When determining, who may enter the shared project information systems, i.e., who is member of the project group, membership of either of the two groups is sufficient. Similarly, if a person is explicitly denied membership of one group, he may not have membership to an equivalent group.

Specific Scenario of DIM for the LEGO Train: We use the distributed engineering of the *LEGO Train* set 31504 as a specific scenario to explain our problem space and solution. Figure 2 illustrates the components of the train. While company A is responsible for engineering technical specifications for the steam engine and chassis, company B develops the cabin. In the following description, we use lower-case roman numbers (i, ii, ...) to indicate aspects of the scenario, which we will later reference for requirement deduction in Sect. 4.

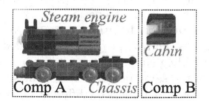

Fig. 2. Two companies jointly building a train. Company A builds the steam engine as well as the chassis, while company B delivers the cabin.

Person 1, an employee of company A, has to work with IT systems of both companies (i). On the one hand, Person 1 needs to work in A's systems to work on the steam engine and the chassis (`a:a-1`). On the other hand, he needs access to information from B regarding mechanical, hydraulic, and electrical assembly interfaces connecting the cabin and the chassis (`b:b-1`). Thus, Person 1 needs two identities, one for each company and acts in the namespaces of both of these two, which we call a **distributed identity**. Certain organizational changes involving Person 1, e.g., if Person 1 switched to another role, department, or even company, should influence the permissions of both identities, `a:a-1` and `b:b-1`, e.g., revoking certain system access rights (ii). As Person 1 is also project leader for the train product, he administrates a project group `a:group-1` at company A.

In company B, an equivalent project group `b:group-1` exists, based in systems of company B. As Person 1 (of company A) is the project leader, he has to administrate both technical groups, `a:group-1` and `b:group-1`, which both refer to the same logical **distributed group** of project members, but, as stated above, with different company namespaces (iii). The workflows describing the various tasks executed by the project group, such as adapting product changes to CAD data, Bill Of Materials, and manuals, require various roles, like design engineer, configuration manager, and quality assurance specialist. These **distributed roles** not only have to be able to be assigned to employees of both companies – and even external third party members – but also need to be able to relate to distributed identities and groups described above as well as distributed information systems of the parties involved (iv).

4   Requirements

From the discussion of the related work in Sect. 2 and their limitations, as well as the features for a DIM motivated by the scenario in Sect. 3, we derive a set of functional and non-functional requirements to a Distributed Identity Management of agents, groups, and, roles. The requirements are in detail:

R1: Unique identifiers for persons, groups, and roles across namespaces. For DIM, persons, groups, and roles must be *uniquely identifiable*, i.e., they must be referenceable across namespaces, such as organizations (companies, universities, social networks, etc.), via globally unambiguous identifiers. This requirement relates to (i) in the scenario.

R2: Distributed identities. Identities uniquely refer to natural persons in namespaces, applications, and/or projects. *Distributed identities* extend the notion of identity by providing support for creating and connecting multiple of such unique identifiers of the same person across namespaces. For example, the same natural person has login identifiers on different IT systems. In the scenario, (ii) describes such as a situation.

R3: Distributed groups. Groups consist of one or more persons and/or other groups [19]. This includes persons and groups from different namespaces, e.g., they can be members of different organizations. In analogy to distributed identities for persons (see R2 above), *distributed groups* require to support multiple identifiers to refer to the same group across namespaces. For example, as discussed in the scenario, shared information systems must be able to process requests regardless of namespace, e.g., querying information about a distributed group, and therefore need to be able to work with distributed identifiers for the (logical) same group. The situation (iii) in the scenario describes this.

R4: Distributed roles. Roles describe a set of tasks and/or responsibilities a person or group this role is assigned to executes and/or holds. A role is, like persons and groups, to be uniquely identified within a system. *Distributed roles* must be connectable and manageable from different namespaces, i.e., it must be possible to have different role identifiers in different namespaces, which are actually referring to the same role, and thus can be used for the same kind of

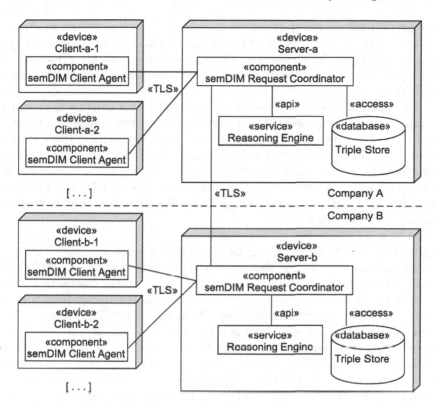

Fig. 3. semDIM Client-Server Architecture featuring two companies, each owning one DIM Server as well as arbitrary amounts of Clients.

authorization. For example, two roles for the membership in the project group **group-1** exist in our scenario (see Fig. 1). One role is defined in the namespace of company A (**a:group-1**) and one in the namespace of company B (**b:group-1**). All agents holding either of these two membership roles belong to the joint *LEGO train* project group. Thus, there are two identifiers (one per company) for the project member role, which are semantically equivalent w. r. t. the project. See (iv) in the scenario.

5   Novel Concept of semDIM

Our approach differs from the state of the art by being able to support distributed management of identities, groups, and roles. In this section, we first describe the resulting, universal client-server architecture. Then, we illustrate a generic use of this architecture. Subsequently, we elaborate on the underlying semantics of our solution in Sect. 6.

We propose a component-based client-server architecture [24] on the Semantic Web, depicted in Fig. 3 as an UML 2 Deployment Diagram[4]. Any activity in DIM, such as creating new groups or adding group members, is represented as a graph, which is transmitted and processed by the semDIM components, running on multiple devices.

Without loss of generality, we assume in the following a basic setup consisting of several clients (Client-a-1, Client-b,1, etc.) and one server per organization (Server-a and Server-b) running on separate logical systems. A triple store on the server is used as persistent storage for valid triples. Triples are valid, if their requirements are met, e.g., a user trying to add a group member actually has the group admin role of that role. The connection between Client and Server is secured with standard transport encryption (TLS) to ensure confidentiality of the transmitted information.

Component View: The **Client Agent** is the software program running on the user's client. Theoretically, the user could read and write requests as RDF graphs manually. But this would be quite impractical. Therefore, the Client Agent takes user input through guided user interaction, processes it into graph form and handles the messaging with and responses from the server. The Client Agent is the only client-side component. All other components run on the Server. The **Request Coordinator** acts as a central component of semDIM. It offers an interface for incoming requests coming from the Client Agents or other servers' Request Coordinators. The Request Coordinator communicates internally with the Reasoning Engine and Triple Store. The **Reasoning Engine** checks for any inconsistencies in the requests received from the Request Coordinator, e.g, if a user not authorized to add a group member tries to do so. The reasoning consists of formal consistency checks regarding the ontology patterns. Here, different OWL reasoning engines can be integrated such as Pellet [23] or Hermit [20]. In addition, the reasoning engines verifies if the requests are valid in terms of the agreed identity management policies, e.g., the policy "only group administrators can add new group members". The **Triple Store** is used as persistent storage of identity information. For the prototype implementation of the architecture, we use RDF4J[5] for SPARQL-Endpoint and triple store management.

Dynamic View: After introducing the components of semDIM, we present the ontology-based message passing between clients and server and server to server. (1) The User (locally) creates new triples, e.g., adding somebody to a group he administrates, via the Client Agent. (2) The Client Agent sends this graph to the Server. The Request Coordinator receives the graph and starts the evaluation process. (3) The Request Coordinator sends the query to validate the prerequisite for accepting the triples in the graph, e.g., if the signer has a necessary role, such as group administrator or namespace owner. (4) The Reasoner component processes already accepted triples from the triple store together with the graph

---

[4] https://www.omg.org/spec/UML/2.5.1/PDF, last accessed: 2020-09-14.
[5] https://rdf4j.org/, last accessed: 2020-09-14.

and decides which triples are valid or invalid. Finally, (5) the Request Coordinator sends triple updates for valid signed triples to the triple store. After the triples have been added to the triple store, they are now used for validating (see step (4)) any future requests.

Secured Server-to-Server communication is modeled as replication of the content of the relevant repository in the triple store, i.e., limited to the data both organization require for the joined project. Different replication strategies can be applied as discussed in [15]. We apply an approach based on ontology patterns to communicate DIM changes across multiple servers. The patterns are briefly described in Sect. 6 and their use is shown in Sect. 7.

6 Knowledge Representation in DIM Using Ontology Design Patterns

For a formal model of DIM, we apply best practises and reuse and combine existing core ontologies [17] for repesenting the information regarding distributed persons, groups, and roles. This ensures strong axiomatization as well as integrateability to systems also building on these ontologies. Especially by using the foundational ontology DOLCE+DnS Ultralight (DUL) [4], our solution provides compatibility to other frameworks relying on DUL-based ontologies, as the common use of shared concepts inherently results in semantic integrateability.

We base the design of our knowledge representation patterns on the methodology of Scherp et al. [17]. We reuse the foundational ontology DUL and the core ontology strukt for distributed workflows [16], InFO for policies [8], and CO-PLM for semantically describing product lifecylce data [18]. We use DUL, as it provides strong semantics and supports pattern-based extensions. An example of such an extension is strukt, which reuses concepts of DUL and extends them by a framework for different types of workflows. We identified the core ontology strukt [16] as basis for modeling distributed workflows as it unifies many different existing models and systems, a generalization that can then directly be leveraged by semDIM.

For semDIM, we combine strukt with the generic ontology design pattern for policy modeling from the core ontology InFO [8]. This enables associating policies with group and role management. Furthermore, semDIM can be combined with other core and domain specific ontologies. For example, as our scenario is set in the PLM context, we integrate CO-PLM [18] for phase-dependent semantic product lifecyle information modeling. This integration allows connecting general DIM entities of identities, groups, roles, as well as DIM policies and workflows with PLM specific concepts. For example, specific files on a file share, which belong to a certain project and are of a specific document type (e.g., design plans, manuals, etc.), may have a policy to only be accessible by project members of certain organizations with a designated role.

Our approach uses DUL's Descriptions and Situations (DnS) pattern to represent semantics between identities of persons, groups, and roles. DnS allows to create descriptive contexts, i.e., `Descriptions`, defining various `Concepts`, such as `Roles`, `Parameters`, and `EventTypes`. These `Descriptions` may be satisfied by multiple relational contexts, called `Situations`, setting entities for the `Concepts` defined in the respective `Descriptions`. For example, a `Situation` might set an `Agent` classified by a `Role`, or an `Event` classified by an `EventType`. By reusing this pattern, we are able to distinguish between descriptive and relational contexts and integrate our concepts into DUL.

7   Evaluation: Application of semDIM Patterns

We evaluate our solution against the requirements stated in Sect. 4. For this, we demonstrate the application of a prototype implementation of semDIM adapted to the scenario from Sect. 3. The following nomenclature helps the reader to recognize which type of entity or property a name refers to: *Agents* are named by a single letter or a short description followed by a hyphen and a number, e.g., `a-1`, `b-1`, `root-a-1`. *Groups* are named similar to agents, but have `group` or `_g` within their name, e.g., `group-1`, `group-2`, `admin-group-1`, `admin-group-2`, `project_g-1`. *Roles* are identified by having `_role` or `_r` in their name, e.g., `admin_role-1`. These conventions only serve readability and are not normative. As the following statements are representatives for actions in different points in time of the project, we introduce the following four project phases: Initiation, Setup, Operations, and Closure.

Example for R1: Namespaces and Unique Identifiers The two companies A and B have unique namespaces, e.g., their publicly registered domain names. Therefore, they own their respective namespace, giving them full read and write access. Every set of triples using identifiers of these namespaces either explicitly states the full identifier to the respective namespace or reuses the prefixes. The companies coin identifiers for their namespace. For example, the URI `https://companyA.example/HR#a-1` defines the employee `a-1`, while the URI `https://companyA.example/HR` models the HR department. The very first triples exchanged by the companies at Project Initiation are the root identities, `root-a-1` and `root-b-1`. Listings 1 and 2 show the triples as created and transmitted by the companies via a secured and trusted channel.

```
1  @prefix a: <https://companyA.example/>.
2  a:root-a-1 a foaf:Person ;
3      semDIM:ownsNamespace a:.
```

Listing 1. Namespaces definitions defined by `a:root-a-1`

```
1  @prefix b: <https://companyB.example/>.
2  b:root-b-1 a foaf:Person;
3      semDIM:ownsNamespace b:.
```

Listing 2. Namespaces definitions defined by `b:root-b-1`

After the exchange, each company holds definitions for its own as well as the other company's namespaces and root identities. They are used to define initial identities and groups. Listing 3 depicts those first identities and groups for company A defined by root-a-1. As they use the namespace a:, they are uniquely identifiable even outside of company A. Similar triples also exist on B's side using the namespace b: (listing not depicted). As shown in the semDIM architecture (see Fig. 3), the triples exchanged by the companies are verified through the reasoning engine and incorporated in the triple stores.

```
1   a:a-1 a foaf:Person.
2   a:a-2 a foaf:Person.
3
4   a:group-1 a foaf:Group.
5   a:group-2 a foaf:Group.
6
7   a:groupAdmins_g-a-1 a foaf:Group;
8       foaf:member a:a-1.
9   a:groupAdmins_g-a-2 a foaf:Group.
10
11  a:group-1 semDIM:administratedBy a:groupAdmins_g-a-1.
12  a:group-2 semDIM:administratedBy a:groupAdmins_g-a-2.
```

Listing 3. First identities and groups defined by `a:root-a-1`

These triples are also exchanged during the Initiation phase. At the end of the Initiation phase, both companies' servers hold the initial namespaces and entities relevant for the project, but there are no connections across companies yet. These are created in the Setup Phase.

Example for R2: Distributed identifiers for agents The identities can be referenced across namespaces, e.g., by connecting two separate identities of the same person in both companies A and B. This is simply done by using the owl:sameAs property as shown in Listing 4: In our scenario, Person 1 belongs only to one company (A), but he needs a separate account, and therefore an additional identifier, in the other company B. In real life settings, such a separation of accounts may also be necessary, if an information system does not allow for recognizing identities outside of its home namespace. This triple is exchanged during the Setup Phase.

```
1   a:a-1 owl:sameAs b:b-1.
```

Listing 4. Identity connection defined by `a:a-1`

Example for R3: Distributed identifiers for groups In Listing 3, line 8 we show a group membership definition. Lines 1–12 define the administration of group-1 and group-2. All of these triples are created by a:root-a-1 and are also transmitted to B's server in the Setup Phase. Groups can also be defined across namespaces, i.e., as distributed groups as Listing 5 demonstrates.

```
1  a:group-1  owl:sameAs  b:group-1.
```

Listing 5. Group connection defined by `a:root-a-1`

Example for R4: Distributed identifiers for roles In the Operations Phase, identity information consistently changes, e.g., new accounts are created and added to groups or roles are assigned. Also, project data not related to IM also gets exchanged now, e.g., `Lego Train` product information in our scenario. Listing 6 shows the RDF data equivalent to a group admin permission assignment. It shows the assignment of the administrator role for group `a:group-1` to `a:a-1` by `root-a-1`. With this role, `a:a-1` can add or remove members to the project group `group-1`, which is one of his essential tasks as project leader.

```
1   a:admin_perm-1 a semDIM:GroupPermission;
2      dul:defines a:namespace_owner-1 , a:group_admin-1,
3         a:group_administration-1 , a:administrated_group_role-1.
4
5   a:namespace_owner-1 a semDIM:AssignerRole;
6         dul:isRoleOf a:root-a-1.
7
8   a:group_admin-1 a semDIM:AssignedRole;
9         dul:isRoleOf a:a-1.
10
11  a:group_administration-1 a semDIM:AssignedTask;
12     dul:isExecutedIn a:admin_action-1.
13
14  a:administrated_group_role-1 a semDIM:AffectedGroupRole;
15        dul:isRoleOf a:group-1.
16
17  a:admin_assign-1 a semDIM:GroupPermissionExecution;
18     dul:isSettingFor a:root-a-1 , a:a-1,
19        a:admin_action-1 , a:group-1.
```

Listing 6. `dul:Role` Assignment defined by `a:root-a-1`

Lastly, in the Closure Phase, the project ends and no further communication between the systems of A and B is expected. Now, each company deletes or archives the triples containing the namespace of the other company to revoke all entity assignments and connections.

We demonstrated the specific use of semDIM in the context of our scenario from Sect. 3. Furthermore, we checked the consistency of the statements in the listings above with the patterns by applying the Hermit reasoner [20]. As our approach relies on semantic technologies, it is easily extensible. Additional features for improving security and functionality, such as certificate based graph signing, are potential topics of future work.

8   Conclusion

We presented semDIM as a solution for Semantic Distributed Identity Management. We elaborated the shortcomings of existing solutions and proposed an approach based on Semantic Web technologies to define and manage not only distributed identities of persons, but also distributed groups, and roles. We demonstrated semDIM at the example of industrial collaboration. A prototypical implementation of semDIM as well as .owl-files of the ontology patterns can be accessed under: https://github.com/FSCHOEN/semDIM.

References

1. Brickley, D., Miller, L.: FOAF vocabulary specification 0.99 (2014). http://xmlns.com/foaf/spec/20140114.html
2. Cirio, L., Cruz, I.F., Tamassia, R.: A role and attribute based access control system using semantic web technologies. In: Meersman, R., Tari, Z., Herrero, P. (eds.) OTM 2007. LNCS, vol. 4806, pp. 1256–1266. Springer, Heidelberg (2007). https://doi.org/10.1007/978-3-540-76890-6_53
3. Gai, K., Qiu, M., Thuraisingham, B., Tao, L.: Proactive attribute-based secure data schema for mobile cloud in financial industry. In: IEEE HPCC, CSS, and ICESS (2015)
4. Gangemi, A.: DOLCE+DnS Ultralite (DUL). ontologydesignpatterns.org (2009). http://ontologydesignpatterns.org/wiki/Ontology:DOLCE+DnS_Ultralite
5. Hu, L., Ying, S., Jia, X., Zhao, K.: Towards an approach of semantic access control for cloud computing. In: Jaatun, M.G., Zhao, G., Rong, C. (eds.) CloudCom 2009. LNCS, vol. 5931, pp. 145–156. Springer, Heidelberg (2009). https://doi.org/10.1007/978-3-642-10665-1_13
6. Kasem-Madani, S., Meier, M.: Security and privacy policy languages: a survey, categorization and gap identification. https://arxiv.org/pdf/1512.00201
7. Kasten, A.: Secure Semantic Web Data Management: Confidentiality, Integrity, and Compliant Availability in Open and Distributed Networks. University Koblenz-Landau (2016)
8. Kasten, A., Scherp, A.: Ontology-based information flow control of network-level internet communication. IJSC 9(01), 1–45 (2015)
9. Kayes, A., Han, J., Colman, A.: An ontological framework for situation-aware access control of software services. Inf. Syst. 53, 253–277 (2015)
10. Kirrane, S., Mileo, A., Decker, S.: Access control and the resource description framework: a survey. Semant. Web 8(2), 311–352 (2017)
11. Mansour, E., et al.: A demonstration of the solid platform for social web applications. In: Proceedings of the 25th International Conference Companion on World Wide Web - WWW 2016 Companion. ACM Press, New York (2016)
12. OASIS: eXtensible Access Control Markup Language Version 3.0. OASIS (2010)
13. Obrst, L., McCandless, D., Ferrell, D.: Fast semantic attribute-role-based access control (ARBAC) in a collaborative environment. In: Proceedings of the 8th IEEE International Conference on Collaborative Computing: Networking, Applications and Worksharing. IEEE (2012)
14. Priebe, T., Dobmeier, W., Kamprath, N.: Supporting attribute-based access control with ontologies. In: First International Conference on Availability, Reliability and Security (ARES 2006) (2006)
15. Rietveld, L.: Replication for linked data. In: Cudré-Mauroux, P., et al. (eds.) ISWC 2012. LNCS, vol. 7650, pp. 415–423. Springer, Heidelberg (2012). https://doi.org/10.1007/978-3-642-35173-0_31

16. Scherp, A., Eißing, D., Staab, S.: strukt—a pattern system for integrating individual and organizational knowledge work. In: Aroyo, L., et al. (eds.) ISWC 2011. LNCS, vol. 7031, pp. 569–584. Springer, Heidelberg (2011). https://doi.org/10.1007/978-3-642-25073-6_36
17. Scherp, A., Saathoff, C., Franz, T., Staab, S.: Designing core ontologies. In: Applied Ontology, vol. 6. IOS Press (2011)
18. Schönteich, F., Kasten, A., Scherp, A.: A pattern-based core ontology for product lifecycle management based on DUL. In: WOP 2018 at ISWC 2018, Monterey, USA. CEUR Workshop Proceedings, CEUR-WS.org (2018)
19. Schwagereit, F., Scherp, A., Staab, S.: Representing Distributed Groups with dgFOAF. In: ESWC 2010, Heraklion, Crete, Greece (2010)
20. Shearer, R., Motik, B., Horrocks, I.: HermiT: a highly-efficient OWL reasoner directions. In: ISWC 2008. Springer, Heidelberg (2008)
21. Shen, H.: A semantic-aware attribute-based access control model for web services. In: Hua, A., Chang, S.-L. (eds.) ICA3PP 2009. LNCS, vol. 5574, pp. 693–703. Springer, Heidelberg (2009). https://doi.org/10.1007/978-3-642-03095-6_65
22. Silva, E.F.: ACROSS-FI: attribute-based access control with distributed policies for future internet. In: ICN. IARIA XPS Press (2015)
23. Sirin, E., Parsia, B., Grau, B.C., Kalyanpur, A., Katz, Y.: Pellet: a practical OWL-DL reasoner. J. Web Seman. 5(2), 51–53 (2007)
24. Szyperski, C., Gruntz, D., Murer, S.: Component software: beyond object-oriented programming, 2nd edn. Component Software Series. Addison-Wesley, London (2003)
25. W3C: WebID 1.0 - Web Identity and Discovery Editor's Draft 05 March 2014. W3C (2014). https://www.w3.org/2005/Incubator/webid/spec/identity/
26. W3C: Decentralized Identifiers (DIDs) v1.0 - Core architecture, data model, and representations - W3C Working Draft 07 September 2020. W3C (2020). https://www.w3.org/TR/did-core/

Telegram: Data Collection, Opportunities and Challenges

Tuja Khaund(✉), Muhammad Nihal Hussain(✉), Mainuddin Shaik(✉),
and Nitin Agarwal(✉)

University of Arkansas At Little Rock, Little Rock, AR 72204, USA
{txkhaund,mnhussain,mxshaik,nxagarwal}@ualr.edu

Abstract. Over the years, social media platforms such as Facebook, Twitter, etc.,
have become a valuable resource for marketing, public relations etc. One emerging
mobile instant messaging medium, Telegram, has recently gained momentum
in countries such as Brazil, Indonesia, Iran, Russia, Ukraine, and Uzbekistan.
While most social media platforms have been studied extensively, Telegram is
still underexplored and a gold mine for researchers and social scientists to explore
and study user behaviors. Moreover, the ease of data collection through its API and
access to historical data makes it a lucrative platform for social computing research.
This paper explores the features of Telegram and presents a methodology to collect
and analyze data. We also demonstrate the viability of the platform as a source of
social computing research by presenting a case study on Ukrainian Parliamentary
members' discourse. We conduct both text and network analysis to gain insights
into political discourse and public opinion. Our findings include use of Telegram
by Ukrainian politicians to connect with their voter base, promote their work
as well as ridicule their peers. As a result, channels are actively disseminating
information on current political affairs and chat groups that discuss views on
Ukrainian government. From our study, we conclude that Telegram is a rich data
source to study social behavior, analyze information campaigns through content
dissemination, etc. This study opens plethora of research opportunities in future
on Telegram.

Keywords: Social network analysis · Sentiment analysis · Telegram · Ukraine ·
Social computing

1 Introduction

Online social networks (OSNs) are dynamic social interaction platforms with billions
of users worldwide. They attract people regardless of their age, gender, socioeconomic
status, etc., and produce a tremendous amount of digital data for analysis [1]. The number
of OSN users is increasing every year. According to the Pew Research Center's survey
report, 65% of adult Americans use at least one social networking site [2]. Information is
rapidly disseminated among these users through online social interactions generating a
huge volume of data that provides the opportunity to study behaviors of digital societies

© Springer Nature Switzerland AG 2021
J. A. Lossio-Ventura et al. (Eds.): SIMBig 2020, CCIS 1410, pp. 513–526, 2021.
https://doi.org/10.1007/978-3-030-76228-5_37

[3]. An in-depth investigation of OSNs is important to enhance the understanding of social and behavioral dynamics, as well as addressing pressing societal issues.

In recent years, Instant Messaging (IM) has become one of the fastest growing services provided by the mobile-based social media networks [4]. Telegram is now a new paradigm between social media and instant messengers. It allows individuals to share news and information, coordinate political activity, and discuss politics [5]. In Russia, Telegram became the news hub for insider information and internal political discussions [6]. Telegram's popularity recently spiked in Ukraine as Amazon's Alexa Website Ranking service puts Telegram in the top 50 websites visited in Ukraine[1]. Telegram is not as strictly scrutinized as other social media outlets such as Facebook or Twitter, so it is hard to differentiate facts from misinformation. In a recent case study, the Atlantic Council's Digital Forensic Research Lab (DFRL) [6] analyzed the role of Telegram posts in the spread of misinformation about an upcoming prisoner exchange between Ukraine and Russia. These posts were subsequently confirmed, erroneously by a Ukrainian government official on Facebook. The DFRL analyzed the dissemination of the unsubstantiated reports and found that they first emerged in several anonymous Telegram channels which were later picked up by news outlets as well as influential public figures.

In this paper, we conduct an exploratory analysis of the various features on Telegram and present a methodology to collect and analyze data. We also demonstrate its viability as a platform for social computing research by presenting a case study on Ukrainian political discourse. Through this case study, we wanted to study the political motivation as well as public opinion on the two presidential candidates, Poroshenko and Zelensky along with other members of the Parliament. Our findings indicate that Ukrainian politicians mainly use Telegram to interact with their base voters. Politicians and their entourage maintain channels that are actively disseminating information related to changing political climate and chat groups that discuss their views on Ukrainian government. We also found information campaigns and use of algorithmic manipulation strategies that were previously detected on other platforms [6, 15]. We also explain the challenges encountered and limitations of the study.

The rest of the paper is organized as follows. In the next section, we explore related work and examine how Telegram has helped other researchers to study group dynamics and misinformation, among other topics. Then we discuss our methodology in Sect. 3, where we explain the data collection methodology and describe the acquired dataset. Section 4 presents case study on Ukrainian political discourse. Finally, we present our findings, limitations and future work in Sect. 5.

2 Literature Review

Existing research revealed how Telegram has been extensively used by individuals, educational organizations, companies and political parties for different purposes. Bradshaw et al. [5] reported evidence of Telegram based disinformation campaigns alongside other chat applications such as WhatsApp and WeChat. They identified evidence of political

---

[1] https://www.alexa.com/siteinfo/telegram.org.

communication strategies such as targeting advertisements to specific segments of the population using demographic information, data on user attitudes, or gaming algorithms through search engine optimization techniques to make their content appear higher in search results. Agur and Frisch [9] explored the catalytic effect of social media on digital and physical activism by interviewing participants in the Hong Kong's 2014 Umbrella Movement. They studied ways in which protesters used digital platforms during the debates about elections for Hong Kong's Chief Executive. While analyzing the extent of activists' social media usage to organize, mobilize, and persuade beyond the movement, authors found Telegram played a significant role because of its robust security features. Protest leaders adopted Telegram for sensitive discussions, and developed guidelines for sensitive deliberations since they were rarely responsive to Twitter DMs (direct messages) or email. However, with Telegram's encrypted channels, it was easier to organize them in person with phones stored in another location to protect against surveillance.

While these studies focused on Telegram, these studies were conducted empirically and the data collection was done through interviews. There is a need for both qualitative and quantitative analysis of information being disseminated on Telegram. Moreover, there is a need to analyze the political campaigns and influence operations on this platform. Our work focuses on bridging this gap by extending our previously published social media data collection methodologies [10–12] to include Telegram and adopt methods from various other studies that emphasize on how to perform 'social media text analytics' when analyzing data from messaging applications and social media platforms in general [13].

Practice of measuring and analyzing public opinion via polling is slowly being replaced by text mining and natural language processing (NLP). Few recent studies have found political opinion expressed via Twitter and official poll data are strongly correlated leading to the suggestion that real-time text mining can be considered as a substitute for traditional polling [14]. Also, political, business and public health data were identified as fertile context for text analytics by Bollier et al. [15]. Al-Ani et al. [16] used NLP techniques to analyze the narratives that were generated by the Egyptian bloggers that were opposing the government's corruption during the uprising of Egyptian revolution. This study found various political narratives and was able to distinguish them using text analysis. They also presented the trends of these counter narratives. In another study, Anstead and O'Loughlin [17] advocated amalgamation of real-time data to study political strategies. Furthermore, a study by Zeng et al. [18] analyzed the political discussion from the perspective of citizens and political institutions using social media analytic techniques. It found that political institutions prefer to actively participate in the political discussion through social media platforms particularly during election campaigns because social media can help reach wider audience and sway political opinions. Simultaneously, it also can be used to build community support for their candidates running for the government office. During the 2008 US presidential campaigns, Wanner et al. [19] applied real-time text mining of news coverage in their study to analyze sentiments around specific candidates and topics. Study on content and sentiment analysis on entertainment industry's social media data found that film's box-office success could be predicted [20]. In the public health area, spread of epidemics and natural calamity have been identified by text mining analyses using quantitative and qualitative approach on social media conversations [21, 22].

3 Methodology

This section elaborates the steps followed to collect and process data successfully. It includes three main steps and a few sub-steps that will help initiate the API, identify relevant data and crawl it. The high-level workflow is depicted in Fig. 1.

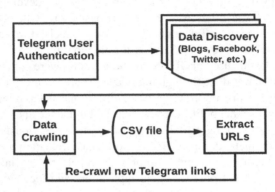

Fig. 1. Data collection methodology

3.1 Setting up Data Collection Scripts

To create a Telegram API that can be utilized to collect data following steps needs to be completed by a user.

1. Create a developer account with a registered phone number with SMS[2].
2. Generate API credentials such as api_id, api_hash, and phone number for user authorization.
3. Authentication: We used Python library Telethon to authenticate the generated keys.

After successful execution, an activation code was sent to the Telegram app to fully enable the API access. Once everything is set up correctly, the API will crawl all messages from groups or channels that the linked Telegram account is a member of.

3.2 Discovery of Relevant Channels and Groups

The most difficult part of the data collection is discovering appropriate channels and groups. Some groups or channels were private while others are so obscure that we could not easily identify them. Their names were in Ukrainian which made searching

---

[2] https://core.telegram.org/api/obtaining_api_id.

quite difficult. We started with a set of channels by scouring blogs, Facebook and other platforms. Later, we snowballed by adding links to data collection that were obtained from Sect. 3.3. The initial data collection started in November 2019 and the latest re-crawl date is February 09, 2020. We found eight active Telegram channels (see Table 1, top) that initiated our automated data collection process. We also identified new Telegram channels (see Table 1, bottom) during our data processing stage (explained in the next section).

Table 1. Telegram channel information

Channel (ID)	Members	Messages
Volodymyr Groysman (*volodymyrgroysman*)	102	37
Андрій Садовий (*andriysadovyi*)	287	158
Верховна Рада України (*verkhovnaradaukrainy*)	546	625
Гриценко 2019 (*grytsenko_2019*)	71	55
ЛЕЩЕНКО ТУТ (*LeshchenkoS*)	16741	633
Олексій Рябчин (*alexrbchnMP*)	302	186
Петро Порошенко (PresidentPoroshenko)	43060	644
Тимошенко Юлія підтримка (*Tymoshenko_Yulia*)	80	28
Мустафа Найем (*mustafanayyem*)	19747	382
Sonya Koshkina (*sonyakoshkina*)	44001	1014
Шабунін депутатам (*Shabunin_RADI*)	1602	43
Володимир Зеленський (Президент України) (*PresidentZelenskij*)	6868	699
Легитимный (*legitimniy*)	66450	3110

3.3 Data Processing and Storage

Using the Telegram API, we extracted information from these channels and groups in the form of message_id, message, from_id (groups only), datetime, reply_to_msg_id (groups only). Note that some of the attributes are only available for groups. The 'message_id' is created by Telegram and is incremented starting from 'message1'. The column 'from_id' is a group-only feature that refers to the username of the group member. Similarly, 'reply_to_msg_id' is also for groups only and includes the 'message_id' of parent message. The 'message' field includes text and, unlike Twitter, there is no restriction on character limit. We found that users use this opportunity to frame the content as well as embed URLs that support their argument making it a perfect platform for discussion and influence operations. We identified the presence of blogs, other social media, and even new Telegram links. We identified a total of 1348 links; extracted and expanded all URLs using urlextract[3]. The collected data is saved to a CSV file and with every re-crawl, the script starts with the last message ID and appends the new data to the existing CSV file[4].

---

[3] https://urlextract.readthedocs.io/en/latest/urlextract.html.

[4] Data and the code are available upon request.

4 Analysis and Findings

Telegram offers two main mediums for users to interact with each other, namely: Group and Channel. Although both channels and groups allow users to send messages, groups provide a forum for discussion enabling users to reply to each other whereas channels only allow channel admins to send messages. We conduct text analysis on both mediums to study content dissemination. Since group members interact with each other, we also conducted social network analysis on their communication network.

4.1 Group Analysis

To conduct social network analysis on a communication network, we identified one chat group called Володимир Зеленський (Volodimir Zelensky) Chat. We found 5210 messages shared by 637 users.

Social Network Analysis. We constructed a communication [user to user] network of the members in the chat group based on the 'reply_to' property. We removed all entries where the 'reply_to_msg_id' field was empty. Although Telegram permanently removes messages deleted by a user, any existing messages that referenced it (or had replied to it) still maintain the reference. We also discarded 80 entries, where the 'message_id' was missing. The final network consisted of 364 nodes and 770 edges as shown in Fig. 2.

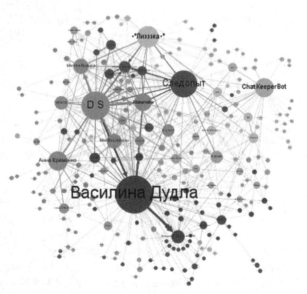

Fig. 2. Commenter-commenter 'reply-to' network. Nodes are colored based on communities.

The reply-to network is a directed network where the direction of the arrow travels from the source node (commenter) to the 'replied-to' node. The nodes are sized based on their out-degree. We applied a modularity based clustering algorithm [23] to detect communities and colored the nodes based on their community class. The modularity score is 0.409 which is moderately low which indicates that communities have sparser connections within its members but more connections to other users in different clusters. The edges are weighted based on the number of replies between them and colored based on their target node which also represents the direction. Edge thickness helps us identify actors who interacted with the most within the network. It also helps us find active users within the chat group. This network had a low network density score of 0.024 suggesting that not all users are connected to each other. However, having network diameter of 8 suggests means that even if users did not interact directly with other users, they were still reachable to each other within a distance of eight nodes. We also calculated out-degree and in-degree centrality measures to list users that reached out to and were reached out by most other users within the network (see Table 2). We listed a few of the top pairs of commenters who interacted the most in the chat group in Table 3.

Table 2. Top five users with out-degree and in-degree centrality measures respectively

User	Type	Value
D S	Out-degree	241
Василина Дудла	Out-degree	155
• °Лизззка•°	Out-degree	96
Следопыт	Out-degree	91
Makemake	Out-degree	84
D S	In-degree	137
Алексей Василевский	In-degree	88
Василина Дудла	In-degree	80
Makemake	In-degree	72
Marinka Pyatnica	In-degree	68

We analyzed the top three active users, Василина Дудла, D S, Makemake and Володимир Зеленський chat's activity on the chat group. For each user, we extracted their messages and conducted sentiment analysis using Linguistic Inquiry and Word Count (LIWC) [24]. We observed that the overall sentiment was positive. Василина Дудла's messages were highly positive while the rest of the users had neutral sentiments. The positive messages were in favor of president Zelenskiy showing praises and respect. Neutral sentiments could suggest either a lack of emotionality or different levels of ambivalence towards the members of the chat group or the content. A sample set of comments along with their translations for our top commenters is listed in Table 4.

While the analysis illustrates the overall sentiment of these users, it has a few limitations. For example, it is hard to detect whether these sentiments are addressed towards a member of the chat group or President Zelensky. Targeted sentiment analysis could help us get better insights on these sentiments that will be conducted in our future work.

To understand what these prominent users are saying, we analyzed word clouds for their chat history (see Fig. 3). For each user, we extracted their messages, translated them, and removed messages which only contained emojis or symbols. We also removed the

Table 3. Top commenter pairs

Commenter	Reply to	Count
Василина Дудла	Володимир Зеленський Chat	29
D S	Makemake	25
D S	Marinka Pyatnica	24
D S	Василина Дудла	22
Василина Дудла	D S	18
Marinka Pyatnica	D S	16
Makemake	D S	16
Станіслав Підвірний	А Д min	16

Table 4. Top users' comments from the Zelenskiy Chat group

Comments	Translation
Підтримую Вас на всі 100% но і підтримуймо разом нашого Президента Зеленського на всі 100% перемога за Україною і українцями удачі з Богом	We support you all 100% but support our President Zelensky together for all 100% victory over Ukraine and Ukrainians good luck with God
Поэтому мы и поддерживаем нашего Президента, чтоб он войну закончил	That is why we support our President to end the war
Я в це вірю і підтримую нашого Президента і його дії Він сильний розумний найкращий на всю Україну і світ	I believe in and support our President and his actions. He is a strong intelligent best in all Ukraine and the world

word 'Ukraine' since it was frequently used and based on the context it was bound to be frequent. Even though words such as war and death appear in our results, prominent words include Zelensky, Support, God, etc. This shows that the top actors were speaking in support of their president and comparing him to God with comments such as "Zelensky is a gift to Ukraine from God", "Poroshenko's death !! @", "Zelensky Power of Ukraine ✊💥", etc. Other discussions include bills introduced by the Ukrainian government, Ukraine-Russia relations, etc. A few comments include "Аа вообще, я думаю, нужно объединиться с Россией в советский союз 👍👍👍(And in general, I think we need to unite with Russia in the Soviet Union)", "как хорошо что наш Президент дружит с Путиным, не то что этот Порошенко (how good that our president is friends with Putin, not that this Poroshenko)", and "All arrangements with the invader and killer Putin should be made only after the full withdrawal of Russian troops from the Donbass, i.e. to carry out a complete de-occupation. And to take the borders under Ukrainian control".

Fig. 3. Word cloud of users', Василина Дудла (top-left), D S (top-right), Makemake (bottom-left) and Володимир Зеленський Chat (bottom-right) messages on Zelenskiy chat group.

4.2 Channel Analysis

Telegram channels have limited forms of interaction between members. The admin is the content producer and its members are the content receivers or audience. Audience can like or dislike a post, but that feature is not enabled in all channels. So, we have ignored the analysis of likes/dislikes for this study. The message content of these channels was of interest. It should be noted that we translated the messages from Ukrainian to English.

Posting Frequency. We constructed timestamp frequency charts of posted messages to identify events of interest based on user activity. For example, the activity of channels Олексій Рябчин (alexrbchnMP), ЛЕЩЕНКО ТУТ (LeshchenkoS) and Мустафа Найем (mustafanayyem) peaked during the months of November and December 2018. A few other months include January 2019, and May 2019. To understand the cause of these spikes, we created word clouds of all the messages that were shared on the channel during those months. We learnt that a new Martial Law was introduced in Ukraine in November 2018 and the majority of the discussion revolved around it. Discussions in February focused on President Poroshenko and his impeachment bill. A few messages covered his speech during the NATO Summit at Brussels, Belgium, but the remaining conversations were predominantly about Zelenskiy's inauguration and his upcoming roles as the new president of Ukraine. Due to space limitations, we are showing posting frequency of two users in Figs. 4 and 5.

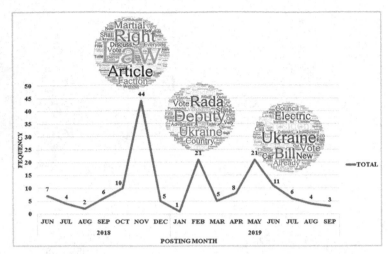

Fig. 4. Frequency of messages posted on the Олексій Рябчин (alexrbchnMP) channel and word clouds of the peak months.

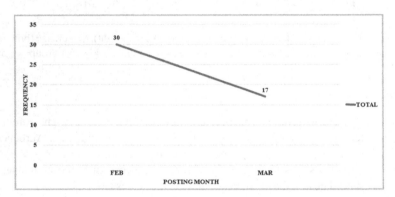

Fig. 5. Frequency of messages posted on the Гриценко 2019 (grytsenko_2019) channel. Active months include Feb–Mar 2019.

We conducted similar analyses on the other channels to understand the overall channels' user activities and observed similar trends in posting during these three months. One channel 'grytsenko_2019' (see Fig. 5) only posted messages during the month of February and May 2019. This shows that some accounts are created specifically to push content during certain events where they can get the maximum exposure to their posts. Although this indicates use of inorganic accounts for information campaigns, it is unclear if these accounts were fully automated bot accounts [25, 26], paid users or a combination of either. Further investigations are needed to classify them.

Cross-media Link Analysis. Upon analyzing the links on our channel list, we found several URLs directed to various social media platforms. There were 159 YouTube links, 8 Instagram links, 113 Facebook links and 36 blogs that were shared on these channels. We extracted these links and ran a quick check to identify common URLs across different channels. This helps understand the different roles social media platforms play in information dissemination - platforms that host the information and the ones that drive users or views to the platform that is hosting the content [8]. This tactic, also known as the cross-media dissemination approach, has been observed in several disinformation campaigns [7]. A few examples are shown in Table 5.

Empirically digging deeper into these, we found YouTube link shared belongs to the official channel of Bihus.Info project, an anti-corruption journalistic investigation team. This video discusses an investigation led by Lesia Ivanova about the secret correspondence of Poroshenko's entourage. The rollbacks and the scheme to steal millions on the defense, Russian smuggling and money laundering with the help of the son of one of the most influential officials and a friend of the President was covered in large scale. The Instagram link is the official account of MP Sergey Leshchenko which was shared to boost his social media presence. The rest of the frequently shared links belong to prominent blogs in Ukraine.

Table 5. Cross-media Information sharing

Channels (ID)	Media	Source
Mustafanayyem, LeshchenkoS	youtube.com/watch?v=lGTf2nUyxfw	YouTube
LeshchenkoS, ravers_party	instagram.com/sergii_leshchenko/	Instagram
alexrbchnMP, LeshchenkoS	blogs.pravda.com.ua	Blog
alexrbchnMP, LeshchenkoS, mustafanayyem, sonyakoshkina	lb.ua	Blog

5 Discussion and Conclusions

Telegram is very popular and growing rapidly in countries such as Brazil, Indonesia, Iran, Russia, Ukraine, and Uzbekistan. Telegram is a rising platform for misinformation and social manipulation. There are several ways researchers can utilize Telegram to conduct studies that can benefit the society. It is a rich source of information and its ability to access historical data gives more flexibility to researchers to conduct an in-depth analyses.

In this study, we presented a methodology to collect data from Telegram messaging platform, explained the features that can be collected and challenges encountered. We also demonstrated its viability as a platform for social computing research through a case study on Ukrainian political discourse. Analysis of these groups and channels helped us understand Ukrainian political affairs and people's reactions to ongoing events. From analysis of the chat group, we found most members were praising their president. Using social network analysis, we identified active members of the groups and through basic textual analysis visualized the overall discussion in the chat group. We also found a variety of terms that correspond to ongoing Ukrainian political affairs. Another insight derived from the analysis was that the commenters were divided in their opinions about Ukraine-Russia relations as well as President Zelenskiy and former President Poroshenko. From analysis of the channels, we found peak in activity around important events where content was pushed at a higher rate. This analysis also helped in detecting popular events quickly and effortlessly. Another insight derived upon analysis of the URLs shared in the channels was channel admins used algorithmic manipulation techniques including cross-media approach for content dissemination. This also shows that platforms such as Telegram serve as vehicles that drive users to the original content generators such as YouTube or blogs.

We encountered several challenges during data discovery, collection, and processing. The majority of the channel names were in Ukrainian that required translation in order to identify them. The Python script required support for skipping large blocks of messages where an admin removed them due to bot spam. Due to the volume of extracted URLs, we had to modify the script to fix or remove broken links as well as speed up the expansion process. We also had to translate all the Ukrainian text to English for our analysis. The dataset was also curated through one chat group and a number of telegram channels, which could be considered limited to some researchers. However, with the existing dataset, we were able to find insights on the political discourse of these channels and chat groups on Telegram.

For immediate future work, we would like to extend our work by expanding our dataset, conducting targeted sentiment analysis and examining community dynamics within the chat groups. We also plan to conduct an in-depth analysis of the content with Topic Modeling. Given Telegram's popularity in certain regions, we plan to investigate cyber-cultural influences on communications, as our long-term research.

Acknowledgements. This research is funded in part by the U.S. National Science Foundation (OIA-1946391, OIA-1920920, IIS-1636933, ACI-1429160, and IIS-1110868), U.S. Office of Naval Research (N00014-10-1-0091, N00014-14-1-0489, N00014-15-P-1187, N00014-16-1-2016, N00014-16-1-2412, N00014-17-1-2675, N00014-17-1-2605, N68335-19-C-0359, N00014-19-1-2336, N68335-20-C-0540), U.S. Air Force Research Lab, U.S. Army Research Office (W911NF-17-S-0002, W911NF-16-1-0189), U.S. Defense Advanced Research Projects Agency (W31P4Q-17-C-0059), Arkansas Research Alliance, the Jerry L. Maulden/Entergy Endowment at the University of Arkansas at Little Rock, and the Australian Department of Defense Strategic Policy Grants Program (SPGP) (award number: 2020-106-094). Any opinions, findings, and conclusions or recommendations expressed in this material are those of the authors and do not necessarily reflect the views of the funding organizations. The researchers gratefully acknowledge the support.

References

1. Raghavan, S.: Digital forensic research: current state of the art. CSI Trans. ICT **1**, 91–114 (2013). https://doi.org/10.1007/s40012-012-0008-7
2. Perrin, A.: Social Media Usage: 2005–2015, Washington, DC. 1 (2015)

3. Ratkiewicz, J., Conover, M., Meiss, M.R., Gonc̦alves, B., Flammini, A., Menczer, F.: Detecting and tracking political abuse in social media. In: Proceedings of the Fifth International AAAI Conference on Weblogs and Social Media, pp. 297–304. The AAAI Press, Barcelona, Catalonia, Spain (2011)

4. Sivabalan, K., Ali, Z.: Mobile Instant Messaging as Collaborative Tool for Language Learning. Int. J. Lang. Educ. Appl. Linguist. **9**, 99–109 (2019). https://doi.org/10.15282/ijleal.v9.297

5. Bradshaw, S., Howard, P.N.: Challenging Truth and Trust: A Global Inventory of Organized Social Media Manipulation, pp. 1–26. Project on Computational Propaganda, Oxford (2018)

6. DFRLab: Ukrainian media jump the gun on Russia-Ukraine prisoner swap. 1 (2019). https://medium.com/dfrlab/ukrainian-media-jump-the-gun-on-russia-ukraine-prisoner-swap-321 6f860bc04

7. Bandeli, K.K., Agarwal, N.: Analyzing the role of media orchestration in conducting disinformation campaigns on blogs. Comput. Math. Organ. Theory. 27 (2018). https://doi.org/10.1007/s10588-018-09288-9

8. Hussain, M.N.: Role of Multiple Social Media Platforms in Online Campaigns, 64 (2019). https://0-search-proquest-com.library.ualr.edu/docview/2377711983?accountid=14482

9. Agur, C., Frisch, N.: Digital disobedience and the limits of persuasion: social media activism in Hong Kong's 2014 Umbrella Movement. Soc. Media Soc. **5**, 12 (2019). https://doi.org/10.1177/2056305119827002

10. Khaund, T., Bandeli, K.K., Walter, O., Agarwal, N.: A novel methodology to identify and collect data from relevant blogs leveraging multiple social media platforms and cyber forensics. In: The Fifth International Conference on Big Data, Small Data, Linked Data and Open Data, pp. 41–45. IARIA XPS Press, Valencia, Spain (2019)

11. Roy, A.K., Agarwal, N.: Automating blog crawling using pattern recognition. In: The Ninth International Conference on Social Media Technologies, Communication, and Informatics, pp. 32–38. IARIA XPS Press, Valencia, Spain (2019)

12. Hussain, M.N., Obadimu, A., Bandeli, K.K., Nooman, M., Al-khateeb, S., Agarwal, N.: A framework for blog data collection: challenges and opportunities. In: The Seventh International Conference on Advances in Information Mining and Management, pp. 35–40. IARIA XPS Press, Venice, Italy (2017)

13. Stieglitz, S., Dang-Xuan, L.: Social media and political communication: a social media analytics framework. Soc. Netw. Anal. Mining **3**(4), 1277–1291 (2012). https://doi.org/10.1007/s13278-012-0079-3

14. O'Connor, B., Balasubramanyan, R., Routledge, B.R., Smith, N.A.: From tweets to polls: linking text sentiment to public opinion time series. In: Proceedings of the Fourth International AAAI Conference on Weblogs and Social Media, pp. 122–129. AAAI Press, Washington, DC (2010)

15. Bollier, D., Firestone, C.M.: The Promise and Peril of Big Data, The Aspen Institute, Aspen, Colorado, p. 66 (2009)

16. Al-Ani, B., Mark, G., Chung, J., Jones, J.: The Egyptian blogosphere: a counter-narrative of the revolution. In: Proceedings of the ACM 2012 Conference on Computer Supported Cooperative Work, pp. 17–26. Association for Computing Machinery, New York, NY, USA (2012). https://doi.org/10.1145/2145204.2145213

17. Anstead, N., O'Loughlin, B.: Semantic Polling: The Ethics of Online Public Opinion, The London School of Economics and Political Science, London, UK, 17 (2012).

18. Zeng, D., Chen, H., Lusch, R., Li, S.-H.: Social media analytics and intelligence. IEEE Intell. Syst. **25**, 13–16 (2010). https://doi.org/10.1109/MIS.2010.151

19. Wanner, F., Rohrdantz, C., Mansmann, F., Oelke, D., Keim, D.A.: Visual sentiment analysis of RSS news feeds featuring the US Presidential Election in 2008. In: Visual Interfaces to the Social and the Semantic Web, pp. 1–8. Konstanzer Online-Publikations-System (KOPS), Sanibel Island, Florida (2009)

20. Asur, S., Huberman, B.A.: Predicting the future with social media. In: 2010 IEEE/WIC/ACM International Conference on Web Intelligence and Intelligent Agent Technology, pp. 492–499 (2010). https://doi.org/10.1109/WI-IAT.2010.63

21. Ashktorab, Z., Brown, C., Nandi, M., Culotta, A.: Tweedr: Mining twitter to inform. In: 11th Proceedings of the International Conference on Information Systems for Crisis Response and Management, p. 5. University Park, Pennsylvania, USA (2014)

22. Chunara, R., Andrews, J.R., Brownstein, J.S.: Social and News Media Enable Estimation of Epidemiological Patterns Early in the 2010 Haitian Cholera Outbreak, 7 (2012). https://doi.org/10.4269/ajtmh.2012.11-0597

23. Blondel, V.D., Guillaume, J.-L., Lambiotte, R., Lefebvre, E.: Fast unfolding of communities in large networks. J. Stat. Mech. Theory Exp. **2008**, 13 (2008). https://doi.org/10.1088/1742-5468/2008/10/P10008

24. Pennebaker, J.W., Boyd, R.L., Jordan, K., Blackburn, K.: The Development and Psychometric Properties of LIWC2015. In: Texas ScholarWorks. p. 26. The University of Texas at Austin, Austin, TX (2015).

25. Khaund, T., Al-Khateeb, S., Tokdemir, S., Agarwal, N.: Analyzing Social Bots and Their Coordination During Natural Disasters. In: Thomson, Robert, Dancy, Christopher, Hyder, Ayaz, Bisgin, Halil (eds.) Social, Cultural, and Behavioral Modeling. LNCS, vol. 10899, pp. 207–212. Springer, Cham (2018). https://doi.org/10.1007/978-3-319-93372-6_23

26. Khaund, T., Bandeli, K.K., Hussain, M.N., Obadimu, A., Al-Khateeb, S., Agarwal, N.: Analyzing social and communication network structures of social bots and humans. In: 2018 IEEE/ACM International Conference on Advances in Social Networks Analysis and Mining (ASONAM), pp. 794–797 (2018). https://doi.org/10.1109/ASONAM.2018.8508665

Graph Theory Applied to International Code of Diseases (ICD) in a Hospital

C. Boldorini Jr.[ID], C. D. G. Euzebio[ID], L. P. Porto[ID], A. S. Martinez[ID],
and E. E. S. Ruiz[✉][ID]

Faculdade de Filosofia, Ciências e Letras de Ribeirão Preto,
Universidade de São Paulo (USP), Av. Bandeirantes, 3900,
Monte Alegre, Ribeirão Preto, SP 14040-901, Brazil
evandro@usp.br
https://www.ffclrp.usp.br/

Abstract. We analyze comorbidity from a set of International Code of Diseases (ICD) records from a tertiary level hospital based on the graph theory. Comorbidity is the simultaneous presence of two or more diseases or conditions in a patient. A total of 36,236 patient health records, containing 80,253 ICD code notifications, have been studied. We show that over 43.0% of all comorbidities can be determined from the dominant graph edges. This study goes beyond a first-order statistical analysis. ICD graph chapters can be used to understand patient flow in hospital specialties and may also be used to quantify inter and intra-relationships among major hospitalization events. Our result could help plan hospital organization arranging sectors highly correlated close together.

Keywords: Data mining · Data science · Disease tracking · Health data interpretation

1 Introduction

A graph is a collection of items, called *vertices* or *nodes*, connected among themselves by *edges* or *links*. The study and research of the graph theory are among the fundamental subjects of discrete mathematics and computational sciences [4]. The Euler's solution of the Königsberg bridge problem, as early as 1735, is known to be the first true proof in graph theory. Graphs may be classified according to the presence of patterns.

Recently, graph theory has been extensively used in the research of natural phenomena and human-made structures. The World Wide Web, social networks, food webs, distribution networks as blood vessels, and electricity are among a large number of examples of structures that resemble graphs. These examples can be seen as graphs with hundreds or even thousands of vertices, and a similar order of number of edges connecting them. Among a vast number of articles and books about this subject, extensive can be seen in articles from Bassett and Sporns [3], Barabási [1,2] Newman [9], and Dorogovtsev [5]. In medicine, graph

© Springer Nature Switzerland AG 2021
J. A. Lossio-Ventura et al. (Eds.): SIMBig 2020, CCIS 1410, pp. 527–539, 2021.
https://doi.org/10.1007/978-3-030-76228-5_38

theory has also been used to predict chronic disease, such as type 2 diabetes [7]. Knowledge graphs have been researched for clinical decision support systems in medicine and self-diagnostic symptom checkers [11]. The temporal graph can capture temporal relationships of the medical events, and it is used as a piece of authoritative information for analytic tasks in healthcare [8].

The analysis of these graphs is a fundamental milestone towards the understanding of the International Code of Diseases ICD codes interrelationships.

Here, the graph theory has been used to analyze patient reports entries of a tertiary hospital codified using the International Code for Diseases (ICD) [12]. One may also see this study as a comorbidity analysis, in other words, an analysis of the simultaneous presence of two diseases or conditions in a patient. This article is organized as follows: The collected data is summarized in Sect. 2. In Sect. 3, the ICD codes are reduced to the referenced chapters they belong to. These ICD chapters correspond to the graph nodes, while the occurrence of multiple entries establishes links among these nodes. Also in this section, graphs formed by these relationships are analyzed. The closing comments and discussions are found in Sect. 4, while the conclusions are presented in Sect. 5.

2   Data Description and First Order Statistics

The tertiary level teaching hospital *Hospital das Clínicas da Faculdade de Medicina de Ribeirão Preto*, (HCFMRP), *Universidade de São Paulo*, keeps hospitalization records of every patient. Annually, a digital summary report of every discharged patient is produced. This summary is formed by a sequence of records (entries) in which a single entry corresponds to a patient admittance at the HCFMRP. These entry records are composed of some demographic fields, and, for the concern of this work, it is also part of these health records.

1. ICD code for the main hospitalization cause (here referred as af_1); followed by
2. up to four secondary (supplementary) ICD (af_i, $2 \leq i \leq 5$) reports.

A summary report has been analyzed. The results are reported in the following section. Prior to the graph analysis, a broader view of these records is presented. The discharged patient summary has been analyzed in terms of entry numbers. It is important to stress that a particular patient might have multiple entries.

A total of 36,236 records have been analyzed. From this total:

- 18,926 (52.2%) records are related to female admissions;
- 17,305 (47.8%) records are related to male; and
- 3 (negligible, <0.001%) records are coded *undetermined sex*;

also,

- 34,665 (95.7%) entries received the code *discharged under medical order*;
- 31 (0.1%) entries are due to escaped patients from the hospital; and

– 1,539 (4.2%) were diseased patients, in which
  • 1,037 (67.4% from 1,539) patients have been submitted to autopsy; while
  • 502 (32.6%) have not.

Each reported ICD code entry has been transformed into the ICD chapter. Table 1 describes the ICD chapters name [12]. Every report entry has at least the main cause of hospitalization ICD code notified, called af_1. In the analyzed summary report, 80,253 ICD notifications have been reported. Table 2 summarizes the number of ICD codes for each entry class, if primary or secondary (supplementary), and it is ordered by *Total* column.

Table 1. ICD-10 chapter list.

ICD chapter	Title
1	Certain infectious and parasitic diseases
2	Neoplasms
3	Diseases of the blood and blood-forming organs and certain disorders involving the immune mechanism
4	Endocrine, nutritional and metabolic diseases
5	Mental and behavioural disorders
6	Diseases of the nervous system
7	Diseases of the eye and adnexa
8	Diseases of the ear and mastoid process
9	Diseases of the circulatory system
10	Diseases of the respiratory system
11	Diseases of the digestive system
12	Diseases of the skin and subcutaneous tissue
13	Diseases of the musculoskeletal system and connective tissue
14	Diseases of the genitourinary system
15	Pregnancy, childbirth and the puerperium
16	Certain conditions originating in the perinatal period
17	Congenital malformations, deformations and chromosomal abnormalities
18	Symptoms, signs and abnormal clinical and laboratory findings, not elsewhere classified
19	Injury, poisoning and certain other consequences of external causes
20	External causes of morbidity and mortality
21	Factors influencing health status and contact with health services
22	Codes for special purposes

The relationship between the number of ICD codes grouped under chapters and their accumulated frequency is pictured in Fig. 1. Notice in Table 2 that there is no entry for Chap. 20, *External causes of morbidity and mortality*, nor for Chap. 22, *Codes for special purposes*. Chapter 22 was not in use during the analyzed period. Also, 51.7% of every ICD are codes related to only six chapters out of 21 possibilities. These six chapter are: 9 (13.5%), 19 (9.3%), 15 (8.3%), 10 (7.3%), 11 (6.8%) and 1 (6.6%), in this order. In a similar way, the last 10 chapters correspond to less than 20.0% (17.6%) of the codes, including Chap. 20. Table 2 also shows that in only two entries, corresponding to Chaps. 4, *Endocrine, nutritional and metabolic diseases*, and 16, *Certain conditions originating in the perinatal period*, the first affection is not the largest sum in the row. This reflects the wide scope of these ICD chapters.

Table 2. Number of ICD codes by chapters, the accumulated number per chapter, their percentage and the accumulated relative frequency (fac). Notice that af_1 is smaller than af_2 in Chaps. 4 and 16. See Fig. 1.

ICD chapter	af_1	af_2	af_3	af_4	af_5	Total	%	fac
9	3606	3293	2149	1121	635	10804	13.5	13.5
19	3887	1808	935	526	269	7425	9.2	22.7
15	3522	1825	877	339	132	6695	8.3	31.0
10	2637	1544	786	480	318	5765	7.2	38.2
11	2741	1246	755	437	275	5454	6.8	45.0
1	1968	1369	939	653	401	5330	6.6	51.6
2	3262	767	355	132	83	4599	5.7	57.4
21	2781	824	488	261	126	4480	5.6	63.0
4	949	1293	1030	654	370	4296	5.3	68.3
14	1968	1265	526	337	188	4284	5.3	73.6
5	1431	1043	663	348	184	3669	4.6	78.2
6	1901	817	346	188	94	3346	4.2	82.4
16	129	1281	809	519	343	3081	3.8	86.2
18	1056	777	344	247	161	2585	3.2	89.4
13	1578	457	190	74	43	2342	2.9	92.3
17	655	423	234	173	100	1585	2.0	94.3
3	515	455	294	182	97	1543	1.9	96.2
7	888	191	65	33	32	1209	1.5	97.7
12	439	274	181	115	65	1074	1.3	99.0
8	322	205	103	35	22	687	0.9	99.9

3   Applying Graph Theory

A particular view of a single summary report record can be regarded as the interrelations among the five possible ICD code entries. For a given record, each

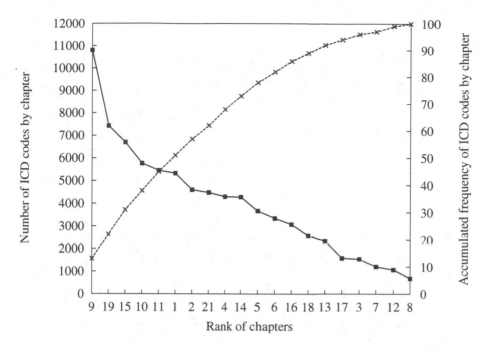

Fig. 1. Number of ICD codes for each chapter and their accumulated frequency. See Table 2.

entry, corresponding to one affection, is transformed into its equivalent ICD chapter. The affection af_1 represents the main hospitalization cause. Using a graph representation, af_1 is related to the other four affections, representing secondary causes. These relationships may be represented as a *star graph*, as seen in Fig. 2.

An edge represents the relationship between two nodes or vertices. For our purposes, only undirected (symmetric) edges have been considered, which means that, for two nodes **A** and **B**, the edge **AB** is the same edge as **BA**. A chapter may be referred to itself, as pictured in Fig. 2, node af_1, if the same chapter appears at least twice in the same record. This is called a *self-tie*, or a *self-link*. If multiple instances of a single chapter occur in the same summary report, only one self-tie is computed. Self-ties will be covered in detail later.

The star graph pictured in Fig. 2 is the building block of a complete graph formed by all the star graphs representing all the patient's summary report, one summary report per line. A weight is assigned to an edge according to the number of records connecting two nodes. Edge weight represents the frequency two chapters had been related in the medical report summary. The matrix of edges weights (adjacency matrix) resulting from all patient summary is presented in Table 3. In this table, each entry represents the edge weight, $w_{i,j}$, between two ICD chapters, chapters i and j. The edge weight may also be interpreted as the strength measure between two chapters.

Table 3. Adjacency matrix representing the entire graph.

Chapters	9	10	19	1	11	21	2	4	14	15	6	5	18	13	3	16	17	12	7	8
9	1516	824	361	574	543	333	363	1055	494	2	314	334	456	204	183	7	67	95	58	25
10	824	1110	194	700	332	148	394	318	168	2	176	145	279	84	270	40	125	95	28	139
19	361	194	2769	128	128	185	164	124	125	10	168	345	123	128	49	1	36	65	43	10
1	574	700	128	475	443	139	169	476	228	19	282	128	355	92	187	14	54	170	34	70
11	543	332	128	443	1623	165	225	301	176	1	79	173	222	53	101	15	70	37	8	8
21	333	148	185	139	165	1165	120	70	149	262	81	56	120	61	49	1235	171	109	25	10
2	363	394	164	169	225	120	2024	208	289	1	117	33	213	49	177	0	23	30	7	17
4	1055	318	124	476	301	70	208	308	312	2	156	136	186	71	63	5	37	79	38	18
14	494	168	125	228	176	149	289	312	1084	2	86	57	156	196	66	2	83	45	2	3
15	2	2	10	19	1	262	1	2	2	3269	3	2	2	0	0	0	0	0	0	0
6	314	176	168	282	79	81	117	156	86	3	1181	291	107	107	24	16	68	24	22	22
5	334	145	345	128	173	56	33	136	57	2	291	1040	114	27	17	3	13	21	13	3
18	456	279	123	355	222	120	213	186	156	2	107	114	303	55	109	7	35	20	6	23
13	204	84	128	92	53	61	49	71	196	0	107	27	55	1058	60	2	22	35	4	5
3	183	270	49	187	101	49	177	63	66	0	24	17	109	60	211	1	14	36	7	16
16	7	40	1	14	15	1235	0	5	2	0	16	3	7	2	1	79	51	9	3	2
17	67	125	36	54	70	171	23	37	83	0	68	13	35	22	14	51	423	10	18	13
12	95	95	65	170	37	109	30	79	45	0	24	21	20	35	36	9	10	214	8	6
7	58	28	43	34	8	25	7	38	2	0	22	13	6	4	7	3	18	8	758	3
8	25	139	10	70	8	10	17	18	3	0	22	3	23	5	16	2	13	6	3	262

Table 4. Self-links per chapter. w corresponds to the total vertice links, $w_{i,i}$ is the actual number of self-links, % is the percentage of self-links in w, and $w' = w - w_{i,i}$.

Vertice	9	19	15	10	11	1	2	21	4	14	5	6	16	18	13	17	3	7	12	8
w	10695	5783	3581	7253	6065	6541	5116	5704	6363	5114	3994	4227	1836	4221	2699	1815	2638	1254	1696	927
$w_{i,i}$	1516	2769	3269	1110	1623	475	2024	1165	308	1084	1040	1181	79	303	1058	423	211	758	214	262
%	14	48	91	15	27	7	40	20	5	21	26	28	4	7	39	23	8	60	13	28
w'	9179	3014	312	6143	4442	6066	3092	4539	6055	4030	2954	3046	1757	3918	1641	1392	2427	496	1482	665

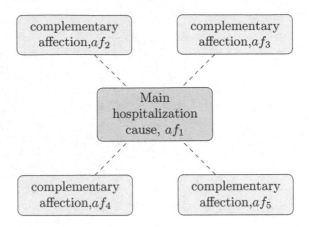

Fig. 2. A sample star graph formed by the relation between main hospitalization cause and the secondary causes.

A complete graph depicting all the vertices, edges and their weights, given by Table 3, can be built. In this graph, every chapter is connected to all others. The exception corresponds to Chap. 20, *External Causes*, due to the absence of codes. Also due to its intricate structure, this full graph is difficult to analyze if all the edges are pictured at once.

According to Hanneman [6], the size of a graph is indexed simply by counting the number of nodes. In an undirected graph, consisting of N nodes, there are $N * (N - 1)/2$ edges at the most, excluding the self-ties. In the constructed ICD graph, with the exception of node 20, every node is linked to all others. The formed graph contains 190 edges, excluding the self-ties, and 210 edges including them. For each edge, a weight is assigned measuring the edge frequency.

3.1   Self-ties Analysis

An important and exciting feature is the high frequency of self-ties in most of the chapters. Despite the expected high number of connections between two distinct chapters, one sees in Table 3 that the number of self-ties $w_{i,i}$ can be much greater than any other $w_{i,j}$, such as Chaps. 9 and 15, which are often referred. It means that once a given record for the primary cause is attributed, most of the secondary causes often belong to the same chapter as the primary one.

Table 4 details the self-ties effect from Table 3. On one hand, Chaps. 15 (91.0%), 7 (70.0%) and 19 (48.0%) might indicate that diseases within these chapters are reported with more details than the others. On the other hand, codes from Chaps. 16 (4.0%) and 4 (5.0%) are most probably reported only as a primary cause of hospitalization and without other outcome, or no other ICD code in the same report.

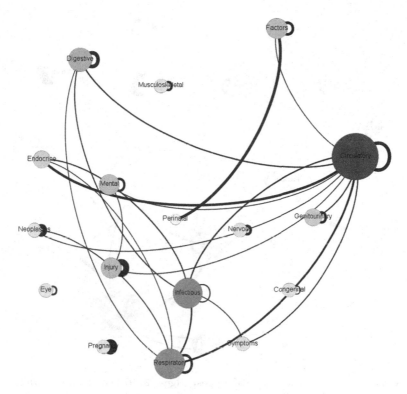

Fig. 3. Graph formed by the top 10.0% largest edges (30.485 connections) corresponding to 45.3% of all links between chapters. Shades of the green color correspond to the number of edges. (Color figure online)

3.2   Cutting Edges: 10%

Apart from the richness of the whole graph formed by the relationships presented in Table 3, a more substantial representation of the strongest chapter connections may be seen in the graph formed only by the top 10.0% more frequent edges (edge weights greater than 314). This corresponds to more than 43.0% of all registered comorbidities. This graph is depicted in Fig. 3, where one notices the importance of Chap. 9 (*Diseases of the circulatory system*) as the most connected one (10.695 edges, 15.9% of all the edges). Figures 3 and 4 have their node size proportional to their degree, and the edge's thickness is equivalent to their weight. From the ICD 21 chapters, only 12 are self-related chapters, i.e. form a principal connected component. This 10.0%-cutoff leaves five chapters without any connections and some of them resemble hospital specialized clinics, such as: the clinics for eye diseases, orthopedics, maternity hospital etc.

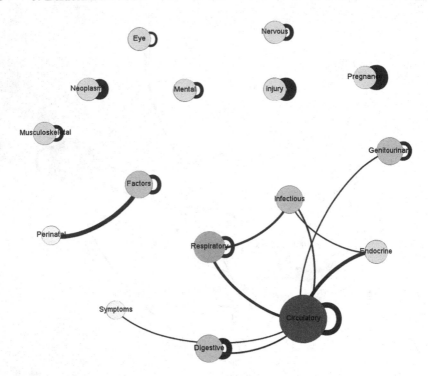

Fig. 4. Graph formed by the top 5.0% largest edges (24.973 connections) which corresponds to 37.1% of all links between chapters. Shades of the green color correspond to the number of edges. (Color figure online)

3.3   The Top 5%

It is remarkable that the edge weights >443 correspond to over 1/3 (37.1%) of all the chapter connections. They form the graph pictured in Fig. 4, where one notice the strong interrelation among ICD Chap. 9 (*Circulatory*), 4 (*Endocrine*) and 1 (*Infectious*). Also the ICD Chap. 10 (*Respiratory*) is strongly connected to Chaps. 9 and 1. Connected to Chap. 9 in the principal connected component are the following chapters: 14, 18 and 11. Notice that Chaps. 21 and 16 are strongly connected between themselves. The other ICD chapters are isolated, being self consistent.

4   Discussions

In the following, we treat in detail the implications of the presented results obtained in the previous section.

Self-ties. From the 21 ICD chapters, 5 chapters have more than 39.0% of self-ties. Considering that these five chapters (*Pregnancy* (15), *Eye* (7), *Injury* (19), *Neoplasms* (2) and *Muskuloskeletal* (13)) are, each one, connected to itself in the top 5.0% graph, we understand this is a clear indication that, within these specialities there is, at least, a refined procedure when reporting affections within these chapters. One may also see a quantitative reason to hospital specialities, such as the later chapter names. The high frequency of self-ties might also indicate an adequate division of the whole variety of affections among the ICD chapters.

10% Cut-off. The 10.0% cut-off should enclose the most frequent activities in this tertiary level hospital and one sees that the majority of the ICD chapters (17) are depicted in Fig. 3. This graph also highlights the weight discrepancy when self-ties are compared to regular edges. There are also many edges with weight just over 300 ($w = 314$ has been the threshold for the 10.0% cut-off). From these edges, we emphasize the weak link between Chap. 21, (*Factors influencing health status and contact with health services*), and the main connected component represented by Chap. 9, *Circulatory*, if compared to the link between Chap. 21 and the *Perinatal*, Chap. 16, ($w = 1235$). Another fragile edge is the link between Chap. 2 (*Neoplasms*) and the *Circulatory* chapter.

Among the nodes forming the principal connected component, eight of them can be considered the most important due to their number of edges. These are: *Circulatory*; *Respiratory*; *Infectious*; *Digestive*; *Neoplasms*; *Endocrine*; *Genitourinary*, and; *Symptoms*.

If self-ties are not considered, the same order is sustained for the first three chapters, unveiling their importance not only within itself but their strong relationship to other chapters. Not considering the self-ties, the *Endocrine* Chapter assumes the fourth place, followed by the *Digestive, Symptoms, Neoplasms* and *Genitourinary*. It is also important to notice that, not considering the self-ties, the *Respiratory* and the *Infectious* chapters have, each one, $\sim$ 48.0% of the *Circulatory* chapter edges, affirming the importance of the latest.

5% Cut-off. From the 8 chapters considered in the 10.0% graph of Fig. 3, the *Neoplasms* Chapter is now detached in the 5.0% graph of Fig. 4. Considering the sum of all the edges from these 7 chapters, from the largest sum to the smallest one, their order is: *Circulatory*; *Respiratory*; *Infectious*; *Digestive*; *Genitourinary*; *Endocrine*, and; *Symptoms*. With the exception of the first chapter (*Circulatory*) this order is not maintained if the self-ties are not considered. In this situation the *Infectious* Chapter assumes the second place, with 44.3% of the *Circulatory* Chapter edges, followed by the *Endocrine* and the *Respiratory* ($\sim$ 38.0%).

Although there are some scientific evidences relating environmental pollution and the increase of respiratory diseases [10] in this hospital region, further analysis are needed to generalize its importance to other areas. We suppose the same observation should be made for the remaining chapters.

Without disregarding the relevance of the *Infectious* (Chap. 4), the *Endocrine, nutritional and metabolic diseases*, is also an important node to this internal graph component. Its importance might be due to the important chronic diseases listed in the ICD chapters, such as diabetes. With the exception of Chap. 17 (*Congenital*), all the other chapters remain from the 10.0% graph mainly due to the self-ties.

General Comments. For both cut-off graphs, as seen in Figs. 3 and 4, the *Circulatory* Chapter counts for the largest connected node. Chapter 9 is the overall most cited chapter (see also Table 2) and has also the largest number of edges (see Table 4). However, the most referred chapter, due to self-ties and chapter connections, is not necessarily the most connected one. This may be caused by the limitation to one link for records with multiple appearances of a single chapter.

If each graph node has the same degree, they form a *regular* graph. If n links randomly (uniformly distributed) connect N nodes, one calls *Erdös-Rényi* graphs. Between the regular and random graphs, there is the class of the *small world* graphs been locally connected with low mean path length [2]. Neither of these graphs seems to describe the graph of Fig. 3. Due to the finitude of data, one cannot classify this graph as a complex network. Nevertheless, one sees nodes with a very high degree compared to the average (hubs).

5　Conclusions

We proposed a novel approach to hospital data analysis using graph theory. A set of 36,236 records of the HCFRMP hospital discharged patient summary was used to represent ICD chapters relationships. The most frequently accessed inter chapters paths have been pictured as graphs and analysed. The importance of Chap. 9, *Diseases of the circulatory system*, has been unveiled not only to the strong relationships to other chapters, but also to the significant number of intrarelationships. We believe this approach could be used to compare possible changes in disease evolution paths due to social, economic and environmental conditions in different periods of time. As for a future study, we intend to pursue, is the expansion of these single chapter nodes as a graph composed of the complete ICD affection codes within it. Also, we propose to characterize formally the obtained graph and consider multiple entries differently from patients with a single admittance.

Acknowledgments. We acknowledge the valuable work of the following staff members of the *Centro de Processamento de Dados Hospitalares*, CPDH, from the *Departamento de Medicina Social* of the *Faculdade de Medicina de Ribeirão Preto* – USP: Ms. Dulce Helena de Brito and Miss Rosane Aparecida Monteiro for the fruitful insights and discussions about the ICD-10. We also wish to express our gratitude to Mr. Gilmar Mazzer for providing us a digital copy of the summary report used and to Carla Fernandes da Silva for drawing the graphs. This study was financed in part by the Coordenação de Aperfeiçoamento de Pessoal de Nível Superior – Brasil (CAPES) – Finance Code 001. ASM acknowledges the support of CNPq (309851/2018-1), Instituto de Ciência e Tecnologia de Sistemas Complexos (INCT–SC/CNPq) e ao Núcleo de Apoio da Física Médica (NAP–FisMed) USP.

References

1. Albert, R.Z., Barabási, A.L.: Statistical mechanics of complex networks. Rev. Mod. Phys. **74**(1), 47–97 (2002). https://doi.org/10.1103/RevModPhys.74.47
2. Barabási, A.L.: Network Science. Cambridge University Press, Cambridge (2016).ISBN: 978-1-07626-6
3. Bassett, D.S., Sporns, O.: Network neuroscience. Nat. Neurosci. **20**(3), 353–364 (2017)
4. Chartrand, G., Zhang, P.: A First Course in Graph Theory. Courier Corporation, North Chelmsford (2013)
5. Dorogovtsev, S.N., Mendes, J.F.F.: Evolution of networks. Adv. Phys. **51**(4), 1079–1187 (2002)
6. Hanneman, R.A., Riddle, M.: A Brief Introduction to Analyzing Social Network Data, chap. 23. SAGE Research Methods (2014). The SAGE Handbook of Social Network Analysis
7. Khan, A., Uddin, S., Srinivasan, U.: Chronic disease prediction using administrative data and graph theory: the case of type 2 diabetes. Expert Syst. Appl. **136**, 230–241 (2019)
8. Liu, C., Wang, F., Hu, J., Xiong, H.: Temporal phenotyping from longitudinal electronic health records: a graph based framework. In: Proceedings of the 21th ACM SIGKDD International Conference on Knowledge Discovery and Data Mining, pp. 705–714 (2015)
9. Newman, M.E.J.: The structure and function of complex networks. SIAM Rev. **45**(2), 167–256 (2003)
10. Roseiro, M.N.V.: Morbidade por problemas respiratórios em Ribeirão Preto-SP, de 1995 a 2001, segundo indicadores ambientais, sociais e econômicos. Master's Thesis, Escola de Enfermagem de Ribeirão Preto, Universidade de São Paulo (2002)
11. Rotmensch, M., Halpern, Y., Tlimat, A., Horng, S., Sontag, D.: Learning a health knowledge graph from electronic medical records. Sci. Rep. **7**(1), 1–11 (2017)
12. WHO, World Health Organization: ICD-10: International Statistical Classification of Diseases and Related Health Problems : Tenth Revision (2004)

CovidStream: Interactive Visualization of Emotions Evolution Associated with Covid-19

Herwin Alayn Huillcen Baca[1]([⊠])(iD),
Flor de Luz Palomino Valdivia[1](iD), Yalmar Ponce Atencio[1](iD),
Manuel J. Ibarra[2](iD), Mario Aquino Cruz[2](iD),
and Melvin Edward Huillcen Baca[3](iD)

[1] José María Arguedas National University, Apurímac, Peru
{hhuillcen,fpalomino,yalmar}@unajma.edu.pe
[2] Micaela Bastidas National University, Apurímac, Peru
[3] Santa María Catholic University, Arequipa, Peru
mhuillcen@ucsm.edu.pe

Abstract. Since the beginning of the pandemic caused by Covid-19, the emotions of humanity have evolved abruptly, mainly for policies adopted by the governments of countries. These policies, since they have a high impact on people's health, need feedback on people's emotional perception and their connections with entities directly related to emotions, to have relevant information for decision making. Given the global social isolation, emotions have been expressed with higher magnitude in comments on social networks, generating a large amount of data that is a source for various investigations. The objective of this work is to design and adapt an interactive visualization tool called CovidStream, for monitoring the evolution of emotions associated with Covid-19 in Peru, for which Visual Analytics, Deep learning, and Sentiment Analysis techniques are combined. This visualization tool allows showing the evolution of the emotions associated with the Covid-19 and its relationships with three entities: persons, places, and organizations, which have an impact on emotions, all in a temporal space dimension. For the visualization of entities and emotions, Peruvian tweets extracted between January and July 2020 were used, all of them with the hashtag #Covid-19. For the classification of emotions, a recurrent neural network model with LSTM architecture was implemented, taking as training and test data the one proposed by SemEval-2018 Task1, corresponding to Spanish tweets labeled with emotions: anger, fear, joy, and sadness.

Keywords: Visual analytics · Deep learning · Sentiment analysis · Time series · Wordcloud · StreamGraph · Emotion classification · Entity recognition · LSTM · Tweets

© Springer Nature Switzerland AG 2021
J. A. Lossio-Ventura et al. (Eds.): SIMBig 2020, CCIS 1410, pp. 540–551, 2021.
https://doi.org/10.1007/978-3-030-76228-5_39

1   Introduction

There are many works [7–10] that classify emotions from comments on social networks, where the results are aimed at obtaining greater accuracy of classification, however, none seeks to establish some kind of relationship or possible cause of these classified emotions.

A comment extracted from a social network contains data that can be analyzed not only to classify them in a category, but also to extract key information, based on recognition of entities. For example, if a comment has been classified as Fear and in turn has identified entities such as Donald Trump, China, and WHO (World Health Organization), it is possible to interpret that the emotion Fear is due to some announcement by Donald Trump about some event in China and that has some implication in the WHO, then there is a better understanding of the nature of the emotion Fear of said comment. According to the best authors, there are no works that shows information about the possible relationships between entities and their emotions; these relationships should be shown in a visualization tool that allows a better perception of the nature of emotions.

Most of the emotions classification works are based on comments in the English language; few works are based on the Spanish language, which constitutes a gap in this field of research. The social isolation policies throughout the planet, caused by the Covid-19, made human interaction, more virtual than physical, through the use of social networks, where opinions and emotions are reflected in higher dimension, which constitutes a rich source for the analysis of comments. However, there are limitations to access these sources, with the social network tweeter being the only one that makes all comments available, almost without restrictions.

Peru is one of the countries most affected by Covid-19 and requires technological platforms that help make the best decisions to mitigate the effects of the pandemic caused by Covid-19. In this way, we design and adapt a visualization tool called CovidStream to visualize the evolution of emotions (anger, fear, joy, and sadness) associated with the Covid-19 in Peru, and to show possible relationships with key entities (persons, places, and organizations), all in a temporal space dimension, to have a better understanding of the nature of emotions.

The investigation took comments from the social network Twitter with the hashtag #Covid-19, between January 1 and July 25, 2020, limited to centralized comments in the city of Lima.

2   Related Work

Wu et al. [4], present an interactive visualization tool called Plexus, which identifies and visualizes people's emotions for two specific topics. The authors take as motivation that in the display of tweets, attributes not only such as the frequency of words can be shown, also the underlying connections of different topics and opinions. The objective of this work was to design and create a visualization tool to present the results of the semantic analysis of tweets, regarding the emotions expressed in the text, so that users can understand the connections between these topics and emotions. They propose as future works, visualize emotions in time series, in such a way to perceive the evolution of emotions in a temporal space. In our work, we take this idea and focus it to visualize the evolution of the emotions associated with Peruvian tweets, regarding the specific topic "covid-19", in a temporal space and show the underlying relationships with entities extracted from each tweet.

Ma'ady et al. [5], took as a reference that visualizing the emotional behavior of clients in a temporal space and recognizing the patterns of emotions, can play a crucial role in decision making. They discussed how emotions fluctuated between patterns and demonstrated how it could be explored in useful visualizations with an appropriate framework. They used tweets from 4 countries: USA, Japan, Indonesia, and Taiwan, to visually analyze emotions and their associated patterns regarding the topic iPhone. A visualized tool was constructed with a two-dimensional heat map that shows the evolution of emotions. We rescue the idea that recognizing the patterns of emotions is essential in decision making.

Mohammad et al. [3], present the solutions to Task 1 of the SemEval-2018 tweet sentiment analysis contest: the objective was to classify the affective state of a person from their tweet. For this, they had tagged datasets in English, Arabic, and Spanish languages, seventy teams from around the world competed. The methods, resources, and tools used by the participating teams are shown, with a focus on the affective state classification techniques. The datasets were made freely available for use in the classification process. It was observed that the technique most used by the teams was LSTM [14]. In our work, we took these techniques as a reference to decide the use of LSTM [14] as a machine learning technique to classify tweets in Spanish. Likewise, we used the available dataset of tweets in Spanish, labeled with emotions: anger, fear, joy, and sadness.

Dang et al. [6], implemented WordStream, an interactive visual tool for demonstrating the evolution of topics. They used two popular techniques: Wordcloud to offer an attractive visualization of the text through font sizes and colors; on the other hand, they used Streamgraph, to visualize the evolution of a topic. Wordstream shows the evolution of a topic in a temporal space dimension, using layers corresponding to entities extracted from texts. It was tested with texts obtained from news web pages, trying to find relationships between entities over time. Our work takes as reference this visualization technique of the evolution of a topic. In our case, the topic is Covid-19, and the layers correspond to emotions and entities (persons, organizations, and places) associated with Peruvian tweets, in such a way to find underlying relationships between emotions and entities over time.

3 Proposal

The proposal has two objectives:

- Design and adapt an interactive visualization tool called CovidStream to display the evolution of emotions associated with Covid-19 in Peru, showing the relationship of emotions (anger, fear, joy, and sadness) and representative entities (persons, places, and organizations), that allow a better understanding of the nature of emotions.

- Implement an emotion classification model for comments from the social network Twitter in Spanish, based on a recurrent neural network with LSTM [14] architecture with training and test data provided by the SemEval-2018 Task1 [3] dataset.

CovidStream is a hybrid solution that mixes Visual Analytics, Deep Learning and Sentiment Analysis techniques, to show the evolution of emotions of a topic that is of global interest: the Covid-19. The CovidStream design is the combination of the StreamGraph and WordCloud visualization techniques, containing four layers:

- **L1:** First layer with a word cloud of the entity persons.
- **L2:** Second layer with a word cloud of the entity places.
- **L3:** Third layer with a word cloud of the entity organizations.
- **L4:** Fourth layer with the emotions word cloud.

The target users are government and non-government entities that need to make decisions about the perception of Peruvians regarding the Covid-19. Our work aims to answer the questions:

- **Q1:** How is the evolution of the emotional perception of Peruvians regarding the Covid-19, over time?
- **Q2:** Who are the persons, places, and organizations that influence the emotional perception of Peruvians, regarding Covid-19, over time?
- **Q3:** What is the evolution of persons, places, and organizations that intervene in the emotions of Peruvians, regarding Covid-19, over time?

There are six interactions between CovidStream and the user:

- **I1:** Show the relationships between emotions and entities, according to the size, location and colors of the words, as well as the evolution isolated by each word.
- **I2:** Show the time evolution of a specific entity or emotion.
- **I3:** Show the relationships between emotions and entities, for each month, between and January and July 2020.
- **I4:** Definition of the number of most ranked words per month, to vary the granularity of the layers.
- **I5:** Definition of the display area, varying the height and width of the graphic, to appreciate more or less detail of the layers.
- **I6:** Word orientation definition.

The Fig. 1 shows the pipeline of our proposal.

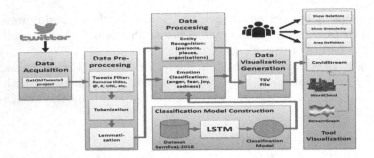

Fig. 1. Pipeline of our proposal.

4 Implementation

4.1 Classification Model Construction

The classification model is based on a recurrent neural network with LSTM [14] architecture. The efficiency of our model was evaluated with the accuracy metric.

Dataset Exploration. A limitation of our work was having tweets tagged with their respective emotions, especially in the Spanish language. However, there is The SemEval-2018 Task 1: Affect in Tweets competition dataset [3], which offers tweets tagged with the emotions fear, angry, joy and sadness, in English, Arabic, and Spanish. We take the training and test dataset corresponding to the EI-oc (emotion intensity to ordinal classification) category. This dataset has 4541 tagged tweets.

Dataset Preprocessing and Tokenization. Tweets were cleaned, through filters: removal of tildes, strange characters, users, hashtags, URLs, etc. Likewise, all words were converted to lowercase. After, we divided each tweet into an array of words, through of tokenization process.

Convert Data to Numeric Vectors. Subsequently, the array of words are transformed into numerical vectors, with the aim of creating a machine learning model for model training. This process is also known as text-to-sequences, in our case we use a vector of size 50.

Built and Train the LSTM Model. The definition of the LSTM [14] model is shown in Fig. 2.

The model was compiled with categorical-cross entropy loss function, adam optimizer, and accuracy metrics. The dataset was divided into 80% for training and 20% for testing, it was subsequently trained with batch-size = 256 and epochs = 50.

```
Layer (type)                    Output Shape          Param #
=================================================================
input_1 (InputLayer)            (None, 50)             0
_____
embedding_1 (Embedding)         (None, 50, 500)        50000000
_____
lstm_1 (LSTM)                   (None, 512)            2074624
_____
dense_1 (Dense)                 (None, 256)            131328
_____
activation_1 (Activation)       (None, 256)            0
_____
dropout_1 (Dropout)             (None, 256)            0
_____
dense_2 (Dense)                 (None, 4)              1028
_____
activation_2 (Activation)       (None, 4)              0
=================================================================
Total params: 52,206,980
Trainable params: 52,206,980
Non-trainable params: 0
```

Fig. 2. Definition of LSTM model.

Test the Model. The model was trained and tested, obtaining an accuracy of 74.64% in the classification of emotions, this result is within the results of The SemEval-2018 Task 1 [3].

4.2 Data Acquisition

The dataset corresponds to Peruvian tweets with the hashtag #Covid-19, taken between January 1 and July 25, 2020, dates that involve the appearance and evolution of Covid-19 in Peru. For the acquisition of tweets, the library GetOldTweets3 [1], available for Python, which allowed to extract tweets at date intervals provided by the user, was found to be more useful than the library "Tweepy" [2], which only allows you to extract tweets from a week old. The tweets correspond to the geographic area of the city of Lima, Peru, taking Lima Centro as a reference, with an area of around 50 km. It was stored in batches of 15 days, in CSV type files.

4.3 Data Preprocessing

Tweet Filter and Tokenization. For each tweet, the following filters were applied: tick removal, lowercase text conversion, elimination of strange characters, and deletion of usernames and URLs. Tokenization, this process consisted of dividing each tweet into an array of words, then creating an array of tweets with each array created.

4.4 Data Processing

Entity Recognition. From the preprocessed data, the process of identifying the entities: persons, organizations, and places of each tweet is carried out; for this, the Spacy [13] library available for Python was used. It is possible that there are tweets that do not have any recognized entity, in which case the tweet is ignored.

Emotion Classification. Each preprocessed tweet was classified with its own emotion; For this, the previously constructed classification model, detailed in Subsect. 4.1, was used.

4.5 Data Visualization Generation

Given the entities and emotions for each tweet, a TSV file with five columns was created: date and time, entity person, entity organization, entity place, and sssociated emotion. If there are two or more entities of the same type, it is separated by "|" character. All the data in the file is ordered, since they are represented in time series.

4.6 Building Tool Visualization

The general interface of CovidStream is shown in Fig. 3, the control panel is displayed on the left for interactions (**I1, I2, I3, I4, I5, I6**), in the central part the four layers are shown (**L1, L2, L3, L4**), to answer the questions (**Q1, Q2, Q3**). CovidStream is available at the link: http://www.unajma.edu.pe/CovidStream/.

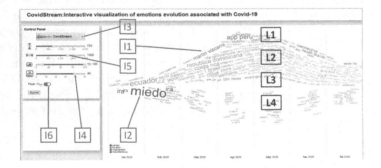

Fig. 3. General interface of CovidStream with interactions and layers.

The CovidStream visualization tool was adapted from WordStream [6], using two techniques:

WordCloud. Designed to optimize the use of space and offer an attractive visualization of words, based on frequency, through sizes and colors. Wordle [12] is the best-known algorithm, is a randomized greedy algorithm to place words. It is greedy since it prioritizes the more frequent words, CovisStream use this technique. There are attempts to integrate temporal constraints into Wordle. Parallel Tag Clouds [15] utilize the parallel coordinates to represent time constraint. At each time step terms are placed in order of importance, based on term frequency. This technique also has a feature that is implemented in CovidStream, which is to display a stream when a term is selected.

StreamGraph. StreamGraph [11] an evolution of ThemeRiver [16], focuses on minimizing the wiggle per layer, to avoid legibility issue in the previous stacked graph, and also improve the aesthetic aspect of the overall graph. CovisStream use this technique and places terms as close to its time step as possible by utilizing space sharing approach between adjacent time steps.

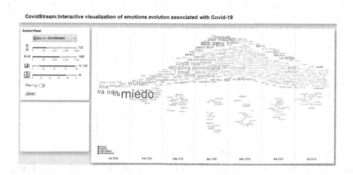

Fig. 4. CovidStream with default interaction parameters.

5 Results

The results were analyzed by answering the questions **Q1**, **Q2**, and **Q3**.

5.1   Q1: How is the Evolution of the Emotional Perception of Peruvians Regarding the Covid-19, Over Time?

When CovidStream is executed, the evolution of emotions is shown, see Fig. 4. It is observed that the emotion Fear (miedo) predominates in size and color **(I1)** over the other emotions, especially between January and February. Better appreciated when using **(I6)**.

However, its evolution cannot be seen in the other months, for which the interaction **(I2)** is used, and an increase is observed from January to April and it is maintained until July, see Fig. 5.

In the same figure, same behavior is observed with the emotions Sadness (tristeza) and Anger (ira), but to a lesser degree than Fear (miedo). In case of the emotion Joy (alegría), its evolution is maintained, except in May.

With this analysis, it can be concluded that Peruvians feel more fear over time, added to sadness and anger. Joy is not a predominant emotion in Peruvians.

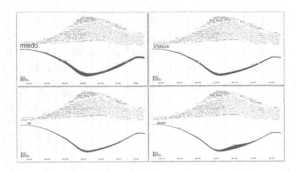

Fig. 5. CovidStream with the evolution of individual emotions.

5.2   Q2: Who are the Persons, Places, and Organizations that Influence the Emotional Perception of Peruvians, Regarding Covid-19, Over Time?

The number of words and the display area influences in the granularity of the layers **(L1, L2, L3)**, for this, we use the interaction **(I4)** referring to the configuration of the number of most ranked words, and **(I5)** related to the CovidStream display area, see Fig. 6. It is observed that in January, the emotion Fear (miedo) has a direct relationship with China and Ecuador places.

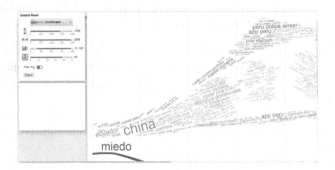

Fig. 6. CovidStream with definition of display area and number of words.

However, the display area is still limited to observe all the relationships, so we use the interaction **(I3)**, referred to showing the relationships by month. In Fig. 7, on relationships in January, it is observed with greater accuracy that the emotion Fear (miedo) is related to the places China, Wuhan, Perú, and Ecuador, with persons as Elizabeth Hinostroza (Minister of Health of Peru) and Martín Vizcarra, and organizations as the Ministry of Health (minsa) and the WHO (oms).

In the same figure, on relationships in March, shows relationships between the emotion "Fear" (miedo) with places Brazil, Colombia, and Italy, with persons as President Martín Vizcarra, organizations as the WHO (oms).

Fig. 7. CovidStream with relationships between emotions and entities in January and March 2020.

5.3 Q3: What is the Time Evolution of Persons, Places, and Organizations that Intervene in the Emotions of Peruvians, Regarding Covid-19, Over Time?

We use the interaction (**I2**), on the evolution of a specific entity, for example, "Fig. 8" shows the individual evolution of the China place, it is observed that there was a high frequency of comments between the months of January and February and then it declined. The same figure shows the individual evolution of the person President Martín Vizcarra, a stable frequency is observed, but with a greater presence in March and June.

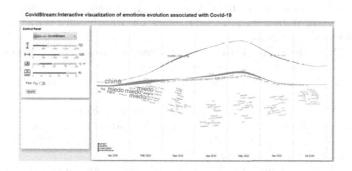

Fig. 8. CovidStream with individual evolution of entities

6   Conclusions

An interactive visualization tool for the evolution of emotions in Peru was designed and implemented, regarding Covid-19; in space temporal dimension. This tool shows the evolution of emotions: fear, sadness, anger, and joy and relates them to entities: persons, places, and organizations, showing the underlying relationships between emotions and their origins. Emotions and entities were identified from Peruvian tweets.

An emotion classification model was built based on a recurrent neural network with LSTM [14] architecture, to classify tweets in Spanish, achieving an accuracy of 74.64%.

References

1. Henrique, J.: GetOldTweets by Python. https://github.com/Jefferson-Henrique/GetOldTweets-python
2. Roesslein, J.: Tweepy: Twitter for Python (2020). https://github.com/tweepy/tweepy
3. Mohammad, S., Bravo-Marquez, F., Salameh, M., Kiritchenko, S.: SemEval-2018 task 1: affect in tweets. In: Proceedings of International Workshop on Semantic Evaluation (SemEval-2018), June 2018
4. Wu, X., Bartram, L., Shaw, C.: Plexus: an interactive visualization tool for analyzing public emotions from Twitter data (2017). arXiv preprint arXiv:1701.06270
5. Ma'ady, M.N.P., Yang, C.K., Kusumawardani, R.P., Suryotrisongko, H.: Temporal exploration in 2D visualization of emotions on Twitter stream. Telkomnika **16**(1), 376–384 (2018)
6. Dang, T., Nguyen, H. N., Pham, V., Johansson, J., Sadlo, F., Marai, G.E.: WordStream: interactive visualization for topic evolution. In: EuroVis (Short Papers), pp. 103–107 (2019)
7. Bravo-Marquez, F., Frank, E., Mohammad, S.M., Pfahringer, B.: Determining word-emotion associations from tweets by multi-label classification. In: 2016 IEEE/WIC/ACM International Conference on Web Intelligence (WI), pp. 536–539. IEEE, October 2016
8. Jabreel, M., Moreno, A.: A deep learning-based approach for multi-label emotion classification in tweets. Appl. Sci. **9**(6), 1123 (2019)
9. Mohammad, S.M., Bravo-Marquez, F.: Emotion intensities in tweets (2017). arXiv preprint arXiv:1708.03696
10. Liew, J.S.Y., Turtle, H.R.: Exploring fine-grained emotion detection in tweets. In: Proceedings of the NAACL Student Research Workshop, pp. 73–80, June 2016
11. Byron, L., Wattenberg, M.: Stacked graphs - geometry and aesthetics. IEEE Trans. Vis. Comput. Graph. **14**(6), 1245–1252 (2008)
12. Viegas, F.B., Wattenberg, M., Feinberg, J.: Participatory visualization with wordle. IEEE Trans. Vis. Comp. Graph. **15**(6), 1137–1144 (2009)
13. Honnibal, M., Johnson, M.: An improved non-monotonic transition system for dependency parsing. In: Proceedings of the 2015 Conference on Empirical Methods in Natural Language Processing, pp. 1373–1378, September 2015
14. Hochreiter, S., Schmidhuber, J.: Long short-term memory. Neural Comput. **9**(8), 1735–1780 (1997)

15. Collins, C., Viégas, F.B., Wattenberg, M.: Parallel tag clouds to explore and ana-lyze faceted text corpora. In: Proceedings of the VAST 09 - IEEE Symposium on Visual Analytics Science and Technology, pp. 91–98 (2009)
16. Havre, S., Hetzler, B., Nowell, L.: ThemeRiver: visualizing theme changes over time. In: Proceedings of IEEE Symposium on Information Visualization 2000, INFOVIS 2000, pp. 115–123 (2000)

Author Index

Printed in the United States
by Baker & Taylor Publisher Services